New York Cannabis Laws and Regulations

2022 Edition

Omar Figueroa

New York Cannabis Laws and Regulations 2022

ISBN 979-8-9856826-4-9

Disclaimer

This publication has been created to provide you with accurate and authoritative information concerning New York cannabis and hemp laws and regulations. It is sold with the understanding that the publisher is not engaged in rendering legal or other professional services. This publication is not a substitute for legal advice of an attorney. If you require legal or other expert advice, you should seek the services of a competent attorney or other professional.

The law is ever changing and sometimes errors happen even with careful attention to detail. If you find any errors, please email us the details at book@omarfigueroa.com with the phrase "Book Error: Confidential" in the subject line. Although this publication is designed to aid in the research and practice of cannabis law, it is recommended that you cross check the New York Legislature website for any change in the law. The URL for the Legislature's website is:

https://assembly.state.ny.us/leg/

Because New York's cannabis and hemp regulations are also evolving, please check for the latest regulatory updates at the Office of Cannabis Management webpage:

https://cannabis.ny.gov/laws-regulations

Also, please keep yourself informed by purchasing the most up-to-date edition of this publication as it comes available.

Colophon

Author: Omar Figueroa, Esq.

Legal and Research Assistant: Tina S. Smith, J.D.

Text Design: Jocelyn Bergen

Cover Design: Ophelia Chong

Cover Image: Ruth Frase

Index: Jennifer Weers

Typeface: PT Serif

Published by Lux Law Publishing

Preface

Governor Andrew Cuomo signed legislation legalizing adult-use cannabis on March 31, 2021. The Marihuana Regulation and Taxation Act (MRTA) created a comprehensive regulatory structure to oversee the licensure, cultivation, production, distribution, sale, and taxation of medical cannabis, adult-use cannabis, and cannabinoid hemp. Adults are allowed to possess up to 3 ounces of cannabis or 24 grams of concentrated cannabis in public, with up to five pounds of cannabis in one's residence. In addition, home cultivation of up to three mature and three immature medical cannabis plants per individual, with a maximum of twelve plants per household is permitted.

New York is the Fourteenth state, not counting the District of Columbia, to legalize cannabis for adult use. This historic change comes seven years after Governor Cuomo signed legislation to permit a medical cannabis program which ended a century of cannabis prohibition in the state. In 1914, New York started restricting cannabis by requiring citizens to get a prescription to use it.

On a national level, Congress passed the Pure Food and Drug Act in 1906. It ensured that citizens were permitted to use cannabis with a prescription. America turned against the herb as it was demonized by opportunists such as Harry Anslinger at a time when an influx of cannabis-using immigrants were arriving. In 1925, the New York Times claimed that a Mexican called Escrado Valle killed six people after running amok in a hospital. Valle had apparently become "crazed from smoking marihuana." In 1927, the New York Times went full Reefer Madness when it published an article with the scary title: "Mexican Family Go Insane." According to doctors, a widow and her four children were driven insane after eating the cannabis plant. The physicians went on to say that the mother would remain insane for the rest of her life. Also, there was "no hope of saving the children's lives."

An era of ludicrous anti-cannabis propaganda began. New York state banned cannabis use completely in 1927. A decade later, the 1937 Marihuana Tax Act effectively prohibited cannabis across the United States.

Common sense started to prevail within New York when the Mayor of New York City, Fiorello La Guardia, assigned a committee to look into cannabis in the city in 1939. (Notably, LaGuardia airport is named after former Mayor La Guardia, whose first name Fiorello means "little flower" in Italian.) Five years later, the La Guardia Report found that the gateway theory was primarily false. It also suggested that cannabis was not widely associated with use by children, addiction, or juvenile delinquency. The report effectively debunked most myths attributed to cannabis. It also revealed the stupidity of the hysteria that surrounded the plant. Sadly, anti-cannabis campaigners such as Anslinger were able to convince the public to dismiss the report.

At this time, New York had a difficult time keeping cannabis under control. The city's Sanitation Department, known as the White Wing Squad, started to cut and burn every cannabis plant they could find, but it wasn't a particularly successful effort. By 1951, there were reports of 10-foot tall cannabis plants spotted in the city's empty lots and the Bronx underpasses. The squad uprooted and destroyed 41,000 pounds of cannabis, including the largest haul from Brooklyn at 17,200 pounds. The news estimated the value of the destroyed crops in that borough alone at approximately $6 million.

In 1969, the United States Supreme Court ruled that the 1937 Marihuana Tax Act was unconstitutional; however, a short time later, the Controlled Substances Act of 1970 scheduled cannabis as a controlled substance. Under federal law, it remains a Schedule I substance today. In 1973, New York Governor Nelson Rockefeller signed legislation that became known as the Rockefeller Drug Laws. This draconian legislation increased the penalty for selling two ounces or possessing four ounces of cannabis. The law also applied to substances such as cocaine, heroin, and morphine, and involved a minimum prison sentence of 15 years with a maximum sentence of 25 years to life.

In 1977, New York decriminalized possession of fewer than 25 grams of cannabis, which helped decrease arrests for simple possession; however, possession in public view remained a misdemeanor. Civil rights advocates stated that this was used as a loophole to unfairly arrest, as police officers conducting suspicionless stop-and-frisks would direct New Yorkers to empty their pockets (sometimes with false promises of no arrest) and then arrest them for the misdemeanor of possession in public view. In response to the continued arrests for cannabis possession, in 2014, New York City Mayor Bill de Blasio directed the NYPD to cease arrests, and instead issue tickets, for small possession even in cases where the 1977 law might allow an arrest, such as cannabis entering "public view" during a stop-and-frisk.

In 2014, Governor Cuomo signed the Compassionate Care Act to establish a comprehensive medical cannabis program in New York. The Department of Health announced the launch of the state's medical cannabis program 18 months later, establishing strict regulatory controls, and ensuring the availability of pharmaceutical-grade medical cannabis products for certified patients.

In 2018, Governor Cuomo urged the New York State Legislature to fund a study on the effects of legalizing cannabis for recreational use. The proposed study would examine a wide variety of issues, including the legal, economic, and social ramifications recreational cannabis could have on New York. The Department of Health completed its study and recommended the legalization of cannabis in New York, citing economic, public health, and public safety benefits. Cuomo stated that New York should "legalize the adult use of recreational cannabis once and for all." The study was followed by an amended Marihuana Regulation and Taxation Act bill, which would legalize and regulate cannabis in the state.

In 2019, New York enacted legislation expanding the decriminalization of recreational use of cannabis, but did not legalize it.

Negotiations between the governor's office and the legislature over the final cannabis legalization bill were finally successful on March 30, 2021, and the Marihuana Regulation and Taxation Act (MRTA) was passed in the New York State Assembly and Senate. Governor Cuomo signed the bill into law the following day. On April 9, 2021, cannabis related criminal records in the state of New York were confirmed to have been expunged by the law as well.

A provision in the Marihuana Regulation and Taxation Act permits local municipalities the opportunity to opt out of the state issuing licenses for marijuana dispensaries and/or on-site consumption lounges within their jurisdiction. The Rockefeller Institute launched the Marijuana Opt-Out Tracker to track the status of the opt-out process. To view which towns, cities, and villages within New York state have made the decision to opt out, you can visit the website at: https://rockinst.org/issue-areas/state-local-government/municipal-opt-out-tracker/.

The Marihuana Regulation and Taxation Act includes provisions to expand the Medical Marihuana Program allowing people with a larger list of medical conditions to access medical cannabis, increasing the number of caregivers allowed per patient, and permitting home cultivation of medical cannabis for patients.

The Marihuana Regulation and Taxation Act also permits the sale of hemp flower in the cannabinoid hemp program, and allows for smokable forms. This expands on the regulatory framework New York established in 2019, for the production and sale of hemp and hemp extract. The program established a state permitting process for growers, processors, and sellers of hemp and hemp extract as well as laboratory testing and labeling of hemp extract products.

The Office of Cannabis Management and Cannabis Control Board are in the process of promulgating additional emergency and proposed final regulations. Adoption of final regulations by the Cannabis Control Board is not anticipated until next year. This edition of the book includes the recently adopted Conditional Adult-Use Retail Dispensary Regulations, Personal Home Cultivation of Medical Cannabis Regulations, Cannabinoid Hemp Regulations, Cannabis Laboratories Emergency Regulations, Adult-Use Packaging and Labeling Proposed Regulations, and the Adult-Use Marketing and Advertising Proposed Regulations. The Conditional Adult-Use

Cultivator and Conditional Adult-Use Processor licenses were statutory enactments through Senate Bill 8084, unlike the Conditional Adult-Use Retail Dispensary license, which was created by the regulators and therefore is not found in the Cannabis Law.

This publication provides a carefully curated compendium of the various laws and regulations governing cannabis and hemp in the Empire State. It is a user-friendly guide that can be used by operators, professionals, and regulators.

This book also includes charts of the separate license types and permits under the Marihuana Regulation and Taxation Act for medical cannabis, adult-use cannabis, and cannabinoid hemp. These charts simplify the comprehensive regulatory structure to help you visualize how the different licenses work together to bring cannabis to the end consumer.

In addition, the book includes the Office of Cannabis Management guidance materials for adult-use conditional cultivators, adult-use conditional processors, packaging, labeling, and true parties of interest.

The New York State Bar Association has released several ethics opinions examining the conflict between state and federal laws concerning cannabis. These opinions are included to help guide lawyers in their counseling of cannabis clients.

We hope you find New York Cannabis Laws and Regulations to be an indispensable tool in your library.

Because New York law is rapidly evolving, we suggest that readers check for the latest changes, amendments, and updates at the New York Legislature's web site:

https://assembly.state.ny.us/leg/

New York's cannabis and hemp regulations are also evolving, so please check for the latest regulatory updates at the Office of Cannabis Management web page:

https://cannabis.ny.gov/laws-regulations

Contents at a Glance

PART 1: LAWS

PART 2: REGULATIONS

Table of Contents

Part 1: Laws

I. Agriculture and Markets Law

ARTICLE 29 GROWTH OF HEMP

II. Alcoholic Beverage Control Law

III. Cannabis Law

ARTICLE 1 SHORT TITLE; LEGISLATIVE FINDINGS AND INTENT; DEFINITIONS

ARTICLE 2 NEW YORK STATE CANNABIS CONTROL BOARD

ARTICLE 3 MEDICAL CANNABIS

ARTICLE 4 ADULT-USE CANNABIS

ARTICLE 5 CANNABINOID HEMP AND HEMP EXTRACT

VI. General Business Law

VII. Labor Law

VIII. Penal Law

PART 3. SPECIFIC OFFENSES

Title K. OFFENSES INVOLVING FRAUD

ARTICLE 179. CRIMINAL DIVERSION OF MEDICAL MARIHUANA

Title M. OFFENSES AGAINST PUBLIC HEALTH AND MORALS

ARTICLE 220. CONTROLLED SUBSTANCES OFFENSES

ARTICLE 222. CANNABIS

IX. Public Health Law

ARTICLE 13-E. REGULATION OF SMOKING AND VAPING IN CERTAIN PUBLIC AREAS

ARTICLE 33. CONTROLLED SUBSTANCES

Title 1. GENERAL PROVISIONS

Title 5-A. MEDICAL USE OF MARIHUANA

Title 6. RECORDS AND REPORTS

ARTICLE 33-A. CONTROLLED SUBSTANCES THERAPEUTIC RESEARCH ACT

ARTICLE 33-B. REGULATION OF CANNABINOID HEMP AND HEMP EXTRACT

X. Social Services Law

XI. State Finance Law

XII. Tax Law

ARTICLE 20-B. EXCISE TAX ON MEDICAL CANNABIS

ARTICLE 20-C. TAX ON ADULT-USE CANNABIS PRODUCTS

XIII. Vehicle and Traffic Law

Part 2: Regulations

Title 1. Department of Agriculture and Markets

Chapter III. Plant Industry

SUBCHAPTER F. INDUSTRIAL HEMP

Part 159. Industrial Hemp Agricultural Pilot Programs

Title 9. Executive Department

SUBTITLE B. DIVISION OF ALCOHOLIC BEVERAGE CONTROL

Chapter II. Rules of the Office of Cannabis Management

PART 114. CANNABINOID HEMP.

PART 115. PERSONAL HOME CULTIVATION OF MEDICAL CANNABIS.

PART 116. CONDITIONAL ADULT-USE RETAIL DISPENSARY

PART 128. ADULT-USE PACKAGING AND LABELING (PROPOSED REGULATIONS)

PART 129. ADULT-USE MARKETING AND ADVERTISING (PROPOSED REGULATIONS)

PART 130. CANNABIS LABORATORIES (EMERGENCY REGULATIONS)

Title 10. Department of Health

Chapter XIII. Medical Use of Marihuana

PART 1004. MEDICAL USE OF MARIHUANA

Part 3: New York State Bar Association Legal Ethics Opinions

Part 4: Charts of License and Permit Types

Part 5: Office of Cannabis Management Guidance

Index

Part 1: Laws

I. Agriculture and Markets Law

ARTICLE 29. GROWTH OF HEMP

Agriculture and Markets Law § 505. Definitions.

As used in this article:

1. "Hemp" means the plant Cannabis sativa L. and any part of such plant, including the seeds thereof and all derivatives, extracts, cannabinoids, isomers, acids, salts, and salts of isomers, whether growing or not, with a delta-9 tetrahydrocannabinol concentration of not more than three-tenths of a percent on a dry weight basis.

2. "Institution of higher education" means:

(a) any of the colleges and universities described in subdivision three of section three hundred fifty-two of the education law;

(b) a college established and operated pursuant to the provisions of article one hundred twenty-six of the education law, and providing two-year or four-year post-secondary programs in general and technical educational subjects and receiving financial assistance from the state;

(c) the city university of New York, as defined in subdivision two of section sixty-two hundred two of the education law; and

(d) a not-for-profit two or four-year university or college given the power to confer associate, baccalaureate or higher degrees in this state by the legislature or by the regents under article five of the education law.

3. "License" means a license, permit or registration issued pursuant to this article.

4. "Processing of hemp in connection with its growing and cultivation" means the growing, cultivation, cloning, harvesting, drying, curing, grinding and trimming of hemp plants.

Agriculture and Markets Law § 506. Growth, sale, distribution, transportation and processing of hemp and products derived from such hemp permitted.

1. Notwithstanding any provision of law to the contrary, hemp and products derived from such hemp are agricultural products which may be grown, cultivated, produced, processed, manufactured, possessed in the state, and sold, distributed, or transported in the state, pursuant to authorization under federal law, the provisions of this article, article thirty-three-B of the public health law or any other state law.

2. Notwithstanding any provision of law to the contrary restricting the growing or cultivating, processing, manufacturing, sale, distribution or transportation of hemp and products derived from such hemp, and subject to authorization of the growth and cultivation of hemp under federal law, the commissioner may: (a) authorize the growing, cultivating, processing and manufacturing of hemp as part of agricultural pilot programs conducted by the department or an institution of higher education to study the growth and cultivation, sale, distribution, transportation, processing and manufacturing of such hemp and products derived from such hemp provided that the sites and programs used for growing or cultivating hemp are authorized by, and registered with, the department; and (b) license the growth and cultivation of hemp, including the processing of hemp in connection with its growing and

cultivation, and the sale of hemp plants or hemp seed.

Agriculture and Markets Law § 507. Prohibitions.

1. Except as authorized by federal and state law, and rules and regulations promulgated thereunder, the growth, cultivation, sale, distribution or export of hemp is prohibited.

2. Hemp produced outside the state and sold or distributed in the state shall meet all standards established for hemp under state law, rules and regulations.

Agriculture and Markets Law § 508. Regulations.

The commissioner is hereby authorized to adopt, amend, promulgate and issue rules and regulations consistent with the provisions of this article, including, but not limited to:

1. The authorization or licensing of any person who may acquire or possess hemp plants or viable seeds, grow or cultivate hemp plants, or sell, purchase, distribute, or transport such plants, plant parts, or seeds;

2. Reasonable license fees and duration of licensure, which shall be at least three years;

3. Maintaining relevant information regarding land on which hemp is produced within the state, including the legal description of the land and its latitude and longitude, for a period of not less than three calendar years;

4. The procedure for testing of hemp produced in the state for delta-9 tetrahydrocannabinol levels, using post decarboxylation, other similarly reliable methods, or any other method authorized by the United States department of agriculture;

5. Procedures for effective disposal of hemp plants or products derived from hemp that are produced in violation of this article or its rules and regulations;

6. Procedures for conducting sampling of hemp to verify that hemp is not produced in violation of this article or its rules and regulations;

7. Such other matters that are necessary or appropriate for the state to obtain approval from the United States department of agriculture to assume primary regulatory authority over the production of hemp, pursuant to federal law;

8. Such other matters that are necessary or appropriate for the administration of agricultural pilot programs of the department or institutions of higher education or the regulation of program participants or their activities;

9. Record keeping and any reporting requirements;

10. Reasonably necessary security measures;

11. Standards, practices or requirements for the growth, cultivation and the processing of hemp in connection with its cultivation, as necessary, depending upon the hemp's intended use; or

12. Such other rules and regulations as the commissioner deems appropriate or necessary.

Agriculture and Markets Law § 509. Hemp grower's authorization, license; fees; requirements.

1. No person shall:

(a) grow, cultivate, process, produce, sell or distribute hemp in the state unless authorized by the commissioner as part of an agricultural research pilot program established under this article; or

(b) grow, cultivate and process hemp in connection with its growing and cultivation or sell hemp plants or hemp seed unless licensed by the commissioner. Mere transportation, such as by common carrier or another entity or individual, does not constitute activity subject to licensing under this article.

2. A hemp grower license does not authorize the processing or retail sale of hemp for human consumption, as defined in section thirty-three hundred ninety-eight of the public health law, unless the licensee also obtains a cannabinoid hemp processor license, cannabinoid hemp retailer license, or any other license required pursuant of article thirty-three-B of the public health law.

3. Applications for licenses, authorizations or a modification thereof, as set out in regulation, shall be upon a form specified by the commissioner, accompanied by a reasonable application fee for new applications or significant modifications to an application, which shall be established by regulation and which may be made non-refundable by regulation.

4. The commissioner may also assess a reasonable authorization or licensing fee established by regulation, scaled to cover the estimated, or if known, actual costs of inspections, regulatory testing and other administrative expenses of the authorized or licensed activity, which fee shall be paid prior to the issuance of the authorization or license.

5. The applicant, if an individual, shall be asked to furnish together with the application evidence of his or her good moral character and, if an entity, the applicant shall be asked to furnish together with the application evidence of the good moral character of the individuals who have or will have substantial responsibility for the licensed or authorized activity and those in control of the entity, including principals, officers, or others exercising such control. The names of such individuals shall be set forth in the application.

6. The applicant shall furnish evidence of his, her or its experience and competency, and that the applicant has adequate facilities, equipment, process controls, testing capability and security, to grow, cultivate and process hemp in connection with its growing and cultivation or to sell hemp plants or hemp seed.

7. The department shall provide an application for renewal of any license issued under this article not less than ninety days prior to the expiration of the current license. A renewal application shall be submitted to the commissioner at least thirty days prior to the expiration of the authorization or license, on a form or forms provided by the commissioner for such purpose.

Agriculture and Markets Law § 510. Granting, suspending or revoking licenses.

After due notice and opportunity to be heard, as established by rules and regulations, the commissioner may decline to grant a new license, impose conditions or limits with respect to the grant of a license, modify an existing license or decline to renew a license, or suspend or revoke a license already granted, whenever the commissioner finds that:

1. A material statement contained in an application is or was false or misleading;

2. The applicant or licensee, or a person in a position of management and control thereof or of the licensed activity, does not have good moral character, necessary experience or competency, adequate facilities, equipment, process controls, testing capability or security, to grow, cultivate and process hemp in connection with its growing and cultivation or to sell hemp plants or hemp seed;

3. After appropriate notice and opportunity, the applicant or licensee has failed to produce any records or provide any information required by this article, the rules and regulations promulgated pursuant thereto or demanded by the commissioner, reasonably related to the administration and enforcement of this article;

4. The applicant or licensee, or any officer, director, partner, or other person exercising any position of management or control thereof has willfully failed to comply with any of the provisions of this article or rules and regulations promulgated pursuant thereto or other law of this state applicable to the licensed activity; or

5. The licensee has failed to comply with its compliance action plan established under section five hundred sixteen of this article.

Agriculture and Markets Law § 511. Proceedings to review.

The action of the commissioner in refusing to grant or renew a license, or in revoking or suspending a license, or in conditioning or limiting the granting or renewal of a license, may be reviewed in the manner provided by article seventy-eight of the civil practice law and rules, and the decision of the commissioner shall be final unless within four months from the date of service thereof upon the party affected thereby a court proceeding is instituted to review such action. The pleadings upon which such review proceeding is instituted shall be served in the manner specified in the civil practice law and rules, unless a different manner of service is provided in an order to show cause granted by the supreme court.

Agriculture and Markets Law § 512. Transferability; change in ownership or control.

1. Licenses issued under this article are not transferable, absent written consent of the commissioner.

2. A license shall become void by a change in ownership, substantial corporate change or change of location or acreage grown without prior written approval of the commissioner. The commissioner may promulgate rules and regulations allowing for certain types of changes in ownership without the need for prior written approval.

Agriculture and Markets Law § 513. Access to criminal history information through the division of criminal justice services.

In connection with the administration of this article, the commissioner is authorized to request, receive and review criminal history information through the division of criminal justice services, referred to as "the division" for the purposes of this section, with respect to any person seeking authorization under this article to undertake a hemp pilot project or a hemp license; and/or each individual who has substantial management responsibility for the authorized or licensed activity or those in control of the entity, including principals, officers, or other such persons. Those persons for whom criminal history information is sought shall promptly submit to the division his or her fingerprints in such form and in such manner as specified by the division, for the purpose of conducting a search identifying criminal convictions and pending criminal charges and returning a report thereon in accordance with the procedures and requirements established by the division pursuant to the provisions of article thirty-five of the executive law, which shall include the payment of the specified processing fees for the cost of the division's full search and retain procedures and a national criminal history record check for such information. The commissioner, or his or her designee, shall submit such fingerprints and the processing fee to the division. The division shall forward to the commissioner a report with respect to the person's previous criminal convictions and pending criminal charges, if any, or a statement that the person has no such previous criminal history according to its files. Fingerprints submitted to the division pursuant to this section may also be submitted to the federal bureau of investigation for a national criminal history record check as described in this section. If additional copies of fingerprints are required, the person to be fingerprinted shall furnish them upon request.

Agriculture and Markets Law § 514. Records.

Every licensee shall keep, in such form as the commissioner may direct, such records as may be required pursuant to rules and regulations promulgated pursuant to this article.

Agriculture and Markets Law § 515. Aids to enforcement.

1. All licensees shall be subject to reasonable inspection by the department and a person who holds a license must make himself or herself, or an agent thereof, available and present for any inspection required by the department. The department shall make reasonable accommodations so that ordinary business is not interrupted, and safety and security procedures are not compromised by the inspection.

2. The commissioner may promulgate rules and regulations to aid in the enforcement of this article, provided such enforcement tools, remedies and/or procedures are available to the commissioner for enforcement with respect to similar licensed practices or prohibited conduct under this chapter, and/or the civil practice law and rules.

Agriculture and Markets Law § 516. Compliance action plan.

If the commissioner determines, after notice and an opportunity to be heard, that a licensee has negligently violated a provision of this article or its rules or regulations, that licensee shall be required to comply with a corrective action plan established by the commissioner to correct the violation by a reasonable date and to periodically report to the commissioner with respect to the licensee's compliance for a period of no less than the next two calendar years following the commencement date of the compliance action plan. Notwithstanding the above, this provision shall not be applicable to a research partner conducting hemp research pursuant to a research partner agreement, the terms of which shall control.

Agriculture and Markets Law § 517. Penalties.

Notwithstanding the provisions of any law to the contrary, except section five hundred sixteen of this article, the failure to comply with a requirement of this article, a rule or regulation promulgated thereunder, or the research agreements entered into by those conducting department authorized research may be punishable by a civil penalty of not more than one thousand dollars for a first violation; not more than five thousand dollars for a second violation within three years; and not more than ten thousand dollars for a third violation and each subsequent violation thereafter, within three years.

Agriculture and Markets Law § 518. Remedies.

The commissioner may institute such action at law or in equity as may be necessary to enforce compliance with any provision of this article or of any rule or regulation applicable thereto or promulgated thereunder in a manner consistent with this chapter and/or the civil practice law and rules.

Agriculture and Markets Law § 519. Hemp economic development.

To the extent the commissioner believes it to be necessary, the commissioner shall consult and cooperate with the New York state urban development corporation with respect to the funding and support of research concerning hemp and businesses involved in growing, cultivating, and processing hemp for food, fiber, cannabinoid content, construction materials and other uses.

Agriculture and Markets Law § 520. Hemp data collection and best farming practices.

1. The commissioner shall have the power to collect and publish data and research concerning, among other things, the growth, cultivation, production and processing methods of hemp and products derived from hemp and work with the New York state college of agriculture and life sciences at Cornell pursuant to section fifty-seven hundred twelve of the education law and Cornell cooperative extension pursuant to section two hundred twenty-four of the county law to promote best farming practices for hemp which are compatible with state water quality and other environmental objectives.

2. The department, in conjunction with the department of environmental conservation, shall promulgate all necessary rules and regulations, as well as a process for approval, governing the safe production of hemp, including, but not limited to, environmental and energy standards and restrictions on the use of pesticides.

3. The department shall, to the extent practicable, share data and documentation related to an agricultural research pilot program with the office of cannabis management.

Agriculture and Markets Law § 521. Severability.

If any provision of this article or the application thereof to any person or circumstances is held invalid, such invalidity shall not affect other provisions or applications of the article which can be given effect without the invalid provision or application, and to this end the provisions of this article are declared to be severable.

II. Alcoholic Beverage Control Law

Alcoholic Beverage Control Law § 102. General prohibitions and restrictions.

1. (a) Except as provided in section seventy-nine-c of this chapter, no alcoholic beverages shall be shipped into the state unless the same shall be consigned to a person duly licensed hereunder to traffic in alcoholic beverages. This prohibition shall apply to all shipments of alcoholic beverages into New York state and includes importation or distribution for commercial purposes, for personal use, or otherwise, and irrespective of whether such alcoholic beverages were purchased within or without the state, provided, however, this prohibition shall not apply to any shipment consigned to a New York resident who has personally purchased alcoholic beverages for his personal use while outside the United States for a minimum period of forty-eight consecutive hours and which he has shipped as consignor to himself as consignee. Purchases made outside the United States by persons other than the purchaser himself, regardless whether made as his agent, or by his authorization or on his behalf, are deemed not to have been personally purchased within the meaning of this paragraph.

(b) Except as provided in section seventy-nine-c of this chapter, no common carrier or other person shall bring or carry into the state any alcoholic beverages, unless the same shall be consigned to a person duly licensed hereunder to traffic in alcoholic beverages, provided, however, that alcoholic beverages may be delivered by a trucking permittee from a steamship or railroad station or terminal to a New York resident who has personally purchased alcoholic beverages for his personal use while outside the United States for a minimum period of forty-eight consecutive hours, and which he has shipped as consignor to himself as consignee, and except as so stated, no trucking permittee shall accept for delivery, deliver or transport from a steamship or railroad station or terminal any shipment of alcoholic beverages consigned to a non-licensed person having his home or business in New York state. Purchases of alcoholic beverages made outside the United States by persons other than the purchaser himself, regardless whether made as his agent, or by his authorization or on his behalf, are deemed not to have been personally purchased within the meaning of this paragraph.

(c) Paragraphs (a) and (b) of this subdivision shall apply to alcoholic beverages, either in the original package or otherwise, whether intended for commercial or personal use, as well as otherwise, and to foreign, interstate, as well as intrastate, shipments or carriage, irrespective of whether such alcoholic beverages were purchased within or without the state.

(d) Nothing in this chapter shall be deemed to exempt from taxation the sale or use of any alcoholic beverages subject to any tax imposed under or pursuant to the authority of the tax law or to grant any other exemption from the provisions of such law.

2. No person holding any license hereunder, other than a license to sell an alcoholic beverage at retail for off-premises consumption or a license or special license to sell an alcoholic beverage at retail for consumption on the premises where such license authorizes the sale of liquor, beer and/or wine on the premises of a catering establishment, hotel, restaurant, club, or recreational facility, shall knowingly employ in connection with his business in any capacity whatsoever, any person, who has been convicted of a felony, or any of the following offenses, who has not subsequent to such conviction received an executive pardon therefor removing any civil disabilities incurred thereby, a certificate of relief from disabilities or a certificate of good conduct pursuant to article twenty-three of the correction law, or other relief from disabilities provided by law, or the written approval of the state liquor authority permitting such employment, to wit:

    (a) Illegally using, carrying or possessing a pistol or other dangerous weapon;

    (b) Making or possessing burglar's instruments;

    (c) Buying or receiving or criminally possessing stolen property;

    (d) Unlawful entry of a building;

    (e) Aiding escape from prison;

    (f) Unlawfully possessing or distributing habit forming narcotic drugs;

    (g) Violating subdivisions six, ten or eleven of section seven hundred twenty-two of the former penal law as in force and effect immediately prior to September first, nineteen hundred sixty-seven, or violating sections 165.25 or 165.30 of the penal law;

    (h) Vagrancy or prostitution; or

    (i) Ownership, operation, possession, custody or control of a still subsequent to July first, nineteen hundred fifty-four.

If, as hereinabove provided, the state liquor authority issues its written approval for the employment by a licensee, in a specified capacity, of a person previously convicted of a felony or any of the offenses above enumerated, such person, may, unless he is subsequently convicted of a felony or any of such offenses, thereafter be employed in the same capacity by any other licensee without the further written approval of the authority unless the prior approval given by the authority is terminated.

The liquor authority may make such rules as it deems necessary to carry out the purpose and intent of this subdivision.

As used in this subdivision, "recreational facility" shall mean: (i) premises that are part of a facility the principal business of which shall be the providing of recreation in the form of golf, tennis, swimming, skiing or boating; and (ii) premises in which the principal business shall be the operation of a theatre, concert hall, opera house, bowling establishment, excursion and sightseeing vessel, or accommodation of athletic events, sporting events, expositions and other similar events or occasions requiring the accommodation of large gatherings of persons.

3-a. No licensee or permittee shall purchase or agree to purchase any alcoholic beverages from any person within the state who is not duly licensed to sell such alcoholic beverage as the case may be, at the time of such agreement and sale nor give any order for any alcoholic beverage to any individual who is not the holder of a solicitor's permit, except as provided for in section eighty-five or ninety-nine-g of this chapter.

3-b. No retail licensee shall purchase, agree to purchase or receive any alcoholic beverage except from a person duly licensed within the state by the liquor authority to sell such alcoholic beverage at the time of such agreement and sale to such retail licensee, except as provided for in section eighty-five or ninety-nine-g of this chapter.

4. No licensee or any of his or its agents, servants or employees shall peddle any liquor and/or wine from house to house by means of a truck or otherwise, where the sale is consummated and delivery made concurrently at the residence or place of business of a consumer. This subdivision shall not prohibit the delivery by a licensee to consumers, pursuant to sales made at the place of business of said licensee.

5. No licensee shall employ any canvasser or solicitor for the purpose of receiving an order from a consumer for any liquor and/or wine at the residence or place of business of such consumer, nor shall any licensee receive or accept any order, for the sale of any liquor and/or wine, which shall be solicited at the residence or place of business of a consumer. This subdivision shall not prohibit the solicitation by a wholesaler of an order from any licensee at the licensed premises of such licensee.

6. No alcoholic beverage shall be released for delivery from any warehouse located within the state, except upon a permit having first been obtained as provided by this chapter. Applications for such permits may be filed at the office of the liquor authority in New York, Albany or Buffalo, whichever is nearest to the location of the warehouse, and shall be upon a form to be prepared by the liquor authority. This provision shall not apply to alcoholic beverages, which are to be released for shipment outside of the state.

7. Each person owning or operating any warehouse located within the state shall keep and maintain as part of his permanent records, treasury department forms fifty-two and fifty-two-a as heretofore required by the United States government.

8. No alcoholic beverage retail licensee shall sell cannabis, as defined in section three of the cannabis law, nor have or possess a license or permit to sell cannabis, on the same premises where alcoholic beverages are sold.

III. Cannabis Law

ARTICLE 1. SHORT TITLE; LEGISLATIVE FINDINGS AND INTENT; DEFINITIONS

Cannabis Law § 1. Short title.

This chapter shall be known and may be cited and referred to as the "cannabis law".

Cannabis Law § 2. Legislative findings and intent.

Legislative findings and intent. The legislature finds that existing marihuana laws have not been beneficial to the welfare of the general public. Existing laws have been ineffective in reducing or curbing marihuana use and have instead resulted in devastating collateral consequences including mass incarceration and other complex generational trauma, that inhibit an otherwise law-abiding citizen's ability to access housing, employment opportunities, and other vital services. Existing laws have also created an illicit market which represents a threat to public health and reduces the ability of the legislature to deter the accessing of marihuana by minors. Existing marihuana laws have disproportionately impacted African-American and Latinx communities.

The intent of this act is to regulate, control, and tax marihuana, heretofore known as cannabis, generate significant new revenue, make substantial investments in communities and people most impacted by cannabis criminalization to address the collateral consequences of such criminalization, prevent access to cannabis by those under the age of twenty-one years, reduce the illegal drug market and reduce violent crime, reduce participation of otherwise law-abiding citizens in the illicit market, end the racially disparate impact of existing cannabis laws, create new industries, protect the environment, improve the state's resiliency to climate change, protect the public health, safety and welfare of the people of the state, increase employment and strengthen New York's agriculture sector.

Nothing in this act is intended to limit the authority of any district, government agency or office or employers to enact and enforce policies pertaining to cannabis in the workplace; to allow driving under the influence of cannabis; to allow individuals to engage in conduct that endangers others; to allow smoking cannabis in any location where smoking tobacco is prohibited; or to require any individual to engage in any conduct that violates federal law or to exempt anyone from any requirement of federal law or pose any obstacle to the federal enforcement of federal law.

The legislature further finds and declares that it is in the best interest of the state to regulate medical cannabis, adult-use cannabis, cannabinoid hemp and hemp extracts under independent entities, known as the cannabis control board and the office of cannabis management.

Cannabis Law § 3. Definitions.

Whenever used in this chapter, unless otherwise expressly stated or unless the context or subject matter requires a different meaning, the following terms shall have the representative meanings hereinafter set forth or indicated:

1. "Applicant" unless otherwise specified in this chapter, shall mean a person applying for any cannabis, medical cannabis or cannabinoid hemp license or permit issued by the New York state cannabis control board pursuant to this chapter that: has a significant presence in New York state, either individually or by having a principal corporate location in the state; is incorporated or otherwise organized under the laws of this state; or a majority of the ownership are residents of this state. For the purposes of this subdivision, "person" means an individual, institution, corporation, government or governmental subdivision or agency, business trust, estate, trust, partnership or association, or any other legal entity.

2. "Cannabinoid" means the phytocannabinoids found in hemp and does not include synthetic cannabinoids as that term is defined in subdivision (g) of schedule I of section thirty-three hundred six of the public health law.

3. "Cannabinoid hemp" means any hemp and any product processed or derived from hemp, that is used for human consumption provided that when such product is packaged or offered for retail sale to a consumer, it shall not have a concentration of more than three tenths of a percent delta-9 tetrahydrocannabinol.

4. "Cannabinoid hemp processor license" means a license granted by the office to process, extract, pack or manufacture cannabinoid hemp or hemp extract into products, whether in intermediate or final form, used for human consumption.

5. "Cannabis" means all parts of the plant of the genus Cannabis, whether growing or not; the seeds thereof; the resin

extracted from any part of the plant; and every compound, manufacture, salt, derivative, mixture, or preparation of the plant, its seeds or resin. It does not include the mature stalks of the plant, fiber produced from the stalks, oil or cake made from the seeds of the plant, any other compound, manufacture, salt, derivative, mixture, or preparation of the mature stalks (except the resin extracted therefrom), fiber, oil, or cake, or the sterilized seed of the plant which is incapable of germination. It does not include hemp, cannabinoid hemp or hemp extract as defined by this section or any drug products approved by the federal Food and Drug Administration.

6. "Cannabis consumer" means a person twenty-one years of age or older acting in accordance with any provision of this chapter.

7. "Cannabis control board" or "board" means the New York state cannabis control board created pursuant to article two of this chapter.

8. "Cannabis flower" means the flower of a plant of the genus Cannabis that has been harvested, dried, and cured, prior to any processing whereby the plant material is transformed into a concentrate, including, but not limited to, concentrated cannabis, or an edible or topical product containing cannabis or concentrated cannabis and other ingredients. Cannabis flower excludes leaves and stem.

9. "Cannabis product" or "adult-use cannabis product" means cannabis, concentrated cannabis, and cannabis-infused products for use by a cannabis consumer.

10. "Cannabis-infused products" means products that have been manufactured and contain either cannabis or concentrated cannabis and other ingredients that are intended for use or consumption.

11. "Cannabis trim" means all parts of the plant of the genus Cannabis other than cannabis flower that have been harvested, dried, and cured, but prior to any further processing.

12. "Caring for" means treating a patient, in the course of which the practitioner has completed a full assessment of the patient's medical history and current medical condition.

13. "Certification" means a certification made under this chapter.

14. "Certified medical use" includes the acquisition, cultivation, manufacture, delivery, harvest, possession, preparation, transfer, transportation, or use of medical cannabis for a certified patient, or the acquisition, administration, cultivation, manufacture, delivery, harvest, possession, preparation, transfer, or transportation of medical cannabis by a designated caregiver or designated caregiver facility, or paraphernalia relating to the administration of cannabis, including whole cannabis flower, to treat or alleviate a certified patient's medical condition or symptoms associated with the patient's medical condition.

15. "Certified patient" means a patient who is a resident of New York state or receiving care and treatment in New York state as determined by the board in regulation, and is certified under this chapter.

16. "Chief equity officer" means the chief equity officer of the office of cannabis management.

17. "Concentrated cannabis" means: (a) the separated resin, whether crude or purified, obtained from cannabis; or (b) a material, preparation, mixture, compound or other substance which contains more than three percent by weight or by volume of total THC, as defined in this section.

18. "Condition" means having one of the following conditions: cancer, positive status for human immunodeficiency virus or acquired immune deficiency syndrome, amyotrophic lateral sclerosis, Parkinson's disease, multiple sclerosis, damage to the nervous tissue of the spinal cord with objective neurological indication of intractable spasticity, epilepsy, inflammatory bowel disease, neuropathies, Huntington's disease, post-traumatic stress disorder, pain that degrades health and functional capability where the use of medical cannabis is an alternative to opioid use, substance use disorder, Alzheimer's, muscular dystrophy, dystonia, rheumatoid arthritis, autism or any other condition certified by the practitioner.

19. "Cultivation" means growing, cloning, harvesting, drying, curing, grading, and trimming of cannabis plants for

sale to certain other categories of cannabis license- and permit-holders.

20. "Delivery" means the direct delivery of cannabis products by a retail licensee, microbusiness licensee, or delivery licensee to a cannabis consumer.

21. "Designated caregiver facility" means a facility that registers with the office to assist one or more certified patients with the acquisition, possession, delivery, transportation or administration of medical cannabis and is a: general hospital or residential health care facility operating pursuant to article twenty-eight of the public health law; an adult care facility operating pursuant to title two of article seven of the social services law; a community mental health residence established pursuant to section 41.44 of the mental hygiene law; a hospital operating pursuant to section 7.17 of the mental hygiene law; a mental hygiene facility operating pursuant to article thirty-one of the mental hygiene law; an inpatient or residential treatment program certified pursuant to article thirty-two of the mental hygiene law; a residential facility for the care and treatment of persons with developmental disabilities operating pursuant to article sixteen of the mental hygiene law; a residential treatment facility for children and youth operating pursuant to article thirty-one of the mental hygiene law; a private or public school; research institution with an internal review board; or any other facility as determined by the board in regulation.

22. "Designated caregiver" means an individual designated by a certified patient in a registry application. A certified patient may designate up to five designated caregivers not counting designated caregiver facilities or designated caregiver facilities' employees.

23. "Designated caregiver facility employee" means an employee of a designated caregiver facility.

24. "Distributor" means any person who sells at wholesale any cannabis product, except medical cannabis, for the sale of which a license is required under the provisions of this chapter.

25. "Executive director" means the executive director of the office of cannabis management.

26. "Form of medical cannabis" means characteristics of the medical cannabis recommended or limited for a particular certified patient, including the method of consumption and any particular strain, variety, and quantity or percentage of cannabis or particular active ingredient, or whole cannabis flower.

27. "Hemp" means the plant Cannabis sativa L. and any part of such plant, including the seeds thereof and all derivatives, extracts, cannabinoids, isomers, acids, salts, and salts of isomers, whether growing or not, with a delta-9 tetrahydrocannabinol concentration (THC) of not more than three-tenths of a percent on a dry weight basis. It shall not include "medical cannabis" as defined in this section.

28. "Hemp extract" means all derivatives, extracts, cannabinoids, isomers, acids, salts, and salts of isomers derived from hemp, used or intended for human consumption, for its cannabinoid content, with a delta-9 tetrahydrocannabinol concentration of not more than an amount determined by the office in regulation. For the purpose of this article, hemp extract excludes (a) any food, food ingredient or food additive that is generally recognized as safe pursuant to federal law; or (b) any hemp extract that is not used for human consumption. Such excluded substances shall not be regulated pursuant to the provisions of this article but are subject to other provisions of applicable state law, rules and regulations.

29. "Labor peace agreement" means an agreement between an entity and a labor organization that, at a minimum, protects the state's proprietary interests by prohibiting labor organizations and members from engaging in picketing, work stoppages, boycotts, and any other economic interference with the entity.

30. "Laboratory testing facility" means any independent laboratory capable of testing cannabis and cannabis products for adult-use and medical-use; cannabinoid hemp and hemp extract; or for all categories of cannabis and cannabis products as per regulations set forth by the state cannabis control board.

31. "License" means a written authorization as provided under this chapter permitting persons to engage in a specified activity authorized pursuant to this chapter.

32. "Licensee" means an individual or an entity who has been granted a license under this chapter.

33. "Medical cannabis" means cannabis as defined in this section, intended for a certified medical use, as determined by the board in consultation with the commissioner of health.

34. "Microbusiness" means a licensee that may act as a cannabis producer for the cultivation of cannabis, a cannabis processor, a cannabis distributor and a cannabis retailer under this article; provided such licensee complies with all requirements imposed by this article on licensed producers, processors, distributors and retailers to the extent the licensee engages in such activities.

35. "Nursery" means a licensee that produces only clones, immature plants, seeds, and other agricultural products used specifically for the planting, propagation, and cultivation of cannabis by licensed adult use cannabis cultivators, microbusinesses, cooperatives and registered organizations.

36. "Office" or "office of cannabis management" means the New York state office of cannabis management.

37. "On-site consumption" means the consumption of cannabis in an area licensed as provided for in this chapter.

38. "Package" means any container or receptacle used for holding cannabis or cannabis products.

39. "Permit" means a permit issued pursuant to this chapter.

40. "Permittee" means any person to whom a permit has been issued pursuant to this chapter.

41. "Practitioner" means a practitioner who is licensed, registered or certified by New York state to prescribe controlled substances within the state. Nothing in this chapter shall be interpreted so as to give any such person authority to act outside their scope of practice as defined by title eight of the education law. Additionally, nothing in this chapter shall be interpreted to allow any unlicensed, unregistered, or uncertified person to act in a manner that would require a license, registration, or certification pursuant to title eight of the education law.

42. "Processor" means a licensee that extracts concentrated cannabis and/or compounds, blends, extracts, infuses, or otherwise manufactures concentrated cannabis or cannabis products, but not the cultivation of the cannabis contained in the cannabis product.

43. "Registered organization" means an organization registered under article three of this chapter.

44. "Registry application" means an application properly completed and filed with the board by a certified patient under article three of this chapter.

45. "Registry identification card" means a document that identifies a certified patient or designated caregiver, as provided under this chapter.

46. "Retail sale" means to solicit or receive an order for, to keep or expose for sale, and to keep with intent to sell, made by any licensed person, whether principal, proprietor, agent, or employee, of any cannabis, cannabis product, cannabinoid hemp or hemp extract product to a cannabis consumer for any purpose other than resale.

47. "Retailer" means any person who sells at retail any cannabis product, the sale of which a license is required under the provisions of this chapter.

48. "Small business" means small business as defined in section one hundred thirty-one of the economic development law, and shall apply for purposes of this chapter where any inconsistencies exist.

49. "Smoking" means the burning of a lighted cigar, cigarette, pipe or any other matter or substance which contains cannabis including the use of an electronic smoking device that creates an aerosol or vapor.

50. "Social and economic equity applicant" means an individual or an entity who is eligible for priority licensing pursuant to the criteria established in article four of this chapter.

51. "Terminally ill" means an individual has a medical prognosis that the individual's life expectancy is approximately one year or less if the illness runs its normal course.

52. "THC" means Delta-9-tetrahydrocannabinol; Delta-8-tetrahydrocannabinol; Delta-10-tetrahydrocannabinol and the optical isomer of such substances.

53. "Total THC" means the sum of the percentage by weight or volume measurement of tetrahydrocannabinolic acid multiplied by 0.877, plus, the percentage by weight or volume measurement of THC.

54. "Warehouse" means and includes a place in which cannabis products are securely housed or stored.

55. "Wholesale" means to solicit or receive an order for, to keep or expose for sale, and to keep with intent to sell, made by any licensed person, whether principal, proprietor, agent, or employee of any adult-use, medical-use cannabis or cannabis product, or cannabinoid hemp and hemp extract product for purposes of resale.

ARTICLE 2. NEW YORK STATE CANNABIS CONTROL BOARD

Cannabis Law § 7. Establishment of the cannabis control board or "board".

1. The cannabis control board is hereby created and shall consist of a chairperson nominated by the governor and with the advice and consent of the senate, with one vote, and four other voting board members as provided for in subdivision two of this section.

2. Appointments. In addition to the chairperson, the governor shall have two direct appointments to the board, and the temporary president of the senate and the speaker of the assembly shall each have one direct appointment to the board. Appointments shall be for a term of three years each and should, to the extent possible, be geographically and demographically representative of the state and communities historically affected by the war on drugs. Board members shall be citizens and permanent residents of this state. The chairperson and the remaining members of such board shall continue to serve as chairperson and members of the board until the expiration of the respective terms for which they were appointed. Upon the expiration of such respective terms the successors of such chairperson and members shall be appointed to serve for a term of three years each and until their successors have been appointed and qualified. The members, except for the chairperson, shall when performing the work of the board, be compensated at a rate of two hundred sixty dollars per day, and together with an allowance for actual and necessary expenses incurred in the discharge of their duties. The chairperson shall receive an annual salary not to exceed an amount appropriated therefor by the legislature, and their expenses actually and necessarily incurred in the performance of their official duties, unless otherwise provided by the legislature. No member or member's spouse or minor child shall have any interest in an entity regulated by the board.

3. Expenses. Each member of the board shall be entitled to their expenses actually and necessarily incurred by them in the performance of their duties.

4. Removal. Any member of the board may be removed by the governor for good cause after notice and an opportunity to be heard. A statement of the good cause for their removal shall be filed by the governor in the office of the secretary of state.

5. Vacancies; quorum.

    (A) In the event of a vacancy caused by the death, resignation, removal or inability to perform his or her duties of any board member, the vacancy shall be filled in the manner as the original appointment for the remainder of the unexpired term.

(B)(i) In the event of a vacancy caused by the death, resignation, removal, or inability to act of the chair, the vacancy shall be filled in the same manner as the original appointment for the remainder of the unexpired term. Notwithstanding any other provision of law to the contrary, the governor shall designate one of the remaining board members to serve as acting chairperson for a period not to exceed six months or until a successor chairperson has been confirmed by the senate. Upon the expiration of the six month term, if the governor has nominated a successor chairperson, but the senate has not acted upon the nomination, the acting chairperson can continue to serve as acting chairperson for an additional ninety days or until the governor's successor chairperson nomination is confirmed by the senate, whichever comes first;

(ii) The governor shall provide immediate written notice to the temporary president of the senate and the speaker of the assembly of the designation of a board member as acting chairperson;

(iii) If (a) the governor has not nominated a successor chairperson upon the expiration of the six month term or (b) the senate does not confirm the governor's successor nomination within the additional ninety days, the board member designated as acting chairperson shall no longer be able to serve as acting chairperson and the governor is prohibited from extending the powers of that acting chairperson or from designating another board member to serve as acting chairperson; and

(iv) A board member serving as the acting chairperson of the cannabis control board shall be deemed a state officer for purposes of section seventy-three of the public officers law.

(C) A majority of the voting board members of the board shall constitute a quorum for the purpose of conducting the business thereof and a majority vote of all the members in office shall be necessary for action. Provided, however, that a board member designated as an acting chairperson pursuant to this chapter shall have only one vote for purposes of conducting the business of the cannabis control board.

6. The cannabis control board and office of cannabis management shall have its principal office in the city of Albany, and maintain branch offices in the cities of New York and Buffalo and such other places as it may deem necessary.

The board shall establish appropriate procedures to ensure that hearing officers are shielded from ex parte communications with alleged violators and their attorneys and from other employees of the office of cannabis management and shall take such other steps as it shall deem necessary and proper to shield its judicial processes from unwarranted and inappropriate communications and attempts to influence.

7. Disqualification of members of the board and employees of the office of cannabis management. No member of the board or any officer, deputy, assistant, inspector or employee or spouse or minor child thereof shall have any interest, direct or indirect, either proprietary or by means of any loan, mortgage or lien, or in any other manner, in or on any premises where cannabis is manufactured or sold; nor shall they have any interest, direct or indirect, in any business wholly or partially devoted to the cultivation, manufacture, distribution, sale, transportation or storage of cannabis, or own any stock in any corporation which has any interest, proprietary or otherwise, direct or indirect, in any premises where cannabis or hemp extract is cultivated or manufactured, distributed, or sold, or in any business wholly or partially devoted to the cultivation, manufacture, distribution, sale, transportation or storage of cannabis or hemp extract or receive any commission or profit whatsoever, direct or indirect, from any person applying for or receiving any license or permit provided for in this chapter, or hold any other public office in the state or in any political subdivision except upon the written permission of the board, such member of the board or office of cannabis management or officer, deputy, assistant, inspector or employee thereof may hold the public office of notary public or member of a community board of education in the city school district of the city of New York. Anyone who violates any of the provisions of this section shall be removed.

Cannabis Law § 8. Establishment of an office of cannabis management.

There is hereby established, within the division of alcoholic beverage control, an independent office of cannabis management, which shall have exclusive jurisdiction to exercise the powers and duties provided by this chapter. The office shall exercise its authority by and through an executive director.

Cannabis Law § 9. Executive director.

The office shall exercise its authority, other than powers and duties specifically granted to the board, by and through an executive director nominated by the governor and with the advice and consent of the senate. The executive director shall serve for a term of three years and once confirmed, may only be removed for good cause with appropriate notice. The executive director of the state office of cannabis management shall receive an annual salary not to exceed an amount appropriated therefor by the legislature and his or her expenses actually and necessarily incurred in the performance of his or her official duties, unless otherwise provided by the legislature.

Cannabis Law § 10. Powers and duties of the cannabis control board.

The cannabis control board or "board" shall have the following functions, powers and duties as provided for in this chapter:

1. Discretion to issue or refuse to issue any registration, license or permit provided for in this chapter, as follows: the chairperson, after receiving a recommendation and relevant application information from the office and providing such information to all board members, shall issue a preliminary determination on whether the license, registration or permit shall be granted, denied, or held for further action. Within fourteen days of the chairperson's preliminary determination, any board member may object to the chairperson's preliminary determination, or request the matter be brought before the full board for consideration. Any preliminary determination by the chairperson shall take effect fourteen days after it has been issued by the chairperson, provided that no board member objects or requests the matter be considered by the full board, as adopted by the board through resolution.

2. Sole discretion to limit, or not to limit, the number of registrations, licenses and permits of each class to be issued within the state or any political subdivision thereof, in a manner that prioritizes social and economic equity applicants with the goal of fifty percent awarded to such applicants, and considers small business opportunities and concerns, avoids market dominance in sectors of the industry, and reflects the demographics of the state.

3. Sole discretion to revoke, cancel or suspend for cause any registration, license, or permit issued under this chapter and/or to impose a civil penalty for cause, after notice and an opportunity for a hearing, against any holder of a registration, license, or permit issued pursuant to this chapter.

4. To fix by rule and regulation the standards and requirements of cultivation, processing, packaging, marketing, and sale of medical cannabis, adult-use cannabis and cannabis product, and cannabinoid hemp and hemp extract, including but not limited to, the ability to regulate excipients, and the types, forms, and concentration of products which may be manufactured and/or processed, in order to ensure the health and safety of the public and the use of proper ingredients and methods in the manufacture of all medical, adult-use, cannabinoid hemp and hemp extract to be sold or consumed in the state and to ensure that products are not packaged, marketed, or otherwise sold in a way which targets minors or promotes increased use or cannabis use disorders.

5. To limit or prohibit, at any time of public emergency and without previous notice or advertisement, the cultivation, processing, distribution or sale of any or all cannabis products, medical cannabis or cannabinoid hemp and hemp extract, for and during the period of such emergency.

6. To hold hearings, subpoena witnesses, compel their attendance, administer oaths, to examine any person under oath and in connection therewith to require the production of any books or records relative to the inquiry. A subpoena issued under this section shall be regulated by the civil practice law and rules.

7. To appoint any necessary directors, deputies, counsels, assistants, investigators, and other employees within the limits provided by appropriation. Directors, deputies and counsels, including the chief equity officer, and confidential secretaries to board members shall be in the exempt class of the civil service. The other assistants, investigators and employees of the office shall all be in the competitive class of the civil service and shall be considered for purposes of article fourteen of the civil service law to be public employees of the state, and shall be assigned to the appropriate bargaining unit. Investigators so employed by the office shall be deemed to be peace officers only for the purposes of enforcing the provisions of this chapter or judgments or orders obtained for violation thereof, with all the powers set forth in section 2.20 of the criminal procedure law. Employees transferred to the office shall be transferred without further examination or qualification to the same or similar titles and shall remain in the same collective bargaining units and shall retain their respective civil service classifications, status and rights pursuant to their collective bargaining units and collective bargaining agreements. Employees serving in positions in newly created titles shall be assigned to the appropriate collective bargaining unit as they would have been assigned to were such titles created prior to the establishment of the office of cannabis management. Any action taken under this subdivision shall be subject to and in accordance with the civil service law. The executive director shall appoint a deputy director for health and safety who shall be a licensed health care practitioner within the state and who shall oversee all clinical aspects of the office.

8. To inspect or provide authorization for the inspection at any time of any premises where medical cannabis, adult-use cannabis or cannabinoid hemp and hemp extract is cultivated, processed, stored, distributed or sold.

9. To prescribe forms of applications for registrations, licenses and permits under this chapter and of all reports deemed necessary by the board.

10. To appoint such advisory groups and committees as deemed necessary to provide assistance to the board to carry out the purposes and objectives of this chapter.

11. To exercise the powers and perform the duties in relation to the administration of the board and the office of cannabis management as are necessary but not specifically vested by this chapter, including but not limited to budgetary and fiscal matters.

12. To develop and establish minimum criteria for certifying employees to work in the cannabis industry in positions requiring advanced training and education.

13. To enter into contracts, memoranda of understanding, and agreements as deemed appropriate to effectuate the policy and purpose of this chapter.

14. To advise the office of cannabis management and/or urban development corporation in making low interest or zero-interest loans to qualified social and economic equity applicants as provided for in this chapter.

15. If public health, safety, or welfare imperatively requires emergency action, and incorporates a finding to that effect in an order, summary suspension of a license may be ordered, effective on the date specified in such order or upon service of a certified copy of such order on the licensee, whichever shall be later, pending proceedings for revocation or other action. These proceedings shall be promptly instituted and determined. In addition, the board may be directed to order the administrative seizure of product, issue a stop order, or take any other action necessary to effectuate and enforce the policy and purpose of this chapter.

16. To draft and provide for public comment and issue regulations, declaratory rulings, guidance and industry advisories.

17. To draft and provide an annual report on the effectiveness of this chapter. The annual report shall be prepared, in consultation with the division of the budget, the urban development corporation, the department of taxation and finance, the department of health, department of agriculture and markets, office of addiction services and supports, office of mental health, New York state police, department of motor vehicles and the division of criminal justice services. The report shall provide, but not be limited to, the following information:

(a) the number of registrations, licenses, and permits applied for by geographic region of the state; the number of registrations, licenses, and permits approved or denied by geographic region of the state;

(b) the economic and fiscal impacts associated with this chapter, including revenue from licensing or other fees, fines and taxation related to the cultivation, distribution and sale of cannabis for medical and adult-use and cannabinoid hemp and hemp extract in this state;

(c) specific programs and progress made by the cannabis control board and the office of cannabis management in achieving the goals of the social and economic equity plan, and other social justice goals including, but not limited to, restorative justice, minority- and women-owned businesses, distressed farmers and service disabled veterans;

(d) demographic data on owners and employees in the medical cannabis, adult-use cannabis and cannabinoid hemp and hemp extract industry;

(e) impacts to public health and safety, including substance use disorder;

(f) impacts associated with public safety, including, but not limited to, traffic-related issues, law enforcement, under-age prevention in relation to accessing adult-use cannabis, and efforts to eliminate the illegal market for cannabis products in New York;

(g) any other information or data deemed significant; and

(h) the board shall make recommendations regarding the appropriate level of taxation of adult-use cannabis, as well as changes necessary to: improve registration, licensing and permitting; promoting and encouraging social and economic equity applicants; improve and protect the public health and safety of New Yorkers; improve access and availability for substance abuse treatment programs; and any other recommendations deemed necessary and appropriate. Such report shall be published on the office's website and presented to the governor, the majority leader of the senate and the speaker of the assembly, no later than January first, two thousand twenty-three and annually thereafter.

18. When an administrative decision is appealed to the board by an applicant, registered organization, licensee or permittee, issue a final determination of the office.

19. Approve the opening of new license application periods, and when new or additional licenses are made available pursuant to this chapter, provided, however, that the initial adult-use cannabis retail dispensary license application period shall be opened for all applicants at the same time.

20. Approve any price quotas or price controls set by the executive director as provided by this chapter.

21. Approve the office's social and economic equity plan pursuant to section eighty-four of this chapter.

22. To enter into tribal-state compacts with the New York state Indian nations and tribes, as defined by section two of the Indian law, authorizing such Indian nations or tribes to acquire, possess, manufacture, sell, deliver, transport, distribute or dispense adult-use cannabis and/or medical cannabis.

23. With the exception of promulgating rules and regulations, the board shall have the power to delegate any functions, powers and duties as provided for in this section to the executive director of the office of cannabis management. Any such delegation shall be through a resolution voted on and approved by the board members.

24. The board shall, two years after the first retail sale pursuant to this chapter, review the impact of licenses issued pursuant to article four of this chapter with substantial market share for any category of licensure, to determine if such licensees are impairing the achievement of the goals of inclusion of social equity licensees, fairness for small businesses and distressed farmers, adequate supplies of cannabis and prevention of dominant marketplace participation in the cannabis industry. The board may modify the terms of the licensee's license consistent with the determination and to better achieve those goals. Any such modification may be appealed by the licensee for a formal hearing as provided in section seventeen of this article. For any licensee such review shall include violations of New York state labor law and labor peace agreements. Further, an existing collective bargaining agreement shall not be

infringed or voided by any licensee who after such review suffers from a reduction in market share.

Cannabis Law § 11. Functions, powers and duties of the executive director; office of cannabis management.

The executive director, as authorized by and through this chapter, shall have the following functions, powers and duties as provided for in this chapter:

1. To exercise the powers and perform the duties in relation to the administration of the office of cannabis management as are not specifically vested by this chapter in, or delegated by, the cannabis control board.

2. To keep records in such form as they may prescribe of all registrations, licenses and permits issued and revoked within the state; such records shall be so kept as to provide ready information as to the identity of all licensees including the names of the officers and directors of corporate licensees and the location of all licensed premises. The executive director may contract to furnish copies of the records of licenses and permits of each class and type issued within the state or any political subdivision thereof, for any license or permit year or term of years not exceeding five years.

3. To inspect or provide for the inspection of any premises where medical cannabis, adult-use cannabis, hemp cannabis are manufactured or sold.

4. To prescribe forms of applications for licenses and permits under this chapter and of all reports deemed necessary by the board.

5. To inspect or provide for the inspection of any licensed or permitted premises where medical, adult-use or hemp is cultivated, processed, stored, distributed or sold.

6. To prescribe forms of applications for registrations, licenses and permits under this chapter and of all reports deemed necessary by the board.

7. To delegate the powers provided in this section to such other officers or employees as may be deemed appropriate by the executive director.

8. To exercise the powers and perform the duties as delegated by the board in relation to the administration of the office as are necessary, including but not limited to budgetary and fiscal matters.

9. To enter into contracts, memoranda of understanding, and agreements to effectuate the policy and purpose of this chapter.

10. To advise and assist the board in carrying out any of its functions, powers and duties.

11. To coordinate across state agencies and departments in order to research and study any changes in cannabis use and the impact that cannabis use and the regulated cannabis industry may have on access to cannabis products, public health, and public safety.

12. To issue guidance and industry advisories.

Cannabis Law § 12. Chief equity officer.

The board, by an affirmative vote of at least four members, shall appoint a chief equity officer. The chief equity officer shall receive an annual salary not to exceed an amount appropriated therefor by the legislature and their expenses actually and necessarily incurred in the performance of official duties, unless otherwise provided by the legislature.

1. The chief equity officer shall assist with the development and implementation of, and ensure the cannabis control

board and the office of cannabis management's continued compliance with, the social and economic equity plan, required to be developed pursuant to article four of this chapter.

2. The chief equity officer shall establish public education programming dedicated to providing communities that have been impacted by cannabis prohibition with information detailing the licensing process and informing individuals of the support and resources that the office can provide to individuals and entities interested in participating in activity licensed under this chapter.

3. The chief equity officer shall provide a report to the board, no later than January first, two thousand twenty-three, and annually thereafter, of their activities in ensuring compliance with the social and economic equity plan, required to be developed pursuant to article four of this chapter, and the board shall provide such report to the legislature.

Cannabis Law § 13. Rulemaking authority.

1. The board shall perform such acts, prescribe such forms and propose such rules, regulations and orders as it may deem necessary or proper to fully effectuate the provisions of this chapter.

2. The board shall, in consultation with the executive director and the chief equity officer, have the authority to promulgate any and all necessary rules and regulations governing the cultivation, manufacture, processing, transportation, distribution, testing, delivery, and sale of medical cannabis, adult-use cannabis, and cannabinoid hemp and hemp extract, including but not limited to the registration of organizations authorized to sell medical cannabis, the licensing and/or permitting of adult-use cannabis cultivators, processors, cooperatives, microbusiness, distributors, laboratories, and retailers, and the licensing of cannabinoid hemp and hemp extract producers and processors pursuant to this chapter, including, but not limited to:

   (a) prescribing forms and establishing application, reinstatement, and renewal fees;

   (b) the qualifications and selection criteria for registration, licensing, or permitting;

   (c) the books and records to be created and maintained by all registered organizations, licensees, and permittees, including the reports to be made thereon to the office, and inspection of any and all books and records maintained by any registered organization, licensee, or permittee and on the premises of any registered organization, licensee, or permittee;

   (d) methods of producing, processing, and packaging cannabis, medical cannabis, cannabis-infused products, concentrated cannabis, and cannabinoid hemp and hemp extract; conditions of sanitation, and standards of ingredients, quality, and identity of cannabis products cultivated, processed, packaged, or sold by any registered organizations and licensees;

   (e) security requirements for medical cannabis and adult-use cannabis retail dispensaries and premises where cannabis products, medical cannabis, and cannabinoid hemp and hemp extract, are cultivated, produced, processed, or stored, and safety protocols for registered organizations, licensees and their employees;

   (f) hearing procedures and additional causes for cancellation, suspension, revocation, and/or civil penalties against any person registered, licensed, or permitted by the board; and

   (g) the circumstances, manner and process by which an applicant, registered organization, licensee, or permittee, may apply to change or alter its previously submitted or approved owners, managers, members, directors, financiers, or interest holders.

3. The board shall promulgate rules and regulations that are designed to:

   (a) prevent the distribution of adult-use cannabis or cannabis product to persons under twenty-one years of age, including the modification of tobacco vaping products for use with cannabis;

(b) prevent the revenue from the sale of cannabis from going to criminal enterprises;

(c) prevent the diversion and inversion of cannabis from this state to other states and from other states into this state, insofar as cannabis remains federally prohibited;

(d) prevent cannabis, hemp, cannabinoid hemp and hemp extract activity that is legal under state law from being used as a cover or pretext for the trafficking of other illegal drugs or other illegal activity;

(e) inform the public about the dangers of driving while impaired and the public health consequences associated with the use of cannabis;

(f) prevent the growing of cannabis on public lands;

(g) inform the public about the prohibition on the possession and use of cannabis on federal property; and

(h) establish application, licensing, and permitting processes which ensure all material owners and interest holders are disclosed and that officials or other individuals with control over the approval of an application, permit, or license do not themselves have any interest in an application, license, or permit.

4. The board, in consultation with the department of agriculture and markets and the department of environmental conservation, shall promulgate necessary rules and regulations governing the safe production of cannabis, including environmental and energy standards and restrictions on the use of pesticides and best practices for water and energy conservation.

5. Emergency rules and regulations: In adopting any emergency rule, the board shall comply with the provisions of subdivision six of section two hundred two of the state administrative procedure act and subdivision three of section one hundred one-a of the executive law; provided, however, that notwithstanding the provisions of such laws:

(a) Such emergency rule may remain in effect for no longer than one hundred twenty days, unless within such time the board complies with the provisions of such laws and adopts the rule as a permanent rule;

(b) If, prior to the expiration of a rule adopted pursuant to this paragraph, the board finds that the readoption of such rule on an emergency basis or the adoption of a substantially similar rule on an emergency basis is necessary for the preservation of the public health, safety or general welfare the agency may only readopt the rule on an emergency basis or adopt a substantially similar rule on an emergency basis if on or before the date of such action the board has also submitted a notice of proposed rule making pursuant to subdivision six of section two hundred two of the state administrative procedure act and subdivision three of section one hundred one-a of the executive law. An emergency rule adopted pursuant to this paragraph may remain in effect for no longer than one hundred twenty days;

(c) An emergency rule adopted pursuant to this subdivision or a substantially similar rule adopted on an emergency basis may remain in effect for no longer than one hundred twenty days, but upon the expiration of such one hundred twenty-day period no further readoptions or adoptions of substantially similar rules shall be permitted for a period of one hundred twenty days. Nothing in this subdivision shall preclude the adoption of such rule by submitting a notice of adoption pursuant to subdivision five of section two hundred two of the state administrative procedure act; and

(d) Strict compliance with the provisions of this subdivision shall be required, and any emergency rule or substantially similar rule that does not so comply shall be void and of no legal effect.

6. The board shall have the authority to promulgate regulations governing the appropriate use and licensure of the manufacturing of cannabinoids, or other compounds contained within the cannabis plant, through any method other than planting, growing, cloning, harvesting, or other traditional means of plant agriculture.

Cannabis Law § 14. State cannabis advisory board.

1. The state cannabis advisory board or "advisory board" is established within the office of cannabis management and directed to work in collaboration with the cannabis control board and the executive director to advise and issue recommendations on the use of medical cannabis, adult-use cannabis and cannabinoid hemp and hemp extract in the state of New York, and shall govern and administer the New York state community grants reinvestment fund pursuant to section 99-kk of the state finance law.

2. The state cannabis advisory board shall consist of thirteen voting appointed members, along with a representative from the department of environmental conservation, the department of agriculture and markets, the office of children and family services, the department of labor, the department of health, the division of housing and community renewal, the office of addiction services and supports, and the department of education, serving as non-voting ex-officio members. The governor shall have seven appointments, the temporary president of the senate and the speaker of the assembly shall each have three appointments to the board. The members shall be appointed to each serve three year terms and in the event of a vacancy, the vacancy shall be filled in the manner of the original appointment for the remainder of the term. The appointed members and representatives shall receive no compensation for their services but shall be allowed their actual and necessary expenses incurred in the performance of their duties as board members.

3. Advisory board members shall have statewide geographic representation that is balanced and diverse in its composition. Appointed members shall have an expertise in public and behavioral health, substance use disorder treatment, effective rehabilitative treatment for adults and juveniles, homelessness and housing, economic development, environmental conservation, job training and placement, criminal justice, and drug policy. Further, the advisory board shall include residents from communities most impacted by cannabis prohibition, people with prior drug convictions, the formerly incarcerated, and representatives from the farming industry, cannabis industry, and organizations serving communities impacted by past federal and state drug policies.

4. The chairperson of the advisory board and the vice chairperson shall be elected from among the members of the advisory board by the members of such advisory board. The vice chairperson shall represent the advisory board in the absence of the chairperson at all official advisory board functions.

5. The advisory board shall make recommendations to the cannabis control board, the office and the legislature on cannabis and hemp cultivation, processing, distribution, transport, social and economic equity in the cannabis and hemp industries, criminal justice, public health and safety concerns, law enforcement related to cannabis and cannabis products, and on the testing and sale of cannabis and cannabis products.

6. The advisory board shall meet as frequently as its business may require. The advisory board shall enact and from time to time may amend bylaws in relation to its meetings and the transaction of its business. A majority of the total number of voting members which the board would have were there no vacancies, shall constitute a quorum and shall be required for the board to conduct business. All meetings of the advisory board shall be conducted in accordance with the provisions of article seven of the public officers law.

Cannabis Law § 15. Disposition of moneys received for license fees.

The board shall establish a scale of application, licensing, and renewal fees, based upon the cost of enforcing this chapter and the size of the cannabis business being licensed, as follows:

1. The board shall charge each registered organization, licensee and permittee a registration, licensure or permit fee, and renewal fee, as applicable. The fees may vary depending upon the nature and scope of the different registration, licensure and permit activities.

2. The total fees assessed pursuant to this chapter shall be set at an amount that will generate sufficient total revenue to, at a minimum, fully cover the total costs of administering this chapter.

3. All registration and licensure fees shall be set on a scaled basis by the board, dependent on the size and capacity of the business and for social and economic equity applicants such fees may be assessed to accomplish the goals of this chapter.

4. The board shall deposit all fees collected in the New York state cannabis revenue fund established pursuant to section ninety-nine-ii of the state finance law.

Cannabis Law § 16. Violations of cannabis laws or regulations; penalties and injunctions.

1. Any person who violates, disobeys or disregards any term or provision of this chapter or of any lawful notice, order or regulation pursuant thereto for which a civil or criminal penalty is not otherwise expressly prescribed by law, shall be liable to the people of the state for a civil penalty of not to exceed five thousand dollars for every such violation.

2. The penalty provided for in subdivision one of this section may be recovered by an action brought by the board in any court of competent jurisdiction.

3. Such civil penalty may be released or compromised by the board before the matter has been referred to the attorney general, and where such matter has been referred to the attorney general, any such penalty may be released or compromised and any action commenced to recover the same may be settled and discontinued by the attorney general with the consent of the board.

4. It shall be the duty of the attorney general upon the request of the board to bring an action for an injunction against any person who violates, disobeys or disregards any term or provision of this chapter or of any lawful notice, order or regulation pursuant thereto; provided, however, that the executive director shall furnish the attorney general with such material, evidentiary matter or proof as may be requested by the attorney general for the prosecution of such an action.

5. It is the purpose of this section to provide additional and cumulative remedies, and nothing herein contained shall abridge or alter rights of action or remedies now or hereafter existing, nor shall any provision of this section, nor any action done by virtue of this section, be construed as estopping the state, persons or municipalities in the exercising of their respective rights.

Cannabis Law § 17. Formal hearings; notice and procedure.

1. The board, or any person designated by them for this purpose, may issue subpoenas and administer oaths in connection with any hearing or investigation under or pursuant to this chapter, and it shall be the duty of the board and any persons designated by them for such purpose to issue subpoenas at the request of and upon behalf of the respondent.

2. The board and those designated by them shall not be bound by the laws of evidence in the conduct of hearing proceedings, but the determination shall be founded upon preponderance of evidence to sustain it.

3. Notice and right of hearing as provided in the state administrative procedure act shall be served at least fifteen days prior to the date of the hearing, provided that, whenever because of danger to the public health, safety or welfare it appears prejudicial to the interests of the people of the state to delay action for fifteen days, the board may serve the respondent with an order requiring certain action or the cessation of certain activities immediately or within a specified period of less than fifteen days.

4. Service of notice of hearing or order shall be made by personal service or by registered or certified mail. Where service, whether by personal service or by registered or certified mail, is made upon an incompetent, partnership, or corporation, it shall be made upon the person or persons designated to receive personal service by article three of the

civil practice law and rules.

5. At a hearing, that to the greatest extent practicable shall be reasonably near the respondent, the respondent may appear personally, shall have the right of counsel, and may cross-examine witnesses against him or her and produce evidence and witnesses on his or her behalf.

6. Following a hearing, the board may make appropriate determinations and issue a final order in accordance therewith.

7. The board may adopt, amend and repeal administrative rules and regulations governing the procedures to be followed with respect to hearings, such rules to be consistent with the policy and purpose of this chapter and the effective and fair enforcement of its provisions.

8. The provisions of this section shall be applicable to all hearings held pursuant to this chapter, except where other provisions of this chapter applicable thereto are inconsistent therewith, in which event such other provisions shall apply.

Cannabis Law § 18. Ethics, transparency and accountability.

No member of the board or office or any officer, deputy, assistant, inspector or employee, or spouse or minor child of such member, officer, assistant, inspector or employee thereof shall have any interest, direct or indirect, either proprietary or by means of any loan, mortgage or lien, or in any other manner, in or on any premises where adult-use cannabis, medical cannabis or cannabinoid hemp and hemp extract is cultivated, processed, distributed or sold; nor shall he or she have any interest, direct or indirect, in any business wholly or partially devoted to the cultivation, processing, distribution, sale, transportation or storage of adult-use cannabis, medical cannabis or cannabinoid hemp and hemp extract, or own any stock in any corporation which has any interest, proprietary or otherwise, direct or indirect, in any premises where adult use cannabis, medical cannabis or cannabinoid hemp and hemp extract is cultivated, processed, distributed or sold, or in any business wholly or partially devoted to the cultivation, processing, distribution, sale, transportation or storage of adult-use cannabis, medical cannabis or cannabinoid hemp and hemp extract, or receive any commission or profit whatsoever, direct or indirect, from any person applying for or receiving any license or permit provided for in this chapter, or hold any other elected public office in the state or in any political subdivision. After notice and opportunity to be heard, anyone found to have knowingly violated any of the provisions of this section shall, after notice, be removed and shall divest themselves of such direct or indirect interests, in addition to any other penalty provided by law.

Cannabis Law § 19. Public health and education campaign.

The office, in consultation with the commissioners of the department of health, office of addiction services and supports, and office of mental health, shall develop and implement a comprehensive public health monitoring, surveillance and education campaign regarding the legalization of adult-use cannabis and the impact of cannabis use on public health and safety. The public health and education campaign shall also include general education to the public about the cannabis law.

Cannabis Law § 20. Establish uniform policies and best practices.

The office shall engage in activities with other states, territories, or jurisdictions in order to coordinate and establish uniform policies and best practices in cannabis regulation. These activities shall prioritize coordination with neighboring and regional states, and may include, but not be limited to, establishing working groups related to laboratory testing, product safety, taxation, road safety, compliance and adherence with federal policies which promote or facilitate cannabis research, commerce and/or regulation, and any other issues identified by the executive director.

ARTICLE 3. MEDICAL CANNABIS

Cannabis Law § 30. Certification of patients.

1. A patient certification may only be issued if:

(a) the patient has a condition, which shall be specified in the patient's health care record;

(b) the practitioner by training or experience is qualified to treat the condition;

(c) the patient is under the practitioner's continuing care for the condition; and

(d) in the practitioner's professional opinion and review of past treatments, the patient is likely to receive therapeutic or palliative benefit from the primary or adjunctive treatment with medical use of cannabis for the condition.

2. The certification shall include: (a) the name, date of birth and address of the patient; (b) a statement that the patient has a condition and the patient is under the practitioner's care for the condition; (c) a statement attesting that all requirements of subdivision one of this section have been satisfied; (d) the date; and (e) the name, address, telephone number, and the signature of the certifying practitioner. The board may require by regulation that the certification shall be on a form provided by the office. The practitioner may state in the certification that, in the practitioner's professional opinion, the patient would benefit from medical cannabis only until a specified date. The practitioner may state in the certification that, in the practitioner's professional opinion, the patient is terminally ill and that the certification shall not expire until the patient dies.

3. In making a certification, the practitioner may consider the form of medical cannabis the patient should consume, including the method of consumption and any particular strain, variety, and quantity or percentage of cannabis or particular active ingredient, and appropriate dosage. The practitioner may state in the certification any recommendation or limitation the practitioner makes, in his or her professional opinion, concerning the appropriate form or forms of medical cannabis and dosage.

4. Every practitioner shall consult the prescription monitoring program registry prior to making or issuing a certification, for the purpose of reviewing a patient's controlled substance history. For purposes of this section, a practitioner may authorize a designee to consult the prescription monitoring program registry on his or her behalf, provided that such designation is in accordance with section thirty-three hundred forty-three-a of the public health law.

5. The practitioner shall give the certification to the certified patient, and place a copy in the patient's health care record.

6. No practitioner shall issue a certification under this section for themselves.

7. A registry identification card based on a certification shall expire one year after the date the certification is signed by the practitioner, except as provided for in subdivision eight of this section.

8. (a) If the practitioner states in the certification that, in the practitioner's professional opinion, the patient would benefit from medical cannabis only until a specified earlier date, then the registry identification card shall expire on that date; (b) if the practitioner states in the certification that in the practitioner's professional opinion the patient is terminally ill and that the certification shall not expire until the patient dies, then the registry identification card shall state that the patient is terminally ill and that the registration card shall not expire until the patient dies; (c) if the practitioner re-issues the certification to terminate the certification on an earlier date, then the registry identification card shall expire on that date and shall be promptly destroyed by the certified patient; (d) if

the certification so provides, the registry identification card shall state any recommendation or limitation by the practitioner as to the form or forms of medical cannabis or dosage for the certified patient; and (e) the board shall make regulations to implement this subdivision.

9. (a) A certification may be a special certification if, in addition to the other requirements for a certification, the practitioner certifies in the certification that the patient's condition is progressive and degenerative or that delay in the patient's certified medical use of cannabis poses a risk to the patient's life or health.

(b) The office shall create the form to be used for a special certification and shall make that form available to be downloaded from the office's website.

10. Prior to issuing a certification a practitioner must complete, at a minimum, a two-hour course as determined by the board in regulation. For the purposes of this article a person's status as a practitioner is deemed to be a "license" for the purposes of section thirty-three hundred ninety of the public health law and shall be subject to the same revocation process.

Cannabis Law § 31. Lawful medical use.

The possession, acquisition, use, delivery, transfer, transportation, or administration of medical cannabis by a certified patient, designated caregiver or the employees of a designated caregiver facility, for certified medical use, shall be lawful under this article provided that:

1. the cannabis that may be possessed by a certified patient shall not exceed a sixty-day supply of the dosage determined by the practitioner, consistent with any guidance and regulations issued by the board, provided that during the last seven days of any sixty-day period, the certified patient may also possess up to such amount for the next sixty-day period;

2. the cannabis that may be possessed by designated caregivers does not exceed the quantities referred to in subdivision one of this section for each certified patient for whom the caregiver possesses a valid registry identification card, up to four certified patients;

3. the cannabis that may be possessed by designated caregiver facilities does not exceed the quantities referred to in subdivision one of this section for each certified patient under the care or treatment of the facility;

4. the form or forms of medical cannabis that may be possessed by the certified patient, designated caregiver or designated caregiver facility pursuant to a certification shall be in compliance with any recommendation or limitation by the practitioner as to the form or forms of medical cannabis or dosage for the certified patient in the certification;

5. the medical cannabis shall be kept in the original package in which it was dispensed under this article, except for the portion removed for immediate consumption for certified medical use by the certified patient; and

6. in the case of a designated caregiver facility, the employee assisting the patient has been designated as such by the designated caregiver facility.

Cannabis Law § 32. Registry identification cards.

1. Upon approval of the certification, the office shall issue registry identification cards for certified patients and designated caregivers. A registry identification card shall expire as provided in this article or as otherwise provided in this section. The office shall begin issuing registry identification cards as soon as practicable after the certifications required by this chapter are granted. The office may specify a form for a registry application, in which case the office shall provide the form on request, reproductions of the form may be used, and the form shall be available for downloading from the board's or office's website.

2. To obtain, amend or renew a registry identification card, a certified patient or designated caregiver shall file a registry application with the office, unless otherwise exempted by the board in regulation. The registry application or renewal application shall include:

(a) in the case of a certified patient:

(i) the patient's certification, a new written certification shall be provided with a renewal application if required by the office;

(ii) the name, address, and date of birth of the patient;

(iii) the date of the certification;

(iv) if the patient has a registry identification card based on a current valid certification, the registry identification number and expiration date of that registry identification card;

(v) the specified date until which the patient would benefit from medical cannabis, if the certification states such a date;

(vi) the name, address, and telephone number of the certifying practitioner;

(vii) any recommendation or limitation by the practitioner as to the form or forms of medical cannabis or dosage for the certified patient;

(viii) if the certified patient designates a designated caregiver, the name, address, and date of birth of the designated caregiver, and other individual identifying information required by the board;

(ix) if the designated caregiver is a cannabis research license holder under this chapter, the name of the organization conducting the research, the address, phone number, name of the individual leading the research or appropriate designee, and other identifying information required by the board; and

(x) other individual identifying information required by the office;

(b) in the case of a designated caregiver:

(i) the name, address, and date of birth of the designated caregiver;

(ii) if the designated caregiver has a registry identification card, the registry identification number and expiration date of that registry identification card; and

(iii) other individual identifying information required by the office;

(c) a statement that a false statement made in the application is punishable under section 210.45 of the penal law;

(d) the date of the application and the signature of the certified patient or designated caregiver, as the case may be;

(e) any other requirements determined by the board.

3. Where a certified patient is under the age of eighteen or otherwise incapable of consent:

(a) The application for a registry identification card shall be made by the person responsible for making health care decisions for the patient.

(b) The designated caregiver shall be: (i) a parent or legal guardian of the certified patient; (ii) a person designated by a parent or legal guardian; (iii) an employee of a designated caregiver facility, including a cannabis research license holder; or (iv) an appropriate person approved by the office upon a sufficient showing that no parent or legal guardian is appropriate or available.

4. No person may be a designated caregiver if the person is under twenty-one years of age unless a sufficient showing is made to the office that the person should be permitted to serve as a designated caregiver. The requirements for such a showing shall be determined by the board.

5. No person may be a designated caregiver for more than four certified patients at one time; provided, however, that this limitation shall not apply to a designated caregiver facility, or cannabis research license holder as defined by this chapter.

6. If a certified patient wishes to change or terminate his or her designated caregiver, for whatever reason, the certified patient shall notify the office as soon as practicable. The office shall issue a notification to the designated caregiver that their registration card is invalid and must be promptly destroyed. The newly designated caregiver must comply with all requirements set forth in this section.

7. If the certification so provides, the registry identification card shall contain any recommendation or limitation by the practitioner as to the form or forms of medical cannabis or dosage for the certified patient.

8. The office shall issue separate registry identification cards for certified patients and designated caregivers as soon as reasonably practicable after receiving a complete application under this section, unless it determines that the application is incomplete or factually inaccurate, in which case it shall promptly notify the applicant.

9. If the application of a certified patient designates an individual as a designated caregiver who is not authorized to be a designated caregiver, that portion of the application shall be denied by the office but that shall not affect the approval of the balance of the application.

10. A registry identification card shall:

(a) contain the name of the certified patient or the designated caregiver as the case may be;

(b) contain the date of issuance and expiration date of the registry identification card;

(c) contain a registry identification number for the certified patient or designated caregiver, as the case may be and a registry identification number;

(d) contain a photograph of the individual to whom the registry identification card is being issued, which shall be obtained by the office in a manner specified by the board in regulations; provided, however, that if the office requires certified patients to submit photographs for this purpose, there shall be a reasonable accommodation of certified patients who are confined to their homes due to their medical conditions and may therefore have difficulty procuring photographs;

(e) be a secure document as determined by the board;

(f) plainly state any recommendation or limitation by the practitioner as to the form or forms of medical cannabis or dosage for the certified patient; and

(g) any other requirements determined by the board.

11. A certified patient or designated caregiver who has been issued a registry identification card shall notify the office of any change in his or her name or address or, with respect to the patient, if he or she ceases to have the condition noted on the certification within ten days of such change. The certified patient's or designated caregiver's registry identification card shall be deemed invalid and shall be promptly destroyed.

12. If a certified patient or designated caregiver loses his or her registry identification card, he or she shall notify the office within ten days of losing the card. The office shall issue a new registry identification card as soon as practicable, which may contain a new registry identification number, to the certified patient or designated caregiver, as the case may be.

13. The office shall maintain a confidential list of the persons to whom it has issued registry identification cards.

Individual identifying information obtained by the office under this article shall be confidential and exempt from disclosure under article six of the public officers law.

14. The board shall verify to law enforcement personnel in an appropriate case whether a registry identification card is valid and any other relevant information necessary to protect patients' rights to medical cannabis by confirming compliance with this article.

15. If a certified patient or designated caregiver willfully violates any provision of this article as determined by the board, his or her certification and registry identification card may be suspended or revoked. This is in addition to any other penalty that may apply.

16. The board shall make regulations for special certifications, which shall include expedited procedures and which may require the applicant to submit additional documentation establishing the clinical basis for the special certification. If the board has not established and made available a form for a registry application or renewal application, then in the case of a special certification, a registry application or renewal application that otherwise conforms with the requirements of this section shall not require the use of a form.

Cannabis Law § 33. Registration as a designated caregiver facility.

1. To obtain, amend or renew a registration as a designated caregiver facility, the facility shall file a registry application with the office. The registry application or renewal application shall include:

> (a) the facility's full name and address;

> (b) operating certificate or license number where appropriate;

> (c) name, title, and signature of an authorized facility representative;

> (d) a statement that the facility agrees to secure and ensure proper handling of all medical cannabis products;

> (e) an acknowledgement that a false statement in the application is punishable under section 210.45 of the penal law; and

> (f) any other information that may be required by the board.

2. Prior to issuing or renewing a designated caregiver facility registration, the office may verify the information submitted by the applicant. The applicant shall provide, at the office's request, such information and documentation, including any consents or authorizations that may be necessary for the office to verify the information.

3. The office shall approve, deny or determine incomplete or inaccurate an initial or renewal application within thirty days of receipt of the application. If the application is approved within the thirty-day period, the office shall issue a registration as soon as is reasonably practicable.

4. An applicant shall have thirty days from the date of a notification of an incomplete or factually inaccurate application to submit the materials required to complete, revise or substantiate information in the application. If the applicant fails to submit the required materials within such thirty-day time period, the application shall be denied by the office.

5. Registrations issued under this section shall remain valid for two years from the date of issuance.

Cannabis Law § 34. Registered organizations.

1. A registered organization shall be a for-profit business entity or not-for-profit corporation organized for the

purpose of acquiring, possessing, manufacturing, selling, delivering, transporting, distributing or dispensing cannabis for certified medical use.

2. The acquiring, possession, manufacture, sale, delivery, transporting, distributing or dispensing of medical cannabis by a registered organization under this article in accordance with its registration under this article or a renewal thereof shall be lawful under this chapter.

3. Each registered organization shall contract with an independent laboratory permitted by the board to test the medical cannabis produced by the registered organization. The board shall approve the laboratories used by the registered organization, including sampling and testing protocols and standards used by the laboratories, and may require that the registered organization use a particular testing laboratory. The board is authorized to issue regulations requiring the laboratory to perform certain tests and services.

4. (a) A registered organization may lawfully, in good faith, sell, deliver, distribute or dispense medical cannabis to a certified patient or designated caregiver upon presentation to the registered organization of a valid registry identification card for that certified patient or designated caregiver. When presented with the registry identification card, the registered organization shall provide to the certified patient or designated caregiver a receipt, which shall state: the name, address, and registry identification number of the registered organization; the name and registry identification number of the certified patient and the designated caregiver, if any; the date the cannabis was sold; any recommendation or limitation by the practitioner as to the form or forms of medical cannabis or dosage for the certified patient; and the form and the quantity of medical cannabis sold. The registered organization shall retain a copy of the registry identification card and the receipt for six years and shall make such records available to the office.

(b) The proprietor of a registered organization shall file or cause to be filed any receipt and certification information with the office by electronic means on a real-time basis as the board shall require by regulation. When filing receipt and certification information electronically pursuant to this paragraph, the proprietor of the registered organization shall dispose of any electronically recorded prescription information in such manner as the board shall by regulation require.

5. (a) No registered organization may sell, deliver, distribute or dispense to any certified patient or designated caregiver a quantity of medical cannabis larger than that individual would be allowed to possess under this chapter.

(b) When dispensing medical cannabis to a certified patient or designated caregiver, the registered organization: (i) shall not dispense an amount greater than a sixty-day supply to a certified patient until the certified patient has exhausted all but a seven day supply provided pursuant to a previously issued certification; and (ii) shall verify the information in subparagraph (i) of this paragraph by consulting the prescription monitoring program registry under this article.

(c) Medical cannabis dispensed to a certified patient or designated caregiver by a registered organization shall conform to any recommendation or limitation by the practitioner as to the form or forms of medical cannabis or dosage for the certified patient.

6. When a registered organization sells, delivers, distributes or dispenses medical cannabis to a certified patient or designated caregiver, it shall provide to that individual a safety insert, developed by the registered organization subject to regulations issued by the board and include, but not be limited to, information on:

    (a) methods for administering medical cannabis,

    (b) any potential dangers stemming from the use of medical cannabis,

    (c) how to recognize what may be problematic usage of medical cannabis and obtain appropriate services or treatment for problematic usage, and

    (d) other information as determined by the board.

7. Registered organizations shall not be managed by or employ anyone who has been convicted within three years of the date of hire, of any felony related to the functions or duties of operating a business, except that if the board determines that the manager or employee is otherwise suitable to be hired, and hiring the manager or employee would not compromise public safety, the board shall conduct a thorough review of the nature of the crime, conviction, circumstances, and evidence of rehabilitation of the manager or employee, and shall evaluate the suitability of the manager or employee based on the evidence found through the review. In determining which offenses are substantially related to the functions or duties of operating a business, the board shall include, but not be limited to, the following:

> (a) a felony conviction involving fraud, money laundering, forgery and other unlawful conduct related to owning and operating a business; and

> (b) a felony conviction for hiring, employing or using a minor in transporting, carrying, selling, giving away, preparing for sale, or peddling, any controlled substance, or selling, offering to sell, furnishing, offering to furnish, administering, or giving any controlled substance to a minor.

A felony conviction for the sale or possession of drugs, narcotics, or controlled substances is not substantially related. This subdivision shall only apply to managers or employees who come into contact with or handle medical cannabis.

8. Manufacturing of medical cannabis by a registered organization shall only be done in a secure facility located in New York state, which may include a greenhouse. The board shall promulgate regulations establishing requirements for such facilities.

9. Dispensing of medical cannabis by a registered organization shall only be done in an indoor, enclosed, secure facility located in New York state. The board shall promulgate regulations establishing requirements for such facilities.

10. A registered organization may contract with a person or entity to provide facilities, equipment or services that are ancillary to the registered organization's functions or activities under this article including, but not limited to, shipping, maintenance, construction, repair, and security, provided that the person or entity shall not perform any function or activity directly involving the planting, growing, tending, harvesting, processing, or packaging of cannabis plants, medical cannabis, or medical cannabis products being produced by the registered organization; or any other function directly involving manufacturing or retailing of medical cannabis. All laws and regulations applicable to such facilities, equipment, or services shall apply to the contract. The registered organization and other parties to the contract shall each be responsible for compliance with such laws and regulations under the contract. The board may make regulations consistent with this article relating to contracts and parties to contracts under this subdivision.

11. A registered organization shall, based on the findings of an independent laboratory, provide documentation of the quality, safety and clinical strength of the medical cannabis manufactured or dispensed by the registered organization to the office and to any person or entity to which the medical cannabis is sold or dispensed.

12. A registered organization shall be deemed to be a "health care provider" for the purposes of title two-D of article two of the public health law.

13. Medical cannabis shall be dispensed to a certified patient or designated caregiver in a sealed and properly labeled package. The labeling shall contain: (a) the information required to be included in the receipt provided to the certified patient or designated caregiver by the registered organization; (b) the packaging date; (c) any applicable date by which the medical cannabis should be used; (d) a warning stating, "This product is for medicinal use only. Women should not consume during pregnancy or while breastfeeding except on the advice of the certifying health care practitioner, and in the case of breastfeeding mothers, including the infant's pediatrician. This product might impair the ability to drive. Keep out of reach of children."; (e) the amount of individual doses contained within; and (f) a warning that the medical cannabis must be kept in the original container in which it was dispensed.

14. The board is authorized to make rules and regulations restricting the advertising and marketing of medical

cannabis.

15. A registered organization shall operate in accordance with minimum operating and recordkeeping requirements determined by the board in regulation.

Cannabis Law § 35. Registering of registered organizations.

1. (a) An applicant for registration as a registered organization under section thirty-four of this article shall include such information prepared in such manner and detail as the board may require, including but not limited to:

(i) a description of the activities in which it intends to engage as a registered organization;

(ii) that the applicant:

(A) is of good moral character;

(B) possesses or has the right to use sufficient land, buildings, and other premises, which shall be specified in the application, and equipment to properly carry on the activity described in the application, or in the alternative posts a bond of not less than two million dollars;

(C) is able to maintain effective security and control to prevent diversion, abuse, and other illegal conduct relating to the cannabis; and

(D) is able to comply with all applicable state laws and regulations relating to the activities in which it intends to engage under the registration;

(iii) that the applicant has entered into a labor peace agreement with a bona fide labor organization that is actively engaged in representing or attempting to represent the applicant's employees and the maintenance of such a labor peace agreement shall be an ongoing material condition of certification;

(iv) the applicant's status as a for-profit business entity or not-for-profit corporation; and

(v) the application shall include the name, residence address and title of each of the officers and directors and the name and residence address of any person or entity that is a member of the applicant. Each such person, if an individual, or lawful representative if a legal entity, shall submit an affidavit with the application setting forth:

(A) any position of management, interest or ownership during the preceding ten years of a ten per centum or greater interest in any other cannabis business, or applicant, located in or outside this state, manufacturing or distributing drugs including indirect management, interest, or ownership of parent companies, subsidiaries, or affiliates;

(B) whether such person or any such business has been convicted of a felony or had a registration or license suspended or revoked in any administrative or judicial proceeding, and if applicable, the history of violations or administrative penalties with respect to any license to cultivate, manufacture, distribute or sell adult-use cannabis or medical cannabis; and

(C) such other information as the board may reasonably require.

2. The applicant shall be under a continuing duty to report to the office any change in facts or circumstances reflected in the application or any newly discovered or occurring fact or circumstance which is required to be included in the application.

3. (a) The board shall grant a registration or amendment to a registration under this section if they are satisfied that:

(i) the applicant will be able to maintain effective control against diversion of cannabis;

(ii) the applicant will be able to comply with all applicable state laws;

(iii) the applicant and its officers are ready, willing and able to properly carry on the manufacturing or distributing activity for which a registration is sought;

(iv) the applicant possesses or has the right to use sufficient land, buildings and equipment to properly carry on the activity described in the application;

(v) it is in the public interest that such registration be granted, including but not limited to:

(A) whether the number of registered organizations in an area will be adequate or excessive to reasonably serve the area;

(B) whether the registered organization is a minority and/or woman owned business enterprise, a service-disabled veteran-owned business, or from communities disproportionally impacted by the enforcement of cannabis prohibition;

(C) whether the registered organization provides education and outreach to practitioners;

(D) whether the registered organization promotes the research and development of medical cannabis and patient outreach;

(E) the affordability of medical cannabis products offered by the registered organization;

(F) whether the registered organization is culturally, linguistically, and medically competent to provide services to unserved and underserved areas; and

(G) whether the registered organization promotes racial, ethnic, and gender diversity in their workforce;

(vi) the applicant and its managing officers are of good moral character;

(vii) the applicant has entered into a labor peace agreement with a bona fide labor organization that is actively engaged in representing or attempting to represent the applicant's employees; and the maintenance of such a labor peace agreement shall be an ongoing material condition of registration; and

(viii) the applicant satisfies any other conditions as determined by the board.

(b) If the board is not satisfied that the applicant should be issued a registration, he or she shall notify the applicant in writing of those factors upon which further evidence is required. Within thirty days of the receipt of such notification, the applicant may submit additional material to the board or demand a hearing, or both.

(c) The fee for a registration under this section shall be an amount determined by the board in regulations; provided, however, if the registration is issued for a period greater than two years the fee shall be increased, pro rata, for each additional month of validity.

(d) Registrations issued under this section shall be effective only for the registered organization and shall specify:

(i) the name and address of the registered organization;

(ii) which activities of a registered organization are permitted by the registration;

(iii) the land, buildings and facilities that may be used for the permitted activities of the registered organization; and

(iv) such other information as the board shall reasonably provide to assure compliance with this article.

(e) Upon application of a registered organization, a registration may be amended to allow the registered organization to relocate within the state or to add or delete permitted registered organization activities or facilities. The fee for such amendment shall be determined by the board in regulation and be based off the administrative burden to process and review the amendment by the office, provided no fee shall be greater than two thousand dollars.

4. A registration issued under this section shall be valid for two years from the date of issue, except that in order to facilitate the renewals of such registrations, the board may upon the initial application for a registration, issue some registrations which may remain valid for a period of time greater than two years but not exceeding an additional eleven months.

5. (a) An application for the renewal of any registration issued under this section shall be filed with the board not more than six months nor less than four months prior to the expiration thereof. A late-filed application for the renewal of a registration may, in the discretion of the board, be treated as an application for an initial license.

(b) The application for renewal shall include such information prepared in the manner and detail as the board may require, including but not limited to:

(i) any material change in the circumstances or factors listed in subdivision one of this section; and

(ii) every known charge or investigation, pending or concluded during the period of the registration, by any governmental or administrative agency with respect to:

(A) each incident or alleged incident involving the theft, loss, or possible diversion of medical cannabis manufactured or distributed by the applicant; and

(B) compliance by the applicant with the laws of the state with respect to the cultivation, manufacture, distribution, or sale of medical cannabis or adult-use cannabis, where applicable.

(c) An applicant for renewal shall be under a continuing duty to report to the board any change in facts or circumstances reflected in the application or any newly discovered or occurring fact or circumstance which is required to be included in the application and to obtain approval prior to any material change in management, interest or ownership.

(d) If the board is not satisfied that the registered organization applicant is entitled to a renewal of the registration, the board shall within a reasonably practicable time as determined by the executive director, serve upon the registered organization or its attorney of record in person or by registered or certified mail an order directing the registered organization to show cause why its application for renewal should not be denied. The order shall specify in detail the respects in which the applicant has not satisfied the board that the registration should be renewed.

(e) Within a reasonably practicable time as determined by the board of such order, the applicant may submit additional material to the board or demand a hearing or both; if a hearing is demanded the board shall fix a date as soon as reasonably practicable.

6. (a) The board shall renew a registration unless he or she determines and finds that:

(i) the applicant is unlikely to maintain or be able to maintain effective control against diversion;

(ii) the applicant is unlikely to comply with all state laws applicable to the activities in which it may engage under the registration;

(iii) it is not in the public interest to renew the registration because the number of registered organizations in an area is excessive to reasonably serve the area;

(iv) the applicant has either violated or terminated its labor peace agreement; or

(v) the applicant has substantively violated the laws of another jurisdiction, in which they operate or have operated a cannabis license or registration, related to the operation of a cannabis business.

(b) For purposes of this section, proof that a registered organization, during the period of its registration, has failed to maintain effective control against diversion, violates any provision of this article, or has knowingly or negligently failed to comply with applicable state laws relating to the activities in which it engages under the registration, may constitute grounds for suspension, termination or limitation of the registered organization's registration or as determined by the board. The registered organization shall also be under a continuing duty to report to the office any material change or fact or circumstance to the information provided in the registered organization's application.

7. The board may suspend or terminate the registration of a registered organization, on grounds and using procedures under this article relating to a license, to the extent consistent with this article. The board shall suspend or terminate the registration in the event that a registered organization violates or terminates the applicable labor peace agreement. Conduct in compliance with this article which may violate conflicting federal law, shall not be grounds to suspend or terminate a registration.

8. A registered organization that manufactures medical cannabis may have no more than four dispensing sites wholly owned and operated by such registered organization. Such registered organization may have an additional four dispensing sites; provided, however, that the first two additional dispensing sites shall be located in underserved or unserved geographic locations, as determined by the board. The board shall ensure that such registered organizations and dispensing sites are geographically distributed across the state and that their ownership reflects the demographics of the state.

9. In coordination with the chief equity officer the board shall register additional registered organizations to provide services to unserved and underserved areas of the state. Pursuant to the social and economic equity plan established by section eighty-seven of this chapter, those additional registered organizations shall be reflective of the demographics of the state, be representative of communities disproportionately impacted by cannabis prohibition, and be culturally, linguistically, and medically competent to serve unserved and underserved areas of the state. The board shall actively promote racial, ethnic, and gender diversity when registering additional registered organizations.

Cannabis Law § 36. Reports of registered organizations.

1. The board shall, by regulation, require each registered organization to file reports by the registered organization during a particular period. The board shall determine the information to be reported and the forms, time, and manner of the reporting.

2. The board shall, by regulation, require each registered organization to adopt and maintain security, tracking, record keeping, record retention and surveillance systems, relating to all medical cannabis at every stage of acquiring, possession, manufacture, sale, delivery, transporting, distributing, or dispensing by the registered organization, subject to regulations of the board.

Cannabis Law § 37. Evaluation; research programs; report by board.

1. The board may provide for the analysis and evaluation of the operation of this article. The board may enter into agreements with one or more persons, not-for-profit corporations or other organizations, for the performance of an evaluation of the implementation and effectiveness of this article.

2. The board may develop, seek any necessary federal approval for, and carry out research programs relating to medical use of cannabis. Participation in any such research program shall be voluntary on the part of practitioners, patients, and designated caregivers.

3. The board shall report every two years, beginning two years after the effective date of this article, to the governor and the legislature on the medical use of cannabis under this article and make appropriate recommendations.

Cannabis Law § 38. Cannabis research license.

1. The board shall establish a cannabis research license that permits a licensee to produce, process, purchase and/or possess cannabis for the following limited research purposes:

(a) to test chemical potency and composition levels;

(b) to conduct clinical investigations of cannabis-derived drug products;

(c) to conduct research on the efficacy and safety of administering cannabis as part of medical treatment; and

(d) to conduct genomic or agricultural research.

2. As part of the application process for a cannabis research license, an applicant must submit to the board a description of the research that is intended to be conducted as well as the amount of cannabis to be grown or purchased. The board shall review an applicant's research project and determine whether it meets the requirements of subdivision one of this section. In addition, the board shall assess the application based on the following criteria:

(a) project quality, study design, value, and impact;

(b) whether the applicant has the appropriate personnel, expertise, facilities and infrastructure, funding, and human, animal, or other approvals in place to successfully conduct the project; and

(c) whether the amount of cannabis to be grown or purchased by the applicant is consistent with the project's scope and goals. If the office determines that the research project does not meet the requirements of subdivision one of this section, the application must be denied.

3. A cannabis research licensee may only sell cannabis grown or within its operation to other cannabis research licensees. The board may revoke a cannabis research license for violations of this section.

4. A cannabis research licensee may contract with an institution of higher education, including but not limited to a hospital within the state university of New York, to perform research in conjunction with such institution. All research projects, entered into under this section must be approved by the board and meet the requirements of subdivision one of this section.

5. In establishing a cannabis research license, the board may adopt regulations on the following:

(a) application requirements;

(b) cannabis research license renewal requirements, including whether additional research projects may be added or considered;

(c) conditions for license revocation;

(d) security measures to ensure cannabis is not diverted to purposes other than research;

(e) amount of plants, useable cannabis, cannabis concentrates, or cannabis-infused products a licensee may have on its premises;

(f) licensee reporting requirements;

(g) conditions under which cannabis grown by licensed cannabis producers and other product types from licensed cannabis processors may be donated to cannabis research licensees; and

(h) any additional requirements deemed necessary by the board.

6. A cannabis research license issued pursuant to this section must be issued in the name of the applicant and specify the location at which the cannabis researcher intends to operate, which must be within the state of New York.

7. The application fee for a cannabis research license shall be determined by the board on an annual basis and may be based on the size, scope and duration of the research proposed.

8. Each cannabis research licensee shall issue an annual report to the board. The board shall review such report and make a determination as to whether the research project continues to meet the research qualifications under this section.

Cannabis Law § 39. Registered organizations and adult-use cannabis.

The board shall have the authority to grant some or all of the registered organizations registered with the department of health and currently registered and in good standing with the office, the ability to obtain adult-use cannabis licenses pursuant to article four of this chapter subject to any fees, rules or conditions prescribed by the board in regulation.

Cannabis Law § 40. Relation to other laws.

1. The provisions of this article shall apply, except that where a provision of this article conflicts with another provision of this chapter, this article shall apply.

2. Medical cannabis shall not be deemed to be a "drug" for purposes of article one hundred thirty-seven of the education law.

Cannabis Law § 41. Home cultivation of medical cannabis.

Certified patients twenty-one years of age or older may cultivate cannabis for personal use. Designated caregivers twenty-one years of age or older, caring for certified patients either younger than twenty-one years of age or whose physical or cognitive impairments prevent them from cultivating cannabis, may cultivate cannabis for use by such patients, provided that no other caregiver is growing for said patient or patients. All cultivation under this section shall be in accordance with section 222.15 of the penal law and any regulations made by the board, provided that the maximum number of cannabis plants a designated caregiver is authorized to grow is proportionately increased for each patient they are growing for.

Cannabis Law § 42. Protections for the medical use of cannabis.

1. Certified patients, designated caregivers, designated caregiver facilities and employees of designated caregiver facilities, practitioners, registered organizations and the employees of registered organizations, and cannabis researchers shall not be subject to arrest, prosecution, or penalty in any manner, or denied any right or privilege, including but not limited to civil penalty or disciplinary action by a business or occupational or professional licensing board or bureau, solely for the certified medical use or manufacture of cannabis, or for any other action or conduct in accordance with this article.

2. Being a certified patient shall be deemed to be having a "disability" under article fifteen of the executive law, section forty-c of the civil rights law, sections 240.00, 485.00, and 485.05 of the penal law, and section 200.50 of the criminal procedure law. This subdivision shall not bar the enforcement of a policy prohibiting an employee from performing his or her employment duties while impaired by a controlled substance. This subdivision shall not require any person or entity to do any act that would put the person or entity in direct violation of federal law or cause it to lose a federal contract or funding.

3. The fact that a person is a certified patient and/or acting in accordance with this article, shall not be a consideration in a proceeding pursuant to applicable sections of the domestic relations law, the social services law

and the family court act.

4. (a) Certification applications, certification forms, any certified patient information contained within a database, and copies of registry identification cards shall be deemed exempt from public disclosure under sections eighty-seven and eighty-nine of the public officers law. Upon specific request by a certified patient to the office, the office shall verify the requesting patient's status as a valid certified patient to the patient's school or employer or other designated party, to ensure compliance with the protections afforded by this section.

(b) The name, contact information, and other information relating to practitioners registered with the board under this article shall be public information and shall be maintained on the board's website accessible to the public in searchable form. However, if a practitioner notifies the board in writing that he or she does not want his or her name and other information disclosed, that practitioner's name and other information shall thereafter not be public information or maintained on the board's website, unless the practitioner cancels the request.

5. A person currently under parole, probation or other state or local supervision, or released on bail awaiting trial may not be punished or otherwise penalized for conduct allowed under this article.

6. Employees who use medical cannabis shall be afforded the same rights, procedures and protections that are available and applicable to injured workers under the workers' compensation law, or any rules or regulations promulgated thereunder, when such injured workers are prescribed medications that may prohibit, restrict, or require the modification of the performance of their duties.

Cannabis Law § 43. Regulations.

The board shall promulgate regulations to implement this article. The cannabis advisory board may make recommendations to the board.

Cannabis Law § 44. Suspend; terminate.

Based upon the recommendation of the board, executive director and/or the superintendent of state police that there is a risk to the public health or safety, the governor may immediately suspend or terminate all licenses issued to registered organizations.

Cannabis Law § 45. Pricing.

Registered organizations shall submit documentation to the executive director of any change in pricing per dose for any medical cannabis product within fifteen days of such change. Prior approval by the executive director shall not be required for any such change; provided however that the board is authorized to modify the price per dose for any medical cannabis product if necessary to maintain public access to appropriate medication.

ARTICLE 4. ADULT-USE CANNABIS

Cannabis Law § 61. License application.

1. Any person may apply to the board for a license to cultivate, process, distribute, deliver or dispense cannabis within this state for sale. Such application shall be in writing and verified and shall contain such information as the board shall require. Such application shall be accompanied by a check or draft for the amount required by this article for such license. If the board shall approve the application, it shall issue a license in such form as shall be determined

by its rules. Such license shall contain a description of the licensed premises and in form and in substance shall be a license to the person therein specifically designated to cultivate, process, distribute, deliver or dispense cannabis in the premises therein specifically licensed.

2. Except as otherwise provided in this article, a separate license shall be required for each facility at which cultivation, processing, distribution or retail dispensing is conducted.

3. An applicant shall not be denied a license under this article based solely on a conviction for a violation of article two hundred twenty or section 240.36 of the penal law, prior to the date article two hundred twenty-one of the penal law took effect, a conviction for a violation of article two hundred twenty-one of the penal law, or a conviction for a violation of article two hundred twenty-two of the penal law after the effective date of this chapter.

Cannabis Law § 62. Information to be requested in applications for licenses.

1. The board shall have the authority to prescribe the manner and form in which an application must be submitted to the office for licensure under this article.

2. The board is authorized to adopt regulations, including by emergency rule, establishing information which must be included on an application for licensure under this article. Such information may include, but is not limited to: information about the applicant's identity, including racial and ethnic diversity; ownership and investment information, including the corporate structure; evidence of good moral character, including the submission of fingerprints by the applicant to the division of criminal justice services; information about the premises to be licensed; financial statements; and any other information prescribed by regulation.

3. All license applications shall be signed by the applicant (if an individual), by a managing member (if a limited liability company), by an officer (if a corporation), or by all partners (if a partnership). Each person signing such application shall verify or affirm it as true under the penalties of perjury.

4. All license or permit applications shall be accompanied by a check, draft or other forms of payment as the board may require or authorize in the amount required by this article for such license or permit.

5. If there are any proposed changes, after the filing of the application or the granting of a license or permit, in any of the facts required to be set forth in such application, a supplemental statement giving notice of such proposed change, cost and source of money involved in the change, duly verified or affirmed, shall be filed with the board at least thirty days prior to such proposed change. Failure to do so shall, if willful and deliberate, be cause for denial or revocation of the license.

6. In giving any notice, or taking any action in reference to a registered organization or licensee of a licensed premises, the board may rely upon the information furnished in such application and in any supplemental statement connected therewith, and such information may be presumed to be correct, and shall be binding upon registered organizations, licensee or licensed premises as if correct. All information required to be furnished in such application or supplemental statements shall be deemed material in any prosecution for perjury, any proceeding to revoke, cancel or suspend any license, and in the board's final determination to approve or deny the license.

7. The board may waive the submission of non-material information or documentation described in this section, the waiver of which would not be inconsistent with the purposes and goals set forth in this article, for any category of license or permit, provided that it shall not be permitted to waive the requirement for submission of any such category of information solely for an individual applicant or applicants.

8. The board pursuant to regulation, may wholly prohibit and/or prescribe specific criteria under which it will consider and allow limited transfers or changes of ownership, interest, or control during the registration or license application period and/or up to two years after an approved applicant commences licensed activities.

Cannabis Law § 63. Fees.

1. The board shall have the authority to charge applicants for licensure under this article a non-refundable application fee. Such fee may be based on the type of licensure sought, cultivation and/or production volume, or any other factors deemed reasonable and appropriate by the board to achieve the policy and purpose of this chapter.

1-a. The board shall also have the authority to assess a registered organization with a one-time special licensing fee for a registered organization adult-use cultivator processor, distributor retail dispensary license. Such fee shall be assessed at an amount to adequately fund social and economic equity and incubator assistance pursuant to this article and paragraph (c) of subdivision three of section ninety-nine-ii of the state finance law. Provided, however, that the board shall not allow registered organizations to dispense adult-use cannabis from more than three of their medical cannabis dispensing locations. The timing and manner in which registered organizations may be granted such authority shall be determined by the board in regulation.

2. The board shall have the authority to charge licensees a biennial license fee. Such fee shall be based on the amount of cannabis to be cultivated, processed, distributed and/or dispensed by the licensee or the gross annual receipts of the licensee for the previous license period, and any other factors deemed reasonable and appropriate by the board.

3. The board shall waive or reduce fees pursuant to this section for social and economic equity applicants.

Cannabis Law § 64. Selection criteria.

1. The board shall develop regulations for use by the office in determining whether or not an applicant should be granted the privilege of an initial adult-use cannabis license, based on, but not limited to, the following criteria:

   (a) the applicant is a social and economic equity applicant;

   (b) the applicant will be able to maintain effective control against the illegal diversion or inversion of cannabis;

   (c) the applicant will be able to comply with all applicable state laws and regulations;

   (d) the applicant and its officers are ready, willing, and able to properly carry on the activities for which a license is sought including with assistance from the social and economic equity and incubator program, if applicable;

   (e) where appropriate and applicable, the applicant possesses or has the right to use sufficient land, buildings, and equipment to properly carry on the activity described in the application or has a plan to do so if qualifying as a social and economic equity applicant;

   (f) the applicant qualifies as a social and economic equity applicant or sets out a plan for benefiting communities and people disproportionally impacted by enforcement of cannabis laws;

   (g) it is in the public interest that such license be granted, taking into consideration, but not limited to, the following criteria:

      (i) that it is a privilege, and not a right, to cultivate, process, distribute, and sell adult-use cannabis;

      (ii) the number, classes, and character of other licenses in proximity to the location and in the particular municipality, subdivision thereof or geographic boundary as established by the board;

      (iii) evidence that all necessary licenses and permits have been or will be obtained from the state and all other relevant governing bodies;

      (iv) effect of the grant of the license on pedestrian or vehicular traffic, and parking, in proximity to the location;

(v) the existing noise level at the location and any increase in noise level that would be generated by the proposed premises;

(vi) the ability to increase climate resiliency and minimize or eliminate adverse environmental impacts, including but not limited to water usage, energy usage, carbon emissions, waste, pollutants, harmful chemicals and single use plastics;

(vii) the effect on the production, price and availability of cannabis and cannabis products;

(viii) the applicant's history of violations and compliance with the laws of another jurisdiction, in which they operate or have operated a cannabis license or registration, related to the operation of a cannabis business;

(ix) the applicant's history of violations related to the operation of a business, including but not limited to, violations related to labor laws, federal occupational safety and health law and tax compliance; and

(x) any other factors specified by law or regulation that are relevant to determine that granting a license would promote public convenience and advantage, public health and safety and the public interest of the state, county or community.

(h) the applicant and its managing officers are of good moral character and do not have an ownership or controlling interest in more licenses or permits than allowed by this chapter, or any regulations promulgated hereunder;

(i) the applicant has entered into a labor peace agreement with a bona-fide labor organization that is actively engaged in representing or attempting to represent the applicant's employees, and the maintenance of such a labor peace agreement shall be an ongoing material condition of licensure. In evaluating applications from entities with twenty-five or more employees, the office shall give consideration to whether applicants have entered into an agreement with a statewide or local bona-fide building and construction trades organization for construction work on its licensed facilities;

(j) the applicant will contribute to communities and people disproportionately harmed by enforcement of cannabis laws through including, but not limited to, the social responsibility framework as provided in section sixty-six of this article and report these contributions to the board;

(k) if the application is for an adult-use cultivator or processor license, the environmental and energy impact, including compliance with energy standards, of the facility to be licensed;

(l) the applicant satisfies any other conditions as determined by the board; and

(m) if the applicant is a registered organization, the organization's maintenance of effort in manufacturing and/or dispensing and/or research of medical cannabis for certified patients and caregivers.

2. If the board is not satisfied that the applicant should be issued a license, the executive director shall notify the applicant in writing of the specific reason or reasons recommended by the board for denial.

3. The state cannabis advisory board shall have the authority to recommend to the board the number of licenses issued pursuant to this article to ensure a competitive market where no licensee is dominant in the statewide marketplace or in any individual category of licensing, to actively promote and potentially license social and economic equity applicants, and carry out the goals of this chapter.

Cannabis Law § 65. Limitations of licensure; duration.

1. No license of any kind may be issued to a person under the age of twenty-one years, nor shall any licensee employ anyone under the age of eighteen years. Any employee eighteen years of age or older but under twenty-one years of

age may not have direct interaction with customers inside a licensed retail store.

2. (a) No licensee shall sell, deliver, or give away or cause or permit or procure to be sold, delivered or given away any cannabis or cannabis product to any person, actually or apparently, under the age of twenty-one years or any visibly intoxicated person.

(b) It shall be an affirmative defense that such person had produced a photographic identification card apparently issued by a governmental entity and that the cannabis had been sold, delivered or given to such person in reasonable reliance upon such identification. In evaluating the applicability of such affirmative defense, the board shall take into consideration any written policy or training adopted and implemented by the licensee to prevent sales to minors.

3. No licensee or permittee shall knowingly sell, deliver or give away or cause or permit or procure to be sold, delivered or given away to a lawful cannabis consumer any amount of cannabis which they know would cause the lawful cannabis consumer to be in violation of this chapter or possession limits established by article two hundred twenty-two of the penal law.

4. The board, on the recommendation of the office shall have the authority to limit, by canopy, plant count, square footage or other means, the amount of cannabis allowed to be grown, processed, distributed or sold by a licensee.

5. All licenses under this article shall expire two years after the date of issue.

Cannabis Law § 66. License renewal.

1. Each license, issued pursuant to this article, may be renewed upon application therefore by the licensee and the payment of the fee for such license as prescribed by this article. In the case of applications for renewals, the board may dispense with the requirements of such statements as it deems unnecessary in view of those contained in the application made for the original license, but in any event the submission of photographs of the licensed premises shall be dispensed with, provided the applicant for such renewal shall file a statement with the board to the effect that there has been no alteration of such premises since the original license was issued. The board may make such rules as it deems necessary, not inconsistent with this chapter, regarding applications for renewals of licenses and permits and the time for making the same.

2. Each applicant must submit to the office documentation of the racial, ethnic, and gender diversity of the applicant's employees and owners prior to a license being renewed. In addition, the board shall consult with the chief equity officer and executive director to create a social responsibility framework agreement that fosters racial, ethnic, and gender diversity in their workplace and make the adherence to such agreement a conditional requirement of license renewal.

3. The board shall provide an application for renewal of a license issued under this article not less than ninety days prior to the expiration of the current license.

4. The board may only issue a renewal license upon receipt of the prescribed renewal application and renewal fee from a licensee if, in addition to the criteria in this section, the licensee's license is not under suspension and has not been revoked.

5. Each applicant must maintain a labor peace agreement with a bona-fide labor organization that is actively engaged in representing or attempting to represent the applicant's employees and the maintenance of such a labor peace agreement shall be an ongoing material condition of licensure.

6. Each applicant must provide evidence of the execution of their plan for benefitting communities and people disproportionally impacted by cannabis law enforcement required for initial licensing pursuant to section sixty-four of this article.

Cannabis Law § 67. Amendments; changes in ownership and organizational structure.

1. Licenses issued pursuant to this article shall specify:

   (a) the name and address of the licensee;

   (b) the activities permitted by the license;

   (c) the land, buildings and facilities that may be used for the licensed activities of the licensee;

   (d) a unique license number issued by the board to the licensee; and

   (e) such other information as the board shall deem necessary to assure compliance with this chapter.

2. Upon application of a licensee to the board, a license may be amended to allow the licensee to relocate within the state, to add or delete licensed activities or facilities, or to amend the ownership or organizational structure of the entity that is the licensee. The board shall establish a fee for such amendments.

3. A license shall become void by a change in ownership, substantial corporate change or location without prior written approval of the board. The board may promulgate regulations allowing for certain types of changes in ownership without the need for prior written approval.

4. For purposes of this section, "substantial corporate change" shall mean:

   (a) for a corporation, a change of fifty-one percent or more of the officers and/or directors, or a transfer of fifty-one percent or more of stock of such corporation, or an existing stockholder obtaining fifty-one percent or more of the stock of such corporation; or

   (b) for a limited liability company, a change of fifty-one percent or more of the managing members of the company, or a transfer of fifty-one percent or more of ownership interest in said company, or an existing member obtaining a cumulative of fifty-one percent or more of the ownership interest in said company; or

   (c) for a partnership, a change of fifty-one percent or more of the managing partners of the company, or a transfer of fifty-one percent or more of ownership interest in said company, or an existing member obtaining a cumulative of fifty-one percent or more of the ownership interest in said company.

Cannabis Law § 68. Adult-use cultivator license.

1. An adult-use cultivator's license shall authorize the acquisition, possession, distribution, cultivation and sale of cannabis from the licensed premises of the adult-use cultivator by such licensee to duly licensed processors in this state. The board may establish regulations allowing licensed adult-use cultivators to perform certain types of minimal processing without the need for an adult-use processor license.

2. For purposes of this section, cultivation shall include, but not be limited to, the agricultural production practices of planting, growing, cloning, harvesting, drying, curing, grading and trimming of cannabis.

3. A person holding an adult-use cultivator's license may apply for, and obtain, one processor's license and one distributor's license solely for the distribution of their own products.

4. A person holding an adult-use cultivator's license may not also hold a retail dispensary license pursuant to this article and no adult-use cannabis cultivator shall have a direct or indirect interest, including by stock ownership, interlocking directors, mortgage or lien, personal or real property, management agreement, share parent companies or affiliated organizations, or any other means, in any premises licensed as an adult-use cannabis retail dispensary or in any business licensed as an adult-use cannabis retail dispensary or in any registered organization registered

pursuant to article three of this chapter.

5. No person may have a direct or indirect financial or controlling interest in more than one adult-use cultivator license issued pursuant to this chapter, provided that one adult-use cultivator license may authorize adult-use cultivation in more than one location pursuant to criteria established by the board in regulation.

Cannabis Law § 68-a. Registered organization adult-use cultivator processor distributor retail dispensary license.

1. A registered organization cultivator processor distributor retail dispensary license shall have the same authorization and conditions as adult-use cultivator, adult-use processor, adult-use distributor and adult-use retail dispensary licenses issued pursuant to this article provided, however that the location of its adult-use dispensaries shall be limited to only three of the organization's medical dispensaries' premises and facilities authorized pursuant to article three of this chapter, and that it may only distribute its own products. Provided further that such registered organization shall maintain its medical cannabis license and continue offering medical cannabis to a degree established by regulation of the board. Such license does not qualify such organization for any other adult-use license.

2. A person holding a registered organization adult-use cultivator processor distributor retail dispensary license may not also hold another retail dispensary license pursuant to this article and no registered organization adult-use cultivator processor distributor retail dispensary shall have a direct or indirect interest, including by stock ownership, interlocking directors, mortgage or lien, personal or real property, management agreement, share parent companies or affiliated organizations, or any other means, in any premises licensed as an adult-use cannabis retail dispensary or in any business licensed as an adult-use cannabis retail dispensary.

Cannabis Law § 68-b. Registered organization adult-use cultivator, processor and distributor license.

A registered organization cultivator, processor and distributor license shall have the same authorization and conditions as an adult-use cultivator, processor, and distributor license, provided, however, that such license does not qualify such organization for any other adult-use license and may only authorize the distribution of the licensee's own products.

Cannabis Law § 68-c. Conditional adult-use cultivator license.

1. A conditional adult-use cultivator license shall be subject to the same authorizations, restrictions and requirements applied to any adult-use cultivator pursuant to section sixty-eight of this article for the duration of the conditional period of the license, as well as to any new terms and conditions imposed by the board and office.

2. To be eligible to apply for a conditional adult-use cultivator license, a cultivator must.

(a) have held a valid industrial hemp grower authorization from the department of agriculture and markets, as of December thirty-first, two thousand twenty-one, which authorized the growing of cannabinoid hemp, and is in good standing with the department of agriculture and markets;

(b) have grown and harvested hemp for at least two of the past four years pursuant to that license and be able to provide proof, as defined by the office, of the amount of hemp planted by the applicant during each of the two years that hemp was grown; and

(c) as an individual applicant have an ownership interest of fifty-one percent or more, or as any other applicant have an ownership interest of fifty-one percent or more of the entity that is the licensee.

3. A conditional adult-use cultivator license shall authorize the cultivation of cannabis outdoors or in a greenhouse with no more than twenty artificial lights unless otherwise authorized by the office. A conditional adult-use cultivator licensee may cultivate up to forty-three thousand five hundred sixty square feet of flowering canopy outdoors or twenty-five thousand square feet of flowering canopy in a greenhouse. A cultivator may cultivate both outdoors and in a greenhouse provided the flowering canopy in a greenhouse is less than twenty-thousand square feet and the total flowering canopy is equal to or less than thirty-thousand square feet.

4. A conditional adult-use cultivator licensee must comply with any environmental standards and requirements mandated by the office.

5. The cultivation of cannabis shall only be permitted within the same or an adjacent county in which the conditional adult-use cultivator licensee had previously been authorized by the department of agriculture and markets to grow hemp.

6. A conditional adult-use cultivator licensee shall have the temporary authority to minimally process and distribute cannabis products, provided that such final products shall be in the form of cannabis flower, without holding an adult-use processor or distributor license established pursuant to sections sixty-nine and seventy-one of this article; provided that the licensee complies with all requirements for the processing and distribution of cannabis products as set out by the board in regulations or in the terms and conditions of the conditional license. Such authority to minimally process and distribute cannabis products expires on June first, two thousand twenty-three. After June first, two thousand twenty-three, any conditional adult-use cultivator seeking to process and distribute cannabis products shall be required to apply for and receive a processor and distributor license to conduct this activity.

7. For the duration of the conditional period of the conditional adult-use cultivator license, the ownership or organizational structure of the entity that is the licensee shall not be amended, except pursuant to the provisions of subdivisions two, three and four of section sixty-seven of this article.

8. The office shall set out specific terms and conditions setting out requirements necessary to be awarded and maintain a conditional adult-use cultivator license, including but not limited to the requirement that a licensee agrees to participate in an environmental sustainability program and a social equity mentorship program. Such mentorship program shall be directed to train individuals interested in becoming licensed cultivators and shall leverage remote and in-person mentees with experience in agriculture business management, sustainable cannabis cultivation, and best practices. Candidates for the mentorship program must be at least eighteen years of age, must be a New York state resident, and must be individuals that would be considered social equity applicants as defined by section eighty-seven of this article. The license terms and conditions set out by the office shall include requirements that a licensee enter into a labor peace agreement with a bona-fide labor organization that is actively engaged in representing or attempting to represent the applicant's employees within six months of licensure, that the maintenance of such labor peace agreement shall be an ongoing material condition of licensure, and that licensees shall meet any other eligibility requirements established by the office.

9. The board shall establish a non-refundable application and license fee, in a manner consistent with section sixty-three of this article, for the conditional adult-use cultivator license. No such license shall be issued after December thirty-first, two thousand twenty-two and such license shall only be valid through June thirtieth, two thousand twenty-four.

10. A conditional adult-use cultivator license shall be deemed to have been surrendered to the board and a conditional adult-use cultivator licensee shall be deemed not to be in good standing, as determined in the discretion of the executive director in a written notice, effective upon delivery to the licensee at the licensee's last known address on file with the office, for reasons including but not limited to:

    (a) failure to abide by all the terms and conditions of the conditional adult-use cultivator license;

    (b) failure to adhere to all requirements set out in regulations and guidance, including those promulgated after receiving the conditional adult-use cultivator license;

(c) failure to submit information, records, or reports;

(d) failure to correct deficiencies in accordance with an approved corrective action plan;

(e) deviation from regulations, licensing terms, or standard operating procedures in a manner that the office determines may jeopardize health or safety of the public, or the quality of products grown or produced;

(f) failure to provide office employees with access to the premises; and

(g) failure to begin operations within six months of the date of the issuance of the license.

11. A licensee whose conditional adult-use cultivator license has been deemed surrendered may within ten days of the delivery date of such notice appeal the determination of the executive director to the board pursuant to subdivision eighteen of section ten of this chapter. The board shall have sole discretion to determine the conduct of the appeal, which shall include notice and an opportunity to be heard. Upon review by the board, the board shall issue a final written determination which may then be reviewed pursuant to section one hundred thirty-five of this chapter and article seventy-eight of the civil practice law and rules.

12. In the event that a conditional adult-use cultivator licensee elects to cease operation of all permitted activities or to surrender its license, the following provisions shall apply:

(a) the conditional adult-use cultivator licensee shall notify the office in writing at least thirty days prior to the anticipated date of closure;

(b) such written notice shall include a proposed plan for closure. The plan shall be subject to office approval and shall include timetables and describe the procedures and actions the licensee shall take to properly destroy or otherwise dispose of all the licensee's supply of cannabis and/or cannabis products; and

(c) the licensee or former licensee must maintain and make available to the office all records related to the cultivation of cannabis for a period of three years.

13. No later than ninety days before the expiration of a conditional adult-use cultivator license, the office shall, pursuant to a request by the licensee, review the conditional adult-use cultivator licensee to determine whether they are in good standing with the office. Good standing shall include, but not be limited to, compliance with subdivision seven of this section. Any licensee found to be in good standing shall be eligible to apply for and receive an adult-use cultivation license, provided the licensee can meet all requirements of the new license. Such a licensee will receive, at minimum, an adult-use cultivator license for the size of flowering canopy that they were licensed to grow pursuant to their conditional adult-use cultivator license or a larger size flowering canopy and authorization to use artificial light as may be set out by the board in regulation. A licensee may not separately apply for any license type under this article permitting the cultivation of adult-use cannabis while holding a conditional adult-use cultivator license.

14. For the purposes of this section, the office has the authority to define terms including but not limited to "greenhouse", "immature plant", "flowering canopy" as part of the terms and conditions of the conditional adult-use cultivator license.

15. Nothing herein shall limit the authority, power, or other rights or remedies of the board or office.

* NB Repealed June 30, 2024

Cannabis Law § 69. Adult-use processor license.

1. A processor's license shall authorize the acquisition, possession, processing and sale of cannabis from the licensed premises of the adult-use cultivator by such licensee to duly licensed processors or distributors. A person holding an adult-use processor's license may apply for, and obtain, one distributor's license solely for the distribution of their

own products.

2. For purposes of this section, processing shall include, but not be limited to, blending, extracting, infusing, packaging, labeling, branding and otherwise making or preparing cannabis products. Processing shall not include the cultivation of cannabis.

3. No processor shall be engaged in any other business on the premises to be licensed; except that a person issued an adult-use cannabis cultivator, processor, and/or distributor license or a processor who has also been issued a hemp grower license by the department of agriculture and markets or a cannabinoid hemp processor license under this chapter may hold and operate all issued licenses on the same premises.

4. No cannabis processor licensee may hold more than one cannabis processor license provided a single license may authorize processor activities at multiple locations, as set out in regulations by the board.

5. No adult-use cannabis processor shall have a direct or indirect interest, including by stock ownership, interlocking directors, mortgage or lien, personal or real property, management agreement, share parent companies or affiliated organizations or any other means, in any premises licensed as an adult-use cannabis retail dispensary or in any business licensed as an adult-use cannabis retail dispensary or in any registered organization registered pursuant to article three of this chapter.

6. Adult-use processor licensees are subject to minimum operating requirements as determined by the board in regulation.

Cannabis Law § 69-a. Conditional adult-use processor license.

1. A conditional adult-use processor license shall be subject to the same authorizations, restrictions and requirements applied to any adult-use processor pursuant to section sixty-nine of this article for the duration of the conditional period of the license, as well as to any new terms and conditions imposed by the board and office.

2. To be eligible to apply for a conditional adult-use processor license, a processor must:

> (a) have applied for a cannabinoid hemp processor license pursuant to section ninety-two of this chapter before January first, two thousand twenty-two;

> (b) hold an active cannabinoid hemp processor license issued by the office; and

> (c) as an individual applicant have an ownership interest of fifty-one percent or more, or as any other applicant have an ownership interest of fifty-one percent or more of the entity that is the licensee.

3. A conditional adult-use processor license shall authorize the processing and manufacturing of cannabis products provided the licensee complies with all requirements for the processing and manufacture of cannabis products as set out by the board. A conditional adult-use processor licensee shall only perform extraction activities if authorized to under the licensee's cannabinoid hemp processor license and all extraction methods are subject to office approval.

4. A conditional adult-use processor licensee must comply with any environmental standards and requirements as mandated by the office.

5. The processing of cannabis shall only be permitted at the same location in which the conditional adult-use processor licensee is authorized to process hemp, unless expressly authorized by the office.

6. A conditional adult-use processor licensee shall have the authority to distribute cannabis products without holding an adult-use distributor license established pursuant to section seventy-one of this article until June first, two thousand twenty-three, provided that the licensee complies with all requirements for the distribution of cannabis products as set out by the office. After June first, two thousand twenty-three, any conditional processor seeking to distribute cannabis products shall be required to apply for and receive a distributor license to conduct this activity.

7. For the duration of the conditional period of the conditional adult-use processor license, the ownership or organizational structure of the entity that is the licensee shall not be amended, except pursuant to the provisions of subdivisions two, three and four of section sixty-seven of this article.

8. The office shall set out specific terms and conditions setting out requirements necessary to be awarded and maintain a conditional adult-use processor license, including but not limited to the requirement that a licensee agrees to participate in an environmental sustainability program and a social equity mentorship program. Such program shall be directed to train individuals interested in becoming licensed processors and shall leverage remote and in-person engagement to provide mentees with experience in processing techniques and good manufacturing practices. Candidates for the mentorship program must be at least eighteen years of age, must be a New York state resident, and must be individuals that would be considered social equity applicants as defined by section eighty-seven of this article. The license terms and conditions set out by the office shall include requirements that a licensee enter into a labor peace agreement with a bona-fide labor organization that is actively engaged in representing or attempting to represent the applicant's employees within six months of licensure, that the maintenance of such labor peace agreement shall be an ongoing material condition of licensure, and that licensees shall meet any other eligibility requirements established by the office.

9. The board shall establish a non-refundable application and license fee, in a manner consistent with section sixty-three of this article, for the conditional adult-use processor license. No such license shall be issued after December thirty-first, two thousand twenty-two and such license shall only be valid through June thirtieth, two thousand twenty-four.

10. A conditional adult-use processor license shall be deemed to have been surrendered to the board and a conditional adult-use processor licensee shall be deemed not to be in good standing, as determined in the discretion of the executive director in a written notice, effective upon delivery to the licensee at the licensee's last known address on file with the office, for reasons including but not limited to:

   (a) failure to abide by all the terms and conditions of the conditional adult-use processor license;

   (b) failure to adhere to all requirements set out in regulations and guidance, including those promulgated after receiving the conditional adult-use processor license;

   (c) failure to submit information, records, or reports;

   (d) failure to correct deficiencies in accordance with an approved corrective action plan;

   (e) deviation from regulations, licensing terms, or standard operating procedures in a manner the office determines may jeopardize health or safety of the public, or the quality of products produced;

   (f) failure to provide office employees with access to the premises; and

   (g) failure to begin operations within six months of the date of the issuance of the license.

11. A licensee whose conditional adult-use processor license has been deemed surrendered may within ten days of the delivery date of such notice appeal the determination of the executive director to the board pursuant to subdivision eighteen of section ten of this chapter. The board shall have sole discretion to determine the conduct of the appeal, which shall include notice and an opportunity to be heard. Upon review by the board, the board shall issue a final written determination which may then be reviewed pursuant to section one hundred thirty-five of this chapter and article seventy-eight of the civil practice law and rules.

12. In the event that a conditional adult-use processor licensee elects to cease operation of all permitted activities or to surrender its license, the following provisions shall apply:

   (a) the conditional adult-use processor licensee shall notify the office in writing at least thirty days prior to the anticipated date of closure;

   (b) such written notice shall include a proposed plan for closure. The plan shall be subject to office approval and shall include timetables and describe the procedures and actions the licensee shall take to properly destroy or otherwise dispose of all the licensee's supply of cannabis and/or cannabis products; and

(c) the licensee or former licensee must maintain and make available to the office all records related to the cultivation of cannabis for a period of three years.

13. No later than ninety days before the expiration of a conditional adult-use processor license, the office shall, pursuant to a request by the licensee, review the conditional adult-use processor licensee to determine whether they are in good standing with the office. Good standing shall include, but not be limited to, compliance with subdivision seven of this section. Any licensee found to be in good standing shall be eligible to apply for and receive an adult-use processor license, provided the licensee can meet all requirements of the new license.

14. For the purposes of this section, the office has the authority to define terms including but not limited to "extraction" as part of the terms and conditions of the conditional adult-use processor license.

15. Nothing in this section shall limit the authority, power, or other rights or remedies of the board or office.

* NB Repealed June 30, 2024

Cannabis Law § 70. Adult-use cooperative license.

1. A cooperative license shall authorize the acquisition, possession, cultivation, processing, distribution and sale from the licensed premises of the adult-use cooperative by such licensee to duly licensed distributors, on-site consumption sites, registered organization and/or retail dispensaries; but not directly to cannabis consumers.

2. To be licensed as an adult-use cooperative, the cooperative must:

(a) be comprised of residents of the state of New York as a limited liability company or limited liability partnership under the laws of the state, or an appropriate business structure as determined and authorized by the board;

(b) subordinate capital, both as regards control over the cooperative undertaking, and as regards the ownership of the pecuniary benefits arising therefrom;

(c) be democratically controlled by the members themselves on the basis of one vote per member;

(d) vest in and allocate with priority to and among the members of all increases arising from their cooperative endeavor in proportion to the members' active participation in the cooperative endeavor; and

(e) the cooperative must operate according to the seven cooperative principles published by the International Cooperative Alliance in nineteen hundred ninety-five.

3. A cooperative member shall be a natural person and shall not be a member of more than one adult-use cooperative licensed pursuant to this section.

4. No natural person or member of an adult-use cooperative license may have a direct or indirect financial or controlling interest in any other adult-use cannabis license issued pursuant to this chapter.

5. No adult-use cannabis cooperative shall have a direct or indirect interest, including by stock ownership, interlocking directors, mortgage or lien, personal or real property, or any other means, in any premises licensed as an adult-use cannabis retail dispensary or in any business licensed as an adult-use cannabis retail dispensary pursuant to this chapter.

6. The board shall promulgate regulations governing cooperative licenses, including, but not limited to, the establishment of canopy limits on the size and scope of cooperative licensees, and other measures designed to incentivize the use and licensure of cooperatives.

Cannabis Law § 71. Adult-use distributor license.

1. A distributor's license shall authorize the acquisition, possession, distribution and sale of cannabis from the licensed premises of a licensed adult-use cultivator, processor, adult-use cooperative, microbusiness, or registered organization authorized pursuant to this chapter to sell adult-use cannabis, to duly licensed retail dispensaries and on-site consumption sites.

2. No distributor shall have a direct or indirect economic interest in any microbusiness, adult-use retail dispensary, adult-use on-site consumption licensee or in any registered organization registered pursuant to article three of this chapter. This restriction shall not prohibit a registered organization authorized pursuant to section thirty-nine of this chapter, from being granted licensure by the board to distribute adult-use cannabis products cultivated and processed by the registered organization to licensed adult-use retail dispensaries.

3. Any distributor with a direct or indirect interest in a licensed cultivator or processor, shall only distribute cannabis or cannabis products cultivated and/or processed by such licensee.

4. Nothing in subdivision two of this section shall prevent a distributor from charging an appropriate fee, authorized by the board, for the distribution of cannabis, including based on the volume of cannabis distributed.

5. Adult-use distributor licensees are subject to minimum operating requirements as determined by the board in regulation.

Cannabis Law § 72. Adult-use retail dispensary license.

1. A retail dispensary license shall authorize the acquisition, possession, sale and delivery of cannabis from the licensed premises of the retail dispensary by such licensee to cannabis consumers.

2. No person may have a direct or indirect financial or controlling interest in more than three adult-use retail dispensary licenses issued pursuant to this chapter.

3. No person holding a retail dispensary license may also hold an adult-use cultivation, processor, microbusiness, cooperative or distributor license pursuant to this article or be registered as a registered organization pursuant to article three of this chapter, except for such organizations licensed pursuant to sections sixty-eight-a and sixty-eight-b of this article.

4. No retail license shall be granted for any premises, unless the applicant shall be the owner thereof, or shall be able to demonstrate possession of the premises within thirty days of final approval of the license through a lease, management agreement or other agreement giving the applicant control over the premises, in writing, for a term not less than the license period.

5. With the exception of delivery or microbusiness licensees, no premises shall be licensed to sell cannabis products, unless said premises shall be located in a store, the principal entrance to which shall be from the street level and located on a public thoroughfare in premises which may be occupied, operated or conducted for business, trade or industry.

6. No cannabis retail licensee shall locate a storefront within five hundred feet of a school grounds as such term is defined in the education law or within two hundred feet of a house of worship.

Cannabis Law § 73. Microbusiness license.

1. A microbusiness license shall authorize the limited cultivation, processing, distribution, delivery, and dispensing of their own adult-use cannabis and cannabis products.

2. A microbusiness licensee may not hold any direct or indirect interest in any other license in this chapter and may only distribute its own cannabis and cannabis products to dispensaries.

3. The size, scope and eligibility criteria of a microbusiness shall be determined in regulation by the board in consultation with the executive director and the chief equity officer. The granting of such licenses shall promote social and economic equity applicants as provided for in this chapter.

Cannabis Law § 74. Delivery license.

A delivery license shall authorize the delivery of cannabis and cannabis products by licensees independent of another adult-use cannabis license, provided that each delivery licensee may have a total of no more than twenty-five individuals, or the equivalent thereof, providing full-time paid delivery services to cannabis consumers per week under one license. For the purposes of this section the state cannabis advisory board shall provide recommendations to the board for the application process, license criteria, and scope of licensed activities for this class of license. No person may have a direct or indirect financial or controlling interest in more than one delivery license. The granting of such licenses shall promote social and economic equity applicants as provided for in this chapter.

Cannabis Law § 75. Nursery license.

1. A nursery license shall authorize the production, sale and distribution of clones, immature plants, seeds, and other agricultural products used specifically for the planting, propagation, and cultivation of cannabis by licensed adult-use cultivators, cooperatives, microbusinesses or registered organizations. For the purposes of this section, the office shall provide recommendations to the board for the application process, license criteria and scope of licensed activities for this class of license. The granting of such licenses shall promote social and economic equity applicants as provided for in this chapter.

2. A person or entity holding an adult-use cultivator's license may apply for, and obtain, one nursery license to sell directly to other cultivators, cooperatives, microbusinesses, or registered organizations.

Cannabis Law § 76. Notification to municipalities of adult-use retail dispensary or on-site consumption license.

1. Not less than thirty days nor more than two hundred seventy days before filing an application for licensure as an adult-use retail dispensary or registered organization adult-use cultivator processor distributor retail dispensary or an on-site consumption licensee, an applicant shall notify the municipality in which the premises is located of such applicant's intent to file such an application.

2. Such notification shall be made to the clerk of the village, town or city, as the case may be, wherein the premises is located. For purposes of this section:

(a) notification need only be given to the clerk of a village when the premises is located within the boundaries of the village; and

(b) in the city of New York, the community board established pursuant to section twenty-eight hundred of the New York city charter with jurisdiction over the area in which the premises is located shall be considered the appropriate public body to which notification shall be given.

3. Such notification shall be made in such form as shall be prescribed by the rules of the board.

4. When a city, town, or village, and in New York city a community board, expresses an opinion for or against the granting of such registration, license or permit application, any such opinion shall be deemed part of the record upon

which the office makes its recommendation to the board to grant or deny the application and the board shall respond in writing to such city, town, village or community board with an explanation of how such opinion was considered in the granting or denial of an application.

5. Such notification shall be made by: (a) certified mail, return receipt requested; (b) overnight delivery service with proof of mailing; or (c) personal service upon the offices of the clerk or community board.

6. The board shall require such notification to be on a standardized form that can be obtained on the internet or from the board and such notification to include:

(a) the trade name or "doing business as" name, if any, of the establishment;

(b) the full name of the applicant;

(c) the street address of the establishment, including the floor location or room number, if applicable;

(d) the mailing address of the establishment, if different than the street address;

(e) the name, address and telephone number of the attorney or representative of the applicant, if any;

(f) a statement indicating whether the application is for:

(i) a new establishment;

(ii) a transfer of an existing licensed business;

(iii) a renewal of an existing license; or

(iv) an alteration of an existing licensed premises;

(g) if the establishment is a transfer or previously licensed premises, the name of the old establishment and such establishment's registration or license number;

(h) in the case of a renewal or alteration application, the registration or license number of the applicant; and

(i) the type of license.

Cannabis Law § 77. Adult-use on-site consumption license; provisions governing on-site consumption licenses.

1. No applicant shall be granted an adult-use on-site consumption license for any premises, unless the applicant shall be the owner thereof, or shall be in possession of said premises under a lease, in writing, for a term not less than the license period except, however, that such license may thereafter be renewed without the requirement of a lease as provided in this section. This subdivision shall not apply to premises leased from government agencies; provided, however, that the appropriate administrator of such government agency provides some form of written documentation regarding the terms of occupancy under which the applicant is leasing said premises from the government agency for presentation to the office at the time of the license application. Such documentation shall include the terms of occupancy between the applicant and the government agency, including, but not limited to, any short-term leasing agreements or written occupancy agreements.

2. No person may have a direct or indirect financial or controlling interest in more than three adult-use on-site consumption licenses issued pursuant to this chapter.

3. No person holding an adult-use on-site consumption license may also hold an adult-use retail dispensary, cultivation, processor, microbusiness, cooperative or distributor license pursuant to this article or be registered as a registered organization pursuant to article three of this chapter.

4. No applicant shall be granted an adult-use on-site consumption license for any premises within five hundred feet of school grounds as such term is defined in the education law or two hundred feet from a house of worship.

5. The board may consider any or all of the following in determining whether public convenience and advantage and the public interest will be promoted by the granting of an adult-use on-site consumption license at a particular location:

(a) that it is a privilege, and not a right, to cultivate, process, distribute, and sell cannabis;

(b) the number, classes, and character of other licenses in proximity to the location and in the particular municipality or subdivision thereof;

(c) evidence that all necessary licenses and permits have been obtained from the state and all other governing bodies;

(d) whether there is a demonstrated need for spaces to consume cannabis;

(e) effect of the grant of the license on pedestrian or vehicular traffic, and parking, in proximity to the location;

(f) the existing noise level at the location and any increase in noise level that would be generated by the proposed premises; and

(g) any other factors specified by law or regulation that are relevant to determine that granting a license would promote public convenience and advantage and the public interest of the community.

6. If the board shall disapprove an application for an on-site consumption license, it shall state and file in its offices the reasons therefor and shall notify the applicant thereof. Such applicant may thereupon apply to the board for a review of such action in a manner to be prescribed by the rules of the board.

7. No adult-use cannabis on-site consumption licensee shall keep upon the licensed premises any adult-use cannabis products except those purchased from a licensed adult-use distributor; registered organization adult-use cultivator processor distributor retail dispenser; registered organization adult-use cultivator, processor and distributor; cooperative, or microbusiness authorized to sell adult-use cannabis, and only in containers approved by the board. Such containers shall have affixed thereto such labels as may be required by the rules of the board. No adult-use on-site consumption licensee shall reuse, refill, tamper with, adulterate, dilute or fortify the contents of any container of cannabis products as received from the manufacturer or distributor.

8. No adult-use on-site consumption licensee shall sell, deliver or give away, or cause or permit or procure to be sold, delivered or given away any cannabis for consumption on the premises where sold in a container or package containing a quantity or number of servings more than authorized by the board.

9. No adult-use on-site consumption licensee shall suffer, permit or promote activities or events on its premises wherein any person shall use such premises for activities including, but not limited to, gambling, exposing or simulating, contests, or fireworks that are prohibited by subdivision six, six-a, six-b, six-c or seven of section one hundred six of the alcoholic beverage control law or any other similar activities the board deems to be prohibited.

10. No premises licensed to sell adult-use cannabis for on-site consumption under this chapter shall be permitted to have any opening or means of entrance or passageway for persons or things between the licensed premises and any other room or place in the building containing the licensed premises, or any adjoining or abutting premises, unless ingress and egress is restricted by an employee, agent of the licensee, or other method approved by the board of controlling access to the facility.

11. Each adult-use on-site consumption licensee shall keep and maintain upon the licensed premises, adequate records of all transactions involving the business transacted by such licensee which shall show the amount of cannabis products, in an applicable metric measurement, purchased by such licensee together with the names, license numbers and places of business of the persons from whom the same were purchased, the amount involved in such purchases, as well as the sales of cannabis products made by such licensee. The board is hereby authorized

to promulgate rules and regulations permitting an on-site licensee operating two or more premises separately licensed to sell cannabis products for on-site consumption to inaugurate or retain in this state methods or practices of centralized accounting, bookkeeping, control records, reporting, billing, invoicing or payment respecting purchases, sales or deliveries of cannabis products, or methods and practices of centralized receipt or storage of cannabis products within this state without segregation or earmarking for any such separately licensed premises, wherever such methods and practices assure the availability, at such licensee's central or main office in this state, of data reasonably needed for the enforcement of this chapter. Such records shall be available for inspection by any authorized representative of the board.

12. All licensed adult-use on-site consumption premises shall be subject to inspection by any peace officer, acting pursuant to his or her special duties, or police officer and by the duly authorized representatives of the board, during the hours when the said premises are open for the transaction of business.

13. An adult-use on-site consumption licensee shall not provide cannabis products to any person under the age of twenty-one. No person under the age of twenty-one shall be permitted on the premises of a cannabis on-site consumption facility.

14. The provisions of article thirteen-E of the public health law restricting the smoking or vaping of cannabis shall not apply to adult-use on-site consumption premises.

Cannabis Law § 78. Record keeping and tracking.

1. The board shall, by regulation, require each licensee pursuant to this article to adopt and maintain security, tracking, record keeping, record retention and surveillance systems, relating to all cannabis at every stage of acquiring, possession, manufacture, sale, delivery, transporting, testing or distributing by the licensee, subject to regulations of the board.

2. Every licensee shall keep and maintain upon the licensed premises, adequate books and records of all transactions involving the licensee and sale of its products, which shall include, but is not limited to, all information required by any rules promulgated by the board. Such regulations may require the utilization of an approved seed-to-sale tracking system compiling a licensee's cannabis inventory and transaction data.

Cannabis Law § 79. Inspections and ongoing requirements.

All licensed or permitted premises, regardless of the type of premises, and all records including but not limited to financial statements and corporate documents, shall be subject to inspection by the office, by the duly authorized representatives of the board, by any peace officer acting pursuant to his or her special duties, or by a police officer. The board shall make reasonable accommodations so that ordinary business is not interrupted and safety and security procedures are not compromised by the inspection. A person who holds a license or permit must make himself or herself, or an agent thereof, available and present for any inspection required by the board. Such inspection may include, but is not limited to, ensuring compliance by the licensee or permittee with all of the requirements of this article, the regulations promulgated pursuant thereto, and other applicable state and local building codes, fire, health, safety, and other applicable regulations.

Cannabis Law § 80. Adult-use cultivators, processors or distributors not to be interested in retail dispensaries.

1. It shall be unlawful for any person authorized to cultivate, process, or distribute under this article to:

(a) be interested directly or indirectly in any premises where any cannabis product is sold at retail, including for on-site consumption; or in any business devoted wholly or partially to the sale or delivery of any cannabis product at retail, including for on-site consumption, by stock ownership, interlocking directors, mortgage or lien or any personal or real property, or by any other means;

(b) make, or cause to be made, any loan to any person engaged in the manufacture or sale of any cannabis product at wholesale or retail;

(c) make any gift or render any service of any kind whatsoever, directly or indirectly, to any person licensed under this chapter which in the judgment of the board may influence such licensee to purchase the product of such cultivator or processor or distributor; or

(d) enter into any contract or agreement with any retail, on-site consumption or delivery licensee whereby such licensee agrees to confine his or her sales to cannabis products manufactured or sold by one or more such cultivator or processors or distributors. Any such contract or agreement shall be void and subject the licenses of all parties concerned to revocation for cause and any applicable administrative enforcement and penalties.

2. The provisions of this section shall not prohibit a registered organization authorized pursuant to section thirty-nine or sixty-eight-a of this chapter, or microbusiness authorized pursuant to section seventy-three of this chapter, from cultivating, processing, or selling adult-use cannabis under this article, at facilities wholly owned and operated by such registered organization or microbusiness, subject to any conditions, limitations or restrictions established by this chapter.

3. The board shall develop rules and regulations in regard to this section.

Cannabis Law § 81. Packaging, labeling, and administration of adult-use cannabis products.

1. The board is hereby authorized to promulgate rules and regulations governing the advertising, branding, marketing, packaging, labeling and unconventional methods of administration or ingestion, of cannabis products, sold or possessed for sale in New York state, including rules pertaining to the accuracy of information and rules restricting marketing and advertising to youth.

2. Such regulations shall include, but not be limited to, requiring that:

(a) packaging meets requirements similar to the federal "poison prevention packaging act of 1970," 15 U.S.C. Sec 1471 et seq.;

(b) prior to delivery or sale at a retailer, cannabis and cannabis products shall be labeled according to regulations and placed in a resealable, child-resistant package; and

(c) packages, labels, shapes and products shall not be made to be attractive to or target persons under the age of twenty-one.

3. Such regulations shall include requiring labels warning consumers of any potential impact on human health resulting from the consumption of cannabis products that shall be affixed to those products when sold, if such labels are deemed warranted by the board and may establish standardized and/or uniform packaging and labeling requirements for adult-use products.

4. Such rules and regulations shall establish methods and procedures for determining serving sizes for cannabis products, active cannabis concentration per serving size, and number of servings per container or package, and the methods of separating or clearly delineating servings within a container or package. Such regulations may also require a nutritional or supplement fact panel that incorporates data regarding serving sizes and potency thereof.

5. Such rules and regulations shall establish approved product types and forms and establish an application and

review process to determine the suitability of new product types and forms, taking into consideration the consumer and public health and safety implications of different product varieties, manufacturing processes, product types and forms, the means and methods of administration associated with specific product types, and any other criteria identified by the board for consideration to protect public health and safety.

6. Such regulations shall also require product labels to accurately display the total THC of each product.

7. The packaging, sale, marketing, branding, advertising, labeling or possession by any licensee of any cannabis product not labeled or offered in conformity with rules and regulations promulgated in accordance with this section shall be grounds for the imposition of a fine, and/or the suspension, revocation or cancellation of a license in accordance with the provisions of this chapter.

Cannabis Law § 82. Laboratory testing.

1. Every processor of adult-use cannabis shall contract with an independent laboratory permitted pursuant to section one hundred twenty-nine of this chapter, to test the cannabis products it produces pursuant to rules and regulations prescribed by the office. The board may assign an approved testing laboratory, which the processor of adult-use cannabis must use, and may establish consortia with neighboring states, to inform best practices, and share laboratory data.

2. Adult-use cannabis processors, microbusinesses, cooperatives and registered organizations shall make laboratory test reports available to licensed distributors, retail dispensaries, and on-site consumption sites for all cannabis products manufactured by the processor or licensee.

3. Licensed retail dispensaries shall maintain accurate documentation of laboratory test reports for each cannabis product offered for sale to cannabis consumers. Such documentation shall be made publicly available by the licensed retail dispensary.

4. Onsite laboratory testing by licensees is permissible subject to regulation; however, such testing shall not be certified by the board and does not exempt the licensee from the requirements of quality assurance testing at a testing laboratory pursuant to this section.

5. An owner of a cannabis laboratory testing permit shall not hold a license, or interest in a license, in any other category within this article and shall not own or have ownership interest in a registered organization registered pursuant to article three of this chapter or a cannabinoid hemp processor license pursuant to article five of this chapter.

6. The board shall have the authority to require any licensee under this article to submit cannabis or cannabis products to one or more independent laboratories for testing and the board may promulgate regulations related to all aspects of third-party testing and quality assurance including but not limited to:

    (a) minimum testing and sampling requirements;

    (b) testing and sampling methodologies;

    (c) testing reporting requirements;

    (d) retesting; and

    (e) product quarantine, hold, recall, and remediation.

Cannabis Law § 83. Provisions governing the cultivation and processing of adult-use cannabis.

1. Cultivation and processing of cannabis shall comply with regulations promulgated by the board governing minimum requirements for adult-use cultivators, nurseries, processors, microbusinesses, cooperatives, registered organizations, and registered organization cultivators.

2. No cultivator or processor of adult-use cannabis shall sell, or agree to sell or deliver in the state any cannabis products, as the case may be, except in originally sealed containers containing quantities in accordance with size standards pursuant to rules adopted by the board. Such containers shall have affixed thereto such labels or other means of tracking and identification as may be required by the rules of the board.

3. No cultivator or processor of adult-use cannabis shall furnish or cause to be furnished to any licensee, any exterior or interior sign, printed, painted, electric or otherwise, except as authorized by the board. The board may make such rules as it deems necessary to carry out the purpose and intent of this subdivision.

4. Cultivators of adult-use cannabis consistent with protecting public health and safety, shall comply with plant cultivation regulations, standards, and guidelines consistent with the provisions applicable to hemp, cannabinoid hemp, and hemp extract and issued by the board, in consultation with the department of environmental conservation and the department of agriculture and markets. Such regulations, standards, and guidelines shall be guided by sustainable farming principles and practices such as organic, regenerative, and integrated pest management models to the extent possible, and shall restrict whenever possible, the use of pesticides to those that are registered by the department of environmental conservation or that specifically meet the United States environmental protection agency registration exemption criteria for minimum risk, used in compliance with rules, regulations, standards and guidelines issued by the department of environmental conservation for pesticides.

5. No cultivator or processor of adult-use cannabis shall transport any cannabis products, except in vehicles owned and operated by such cultivator or processor, or hired by such cultivator or processor and operated by a trucking or transportation company registered with the office, and shall only make deliveries at the licensed premises of the purchaser.

6. No cultivator or processor of adult-use cannabis, including an adult-use cannabis cooperative, microbusiness, or registered organization may offer any incentive, payment or other benefit to a licensed cannabis distributor or retail dispensary in return for carrying the cultivator, processor, cooperative, microbusiness or registered organization products, or preferential shelf placement.

7. All cannabis products shall be processed in accordance with good manufacturing practices for the product category, pursuant to either Part 111 or Part 117 of Title 21 of the Code of Federal Regulations, as may be modified by the board in regulation.

8. No processor of adult-use cannabis shall produce any product which, in the discretion of the board, is designed to appeal to anyone under the age of twenty-one years.

9. The use or integration of alcoholic beverages or nicotine in cannabis products is strictly prohibited.

10. The board shall promulgate regulations governing the minimum requirements for the secure transport of adult-use cannabis.

Cannabis Law § 84. Provisions governing the distribution of adult-use cannabis.

1. No distributor shall sell, or agree to sell or deliver any cannabis products, as the case may be, in any container, except in a sealed package. Such containers shall have affixed thereto such labels as may be required by the rules of the board.

2. No distributor shall deliver any cannabis products, except in vehicles owned and operated by such distributor, or hired and operated by such distributor from a trucking or transportation company registered with the board, and

shall only make deliveries at the licensed premises of the purchaser.

3. Each distributor shall keep and maintain upon the licensed premises, adequate books and records of all transactions involving the business transacted by such distributor, which shall show the amount of cannabis products purchased by such distributor and the total THC content of purchased cannabis products as reflected on the product labels together with the names, license numbers and places of business of the persons from whom the same was purchased and the amount involved in such purchases, as well as the amount of cannabis products sold by such distributor together and the total THC content of cannabis products sold as reflected on the final product labels, with the names, addresses, and license numbers of such purchasers and any other information required in regulation. Each sale shall be recorded separately on a numbered invoice, which shall have printed thereon the number, the name of the licensee, the address of the licensed premises, and the current license number. Such distributor shall deliver to the purchaser a true duplicate invoice stating the name and address of the purchaser, the quantity of cannabis products, the total THC content of cannabis products sold as reflected on the product labels, description by brands and the price of such cannabis products, and a true, accurate and complete statement of the terms and conditions on which such sale is made. Such books, records and invoices shall be kept for a period of five years and shall be available for inspection by any authorized representative of the board.

4. No distributor shall furnish or cause to be furnished to any licensee, any exterior or interior sign, printed, painted, electric or otherwise, unless authorized by the board.

5. No distributor shall provide any discount, rebate or customer loyalty program to any licensed retailer, except as otherwise authorized by the board.

6. The board is authorized to promulgate regulations establishing a maximum margin for which a distributor may mark up a cannabis product for sale to a retail dispensary. Any adult-use cannabis product sold by a distributor for more than the maximum markup allowed in regulation, shall be unlawful.

7. Each distributor shall keep and maintain upon the licensed premises, adequate books and records to demonstrate the distributor's actual cost of doing business, using accounting standards and methods regularly employed in the determination of costs for the purpose of federal income tax reporting, for the total operation of the licensee. Such books, records and invoices shall be kept for a period of five years and shall be available for inspection by any authorized representative of the office for use in determining the maximum markup allowed in regulation pursuant to subdivision six of this section.

Cannabis Law § 85. Provisions governing adult-use cannabis retail dispensaries.

1. No cannabis retail licensee shall sell, deliver, or give away or cause or permit or procure to be sold, delivered or given away any cannabis to any person, actually or apparently, under the age of twenty-one years or, any visibly intoxicated person.

2. Valid proof of age is required for each transaction. No licensee, or agent or employee of such licensee shall accept as written evidence of age by any such person for the purchase of any cannabis or cannabis product, any documentation other than: (a) a valid driver's license or non-driver identification card issued by the commissioner of motor vehicles, the federal government, any United States territory, commonwealth or possession, the District of Columbia, a state government within the United States or a provincial government of the dominion of Canada, or (b) a valid passport issued by the United States government or any other country, or (c) an identification card issued by the armed forces of the United States. Upon the presentation of such driver's license or non-driver identification card issued by a governmental entity, such licensee or agent or employee thereof may perform a transaction scan as a precondition to the sale of any cannabis or cannabis product. Nothing in this section shall prohibit a licensee or agent or employee from performing such a transaction scan on any of the other documents listed in this subdivision if such documents include a bar code or magnetic strip that may be scanned by a device capable of deciphering any

electronically readable format. In instances where the information deciphered by the transaction scan fails to match the information printed on the driver's license or non-driver identification card presented by the card holder, or if the transaction scan indicates that the information is false or fraudulent, the attempted purchase of the cannabis or cannabis product shall be denied.

3. No cannabis retail licensee shall sell alcoholic beverages, nor have or possess a license or permit to sell alcoholic beverages, on the same premises where cannabis products are sold.

4. No sign of any kind printed, painted or electric, advertising any brand shall be permitted on the exterior or interior of such premises, except by permission of the board.

5. No cannabis retail licensee shall sell or deliver any cannabis products to any person with knowledge of, or with reasonable cause to believe, that the person to whom such cannabis products are being sold, has acquired the same for the purpose of selling or giving them away in violation of the provisions of this chapter or in violation of the rules and regulations of the board.

6. All premises licensed under this section shall be subject to inspection by any peace officer described in subdivision four of section 2.10 of the criminal procedure law acting pursuant to his or her special duties, or police officer or any duly authorized representative of the board. All licensees shall be subject to reasonable inspection by the office and a person who holds a license must make himself or herself, or an agent thereof, available and present for any inspection required by the office. The office shall make reasonable accommodations so that ordinary business is not interrupted, and safety and security procedures are not compromised by the inspection.

7. No cannabis retail licensee shall be interested, directly or indirectly, in any cultivator, processor, distributor or microbusiness operator licensed pursuant to this article, by stock ownership, interlocking directors, mortgage or lien on any personal or real property or by any other means. Any lien, mortgage or other interest or estate, however, now held by such retailer on or in the personal or real property of such manufacturer or distributor, which mortgage, lien, interest or estate was acquired on or before December thirty-first, two thousand nineteen, shall not be included within the provisions of this subdivision; provided, however, the burden of establishing the time of the accrual of the interest comprehended by this subdivision, shall be upon the person who claims to be entitled to the protection and exemption afforded hereby.

8. No cannabis retail licensee shall make or cause to be made any loan to any person engaged in the cultivation, processing or distribution of cannabis pursuant to this article.

9. Each cannabis retail licensee shall designate the price of each item of cannabis by attaching to or otherwise displaying immediately adjacent to each such item displayed in the interior of the licensed premises where sales are made a price tag, sign or placard setting forth the price at which each such item is offered for sale therein.

10. No person licensed to sell cannabis products at retail, shall allow or permit any gambling, or offer any gambling on the licensed premises, or allow or permit illicit drug activity on the licensed premises.

11. All adult-use dispensing facilities shall make educational materials and resources available to cannabis consumers at the point of sale, as prescribed by the board.

12. The board is authorized, to promulgate regulations governing licensed adult-use dispensing facilities, including but not limited to, the hours of operation, size and location of the licensed facility, types and concentration of product servings offered and establishing a minimum and maximum margin for retail dispensary markups of cannabis product or products before selling to a cannabis consumer. It shall be unlawful for any retail dispensary to sell any adult-use cannabis product for less than the minimum markup allowed in regulation.

Cannabis Law § 86. Adult-use cannabis advertising and marketing.

1. The board shall promulgate rules and regulations governing the form and content of advertising and marketing of licensed cannabis and any cannabis products or services.

2. The board shall promulgate regulations for advertising and marketing content including but not limited to explicit rules prohibiting advertising that:

(a) is false, deceptive, or misleading;

(b) promotes overconsumption;

(c) depicts consumption;

(d) is designed in any way to appeal to children or other minors;

(e) is within or is readily observed within five hundred feet of the perimeter of a school grounds, playground, child day care providers, public park, or library;

(f) is in public transit vehicles and stations;

(g) is in the form of an unsolicited internet pop-up;

(h) is on publicly owned or operated property;

(i) makes medical claims or promotes adult-use cannabis for a medical or wellness purpose;

(j) promotes or implements discounts, coupons, or other means of selling adult-use cannabis products below market value or whose discount would subvert local and state tax collections;

(k) is in the form of a billboard; or

(l) fails to satisfy any other advertising or marketing rule or regulations promulgated by the board related to marketing or advertising, not inconsistent with this chapter.

3. The board shall promulgate explicit rules prohibiting all marketing strategies and implementation including, but not limited to, branding, packaging, labeling, location of cannabis retailers, and advertisements that are designed to:

(a) appeal to persons less then twenty-one years of age and/or populations at-risk of increased adverse health consequences as determined by the board in regulation; or

(b) disseminate false or misleading information to customers.

4. The board shall promulgate regulations requiring that:

(a) all advertisements and marketing accurately and legibly identify the party or other business responsible for its content; and

(b) any broadcast, cable, radio, print and digital communications advertisements only be placed where the audience is reasonably expected to be twenty-one years of age or older, as determined by reliable, up-to-date audience composition data. The burden of proving this requirement lies with the party that has paid for or facilitated the advertisement.

5. The board may establish procedures to review and enforce advertising and marketing requirements.

Cannabis Law § 87. Social and economic equity, minority and women-owned businesses, distressed farmers and service-disabled veterans; incubator program.

1. The board, in consultation with the chief equity officer and executive director, and after receiving public input shall create and implement a social and economic equity plan and actively promote applicants from communities disproportionately impacted by cannabis prohibition, and promote racial, ethnic, and gender diversity when issuing licenses for adult-use cannabis related activities, including mentoring potential applicants, by prioritizing consideration of applications by applicants who are from communities disproportionately impacted by the enforcement of cannabis prohibition or who qualify as a minority or women-owned business, distressed farmers, or service-disabled veterans. Such qualifications shall be determined by the board, with recommendations from the state cannabis advisory board, the chief equity officer and executive director, by regulation.

2. The board's social and economic equity plan shall also promote diversity in commerce, ownership and employment, and opportunities for social and economic equity in the adult-use cannabis industry. A goal shall be established to award fifty percent of adult-use cannabis licenses to social and economic equity applicants and ensure inclusion of:

(a) individuals from communities disproportionately impacted by the enforcement of cannabis prohibition;

(b) minority-owned businesses;

(c) women-owned businesses;

(d) minority and women-owned businesses, as defined in paragraph (d) of subdivision five of this section;

(e) distressed farmers, as defined in subdivision five of this section; and

(f) service-disabled veterans.

3. The social and economic equity plan shall require the consideration of additional criteria in its licensing determinations. Under the social and economic equity plan, extra priority shall be given to applications that demonstrate that an applicant:

(a) is a member of a community disproportionately impacted by the enforcement of cannabis prohibition;

(b) has an income lower than eighty percent of the median income of the county in which the applicant resides; and

(c) was convicted of a marihuana-related offense prior to the effective date of this chapter, or had a parent, guardian, child, spouse, or dependent, or was a dependent of an individual who, prior to the effective date of this chapter, was convicted of a marihuana-related offense.

4. The board in consultation with the cannabis advisory board and the chief equity officer, shall also create an incubator program to encourage social and economic equity applicants to apply and, if granted an adult-use cannabis license, permit or registration, the program shall provide direct support in the form of counseling services, education, small business coaching and financial planning, and compliance assistance.

5. For the purposes of this section, the following definitions shall apply:

(a) "Minority-owned business" shall mean a business enterprise, including a sole proprietorship, partnership, limited liability company or corporation that is:

(i) at least fifty-one percent owned by one or more minority group members;

(ii) an enterprise in which such minority ownership is real, substantial and continuing;

(iii) an enterprise in which such minority ownership has and exercises the authority to control independently the day-to-day business decisions of the enterprise;

(iv) an enterprise authorized to do business in this state and independently owned and operated; and

(v) an enterprise that is a small business.

(b) "Minority group member" shall mean a United States citizen or permanent resident alien who is and can demonstrate membership in one of the following groups:

(i) black persons having origins in any of the black African racial groups;

(ii) Hispanic persons of Mexican, Puerto Rican, Dominican, Cuban, Central or South American of either Indian or Hispanic origin, regardless of race;

(iii) Native American or Alaskan native persons having origins in any of the original peoples of North America; or

(iv) Asian and Pacific Islander persons having origins in any of the far east countries, south east Asia, the Indian subcontinent or the Pacific islands.

(c) "Women-owned business" shall mean a business enterprise, including a sole proprietorship, partnership, limited liability company or corporation that is:

(i) at least fifty-one percent owned by one or more United States citizens or permanent resident aliens who are women;

(ii) an enterprise in which the ownership interest of such women is real, substantial and continuing;

(iii) an enterprise in which such women ownership has and exercises the authority to control independently the day-to-day business decisions of the enterprise;

(iv) an enterprise authorized to do business in this state and independently owned and operated; and

(v) an enterprise that is a small business.

(d) A firm owned by a minority group member who is also a woman may be defined as a minority-owned business, a women-owned business, or both.

(e) "Distressed farmer" shall mean: (i) a New York state resident or business enterprise, including a sole proprietorship, partnership, limited liability company or corporation, that meets the small farm classification developed by the Economic Research Service of the United States Department of Agriculture, has filed a schedule F with farm receipts for the last three years, qualifies for an agriculture assessment and meets other qualifications defined in regulation by the board to demonstrate that they operate a farm operation as defined in section three hundred one of the agriculture and markets law and has been disproportionately impacted, including but not limited to incurring operating losses, by low commodity prices and faces the loss of farmland through development or suburban sprawl and meets any other qualifications as defined in regulation by board; or (ii) a New York state resident or business enterprise, including a sole proprietorship, partnership, limited liability company or corporation, that is a small farm operator and a member of a group that has been historically underrepresented in farm ownership and meets any other qualifications as defined in regulation by board.

(f) "Service-disabled veterans" shall mean persons qualified under article seventeen-B of the executive law.

(g) "Communities disproportionately impacted" shall mean, but not be limited to, a history of arrests, convictions, and other law enforcement practices in a certain geographic area, such as, but not limited to, precincts, zip codes, neighborhoods, and political subdivisions, reflecting a disparate enforcement of cannabis prohibition during a certain time period, when compared to the rest of the state. The board shall, with recommendations from the state cannabis advisory board, the chief equity officer and executive director, issue guidelines to determine how to assess which communities have been disproportionately impacted and how to assess if someone is a member of a community disproportionately impacted.

6. The board shall actively promote applicants that foster racial, ethnic, and gender diversity in their workforce.

7. Licenses issued under the social and economic equity plan shall not be transferred or sold within the first three years of issue, except to a qualified social and economic equity applicant and with the prior written approval of the board. In the event a social and economic equity applicant seeks to transfer or sell their license at any point after issue and the transferee is to a person or entity that does not qualify as a social and economic equity applicant, the transfer agreement shall require the new license holder to pay to the board any outstanding amount owed by the transferor to the board as repayment of any loan issued by the board as well as any other fee or assessment as determined by the board.

Cannabis Law § 88. Data collection and reporting.

The board shall collect demographic data on owners and employees in the adult-use cannabis industry and shall annually publish such data in its annual report.

Cannabis Law § 89. Regulations.

The board shall promulgate regulations with recommendations from the state cannabis advisory board to implement this article.

ARTICLE 5. CANNABINOID HEMP AND HEMP EXTRACT

Cannabis Law § 90. Definitions.

As used in this article, the following terms shall have the following meanings, unless the context clearly requires otherwise:

1. "Cannabinoid" means the phytocannabinoids found in hemp and does not include synthetic cannabinoids as that term is defined in subdivision (g) of schedule I of section thirty-three hundred six of the public health law.

2. "Cannabinoid hemp" means any hemp and any product processed or derived from hemp, that is used for human consumption provided that when such product is packaged or offered for retail sale to a consumer, it shall not have a concentration of more than three tenths of one percent delta-9 tetrahydrocannabinol.

3. "Used for human consumption" means intended by the manufacturer or distributor to be: (a) used for human consumption for its cannabinoid content; or (b) used in, on or by the human body for its cannabinoid content.

4. "Hemp" means the plant Cannabis sativa L. and any part of such plant, including the seeds thereof and all derivatives, extracts, cannabinoids, isomers, acids, salts, and salts of isomers, whether growing or not, with a delta-9 tetrahydrocannabinol concentration (THC) of not more than three-tenths of a percent on a dry weight basis. It shall not include "medical cannabis" as defined in section three of this chapter.

5. "Hemp extract" means all derivatives, extracts, cannabinoids, isomers, acids, salts, and salts of isomers derived from hemp, used or intended for human consumption, for its cannabinoid content, with a delta-9 tetrahydrocannabinol concentration of not more than an amount determined by the board in regulation. For the purpose of this article, hemp extract excludes (a) any food, food ingredient or food additive that is generally recognized as safe pursuant to federal law; or (b) any hemp extract that is not used for human consumption. Such excluded substances shall not be regulated pursuant to the provisions of this article but are subject to other provisions of applicable state law, rules and regulations.

6. "License" means a license issued pursuant to this article.

7. "Cannabinoid hemp processor license" means a license granted by the board to process, extract, pack or manufacture cannabinoid hemp or hemp extract into products, whether in intermediate or final form, used for human consumption.

8. "Processing" means extracting, preparing, treating, modifying, compounding, manufacturing or otherwise manipulating cannabinoid hemp to concentrate or extract its cannabinoids, or creating product, whether in intermediate or final form, used for human consumption. For purposes of this article, processing does not include:

(a) growing, cultivation, cloning, harvesting, drying, curing, grinding or trimming when authorized pursuant to article twenty-nine of the agriculture and markets law; or

(b) mere transportation, such as by common carrier or another entity or individual.

9. "Cannabinoid hemp flower" means the flower of the plant Cannabis sativa L. that has been harvested, dried, and cured, with a delta-9 tetrahydrocannabinol concentration of not more than three-tenths of one percent, on a dry weight basis, prior to any processing.

10. "Cannabinoid hemp flower product" means cannabinoid hemp flower that has been minimally processed consistent with the requirements of this article, intended for retail sale to consumers.

Cannabis Law § 91. Rulemaking authority.

The board may make regulations pursuant to this article for the processing, distribution, marketing, transportation and sale of cannabinoid hemp and hemp extracts used for human consumption, which may include, but not be limited to:

1. Specifying forms, establishing application, reasonable administration and renewal fees, or license duration;

2. Establishing the qualifications and criteria for licensing, as authorized by law;

3. The books and records to be created and maintained by licensees and lawful procedures for their inspection;

4. Any reporting requirements;

5. Methods and standards of processing, labeling, packaging and marketing of cannabinoid hemp, hemp extract and products derived therefrom;

6. Procedures for how cannabinoid hemp, hemp extract or ingredients, additives, or products derived therefrom can be deemed as acceptable for sale in the state;

7. Provisions governing the modes and forms of administration, including inhalation;

8. Procedures for determining whether cannabinoid hemp, hemp extract or ingredients, additives, or products derived therefrom produced outside the state or within the state meet the standards and requirements of this article and can therefore be sold within the state;

9. Procedures for the granting, cancellation, revocation or suspension of licenses, consistent with the state administrative procedures act;

10. Restrictions governing the advertising and marketing of cannabinoid hemp, hemp extract and products derived therefrom;

11. Any other regulations necessary to implement this article;

12. Nothing in this article shall prevent the sale of cannabinoid hemp flower; provided however, that any cannabinoid

hemp flower product sold shall be limited to a person over twenty-one years of age and shall be subject to regulations promulgated by the board; provided further that such regulations shall not unduly restrict the availability of cannabinoid hemp flower; and

13. Any cannabinoid hemp flower product clearly labeled or advertised for the purposes of smoking, or in the form of a cigarette, cigar, or pre-roll, or packaged or combined with other items designed to facilitate smoking such as rolling papers or pipes, shall only be offered for sale in adult-use cannabis retail dispensaries licensed pursuant to article four of this chapter.

Cannabis Law § 92. Cannabinoid hemp processor license.

1. Persons processing cannabinoid hemp or hemp extract used for human consumption, whether in intermediate or final form, shall be required to obtain a cannabinoid hemp processor license from the board.

2. A cannabinoid hemp processor license authorizes one or more specific activities related to the processing of cannabinoid hemp into products used for human consumption, whether in intermediate or final form, and the distribution or sale thereof by the licensee. Nothing herein shall prevent a cannabinoid hemp processor from processing, extracting and processing hemp products not to be used for human consumption.

3. Persons authorized to grow hemp pursuant to article twenty-nine of the agriculture and markets law are not authorized to engage in processing of cannabinoid hemp or hemp extract without first being licensed as a cannabinoid hemp processor under this article.

4. This article shall not apply to hemp, cannabinoid hemp, hemp extracts or products derived therefrom that are not used for human consumption. This article also shall not apply to hemp, cannabinoid hemp, hemp extracts or products derived therefrom that have been deemed generally recognized as safe pursuant to federal law.

5. The board shall have the authority to set reasonable fees for such license, to limit the activities permitted by such license, to establish the period during which such license is authorized, which shall be two years or more, and to make rules and regulations necessary to implement this section.

6. Any person holding an active research partnership agreement with the department of agriculture and markets, authorizing that person to process cannabinoid hemp, shall be awarded licensure under this section, provided that the research partner is actively performing research pursuant to such agreement and is able to demonstrate compliance with this article, as determined by the board, after notice and an opportunity to be heard.

Cannabis Law § 93. Cannabinoid hemp retailer license.

1. Retailers selling cannabinoid hemp, in final form to consumers within the state, shall be required to obtain a cannabinoid hemp retailer license from the board.

2. The board shall have the authority to set reasonable fees for such license, to establish the period during which such license is authorized, which shall be one year or more, and to make rules and regulations necessary to implement this section.

Cannabis Law § 94. Cannabinoid license applications.

1. Persons shall apply for a license under this article by submitting an application upon a form supplied by the board, providing all the relevant requested information, verified by the applicant or an authorized representative of the applicant.

2. A separate license shall be required for each facility at which processing or retail sales are conducted; however, an

applicant may submit one application for separate licensure at multiple locations.

3. Each applicant shall remit with its application the fee for each requested license, which shall be a reasonable fee.

Cannabis Law § 95. Information to be requested in applications for licenses.

1. The board may specify the manner and form in which an application shall be submitted to the board for licensure under this article.

2. The board may adopt regulations establishing what relevant information shall be included on an application for licensure under this article. Such information may include, but is not limited to: information about the applicant's identity; ownership and investment information, including the corporate structure; evidence of good moral character; financial statements; information about the premises to be licensed; information about the activities to be licensed; and any other relevant information specified in regulation.

3. All license applications shall be signed by the applicant if an individual, by a managing partner if a limited liability company, by an officer if a corporation, or by all partners if a partnership. Each person signing such application shall verify it as true under the penalties of perjury.

4. All license applications shall be accompanied by a check, draft or other forms of payment as the board may require or authorize in the reasonable amount required by this article for such license.

5. If there be any change, after the filing of the application or the granting, modification or renewal of a license, in any of the material facts required to be set forth in such application, a supplemental statement giving notice of such change, duly verified, shall be filed with the board within ten days after such change. Failure to do so, if willful and deliberate, may be grounds for revocation of the license.

Cannabis Law § 96. Fees.

The board may charge licensees a reasonable license fee. Such fee may be based on the activities permitted by the license, the amount of cannabinoid hemp or hemp extract to be processed or extracted by the licensee, the gross annual receipts of the licensee for the previous license period, or any other factors reasonably deemed appropriate by the board.

Cannabis Law § 97. Selection criteria.

1. The applicant, if an individual or individuals, shall furnish evidence of the individual's good moral character, and if an entity, the applicant shall furnish evidence of the good moral character of the individuals who have or will have substantial responsibility for the licensed or authorized activity and those in control of the entity, including principals, officers, or others with such control.

2. The applicant shall furnish evidence of the applicant's experience and competency, and that the applicant has or will have adequate facilities, equipment, process controls, and security to undertake those activities for which licensure is sought.

3. The applicant shall furnish evidence of his, her or its ability to comply with all applicable state and local laws, rules and regulations.

4. If the board is not satisfied that the applicant should be issued a license, the board shall notify the applicant in writing of the specific reason or reasons for denial.

5. No license pursuant to this article may be issued to an individual under the age of eighteen years.

Cannabis Law § 98. License renewal.

1. Each license, issued pursuant to this article, may be renewed upon application therefor by the licensee and the payment of the reasonable fee for such license as specified by this article.

2. In the case of applications for renewals, the board may dispense with the requirements of such statements as it deems unnecessary in view of those contained in the application made for the original license.

3. The board shall provide an application for renewal of any license issued under this article not less than ninety days prior to the expiration of the current license.

4. The board may only issue a renewal license upon receipt of the specified renewal application and renewal fee from a licensee if, in addition to the selection criteria set out in this article, the licensee's license is not under suspension and has not been revoked.

Cannabis Law § 99. Form of license.

Licenses issued pursuant to this article shall specify:

1. The name and address of the licensee;

2. The activities permitted by the license;

3. The land, buildings and facilities that may be used for the licensed activities of the licensee;

4. A unique license number issued by the board to the licensee; and

5. Such other information as the board shall deem necessary to assure compliance with this article.

Cannabis Law § 100. Transferability; amendment to license; change in ownership or control.

1. Licenses issued under this article are not transferable, absent written consent of the board.

2. Upon application of a licensee, a license may be amended to add or delete permitted activities.

3. A license shall become void by a change in ownership, substantial corporate change or change of location without prior written approval of the board. The board may make regulations allowing for certain types of changes in ownership without the need for prior written approval.

Cannabis Law § 101. Granting, suspending or revoking licenses.

After due notice and an opportunity to be heard, established by rules and regulations, the board may decline to grant a new license, impose conditions or limits with respect to the grant of a license, modify an existing license or decline to renew a license, and may suspend or revoke a license already granted after due notice and an opportunity to be heard, as established by rules and regulations, whenever the board finds that:

1. A material statement contained in an application is or was false or misleading;

2. The applicant or licensee, or a person in a position of management and control thereof or of the licensed activity, does not have good moral character, necessary experience or competency, adequate facilities, equipment, process controls, or security to process, distribute, transport or sell cannabinoid hemp, hemp extract or products derived therefrom;

3. After appropriate notice and opportunity, the applicant or licensee has failed or refused to produce any records or provide any information required by this article or the regulations promulgated pursuant thereto;

4. The licensee has conducted activities outside of those activities permitted on its license; or

5. The applicant or licensee, or any officer, director, partner, or any other person exercising any position of management or control thereof or of the licensed activity has willfully failed to comply with any of the provisions of this article or regulations under it and other laws of this state applicable to the licensed activity.

Cannabis Law § 102. Record keeping and tracking.

Every licensee shall keep, in such form as the board may direct, such relevant records as may be required pursuant to regulations under this article.

Cannabis Law § 103. Packaging and labeling of cannabinoid hemp and hemp extract.

1. Cannabinoid hemp processors shall be required to provide appropriate label warning to consumers, and restricted from making unapproved label claims, as determined by the board, concerning the potential impact on or benefit to human health resulting from the use of cannabinoid hemp, hemp extract and products derived therefrom for human consumption, which labels shall be affixed to those products when sold, pursuant to rules and regulations that the board may adopt.

2. The board may, by rules and regulations, require processors to establish a code, including, but not limited to QR code, for labels and establish methods and procedures for determining, among other things, serving sizes or dosages for cannabinoid hemp, hemp extract and products derived therefrom, active cannabinoid concentration per serving size, number of servings per container, and the growing region, state or country of origin if not from the United States. Such rules and regulations may require an appropriate fact panel that incorporates data regarding serving sizes and potency thereof.

3. The packaging, sale, or possession of products derived from cannabinoid hemp or hemp extract used for human consumption not labeled or offered in conformity with regulations under this section shall be grounds for the seizure or quarantine of the product, the imposition of a civil penalty against a processor or retailer, and the suspension, revocation or cancellation of a license, in accordance with this article.

Cannabis Law § 104. Processing of cannabinoid hemp and hemp extract.

1. No processor shall sell or agree to sell or deliver in the state any cannabinoid hemp, hemp extract or product derived therefrom, used for human consumption, except in sealed containers containing quantities in accordance with size standards pursuant to rules adopted by the board. Such containers shall have affixed thereto such labels as may be required by the rules of the board.

2. Processors shall take such steps necessary to ensure that the cannabinoid hemp or hemp extract used in their processing operation has only been grown with pesticides that are registered by the department of environmental

conservation or that specifically meet the United States environmental protection agency registration exemption criteria for minimum risk, used in compliance with rules, regulations, standards and guidelines issued by the department of environmental conservation for pesticides.

3. All cannabinoid hemp, hemp extract and products derived therefrom used for human consumption shall be extracted and processed in accordance with good manufacturing processes pursuant to Part 117 or Part 111 of title 21 of the code of federal regulations, as may be defined, modified and decided upon by the board in rules or regulations.

4. As necessary to protect human health, the board shall have the authority to: (a) regulate and prohibit specific ingredients, excipients or methods used in processing cannabinoid hemp, hemp extract and products derived therefrom; and (b) prohibit, or expressly allow, certain products or product classes derived from cannabinoid hemp or hemp extract, to be processed.

Cannabis Law § 105. Laboratory testing.

Every cannabinoid hemp processor shall contract with an independent commercial laboratory to test the hemp extract and products produced by the licensed processor. The board shall establish the necessary qualifications or certifications required for such laboratories used by licensees. The board is authorized to issue rules and regulations consistent with this article establishing the testing required, the reporting of testing results and the form for reporting such laboratory testing results. The board has authority to require licensees to submit any cannabinoid hemp, hemp extract or product derived therefrom, processed or offered for sale within the state, for testing by the board. This section shall not obligate the board, in any way, to perform any testing on hemp, cannabinoid hemp, hemp extract or product derived therefrom.

Cannabis Law § 106. New York hemp product.

The board may establish and adopt official grades and standards for cannabinoid hemp, hemp extract and products derived therefrom, as the board may deem advisable, which are produced for sale in this state and, from time to time, may amend or modify such grades and standards.

Cannabis Law § 107. Penalties.

Notwithstanding the provision of any law to the contrary, the failure to comply with a requirement of this article, or a regulation thereunder, may be punishable by a civil penalty of not more than one thousand dollars for a first violation; not more than five thousand dollars for a second violation within three years; and not more than ten thousand dollars for a third violation and each subsequent violation thereafter, within three years.

Cannabis Law § 108. Hemp workgroup.

The board, in consultation with the commissioner of the department of agriculture and markets, may appoint a New York state hemp and hemp extract workgroup, composed of growers, researchers, producers, processors, manufacturers and trade associations, to make recommendations for the industrial hemp and cannabinoid hemp programs, state and federal policies and policy initiatives, and opportunities for the promotion and marketing of cannabinoid hemp and hemp extract as consistent with federal and state laws, rules and regulations.

Cannabis Law § 109. Prohibitions.

1. Except as authorized by the United States food and drug administration, the processing of cannabinoid hemp or

hemp extract used for human consumption is prohibited within the state unless the processor is licensed under this article.

2. Cannabinoid hemp and hemp extracts used for human consumption and grown or processed outside the state shall not be distributed or sold at retail within the state, unless they meet all standards established for cannabinoid hemp under state law and regulations.

3. The retail sale of cannabinoid hemp is prohibited in this state unless the retailer is licensed under this article.

Cannabis Law § 110. Special use permits.

The board shall have the authority to issue temporary permits for carrying on any activity related to cannabinoid hemp, hemp extract and products derived therefrom, licensed under this article. The board may set reasonable fees for such permits, to establish the periods during which such permits are valid, and to make rules and regulations to implement this section.

Cannabis Law § 111. Severability.

If any provision of this article or the application thereof to any person or circumstances is held invalid, such invalidity shall not affect other provisions or applications of this article which can be given effect without the invalid provision or application, and to this end the provisions of this article are declared to be severable.

ARTICLE 6. GENERAL PROVISIONS

Cannabis Law § 125. General prohibitions and restrictions.

1. No person shall cultivate, process, distribute for sale or sell at wholesale or retail or deliver to consumers any cannabis, cannabis product, medical cannabis or cannabinoid hemp or hemp extract product within the state without obtaining the appropriate registration, license, or permit therefor required by this chapter unless otherwise authorized by law.

2. No registered organization, licensee, or permittee or other entity under the jurisdiction of the board shall sell, or agree to sell or deliver in this state any cannabis or cannabinoid hemp or hemp extract for the purposes of resale to any person who is not duly registered, licensed or permitted pursuant to this chapter to sell such product, at wholesale or retail, as the case may be, at the time of such agreement and sale.

3. No registered organization, licensee, or permittee or other entity under the jurisdiction of the board shall employ, or permit to be employed, or shall allow to work, on any premises registered or licensed for retail sale hereunder, any person under the age of eighteen years in any capacity where the duties of such person require or permit such person to sell, dispense or handle cannabis. Any employee eighteen years of age or older and under twenty-one years of age may not have direct interaction with customers inside a licensed retail store.

4. No registered organization, licensee, or permittee, or other entity under the jurisdiction of the board, shall sell, deliver or give away, or cause, permit or procure to be sold, delivered or given away any cannabis, cannabis product, or medical cannabis on credit; except that a registered organization, licensee or permittee may accept third party credit cards for the sale of any cannabis, cannabis product, or medical cannabis for which it is registered, licensed or permitted to dispense or sell to patients or cannabis consumers. This includes, but is not limited to, any consignment sale of any kind.

5. No registered organization, licensee, or permittee, or other entity under the jurisdiction of the board, shall cease

to be operated as a bona fide or legitimate premises within the contemplation of the registration, license, or permit issued for such premises, as determined within the judgment of the board.

6. No registered organization, licensee, or permittee, or other entity under the jurisdiction of the board, shall refuse, nor any person holding a registration, license, or permit refuse, nor any officer or director of any corporation or organization holding a registration, license, or permit refuse, to appear and/or testify under oath at an inquiry or hearing held by the board, with respect to any matter bearing upon the registration, license, or permit, the conduct of any people at the licensed premises, or bearing upon the character or fitness of such registrant, licensee, or permittee, or other entity under the jurisdiction of the board, to continue to hold any registration, license, or permit. Nor shall any of the above offer false testimony under oath at such inquiry or hearing.

7. No registered organization, licensee, or permittee, or other entity under the jurisdiction of the board, shall engage, participate in, or aid or abet any violation of any provision of this chapter, or the rules or regulations of the board.

8. It shall be the responsibility of the registered organization, licensee or permittee, or other entity under the jurisdiction of the board, to exercise adequate supervision over the registered, licensed or permitted location. Persons registered, licensed, or permitted shall be held strictly accountable for any and all violations that occur upon any registered, licensed, or permitted premises, and for any and all violations committed by or permitted by any manager, agent or employee of such registered, licensed, or permitted person.

9. As it is a privilege under the law to be registered, licensed, or permitted to cultivate, process, distribute, or sell cannabis, the board may impose any such further restrictions upon any registrant, licensee, or permittee in particular instances as it deems necessary to further state policy and best serve the public interest. A violation or failure of any person registered, licensed, or permitted to comply with any condition, stipulation, or agreement, upon which any registration, license, or permit was issued or renewed by the board may, in accordance with this chapter subject the registrant, licensee, or permittee to suspension, cancellation, revocation, and/or civil penalties in accordance with this chapter, as determined by the board.

10. No adult-use cannabis or medical cannabis may be imported to, or exported out of, New York state by a registered organization, licensee or person holding a license and/or permit pursuant to this chapter, until such time as it may become legal to do so under federal law. Should it become legal to do so under federal law, the board may promulgate such rules and regulations as it deems necessary to protect the public and the policy of the state, including but not limited to prioritize and promote New York cannabis. Further, all such cannabis or cannabis products must be distributed in a manner consistent with the provisions of this chapter.

11. No registered organization, licensee or any of its agents, servants or employees shall sell any cannabis product, or medical cannabis from house to house by means of a truck or otherwise, where the sale is consummated and delivery made concurrently at the residence or place of business of a cannabis consumer. This subdivision shall not prohibit the delivery by a registered organization to certified patients or their designated caregivers, pursuant to article three of this chapter.

12. No licensee shall employ any canvasser or solicitor for the purpose of receiving an order from a certified patient, designated caregiver or cannabis consumer for any cannabis product, or medical cannabis at the residence or place of business of such patient, caregiver or consumer, nor shall any licensee receive or accept any order, for the sale of any cannabis product, or medical cannabis which shall be solicited at the residence or place of business of a patient, caregiver or consumer. This subdivision shall not prohibit the solicitation by a distributor of an order from any licensee at the licensed premises of such licensee.

Cannabis Law § 126. License to be confined to premises licensed; premises for which no license shall be granted; transporting cannabis.

1. A registration, license, or permit issued to any person, pursuant to this chapter, for any registered, licensed, or permitted premises shall not be transferable to any other person, to any other location or premises, or to any other building or part of the building containing the licensed premises except in the discretion of the office. All privileges granted by any registration, license, or permit shall be available only to the person therein specified, and only for the premises licensed and no other except if authorized by the board. Provided, however, that the provisions of this section shall not be deemed to prohibit the amendment of a registration or license as provided for in this chapter. A violation of this section shall subject the registration, license, or permit to revocation for cause.

2. Where a registration or license for premises has been revoked, the board in its discretion may refuse to issue a registration, license, or permit under this chapter, for a period of up to five years after such revocation, for such premises or for any part of the building containing such premises and connected therewith.

3. In determining whether to issue such a proscription against granting any registration, license, or permit for such five-year period, in addition to any other factors deemed relevant to the board, the board shall, in the case of a license revoked due to the sale of cannabis to a person under the age of twenty-one not otherwise authorized by this chapter, determine whether the proposed subsequent licensee has obtained such premises through an arm's length transaction, and, if such transaction is not found to be an arm's length transaction, the office shall deny the issuance of such license.

4. For purposes of this section, "arm's length transaction" shall mean a sale of a fee of all undivided interests in real property, lease, management agreement, or other agreement giving the applicant control over the cannabis at the premises, or any part thereof, in the open market, between an informed and willing buyer and seller where neither is under any compulsion to participate in the transaction, unaffected by any unusual conditions indicating a reasonable possibility that the sale was made for the purpose of permitting the original licensee to avoid the effect of the revocation. The following sales shall be presumed not to be arm's length transactions unless adequate documentation is provided demonstrating that the sale, lease, management agreement, or other agreement giving the applicant control over the cannabis at the premises, was not conducted, in whole or in part, for the purpose of permitting the original licensee to avoid the effect of the revocation:

   (a) a sale between relatives;

   (b) a sale between related companies or partners in a business; or

   (c) a sale, lease, management agreement, or other agreement giving the applicant control over the cannabis at the premises, affected by other facts or circumstances that would indicate that the sale, lease, management agreement, or other agreement giving the applicant control over the cannabis at the premises, is entered into for the primary purpose of permitting the original licensee to avoid the effect of the revocation.

5. No registered organization, licensee or permittee shall transport cannabis products or medical cannabis except in vehicles owned and operated by such registered organization, licensee or permittee, or hired and operated by such registered organization, licensee or permittee from a trucking or transportation company permitted and registered with the board.

6. No common carrier or person operating a transportation facility in this state, other than the United States government, shall knowingly receive for transportation or delivery within the state any cannabis products or medical cannabis unless the shipment is accompanied by a copy of a bill of lading, or other document, showing the name and address of the consignor, the name and address of the consignee, the date of the shipment, and the quantity and kind of cannabis products or medical cannabis contained therein.

Cannabis Law § 127. Protections for the use of cannabis; unlawful discriminations prohibited.

1. No person, registered organization, licensee or permittee, employees, or their agents shall be subject to arrest,

prosecution, or penalty in any manner, or denied any right or privilege, including but not limited to civil liability or disciplinary action by a business or occupational or professional licensing board or office, solely for conduct permitted under this chapter. For the avoidance of doubt, the appellate division of the supreme court of the state of New York, and any disciplinary or character and fitness committees established by law are occupational and professional licensing boards within the meaning of this section. State or local law enforcement agencies shall not cooperate with or provide assistance to the government of the United States or any agency thereof in enforcing the federal controlled substances act solely for actions consistent with this chapter, except as pursuant to a valid court order.

2. No landlord may refuse to lease to and may not otherwise penalize an individual solely for conduct authorized under this chapter, except:

(a) if failing to do so would cause the landlord to lose a monetary or licensing related benefit under federal law or regulations; or

(b) if a property has in place a smoke-free policy, it is not required to permit the smoking of cannabis products on its premises, provided no such restriction may be construed to limit the certified medical use of cannabis.

2-a. No school, college or university may refuse to enroll and may not otherwise penalize a person solely for conduct allowed under this chapter, except:

(a) if failing to do so would cause the school, college or university to lose a monetary or licensing related benefit under federal law or regulations; or

(b) if the school, college or university has adopted a code of conduct prohibiting cannabis use on the basis of a sincere religious belief of the school, college or university.

3. For the purposes of medical care, including organ transplants, a certified patient's authorized use of medical cannabis must be considered the equivalent of the use of any other medication under the direction of a practitioner and does not constitute the use of an illicit substance or otherwise disqualify a registered qualifying patient from medical care.

4. An employer shall adhere to policies regarding cannabis use in accordance with section two hundred one-d of the labor law.

5. No person may be denied custody of or visitation or parenting time with a minor under the family court act, domestic relations law or social services law, solely for conduct permitted under this chapter including, but not limited to, section 222.05 or 222.15 of the penal law, unless it is in the best interest of the child and the child's physical, mental or emotional condition has been impaired, or is in imminent danger of becoming impaired as a result of the person's behavior as established by a fair preponderance of the evidence. For the purposes of this section, this determination cannot be based solely on whether, when, and how often a person uses cannabis without separate evidence of harm.

6. A person currently under parole, probation or other state supervision, or released on recognizance, non-monetary conditions, or bail prior to being convicted, shall not be punished or otherwise penalized for conduct allowed under this chapter unless the terms and conditions of said parole, probation, or state supervision explicitly prohibit a person's cannabis use or any other conduct otherwise allowed under this chapter. A person's use of cannabis or conduct under this chapter shall not be prohibited unless it has been shown by clear and convincing evidence that the prohibition is reasonably related to the underlying crime. Nothing in this provision shall restrict the rights of a certified medical patient.

Cannabis Law § 128. Permits, registrations and licenses.

1. No permit, registration or license shall be transferable or assignable except that notwithstanding any other

provision of law, the permit, registration or license of a sole proprietor converting to corporate form, where such proprietor becomes the sole stockholder and only officer and director of such new corporation, may be transferred to the subject corporation if all requirements of this chapter remain the same with respect to such permit, registration or license as transferred and, further, the registered organization or licensee shall transmit to the board, within ten days of the transfer of license allowable under this subdivision, on a form prescribed by the board, notification of the transfer of such license.

2. No permit, registration or license shall be pledged or deposited as collateral security for any loan or upon any other condition; and any such pledge or deposit, and any contract providing therefor, shall be void.

3. Permits, registrations and licenses issued under this chapter shall contain, in addition to any further information or material to be prescribed by the rules and regulations of the board, the following information:

(a) name of the person to whom the license is issued;

(b) type of license and what type of cannabis commerce is thereby permitted;

(c) description by street and number, or otherwise, of licensed premises; and

(d) a statement in substance that such license shall not be deemed a property or vested right, and that it may be revoked at any time pursuant to law.

Cannabis Law § 129. Laboratory testing permits.

1. The board shall approve and permit one or more independent cannabis testing laboratories to test medical cannabis, adult-use cannabis and/or cannabinoid hemp or hemp extract.

2. To be permitted as an independent cannabis laboratory, a laboratory must apply to the office, on a form and in a manner prescribed by the office, which may include a reasonable fee, and must demonstrate the following to the satisfaction of the board:

(a) the owners and directors of the laboratory are of good moral character;

(b) the laboratory and its staff has the skills, resources and expertise needed to accurately and consistently perform all of the testing required for adult-use cannabis, medical cannabis and/or cannabinoid hemp or hemp extract;

(c) the laboratory has in place and will maintain adequate policies, procedures, and facility security to ensure proper: collection, labeling, accessioning, preparation, analysis, result reporting, disposal and storage of adult-use cannabis, and/or medical cannabis;

(d) for the testing of cannabis, the laboratory is physically located in New York state; and

(e) the laboratory meets any and all requirements prescribed by this chapter and by the board in regulation.

3. The owner of a laboratory testing permit under this section shall not hold a permit, registration or license in any category of this chapter and shall not have any direct or indirect ownership interest in such registered organization or licensee. No board member, officer, manager, owner, partner, principal stakeholder or member of a registered organization or licensee under this chapter, or such person's immediate family member, shall have an interest or voting rights in any laboratory testing permittee.

4. The board shall require that the permitted laboratory report testing results to the board in a manner, form and timeframe as determined by the office.

5. The board is authorized to promulgate regulations, establishing minimum operating and testing requirements, and requiring permitted laboratories to perform certain tests and services.

6. A laboratory granted a laboratory testing permit under this chapter shall not required to be licensed by the federal drug enforcement agency.

7. The board is authorized to enter into contracts or memoranda of understanding with any other state for the purposes of aligning laboratory testing requirements or establishing best practices in testing of cannabis.

Cannabis Law § 130. Special use permits.

The board shall have the authority to issue temporary permits for carrying on activities consistent with the policy and purpose of this chapter with respect to cannabis. No special use permit shall extend for a period longer than ninety days and shall not be renewable, except where a permit is being issued to a licensee as defined in article four of this chapter. A special use permit shall be issued pursuant to an abbreviated application process. The special use permit holder shall have ninety days in which to become fully licensed by satisfying all of the remaining conditions for licensure which were not required for the issuance of the special use permit.

The board may set reasonable fees for such permits and make rules and regulations to implement this section.

1. Industrial cannabis permit - to purchase cannabis from one of the entities licensed by the board for use in the manufacture and sale of any of the following, when such cannabis is not otherwise suitable for consumption purposes, namely: (a) apparel, energy, paper, and tools; (b) scientific, chemical, mechanical and industrial products; or (c) any other industrial use as determined by the board in regulation.

2. Trucking permit - to allow for the trucking or transportation of cannabis products, or medical cannabis by a person other than a registered organization or licensee under this chapter.

3. Warehouse permit - to allow for the storage of cannabis, cannabis products, or medical cannabis at a location not otherwise registered or licensed by the office.

4. Packaging permit - to authorize a licensed cannabis distributor to sort, package, label and bundle cannabis products from one or more registered organizations or licensed processors, on the premises of the licensed cannabis distributor or at a warehouse for which a permit has been issued under this section.

Cannabis Law § 131. Local opt-out; municipal control and preemption.

1. The licensure and establishment of a retail dispensary license and/or on-site consumption license under the provisions of article four of this chapter authorizing the retail sale of adult-use cannabis to cannabis consumers shall not be applicable to a town, city or village which, after the effective date of this chapter, and, on or before the later of December thirty-first, two thousand twenty-one or nine months after the effective date of this section, adopts a local law, subject to permissive referendum governed by section twenty-four of the municipal home rule law, requesting the cannabis control board to prohibit the establishment of such retail dispensary licenses and/or on-site consumption licenses contained in article four of this chapter, within the jurisdiction of the town, city or village. Provided, however, that any town law shall apply to the area of the town outside of any village within such town. No local law may be adopted after the later of December thirty-first, two thousand twenty-one or nine months after the effective date of this section prohibiting the establishment of retail dispensary licenses and/or on-site consumption licenses; provided, however, that a local law repealing such prohibition may be adopted after such date.

2. Except as provided for in subdivision one of this section, all county, town, city and village governing bodies are hereby preempted from adopting any law, rule, ordinance, regulation or prohibition pertaining to the operation or licensure of registered organizations, adult-use cannabis licenses or cannabinoid hemp licenses. However, towns, cities and villages may pass local laws and regulations governing the time, place and manner of the operation of licensed adult-use cannabis retail dispensaries and/or on-site consumption site, provided such law or regulation does

not make the operation of such licensed retail dispensaries or on-site consumption sites unreasonably impracticable as determined by the board.

Cannabis Law § 131-a. Office to be necessary party to certain proceedings.

The office shall be made a party to all actions and proceedings affecting in any manner the possession, ownership or transfer of a registration, license or permit to operate within a municipality and to all such injunction proceedings.

Cannabis Law § 132. Penalties for violation of this chapter.

1. Any person who cultivates for sale or sells cannabis, cannabis products, or medical cannabis without having an appropriate registration, license or permit therefor, or whose registration, license, or permit has been revoked, surrendered or cancelled, may be subject to prosecution in accordance with article two hundred twenty-two of the penal law.

2. Any registered organization or licensee, who has received notification of a registration or license suspension pursuant to the provisions of this chapter, who sells cannabis, cannabis products, medical cannabis or cannabinoid hemp or hemp extract during the suspension period, shall be subject to prosecution as provided in article two hundred twenty-two of the penal law, and upon conviction thereof under this section may be subject to a civil penalty of not more than five thousand dollars.

3. Any person who shall knowingly make any materially false statement in the application for a registration, license or a permit under this chapter may be subject to license or registration suspension, revocation, or denial subject to the board, and may be subject to a civil penalty of not more than two thousand dollars.

4. Any person under the age of twenty-one found to be in possession of cannabis or cannabis products who is not a certified patient pursuant to article three of this chapter shall be in violation of this chapter and shall be subject to the following penalty:

(a) (i) The person shall be subject to a civil penalty of not more than fifty dollars. The civil penalty shall be payable to the office of cannabis management.

(ii) Any identifying information provided by the enforcement agency for the purpose of facilitating payment of the civil penalty shall not be shared or disclosed under any circumstances with any other agency or law enforcement division.

(b) The person shall, upon payment of the required civil penalty, be provided with information related to the dangers of underage use of cannabis and information related to cannabis use disorder by the office.

(c) The issuance and subsequent payment of such civil penalty shall in no way qualify as a criminal accusation, admission of guilt, or a criminal conviction and shall in no way operate as a disqualification of any such person from holding public office, attaining public employment, or as a forfeiture of any right or privilege.

5. Cannabis recovered from individuals who are found to be in violation of this chapter may after notice and opportunity for a hearing be considered a nuisance and shall be disposed of or destroyed.

6. After due notice and opportunity to be heard, as established by rules and regulations, nothing in this section shall prohibit the board from suspending, revoking, or denying a license, permit, registration, or application in addition to the penalties prescribed in this section.

Cannabis Law § 133. Revocation of registrations, licenses and permits for cause; procedure for revocation or cancellation.

1. Any registration, license or permit issued pursuant to this chapter may be revoked, cancelled, suspended and/or subjected to the imposition of a civil penalty for cause.

2. There shall be a rebuttable presumption of revocation for the following causes:

   (a) conviction of the registered organization, licensee, permittee or his or her agent or employee for selling any illicit cannabis on the premises registered, licensed or permitted; or

   (b) for transferring, assigning or hypothecating a registration, license or permit without prior written approval of the office.

3. Notwithstanding the issuance of a registration, license or permit by way of renewal, the board may revoke, cancel or suspend such registration, license or permit and/or may impose a civil penalty against any holder of such registration, license or permit, as prescribed by this section, for causes or violations occurring during the license period immediately preceding the issuance of such registration, license or permit.

4. (a) As used in this section, the term "for cause" shall also include the existence of a sustained and continuing pattern of misconduct, failure to adequately prevent diversion or disorder on or about the registered, licensed or permitted premises, or in the area in front of or adjacent to the registered or licensed premises, or in any parking lot provided by the registered organization or licensee for use by registered organization or licensee's patrons, which significantly adversely affects or tends to significantly adversely affect the protection, health, welfare, safety, or repose of the inhabitants of the area in which the registered or licensed premises is located.

(b) (i) As used in this section, the term "for cause" shall also include deliberately misleading the board or office of cannabis management:

   (A) as to the nature and character of the business to be operated by the registered organization, licensee or permittee; or

   (B) by substantially altering the nature or character of such business during the registration or licensing period without seeking appropriate approvals from the board.

(ii) As used in this subdivision, the term "substantially altering the nature or character" of such business shall mean any significant and material alteration in the scope of business activities conducted by a registered organization, licensee or permittee that would require obtaining an alternate form of registration, license or permit.

5. As used in this chapter, the existence of a sustained and continuing pattern of misconduct or disorder on or about the premises may be presumed upon the sixth incident reported to the board by a law enforcement agency, or discovered by the board during the course of any investigation, of misconduct or disorder on or about the premises or related to the operation of the premises, absent clear and convincing evidence of either fraudulent intent on the part of any complainant or a factual error with respect to the content of any report concerning such complaint relied upon by the board.

6. Any registration, license or permit issued by the board pursuant to this chapter may be revoked, cancelled or suspended and/or be subjected to the imposition of a monetary penalty set forth in this chapter in the manner prescribed by this section.

7. The board may on its own initiative, or on complaint of any person, institute proceedings to revoke, cancel or suspend any adult-use cannabis retail dispensary license or adult-use cannabis on-site consumption license and may impose a civil penalty against the licensee after a hearing at which the licensee shall be given an opportunity to be heard. Such hearing shall be held in such manner and upon such notice as may be prescribed in regulation by the board.

8. All other registrations, licenses or permits issued under this chapter may be revoked, cancelled, suspended and/or made subject to the imposition of a civil penalty by the office after a hearing to be held in such manner and upon such notice as may be prescribed in regulation by the board.

9. Where a licensee or permittee is convicted of two or more qualifying offenses within a five-year period, the office, upon receipt of notification of such second or subsequent conviction, shall, in addition to any other sanction or civil or criminal penalty imposed pursuant to this chapter, impose on such licensee a civil penalty not to exceed ten thousand dollars. For purposes of this subdivision, a qualifying offense shall mean the sale of cannabis to a person under the age of twenty-one not otherwise authorized by this chapter. For purposes of this subdivision only, a conviction of a licensee or an employee or agent of such licensee shall constitute a conviction of such licensee.

10. The board may adopt rules and regulations based on federal guidance, provided those rules and regulations are designed to comply with federal guidance and mitigate federal enforcement against the registrations, licenses, or permits issued under this chapter, or the cannabis industry as a whole. This may include regulations which permit the sharing of licensee, registrant, or permit holder information with designated banking or financial institutions, provided these regulations are designed to aid cannabis industry participants' access to banking and financial services.

Cannabis Law § 134. Lawful actions pursuant to this chapter.

1. Contracts related to the operation of registered organizations, licenses and permits under this chapter shall be lawful and shall not be deemed unenforceable on the basis that the actions permitted pursuant to the registration, license or permit are prohibited by federal law.

2. The following actions are not unlawful as provided under this chapter, shall not be an offense under any state or local law, and shall not result in any civil penalty, fine, seizure, or forfeiture of assets, or be the basis for detention or search against any person acting in accordance with this chapter:

(a) Actions of a registered organization, licensee, or permittee, or the employees or agents of such registered organization, licensee or permittee, as permitted by this chapter and consistent with rules and regulations of the office, pursuant to a valid registration, license or permit issued by the board.

(b) Actions of those who allow property to be used by a registered organization, licensee, or permittee, or the employees or agents of such registered organization, licensee or permittee, as permitted by this chapter and consistent with rules and regulations of the office, pursuant to a valid registration, license or permit issued by the board.

(c) Actions of any person or entity, their employees, or their agents providing a service to a registered organization, licensee, permittee or a potential registered organization, licensee, or permittee, as permitted by this chapter and consistent with rules and regulations of the office, relating to the formation of a business.

(d) The purchase, cultivation, possession, or consumption of cannabis and medical cannabis, as permitted by law, and consistent with rules and regulations of the board.

Cannabis Law § 135. Review by courts.

An action by the board shall be subject to review by the supreme court in the manner provided in article seventy-eight of the civil practice law and rules including, but not limited to:

(a) Refusal by the board to issue a registration, license, or a permit.

(b) The revocation, cancellation or suspension of a registration, license, or permit by the board.

(c) The failure or refusal by the board to render a decision upon any application or hearing submitted to or held by the board within sixty days after such submission or hearing.

(d) The transfer by the board of a registration, license, or permit to any other entity or premises, or the failure or refusal by the board to approve such a transfer.

(e) Refusal to approve alteration of premises.

(f) Refusal to approve a corporate change in stockholders, stockholdings, officers or directors.

Cannabis Law § 136. Illicit cannabis.

1. "Illicit cannabis" means and includes any cannabis flower, concentrated cannabis and cannabis product on which any tax required to have been paid under any applicable state law, has not been paid. Illicit cannabis shall not include any cannabis lawfully possessed in accordance with this chapter or the penal law.

2. Any person holding a license, permit or registration under this chapter who shall knowingly possess or have under his or her control any cannabis known by the person to be illicit cannabis is guilty of a class B misdemeanor.

3. Any person holding a license, permit or registration pursuant to this chapter who shall knowingly barter, exchange, give or sell, or offer to barter, exchange, give or sell any cannabis known by the person to be illicit cannabis is guilty of a misdemeanor.

4. Any person holding a license, permit or registration pursuant to this chapter who shall knowingly possess or have under his or her control or transport any cannabis known by the person to be illicit cannabis with intent to barter, exchange, give or sell such cannabis is guilty of a class B misdemeanor.

5. Any person who, being the owner, lessee or occupant of any room, shed, tenement, booth, building, float, vessel or part thereof who knowingly permits the same to be used for the cultivation, processing, distribution, purchase, sale, warehousing or transportation of any cannabis, in violation of a possession limit in the penal law, known by the person to be illicit cannabis, is guilty of a violation.

Cannabis Law § 137. Persons forbidden to traffic cannabis; certain officials not to be interested in manufacture or sale of cannabis products.

1. The following are forbidden to traffic in cannabis except in extraordinary circumstances as determined by the board:

(a) An individual who has been convicted of an offense related to the functions or duties of owning and operating a business within three years of the application date, except that if the board determines that the owner or licensee is otherwise suitable to be issued a license, and the board determines granting the license is not inconsistent with public safety, the board shall conduct a thorough review of the nature of the crime, conviction, circumstances and evidence of rehabilitation of the owner in accordance with article twenty-three-A of the correction law, and shall evaluate the suitability of the owner or licensee to be issued a license based on the evidence found through the review. In determining which offenses are substantially related to the functions or duties of owning and operating a business, the board shall include, but not be limited to, the following:

(i) a felony conviction within the past five years involving fraud, money laundering, forgery or other unlawful conduct related to owning and operating a business; and

(ii) a felony conviction within the past five years for hiring, employing, or using a minor in transporting, carrying, selling, giving away, preparing for sale, or peddling, any controlled substance to a minor; or selling, offering to sell, furnishing, offering to furnish, administering, or giving any controlled substance to a minor.

(b) A person under the age of twenty-one years;

(c) A partnership or a corporation, unless each member of the partnership, or each of the principal officers and directors of the corporation, is a citizen of the United States or a person lawfully admitted for permanent residence in the United States, not less than twenty-one years of age; provided however that a corporation which otherwise conforms to the requirements of this section and chapter may be licensed if each of its principal officers and more than one-half of its directors are citizens of the United States or persons lawfully admitted for permanent residence in the United States; and provided further that a corporation organized under the not-for-profit corporation law or the education law which otherwise conforms to the requirements of this section and chapter may be licensed if each of its principal officers and directors are not less than twenty-one years of age; and provided, further, that a corporation organized under the not-for-profit corporation law or the education law and located on the premises of a college as defined by section two of the education law which otherwise conforms to the requirements of this section and chapter may be licensed if each of its principal officers and each of its directors are not less than twenty-one years of age;

(d) A person who shall have had any registration or license issued under this chapter revoked for cause, until the expiration of one year from the date of such revocation;

(e) A person not registered or licensed under the provisions of this chapter, who has been convicted of a misdemeanor or felony in violation of this chapter, until the expiration of one year from the date of such conviction; or

(f) A corporation or partnership, if any officer and director or any partner, while not licensed under the provisions of this chapter, has been convicted of a misdemeanor or felony in violation of this chapter, or has had a registration or license issued under this chapter revoked for cause, until the expiration of up to one year from the date of such conviction or revocation as determined by the board.

2. Except as may otherwise be provided for in regulation, it shall be unlawful for any chief of police, police officer or subordinate of any police department in the state, to be either directly or indirectly interested in the cultivation, processing, distribution, or sale of cannabis products or to offer for sale, or recommend to any registered organization or licensee any cannabis products. A person may not be denied any registration or license granted under the provisions of this chapter solely on the grounds of being the spouse or domestic partner of a public servant described in this section. The solicitation or recommendation made to any registered organization or licensee, to purchase any cannabis products by any police official or subordinate as hereinabove described, shall be presumptive evidence of the interest of such official or subordinate in the cultivation, processing, distribution, or sale of cannabis products.

3. No elected village officer shall be subject to the limitations set forth in subdivision two of this section unless such elected village officer shall be assigned duties directly relating to the operation or management of the police department.

Cannabis Law § 138. Access to criminal history information through the division of criminal justice services.

In connection with the administration of this chapter, the board is authorized to request, receive and review criminal history information through the division of criminal justice services with respect to any person seeking a registration, license, permit or authorization to cultivate, process, distribute or sell medical cannabis, adult-use cannabis, cannabinoid hemp or hemp extract. At the board's request, each person, member, principal and/or officer of the applicant shall submit to the board his or her fingerprints in such form and in such manner as specified by the division, for the purpose of conducting a criminal history search identifying criminal convictions and pending criminal charges and returning a report thereon in accordance with the procedures and requirements established by the division pursuant to the provisions of article thirty-five of the executive law, which shall include the payment of the reasonable prescribed processing fees for the cost of the division's full search and retain procedures and a national criminal history record check. The board, or their designee, shall submit such fingerprints and the processing fee to the division. The division shall forward to the board a report with respect to the applicant's previous criminal history, if any, or a statement that the applicant has no previous criminal history according to its files. Fingerprints submitted to the division pursuant to this subdivision may also be submitted to the federal bureau of investigation for a national criminal history record check. If additional copies of fingerprints are required, the applicant shall furnish them upon request. Upon receipt of such criminal history information, the board shall provide such applicant with a copy of such criminal history information, together with a copy of article twenty-three-A of the correction law, and inform such applicant of his or her right to seek correction of any incorrect information contained in such criminal history information pursuant to regulations and procedures established by the division of criminal justice services.

Cannabis Law § 138-a. Injunction for unlawful manufacturing, sale, or distribution of cannabis.

The office of cannabis management shall have the authority to request an injunction against any person who is unlawfully cultivating, processing, distributing or selling cannabis in this state without obtaining the appropriate registration, license, or permit therefor, in accordance with this chapter and any applicable state law.

Cannabis Law § 139. Severability.

If any provision of this chapter or application thereof to any person or circumstances is held invalid, such invalidity shall not affect other provisions or applications of this chapter that can be given effect without the invalid provision or application, and to this end the provisions of this chapter are declared severable.

IV. Criminal Procedure Law

Criminal Procedure Law § 160.50. Order upon termination of criminal action in favor of the accused.

1. Upon the termination of a criminal action or proceeding against a person in favor of such person, as defined in subdivision three of this section, unless the district attorney upon motion with not less than five days notice to such person or his or her attorney demonstrates to the satisfaction of the court that the interests of justice require otherwise, or the court on its own motion with not less than five days notice to such person or his or her attorney determines that the interests of justice require otherwise and states the reasons for such determination on the record, the record of such action or proceeding shall be sealed and the clerk of the court wherein such criminal action or proceeding was terminated shall immediately notify the commissioner of the division of criminal justice services and the heads of all appropriate police departments and other law enforcement agencies that the action has been terminated in favor of the accused, and unless the court has directed otherwise, that the record of such action or proceeding shall be sealed. Upon receipt of notification of such termination and sealing:

  (a) every photograph of such person and photographic plate or proof, and all palmprints and fingerprints taken or made of such person pursuant to the provisions of this article in regard to the action or proceeding terminated, except a dismissal pursuant to section 170.56 or 210.46 of this chapter, and all duplicates and copies thereof, except a digital fingerprint image where authorized pursuant to paragraph (e) of this subdivision, shall forthwith be, at the discretion of the recipient agency, either destroyed or returned to such person, or to the attorney who represented such person at the time of the termination of the action or proceeding, at the address given by such person or attorney during the action or proceeding, by the division of criminal justice services and by any police department or law enforcement agency having any such photograph, photographic plate or proof, palmprint or fingerprints in its possession or under its control;

(b) any police department or law enforcement agency, including the division of criminal justice services, which transmitted or otherwise forwarded to any agency of the United States or of any other state or of any other jurisdiction outside the state of New York copies of any such photographs, photographic plates or proofs, palmprints and fingerprints, including those relating to actions or proceedings which were dismissed pursuant to section 170.56 or 210.46 of this chapter, shall forthwith formally request in writing that all such copies be destroyed or returned to the police department or law enforcement agency which transmitted or forwarded them, and, if returned, such department or agency shall, at its discretion, either destroy or return them as provided herein, except that those relating to dismissals pursuant to section 170.56 or 210.46 of this chapter shall not be destroyed or returned by such department or agency;

(c) all official records and papers, including judgments and orders of a court but not including published court decisions or opinions or records and briefs on appeal, relating to the arrest or prosecution, including all duplicates and copies thereof, on file with the division of criminal justice services, any court, police agency, or prosecutor's office shall be sealed and not made available to any person or public or private agency;

(d) such records shall be made available to the person accused or to such person's designated agent, and shall be made available to (i) a prosecutor in any proceeding in which the accused has moved for an order pursuant to section 170.56 or 210.46 of this chapter, or (ii) a law enforcement agency upon ex parte motion in any superior court, or in any district court, city court or the criminal court of the city of New York provided that such court sealed the record, if such agency demonstrates to the satisfaction of the court that justice requires that such records be made available to it, or (iii) any state or local officer or agency with responsibility for the issuance of licenses to possess guns, when the accused has made application for such a license, or (iv) the New York state department of corrections and community supervision when the accused is on parole supervision as a result of conditional release or a parole release granted by the New York state board of parole, and the arrest which is the subject of the inquiry is one which occurred while the accused was under such supervision, or (v) any prospective employer of a police officer or peace officer as those terms are defined in subdivisions thirty-three and thirty-four of section 1.20 of this chapter, in relation to an application for employment as a police officer or peace officer; provided, however, that every person who is an applicant for the position of police officer or peace officer shall be furnished with a copy of all records obtained under this paragraph and afforded an opportunity to make an explanation thereto, or (vi) the probation department responsible for supervision of the accused when the arrest which is the subject of the inquiry is one which occurred while the accused was under such supervision; and

(e) where fingerprints subject to the provisions of this section have been received by the division of criminal justice services and have been filed by the division as digital images, such images may be retained, provided that a fingerprint card of the individual is on file with the division which was not sealed pursuant to this section or section 160.55 of this article.

2. A report of the termination of the action or proceeding in favor of the accused shall be sufficient notice of sealing to the commissioner of the division of criminal justice services unless the report also indicates that the court directed that the record not be sealed in the interests of justice. Where the court has determined pursuant to subdivision one of this section that sealing is not in the interest of justice, the clerk of the court shall include notification of that determination in any report to such division of the disposition of the action or proceeding.

3. For the purposes of subdivision one of this section, a criminal action or proceeding against a person shall be considered terminated in favor of such person where:

(a) an order dismissing the entire accusatory instrument against such person pursuant to article four hundred seventy was entered; or

(b) an order to dismiss the entire accusatory instrument against such person pursuant to section 170.30, 170.50, 170.55, 170.56, 180.70, 210.20, 210.46 or 210.47 of this chapter was entered or deemed entered, or an order terminating the prosecution against such person was entered pursuant to section 180.85 of this chapter, and the people have not appealed from such order or the determination of an appeal or appeals by the people from such order has been against the people; or

(c) a verdict of complete acquittal was made pursuant to section 330.10 of this chapter; or

(d) a trial order of dismissal of the entire accusatory instrument against such person pursuant to section 290.10 or 360.40 of this chapter was entered and the people have not appealed from such order or the determination of an appeal or appeals by the people from such order has been against the people; or

(e) an order setting aside a verdict pursuant to section 330.30 or 370.10 of this chapter was entered and the people have not appealed from such order or the determination of an appeal or appeals by the people from such order has been against the people and no new trial has been ordered; or

(f) an order vacating a judgment pursuant to section 440.10 of this chapter was entered and the people have not appealed from such order or the determination of an appeal or appeals by the people from such order has been against the people, and no new trial has been ordered; or

(g) an order of discharge pursuant to article seventy of the civil practice law and rules was entered on a ground which invalidates the conviction and the people have not appealed from such order or the determination of an appeal or appeals by the people from such order has been against the people; or

(h) where all charges against such person are dismissed pursuant to section 190.75 of this chapter. In such event, the clerk of the court which empaneled the grand jury shall serve a certification of such disposition upon the division of criminal justice services and upon the appropriate police department or law enforcement agency which upon receipt thereof, shall comply with the provisions of paragraphs (a), (b), (c) and (d) of subdivision one of this section in the same manner as is required thereunder with respect to an order of a court entered pursuant to said subdivision one; or

(i) prior to the filing of an accusatory instrument in a local criminal court against such person, the prosecutor elects not to prosecute such person. In such event, the prosecutor shall serve a certification of such disposition upon the division of criminal justice services and upon the appropriate police department or law enforcement agency which, upon receipt thereof, shall comply with the provisions of paragraphs (a), (b), (c) and (d) of subdivision one of this section in the same manner as is required thereunder with respect to an order of a court entered pursuant to said subdivision one.

(j) following the arrest of such person, the arresting police agency, prior to the filing of an accusatory instrument in a local criminal court but subsequent to the forwarding of a copy of the fingerprints of such person to the division of criminal justice services, elects not to proceed further. In such event, the head of the arresting police agency shall serve a certification of such disposition upon the division of criminal justice services which, upon receipt thereof, shall comply with the provisions of paragraphs (a), (b), (c) and (d) of subdivision one of this section in the same manner as is required thereunder with respect to an order of a court entered pursuant to said subdivision one.

(k) (i) The conviction was for a violation of article two hundred twenty or section 240.36 of the penal law prior to the effective date of article two hundred twenty-one of the penal law, and the sole controlled substance involved was marihuana and the conviction was only for a misdemeanor and/or violation; or

(ii) the conviction is for an offense defined in section 221.05 or 221.10 of the penal law prior to the effective date of chapter one hundred thirty-two of the laws of two thousand nineteen; or

(iii) the conviction is for an offense defined in former section 221.05 221.10, 221.15, 221.20, 221.35, or 221.40 of the penal law; or

(iv) the conviction was for an offense defined in section 240.37 of the penal law; or

(v) the conviction was for a violation of section 220.03 or 220.06 of the penal law prior to the effective date of the chapter of the laws of two thousand twenty-one that amended this paragraph, and the sole controlled substance involved was concentrated cannabis; or

(vi) the conviction was for an offense defined in section 222.10, 222.15, 222.25 or 222.45 of the penal law.

No defendant shall be required or permitted to waive eligibility for sealing or expungement pursuant to this section as part of a plea of guilty, sentence or any agreement related to a conviction for a violation of section 222.10, 222.15, 222.25 or 222.45 of the penal law and any such waiver shall be deemed void and wholly unenforceable.

(l) An order dismissing an action pursuant to section 215.40 of this chapter was entered.

4. A person in whose favor a criminal action or proceeding was terminated, as defined in paragraph (a) through (h) of subdivision two of this section, prior to the effective date of this section, may upon motion apply to the court in which such termination occurred, upon not less than twenty days notice to the district attorney, for an order granting to such person the relief set forth in subdivision one of this section, and such order shall be granted unless the district attorney demonstrates to the satisfaction of the court that the interests of justice require otherwise. A person in whose favor a criminal action or proceeding was terminated, as defined in paragraph (i) or (j) of subdivision two of this section, prior to the effective date of this section, may apply to the appropriate prosecutor or police agency for a certification as described in said paragraph (i) or (j) granting to such person the relief set forth therein, and such certification shall be granted by such prosecutor or police agency.

5. (a) Expungement of certain marihuana-related records. A conviction for an offense described in paragraph (k) of subdivision three of this section shall, on and after the effective date of this paragraph, in accordance with the provisions of this paragraph, be vacated and dismissed, and all records of such conviction or convictions and related to such conviction or convictions shall be expunged, as described in subdivision forty-five of section 1.20 of this chapter, and the matter shall be considered terminated in favor of the accused and deemed a nullity, having been rendered by this paragraph legally invalid. All such records for an offense described in this paragraph where the conviction was entered on or before the effective date of the chapter of the laws of 2019 that amended this paragraph shall be expunged promptly and, in any event, no later than one year after such effective date.

(b) Duties of certain state officials and law enforcement agencies. Commencing upon the effective date of this paragraph:

(i) the chief administrator of the courts shall promptly notify the commissioner of the division of criminal justice services and the heads of all appropriate police departments, district attorney's offices and other law enforcement agencies of all convictions that have been vacated and dismissed pursuant to paragraph (a) of this subdivision and that all records related to such convictions shall be expunged and the matter shall be considered terminated in favor of the accused and deemed a nullity, having been rendered legally invalid. Upon receipt of notification of such vacatur, dismissal and expungement, all records relating to such conviction or convictions, or the criminal action or proceeding, as the case may be, shall be marked as expunged by conspicuously indicating on the face of the record and on each page or at the beginning of the digitized file of the record that the record has been designated as expunged. Upon the written request of the individual whose case has been expunged or their designated agent, such records shall be destroyed. Such records and papers shall not be made available to any person, except the individual whose case has been expunged or such person's designated agent; and

(ii) where automatic vacatur, dismissal, and expungement, including record destruction if requested, is required by this subdivision but any record of the court system in this state has not yet been updated to reflect same

(A) notwithstanding any other provision of law except as provided in paragraph (d) of subdivision one of this section and paragraph (e) of subdivision four of section eight hundred thirty-seven of the executive law: (1) when the division of criminal justice services conducts a search of its criminal history records, maintained pursuant to subdivision six of section eight hundred thirty-seven of the executive law, and returns a report thereon, all references to a conviction for an offense described in paragraph (k) of subdivision three of this section shall be excluded from such report; and (2) the chief administrator of the courts shall develop and promulgate rules as may be necessary to ensure that no written or electronic report of a criminal history record search conducted by the office of court administration contains information relating to a conviction for an offense described in paragraph (k) of subdivision three of this section; and (B) where court records relevant to such matter cannot be located or have been destroyed, and a person or the person's attorney presents to an appropriate court employee a fingerprint record of the New York state division of criminal justice services, or a copy of a court disposition record or other relevant court record, which indicates that a criminal action or proceeding against such person was terminated by conviction of an offense described in paragraph (k) of subdivision three of this section, then promptly, and in any event within thirty days after such notice to such court employee, the chief administrator of the courts or his or her designee shall assure that such vacatur, dismissal, and expungement, including record destruction if requested, have been completed in accordance with subparagraph (i) of this paragraph.

(c) Vacatur, dismissal and expungement as set forth in this subdivision is without prejudice to any person or such person's attorney seeking further relief pursuant to article four hundred forty of this chapter or any other law. Nothing in this section is intended or shall be interpreted to diminish or abrogate any right or remedy otherwise available to any person.

(d) The office of court administration, in conjunction with the division of criminal justice services, shall develop an affirmative information campaign and widely disseminate to the public, through its website, public service announcements and other means, in multiple languages and through multiple outlets, information concerning the expungement, vacatur and resentencing of marihuana convictions established by the chapter of the laws of two thousand nineteen that added this paragraph, including, but not limited to, the automatic expungement of certain past convictions, the means by which an individual may file a motion for vacatur, dismissal and expungement of certain past convictions, and the impact of such changes on such person's criminal history records.

V. Education Law

Education Law § 6815. Adulterating, misbranding and substituting.

1. Adultered drugs. A drug or device shall be deemed to be adulterated:

a. (1) If it consists in whole or in part of any filthy, putrid, or decomposed substance; or (2) if it has been prepared, packed, or held under insanitary conditions whereby it may have been contaminated with filth, or whereby it may have been rendered injurious to health; or (3) if it is a drug and its container is composed, in whole or in part, of any poisonous or deleterious substance which may render the contents injurious to health; or (4) if it is a drug and it bears or contains, for purposes of coloring only, a coal-tar color other than one from a batch that has been certified in accordance with regulations provided in this article.

b. If it purports to be, or is represented as, a drug the name of which is recognized in an official compendium, and its strength differs from, or its quality or purity falls below, the standard set forth in such compendium. Such determination as to strength, quality or purity shall be made in accordance with the tests or methods of assay set forth in such compendium, or, in the absence or inadequacy of such tests or methods of assay, then in accordance with tests or methods of assay prescribed by regulations of the board of pharmacy as promulgated under this article. Deviations from the official assays may be made in the quantities of samples and reagents employed, provided they are in proportion to the quantities stated in the official compendium. No drug defined in an official compendium shall be deemed to be adulterated under this paragraph because (1) it exceeds the standard of strength therefor set forth in such compendium, if such difference is plainly stated on its label; or (2) it falls below the standard of strength, quality, or purity therefor set forth in such compendium if such difference is plainly stated on its label, except that this clause shall apply only to such drugs, or classes of drugs, as are specified in regu- lations which the board shall promulgate when, as applied to any drug, or class of drugs, the prohibition of such difference is not necessary for the protection of the public health. Whenever a drug is recognized in both the United States pharmacopoeia and the homeopathic pharmacopoeia of the United States, it shall be subject to the requirements of the United States pharmacopoeia unless it is labeled and offered for sale as a homeopathic drug, in which case it shall be subject to the provisions of the homeopathic pharmacopoeia of the United States and not to those of the United States pharmacopoeia.

c. If it is not subject to the provisions of paragraph b of this subdivision and its strength differs from, or its purity or quality falls below, that which it purports or is represented to possess.

d. If it is a drug and any substance has been (1) mixed or packed therewith so as to reduce its quality or strength or (2) substituted wholly or in part therefor.

e. If it is sold under or by a name not recognized in or according to a formula not given in the United States pharmacopoeia or the national formulary but that is found in some other standard work on pharmacology recognized by the board, and it differs in strength, quality or purity from the strength, quality or purity required, or the formula prescribed in, the standard work.

2. Misbranded and substituted drugs and devices. A drug or device shall be deemed to be misbranded:

a. If its labeling is false or misleading in any particular.

b. If in package form, unless it bears a label containing (1) the name and place of business of the manufacturer, packer, or distributor; and (2) an accurate statement of the quantity of the contents in terms of weight, measure, or numerical count: Provided, that under clause (2) of this paragraph the board may establish reasonable variations as to quantity and exemptions as to small packages.

c. If any word, statement, or other information required by or under authority of this article to appear on the label or labeling is not prominently placed thereon with such conspicuousness (as compared with other words, statements, designs, or devices, in the labeling) and in such terms as to render it likely to be read and understood by the ordinary individual under customary conditions of purchase and use.

d. If it is for use by man and contains any quantity of the narcotic or hypnotic substance alpha eucaine, barbituric acid, beta eucaine, bromal, cannabis, carbromal, chloral, coca, cocaine, codeine, heroin, marihuana, morphine, opium, paraldehyde, peyote, or sulphonmethane; or any chemical derivative of such substance, which derivative has been by the secretary, after investigation, found to be, and by regulations under this article, or by regulations promulgated by the board, designated as, habit forming; unless its label bears the name and quantity, or proportion, of such substance or derivative and in juxtaposition therewith the statement "Warning--May be habit forming."

e. If it is a drug and is not designated solely by a name recognized in an official compendium unless its label bears (1) the common or usual name of the drug, if such there be; and (2) in case it is fabricated from two or more ingredients, the common or usual name of each active ingredient, including the kind and quantity by percentage or amount of any alcohol, and also including, whether active or not, the name and quantity or proportion of any bromides, ether, chloroform, acetanilid, acetphenetidin, amidopyrine, antipyrine, atropine, hyoscine, hyoscyamine, arsenic, digitalis, digitalis glucosides, mercury, ouabain, strophanthin, strychnine, thyroid, or any derivative or preparation of any such substances, contained therein: Provided, that, to the extent that compliance with the requirements of clause (2) of this paragraph is impracticable, exemptions shall be established by regulations promulgated by the board.

f. Unless its labeling bears (1) adequate directions for use; and (2) such adequate warnings against use in those pathological conditions or by children where its use may be dangerous to health, or against unsafe dosage or methods or duration of administration or application, in such manner and form, as are necessary for the protection of users: Provided, that, where any requirement of clause (1) of this paragraph, as applied to any drug or device, is not necessary for the protection of the public health, the board shall promulgate regulations exempting such drug or device from such requirement.

g. If it purports to be a drug the name of which is recognized in an official compendium, unless it is packaged and labeled as prescribed therein: Provided, that, the method of packing may be modified with the consent of the secretary in accordance with regulations promulgated by the board. Whenever a drug is recognized in both the United States pharmacopoeia and the homeopathic pharmacopoeia of the United States, it shall be subject to the requirements of the United States pharmacopoeia with respect to packaging and labeling unless it is labeled and offered for sale as a homeopathic drug, in which case it shall be subject to the provisions of the homeopathic pharmacopoeia of the United States, and not to those of the United States pharmacopoeia.

h. (1) If it is a drug and its container is so made, formed or filled as to be misleading; (2) if it is an imitation of another drug; (3) if it is offered for sale under the name of another drug; or (4) if it bears a copy, counterfeit, or colorable imitation of the trademark, label, container or identifying name or design of another drug.

i. If it is dangerous to health when used in the dosage, or with the frequency or duration prescribed, recommended or suggested in the labeling thereof.

j. Except as required by article thirty-three of the public health law, the labeling provisions of this article shall not apply to the compounding and dispensing of drugs on the written prescription of a physician, a dentist, a podiatrist or a veterinarian, which prescription when filled shall be kept on file for at least five years by the pharmacist or druggist. Such drug shall bear a label containing the name and place of business of the dispenser, the serial number and date of the prescription, directions for use as may be stated in the prescription, name and address of the patient and the name of the physician or other practitioner authorized by law to issue the prescription. In addition, such label shall contain the proprietary or brand name of the drug and, if applicable, the strength of the contents, unless the person issuing the prescription explicitly states on the prescription, in his own handwriting, that the name of the drug and the strength thereof should not appear on the label.

VI. General Business Law

General Business Law § 853. Enforcement; limitation of scope.

1. The attorney general or any state or local health officer, town, village or city attorney, or the chief executive officer of a municipality may institute an action in a court of competent jurisdiction to enjoin any activity prohibited pursuant to section eight hundred fifty-one of this chapter. If such court finds that any person, firm or corporation has sold or offered for sale any drug-related paraphernalia, it shall assess civil penalties against such person, firm or corporation in an amount not less than one thousand dollars nor more than ten thousand dollars for each such violation.

2. This article shall not apply to any sale, furnishing or possession which is lawful under section 3381 of the public health law.

* 3. This article shall not apply to any sale, furnishing or possession which is for a lawful purpose under the cannabis law.

* NB Repealed July 5, 2028

VII. Labor Law

Labor Law § 201-d. Discrimination against the engagement in certain activities.

1. Definitions. As used in this section:

   a. "Political activities" shall mean (i) running for public office, (ii) campaigning for a candidate for public office, or (iii) participating in fund-raising activities for the benefit of a candidate, political party or political advocacy group;

   b. "Recreational activities" shall mean any lawful, leisure-time activity, for which the employee receives no compensation and which is generally engaged in for recreational purposes, including but not limited to sports, games, hobbies, exercise, reading and the viewing of television, movies and similar material;

   c. "Work hours" shall mean, for purposes of this section, all time, including paid and unpaid breaks and meal periods, that the employee is suffered, permitted or expected to be engaged in work, and all time the employee is actually engaged in work. This definition shall not be referred to in determining hours worked for which an employee is entitled to compensation under any law including article nineteen of this chapter.

2. Unless otherwise provided by law, it shall be unlawful for any employer or employment agency to refuse to hire, employ or license, or to discharge from employment or otherwise discriminate against an individual in compensation, promotion or terms, conditions or privileges of employment because of:

   a. an individual's political activities outside of working hours, off of the employer's premises and without use of the employer's equipment or other property, if such activities are legal, provided, however, that this paragraph shall not apply to persons whose employment is defined in paragraph six of subdivision (a) of section seventy-nine-h of the civil rights law, and provided further that this paragraph shall not apply to persons who would otherwise be prohibited from engaging in political activity pursuant to chapter 15 of title 5 and subchapter III of chapter 73 of title 5 of the USCA;

   b. an individual's legal use of consumable products, including cannabis in accordance with state law, prior to the beginning or after the conclusion of the employee's work hours, and off of the employer's premises and without use of the employer's equipment or other property;

   c. an individual's legal recreational activities, including cannabis in accordance with state law, outside work hours, off of the employer's premises and without use of the employer's equipment or other property; or

   d. an individual's membership in a union or any exercise of rights granted under Title 29, USCA, Chapter 7 or under article fourteen of the civil service law.

3. The provisions of subdivision two of this section shall not be deemed to protect activity which:

   a. creates a material conflict of interest related to the employer's trade secrets, proprietary information or other proprietary or business interest;

   b. with respect to employees of a state agency as defined in sections seventy-three and seventy-four of the public officers law respectively, is in knowing violation of subdivision two, three, four, five, seven, eight or twelve of section seventy-three or of section seventy-four of the public officers law, or of any executive order, policy, directive, or other rule which has been issued by the attorney general regulating outside employment or activities that could conflict with employees' performance of their official duties;

   c. with respect to employees of any employer as defined in section twenty-seven-a of this chapter, is in knowing violation of a provision of a collective bargaining agreement concerning ethics, conflicts of interest, potential conflicts of interest, or the proper discharge of official duties;

   d. with respect to employees of any employer as defined in section twenty-seven-a of this chapter who are not subject to section seventy-three or seventy-four of the public officers law, is in knowing violation of article eighteen of the general municipal law or any local law, administrative code provision, charter provision or rule or directive of the mayor or any agency head of a city having a population of one million or more, where such law, code provision, charter provision, rule or directive concerns ethics, conflicts of interest, potential conflicts of interest, or the proper discharge of official duties and otherwise covers such employees; and

e. with respect to employees other than those of any employer as defined in section twenty-seven-a of this chapter, violates a collective bargaining agreement or a certified or licensed professional's contractual obligation to devote his or her entire compensated working hours to a single employer, provided however that the provisions of this paragraph shall apply only to professionals whose compensation is at least fifty thousand dollars for the year nineteen hundred ninety-two and in subsequent years is an equivalent amount adjusted by the same percentage as the annual increase or decrease in the consumer price index.

4. Notwithstanding the provisions of subdivision three of this section, an employer shall not be in violation of this section where the employer takes action based on the belief either that: (i) the employer's actions were required by statute, regulation, ordinance or other governmental mandate, (ii) the employer's actions were permissible pursuant to an established substance abuse or alcohol program or workplace policy, professional contract or collective bargaining agreement, or (iii) the individual's actions were deemed by an employer or previous employer to be illegal or to constitute habitually poor performance, incompetency or misconduct.

4-a. Notwithstanding the provisions of subdivision three or four of this section, an employer shall not be in violation of this section where the employer takes action related to the use of cannabis based on the following:

(i) the employer's actions were required by state or federal statute, regulation, ordinance, or other state or federal governmental mandate;

(ii) the employee is impaired by the use of cannabis, meaning the employee manifests specific articulable symptoms while working that decrease or lessen the employee's performance of the duties or tasks of the employee's job position, or such specific articulable symptoms interfere with an employer's obligation to provide a safe and healthy work place, free from recognized hazards, as required by state and federal occupational safety and health law; or

(iii) the employer's actions would require such employer to commit any act that would cause the employer to be in violation of federal law or would result in the loss of a federal contract or federal funding.

5. Nothing in this section shall apply to persons who, on an individual basis, have a professional service contract with an employer and the unique nature of the services provided is such that the employer shall be permitted, as part of such professional service contract, to limit the off-duty activities which may be engaged in by such individual.

6. Nothing in this section shall prohibit an organization or employer from offering, imposing or having in effect a health, disability or life insurance policy that makes distinctions between employees for the type of coverage or the price of coverage based upon the employees' recreational activities or use of consumable products, provided that differential premium rates charged employees reflect a differential cost to the employer and that employers provide employees with a statement delineating the differential rates used by the carriers providing insurance for the employer, and provided further that such distinctions in type or price of coverage shall not be utilized to expand, limit or curtail the rights or liabilities of any party with regard to a civil cause of action.

7. a. Where a violation of this section is alleged to have occurred, the attorney general may apply in the name of the people of the state of New York for an order enjoining or restraining the commission or continuance of the alleged unlawful acts. In any such proceeding, the court may impose a civil penalty in the amount of three hundred dollars for the first violation and five hundred dollars for each subsequent violation.

b. In addition to any other penalties or actions otherwise applicable pursuant to this chapter, where a violation of this section is alleged to have occurred, an aggrieved individual may commence an action for equitable relief and damages.

VIII. Penal Law

PART 3. SPECIFIC OFFENSES

Title K. OFFENSES INVOLVING FRAUD

ARTICLE 179. CRIMINAL DIVERSION OF MEDICAL MARIHUANA

Penal Law § 179.00. Criminal diversion of medical cannabis; definitions.

* NB Repealed July 5, 2028

The following definitions are applicable to this article:

1. "Medical cannabis" means medical cannabis as defined in section three of the cannabis law.

2. "Certification" means a certification, made under section thirty of the cannabis law.

Penal Law § 179.05. Criminal diversion of medical cannabis; limitations.

* NB Repealed July 5, 2028

The provisions of this article shall not apply to:

1. a practitioner authorized to issue a certification who acted in good faith in the lawful course of his or her profession; or

2. a registered organization as that term is defined in section thirty-four of the cannabis law who acted in good faith in the lawful course of the practice of pharmacy; or

3. a person who acted in good faith seeking treatment for a medical condition or assisting another person to obtain treatment for a medical condition.

Penal Law § 179.10. Criminal diversion of medical cannabis in the first degree.

* NB Repealed July 5, 2028

A person is guilty of criminal diversion of medical cannabis in the first degree when he or she is a practitioner, as that term is defined in section three of the cannabis law, who issues a certification with knowledge of reasonable grounds to know that (i) the recipient has no medical need for it, or (ii) it is for a purpose other than to treat a condition as defined in section three of the cannabis law.

Criminal diversion of medical cannabis in the first degree is a class E felony.

Penal Law § 179.11. Criminal diversion of medical cannabis in the second degree.

* NB Repealed July 5, 2028

A person is guilty of criminal diversion of medical cannabis in the second degree when he or she sells, trades, delivers, or otherwise provides medical cannabis to another with knowledge or reasonable grounds to know that the recipient is not registered under article three of the cannabis law.

Criminal diversion of medical cannabis in the second degree is a class B misdemeanor.

Penal Law § 179.15. Criminal retention of medical cannabis.

* NB Repealed July 5, 2028

A person is guilty of criminal retention of medical cannabis when, being a certified patient or designated caregiver, as those terms are defined in section three of the cannabis law, he or she knowingly obtains, possesses, stores or maintains an amount of cannabis in excess of the amount he or she is authorized to possess under the provisions of article three of the cannabis law.

Criminal retention of medical cannabis shall be punishable as provided in section 222.25 of this chapter.

Title M. OFFENSES AGAINST PUBLIC HEALTH AND MORALS

ARTICLE 220. CONTROLLED SUBSTANCES OFFENSES

Penal Law § 220.00. Controlled substances; definitions.

1. "Sell" means to sell, exchange, give or dispose of to another, or to offer or agree to do the same.

2. "Unlawfully" means in violation of article thirty-three of the public health law.

3. "Ounce" means an avoirdupois ounce as applied to solids or semisolids, and a fluid ounce as applied to liquids.

4. "Pound" means an avoirdupois pound.

5. "Controlled substance" means any substance listed in schedule I, II, III, IV or V of section thirty-three hundred six of the public health law.

7. "Narcotic drug" means any controlled substance listed in schedule I(b), I(c), II(b) or II(c) other than methadone.

8. "Narcotic preparation" means any controlled substance listed in schedule II(b-1), III(d) or III(e).

9. "Hallucinogen" means any controlled substance listed in paragraphs (5), (17), (18), (19), (20) and (21) of subdivision (d) of schedule I of section thirty-three hundred six of the public health law.

10. "Hallucinogenic substance" means any controlled substance listed in schedule I(d) other than concentrated cannabis, lysergic acid diethylamide, or an hallucinogen.

11. "Stimulant" means any controlled substance listed in schedule I(f),II(d).

12. "Dangerous depressant" means any controlled substance listed in schedule I(e)(2), (3), II(e), III(c)(3) or IV(c)(2), (31), (32), (40).

13. "Depressant" means any controlled substance listed in schedule IV(c) except (c)(2), (31), (32), (40).

14. "School grounds" means (a) in or on or within any building, structure, athletic playing field, playground or land contained within the real property boundary line of a public or private elementary, parochial, intermediate, junior high, vocational, or high school, or (b) any area accessible to the public located within one thousand feet of the real property boundary line comprising any such school or any parked automobile or other parked vehicle located within one thousand feet of the real property boundary line comprising any such school. For the purposes of this section an "area accessible to the public" shall mean sidewalks, streets, parking lots, parks, playgrounds, stores and restaurants.

15. "Prescription for a controlled substance" means a direction or authorization, by means of an official New York state prescription form, a written prescription form or an oral prescription, which will permit a person to lawfully obtain a controlled substance from any person authorized to dispense controlled substances.

16. For the purposes of sections 220.70, 220.71, 220.72, 220.73, 220.74, 220.75 and 220.76 of this article:

(a) "Precursor" means ephedrine, pseudoephedrine, or any salt, isomer or salt of an isomer of such substances.

(b) "Chemical reagent" means a chemical reagent that can be used in the manufacture, production or preparation of methamphetamine.

(c) "Solvent" means a solvent that can be used in the manufacture, production or preparation of methamphetamine.

(d) "Laboratory equipment" means any items, components or materials that can be used in the manufacture, preparation or production of methamphetamine.

(e) "Hazardous or dangerous material" means any substance, or combination of substances, that results from or is used in the manufacture, preparation or production of methamphetamine which, because of its quantity, concentration, or physical or chemical characteristics, poses a substantial risk to human health or safety, or a substantial danger to the environment.

17. "School bus" means every motor vehicle owned by a public or governmental agency or private school and operated for the transportation of pupils, teachers and other persons acting in a supervisory capacity, to or from school or school activities or privately owned and operated for compensation for the transportation of pupils, children of pupils, teachers and other persons acting in a supervisory capacity to or from school or school activities.

18. "Controlled substance organization" means four or more persons sharing a common purpose to engage in conduct that constitutes or advances the commission of a felony under this article.

19. "Director" means a person who is the principal administrator, organizer, or leader of a controlled substance organization or one of several principal administrators, organizers, or leaders of a controlled substance organization.

20. "Profiteer" means a person who: (a) is a director of a controlled substance organization; (b) is a member of a controlled substance organization and has managerial responsibility over one or more other members of that organization; or (c) arranges, devises or plans one or more transactions constituting a felony under this article so as to obtain profits or expected profits. A person is not a profiteer if he or she is acting only as an employee; or if he or she is acting as an accommodation to a friend or relative; or if he or she is acting only under the direction and control of others and exercises no substantial, independent role in arranging or directing the transactions in question.

Penal Law § 220.78. Witness or victim of drug or alcohol overdose.

1. A person who, in good faith, seeks health care for someone who is experiencing a drug or alcohol overdose or other life threatening medical emergency shall not be charged or prosecuted for a controlled substance offense under this article or a cannabis offense under article two hundred twenty-two of this title, other than an offense involving sale for consideration or other benefit or gain, or charged or prosecuted for possession of alcohol by a person under age twenty-one years under section sixty-five-c of the alcoholic beverage control law, or for possession of drug paraphernalia under article thirty-nine of the general business law, with respect to any controlled substance, cannabis, alcohol or paraphernalia that was obtained as a result of such seeking or receiving of health care.

2. A person who is experiencing a drug or alcohol overdose or other life threatening medical emergency and, in good faith, seeks health care for himself or herself or is the subject of such a good faith request for health care, shall not be charged or prosecuted for a controlled substance offense under this article or a cannabis offense under article two hundred twenty-two of this title, other than an offense involving sale for consideration or other benefit or gain, or charged or prosecuted for possession of alcohol by a person under age twenty-one years under section sixty-five-c of the alcoholic beverage control law, or charged or prosecuted for possession of cannabis or concentrated cannabis by a person under the age of twenty-one under section one hundred thirty-two of the cannabis law, or for possession of drug paraphernalia under article thirty-nine of the general business law, with respect to any substance, cannabis, alcohol or paraphernalia that was obtained as a result of such seeking or receiving of health care.

3. Definitions. As used in this section the following terms shall have the following meanings:

> (a) "Drug or alcohol overdose" or "overdose" means an acute condition including, but not limited to, physical illness, coma, mania, hysteria or death, which is the result of consumption or use of a controlled substance or alcohol and relates to an adverse reaction to or the quantity of the controlled substance or alcohol or a substance with which the controlled substance or alcohol was combined; provided that a patient's condition shall be deemed to be a drug or alcohol overdose if a prudent layperson, possessing an average knowledge of medicine and health, could reasonably believe that the condition is in fact a drug or alcohol overdose and (except as to death) requires health care.

> (b) "Health care" means the professional services provided to a person experiencing a drug or alcohol overdose by a health care professional licensed, registered or certified under title eight of the education law or article thirty of the public health law who, acting within his or her lawful scope of practice, may provide diagnosis, treatment or emergency services for a person experiencing a drug or alcohol overdose.

4. It shall be an affirmative defense to a criminal sale controlled substance offense under this article or a criminal sale of cannabis offense under article two hundred twenty-two of this title, not covered by subdivision one or two of this section, with respect to any controlled substance or cannabis which was obtained as a result of such seeking or receiving of health care, that:

> (a) the defendant, in good faith, seeks health care for someone or for him or herself who is experiencing a drug or alcohol overdose or other life threatening medical emergency; and

> (b) the defendant has no prior conviction for the commission or attempted commission of a class A-I, A-II or B felony under this article.

5. Nothing in this section shall be construed to bar the admissibility of any evidence in connection with the investigation and prosecution of a crime with regard to another defendant who does not independently qualify for the bar to prosecution or for the affirmative defense; nor with regard to other crimes committed by a person who otherwise qualifies under this section; nor shall anything in this section be construed to bar any seizure pursuant to law, including but not limited to pursuant to section thirty-three hundred eighty-seven of the public health law.

6. The bar to prosecution described in subdivisions one and two of this section shall not apply to the prosecution of a class A-I felony under this article, and the affirmative defense described in subdivision four of this section shall not apply to the prosecution of a class A-I or A-II felony under this article.

ARTICLE 222. CANNABIS

Penal Law § 222.00. Cannabis; definitions.

1. "Cannabis" means all parts of the plant of the genus Cannabis, whether growing or not; the seeds thereof; the resin extracted from any part of the plant; and every compound, manufacture, salt, derivative, mixture, or preparation of the plant, its seeds or resin. It does not include the mature stalks of the plant, fiber produced from the stalks, oil or cake made from the seeds of the plant, any other compound, manufacture, salt, derivative, mixture, or preparation of the mature stalks (except the resin extracted therefrom), fiber, oil, or cake, or the sterilized seed of the plant which is incapable of germination. It does not include hemp, cannabinoid hemp or hemp extract as defined in section three of the cannabis law or drug products approved by the Federal Food and Drug Administration.

2. "Concentrated cannabis" means:

    (a) the separated resin, whether crude or purified, obtained from a plant of the genus Cannabis; or

    (b) a material, preparation, mixture, compound or other substance which contains more than three percent by weight of delta-9 tetrahydrocannabinol, or its isomer, delta-8 dibenzopyran numbering system, or delta-1 tetrahydrocannabinol or its isomer, delta 1 (6) monoterpene numbering system.

3. For the purposes of this article, "sell" shall mean to sell, exchange or dispose of for compensation. "Sell" shall not include the transfer of cannabis or concentrated cannabis between persons twenty-one years of age or older without compensation in the quantities authorized in paragraph (b) of subdivision one of section 222.05 of this article.

4. For the purposes of this article, "smoking" shall have the same meaning as that term is defined in section three of the cannabis law.

Penal Law § 222.05. Personal use of cannabis.

Notwithstanding any other provision of law to the contrary:

1. The following acts are lawful for persons twenty-one years of age or older:

    (a) possessing, displaying, purchasing, obtaining, or transporting up to three ounces of cannabis and up to twenty-four grams of concentrated cannabis;

    (b) transferring, without compensation, to a person twenty-one years of age or older, up to three ounces of cannabis and up to twenty-four grams of concentrated cannabis;

    (c) using, smoking, ingesting, or consuming cannabis or concentrated cannabis unless otherwise prohibited by state law;

    (d) possessing, using, displaying, purchasing, obtaining, manufacturing, transporting or giving to any person twenty-one years of age or older cannabis paraphernalia or concentrated cannabis paraphernalia;

    (e) planting, cultivating, harvesting, drying, processing or possessing cultivated cannabis in accordance with section 222.15 of this article; and

    (f) assisting another person who is twenty-one years of age or older, or allowing property to be used, in any of the acts described in paragraphs (a) through (e) of this subdivision.

2. Cannabis, concentrated cannabis, cannabis paraphernalia or concentrated cannabis paraphernalia involved in any way with conduct deemed lawful by this section are not contraband nor subject to seizure or forfeiture of assets under article four hundred eighty of this chapter, section thirteen hundred eleven of the civil practice law and rules,

or other applicable law, and no conduct deemed lawful by this section shall constitute the basis for approach, search, seizure, arrest or detention.

3. Except as provided in subdivision four of this section, in any criminal proceeding including proceedings pursuant to section 710.20 of the criminal procedure law, no finding or determination of reasonable cause to believe a crime has been committed shall be based solely on evidence of the following facts and circumstances, either individually or in combination with each other:

(a) the odor of cannabis;

(b) the odor of burnt cannabis;

(c) the possession of or the suspicion of possession of cannabis or concentrated cannabis in the amounts authorized in this article;

(d) the possession of multiple containers of cannabis without evidence of concentrated cannabis in the amounts authorized in this article;

(e) the presence of cash or currency in proximity to cannabis or concentrated cannabis; or

(f) the planting, cultivating, harvesting, drying, processing or possessing cultivated cannabis in accordance with section 222.15 of this article.

4. Paragraph (b) of subdivision three of this section shall not apply when a law enforcement officer is investigating whether a person is operating a motor vehicle, vessel or snowmobile while impaired by drugs or the combined influence of drugs or of alcohol and any drug or drugs in violation of subdivision four or subdivision four-a of section eleven hundred ninety-two of the vehicle and traffic law, or paragraph (e) of subdivision two of section forty-nine-a of the navigation law, or paragraph (d) of subdivision one of section 25.24 of the parks, recreation and historic preservation law. During such investigations, the odor of burnt cannabis shall not provide probable cause to search any area of a vehicle that is not readily accessible to the driver and reasonably likely to contain evidence relevant to the driver's condition.

Penal Law § 222.10. Restrictions on cannabis use.

Unless otherwise authorized by law or regulation, no person shall:

1. smoke or vape cannabis in a location where smoking or vaping cannabis is prohibited pursuant to article thirteen-E of the public health law; or

2. smoke, vape or ingest cannabis or concentrated cannabis in or upon the grounds of a school, as defined in subdivision ten of section eleven hundred twenty-five of the education law or in or on a school bus, as defined in section one hundred forty-two of the vehicle and traffic law; provided, however, provisions of this subdivision shall not apply to acts that are in compliance with article three of the cannabis law.

Notwithstanding any other section of law, violations of restrictions on cannabis use are subject to a civil penalty not exceeding twenty-five dollars or an amount of community service not exceeding twenty hours.

Penal Law § 222.15. Personal cultivation and home possession of cannabis.

1. Except as provided for in section forty-one of the cannabis law, and unless otherwise authorized by law or regulation, no person may:

(a) plant, cultivate, harvest, dry, process or possess more than three mature cannabis plants and three immature cannabis plants at any one time; or

(b) plant, cultivate, harvest, dry, process or possess, within his or her private residence, or on the grounds of his or her private residence, more than three mature cannabis plants and three immature cannabis plants at any one time; or

(c) being under the age of twenty-one, plant, cultivate, harvest, dry, process or possess cannabis plants.

2. No more than six mature and six immature cannabis plants may be cultivated, harvested, dried, or possessed within any private residence, or on the grounds of a person's private residence.

3. The personal cultivation of cannabis shall only be permitted within, or on the grounds of, a person's private residence.

4. Any mature or immature cannabis plant described in paragraph (a) or (b) of subdivision one of this section, and any cannabis produced by any such cannabis plant or plants cultivated, harvested, dried, processed or possessed pursuant to paragraph (a) or (b) of subdivision one of this section shall, unless otherwise authorized by law or regulation, be stored within such person's private residence or on the grounds of such person's private residence. Such person shall take reasonable steps designed to ensure that such cultivated cannabis is in a secured place and not accessible to any person under the age of twenty-one.

5. Notwithstanding any law to the contrary, a person may lawfully possess up to five pounds of cannabis in their private residence or on the grounds of such person's private residence. Such person shall take reasonable steps designed to ensure that such cannabis is in a secured place not accessible to any person under the age of twenty-one.

6. A county, town, city or village may enact and enforce regulations to reasonably regulate the actions and conduct set forth in subdivision one of this section; provided that:

(a) a violation of any such a regulation, as approved by such county, town, city or village enacting the regulation, may constitute no more than an infraction and may be punishable by no more than a discretionary civil penalty of two hundred dollars or less; and

(b) no county, town, city or village may enact or enforce any such regulation or regulations that may completely or essentially prohibit a person from engaging in the action or conduct authorized by subdivision one of this section.

A violation of this section, other than paragraph (a) of subdivision six of this section, may be subject to a civil penalty of up to one hundred twenty-five dollars per violation.

7. The office of cannabis management shall issue regulations for the home cultivation of cannabis. The office of cannabis management shall enact, and may enforce, regulations to regulate the actions and conduct set forth in this section including requirements for, or restrictions and prohibitions on, the use of any compressed flammable gas solvents such as propane, butane, or other hexane gases for cannabis processing; or other forms of home cultivation, manufacturing, or cannabinoid production and processing, which the office determines poses a danger to public safety; and to ensure the home cultivation of cannabis is for personal use by an adult over the age of twenty-one in possession of cannabis plants, and not utilized for unlicensed commercial or illicit activity, provided any regulations issued by the office shall not completely or essentially prohibit a person from engaging in the action or conduct authorized by this section.

8. The office of cannabis management may issue guidance or advisories for the education and promotion of safe practices for activities and conduct authorized in subdivision one of this section.

9. Subdivisions one through five of this section shall not take effect until such a time as the office of cannabis management has issued regulations governing the home cultivation of cannabis. The office shall issue rules and regulations governing the home cultivation of cannabis by certified patients as defined in section three of the

cannabis law, no later than six months after the effective date of this article and shall issue rules and regulations governing the home cultivation of cannabis for cannabis consumers as defined by section three of the cannabis law no later than eighteen months following the first authorized retail sale of adult-use cannabis products to a cannabis consumer.

Penal Law § 222.20. Licensing of cannabis production and distribution; defense.

In any prosecution for an offense involving cannabis under this article or an authorized local law, it is a defense that the defendant was engaged in such activity in compliance with the cannabis law.

Penal Law § 222.25. Unlawful possession of cannabis.

A person is guilty of unlawful possession of cannabis when he or she knowingly and unlawfully possesses cannabis and such cannabis weighs more than three ounces or concentrated cannabis and such concentrated cannabis weighs more than twenty-four grams.

Unlawful possession of cannabis is a violation punishable by a fine of not more than one hundred twenty-five dollars.

Penal Law § 222.30. Criminal possession of cannabis in the third degree.

A person is guilty of criminal possession of cannabis in the third degree when he or she knowingly and unlawfully possesses:

1. cannabis and such cannabis weighs more than sixteen ounces; or

2. concentrated cannabis and such concentrated cannabis weighs more than five ounces.

Criminal possession of cannabis in the third degree is a class A misdemeanor.

Penal Law § 222.35. Criminal possession of cannabis in the second degree.

A person is guilty of criminal possession of cannabis in the second degree when he or she knowingly and unlawfully possesses:

1. cannabis and such cannabis weighs more than five pounds; or

2. concentrated cannabis and such concentrated cannabis weighs more than two pounds.

Criminal possession of cannabis in the second degree is a class E felony.

Penal Law § 222.40. Criminal possession of cannabis in the first degree.

A person is guilty of criminal possession of cannabis in the first degree when he or she knowingly and unlawfully possesses:

1. cannabis and such cannabis weighs more than ten pounds; or

2. concentrated cannabis and such concentrated cannabis weighs more than four pounds.

Criminal possession of cannabis in the first degree is a class D felony.

Penal Law § 222.45. Unlawful sale of cannabis.

A person is guilty of unlawful sale of cannabis when he or she knowingly and unlawfully sells cannabis or concentrated cannabis.

Unlawful sale of cannabis is a violation punishable by a fine of not more than two hundred fifty dollars.

Penal Law § 222.50. Criminal sale of cannabis in the third degree.

A person is guilty of criminal sale of cannabis in the third degree when:

1. he or she knowingly and unlawfully sells more than three ounces of cannabis or more than twenty-four grams of concentrated cannabis; or

2. being twenty-one years of age or older, he or she knowingly and unlawfully sells or gives, or causes to be given or sold, cannabis or concentrated cannabis to a person less than twenty-one years of age; except that in any prosecution under this subdivision, it is a defense that the defendant was less than three years older than the person under the age of twenty-one at the time of the offense. This subdivision shall not apply to designated caregivers, practitioners, employees of a registered organization or employees of a designated caregiver facility acting in compliance with article three of the cannabis law.

Criminal sale of cannabis in the third degree is a class A misdemeanor.

Penal Law § 222.55. Criminal sale of cannabis in the second degree.

A person is guilty of criminal sale of cannabis in the second degree when:

1. he or she knowingly and unlawfully sells more than sixteen ounces of cannabis or more than five ounces of concentrated cannabis; or

2. being twenty-one years of age or older, he or she knowingly and unlawfully sells or gives, or causes to be given or sold, more than three ounces of cannabis or more than twenty-four grams of concentrated cannabis to a person less than eighteen years of age. This subdivision shall not apply to designated caregivers, practitioners, employees of a registered organization or employees of a designated caregiver facility acting in compliance with article three of the cannabis law.

Criminal sale of cannabis in the second degree is a class E felony.

Penal Law § 222.60. Criminal sale of cannabis in the first degree.

A person is guilty of criminal sale of cannabis in the first degree when he or she knowingly and unlawfully sells more than five pounds of cannabis or more than two pounds of concentrated cannabis.

Criminal sale of cannabis in the first degree is a class D felony.

Penal Law § 222.65. Aggravated criminal sale of cannabis.

A person is guilty of aggravated criminal sale of cannabis when he or she knowingly and unlawfully sells cannabis or concentrated cannabis weighing one hundred pounds or more.

Aggravated criminal sale of cannabis is a class C felony.

IX. Public Health Law

Public Health Law § 1399-n. Definitions.

For purposes of this article:

1. "Bar" means any area, including outdoor seating areas, devoted to the sale and service of alcoholic beverages for on-premises consumption and where the service of food is only incidental to the consumption of such beverages.

2. "Employer" means any person, partnership, association, limited liability company, corporation or nonprofit entity which employs one or more persons, including the legislative, executive and judicial branches of state government and any political subdivision of the state.

3. "Food service establishment" means any area, including outdoor seating areas, or portion thereof in which the business is the sale of food for on-premises consumption.

4. "Membership association" means a not-for-profit entity which has been created or organized for a charitable, philanthropic, educational, political, social or other similar purpose.

5. "Place of employment" means any indoor area or portion thereof under the control of an employer in which employees of the employer perform services, and shall include, but not be limited to, offices, school grounds, retail stores, banquet facilities, theaters, food stores, banks, financial institutions, factories, warehouses, employee cafeterias, lounges, auditoriums, gymnasiums, restrooms, elevators, hallways, museums, libraries, bowling establishments, employee medical facilities, rooms or areas containing photocopying equipment or other office equipment used in common, and company vehicles.

6. "School grounds" means any building, structure, and surrounding outdoor grounds contained within a public or private pre-school, nursery school, elementary or secondary school's legally defined property boundaries as registered in a county clerk's office, and any vehicles used to transport children or school personnel.

7. "Retail tobacco business" means a sole proprietorship, limited liability company, corporation, partnership or other enterprise in which the primary activity is the retail sale of tobacco products and accessories, and in which the sale of other products is merely incidental.

8. "Smoking" means the burning of a lighted cigar, cigarette, pipe or any other matter or substance which contains tobacco or cannabis as defined in section 222.00 of the penal law, or cannabinoid hemp as defined in section three of the cannabis law.

9. "Vaping" means the use of an electronic cigarette.

10. "Electronic cigarette" shall have the same meaning as in subdivision thirteen of section thirteen hundred ninety-nine-aa of this chapter.

11. "Retail electronic cigarette store" means a retail store devoted primarily to the sale of electronic cigarettes, and in which the sale of other products is merely incidental. The sale of such other products shall be considered incidental if such sales generate less than twenty-five percent of the total annual gross sales.

Public Health Law § 1399-o. Smoking and vaping restrictions.

1. Smoking and vaping shall not be permitted and no person shall smoke or vape in the following indoor areas:

a. places of employment;

b. bars;

c. food service establishments, except as provided in subdivision six of section thirteen hundred ninety-nine-q of this article;

d. enclosed indoor areas open to the public containing a swimming pool;

e. public means of mass transportation, including subways, underground subway stations, and when occupied by passengers, buses, vans, taxicabs and limousines;

f. ticketing, boarding and waiting areas in public transportation terminals;

g. youth centers and facilities for detention as defined in sections five hundred twenty-seven-a and five hundred three of the executive law;

h. any facility that provides child care services as defined in section four hundred ten-p of the social services law, provided, however, that rooms in such a facility that is a private home shall be regulated by this paragraph as follows:

(i) when such private home is not required to be licensed or registered for such services by the office of children and family services, rooms in such home are excluded from the prohibition of this paragraph during periods when children receiving such services are not present; and

(ii) when such private home is required to be licensed or registered for such services by the office of children and family services, rooms in such home are included within the prohibition of this paragraph, regardless of whether or not children receiving such services are present.

i. child day care centers as defined in section three hundred ninety of the social services law and child day care centers licensed by the city of New York;

j. group homes for children as defined in section three hundred seventy-one of the social services law;

k. public institutions for children as defined in section three hundred seventy-one of the social services law;

l. residential treatment facilities for children and youth as defined in section 1.03 of the mental hygiene law;

m. all public and private colleges, universities and other educational and vocational institutions, including dormitories, residence halls, and other group residential facilities that are owned or operated by such colleges, universities and other educational and vocational institutions, except that these restrictions shall not apply in any off-campus residential unit occupied by a person who is not enrolled as an undergraduate student in such college, university or other educational or vocational institution;

n. general hospitals and residential health care facilities as defined in article twenty-eight of this chapter, and other health care facilities licensed by the state in which persons reside; provided, however, that the provisions of this subdivision shall not prohibit smoking and vaping by patients in separate enclosed rooms of residential health care facilities, adult care facilities established or certified under title two of article seven of the social services law, community mental health residences established under section 41.44 of the mental hygiene law, or facilities where day treatment programs are provided, which are designated as smoking and vaping rooms for patients of such facilities or programs;

o. commercial establishments used for the purpose of carrying on or exercising any trade, profession, vocation or charitable activity;

p. indoor arenas;

q. zoos; and

r. bingo facilities.

2. Smoking and vaping shall not be permitted and no person shall smoke or vape in the following outdoor areas:

a. ticketing, boarding or platform areas of railroad stations operated by the metropolitan transportation authority or its subsidiaries.

b. on the grounds of general hospitals and residential health care facilities as defined in article twenty-eight of this chapter, within fifteen feet of a building entrance or exit or within fifteen feet of the entrance to or exit from the grounds of any such general hospital or residential health care facility. This subdivision shall not prohibit smoking and vaping by a patient or a visitor or guest of a patient of a residential health care facility in a separate area on the grounds designated as a smoking and vaping area by the residential health care facility, provided such designated smoking and vaping area is not within thirty feet of any building structure (other than a non-residential structure wholly contained within the designated smoking and vaping area), including any overhang, canopy, awning, entrance, exit, window, intake or exhaust.

3. Smoking and vaping shall not be permitted and no person shall smoke or vape within one hundred feet of the entrances, exits or outdoor areas of any public or private elementary or secondary schools; provided, however, that the provisions of this subdivision shall not apply to smoking or vaping in a residence, or within the real property boundary lines of such residential real property. The provisions of section thirteen hundred ninety-nine-p of this article shall not apply to this subdivision.

4. Smoking and vaping shall not be permitted and no person shall smoke or vape within one hundred feet of the entrances, exits or outdoor areas of any after-school program licensed or registered pursuant to section three hundred ninety of the social services law; provided, however, that the provisions of this subdivision shall only apply on those days and during those hours in which such after-school programs are operational; and provided, further, that the provisions of this subdivision shall not apply to smoking or vaping in a residence, or within the real property boundary lines of such residential real property.

5. a. Use of an electronic cigarette or e-cigarette shall not be permitted on school grounds, as defined in subdivision six of section thirteen hundred ninety-nine-n of this article.

b. "Electronic cigarette" or "e-cigarette" shall have the same meaning as in subdivision thirteen of section thirteen hundred ninety-nine-aa of this chapter.

6. Smoking shall not be permitted and no person shall smoke within one hundred feet of the entrances, exits or outdoor areas of any public or association library as defined in subdivision two of section two hundred fifty-three of the education law; provided, however, that the provisions of this subdivision shall not apply to smoking in a residence, or within the real property boundary lines of such residential real property.

Public Health Law § 1399-o-1. Smoking and vaping restrictions; certain outdoor areas.

1. Smoking and vaping shall not be permitted and no person shall smoke or vape during the hours between sunrise and sunset, when one or more persons under the age of twelve are present at any playground. For the purposes of this section, the term "playground" means an improved area designed, equipped, and set aside for play of six or more children which is not intended for use as an athletic playing field or athletic court, and shall include any play equipment, surfacing, fencing, signs, internal pathways, internal land forms, vegetation, and related structures. Playgrounds or playground equipment constructed upon one, two and three-family residential real property are exempt from the requirements of this section. This section shall not apply to any playground located within the city of New York.

2. No police officer, peace officer, regulatory officer or law enforcement official may arrest, ticket, stop or question any person based solely or in part on an alleged violation of subdivision one of this section, nor may an alleged violation of subdivision one of this section support probable cause to conduct any search or limited search of any person or his or her immediate surroundings.

Public Health Law § 1399-o-2. Smoking restrictions; certain outdoor areas.

1. Smoking shall not be permitted and no person shall smoke in any public park.

2. For the purposes of this section "park" shall mean:

> (a) public parks, beaches, pools, boardwalks, marinas, playgrounds, recreation centers, and group camps; and

> (b) equipment, buildings and facilities now or hereafter under the jurisdiction, charge or control of any state or local government agency or department that are located at or on any property described in paragraph (a) of this subdivision; provided, however, that for the purposes of this section the term public park shall not include the Adirondack park or the Catskill park as those terms are defined in section 9-0101 of the environmental conservation law.

3. The provisions of this section shall not apply to: (a) the sidewalks immediately adjoining parks, squares and public places; (b) any pedestrian route through any park strip, median or mall that is adjacent to vehicular traffic; (c) parking lots or roadways; (d) theatrical productions; and (e) any portion of a park that is not used for park purposes, except when smoking has been specifically prohibited in a state park or portion thereof by the office of parks, recreation and historic preservation. This subdivision shall not limit the applicability of any other laws to such places.

* NB Effective October 13, 2022

Public Health Law § 1399-p. Posting of signs.

1. "Smoking" or "No Smoking" signs, or "Vaping" or "No Vaping" signs, or the international "No Smoking" symbol, which consists of a pictorial representation of a burning cigarette enclosed in a circle with a bar across it, shall be prominently posted and properly maintained where smoking and vaping are regulated by this article, by the owner, operator, manager or other person having control of such area.

2. The owner, operator or manager of a hotel or motel that chooses to develop and implement a smoking and vaping policy for rooms rented to guests shall post a notice at the reception area of the establishment as to the availability, upon request, of rooms in which no smoking and vaping are allowed.

3. The provisions of this section shall apply to after-school programs that are subject to the provisions of subdivision four of section thirteen hundred ninety-nine-o of this article, provided that signs posted pursuant to this subdivision shall specify the specific time period during which smoking and vaping shall be prohibited.

Public Health Law § 1399-q. Smoking and vaping restrictions inapplicable.

1. This article shall not apply to:

(a) Private homes and private residences;

(b) Private automobiles;

(c) A hotel or motel room rented to one or more guests;

(d) Retail tobacco businesses;

(e) Membership associations; provided, however, that smoking and vaping shall only be allowed in membership associations in which all of the duties with respect to the operation of such association, including, but not limited to, the preparation of food and beverages, the service of food and beverages, reception and secretarial work, and the security services of the membership association are performed by members of such membership association who do not receive compensation of any kind from the membership association or any other entity for the performance of such duties;

(f) Cigar bars that, in the calendar year ending December thirty-first, two thousand two, generated ten percent or more of its total annual gross income from the on-site sale of tobacco products and the rental of on-site humidors, not including any sales from vending machines, and is registered with the appropriate enforcement officer, as defined in subdivision one of section thirteen hundred ninety-nine-t of this article. Such registration shall remain in effect for one year and shall be renewable only if: (a) in the preceding calendar year, the cigar bar generated ten percent or more of its total annual gross income from the on-site sale of tobacco products and the rental of on-site humidors, and (b) the cigar bar has not expanded its size or changed its location from its size or location since December thirty-first, two thousand two;

(g) Outdoor dining areas of food service establishments with no roof or other ceiling enclosure; provided, however, that smoking and vaping may be permitted in a contiguous area designated for smoking and vaping so long as such area: (a) constitutes no more than twenty-five percent of the outdoor seating capacity of such food service establishment, (b) is at least three feet away from the outdoor area of such food service establishment not designated for smoking and vaping, and (c) is clearly designated with written signage as a smoking and vaping area;

(h) Enclosed rooms in food service establishments, bars, catering halls, convention halls, hotel and motel conference rooms, and other such similar facilities during the time such enclosed areas or rooms are being used exclusively for functions where the public is invited for the primary purpose of promoting and sampling tobacco products or electronic cigarettes, and the service of food and drink is incidental to such purpose, provided that the sponsor or organizer gives notice in any promotional material or advertisements that smoking and vaping will not be restricted, and prominently posts notice at the entrance of the facility and has provided notice of such function to the appropriate enforcement officer, as defined in subdivision one of section thirteen hundred ninety-nine-t of this article, at least two weeks prior to such function. The enforcement officer shall keep a record of all tobacco sampling events, and such record shall be made available for public inspection. No such facility shall permit smoking and vaping under this subdivision for more than two days in any calendar year; (i) Retail electronic cigarette stores, provided however, that such stores may only permit the use of electronic cigarettes; and

(j) Adult-use on-site consumption premises authorized pursuant to article four of the cannabis law, provided however, that such locations may only permit the smoking or vaping of cannabis.

2. The restrictions of this article on the smoking or vaping of cannabis shall continue to apply to those locations identified in paragraphs (b), (d), (f), (g), (h) and (i) of subdivision one of this section.

Public Health Law § 1399-r. General provisions.

1. Nothing in this article shall be construed to deny the owner, operator or manager of a place covered by this article the right to designate the entire place, or any part thereof, as a nonsmoking and nonvaping area.

2. The provisions of this article shall apply to the legislative, executive and judicial branches of state government and any political subdivision of the state.

3. Smoking and vaping may not be permitted where prohibited by any other law, rule, or regulation of any state agency or any political subdivision of the state. Nothing herein shall be construed to restrict the power of any county, city, town, or village to adopt and enforce additional local law, ordinances, or regulations which comply with at least the minimum applicable standards set forth in this article.

Public Health Law § 1399-s. Violations.

1. It shall be unlawful for any person, firm, limited liability company, corporation or other entity that owns, manages, operates or otherwise controls the use of an area in which smoking and vaping is prohibited or restricted pursuant to section thirteen hundred ninety-nine-o of this article to fail to comply with the provisions of this article. For violations of this subdivision, it shall be an affirmative defense that during the relevant time period actual control of the area was not exercised by the respondent, but rather by a lessee, the sublessee or any other person. To establish an affirmative defense, the respondent shall submit an affidavit and may submit any other relevant proof indicating that the respondent did not exercise actual control of said area during the relevant time period. Such affidavit and other proof shall be mailed by certified mail to the appropriate enforcement officer within thirty days of receipt of such notice of violation.

2. It shall be unlawful for an employer whose place of employment is subject to subdivision one of section thirteen hundred ninety-nine-o of this article to fail to comply with the provisions of such subdivision. For violations of such subdivision, it shall be an affirmative defense that the employer has made good faith efforts to ensure that employees comply with the provisions of this article.

3. It shall be unlawful for any person to smoke or vape in any area where smoking and vaping is prohibited or restricted under section thirteen hundred ninety-nine-o of this article.

Public Health Law § 1399-t. Enforcement.

1. For the purpose of this article the term "enforcement officer" shall mean the board of health of a county or part county health district established pursuant to title three of article three of this chapter, or in the absence thereof, an officer of a county designated for such purpose by resolution of the elected county legislature or board of supervisors adopted within sixty days after the effective date of this article. Any such designation shall be filed with the commissioner within thirty days after adoption. If no such designation is made, the county will be deemed to have designated the department as its enforcement officer. Any county that does not designate an enforcement officer during the time period specified above may do so at any time, thereafter, such designation will be effective thirty days after it is filed with the commissioner. The enforcement officer shall have sole jurisdiction to enforce the provisions of this article on a county-wide basis pursuant to rules and regulations promulgated by the commissioner. In a city with a population of more than one million the enforcement officer shall be the department of health and mental hygiene of such city which shall have sole jurisdiction to enforce the provisions of this article in such city.

2. If the enforcement officer determines after a hearing that a violation of this article has occurred, a civil penalty may be imposed by the enforcement officer pursuant to section thirteen hundred ninety-nine-v of this article. When the enforcement officer is the commissioner, the hearing shall be conducted pursuant to the provisions of section twelve-a of this chapter. When the enforcement officer is a board of health or in a city with a population of more than

one million, the department of health and mental hygiene, or an officer designated to enforce the provisions of this article, the hearing shall be conducted pursuant to procedures set forth in the county sanitary code, or health code of such city, or in the absence thereof, pursuant to procedures established by the elected county legislature or board of supervisors. No other penalty, fine or sanction may be imposed, provided that nothing herein shall be construed to prohibit an enforcement officer from commencing a proceeding for injunctive relief to compel compliance with this article.

3. Any person who desires to register a complaint under this article may do so with the appropriate enforcement officer.

4. The owner, manager, operator or other person having control of any area subject to the provisions of this article, shall inform, or shall designate an agent who shall be responsible for informing individuals smoking or vaping in an area in which smoking or vaping is not permitted that they are in violation of this article.

5. Any person aggrieved by the decision of an enforcement officer other than the commissioner may appeal to the commissioner to review such decision within thirty days of such decision. The decision of any enforcement officer shall be reviewable pursuant to article seventy-eight of the civil practice law and rules.

6. The enforcement officer, subsequent to any appeal having been finally determined, may bring an action to recover the civil penalty provided in section thirteen hundred ninety-nine-v of this article in any court of competent jurisdiction.

7. An enforcement officer who discovers a retail dealer who or which does not display a retail dealer certificate of license or registration from the department of taxation and finance issued pursuant to section four hundred eighty-a of the tax law shall notify the commissioner of taxation and finance within thirty days of the name and address of any such establishment so that the commissioner of taxation and finance can take appropriate action.

Public Health Law § 1399-u. Waiver.

1. The enforcement officer may grant a waiver from the application of a specific provision of this article, provided that prior to the granting of any such waiver the applicant for a waiver shall establish that:

   (a) compliance with a specific provision of this article would cause undue financial hardship; or

   (b) other factors exist which would render compliance unreasonable.

2. Every waiver granted shall be subject to such conditions or restrictions as may be necessary to minimize the adverse effects of the waiver upon persons subject to an involuntary exposure to second-hand smoke or vaping and to ensure that the waiver is consistent with the general purpose of this article.

Public Health Law § 1399-v. Penalties.

The commissioner may impose a civil penalty for a violation of this article in an amount not to exceed that set forth in subdivision one of section twelve of this chapter. Any other enforcement officer may impose a civil penalty for a violation of this article in an amount not to exceed that set forth in paragraph (f) of subdivision one of section three hundred nine of this chapter. Notwithstanding the foregoing provisions, a violation of the provisions of section thirteen hundred ninety-nine-o-two of this article shall be punishable by a civil penalty of fifty dollars for each violation.

* NB Effective October 13, 2022

Public Health Law § 1399-w. Limitation of causes of action.

An employer, administrator, manager, owner or operator of any indoor area, food service establishment, or place of employment regulated by this article who complies or fails to comply with the provisions of this article shall not be subject to any legal liability or action solely as a result of such compliance or noncompliance except as provided in section thirteen hundred ninety-nine-v of this article. Nothing in any other section of this article shall be construed to create, impair, alter, limit, modify, enlarge, abrogate or restrict any theory of liability upon which any person may be held liable to any other person for exposure to smoke or vaping.

Public Health Law § 1399-x. Rules and regulations.

The commissioner shall not promulgate any rules or regulations to effectuate the provisions of section thirteen hundred ninety-nine-n, paragraph f of subdivision one of section thirteen hundred ninety-nine-o or subdivision one of section thirteen hundred ninety-nine-p of this article. The commissioner shall not promulgate any rules or regulations that create, limit or enlarge any smoking or vaping restrictions.

ARTICLE 33. CONTROLLED SUBSTANCES

Title 1. GENERAL PROVISIONS

Public Health Law § 3306. Schedules of controlled substances.

There are hereby established five schedules of controlled substances, to be known as schedules I, II, III, IV and V respectively. Such schedules shall consist of the following substances by whatever name or chemical designation known:

Schedule I.

(a) Schedule I shall consist of the drugs and other substances, by whatever official name, common or usual name, chemical name, or brand name designated, listed in this section.

(b) Opiates. Unless specifically excepted or unless listed in another schedule, any of the following opiates, including their isomers, esters, ethers, salts, and salts of isomers, esters, and ethers, whenever the existence of such isomers, esters, ethers and salts is possible within the specific chemical designation (for purposes of 3-methylfentanyl only, the term isomer includes the optical and geometric isomers):

   (1) Acetyl-alpha-methylfentanyl (N-{1-(-methyl-2-phenethyl) -4-piperidinyl} -N-phenylacetamide.

   (2) Acetylmethadol.

   (3) Allylprodine.

   (4) Alphacetylmethadol (except levo- alphacetylmethadol also known as levo-alpha-acetylmethadol, levomethadylacetate or LAAM).

   (5) Alphameprodine.

   (6) Alphamethadol.

   (7) Alpha-methylfentanyl (N-{1-(alpha-methyl-beta-phenyl) ethyl-4-piperidyl} propionanilide; 1-(1-methyl-2-phenylethyl) -4-(N-propanilido) piperidine).

   (8) Alpha-methylthiofentanyl (N-{1-methyl-2)2-thienyl) ethyl-4-piperidinyl} -N-phenylpropanamide).

   (9) Beta-hydroxyfentanyl (N-{1-2 (2-hydroxy-2-phenethyl)- 4-piperidinyl} -N-phenylpropanamide).

(10) Beta-hydroxy-3-methylfentanyl (other name: N-{1- (2-hydroxy-2-phenethyl) -3-methyl -4-piperidinyl} -N-phenylpropanamide.

(11) Benzethidine.

(12) Betacetylmethadol.

(13) Betameprodine.

(14) Betamethadol.

(15) Betaprodine.

(16) Clonitazene.

(17) Dextromoramide.

(18) Diampromide.

(19) Diethylthiambutene.

(20) Difenoxin.

(21) Dimenoxadol.

(22) Dimepheptanol.

(23) Dimethylthiambutene.

(24) Dioxaphetyl butyrate.

(25) Dipipanone.

(26) Ethylmethylthiambutene.

(27) Etonitazene.

(28) Etoxeridine.

(29) Furethidine.

(30) Hydroxypethidine.

(31) Ketobemidone.

(32) Levomoramide.

(33) Levophenacylmorphan.

(34) 3-Methylfentanyl (N-{3-methy1-1- (2- phenylethyl -4-piperidyl} -N-phenylpropanamide).

(35) 3-Methylthiofentanyl (N-{3-methyl-1- (2-thienyl)ethyl -4-piperidinyl} -N-phenylpropanamide).

(36) Morpheridine.

(37) MPPP (1-methyl -4-phenyl -4-propionoxypiperidine).

(38) Noracymethadol.

(39) Norlevorphanol.

(40) Normethadone.

(41) Norpipanone.

(42) Para-fluorofentanyl (N- (4-fluorophenyl) -N-{1- (2-phenethyl) -4-piperidinyl} -propanamide.

(43) PEPAP (1- (-2-phenethyl) -4-phenyl -4-acetoxypiperidine.

(44) Phenadoxone.

(45) Phenampromide.

(46) Phenomorphan.

(47) Phenoperidine.

(48) Piritramide.

(49) Proheptazine.

(50) Properidine.

(51) Propiram.

(52) Racemoramide.

(53) Thiofentanyl (N-phenyl-N-{1- (2-thienyl) ethyl -4- piperidinyl} -propanamide.

(54) Tilidine.

(55) Trimeperidine.

(56) 3,4-dichloro-N-{(1-dimethylamino)cyclohexylmethyl}benzamide. Some trade or other names: AH-7921.

(57) N-(1-phenethylpiperidin-4-yl)-N-phenylacetamide. Some trade or other names: Acetyl Fentanyl.

(58) N-(1-phenethylpiperidin-4-yl)-N-phenylbutyramide. Other name: Butyryl Fentanyl.

(59) N-{1-{2-hydroxy-2-(thiophen-2-yl)ethyl}piperidin-4-yl}-N-phenylp- ropionamide. Other name: Beta-Hydroxythiofentanyl.

(60) N-(1-phenethylpiperidin-4-yl)-N-phenylfuran-2-carboxamide. Other name: Furanyl Fentanyl.

(61) 3,4-Dichloro-N-{2-(dimethylamino) cyclohexyl}-N-methylbenzamide. Other name: U-47700.

(62) N-(1-phenethylpiperidin-4-yl)-N-phenylacrylamide. Other names: Acryl Fentanyl or Acryloylfentanyl.

(63) N-(4-fluorophenyl)-N-(1-phenethylpiperidin-4-yl)isobutyramide. Other names: 4-fluoroisobutyryl fentanyl, para-fluoroisobutyryl fentanyl.

(64) N-(2-fluorophenyl)-N-(1-phenethylpiperidin-4-yl)propionamide. Other names: ortho-fluorofentanyl or 2-fluorofentanyl.

(65) N-(1-phenethylpiperidin-4-yl)-N-phenyltetrahydrofuran-2-carbox- amide. Other name: tetrahydrofuranyl fentanyl.

(66) 2-methoxy-N-(1-phenethylpiperidin-4-yl)-N-phenylacetamide. Other name: methoxyacetyl fentanyl.

(67) N-(1-phenethylpiperidin-4-yl)-N-phenylcyclopropanecarboxamide. Other name: cyclopropyl fentanyl.

(68) N-(4-fluorophenyl)-N-(1-phenethylpiperidin-4-yl)butyramide. Other name: para-fluorobutyrylfentanyl.

(69) N-(2-fluorophenyl)-2-methoxy-N-(1-phenethylpiperidin-4-yl)acetam- ide. Other name: Ocfentanil.

(70) 1-cyclohexyl-4-(1,2-diphenylethyl)piperazine. Other name: MT-45.

(c) Opium derivatives. Unless specifically excepted or unless listed in another schedule, any of the following opium derivatives, its salts, isomers, and salts of isomers whenever the existence of such salts, isomers, and salts of isomers is possible within the specific chemical designation:

(1) Acetorphine.

(2) Acetyldihydrocodeine.

(3) Benzylmorphine.

(4) Codeine methylbromide.

(5) Codeine-N-oxide.

(6) Cyprenorphine.

(7) Desomorphine.

(8) Dihydromorphine.

(9) Drotebanol.

(10) Etorphine (except hydrochloride salt).

(11) Heroin.

(12) Hydromorphinol.

(13) Methyldesorphine.

(14) Methyldihydromorphine.

(15) Morphine methylbromide.

(16) Morphine methylsulfonate.

(17) Morphine-N-oxide.

(18) Myrophine.

(19) Nicocodeine.

(20) Nicomorphine.

(21) Normorphine.

(22) Pholcodine.

(23) Thebacon.

(d) Hallucinogenic substances. Unless specifically excepted or unless listed in another schedule, any material, compound, mixture, or preparation, which contains any quantity of the following hallucinogenic substances, or which contains any of its salts, isomers, and salts of isomers whenever the existence of such salts, isomers, and salts of isomers is possible within the specific chemical designation (for purposes of this paragraph only, the term "isomer" includes the optical, position and geometric isomers):

(EXPLANATION--Within the following chemical designations, character symbol substitutions were made from the original text: "@" = Greek alpha, "&" =   Greek beta, "'" = prime mark and "∧" = triangle.)

(1) 4-bromo-2, 5-dimethoxy-amphetamine Some trade or other names: 4-bromo-2, 5-dimethoxy-@-methylphenethylamine; 4-bromo-2, 5-DMA.

(2) 2, 5-dimethoxyamphetamine Some trade or other names: 2, 5-dimethoxy-@-methylphenethylamine; 2, 5-DMA.

(3) 4-methoxyamphetamine Some trade or other names: 4-methoxy-@-methylphenethylamine; paramethoxyamphetamine, PMA.

(4) 5-methoxy-3, 4-methylenedioxy - amphetamine.

(5) 4-methyl-2, 5-dimethoxy-amphetamine Some trade and other names: 4-methyl-2, 5-dimethoxy-@-methylphenethylamine; "DOM"; and "STP".

(6) 3, 4-methylenedioxy amphetamine.

(7) 3, 4, 5-trimethoxy amphetamine.

(8) Bufotenine Some trade and other names: 3-(&-dimethylaminoethyl)-5 hydroxindole; 3-(2-dimethylaminoethyl)- 5-indolol; N, N-dimethylserotonin; -5-hydroxy-N, N-dimethyltryptamine; mappine.

(9) Diethyltryptamine Some trade and other names: N, N-diethyltryptamine; DET.

(10) Dimethyltryptamine Some trade or other names: DMT.

(11) Ibogane Some trade and other names: 7-ethyl-6, 6&, 7, 8, 9, 10, 12, 13-octahydro-2-methoxy-6, 9-methano-5h-pyrido {1',2':1,2} azepino {5,4-b} indole: tabernanthe iboga.

(12) Lysergic acid diethylamide.

(13) Mescaline.

(14) Parahexyl. Some trade or other names: 3-Hexyl-1-hydroxy- 7,8,9,10-tetra hydro-6,6,9-trimethyl-6H-dibenfo{b,d} pyran.

(15) Peyote. Meaning all parts of the plant presently classified botanically as Lophophora williamsii Lemaire, whether growing or not, the seeds thereof, any extract from any part of such plant, and every compound, manufacture, salts, derivative, mixture, or preparation of such plant, its seeds or extracts.

(16) N-ethyl-3-piperidyl benzilate.

(17) N-methyl-3-piperidyl benzilate.

(18) Psilocybin.

(19) Psilocyn.

(20) Tetrahydrocannabinols. Synthetic tetrahydrocannabinols not derived from the cannabis plant that are equivalents of the substances contained in the plant, or in the resinous extractives of cannabis, sp. and/or synthetic substances, derivatives, and their isomers with similar chemical structure and pharmacological activity such as the following:

> delta 1 cis or trans tetrahydrocannabinol, and their optical isomers

> delta 6 cis or trans tetrahydrocannabinol, and their optical isomers

> delta 3, 4 cis or trans tetrahydrocannabinol, and its optical isomers (since nomenclature of these substances is not internationally standardized, compounds of these structures, regardless of numerical

designation of atomic positions covered). Any Federal Food and Drug Administration approved product containing tetrahydrocannabinol shall not be considered a synthetic tetrahydrocannabinol.

(21) Ethylamine analog of phencyclidine. Some trade or other names: N-ethyl-1-phenylcyclohexylamine, (1-phenylcyclohexyl) ethylamine, N-(1-phenylcyclohexyl) ethylamine cyclohexamine, PCE.

(22) Pyrrolidine analog of phencyclidine. Some trade or other names 1-(1-phenylcyclohexyl)-pyrrolidine; PCPy, PHP.

(23) Thiophene analog of phencyclidine. Some trade or other names: 1-{1-(2-thienyl)-cyclohexyl}-piperidine, 2-thienylanalog of phencyclidine, TPCP, TCP.

(24) 3,4-methylenedioxymethamphetamine (MDMA).

(25) 3,4-methylendioxy-N-ethylamphetamine (also known as N-ethyl-alpha-methyl-3,4 (methylenedioxy) phenethylamine, N-ethyl MDA, MDE, MDEA.

(26) N-hydroxy-3,4-methylenedioxyamphetamine (also known as N-hydroxy-alpha-methyl-3,4 (methylenedioxy) phenethylamine, and N-hydroxy MDA.

(27) 1-{1- (2-thienyl) cyclohexyl} pyrrolidine. Some other names: TCPY.

(28) Alpha-ethyltryptamine. Some trade or other names: etryptamine; Monase; Alpha-ethyl-1H-indole-3-ethanamine; 3- (2-aminobutyl) indole; Alpha-ET or AET.

(29) 2,5-dimethoxy-4-ethylamphetamine. Some trade or other names: DOET.

(30) 4-Bromo-2,5-dimethoxyphenethylamine. Some trade or other names: 2-(4-bromo-2,5-dimethoxyphenyl)-1-aminoethane; alpha-desmethyl DOB; 2C-B, Nexus.

(31) 2,5-dimethoxy-4-(n)-propylthiophenethylamine (2C-T-7), its optical isomers, salts and salts of isomers.

(33) 2-(4-iodo-2,5-dimethoxyphenyl)-N-(2-methoxybenzyl)ethanamine, also known as 25I-NBOMe; 2C-I-NBOMe; 25I; or Cimbi-5.

(34) 2-(4-chloro-2,5-dimethoxyphenyl)-N-(2-methoxybenzyl)ethanamine, also known as 25 CNBOMe; 2C-C-NBOMe; 25C; or Cimbi-82.

(35) 2-(4-bromo-2,5-dimethoxyphenyl)-N-(2-methoxybenzyl)ethanamine, also known as, 25 BNBOMe; 2C-B-NBOMe; Cimbi-36.

(36) 5-methoxy-N,N-dimethyltryptamine.

(37) Alpha-methyltryptamine. Some trade or other names: AMT.

(38) 5-methoxy-N,N-diisopropyltryptamine. Some trade or other names: 5-MeO-DIPT.

(e) Depressants. Unless specifically excepted or unless listed in another schedule, any material, compound, mixture, or preparation which contains any quantity of the following substances having a depressant effect on the central nervous system, including its salts, isomers, and salts of isomers whenever the existence of such salts, isomers, and salts of isomers is possible within the specific chemical designation:

(1) Mecloqualone.

(2) Methaqualone.

(3) Phencyclidine.

(4) Gamma hydroxybutyric acid, and salt, hydroxybutyric compound, derivative or preparation of gamma

hydroxybutyric acid, including any isomers, esters and ethers and salts of isomers, esters and ethers of gamma hydroxybutyric acid, except gamma-butyrolactone, whenever the existence of such isomers, esters and ethers and salts is possible within the specific chemical.

(5) Gamma-butyrolactone, including butyrolactone; butyrolactone gamma; 4-butyrolactone; 2(3H)-furanone dihydro; dihydro-2(3H)-furanone; tetrahydro-2-furanone; 1,2-butanolide; 1,4-butanolide; 4-butanolide; gamma-hydroxybutyric acid lactone; 3-hydroxybutyric acid lactone and 4-hydroxybutanoic acid lactone with Chemical Abstract Service number (96-48-0) when any such substance is intended for human consumption.

(6) 1,4 butanediol, including butanediol; butane-1,4-diol; 1,4-butylene glyco; butylene glycol; 1,4-dihydroxybutane; 1,4-tetramethylene glycol; tetramethylene glycol; tetramethylene Abstract Service number (110-63-4) when any such substance is intended for human consumption.

(f) Stimulants. Unless specifically excepted or unless listed in another schedule, any material, compound, mixture, or preparation which contains any quantity of the following substances having a stimulant effect on the central nervous system, including its salts, isomers, and salts of isomers:

(1) Fenethylline.

(2) N-ethylamphetamine.

(3) (+ -)cis-4-methylaminorex ((+ -)cis-4,5-dihydro-4-methyl -5-phenyl -2-oxazolamine).

(4) N,N-dimethylamphetamine (also known as N,N-alpha- trimethyl-benzeneethanamine; N,N-alpha-trimethylphenethylamine).

(5) Methcathinone (some other names: 2-(methylamino) - propiophenone; alpha-(methylamino) propiophenone; 2-(methylamino) -1-phenylpropan- 1-one; alpha-N- methylaminopropiophenone; monomethylpropion; ephedrone, N-methylcathinone, methylcathinone; AL-464; AL-422; AL-463 and UR1432), its salts, optical isomers and salts of optical isomers.

(6) Aminorex. Some other names: aminoxaphen; 2-amino-5-phenyl -2-oxazoline; or 4,5-dihydro-5-phenyl-2-oxazolamine.

(7) Cathinone. Some trade or other names: 2-amino-1-phenyl-1-propanone, alpha-aminopropiophenone, 2-aminopropiophenone, and norephedrone.

(8) N-benzylpiperazine (some other names: BZP; 1-benzylpiperazine), its optical isomers, salts and salts of isomers.

(9) 4-methyl-N-methylcathinone or 4-Methylmethcathinone, also known as Mephedrone.

(10) 3,4-methylenedioxypyrovalerone or Methylenedioxypyrovalerone, also known as MDPV.

(11) 3,4-methylenedioxy-N-methylcathinone (some other names: methylone).

(12) 4-Methoxymethcathinone.

(13) 3-Fluoromethcathinone.

(14) 4-Fluoromethcathinone.

(15) Ethylpropion (Ethcathinone).

(16) 2-(2,5-Dimethoxy-4-ethylphenyl)ethanamine (2C-E).

(17) 2-(2,5-Dimethoxy-4-methylphenyl)ethanamine (2C-D).

(18) 2-(4-Chloro-2,5-dimethoxyphenyl)ethanamine (2C-C).

(19) 2-(4-Iodo-2,5-dimethoxyphenyl)ethanamine (2C-I).

(20) 2-{4-(Ethylthio)-2,5-dimethoxyphenyl}ethanamine (2C-T-2).

(21) 2-{4-(Isopropylthio)-2,5-dimethoxyphenyl}ethanamine (2C-T-4).

(22) 2-(2,5-Dimethoxyphenyl)ethanamine (2C-H).

(23) 2-(2,5-Dimethoxy-4-nitro-phenyl)ethanamine (2C-N).

(24) 2-(2,5-Dimethoxy-4-(n)-propylphenyl)ethanamine (2C-P).

(g) Synthetic cannabinoids. Unless specifically excepted or unless listed in another schedule, any material, compound, mixture, or preparation, which contains any quantity of the following synthetic cannabinoid substances, or which contains any of its salts, isomers, and salts of isomers whenever the existence of such salts, isomers, and salts of isomers is possible within the specific chemical designation (for purposes of this paragraph only, the term "isomer" includes the optical, position and geometric isomers):

(1) (1-pentyl-1H-indol-3-yl)(2,2,3,3-tetramethylcyclopropyl) methanone. Some trade or other names: UR-144.

(2) {1-(5-fluro-pentyl)-1H-indol-3-yl}(2,2,3,3-tetramethylcyclopropyl) methanone. Some trade names or other names: 5-fluoro-UR-144, XLR11.

(3) N-(1-adamantyl)-1-pentyl-1H-indazole-3-carboxamide. Some trade or other names: APINACA, AKB48.

(4) quinolin-8-yl 1-pentyl-1H-indole-3-carboxylate. Some trade or other names: PB-22; QUPIC.

(5) quinolin-8-yl 1-(5-fluoropentyl)-1H-indole-3-carboxylate. Some trade or other names: 5-fluoro-PB-22; 5F-PB-22.

(6) N-(1-amino-3-methyl-1-oxobutan-2-yl)-1-(4-fluorobenzyl)-1H-indazo- le-3-carboxamide. Some trade or other names: AB-FUBINACA.

(7) N-(1-amino-3,3-dimethyl-1-oxobutan-2-yl)-1-pentyl-1H-indazole-3- carboxamide. Some trade or other names: ADB-PINACA.

(8) N-(1-amino-3-methyl-1-oxobutan-2-yl)-1-(cyclohexylmethyl)-1H- indazole-3-carboxamide. Some trade or other names: AB-CHMINACA.

(9) N-(1-amino-3-methyl-1-oxobutan-2-yl)-1-pentyl-1H-indazole-3- carboxamide. Some trade or other names: AB-PINACA.

(10) {1-(5-fluoropentyl)-1H-indazol-3-yl}(naphthalen-1-y1)methanone. Some trade or other names: THJ-2201.

(h) (1) Cannabimimetic agents. Unless specifically exempted or unless listed in another schedule, any material, compound, mixture, or preparation that is not approved by the federal food and drug administration (FDA) which contains any quantity of cannabimimetic agents, or which contains their salts, isomers, and salts of isomers whenever the existence of such salts, isomers, and salts of isomers is possible within the specific chemical designation.

(2) As used in this subdivision, the term "cannabimimetic agents" means any substance that is a cannabinoid receptor type 1 (CB1 receptor) agonist as demonstrated by binding studies and functional assays within any of the following structural classes:

(i) 2-(3-hydroxycyclohexyl)phenol with substitution at the 5-position of the phenolic ring by alkyl or alkenyl, whether or not substituted on the cyclohexyl ring to any extent.

(ii) 3-(1-naphthoyl)indole or 3-(1-naphthylmethane)indole by substitution at the nitrogen atom of the indole ring, whether or not further substituted on the indole ring to any extent, whether or not substituted on the naphthoyl or naphthyl ring to any extent.

(iii) 3-(1-naphthoyl)pyrrole by substitution at the nitrogen atom of the pyrrole ring, whether or not further substituted in the pyrrole ring to any extent, whether or not substituted on the naphthoyl ring to any extent.

(iv) 1-(1-naphthylmethylene)indene by substitution of the 3-position of the indene ring, whether or not further substituted in the indene ring to any extent, whether or not substituted on the naphthyl ring to any extent.

(v) 3-phenylacetylindole or 3-benzoylindole by substitution at the nitrogen atom of the indole ring, whether or not further substituted in the indole ring to any extent, whether or not substituted on the phenyl ring to any extent.

(3) Such term includes:

(i) 5-(1,1-dimethylheptyl)-2-{(1R,3S)-3-hydroxycyclohexyl}-phenol (CP-47,497);

(ii) 5-(1,1-dimethyloctyl)-2-{(1R,3S)-3-hydroxycyclohexyl}-phenol (cannabicyclohexanol or CP-47,497 C8-homolog);

(iii) 1-pentyl-3-(1-naphthoyl)indole (JWH-018 and AM678);

(iv) 1-butyl-3-(1-naphthoyl)indole (JWH-073);

(v) 1-hexyl-3-(1-naphthoyl)indole (JWH-019);

(vi) 1-{2-(4-morpholinyl)ethyl}-3-(1-naphthoyl)indole (JWH-200);

(vii) 1-pentyl-3-(2-methoxyphenylacetyl)indole (JWH-250);

(viii) 1-pentyl-3-{1-(4-methoxynaphthoyl)}indole (JWH-081);

(ix) 1-pentyl-3-(4-methyl-1-naphthoyl)indole (JWH-122);

(x) 1-pentyl-3-(4-chloro-1-naphthoyl)indole (JWH-398);

(xi) 1-(5-fluoropentyl)-3-(1-naphthoyl)indole (AM2201);

(xii) 1-(5-fluoropentyl)-3-(2-iodobenzoyl)indole (AM694);

(xiii) 1-pentyl-3-{(4-methoxy)-benzoyl}indole (SR-19 and RCS-4);

(xiv) 1-cyclohexylethyl-3-(2-methoxyphenylacetyl)indole (SR-18 and RCS-8); and

(xv) 1-pentyl-3-(2-chlorophenylacetyl)indole (JWH-203).

Schedule II.

(a) Schedule II shall consist of the drugs and other substances, by whatever official name, common or usual name, chemical name, or brand name designated, listed in this section.

(b) Substances, vegetable origin or chemical synthesis. Unless specifically excepted or unless listed in another schedule, any of the following substances whether produced directly or indirectly by extraction from substances of vegetable origin, or independently by means of chemical synthesis, or by a combination of extraction and chemical synthesis:

(1) Opium and opiate, and any salt, compound, derivative, or preparation of opium or opiate, excluding apomorphine, dextrorphan, nalbuphine, nalmefene, naloxone, and naltrexone, and their respective salts, but including the following:

1. Raw opium.

2. Opium extracts.

3. Opium fluid.

4. Powdered opium.

5. Granulated opium.

6. Tincture of opium.

7. Codeine.

8. Ethylmorphine.

9. Etorphine hydrochloride.

10. Hydrocodone (also known as dihydrocodeinone).

11. Hydromorphone.

12. Metopon.

13. Morphine.

14. Oxycodone.

15. Oxymorphone.

16. Thebaine.

17. Dihydroetorphine.

18. Oripavine.

(2) Any salt, compound, derivative, or preparation thereof which is chemically equivalent or identical with any of the substances referred to in this section, except that these substances shall not include the isoquinoline alkaloids of opium.

(3) Opium poppy and poppy straw.

(4) Coca leaves and any salt, compound, derivative, or preparation of coca leaves, and any salt, compound, derivative, or preparation thereof which is chemically equivalent or identical with any of these substances including cocaine and ecgonine, their salts, isomers, and salts of isomers, except that the substances shall not include: (A) decocainized coca leaves or extraction of coca leaves, which extractions do not contain cocaine or ecgonine; or (B) {123I} ioflupane.

(5) Concentrate of poppy straw (the crude extract of poppy straw in either liquid, solid or powder form which contains the phenanthrene alkaloids of the opium poppy).

(b-1) Unless specifically excepted or unless listed in another schedule, any material, compound, mixture, or preparation containing any of the following, or their salts calculated as the free anhydrous base or alkaloid, in limited quantities as set forth below:

(1) Not more than three hundred milligrams of dihydrocodeinone (hydrocodone) per one hundred milliliters or not more than fifteen milligrams per dosage unit, with a fourfold or greater quantity of an isoquinoline alkaloid of opium.

(2) Not more than three hundred milligrams of dihydrocodeinone (hydrocodone) per one hundred milliliters or not more than fifteen milligrams per dosage unit, with one or more active nonnarcotic ingredients in recognized therapeutic amounts.

(c) Opiates. Unless specifically excepted or unless in another schedule any of the following opiates, including its isomers, esters, ethers, salts and salts of isomers, esters and ethers whenever the existence of such isomers, esters, ethers, and salts is possible within the specific chemical designation, dextrorphan and levopropoxyphene excepted:

(1) Alfentanil.

(2) Alphaprodine.

(3) Anileridine.

(4) Bezitramide.

(5) Bulk dextropropoxyphene (non-dosage forms).

(6) Carfentanil.

(7) Dihydrocodeine.

(8) Diphenoxylate.

(9) Fentanyl.

(10) Isomethadone.

(11) Levo-alphacetylmethadol (also known as levo-alpha-acetylmethadol, levomethadylacetate or LAAM).

(12) Levomethorphan.

(13) Levorphanol.

(14) Metazocine.

(15) Methadone.

(16) Methadone-intermediate, 4-cyano-2-dimethylamino-4, 4-diphenyl butane.

(17) Moramide-intermediate, 2-methyl-3-morpholino-1, 1--diphenylpropane--carboxylic acid.

(18) Pethidine (meperidine).

(19) Pethidine-intermediate-A, 4-cyano-1-methyl-4-phenylpiperidine.

(20) Pethidine-intermediate-B, ethyl-4-phenylpiperidine-4-carboxylate.

(21) Pethidine-intermediate-C, 1--methyl--4-- phenylpiperidine--4-- carboxylic acid.

(22) Phenazocine.

(23) Piminodine.

(24) Racemethorphan.

(25) Racemorphan.

(26) Sufentanil.

(27) Remifentanil.

(28) Tapentadol.

(29) Thiafentanil.

(d) Stimulants. Unless specifically excepted or unless listed in another schedule, any material, compound, mixture, or preparation which contains any quantity of the following substances having a stimulant effect on the central nervous system, including its salts, isomers, and salts of isomers:

   (1) Amphetamine.

   (2) Methamphetamine.

   (3) Phenmetrazine.

   (4) Methylphenidate.

   (5) Lisdexamfetamine.

(e) Depressants. Unless specifically excepted or unless listed in another schedule, any material, compound, mixture, or preparation which contains any quantity of the following substances having a depressant effect on the central nervous system, including its salts, isomers, and salts of isomers whenever the existence of such salts, isomers, and salts of isomers is possible within the specific chemical designation:

   (1) Amobarbital.

   (2) Glutethimide.

   (3) Pentobarbital.

   (4) Secobarbital.

(f) Hallucinogenic substances.

   Nabilone: Another name for nabilone: (+,-)-trans -3-(1,1-dimethylheptyl)-6, 6a, 7, 8, 10, 10a-hexahydro-1-hydroxy-6, 6-dimethyl-9H-dibenzo{b,d}pyran-9-one.

(g) Immediate precursors. Unless specifically excepted or unless listed in another schedule, any material, compound, mixture or preparation which contains any quantity of the following substances:

   (1) Immediate precursor to amphetamine and methamphetamine:

      (i) Phenylacetone Some trade or other names: phenyl-2-propanone; P2P; benzyl methyl ketone; methyl benzyl ketone;

   (2) Immediate precursors to phencyclidine (PCP):

      (i) 1-phenylcyclohexylamine;

      (ii) 1-piperidinocyclohexanecarbonitrile (PCC).

   (3) Immediate precursor to fentanyl:

      (i) 4-anilino-N-phenethyl-4-piperidine (ANPP).

(h) Anabolic steroids. Unless specifically excepted or unless listed in another schedule, "anabolic steroid" shall mean any drug or hormonal substance, chemically and pharmacologically related to testosterone (other than estrogens, progestins, corticosteroids and dehydroepiandrosterone) and includes:

   (1) 3{beta}, 17-dihydroxy-5a-androstane.

   (2) 3{alpha}, 17{beta}-dihydroxy-5a-androstane.

   (3) 5{alpha}-androstan-3,17-dione.

(4) 1-androstenediol (3{beta},17{beta}-dihydroxy-5{alpha}-androst-1- ene).

(5) 1-androstenediol (3{alpha},17{beta}-dihydroxy-5{alpha}-androst-1- ene).

(6) 4-androstenediol (3{beta}, 17{beta}-dihydroxy-androst-4-ene).

(7) 5-androstenediol (3{beta}, 17{beta}-dihydroxy-androst-5-ene).

(8) 1-androstenedione ({5{alpha}}-androst-1-en-3,17-dione).

(9) 4-androstenedione (androst-4-en-3,17-dione).

(10) 5-androstenedione (androst-5-en-3,17-dione).

(11) Bolasterone (7{alpha},17{alpha}-dimethyl-17{beta}-hydroxyandrost- 4-en-3-one).

(12) Boldenone (17{beta}-hydroxyandrost-1, 4,-diene-3-one).

(13) Boldione (androsta-1,4-diene-3,17-dione).

(14) Calusterone (7{beta}, 17{alpha}-dimethyl-17{beta}-hydroxyandrost- 4-en-3-one).

(15) Clostebol (4-chloro-17{beta}-hydroxyandrost-4-en-3-one).

(16) Dehydrochloromethyltestosterone (4-chloro-17{beta}-hydroxy-17 {alpha}-methyl-androst-1, 4-dien-3-one).

(17) {Delta} 1-dihydrotestosterone (a.k.a. '1-testosterone') (17 {beta}-hydroxy-5{alpha}-androst-1-en-3-one).

(18) 4-dihydrotestosterone (17{beta}-hydroxy-androstan-3-one).

(19) Drostanolone (17{beta}-hydroxy-2{alpha}-methyl-5{alpha} -androstan-3-one).

(20) Ethylestrenol (17{alpha}-ethyl-17{beta}-hydroxyestr- 4-ene).

(21) Fluoxymesterone (9-fluoro-17{alpha}-methyl-11{beta}, 17 {beta}- dihydroxyandrost-4-en-3-one).

(22) Formebolone (2-formyl-17{alpha}-methyl-11{alpha}, 17{beta}-dihydroxyandrost-1, 4-dien-3-one).

(23) Furazabol (17{alpha}-methyl-17{beta}-hydroxyandrostano {2, 3-c}-furazan).

(24) 13{beta}-ethyl-17{beta}-hyroxygon-4-en-3-one.

(25) 4-hydroxytestosterone (4, 17{beta}-dihydroxy-androst-4-en-3-one).

(26) 4-hydroxy-19-nortestosterone (4,17{beta}-dihydroxy-estr-4-en-3-one).

(27) desoxymethyltestosterone (17{alpha}-methyl-5{alpha}-androst-2-en-17{beta}-ol) (a.k.a., madol).

(28) Mestanolone (17{alpha}-methyl-17{beta}-hydroxy- 5-androstan-3-one).

(29) Mesterolone (1{alpha} methyl-17{beta}-hydroxy- {5{alpha}}-androstan-3-one).

(30) Methandienone (17{alpha}-methyl-17{beta}-hydroxyandrost-1, 4-dien-3-one).

(31) Methandriol (17{alpha}-methyl-3{beta}, 17{beta}-dihydroxyandrost-5-ene).

(32) Methenolone (1-methyl-17{beta}-hydroxy-5{alpha}-androst- 1-en-3-one).

(33) 17{alpha}-methyl-3{beta},17{beta}-dihydroxy-5a-androstane.

(34) 17{alpha}-methyl-3{alpha}, 17{beta}-dihydroxy- 5a-androstane.

(35) 17{alpha}-methyl-3{beta}, 17{beta}-dihydroxyandrost-4-ene.

(36) 17{alpha}-methyl-4-hydroxynandrolone (17{alpha}-methyl-4- hydroxy-17{beta}-hydroxyestr-4-en-3-one).

(37) Methyldienolone (17{alpha}-methyl-17{beta}-hydroxyestra- 4,9(10)-dien-3-one).

(38) Methyltrienolone (17{alpha}-methyl-17{beta}-hydroxyestra-4, 9-11-trien-3-one).

(39) Methyltestosterone (17{alpha}-methyl-17{beta}-hydroxyandrost- 4-en-3-one).

(40) Mibolerone (7{alpha},17{alpha}-dimethyl-17{beta}-hydroxyestr- 4-en-3-one).

(41) 17{alpha}-methyl-{Delta} 1-dihydrotestosterone (17b{beta}-hydroxy-17{alpha}-methyl-5{alpha}-androst-1-en-3-one) (a.k.a. '17-{alpha}-methyl-1-testosterone').

(42) Nandrolone(17{beta}-hydroxyestr-4-en-3-one).

(43) 19-nor-4-androstenediol (3{beta},17{beta}-dihydroxyestr -4-ene).

(44) 19-nor-4-androstenediol (3{alpha},17{beta}-dihydroxyestr-4-ene).

(45) 19-nor-5-androstenediol (3{beta},17{beta}-dihydroxyestr -5-ene).

(46) 19-nor-5-androstenediol (3{alpha},17{beta}-dihydroxyestr-5-ene).

(47) 19-nor-4,9(10)-androstadienedione (estra-4,9(10)-diene-3,17-dione).

(48) 19-nor-4-androstenedione (estr-4-en-3,17-dione).

(49) 19-nor-5-androstenedione (estr-5-en-3,17-dione).

(50) Norbolethone (13{beta}, 17{alpha}-diethyl-17{beta} -hydroxygon-4-en-3-one).

(51) Norclostebol (4-chloro-17{beta}-hydroxyestr-4-en-3-one).

(52) Norethandrolone (17{alpha}-ethyl-17{beta}-hydroxyestr- 4-en-3-one).

(53) Normethandrolone (17{alpha}-methyl-17{beta} -hydroxyestr-4-en-3-one).

(54) Oxandrolone (17{alpha}-methyl-17{beta}-hydroxy-2-oxa- {5{alpha}}-androstan-3-one).

(55) Oxymesterone (17{alpha}-methyl-4, 17{beta}-dihydroxy androst-4-en-3-one).

(56) Oxymetholone (17 {alpha}-methyl-2-hydroxymethylene-17 {beta}-hydroxy-{5{alpha}}- androstan-3-one).

(57) Stanozolol (17{alpha}-methyl-17{beta}-hydroxy-{5{alpha}}- androst-2-eno{3, 2-c}-pyrazole).

(58) Stenbolone (17{beta}-hydroxy-2-methyl-{5{alpha}}-androst- 1-en-3-one).

(59) Testolactone (13-hydroxy-3-oxo-13, 17-secoandrosta-1, 4-dien-17-oic acid lactone).

(60) Testosterone (17{beta}-hydroxyandrost-4-en-3-one).

(61) Tetrahydrogestrinone (13{beta}, 17{alpha}-diethyl -17{beta}-hydroxygon-4, 9, 11-trien-3-one).

(62) Trenbolone (17{beta}-hydroxyestr-4, 9, 11-trien-3-one).

(63) Any salt, ester or ether of a drug or substance described or listed in this subdivision.

(i) Subdivision (h) of this section shall not include any substance containing anabolic steroids expressly intended for administration through implants to cattle or other nonhuman species and that are approved by the federal food and drug administration solely for such use. Any individual who knowingly and willfully administers to himself or another person, prescribes, dispenses or distributes such substances for other than implantation to cattle or nonhuman species shall be subject to the same penalties as a practitioner who violates the provisions of this section or any other penalties prescribed by law.

Schedule III.

(a) Schedule III shall consist of the drugs and other substances, by whatever official name, common or usual name, chemical name, or brand name designated, listed in this section.

(b) Stimulants. Unless specifically excepted or unless listed in another schedule, any material, compound, mixture, or preparation which contains any quantity of the following substances having a stimulant effect on the central nervous system, including its salts, isomers (whether optical, position, or geometric), and salts of such isomers whenever the existence of such salts, isomers, and salts of isomers is possible within the specific chemical designation:

(1) Those compounds, mixtures, or preparations in dosage unit form containing any stimulant substances listed in schedule II which compounds, mixtures, or preparations were listed on August twenty-five, nineteen hundred seventy-one, as excepted compounds under title twenty-one, section 308.32 of the code of federal regulations and any other drug of the quantitive composition shown in that list for those drugs or which is the same except that it contains a lesser quantity of controlled substances.

(2) Benzphetamine.

(3) Chlorphentermine.

(4) Clortermine.

(6) Phendimetrazine.

(c) Depressants. Unless specifically excepted or unless listed in another schedule, any material, compound, mixture, or preparation which contains any quantity of the following substances having a depressant effect on the central nervous system, including its salts, isomers, and salts of isomers:

(1) Any compound, mixture or preparation containing:

(i) Amobarbital;

(ii) Secobarbital;

(iii) Pentobarbital; or any salt thereof and one or more other active medicinal ingredients which are not listed in any schedule.

(2) Any suppository dosage form containing:

(i) Amobarbital;

(ii) Secobarbital;

(iii) Pentobarbital; or any salt of any of these drugs and approved by the federal food and drug administration for marketing only as a suppository.

(3) Any substance which contains any quantity of a derivative of barbituric acid or any salt thereof.

(4) Chlorhexadol.

(5) Lysergic acid.

(6) Lysergic acid amide.

(7) Methyprylon.

(8) Sulfondiethylmethane.

(9) Sulfonethylmethane.

(10) Sulfonmethane.

(11) Tiletamine and zolazepam or any salt thereof. Some trade or other names for a tiletamine-zolazepam combination product: Telazol. Some trade or other names for tiletamine: 2-(ethylamino) -2-(2-thienyl) -cyclohexanone. Some trade or other names for zolazepam: 4-(2-fluorophenyl) -6,8-dihydro -1, 3, 8i-trimethylpyrazolo-{3,4-e} {1,4} -diazepin-7(1H)-one, flupyrazapon.

(12) Gamma hydroxybutyric acid, and salt, hydroxybutyric compound, derivative or preparation of gamma hydroxybutyric acid, including any isomers, esters and ethers and salts of isomers, esters and ethers of gamma hydroxybutyric acid, contained in a drug product for which an application has been approved under section 505 of the federal food, drug and cosmetic act.

(13) Ketamine, its salts, isomers and salts of isomers (some other names for ketamine: (±)-2-(2-chlorophenyl)-2-(methylamino)- cyclohexanone).

(14) Embutramide.

(d) Nalorphine.

(e) Narcotic drugs. Unless specifically excepted or unless listed in another schedule, any material, compound, mixture, or preparation containing any of the following narcotic drugs, or their salts calculated as the free anhydrous base or alkaloid, in limited quantities as set forth below:

(1) Not more than 1.8 grams of codeine per one hundred milliliters or not more than ninety milligrams per dosage unit, with an equal or greater quantity of an isoquinoline alkaloid of opium.

(2) Not more than 1.8 grams of codeine per one hundred milliliters or not more than ninety milligrams per dosage unit, with one or more active, nonnarcotic ingredients in recognized therapeutic amounts.

(3) Not more than 1.8 grams of dihydrocodeine per one hundred milliliters or not more than ninety milligrams per dosage unit, with one or more active nonnarcotic ingredients in recognized therapeutic amounts.

(4) Not more than three hundred milligrams of ethylmorphine per one hundred milliliters or not more than fifteen milligrams per dosage unit, with one or more active, nonnarcotic ingredients in recognized therapeutic amounts.

(5) Not more than five hundred milligrams of opium per one hundred milliliters or per one hundred grams or not more than twenty-five milligrams per dosage unit, with one or more active, nonnarcotic ingredients in recognized therapeutic amounts.

(6) Not more than fifty milligrams of morphine per one hundred milliliters or per one hundred grams, with one or more active, nonnarcotic ingredients in recognized therapeutic amounts.

(7) Buprenorphine in any quantities.

(f) Dronabinol (synthetic) in sesame oil and encapsulated in a soft gelatin capsule in a U.S. Food and Drug Administration approved product.

Some other names for dronabinol include: (6aR-trans)-6a, 7, 8, 10a-tetrahydro-6, 6, 9-trimethyl-3-pentyl-6H-dibenzo{b,d} pyran-1-o1, or (-)-delta-9-(trans) - tetrahydrocannabinol.

(g) Chorionic gonadotropin.

(1) Unless specifically excepted or unless listed in another schedule any material, compound, mixture, or

preparation which contains any amount of chorionic gonadotropin.

(2) Paragraph one of this subdivision shall not include any substance containing chorionic gonadotropin expressly intended for administration through implants or injection to cattle or other nonhuman species and that are approved by the federal food and drug administration solely for such use. Any individual who knowingly and willfully administers to himself or another person, prescribes, dispenses or distributes such substances for other than implantation or injection to cattle or nonhuman species shall be subject to the same penalties as a practitioner who violates the provisions of this section or any other penalties prescribed by law.

Schedule IV.

(a) Schedule IV shall consist of the drugs and other substances, by whatever official name, common or usual name, chemical name, or brand name designated, listed in this section.

(b) Narcotic drugs. Unless specifically excepted or unless listed in another schedule, any material, compound, mixture, or preparation containing any of the following narcotic drugs, or their salts calculated as the free anhydrous base or alkaloid, in limited quantities as set forth below:

(1) Not more than one milligram of difenoxin and not less than twenty-five micrograms of atropine sulfate per dosage unit.

(2) Dextropropoxyphene (alpha-(+)-4-dimethylamino-1, 2-diphenyl-3- methyl-2-propionoxybutane).

(c) Depressants. Unless specifically excepted or unless listed in another schedule, any material, compound, mixture, or preparation which contains any quantity of the following substances, including its salts, isomers, and salts of isomers whenever the existence of such salts, isomers, and salts of isomers is possible within the specific chemical designation:

(1) Alprazolam.

(2) Barbital.

(3) Bromazepam.

(4) Camazepam.

(5) Chloral betaine.

(6) Chloral hydrate.

(7) Chlordiazepoxide.

(8) Clobazam.

(9) Clonazepam.

(10) Clorazepate.

(11) Clotiazepam.

(12) Cloxazolam.

(13) Delorazepam.

(14) Diazepam.

(15) Estazolam.

(16) Ethchlorvynol.

(17) Ethinamate.

(18) Ethyl Loflazepate.

(19) Fludiazepam.

(20) Flunitrazepam.

(21) Flurazepam.

(22) Halazepam.

(23) Haloxazolam.

(24) Ketazolam.

(25) Loprazolam.

(26) Lorazepam.

(27) Lormetazepam.

(28) Mebutamate.

(29) Medazepam.

(30) Meprobamate.

(31) Methohexital.

(32) Methylphenobarbital (mephobarbital).

(33) Nimetazepam.

(34) Nitrazepam.

(35) Nordiazepam.

(36) Oxazepam.

(37) Oxazolam.

(38) Paraldehyde.

(39) Petrichoral.

(40) Phenobarbital.

(41) Pinazepam.

(42) Prazepam.

(43) Temazepam.

(44) Tetrazepam.

(45) Triazolam.

(46) Midazolam.

(47) Quazepam.

(48) Zolpidem.

(49) Dichloralphenazone.

(50) Zaleplon.

(51) Zopiclone (eszopiclone).

(52) Fospropofol.

(53) Carisoprodol.

* (d) Fenfluramine. Any material, compound, mixture, or preparation which contains any quantity of the following substances, including its salts, isomers (whether optical, position, or geometric), and salts of such isomers, whenever the existence of such salts, isomers and salts of isomers is possible:

(1) Fenfluramine.

* NB Repealed upon the removal of fenfluramine and its salts and isomers from Schedule IV of the federal Controlled Substances Act

(e) Stimulants. Unless specifically excepted or unless listed in another schedule, any material, compound, mixture, or preparation which contains any quantity of the following substances having a stimulant effect on the central nervous system, including its salts, isomers, and salts of such isomers:

(1) Cathine ((+) - norpseudoephedrine).

(2) Diethylpropion.

(3) Fencamfamin.

(4) Fenproporex.

(5) Mazindol.

(6) Mefenorex.

(7) Pemoline (including organometallic complexes and chelates thereof).

(8) Phentermine.

(9) Pipradrol.

(10) SPA((-))-1-dimethylamino-1, 2-diphenylethane).

(11) Modafinil.

(12) Sibutramine.

(f) Other substances. Unless specifically excepted or unless listed in another schedule, any material, compound, mixture or preparation which contains any quantity of the following substances, including its salts:

(1) Pentazocine.

(2) Butorphanol (including its optical isomers).

(3) Tramadol in any quantities.

Schedule V.

(a) Schedule V shall consist of the drugs and other substances, by whatever official name, common or usual name, chemical name, or brand name designated, listed in this section.

(b) Narcotic drugs containing nonnarcotic active medicinal ingredients. Any compound, mixture, or preparation containing any of the following narcotic drugs, or their salts calculated as the free anhydrous base or alkaloid, in limited quantities as set forth below, which shall include one or more nonnarcotic active medicinal ingredients in sufficient proportion to confer upon the compound, mixture, or preparation valuable medicinal qualities other than those possessed by narcotic drugs alone:

(1) Not more than two hundred milligrams of codeine per one hundred milliliters or per one hundred grams.

(2) Not more than one hundred milligrams of dihydrocodeine per one hundred milliliters or per one hundred grams.

(3) Not more than one hundred milligrams of ethylmorphine per one hundred milliliters or per one hundred grams.

(4) Not more than 2.5 milligrams of diphenoxylate and not less than twenty-five micrograms of atropine sulfate per dosage unit.

(5) Not more than one hundred milligrams of opium per one hundred milliliters or per one hundred grams.

(6) Not more than 0.5 milligram of difenoxin and not less than twenty-five micrograms of atropine sulfate per dosage unit.

(c) Stimulants. Unless specifically exempted or excluded or unless listed in another schedule, any material, compound, mixture, or preparation which contains any quantity of the following substances having a stimulant effect on the central nervous system, including its salts, isomers and salts of isomers:

(1) Pyrovalerone.

(d) Depressants. Unless specifically exempted or excluded or unless listed in another schedule, any material, compound, mixture, or preparation which contains any quantity of the following substances having a depressant effect on the central nervous system, including its salts, isomers, and salts of isomers:

(1) Ezogabine {N-{2-amino-4-(4-fluorobenzylamino)-phenyl}-carbamic acid ethyl ester}.

(2) Lacosamide {(R)-2-acetoamido-N-benzyl-3-methoxy-propionamide}.

(3) Pregabalin {(S)-3-(aminomethyl)-5-methylhexanoic acid}.

Title 5-A. MEDICAL USE OF MARIHUANA

Public Health Law § 3360. Definitions.

* NB Repealed July 5, 2028 and Repealed 6 months after the full cannabis control board created by Article 2 of the cannabis law has been appointed

As used in this title, the following terms shall have the following meanings, unless the context clearly requires otherwise:

1. "Certified medical use" means the acquisition, possession, use, or, transportation of medical marihuana by a certified patient, or the acquisition, possession, delivery, transportation or administration of medical marihuana by a designated caregiver, for use as part of the treatment of the patient's serious condition, as authorized in a certification under this title including enabling the patient to tolerate treatment for the serious condition. A certified medical use does not include smoking.

2. "Caring for" means treating a patient, in the course of which the practitioner has completed a full assessment of the patient's medical history and current medical condition.

3. "Certified patient" means a patient who is a resident of New York state or receiving care and treatment in New York state as determined by the commissioner in regulation, and is certified under section thirty-three hundred sixty-one of this title.

4. "Certification" means a certification, made under section thirty-three hundred sixty-one of this title.

5. "Designated caregiver" means the individual designated by a certified patient in a registry application. A certified patient may designate up to two designated caregivers.

6. "Public place" means a public place as defined in regulation by the commissioner.

7. (a) "Serious condition" means:

   (i) having one of the following severe debilitating or life-threatening conditions: cancer, positive status for human immunodeficiency virus or acquired immune deficiency syndrome, amyotrophic lateral sclerosis, Parkinson's disease, multiple sclerosis, damage to the nervous tissue of the spinal cord with objective neurological indication of intractable spasticity, epilepsy, inflammatory bowel disease, neuropathies, Huntington's disease, post-traumatic stress disorder, pain that degrades health and functional capability where the use of medical marihuana is an alternative to opioid use, substance use disorder, or as added by the commissioner; and

   (ii) any of the following conditions where it is clinically associated with, or a complication of, a condition under this paragraph or its treatment: cachexia or wasting syndrome; severe or chronic pain; severe nausea; seizures; severe or persistent muscle spasms; or such conditions as are added by the commissioner.

   (b) No later than eighteen months from the effective date of this section, the commissioner shall determine whether to add the following serious conditions: Alzheimer's, muscular dystrophy, dystonia, post-traumatic stress disorder and rheumatoid arthritis.

8. "Medical marihuana" means marihuana as defined in subdivision twenty-one of section thirty-three hundred two of this article, intended for a certified medical use, as determined by the commissioner in his or her sole discretion. Any form of medical marihuana not approved by the commissioner is expressly prohibited.

9. "Registered organization" means a registered organization under sections thirty-three hundred sixty-four and thirty-three hundred sixty-five of this title.

10. "Registry application" means an application properly completed and filed with the department by a certified patient under section thirty-three hundred sixty-three of this title.

11. "Registry identification card" means a document that identifies a certified patient or designated caregiver, as provided under section thirty-three hundred sixty-three of this title.

12. "Practitioner" means a practitioner who (i) is a physician licensed by New York state and practicing within the state, (ii) who by training or experience is qualified to treat a serious condition as defined in subdivision seven of this section; and (iii) has completed a two to four hour course as determined by the commissioner in regulation and registered with the department; provided however, a registration shall not be denied without cause. Such course may count toward board certification requirements. The commissioner shall consider the inclusion of nurse practitioners under this title based upon considerations including access and availability. After such consideration the commissioner is authorized to deem nurse practitioners as practitioners under this title.

13. "Terminally ill" means an individual has a medical prognosis that the individual's life expectancy is approximately one year or less if the illness runs its normal course.

14. "Labor peace agreement" means an agreement between an entity and a labor organization that, at a minimum,

protects the state's proprietary interests by prohibiting labor organizations and members from engaging in picketing, work stoppages, boycotts, and any other economic interference with the registered organization's business.

15. "Individual dose" means a single measure of raw medical marihuana or non-infused concentrates to be determined and clearly identified by a patient's practitioner for the patient's specific certified condition. For ingestible or sub-lingual medical marihuana products, no individual dose may contain more than ten milligrams of tetrahydrocannabinol.

16. "Form of medical marihuana" means characteristics of the medical marihuana recommended or limited for a particular certified patient, including the method of consumption and any particular strain, variety, and quantity or percentage of marihuana or particular active ingredient.

17. "Applicant" means a for-profit entity or not-for-profit corporation and includes: board members, officers, managers, owners, partners, principal stakeholders and members who submit an application to become a registered organization.

18. "Special certification" means a special certification made under subdivision nine of section thirty-three hundred sixty-one of this title.

Public Health Law § 3361. Certification of patients.

* NB Repealed July 5, 2028 and Repealed 6 months after the full cannabis control board created by Article 2 of the cannabis law has been appointed

1. A patient certification may only be issued if: (a) a practitioner has been registered with the department to issue a certification as determined by the commissioner; (b) the patient has a serious condition, which shall be specified in the patient's health care record; (c) the practitioner by training or experience is qualified to treat the serious condition; (d) the patient is under the practitioner's continuing care for the serious condition; and (e) in the practitioner's professional opinion and review of past treatments, the patient is likely to receive therapeutic or palliative benefit from the primary or adjunctive treatment with medical use of marihuana for the serious condition.

2. The certification shall include (a) the name, date of birth and address of the patient; (b) a statement that the patient has a serious condition and the patient is under the practitioner's care for the serious condition; (c) a statement attesting that all requirements of subdivision one of this section have been satisfied; (d) the date; and (e) the name, address, federal registration number, telephone number, and the handwritten signature of the certifying practitioner. The commissioner may require by regulation that the certification shall be on a form provided by the department. The practitioner may state in the certification that, in the practitioner's professional opinion, the patient would benefit from medical marihuana only until a specified date. The practitioner may state in the certification that, in the practitioner's professional opinion, the patient is terminally ill and that the certification shall not expire until the patient dies.

3. In making a certification, the practitioner shall consider the form of medical marihuana the patient should consume, including the method of consumption and any particular strain, variety, and quantity or percentage of marihuana or particular active ingredient, and appropriate dosage. The practitioner shall state in the certification any recommendation or limitation the practitioner makes, in his or her professional opinion, concerning the appropriate form or forms of medical marihuana and dosage.

4. Every practitioner shall consult the prescription monitoring drug program registry prior to making or issuing a certification, for the purpose of reviewing a patient's controlled substance history. For purposes of this section, a practitioner may authorize a designee to consult the prescription monitoring program registry on his or her behalf, provided that such designation is in accordance with section thirty-three hundred forty-three-a of this article.

5. The practitioner shall give the certification to the certified patient, and place a copy in the patient's health care record.

6. No practitioner shall issue a certification under this section for himself or herself.

7. A registry identification card based on a certification shall expire one year after the date the certification is signed by the practitioner.

8. (a) If the practitioner states in the certification that, in the practitioner's professional opinion, the patient would benefit from medical marihuana only until a specified earlier date, then the registry identification card shall expire on that date;

(b) If the practitioner states in the certification that in the practitioner's professional opinion the patient is terminally ill and that the certification shall not expire until the patient dies, then the registry identification card shall state that the patient is terminally ill and that the registration card shall not expire until the patient dies;

(c) If the practitioner re-issues the certification to terminate the certification on an earlier date, then the registry identification card shall expire on that date and shall be promptly returned by the certified patient to the department;

(d) If the certification so provides, the registry identification card shall state any recommendation or limitation by the practitioner as to the form or forms of medical marihuana or dosage for the certified patient; and

(e) The commissioner shall make regulations to implement this subdivision.

9.(a) A certification may be a special certification if, in addition to the other requirements for a certification, the practitioner certifies in the certification that the patient's serious condition is progressive and degenerative or that delay in the patient's certified medical use of marihuana poses a serious risk to the patient's life or health.

(b) The department shall create the form to be used for a special certification and shall make that form available to be downloaded from the department's website.

Public Health Law § 3362. Lawful medical use.

* NB Repealed July 5, 2028 and Repealed 6 months after the full cannabis control board created by Article 2 of the cannabis law has been appointed

1. The possession, acquisition, use, delivery, transfer, transportation, or administration of medical marihuana by a certified patient or designated caregiver possessing a valid registry identification card, for certified medical use, shall be lawful under this title; provided that:

> (a) the marihuana that may be possessed by a certified patient shall not exceed a thirty day supply of the dosage as determined by the practitioner, consistent with any guidance and regulations issued by the commissioner, provided that during the last seven days of any thirty day period, the certified patient may also possess up to such amount for the next thirty day period;

> (b) the marihuana that may be possessed by designated caregivers does not exceed the quantities referred to in paragraph (a) of this subdivision for each certified patient for whom the caregiver possesses a valid registry identification card, up to five certified patients;

> (c) the form or forms of medical marihuana that may be possessed by the certified patient or designated caregiver pursuant to a certification shall be in compliance with any recommendation or limitation by the practitioner as to the form or forms of medical marihuana or dosage for the certified patient in the certification; and

> (d) the medical marihuana shall be kept in the original package in which it was dispensed under subdivision twelve of section thirty-three hundred sixty-four of this title, except for the portion removed for immediate consumption for certified medical use by the certified patient.

2. Notwithstanding subdivision one of this section:

(a) possession of medical marihuana shall not be lawful under this title if it is smoked, consumed, vaporized, or grown in a public place, regardless of the form of medical marihuana stated in the patient's certification.

(b) a person possessing medical marihuana under this title shall possess his or her registry identification card at all times when in immediate possession of medical marihuana.

Public Health Law § 3363. Registry identification cards.

* NB Repealed July 5, 2028 and Repealed 6 months after the full cannabis control board created by Article 2 of the cannabis law has been appointed

1. Upon approval of the certification, the department shall issue registry identification cards for certified patients and designated caregivers. A registry identification card shall expire as provided in section thirty-three hundred sixty-one of this title or as otherwise provided in this section. The department shall begin issuing registry identification cards as soon as practicable after the certifications required by section thirty-three hundred sixty-nine-b are granted. The department may specify a form for a registry application, in which case the department shall provide the form on request, reproductions of the form may be used, and the form shall be available for downloading from the department's website.

2. To obtain, amend or renew a registry identification card, a certified patient or designated caregiver shall file a registry application with the department. The registry application or renewal application shall include:

(a) in the case of a certified patient:

(i) the patient's certification (a new written certification shall be provided with a renewal application);

(ii) the name, address, and date of birth of the patient;

(iii) the date of the certification;

(iv) if the patient has a registry identification card based on a current valid certification, the registry identification number and expiration date of that registry identification card;

(v) the specified date until which the patient would benefit from medical marihuana, if the certification states such a date;

(vi) the name, address, federal registration number, and telephone number of the certifying practitioner;

(vii) any recommendation or limitation by the practitioner as to the form or forms of medical marihuana or dosage for the certified patient; and

(viii) other individual identifying information required by the department;

(b) in the case of a certified patient, if the patient designates a designated caregiver, the name, address, and date of birth of the designated caregiver, and other individual identifying information required by the department;

(c) in the case of a designated caregiver:

(i) the name, address, and date of birth of the designated caregiver;

(ii) if the designated caregiver has a registry identification card, the registry identification number and expiration date of that registry identification card; and

(iii) other individual identifying information required by the department;

(d) a statement that a false statement made in the application is punishable under section 210.45 of the penal law;

(e) the date of the application and the signature of the certified patient or designated caregiver, as the case may be;

(f) a fifty dollar application fee, provided, that the department may waive or reduce the fee in cases of financial hardship; and

(g) any other requirements determined by the commissioner.

3. Where a certified patient is under the age of eighteen:

(a) The application for a registry identification card shall be made by an appropriate person over twenty-one years of age. The application shall state facts demonstrating that the person is appropriate.

(b) The designated caregiver shall be (i) a parent or legal guardian of the certified patient, (ii) a person designated by a parent or legal guardian, or (iii) an appropriate person approved by the department upon a sufficient showing that no parent or legal guardian is appropriate or available.

4. No person may be a designated caregiver if the person is under twenty-one years of age unless a sufficient showing is made to the department that the person should be permitted to serve as a designated caregiver. The requirements for such a showing shall be determined by the commissioner.

5. No person may be a designated caregiver for more than five certified patients at one time.

6. If a certified patient wishes to change or terminate his or her designated caregiver, for whatever reason, the certified patient shall notify the department as soon as practicable. The department shall issue a notification to the designated caregiver that their registration card is invalid and must be promptly returned to the department. The newly designated caregiver must comply with all requirements set forth in this section.

7. If the certification so provides, the registry identification card shall contain any recommendation or limitation by the practitioner as to the form or forms of medical marihuana or dosage for the certified patient.

8. The department shall issue separate registry identification cards for certified patients and designated caregivers as soon as reasonably practicable after receiving a complete application under this section, unless it determines that the application is incomplete or factually inaccurate, in which case it shall promptly notify the applicant.

9. If the application of a certified patient designates an individual as a designated caregiver who is not authorized to be a designated caregiver, that portion of the application shall be denied by the department but that shall not affect the approval of the balance of the application.

10. A registry identification card shall:

(a) contain the name of the certified patient or the designated caregiver as the case may be;

(b) contain the date of issuance and expiration date of the registry identification card;

(c) contain a registry identification number for the certified patient or designated caregiver, as the case may be and a registry identification number;

(d) contain a photograph of the individual to whom the registry identification card is being issued, which shall be obtained by the department in a manner specified by the commissioner in regulations; provided, however, that if the department requires certified patients to submit photographs for this purpose, there shall be a reasonable accommodation of certified patients who are confined to their homes due to their medical conditions and may therefore have difficulty procuring photographs;

(e) be a secure document as determined by the department;

(f) plainly state any recommendation or limitation by the practitioner as to the form or forms of medical marihuana or dosage for the certified patient; and

(g) any other requirements determined by the commissioner.

11. A certified patient or designated caregiver who has been issued a registry identification card shall notify the department of any change in his or her name or address or, with respect to the patient, if he or she ceases to have the serious condition noted on the certification within ten days of such change. The certified patient's or designated caregiver's registry identification card shall be deemed invalid and shall be returned promptly to the department.

12. If a certified patient or designated caregiver loses his or her registry identification card, he or she shall notify the department and submit a twenty-five dollar fee within ten days of losing the card to maintain the registration. The department may establish higher fees for issuing a new registry identification card for second and subsequent replacements for a lost card, provided, that the department may waive or reduce the fee in cases of financial hardship. The department shall issue a new registry identification card as soon as practicable, which may contain a new registry identification number, to the certified patient or designated caregiver, as the case may be. The certified patient or designated caregiver shall not be able to obtain medical marihuana until the certified patient receives a new card.

13. The department shall maintain a confidential list of the persons to whom it has issued registry identification cards. Individual identifying information obtained by the department under this title shall be confidential and exempt from disclosure under article six of the public officers law. Notwithstanding this subdivision, the department may notify any appropriate law enforcement agency of information relating to any violation or suspected violation of this title.

14. The department shall verify to law enforcement personnel in an appropriate case whether a registry identification card is valid.

15. If a certified patient or designated caregiver willfully violates any provision of this title as determined by the department, his or her registry identification card may be suspended or revoked. This is in addition to any other penalty that may apply.

16. The commissioner shall make regulations for special certifications, which shall include expedited procedures and which may require the applicant to submit additional documentation establishing the clinical basis for the special certification. If the department has not established and made available a form for a registry application or renewal application and determined the application fee if any, or established and made available a form for a registry application or renewal application and determined the application fee for a special certification, then in the case of a special certification, a registry application or renewal application that otherwise conforms with the requirements of this section shall not require the use of a form or the payment of an application fee.

Public Health Law § 3364. Registered organizations.

* NB Repealed July 5, 2028 and Repealed 6 months after the full cannabis control board created by Article 2 of the cannabis law has been appointed

1. A registered organization shall be a for-profit business entity or not-for-profit corporation organized for the purpose of acquiring, possessing, manufacturing, selling, delivering, transporting, distributing or dispensing marihuana for certified medical use.

2. The acquiring, possession, manufacture, sale, delivery, transporting, distributing or dispensing of marihuana by a registered organization under this title in accordance with its registration under section thirty-three hundred sixty-five of this title or a renewal thereof shall be lawful under this title.

3. Each registered organization shall contract with an independent laboratory to test the medical marihuana produced by the registered organization. The commissioner shall approve the laboratory and require that the

laboratory report testing results in a manner determined by the commissioner. The commissioner is authorized to issue regulation requiring the laboratory to perform certain tests and services.

4. (a) A registered organization may lawfully, in good faith, sell, deliver, distribute or dispense medical marihuana to a certified patient or designated caregiver upon presentation to the registered organization of a valid registry identification card for that certified patient or designated caregiver. When presented with the registry identification card, the registered organization shall provide to the certified patient or designated caregiver a receipt, which shall state: the name, address, and registry identification number of the registered organization; the name and registry identification number of the certified patient and the designated caregiver (if any); the date the marihuana was sold; any recommendation or limitation by the practitioner as to the form or forms of medical marihuana or dosage for the certified patient; and the form and the quantity of medical marihuana sold. The registered organization shall retain a copy of the registry identification card and the receipt for six years.

(b) The proprietor of a registered organization shall file or cause to be filed any receipt and certification information with the department by electronic means on a real time basis as the commissioner shall require by regulation. When filing receipt and certification information electronically pursuant to this paragraph, the proprietor of the registered organization shall dispose of any electronically recorded prescription information in such manner as the commissioner shall by regulation require.

5. (a) No registered organization may sell, deliver, distribute or dispense to any certified patient or designated caregiver a quantity of medical marihuana larger than that individual would be allowed to possess under this title.

(b) When dispensing medical marihuana to a certified patient or designated caregiver, the registered organization (i) shall not dispense an amount greater than a thirty day supply to a certified patient until the certified patient has exhausted all but a seven day supply provided pursuant to a previously issued certification, and (ii) shall verify the information in subparagraph (i) of this paragraph by consulting the prescription monitoring program registry under section thirty-three hundred forty-three-a of this article.

(c) Medical marihuana dispensed to a certified patient or designated caregiver by a registered organization shall conform to any recommendation or limitation by the practitioner as to the form or forms of medical marihuana or dosage for the certified patient.

6. When a registered organization sells, delivers, distributes or dispenses medical marihuana to a certified patient or designated caregiver, it shall provide to that individual a safety insert, which will be developed and approved by the commissioner and include, but not be limited to, information on:

    (a) methods for administering medical marihuana in individual doses,

    (b) any potential dangers stemming from the use of medical marihuana,

    (c) how to recognize what may be problematic usage of medical marihuana and obtain appropriate services or treatment for problematic usage, and

    (d) other information as determined by the commissioner.

7. Registered organizations shall not be managed by or employ anyone who has been convicted of any felony of sale or possession of drugs, narcotics, or controlled substances provided that this subdivision only applies to (a) managers or employees who come into contact with or handle medical marihuana, and (b) a conviction less than ten years (not counting time spent in incarceration) prior to being employed, for which the person has not received a certificate of relief from disabilities or a certificate of good conduct under article twenty-three of the correction law.

8. Manufacturing of medical marihuana by a registered organization shall only be done in an indoor, enclosed, secure facility located in New York state, which may include a greenhouse. The commissioner shall promulgate regulations establishing requirements for such facilities.

9. Dispensing of medical marihuana by a registered organization shall only be done in an indoor, enclosed, secure

facility located in New York state, which may include a greenhouse. The commissioner shall promulgate regulations establishing requirements for such facilities.

10. A registered organization shall determine the quality, safety, and clinical strength of medical marihuana manufactured or dispensed by the registered organization, and shall provide documentation of that quality, safety and clinical strength to the department and to any person or entity to which the medical marihuana is sold or dispensed.

11. A registered organization shall be deemed to be a "health care provider" for the purposes of title two-D of article two of this chapter.

12. Medical marihuana shall be dispensed to a certified patient or designated caregiver in a sealed and properly labeled package. The labeling shall contain: (a) the information required to be included in the receipt provided to the certified patient or designated caregiver by the registered organization; (b) the packaging date; (c) any applicable date by which the medical marihuana should be used; (d) a warning stating, "This product is for medicinal use only. Women should not consume during pregnancy or while breastfeeding except on the advice of the certifying health care practitioner, and in the case of breastfeeding mothers, including the infant's pediatrician. This product might impair the ability to drive. Keep out of reach of children."; (e) the amount of individual doses contained within; and (f) a warning that the medical marihuana must be kept in the original container in which it was dispensed.

13. The commissioner is authorized to make rules and regulations restricting the advertising and marketing of medical marihuana, which shall be consistent with the federal regulations governing prescription drug advertising and marketing.

Public Health Law § 3365. Registering of registered organizations.

* NB Repealed July 5, 2028 and Repealed 6 months after the full cannabis control board created by Article 2 of the cannabis law has been appointed

1. Application for initial registration.

    (a) An applicant for registration as a registered organization under section thirty-three hundred sixty-four of this title shall include such information prepared in such manner and detail as the commissioner may require, including but not limited to:

        (i) a description of the activities in which it intends to engage as a registered organization;

        (ii) that the applicant:

            (A) is of good moral character;

            (B) possesses or has the right to use sufficient land, buildings, and other premises (which shall be specified in the application) and equipment to properly carry on the activity described in the application, or in the alternative posts a bond of not less than two million dollars;

            (C) is able to maintain effective security and control to prevent diversion, abuse, and other illegal conduct relating to the marihuana;

            (D) is able to comply with all applicable state laws and regulations relating to the activities in which it intends to engage under the registration;

        (iii) that the applicant has entered into a labor peace agreement with a bona-fide labor organization that is actively engaged in representing or attempting to represent the applicant's employees. The maintenance of such a labor peace agreement shall be an ongoing material condition of certification.

(iv) the applicant's status under subdivision one of section thirty-three hundred sixty-four of this title; and

(v) the application shall include the name, residence address and title of each of the officers and directors and the name and residence address of any person or entity that is a member of the applicant. Each such person, if an individual, or lawful representative if a legal entity, shall submit an affidavit with the application setting forth:

(A) any position of management or ownership during the preceding ten years of a ten per centum or greater interest in any other business, located in or outside this state, manufacturing or distributing drugs;

(B) whether such person or any such business has been convicted of a felony or had a registration or license suspended or revoked in any administrative or judicial proceeding; and

(C) such other information as the commissioner may reasonably require.

2. Duty to report. The applicant shall be under a continuing duty to report to the department any change in facts or circumstances reflected in the application or any newly discovered or occurring fact or circumstance which is required to be included in the application.

3. Granting of registration.

(a) The commissioner shall grant a registration or amendment to a registration under this section if he or she is satisfied that:

(i) the applicant will be able to maintain effective control against diversion of marihuana;

(ii) the applicant will be able to comply with all applicable state laws;

(iii) the applicant and its officers are ready, willing and able to properly carry on the manufacturing or distributing activity for which a registration is sought;

(iv) the applicant possesses or has the right to use sufficient land, buildings and equipment to properly carry on the activity described in the application;

(v) it is in the public interest that such registration be granted; the commissioner may consider whether the number of registered organizations in an area will be adequate or excessive to reasonably serve the area;

(vi) the applicant and its managing officers are of good moral character;

(vii) the applicant has entered into a labor peace agreement with a bona-fide labor organization that is actively engaged in representing or attempting to represent the applicant's employees; and

(viii) the applicant satisfies any other conditions as determined by the commissioner.

(b) If the commissioner is not satisfied that the applicant should be issued a registration, he or she shall notify the applicant in writing of those factors upon which further evidence is required. Within thirty days of the receipt of such notification, the applicant may submit additional material to the commissioner or demand a hearing, or both.

(c) The fee for a registration under this section shall be a reasonable amount determined by the department in regulations; provided, however, if the registration is issued for a period greater than two years the fee shall be increased, pro rata, for each additional month of validity.

(d) Registrations issued under this section shall be effective only for the registered organization and shall specify:

(i) the name and address of the registered organization;

(ii) which activities of a registered organization are permitted by the registration;

(iii) the land, buildings and facilities that may be used for the permitted activities of the registered organization; and

(iv) such other information as the commissioner shall reasonably provide to assure compliance with this title.

(e) Upon application of a registered organization, a registration may be amended to allow the registered organization to relocate within the state or to add or delete permitted registered organization activities or facilities. The fee for such amendment shall be two hundred fifty dollars.

4. A registration issued under this section shall be valid for two years from the date of issue, except that in order to facilitate the renewals of such registrations, the commissioner may upon the initial application for a registration, issue some registrations which may remain valid for a period of time greater than two years but not exceeding an additional eleven months.

5. Applications for renewal of registrations.

(a) An application for the renewal of any registration issued under this section shall be filed with the department not more than six months nor less than four months prior to the expiration thereof. A late-filed application for the renewal of a registration may, in the discretion of the commissioner, be treated as an application for an initial license.

(b) The application for renewal shall include such information prepared in the manner and detail as the commissioner may require, including but not limited to:

(i) any material change in the circumstances or factors listed in subdivision one of this section; and

(ii) every known charge or investigation, pending or concluded during the period of the registration, by any governmental or administrative agency with respect to:

(A) each incident or alleged incident involving the theft, loss, or possible diversion of marihuana manufactured or distributed by the applicant; and

(B) compliance by the applicant with the laws of the state with respect to any substance listed in section thirty-three hundred six of this article.

(c) An applicant for renewal shall be under a continuing duty to report to the department any change in facts or circumstances reflected in the application or any newly discovered or occurring fact or circumstance which is required to be included in the application.

(d) If the commissioner is not satisfied that the applicant is entitled to a renewal of the registration, he or she shall within a reasonably practicable time as determined by the commissioner, serve upon the applicant or his or her attorney of record in person or by registered or certified mail an order directing the applicant to show cause why his or her application for renewal should not be denied. The order shall specify in detail the respects in which the applicant has not satisfied the commissioner that the registration should be renewed.

(e) Within a reasonably practicable time as determined by the commissioner of such order, the applicant may submit additional material to the commissioner or demand a hearing or both. If a hearing is demanded the commissioner shall fix a date as soon as reasonably practicable.

6. Granting of renewal of registrations.

(a) The commissioner shall renew a registration unless he or she determines and finds that:

(i) the applicant is unlikely to maintain or be able to maintain effective control against diversion; or

(ii) the applicant is unlikely to comply with all state laws applicable to the activities in which it may engage under the registration; or

(iii) it is not in the public interest to renew the registration because the number of registered organizations in an area is excessive to reasonably serve the area; or

(iv) the applicant has either violated or terminated its labor peace agreement.

(b) For purposes of this section, proof that a registered organization, during the period of its registration, has failed to maintain effective control against diversion, violates any provision of this article, or has knowingly or negligently failed to comply with applicable state laws relating to the activities in which it engages under the registration, shall constitute grounds for suspension or termination of the registered organization's registration as determined by the commissioner. The registered organization shall also be under a continuing duty to report to the department any material change or fact or circumstance to the information provided in the registered organization's application.

7. The department may suspend or terminate the registration of a registered organization, on grounds and using procedures under this article relating to a license, to the extent consistent with this title. The department shall suspend or terminate the registration in the event that a registered organization violates or terminates the applicable labor peace agreement. Conduct in compliance with this title which may violate conflicting federal law, shall not be grounds to suspend or terminate a registration.

8. The department shall begin issuing registrations for registered organizations as soon as practicable after the certifications required by section thirty-three hundred sixty-nine-b of this title are given.

9. The commissioner shall register no more than five registered organizations that manufacture medical marihuana with no more than four dispensing sites wholly owned and operated by such registered organization. The commissioner shall ensure that such registered organizations and dispensing sites are geographically distributed across the state. The commission may register additional registered organizations.

Public Health Law § 3365-a. Expedited registration of registered organizations.

* NB Repealed July 5, 2028 and Repealed 6 months after the full cannabis control board created by Article 2 of the cannabis law has been appointed

1. There is hereby established in the department an emergency medical marihuana access program (referred to in this section as the "program") under this section. The purpose of the program is to expedite the availability of medical marihuana to avoid suffering and loss of life, during the period before full implementation of and production under this title, especially in the case of patients whose serious condition is progressive and degenerative or is such that delay in the patient's medical use of marihuana poses a serious risk to the patient's life or health. The commissioner shall implement the program as expeditiously as practicable, including by emergency regulation.

2. The department shall begin accepting and acting on applications under this section for registered organizations as soon as practicable after the effective date of this section.

3. For the purposes of this section, and for specified limited times, the commissioner may waive or modify the requirements of this article relating to registered organizations, consistent with the legislative intent and purpose of this title and this section. Where an entity seeking to be a registered organization under the program operates in a jurisdiction other than the state of New York, under licensure or other governmental recognition of that jurisdiction, and the laws of that jurisdiction are acceptable to the commissioner as consistent with the legislative intent and purpose of this title and this section, then the commissioner may accept that licensure or recognition as wholly or

partially satisfying the requirements of this title, for purposes of the registration and operation of the registered organization under the program and this section.

4. In considering an application for registration as a registered organization under this section, the commissioner shall give preference to the following:

(a) an applicant that is currently producing or providing or has a history of producing or providing medical marihuana in another jurisdiction in full compliance with the laws of the jurisdiction;

(b) an applicant that is able and qualified to both produce, distribute, and dispense medical marihuana to patients expeditiously;

(c) an applicant that proposes a location or locations for dispensing by the registered organization, which ensure, to the greatest extent possible, that certified patients with a special certification have access to a registered organization.

5. The commissioner may make regulations under this section:

(a) limiting registered organizations registered under this section to serving patients with special certifications;

(b) limiting the allowable levels of cannabidiol and tetrahydrocannabinol that may be contained in medical marihuana authorized under the program, based on therapeutics and patient safety.

6. A registered organization under this section may apply under section thirty-three hundred sixty-five of this title to receive or renew registration.

Public Health Law § 3366. Reports by registered organizations.

* NB Repealed July 5, 2028 and Repealed 6 months after the full cannabis control board created by Article 2 of the cannabis law has been appointed

1. The commissioner shall, by regulation, require each registered organization to file reports by the registered organization during a particular period. The commissioner shall determine the information to be reported and the forms, time, and manner of the reporting.

2. The commissioner shall, by regulation, require each registered organization to adopt and maintain security, tracking, record keeping, record retention and surveillance systems, relating to all medical marihuana at every stage of acquiring, possession, manufacture, sale, delivery, transporting, distributing, or dispensing by the registered organization, subject to regulations of the commissioner.

Public Health Law § 3367. Evaluation; research programs; report by department.

* NB Repealed July 5, 2028 and Repealed 6 months after the full cannabis control board created by Article 2 of the cannabis law has been appointed

1. The commissioner may provide for the analysis and evaluation of the operation of this title. The commissioner may enter into agreements with one or more persons, not-for-profit corporations or other organizations, for the performance of an evaluation of the implementation and effectiveness of this title.

2. The department may develop, seek any necessary federal approval for, and carry out research programs relating to medical use of marihuana. Participation in any such research program shall be voluntary on the part of practitioners, patients, and designated caregivers.

3. The department shall report every two years, beginning two years after the effective date of this title, to the governor and the legislature on the medical use of marihuana under this title and make appropriate recommendations.

Public Health Law § 3368. Relation to other laws.

*NB Repealed July 5, 2028 and Repealed 6 months after the full cannabis control board created by Article 2 of the cannabis law has been appointed

1. (a) The provisions of this article shall apply to this title, except that where a provision of this title conflicts with another provision of this article, this title shall apply.

(b) Medical marihuana shall not be deemed to be a "drug" for purposes of article one hundred thirty-seven of the education law.

2. Nothing in this title shall be construed to require an insurer or health plan under this chapter or the insurance law to provide coverage for medical marihuana. Nothing in this title shall be construed to require coverage for medical marihuana under article twenty-five of this chapter or article five of the social services law.

Public Health Law § 3369. Protections for the medical use of marihuana.

*NB Repealed July 5, 2028 and Repealed 6 months after the full cannabis control board created by Article 2 of the cannabis law has been appointed

1. Certified patients, designated caregivers, practitioners, registered organizations and the employees of registered organizations shall not be subject to arrest, prosecution, or penalty in any manner, or denied any right or privilege, including but not limited to civil penalty or disciplinary action by a business or occupational or professional licensing board or bureau, solely for the certified medical use or manufacture of marihuana, or for any other action or conduct in accordance with this title.

2. Non-discrimination. Being a certified patient shall be deemed to be having a "disability" under article fifteen of the executive law (human rights law), section forty-c of the civil rights law, sections 240.00, 485.00, and 485.05 of the penal law, and section 200.50 of the criminal procedure law. This subdivision shall not bar the enforcement of a policy prohibiting an employee from performing his or her employment duties while impaired by a controlled substance. This subdivision shall not require any person or entity to do any act that would put the person or entity in violation of federal law or cause it to lose a federal contract or funding.

3. The fact that a person is a certified patient and/or acting in accordance with this title, shall not be a consideration in a proceeding pursuant to applicable sections of the domestic relations law, the social services law and the family court act.

4. (a) Certification applications, certification forms, any certified patient information contained within a database, and copies of registry identification cards shall be deemed exempt from public disclosure under sections eighty-seven and eighty-nine of the public officers law.

(b) The name, contact information, and other information relating to practitioners registered with the department under this title shall be public information and shall be maintained by the commissioner on the department's website accessible to the public in searchable form. However, if a practitioner notifies the department in writing that he or she does not want his or her name and other information disclosed, that practitioner's name and other information shall thereafter not be public information or maintained on the department's website, unless the practitioner cancels the request.

Public Health Law § 3369-a. Regulations.

*NB Repealed July 5, 2028 and Repealed 6 months after the full cannabis control board created by Article 2 of the cannabis law has been appointed

The commissioner shall make regulations to implement this title.

Public Health Law § 3369-b. Effective date.

*NB Repealed July 5, 2028 and Repealed 6 months after the full cannabis control board created by Article 2 of the cannabis law has been appointed

Registry identification cards or registered organization registrations shall be issued or become effective no later than eighteen months from signing or until such time as the commissioner and the superintendent of state police certify that this title can be implemented in accordance with public health and safety interests, whichever event comes later. Prior to making a general certification under this section, the commissioner and the superintendent of state police may make a certification limited to accommodating expedited access for patients with special certifications and for registered organizations under the emergency medical marihuana access program under section thirty-three hundred sixty-five-a of this title.

Public Health Law § 3369-c. Suspend; terminate.

*NB Repealed July 5, 2028 and Repealed 6 months after the full cannabis control board created by Article 2 of the cannabis law has been appointed

Based upon the recommendation of the commissioner and/or the superintendent of state police that there is a risk to the public health or safety, the governor may immediately terminate all licenses issued to registered organizations.

Public Health Law § 3369-d. Pricing.

*NB Repealed July 5, 2028 and Repealed 6 months after the full cannabis control board created by Article 2 of the cannabis law has been appointed

1. Every sale of medical marihuana shall be at the price determined by the commissioner. Every charge made or demanded for medical marihuana not in accordance with the price determined by the commissioner, is prohibited.

2. The commissioner is hereby authorized to set the per dose price of each form of medical marihuana sold by any registered organization. In setting the per dose price of each form of medical marihuana, the commissioner shall consider the fixed and variable costs of producing the form of marihuana and any other factor the commissioner, in his or her discretion, deems relevant to determining the per dose price of each form of medical marihuana.

Public Health Law § 3369-e. Severability.

*NB Repealed July 5, 2028 and Repealed 6 months after the full cannabis control board created by Article 2 of the cannabis law has been appointed

If any clause, sentence, paragraph, section or part of this act shall be adjudged by any court of competent jurisdiction to be invalid, the judgment shall not affect, impair, or invalidate the remainder thereof, but shall be confined in its operation to the clause, sentence, paragraph, section or part thereof directly involved in the controversy in which the judgment shall have been rendered.

Title 6. RECORDS AND REPORTS

Public Health Law § 3371. Confidentiality of certain records, reports, and information.

1. No person, who has knowledge by virtue of his or her office of the identity of a particular patient or research subject, a manufacturing process, a trade secret or a formula shall disclose such knowledge, or any report or record thereof, except:

(a) to another person employed by the department, for purposes of executing provisions of this article;

(b) pursuant to judicial subpoena or court order in a criminal investigation or proceeding;

(c) to an agency, department of government, or official board authorized to regulate, license or otherwise supervise a person who is authorized by this article to deal in controlled substances, or in the course of any investigation or proceeding by or before such agency, department or board;

(d) to the prescription monitoring program registry and to authorized users of such registry as set forth in subdivision two of this section;

(e) to a practitioner to inform him or her that a patient may be under treatment with a controlled substance by another practitioner for the purposes of subdivision two of this section, and to facilitate the department's review of individual challenges to the accuracy of controlled substances histories pursuant to subdivision six of section thirty-three hundred forty-three-a of this article;

(f) to a pharmacist to provide information regarding prescriptions for controlled substances presented to the pharmacist for the purposes of subdivision two of this section and to facilitate the department's review of individual challenges to the accuracy of controlled substances histories pursuant to subdivision six of section thirty-three hundred forty-three-a of this article;

(g) to the deputy attorney general for medicaid fraud control, or his or her designee, in furtherance of an investigation of fraud, waste or abuse of the Medicaid program, pursuant to an agreement with the department

(h) to a local health department for the purpose of conducting public health research or education: (i) pursuant to an agreement with the commissioner; (ii) when the release of such information is deemed appropriate by the commissioner; (iii) for use in accordance with measures required by the commissioner to ensure that the security and confidentiality of the data is protected; and (iv) provided that disclosure is restricted to individuals within the local health department who are engaged in the research or education;

(i) to a medical examiner or coroner who is an officer of or employed by a state or local government, pursuant to his or her official duties; and

(j) to an individual for the purpose of providing such individual with his or her own controlled substance history or, in appropriate circumstances, in the case of a patient who lacks capacity to make health care decisions, a person who has legal authority to make such decisions for the patient and who would have legal access to the patient's health care records, if requested from the department pursuant to subdivision six of section thirty-three hundred forty-three-a of this article or from a treating practitioner pursuant to subparagraph (iv) of paragraph (a) of subdivision two of this section.

* 2. The prescription monitoring program registry may be accessed, under such terms and conditions as are established by the department for purposes of maintaining the security and confidentiality of the information contained in the registry, by:

(a) a practitioner, or a designee authorized by such practitioner pursuant to paragraph (b) of subdivision two of section thirty-three hundred forty-three-a, section thirty-three hundred sixty-one of this article or section thirty of the cannabis law, for the purposes of: (i) informing the practitioner that a patient may be under treatment with a controlled substance by another practitioner; (ii) providing the practitioner with notifications of controlled substance activity as deemed relevant by the department, including but not limited to a notification made available on a monthly or other periodic basis through the registry of controlled substances activity pertaining to his or her patient; (iii) allowing the practitioner, through consultation of the prescription monitoring program registry, to review his or her patient's controlled substances history as required by section thirty-three hundred forty-three-a, section thirty-three hundred sixty-one of this article or section thirty of the cannabis law; and (iv) providing to his or her patient, or person authorized pursuant to paragraph (j) of subdivision one of this section, upon request, a copy of such patient's controlled substance history as is available to the practitioner through the prescription monitoring program registry; or

(b) a pharmacist, pharmacy intern or other designee authorized by the pharmacist pursuant to paragraph (b) of subdivision three of section thirty-three hundred forty-three-a of this article, for the purposes of: (i) consulting the prescription monitoring program registry to review the controlled substances history of an individual for whom one or more prescriptions for controlled substances or certifications for cannabis is presented to the pharmacist, pursuant to section thirty-three hundred forty-three-a of this article; and (ii) receiving from the department such notifications of controlled substance activity as are made available by the department; or

(c) an individual employed by a registered organization as defined in section three of the cannabis law, for the purpose of consulting the prescription monitoring program registry to review the controlled substances history of an individual for whom one or more certifications for cannabis is presented to that registered organization, pursuant to section thirty-three hundred sixty-four of this article or section thirty-four of the cannabis law. Unless otherwise authorized by this article or by the cannabis law, an individual employed by a registered organization will be provided access to the prescription monitoring program in the sole discretion of the commissioner.

* NB Effective until July 5, 2028

* 2. The prescription monitoring program registry may be accessed, under such terms and conditions as are established by the department for purposes of maintaining the security and confidentiality of the information contained in the registry, by:

(a) a practitioner, or a designee authorized by such practitioner pursuant to paragraph (b) of subdivision two of section thirty-three hundred forty-three-a of this article, for the purposes of: (i) informing the practitioner that a patient may be under treatment with a controlled substance by another practitioner; (ii) providing the practitioner with notifications of controlled substance activity as deemed relevant by the department, including but not limited to a notification made available on a monthly or other periodic basis through the registry of controlled substances activity pertaining to his or her patient; (iii) allowing the practitioner, through consultation of the prescription monitoring program registry, to review his or her patient's controlled substances history as required by section thirty-three hundred forty-three-a of this article; and (iv) providing to his or her patient, or person authorized pursuant to paragraph (j) of subdivision one of this section, upon request, a copy of such patient's controlled substance history as is available to the practitioner through the prescription monitoring program registry; or

(b) a pharmacist, pharmacy intern or other designee authorized by the pharmacist pursuant to paragraph (b) of subdivision three of section thirty-three hundred forty-three-a of this article, for the purposes of: (i) consulting the prescription monitoring program registry to review the controlled substances history of an individual for whom one or more prescriptions for controlled substances is presented to the pharmacist, pursuant to section thirty-three hundred forty-three-a of this article; and (ii) receiving from the department such notifications of controlled substance activity as are made available by the department.

* NB Effective July 5, 2028

3. Where it has reason to believe that a crime related to the diversion of controlled substances has been committed,

the department may notify appropriate law enforcement agencies and provide relevant information about the suspected criminal activity, including controlled substances prescribed or dispensed, as reasonably appears to be necessary. The department shall keep a record of the information provided, including, but not limited to: the specific information provided and the agency to which such information was provided, including the name and title of the person to whom such information was provided and an attestation from such person that he or she has authority to receive such information.

4. In the course of any proceeding where such information is disclosed, except when necessary to effectuate the rights of a party to the proceeding, the court or presiding officer shall take such action as is necessary to insure that such information, or record or report of such information is not made public.

ARTICLE 33-A. CONTROLLED SUBSTANCES THERAPEUTIC RESEARCH ACT

Public Health Law § 3397-a. Legislative findings.

The legislature finds that recent research has shown that the use of marijuana may alleviate the nausea and ill-effects of cancer chemotherapy, may alleviate the ill-effects of glaucoma and may have other therapeutic uses. The legislature further finds that there is a need for further research and experimentation with regard to the use of marijuana for therapeutic purposes under strictly controlled circumstances. It is for such research programs that the controlled substances therapeutic research act is hereby enacted.

Public Health Law § 3397-b. Definitions.

1. "Cannabis" means cannabis as defined in section 222.00 of the penal law and shall also include tetrahydrocannabinols or a chemical derivative of tetrahydrocannabinol.

2. "Physician" means a person licensed to practice medicine in the state of New York including a person authorized to practice medicine in a federal medical facility in the state.

3. "Hospital" means a hospital as defined in section twenty-eight hundred one of this chapter.

Public Health Law § 3397-c. Antonio G. Olivieri controlled substances therapeutic research program established; participation.

1. The Antonio G. Olivieri controlled substances therapeutic research program is hereby established in the department of health. The commissioner shall promulgate rules and regulations necessary for the proper administration of the controlled substances therapeutic research act. In such promulgation, the commissioner shall take into consideration those pertinent rules and regulations promulgated by the drug enforcement administration, food and drug administration and the national institute on drug abuse.

2. Participation in the Antonio G. Olivieri controlled substances therapeutic research program shall be limited to cancer patients, glaucoma patients and patients afflicted with other diseases as such diseases are approved by the commissioner. Such patient shall be certified by a physician to and approved by a patient qualification review board or committee in the manner provided by this article. Physician certification and board or committee approval shall be limited to such patients who are involved in a life-threatening or sense-threatening situation. Patients seeking participation in such program may seek the advice and shall be entitled to be advised by appropriate medical personnel concerning the medical efficacy of treatment with conventional controlled substances.

3. The commissioner, on behalf of the department, shall apply to the food and drug administration for an investigational new drug permit within ninety days after the effective date of this section.

Public Health Law § 3397-d. State patient qualification review board; composition; powers and duties.

1. The commissioner shall appoint a state patient qualification review board of no less than three nor more than five members. The state patient qualification review board shall be comprised of:

(a) A physician licensed to practice medicine in New York and certified by the American board of ophthalmology;

(b) A physician licensed to practice medicine in New York and certified by the American board of internal medicine and also certified in the subspecialty of medical oncology;

(c) A physician licensed to practice medicine in New York and certified in psychiatry by the American board of psychiatry and neurology; and

(d) Any other members that the commissioner may deem necessary.

2. Members of such board shall be appointed for three year terms except that the term of those first appointed shall be arranged so that as nearly as possible an equal number shall terminate annually. A vacancy occurring during a term shall be filled by an appointment by the commissioner for the unexpired term. The commissioner shall designate the chairman of the board. Any member may be removed from the board at the pleasure of the commissioner.

3. Each member of the board shall receive up to one hundred fifty dollars as prescribed by the commissioner for each day devoted to board work not to exceed forty-five hundred dollars in any one year, and shall be reimbursed for necessary expenses.

Public Health Law § 3397-e. Patient participation in program; procedure.

1. Any hospital may establish a hospital patient qualification review committee subject to the rules and regulations promulgated by the commissioner. A hospital may designate a hospital human research review committee as set forth in section twenty-four hundred forty-four of this chapter to serve as a hospital patient qualification review committee.

2. Any physician may recommend a patient for participation in the Antonio G. Olivieri controlled substances therapeutic research program to the hospital patient qualification review committee for the hospital wherein such patient has received medical treatment.

3. The hospital patient qualification review committee shall review each recommendation and shall submit approved patient applications to the state patient qualification review board.

4. The state patient qualification review board shall review all physician applicants for the Antonio G. Olivieri controlled substances therapeutic research program and certify or refuse to certify their participation in the program.

5. The state patient qualification review board may delegate to a hospital patient qualification review committee the authority to approve or disapprove a patient's participation in such program.

6. A patient shall not be eligible to participate in such program without the approval of the state patient qualification

review board or the hospital patient qualification review committee delegated pursuant to subdivision five of this section.

7. The hospital human research review committee shall review each human research project proposed hereunder and shall certify to the hospital patient qualification review committee that such project meets the requirements of this article and article twenty-four-A of this chapter.

Public Health Law § 3397-f. Antonio G. Olivieri controlled substances therapeutic research program; distribution.

1. The commissioner shall obtain marijuana through whatever means he deems most appropriate, consistent with regulations promulgated by the national institute on drug abuse, the food and drug administration and the drug enforcement administration and pursuant to the provisions of this article.

2. If, within a reasonable time, the commissioner is unable to obtain controlled substances pursuant to subdivision one of this section, he shall conduct an inventory of available sources of such drugs, including but not limited to the New York state police bureau of criminal investigation and local law enforcement officials. Said inventory shall be for the purpose of determining the feasibility of obtaining controlled substances for use in the program. Upon conducting said inventory, the commissioner shall contract with the available source for the receipt of controlled substances.

3. The commissioner shall cause such marijuana to be transferred to a hospital for distribution to the certified patient pursuant to this article.

ARTICLE 33-B. REGULATION OF CANNABINOID HEMP AND HEMP EXTRACT

Public Health Law § 3398. Definitions.

* NB Repealed 6 months after the full cannabis control board created by Article 2 of the cannabis law has been appointed

As used in this article, the following terms shall have the following meanings, unless the context clearly requires otherwise:

1. "Cannabinoid" means the phytocannabinoids found in hemp and does not include synthetic cannabinoids as that term is defined in subdivision (g) of schedule I of section thirty-three hundred six of this chapter.

2. "Cannabinoid hemp" means any hemp and any product processed or derived from hemp, that is used for human consumption provided that when such product is packaged or offered for retail sale to a consumer, it shall not have a concentration of more than three tenths of a percent delta-9 tetrahydrocannabinol.

3. "Used for human consumption" means intended by the manufacturer or distributor to be: (a) used for human consumption for its cannabinoid content; or (b) used in, on or by the human body for its cannabinoid content.

4. "Hemp" means the plant Cannabis sativa L. and any part of such plant, including the seeds thereof and all derivatives, extracts, cannabinoids, isomers, acids, salts, and salts of isomers, whether growing or not, with a delta-9 tetrahydrocannabinol concentration (THC) of not more than three-tenths of a percent on a dry weight basis. It shall not include "medical marihuana" as defined in subdivision eight of section thirty-three hundred sixty of this chapter.

5. "Hemp extract" means all derivatives, extracts, cannabinoids, isomers, acids, salts, and salts of isomers

derived from hemp, used or intended for human consumption, for its cannabinoid content, with a delta-9 tetrahydrocannabinol concentration of not more than an amount determined by the department in regulation. For the purpose of this article, hemp extract excludes (a) any food, food ingredient or food additive that is generally recognized as safe pursuant to federal law; or (b) any hemp extract that is not used for human consumption. Such excluded substances shall not be regulated pursuant to the provisions of this article but are subject to other provisions of applicable state law, rules and regulations.

6. "License" means a license issued pursuant to this article.

7. "Cannabinoid hemp processor license" means a license granted by the department to process, extract, pack or manufacture cannabinoid hemp or hemp extract into products, whether in intermediate or final form, used for human consumption.

8. "Processing" means extracting, preparing, treating, modifying, compounding, manufacturing or otherwise manipulating cannabinoid hemp to concentrate or extract its cannabinoids, or creating product, whether in intermediate or final form, used for human consumption. For purposes of this article, processing does not include:

> (a) growing, cultivation, cloning, harvesting, drying, curing, grinding or trimming when authorized pursuant to article twenty-nine of the agriculture and markets law; or

> (b) mere transportation, such as by common carrier or another entity or individual.

Public Health Law § 3398-a. Rulemaking authority.

* NB Repealed 6 months after the full cannabis control board created by Article 2 of the cannabis law has been appointed

The commissioner may make regulations pursuant to this article for the processing, distribution, marketing, transportation and sale of cannabinoid hemp and hemp extracts used for human consumption, which may include, but not be limited to:

1. Specifying forms, establishing application, reasonable administration and renewal fees, or license duration;

2. Establishing the qualifications and criteria for licensing, as authorized by law;

3. The books and records to be created and maintained by licensees and lawful procedures for their inspection;

4. Any reporting requirements;

5. Methods and standards of processing, labeling, packaging and marketing of cannabinoid hemp, hemp extract and products derived therefrom;

6. Procedures for how cannabinoid hemp, hemp extract or ingredients, additives, or products derived therefrom can be deemed as acceptable for sale in the state;

7. Provisions governing the modes and forms of administration, including inhalation;

8. Procedures for determining whether cannabinoid hemp, hemp extract or ingredients, additives, or products derived therefrom produced outside the state or within the state meet the standards and requirements of this article and can therefore be sold within the state;

9. Procedures for the granting, cancellation, revocation or suspension of licenses, consistent with the state administrative procedures act;

10. Restrictions governing the advertising and marketing of cannabinoid hemp, hemp extract and products derived therefrom; and

11. Any other regulations necessary to implement this article.

Public Health Law § 3398-b. Cannabinoid hemp processor license.

* NB Repealed 6 months after the full cannabis control board created by Article 2 of the cannabis law has been appointed

1. Persons processing cannabinoid hemp or hemp extract used for human consumption, whether in intermediate or final form, shall be required to obtain a cannabinoid hemp processor license from the department.

2. A cannabinoid hemp processor license authorizes one or more specific activities related to the processing of cannabinoid hemp into products used for human consumption, whether in intermediate or final form, and the distribution or sale thereof by the licensee. Nothing herein shall prevent a cannabinoid hemp processor from processing, extracting and processing hemp products not to be used for human consumption.

3. Persons authorized to grow hemp pursuant to article twenty-nine of the agriculture and markets law are not authorized to engage in processing of cannabinoid hemp or hemp extract without first being licensed as a cannabinoid hemp processor under this article.

4. This article shall not apply to hemp, cannabinoid hemp, hemp extracts or products derived therefrom that are not used for human consumption. This article also shall not apply to hemp, cannabinoid hemp, hemp extracts or products derived therefrom that have been deemed generally recognized as safe pursuant to federal law.

5. The commissioner shall have the authority to set reasonable fees for such license, to limit the activities permitted by such license, to establish the period during which such license is authorized, which shall be two years or more, and to make rules and regulations necessary to implement this section.

6. Any person holding an active research partnership agreement with the department of agriculture and markets, authorizing that person to process cannabinoid hemp, shall be awarded licensure under this section, provided that the research partner is actively performing research pursuant to such agreement and is able to demonstrate compliance with this article, as determined by the department, after notice and an opportunity to be heard.

Public Health Law § 3398-c. Cannabinoid hemp retailer license.

* NB Repealed 6 months after the full cannabis control board created by Article 2 of the cannabis law has been appointed

1. Retailers selling cannabinoid hemp, in final form to consumers within the state, shall be required to obtain a cannabinoid hemp retailer license from the department.

2. The commissioner shall have the authority to set reasonable fees for such license, to establish the period during which such license is authorized, which shall be one year or more, and to make rules and regulations necessary to implement this section.

Public Health Law § 3398-d. Cannabinoid license applications.

* NB Repealed 6 months after the full cannabis control board created by Article 2 of the cannabis law has been appointed

1. Persons shall apply for a license under this article by submitting an application upon a form supplied by

the department, providing all the relevant requested information, verified by the applicant or an authorized representative of the applicant.

2. A separate license shall be required for each facility at which processing or retail sales are conducted; however, an applicant may submit one application for separate licensure at multiple locations.

3. Each applicant shall remit with its application the fee for each requested license, which shall be a reasonable fee.

Public Health Law § 3398-e. Information to be requested in applications for licenses.

*NB Repealed 6 months after the full cannabis control board created by Article 2 of the cannabis law has been appointed

1. The commissioner may specify the manner and form in which an application shall be submitted to the department for licensure under this article.

2. The commissioner may adopt regulations establishing what relevant information shall be included on an application for licensure under this article. Such information may include, but is not limited to: information about the applicant's identity; ownership and investment information, including the corporate structure; evidence of good moral character; financial statements; information about the premises to be licensed; information about the activities to be licensed; and any other relevant information specified in regulation.

3. All license applications shall be signed by the applicant if an individual, by a managing partner if a limited liability company, by an officer if a corporation, or by all partners if a partnership. Each person signing such application shall verify it as true under the penalties of perjury.

4. All license applications shall be accompanied by a check, draft or other forms of payment as the department may require or authorize in the reasonable amount required by this article for such license.

5. If there be any change, after the filing of the application or the granting, modification or renewal of a license, in any of the material facts required to be set forth in such application, a supplemental statement giving notice of such change, duly verified, shall be filed with the department within ten days after such change. Failure to do so, if willful and deliberate, may be grounds for revocation of the license.

Public Health Law § 3398-f. Fees.

*NB Repealed 6 months after the full cannabis control board created by Article 2 of the cannabis law has been appointed

The department may charge licensees a reasonable license fee. Such fee may be based on the activities permitted by the license, the amount of cannabinoid hemp or hemp extract to be processed or extracted by the licensee, the gross annual receipts of the licensee for the previous license period, or any other factors reasonably deemed appropriate by the department.

Public Health Law § 3398-g. Selection criteria.

*NB Repealed 6 months after the full cannabis control board created by Article 2 of the cannabis law has been appointed

1. The applicant, if an individual or individuals, shall furnish evidence of the individual's good moral character, and

if an entity, the applicant shall furnish evidence of the good moral character of the individuals who have or will have substantial responsibility for the licensed or authorized activity and those in control of the entity, including principals, officers, or others with such control.

2. The applicant shall furnish evidence of the applicant's experience and competency, and that the applicant has or will have adequate facilities, equipment, process controls, and security to undertake those activities for which licensure is sought.

3. The applicant shall furnish evidence of his, her or its ability to comply with all applicable state and local laws, rules and regulations.

4. If the commissioner is not satisfied that the applicant should be issued a license, the commissioner shall notify the applicant in writing of the specific reason or reasons for denial.

5. No license pursuant to this article may be issued to an individual under the age of eighteen years.

Public Health Law § 3398-h. License renewal.

* NB Repealed 6 months after the full cannabis control board created by Article 2 of the cannabis law has been appointed

1. Each license, issued pursuant to this article, may be renewed upon application therefor by the licensee and the payment of the reasonable fee for such license as specified by this article.

2. In the case of applications for renewals, the department may dispense with the requirements of such statements as it deems unnecessary in view of those contained in the application made for the original license.

3. The department shall provide an application for renewal of any license issued under this article not less than ninety days prior to the expiration of the current license.

4. The department may only issue a renewal license upon receipt of the specified renewal application and renewal fee from a licensee if, in addition to the selection criteria set out in this article, the licensee's license is not under suspension and has not been revoked.

Public Health Law § 3398-i. Form of license.

* NB Repealed 6 months after the full cannabis control board created by Article 2 of the cannabis law has been appointed

Licenses issued pursuant to this article shall specify:

1. The name and address of the licensee;

2. The activities permitted by the license;

3. The land, buildings and facilities that may be used for the licensed activities of the licensee;

4. A unique license number issued by the department to the licensee; and

5. Such other information as the commissioner shall deem necessary to assure compliance with this chapter.

Public Health Law § 3398-j. Transferability; amendment to license; change in ownership or control.

1. Licenses issued under this article are not transferable, absent written consent of the commissioner.

2. Upon application of a licensee, a license may be amended to add or delete permitted activities.

3. A license shall become void by a change in ownership, substantial corporate change or change of location without prior written approval of the commissioner. The commissioner may make regulations allowing for certain types of changes in ownership without the need for prior written approval.

Public Health Law § 3398-k. Granting, suspending or revoking licenses.

*NB Repealed 6 months after the full cannabis control board created by Article 2 of the cannabis law has been appointed

After due notice and an opportunity to be heard, established by rules and regulations, the commissioner may decline to grant a new license, impose conditions or limits with respect to the grant of a license, modify an existing license or decline to renew a license, and may suspend or revoke a license already granted after due notice and an opportunity to be heard, as established by rules and regulations, whenever the commissioner finds that:

1. A material statement contained in an application is or was false or misleading;

2. The applicant or licensee, or a person in a position of management and control thereof or of the licensed activity, does not have good moral character, necessary experience or competency, adequate facilities, equipment, process controls, or security to process, distribute, transport or sell cannabinoid hemp, hemp extract or products derived therefrom;

3. After appropriate notice and opportunity, the applicant or licensee has failed or refused to produce any records or provide any information required by this article or the regulations promulgated pursuant thereto;

4. The licensee has conducted activities outside of those activities permitted on its license; or

5. The applicant or licensee, or any officer, director, partner, or any other person exercising any position of management or control thereof or of the licensed activity has willfully failed to comply with any of the provisions of this article or regulations under it and other laws of this state applicable to the licensed activity.

Public Health Law § 3398-l. Record keeping and tracking.

*NB Repealed 6 months after the full cannabis control board created by Article 2 of the cannabis law has been appointed

Every licensee shall keep, in such form as the commissioner may direct, such relevant records as may be required pursuant to regulations under this article.

Public Health Law § 3398-m. Packaging and labeling of cannabinoid hemp and hemp extract.

*NB Repealed 6 months after the full cannabis control board created by Article 2 of the cannabis law has been appointed

1. Cannabinoid hemp processors shall be required to provide appropriate label warning to consumers, and restricted from making unapproved label claims, as determined by the department, concerning the potential impact on or benefit to human health resulting from the use of cannabinoid hemp, hemp extract and products derived therefrom for human consumption, which labels shall be affixed to those products when sold, pursuant to rules and regulations that the department may adopt.

2. The department may, by rules and regulations, require processors to establish a code, including, but not limited to QR code, for labels and establish methods and procedures for determining, among other things, serving sizes or dosages for cannabinoid hemp, hemp extract and products derived therefrom, active cannabinoid concentration per serving size, number of servings per container, and the growing region, state or country of origin if not from the United States. Such rules and regulations may require an appropriate fact panel that incorporates data regarding serving sizes and potency thereof.

3. The packaging, sale, or possession of products derived from cannabinoid hemp or hemp extract used for human consumption not labeled or offered in conformity with regulations under this section shall be grounds for the seizure or quarantine of the product, the imposition of a civil penalty against a processor or retailer, and the suspension, revocation or cancellation of a license, in accordance with this article.

Public Health Law § 3398-n. Processing of cannabinoid hemp and hemp extract.

* NB Repealed 6 months after the full cannabis control board created by Article 2 of the cannabis law has been appointed

1. No processor shall sell or agree to sell or deliver in the state any cannabinoid hemp, hemp extract or product derived therefrom, used for human consumption, except in sealed containers containing quantities in accordance with size standards pursuant to rules adopted by the commissioner. Such containers shall have affixed thereto such labels as may be required by the rules of the department.

2. Processors shall take such steps necessary to ensure that the cannabinoid hemp or hemp extract used in their processing operation has only been grown with pesticides that are registered by the department of environmental conservation or that specifically meet the United States environmental protection agency registration exemption criteria for minimum risk, used in compliance with rules, regulations, standards and guidelines issued by the department of environmental conservation for pesticides.

3. All cannabinoid hemp, hemp extract and products derived therefrom used for human consumption shall be extracted and processed in accordance with good manufacturing processes pursuant to Part 117 or Part 111 of title 21 of the code of federal regulations, as may be defined, modified and decided upon by the commissioner in rules or regulations.

4. As necessary to protect human health, the department shall have the authority to: (a) regulate and prohibit specific ingredients, excipients or methods used in processing cannabinoid hemp, hemp extract and products derived therefrom; and (b) prohibit, or expressly allow, certain products or product classes derived from cannabinoid hemp or hemp extract, to be processed.

Public Health Law § 3398-o. Laboratory testing.

* NB Repealed 6 months after the full cannabis control board created by Article 2 of the cannabis law has been appointed

Every cannabinoid hemp processor shall contract with an independent commercial laboratory to test the hemp extract and products produced by the licensed processor. The commissioner shall establish the necessary qualifications or certifications required for such laboratories used by licensees. The commissioner is authorized to issue rules and regulations consistent with this article establishing the testing required, the reporting of testing results and the form for reporting such laboratory testing results. The department has authority to require licensees to submit any cannabinoid hemp, hemp extract or product derived therefrom, processed or offered for sale within the state, for testing by the department. This section shall not obligate the department, in any way, to perform any testing on hemp, cannabinoid hemp, hemp extract or product derived therefrom.

Public Health Law § 3398-p. New York hemp product.

* NB Repealed 6 months after the full cannabis control board created by Article 2 of the cannabis law has been appointed

The commissioner may establish and adopt official grades and standards for cannabinoid hemp, hemp extract and products derived therefrom, as he or she may deem advisable, which are produced for sale in this state and, from time to time, may amend or modify such grades and standards.

Public Health Law § 3398-q. Penalties.

* NB Repealed 6 months after the full cannabis control board created by Article 2 of the cannabis law has been appointed

Notwithstanding the provision of any law to the contrary, the failure to comply with a requirement of this article, or a regulation thereunder, may be punishable by a civil penalty of not more than one thousand dollars for a first violation; not more than five thousand dollars for a second violation within three years; and not more than ten thousand dollars for a third violation and each subsequent violation thereafter, within three years.

Public Health Law § 3398-r. Hemp workgroup.

* NB Repealed 6 months after the full cannabis control board created by Article 2 of the cannabis law has been appointed

The commissioner, in consultation with the commissioner of the department of agriculture and markets, may appoint a New York state hemp and hemp extract workgroup, composed of growers, researchers, producers, processors, manufacturers and trade associations, to make recommendations for the industrial hemp and cannabinoid hemp programs, state and federal policies and policy initiatives, and opportunities for the promotion and marketing of cannabinoid hemp and hemp extract as consistent with federal and state laws, rules and regulations.

Public Health Law § 3398-s. Prohibitions.

* NB Repealed 6 months after the full cannabis control board created by Article 2 of the cannabis law has been appointed

1. Except as authorized by the United States food and drug administration, the processing of cannabinoid hemp or hemp extract used for human consumption is prohibited within the state unless the processor is licensed under this article.

2. Cannabinoid hemp and hemp extracts used for human consumption and grown or processed outside the state shall not be distributed or sold at retail within the state, unless they meet all standards established for cannabinoid hemp under state law and regulations.

3. The retail sale of cannabinoid hemp is prohibited in this state unless the retailer is licensed under this article.

Public Health Law § 3398-t. Special use permits.

* NB Repealed 6 months after the full cannabis control board created by Article 2 of the cannabis law has been appointed

The commissioner shall have the authority to issue temporary permits for carrying on any activity related to cannabinoid hemp, hemp extract and products derived therefrom, licensed under this article. The commissioner may set reasonable fees for such permits, to establish the periods during which such permits are valid, and to make rules and regulations to implement this section.

Public Health Law § 3398-u. Severability.

* NB Repealed 6 months after the full cannabis control board created by Article 2 of the cannabis law has been appointed

If any provision of this article or the application thereof to any person or circumstances is held invalid, such invalidity shall not affect other provisions or applications of this article which can be given effect without the invalid provision or application, and to this end the provisions of this article are declared to be severable.

X. Social Services Law

Social Services Law § 132. Investigation of applications.

1. When an application for assistance or care is received, or a social services official is informed that a person is in need of public assistance and care, an investigation and record shall be made of the circumstances of such person. The object of such investigations shall be to secure the facts necessary to determine whether such person is in need of public assistance or care and what form thereof and service he or she should receive. Information shall be sought as to the residence of such person, the name, age, religious faith, physical condition, earnings or other income, and ability to work of all members of the family, the cause of the person's condition, the ability and willingness of the family, relatives, friends and church to assist, and such other facts as may be useful in determining the treatment which will be helpful to such person. However, nothing in this subdivision or elsewhere in this chapter contained shall be construed to require a social services official to communicate with or require assistance from any person or persons liable by law to contribute to the support of a woman pregnant with, or the mother of, an out of wedlock child, in need of care away from home during pregnancy and during and after delivery, in the case where the surrender of the child to the social services official is under consideration, for such period as may be necessary for such mother and official to decide whether the child will be surrendered for adoption to such official, which period shall not extend beyond ninety days after birth of the child. Except where the welfare official is in possession of positive proof that the applicant is receiving or is eligible to receive unemployment insurance benefits and the amount thereof such investigations shall include written request to the commissioner of labor or his or her duly authorized officer charged with administration of the unemployment insurance law for information as to the status of such person in respect to unemployment insurance benefits.

2. (a) All applications received by a town social services officer shall be forwarded to the county commissioner immediately and all such applications shall be investigated by the staff of the county commissioner. After investigation the county commissioner shall return to the town social services officer every application for safety net assistance made by a person residing or found in such town, together with his or her recommendation as to

the eligibility of the applicant and the amount of assistance to be granted, if any. In addition thereto, the county commissioner shall keep the town social services officer currently informed of persons residing in his or her town who are receiving any form of public assistance and care other than safety net assistance.

(b) In a city social services district, investigation of applications shall be made by the city commissioner of social services and his staff.

(c) In a city which is functioning under section seventy-four-a of this chapter, investigation shall be made by the county commissioner of social services and his staff.

3. The commissioner of the department of family assistance shall provide by regulation for methods of determining eligibility for public assistance and care, other than medical assistance, to be utilized by all social services officials. Such regulations shall provide for methods of verifying information supplied by or about recipients with information contained in the wage reporting system established pursuant to section one hundred seventy-one-a of the tax law and similar systems in other geographically contiguous states, and, to the degree mandated by federal law with the non-wage income file maintained by the United States internal revenue service, with the benefits and earnings data exchange maintained by the United States department of health and human services, and with the unemployment insurance benefit file.

4. (a) Investigation into the cause of the condition of a head of household or of any adult applicant or recipient and the treatment which will be helpful to such person shall include a screening for alcohol and/or substance abuse using a standardized screening instrument to be developed by the office of addiction services and supports in consultation with the department. Such screening shall be performed by a social services district at the time of application and periodically thereafter but not more frequently than every six months, unless the district has reason to believe that an applicant or recipient is abusing or dependent on alcohol or drugs, in accordance with regulations promulgated by the department. Such screening may be conducted by telephone or other digital means at the request of the applicant or recipient.

(b) When the screening process indicates that there is reason to believe that an applicant or recipient is abusing or dependent on alcohol or drugs, the social services district shall require a formal alcohol or substance abuse assessment, which may include drug testing, to be performed by an alcohol and/or substance abuse professional credentialed by the office of addiction services and supports. Provided however, if the applicant or recipient tests positive for the presence of cannabis, the positive result alone shall not be sufficient to establish a dependence for purposes of requiring an individual to participate in a treatment program pursuant to paragraph (c) of this subdivision. The assessment may be performed directly by the district or pursuant to contract with the district. Such assessment may be conducted by telephone or other digital means at the request of the applicant or recipient.

(c) The social services official shall refer applicants and recipients whom it determines are presently unable to work by reason of their need for treatment for alcohol or substance abuse based on the formal assessment to a treatment program licensed or certified by the office of alcoholism and substance abuse services or operated by the United States office of veterans affairs and determined by the social services official to meet the rehabilitation needs of the individual. When residential treatment is appropriate for a single custodial parent, the social services official shall make diligent efforts to refer the parent to a program that would allow the family to remain intact for the duration of the treatment.

(d) A person who fails to participate in the screening or in the assessment shall be ineligible for public assistance. Other members of a household which includes a person who has failed to participate in the screening or assessment shall, if otherwise eligible, receive public assistance only through safety net assistance if they are otherwise eligible for public assistance.

(e) A person referred to a treatment program pursuant to paragraph (c) of this subdivision, and the household with which he or she resides shall receive safety net assistance while the person is participating in such treatment, if the household is otherwise eligible for public assistance. If a person referred to treatment cannot participate in that treatment because treatment is not presently available, that person and the household with which he or she resides shall receive safety net assistance if the household is otherwise eligible for public assistance.

(f) If an applicant or recipient is required, pursuant to paragraph (c) of this subdivision, to participate in an appropriate rehabilitation program and refuses to participate in such program without good cause or leaves such program prior to completion of the program without good cause, provided that program completion shall be solely determined by the guidelines and rules of such rehabilitation program, or if an applicant or recipient has been suspended from the receipt of social security disability benefits or supplemental security income benefits by reason of noncompliance with requirements of the federal social security administration for treatment for substance abuse or alcohol abuse, the person will be disqualified from receiving public assistance as follows:

(i) for the first failure to participate in or complete the program, until the failure ceases or for forty-five days, whichever period of time is longer;

(ii) for the second such failure, until the failure ceases or for one hundred twenty days, whichever period of time is longer; and

(iii) for the third and subsequent failures, until the failure ceases or for one hundred eighty days, whichever period is longer.

Good cause shall be defined in regulations by the commissioner.

The household with which the person resides shall continue to receive safety net assistance if otherwise eligible.

(g) Persons disqualified from receiving public assistance pursuant to paragraph (f) of this subdivision who would otherwise be eligible for public assistance and who return to required treatment prior to the end of the disqualification period and are receiving residential care as defined in paragraph (d) of subdivision three of section two hundred nine of this chapter shall be eligible for safety net assistance.

(h) Notwithstanding any inconsistent provision of section one hundred thirty-one-o of this article, if a recipient required to participate in an appropriate treatment program pursuant to paragraph (c) of this subdivision receives a personal needs allowance, such allowance shall be made as a restricted payment to the treatment program and shall be a conditional payment. If such recipient leaves the treatment program prior to the completion of such program, any accumulated personal needs allowance will be considered an overpayment and returned to the social services district which provided the personal needs allowance.

(i) Compliance with the provisions of this subdivision shall not be required as a condition of applying for or receiving medical assistance.

Social Services Law § 488. Definitions.

As used in this article, the following terms shall have the following meanings:

1. "Reportable incident" shall mean the following conduct that a mandated reporter is required to report to the vulnerable persons' central register:

(a) "Physical abuse," which shall mean conduct by a custodian intentionally or recklessly causing, by physical contact, physical injury or serious or protracted impairment of the physical, mental or emotional condition of a service recipient or causing the likelihood of such injury or impairment. Such conduct may include but shall not be limited to: slapping, hitting, kicking, biting, choking, smothering, shoving, dragging, throwing, punching, shaking, burning, cutting or the use of corporal punishment. Physical abuse shall not include reasonable emergency interventions necessary to protect the safety of any person.

(b) "Sexual abuse," which shall mean any conduct by a custodian that subjects a person receiving services to any offense defined in article one hundred thirty or section 255.25, 255.26 or 255.27 of the penal law; or any conduct or communication by such custodian that allows, permits, uses or encourages a service recipient to engage in any act described in articles two hundred thirty or two hundred sixty-three of the penal law. For purposes of this paragraph only, a person with a developmental disability who is or was receiving services and is also an employee or volunteer of a service provider shall not be considered a custodian if he or she has sexual contact with another service recipient who is a consenting adult who has consented to such contact.

(c) "Psychological abuse," which shall mean conduct by a custodian intentionally or recklessly causing, by verbal or non-verbal conduct, a substantial diminution of a service recipient's emotional, social or behavioral development or condition, supported by a clinical assessment performed by a physician, psychologist, psychiatric nurse practitioner, licensed clinical or master social worker or licensed mental health counselor, or causing the likelihood of such diminution. Such conduct may include but shall not be limited to intimidation, threats, the display of a weapon or other object that could reasonably be perceived by a service recipient as a means for infliction of pain or injury, in a manner that constitutes a threat of physical pain or injury, taunts, derogatory comments or ridicule.

(d) "Deliberate inappropriate use of restraints," which shall mean the use of a restraint when the technique that is used, the amount of force that is used or the situation in which the restraint is used is deliberately inconsistent with a service recipient's individual treatment plan or behavioral intervention plan, generally accepted treatment practices and/or applicable federal or state laws, regulations or policies, except when the restraint is used as a reasonable emergency intervention to prevent imminent risk of harm to a person receiving services or to any other person. For purposes of this subdivision, a "restraint" shall include the use of any manual, pharmacological or mechanical measure or device to immobilize or limit the ability of a person receiving services to freely move his or her arms, legs or body.

(e) "Use of aversive conditioning," which shall mean the application of a physical stimulus that is intended to induce pain or discomfort in order to modify or change the behavior of a person receiving services in the absence of a person-specific authorization by the operating, licensing or certifying state agency pursuant to governing state agency regulations. Aversive conditioning may include but is not limited to, the use of physical stimuli such as noxious odors, noxious tastes, blindfolds, the withholding of meals and the provision of substitute foods in an unpalatable form and movement limitations used as punishment, including but not limited to helmets and mechanical restraint devices.

(f) "Obstruction of reports of reportable incidents," which shall mean conduct by a custodian that impedes the discovery, reporting or investigation of the treatment of a service recipient by falsifying records related to the safety, treatment or supervision of a service recipient, actively persuading a mandated reporter from making a report of a reportable incident to the statewide vulnerable persons' central register with the intent to suppress the reporting of the investigation of such incident, intentionally making a false statement or intentionally withholding material information during an investigation into such a report; intentional failure of a supervisor or manager to act upon such a report in accordance with governing state agency regulations, policies or procedures; or, for a mandated reporter who is a custodian as defined in subdivision two of this section, failing to report a reportable incident upon discovery.

(g) "Unlawful use or administration of a controlled substance," which shall mean any administration by a custodian to a service recipient of: a controlled substance as defined by article thirty-three of the public health law, without a prescription; or other medication not approved for any use by the federal food and drug administration, except for the administration of medical cannabis when such administration is in accordance with article three of the cannabis law, and any regulations promulgated thereunder, as well as the policies or procedures of the facility or provider agency governing such custodians. It also shall include a custodian unlawfully using or distributing a controlled substance as defined by article thirty-three of the public health law, at the workplace or while on duty.

(h) "Neglect," which shall mean any action, inaction or lack of attention that breaches a custodian's duty and that results in or is likely to result in physical injury or serious or protracted impairment of the physical, mental or emotional condition of a service recipient. Neglect shall include, but is not limited to: (i) failure to provide proper supervision, including a lack of proper supervision that results in conduct between persons receiving services that would constitute abuse as described in paragraphs (a) through (g) of this subdivision if committed by a custodian; (ii) failure to provide adequate food, clothing, shelter, medical, dental, optometric or surgical care, consistent with the rules or regulations promulgated by the state agency operating, certifying or supervising the facility or provider agency, provided that the facility or provider agency has reasonable access to the provision of such services and that necessary consents to any such medical, dental, optometric or surgical treatment have been sought and obtained from the appropriate individuals; or (iii) failure to provide access to educational instruction, by a custodian with a duty to ensure that an individual receives access to such instruction in accordance with the provisions of part one of article sixty-five of the education law and/or the individual's individualized education program.

(i) "Significant incident" shall mean an incident, other than an incident of abuse or neglect, that because of its severity or the sensitivity of the situation may result in, or has the reasonably foreseeable potential to result in, harm to the health, safety or welfare of a person receiving services and shall include but shall not be limited to:

(1) conduct between persons receiving services that would constitute abuse as described in paragraphs (a) through (g) of this subdivision if committed by a custodian; or

(2) conduct on the part of a custodian, which is inconsistent with a service recipient's individual treatment plan or individualized educational program, generally accepted treatment practices and/or applicable federal or state laws, regulations or policies and which impairs or creates a reasonably foreseeable potential to impair the health, safety or welfare of a person receiving services, including but not limited to:

(A) unauthorized seclusion, which shall mean the placement of a person receiving services in a room or area from which he or she cannot, or perceives that he or she cannot, leave at will;

(B) unauthorized use of time-out, which shall mean the use of a procedure in which a person receiving services is removed from regular programming and isolated in a room or area for the convenience of a custodian, or as a substitute for programming but shall not include the use of a time-out as an emergency intervention to protect the health or safety of the individual or other persons;

(C) except as provided for in paragraph (g) of subdivision one of this section, the administration of a prescribed or over-the-counter medication, which is inconsistent with a prescription or order issued for a service recipient by a licensed, qualified health care practitioner, and which has an adverse effect on a service recipient. For purposes of this paragraph, "adverse effect" shall mean the unanticipated and undesirable side effect from the administration of a particular medication which unfavorably affects the well-being of a service recipient;

(D) inappropriate use of restraints, which shall mean the use of a restraint when the technique that is used, the amount of force that is used or the situation in which the restraint is used is inconsistent with a service recipient's individual plan, generally accepted treatment practices and/or applicable federal or state laws, regulations or policies. For the purposes of this subdivision, a "restraint" shall include the use of any manual, pharmacological or mechanical measure or device to immobilize or limit the ability of a person receiving services to freely move his or her arms, legs or body; or

(3) any other conduct identified in regulations of the state oversight agency, pursuant to guidelines or standards established by the executive director.

2. "Custodian" means a director, operator, employee or volunteer of a facility or provider agency; or a consultant or an employee or volunteer of a corporation, partnership, organization or governmental entity which provides goods or services to a facility or provider agency pursuant to contract or other arrangement that permits such person to have regular and substantial contact with individuals who are cared for by the facility or provider agency.

3. "Executive director" shall mean the executive director of the justice center for the protection of people with special needs as established by article twenty of the executive law.

4. "Facility" or "provider agency" shall mean:

(a) a facility or program in which services are provided and which is operated, licensed or certified by the office of mental health, the office for people with developmental disabilities or the office of addiction services and supports, including but not limited to psychiatric centers, inpatient psychiatric units of a general hospital, developmental centers, intermediate care facilities, community residences, group homes and family care homes, provided, however, that such term shall not include a secure treatment facility as defined in section 10.03 of the mental hygiene law, services defined in paragraphs four and five of subdivision (a) of section 16.03 of the mental hygiene law, or services provided in programs or facilities that are operated by the office of mental health and located in state correctional facilities under the jurisdiction of the department of corrections and community supervision;

(b) any program or facility that is operated by the office of children and family services for juvenile delinquents or juvenile offenders placed in the custody of the commissioner of such office and any residential programs or facilities licensed or certified by the office of children and family services, excluding foster family homes and residential programs for victims of domestic violence;

(c) adult care facilities, which shall mean adult homes or enriched housing programs licensed pursuant to article seven of this chapter: (i) (A) that have a licensed capacity of eighty or more beds; and (B) in which at least twenty-five percent of the residents are persons with serious mental illness as defined by subdivision fifty-two of section 1.03 of the mental hygiene law; (ii) but not including an adult home or enriched housing program which is authorized to operate fifty-five percent or more of its total licensed capacity of beds as assisted living program beds pursuant to section four hundred sixty-one-l of this chapter;

(d) any overnight, summer day and traveling summer day camps for children with developmental disabilities as defined in regulations promulgated by the commissioner of health; or

(e) the New York state school for the blind and the New York state school for the deaf, which operate pursuant to articles eighty-seven and eighty-eight of the education law; an institution for the instruction of the deaf and the blind which has a residential component and is subject to the visitation of the commissioner of education pursuant to article eighty-five of the education law with respect to its day and residential components; special act school districts serving students with disabilities; or in-state private schools which have been approved by the commissioner of education for special education services or programs, and which have a residential program.

4-a. "State oversight agency" shall mean the state agency that operates, licenses or certifies an applicable facility or provider agency; provided however that such term shall only include the following entities: the office of mental health, the office for people with developmental disabilities, the office of alcoholism and substance abuse services, the office of children and family services, the department of health and the state education department. "State oversight agency" does not include agencies that are certification agencies pursuant to federal law or regulation.

5. "Mandated reporter" shall mean a custodian or a human services professional, but shall not include a service recipient.

5-a. "Human services professional" shall mean any: physician; registered physician assistant; surgeon; medical examiner; coroner; dentist; dental hygienist; osteopath; optometrist; chiropractor; podiatrist; resident; intern; psychologist; registered nurse; licensed practical nurse; nurse practitioner; social worker; emergency medical technician; licensed creative arts therapist; licensed marriage and family therapist; licensed mental health counselor; licensed psychoanalyst; licensed behavior analyst; certified behavior analyst assistant; licensed speech/language pathologist or audiologist; licensed physical therapist; licensed occupational therapist; hospital personnel engaged in the admission, examination, care or treatment of persons; Christian Science practitioner; school official, which includes but is not limited to school teacher, school guidance counselor, school psychologist, school social worker, school nurse, school administrator or other school personnel required to hold a teaching or administrative license or certificate; full or part-time compensated school employee required to hold a temporary coaching license or professional coaching certificate; social services worker; any other child care or foster care worker; mental health professional; person credentialed by the office of alcoholism and substance abuse services; peace officer; police officer; district attorney or assistant district attorney; investigator employed in the office of a district attorney; or other law enforcement official.

6. "Physical injury" and "impairment of physical condition" shall mean any confirmed harm, hurt or damage resulting in a significant worsening or diminution of an individual's physical condition.

7. "Delegate investigatory entity" shall mean a facility or provider agency, or any other entity authorized by the regulations of a state oversight agency or the justice center for the protection of people with special needs to conduct an investigation of a reportable incident.

8. "Justice center" shall mean the justice center for the protection of people with special needs.

9. "Person receiving services," or "service recipient" shall mean an individual who resides or is an inpatient in a residential facility or who receives services from a facility or provider agency.

10. "Personal representative" shall mean a person authorized under state, tribal, military or other applicable law to act on behalf of a vulnerable person in making health care decisions or, for programs that serve children under the jurisdiction of the state education department or the office of children and family services, the service recipient's parent, guardian or other person legally responsible for such person.

11. "Abuse or neglect" shall mean the conduct described in paragraphs (a) through (h) of subdivision one of this section.

12. "Subject of the report" shall mean a custodian, as defined in subdivision two of this section, who is reported to the vulnerable persons' central register for the alleged abuse or neglect of a vulnerable person as defined in subdivision eleven of this section.

13. "Other persons named in the report" shall mean and be limited to the following persons who are named in a report to the vulnerable persons' central register other than the subject of the report: the service recipient whose care and treatment is the concern of a report to the vulnerable persons' central register, and the personal representative, if any, as defined in subdivision ten of this section.

14. "Vulnerable persons' central register" shall mean the statewide central register of reportable incidents involving vulnerable persons, which shall operate in accordance with section four hundred ninety-two of this article.

15. "Vulnerable person" shall mean a person who, due to physical or cognitive disabilities, or the need for services or placement, is receiving services from a facility or provider agency.

16. "Intentionally" and "recklessly" shall have the same meanings as provided in subdivisions one and three of section 15.05 of the penal law.

Social Services Law § 490. Incident management programs.

1. Each state oversight agency, as defined in this article, shall promulgate regulations approved by the justice center, that contain procedures and requirements consistent with guidelines and standards developed by the justice center, addressing the following issues relating to an incident management program; provided, however, that regulations of the state education department need not be approved by the justice center, but shall be developed in consultation with the justice center:

(a) all reportable incidents are identified and reported in a timely manner in accordance with this article;

(b) all reportable incidents are promptly investigated;

(c) individual reportable incidents, and incident patterns and trends, are reviewed to identify and implement preventive and corrective actions, which may include, but shall not be limited to, staff retraining or any appropriate disciplinary action allowed by law or contract, as well as opportunities for improvement;

(d) patterns and trends in the reporting and response to allegations of reportable incidents are reviewed and plans of improvement are timely developed based on such reviews;

(e) information regarding individual reportable incidents, incident patterns and trends, and patterns and trends in the reporting and response to reportable incidents is shared, consistent with applicable law, with the justice center, in the form and manner required by the justice center and, for facilities or provider agencies that are not state operated, with the applicable state oversight agency which shall provide such information to the justice center;

(f) incident review committees are established; provided, however, that the regulations may authorize an exemption from this requirement, when appropriate, based on the size of the facility or provider agency or other relevant factors. Such committees shall be composed of members of the governing body of the facility or provider agency and other persons identified by the director of the facility or provider agency, including some members of the following: direct support staff, licensed health care practitioners, service recipients and representatives of family, consumer and other advocacy organizations, but not the director of the facility or provider agency. Such committee shall meet regularly to: (i) review the timeliness, thoroughness and appropriateness of the facility or provider agency's responses to reportable incidents; (ii) recommend additional opportunities for improvement to the director of the facility or provider agency, if appropriate; (iii) review incident trends and patterns concerning reportable incidents; and (iv) make recommendations to the director of the facility or provider agency to assist in reducing reportable incidents. Members of the committee shall be trained in confidentiality laws and regulations, and shall comply with section seventy-four of the public officers law; and

(g) safe storage, administration, and diversion prevention policies regarding controlled substances and medical cannabis.

2. Notwithstanding any other provision of law, except as may be provided by section 33.25 of the mental hygiene law, records, reports or other information maintained by the justice center, state oversight agencies, delegate investigatory entities, and facilities and provider agencies regarding the deliberations of an incident review committee shall be confidential, provided that nothing in this article shall be deemed to diminish or otherwise derogate the legal privilege afforded to proceedings, records, reports or other information relating to a quality assurance function, including the investigation of an incident reported pursuant to section 29.29 of the mental hygiene law, as provided in section sixty-five hundred twenty-seven of the education law. For purposes of this section, a quality assurance function is a process for systematically monitoring and evaluating various aspects of a program, service or facility to ensure that standards of care are being met.

3. No member of an incident review committee performing a quality assurance function shall be permitted or required to testify in a judicial or administrative proceeding with respect to quality assurance findings, recommendations, evaluations, opinions or actions taken, except that this provision is not intended to relieve any state oversight agency, delegate investigatory entity, facility or provider agency, or an agent thereof, from liability arising from treatment of a service recipient.

4. There shall be no monetary liability on the part of, and no cause of action for damages shall arise against, any person on account of participating in good faith and with reasonable care in the communication of information in the possession of such person to an incident review committee, or on account of any recommendation or evaluation regarding the conduct or practices of any custodian that is made in good faith and with reasonable care.

5. With respect to the implementation of incident management plans in residential schools or facilities located outside of New York state, each state oversight agency shall require that: (a) the justice center, the applicable state

oversight agency and any local social services district and/or local educational agency placing an individual with such facility or school or state agency funding the placement of an individual or student be notified immediately of any allegation of abuse or neglect involving that individual or student; (b) an investigation be conducted by the justice center, or where that is not practicable, by a state agency or other entity authorized or required to investigate complaints of abuse or neglect under the laws of the state in which the facility or school is located; and (c) the findings of such investigation be forwarded to the justice center and each placing entity or funding agency in New York state within ninety days. Failure to comply with the requirements of this section shall be grounds for revocation or suspension of the license or approval of the out of state facility or school.

6. Records of facilities or provider agencies not otherwise subject to article six of the public officers law shall be made available for public inspection and copying, when such records relate to abuse and neglect of vulnerable persons, to the same extent that those records would be available from a state agency, as defined in such article. Requests for such records shall be made in writing to the justice center. The justice center may deny access to records of such facilities or provider agencies, or portions thereof, that the justice center determines would be exempt from disclosure by a state agency pursuant to such article. The requesting party may appeal a denial of access to such records to the executive director of the justice center. A requesting party denied access to a record in such appeal determination may bring a proceeding for review of such denial pursuant to article seventy-eight of the civil practice law and rules. The executive director of the justice center shall promulgate regulations, consistent with the provisions of article six of the public officers law providing for the prompt response to such requests. Facilities or provider agencies covered by this subdivision shall cooperate with the justice center and provide any records that the justice center deems subject to disclosure.

XI. State Finance Law

State Finance Law § 89-h. Medical cannabis trust fund.

* NB Repealed July 5, 2028

1. There is hereby established in the joint custody of the state comptroller and the commissioner of taxation and finance a special fund to be known as the "medical cannabis trust fund."

2. The medical cannabis trust fund shall consist of all moneys required to be deposited in the medical cannabis trust fund pursuant to the provisions of section four hundred ninety of the tax law.

3. The moneys in the medical cannabis trust fund shall be kept separate and shall not be commingled with any other moneys in the custody of the commissioner of taxation and finance and the state comptroller.

4. The moneys of the medical cannabis trust fund, following appropriation by the legislature, shall be allocated upon a certificate of approval of availability by the director of the budget as follows: (a) Twenty-two and five-tenths percent of the monies shall be transferred to the counties in New York state in which the medical cannabis was manufactured and allocated in proportion to the gross sales originating from medical cannabis manufactured in each such county; (b) twenty-two and five-tenths percent of the moneys shall be transferred to the counties in New York state in which the medical cannabis was dispensed and allocated in proportion to the gross sales occurring in each such county; (c) five percent of the monies shall be transferred to the office of addiction services and supports, which shall use that revenue for additional drug abuse prevention, counseling and treatment services; (d) five percent of the revenue received by the department shall be transferred to the division of criminal justice services, which shall use that revenue for a program of discretionary grants to state and local law enforcement agencies that demonstrate a need relating to article three of the cannabis law; said grants could be used for personnel costs of state and local law enforcement agencies; and (e) forty-five percent of the monies shall be deposited to the New York state cannabis revenue fund. For purposes of this subdivision, the city of New York shall be deemed to be a county.

State Finance Law § 99-ii. New York state cannabis revenue fund.

1. There is hereby established in the joint custody of the state comptroller and the commissioner of taxation and finance a special fund to be known as the "New York state cannabis revenue fund".

2. Such fund shall consist of all revenues received by the department of taxation and finance, pursuant to the provisions of article twenty-C of the tax law and all other moneys credited or transferred thereto from any other fund or source pursuant to law. Nothing contained in this section shall prevent the state from receiving grants, gifts or bequests for the purposes of the fund as defined in this section and depositing them into the fund according to law.

2-a. Revenues deposited into this fund pursuant to section fifteen of the cannabis law shall first be used to reimburse the state general fund for any funds transferred to this fund from the state general fund for the purposes of supporting expenditures authorized under paragraph (d) of subdivision three of this section.

3. The moneys in such fund shall be expended for the following purposes:

(a) Reasonable costs incurred by the department of taxation and finance for administering and collecting the taxes imposed by this part.

(b) Reasonable costs incurred by the office of cannabis management and the cannabis control board for implementing, administering, and enforcing the marihuana regulation and taxation act.

(c) Actual and necessary costs incurred by the office of cannabis management and the cannabis control board, and the urban development corporation, related to the administration of incubators and other assistance to qualified social and economic equity applicants including the administration, capitalization, and provision of low and zero interest loans to such applicants pursuant to section sixteen-ee of the urban development corporation act. Such costs shall be paid out of revenues received, including, but not limited to, from special one-time fees paid by registered organizations pursuant to section sixty-three of the cannabis law.

(d) subject to available appropriations and providing that no more than fifty million dollars in funding, shall be made available, whether directly or indirectly for investment in a private debt or equity fund formed pursuant to subdivision thirty-two of section one thousand six hundred seventy-eight of the public authorities law or to cover capital costs associated with establishing conditional adult-use cannabis retail dispensaries for operation by social equity licensees duly licensed pursuant to article two of the cannabis law. Such capital costs shall include all costs, including closely related ancillary costs, related to the leasing, planning, design, construction, reconstruction, rehabilitation, improvement, furnishing, and equipping of such adult-use cannabis retail dispensaries, to the extent such work has been undertaken or costs for such work incurred by: (i) the office of cannabis management and the cannabis control board, (ii) the dormitory authority of the state of New York, or any subsidiary thereof, under agreement with the office of cannabis management and the cannabis control board, or with the private debt or equity fund formed pursuant to subdivision thirty-two of section one thousand six hundred seventy-eight of the public authorities law, or (iii) the private debt or equity fund formed pursuant to subdivision thirty-two of section one thousand six hundred seventy-eight of the public authorities law. Any repayment of the state's investment by the fund, as authorized in this paragraph shall be deposited in the New York state cannabis revenue fund.

(e) Beginning with the two thousand twenty-two--two thousand twenty-three fiscal year and continuing through the two thousand thirty-two--two thousand thirty-three fiscal year, the commissioner of taxation and finance shall annually disburse the following sums for the purposes of data collection and reporting:

(i) Reasonable costs incurred by the office of cannabis management to track and report data related to the licensing of cannabis businesses, including the geographic location, structure, and function of licensed cannabis businesses, and demographic data, including race, ethnicity, and gender, of applicants and license holders. The cannabis control board shall publish reports on its findings annually and shall make the reports available to the public.

(ii) Reasonable costs incurred by the department of criminal justice services to track and report data related to any infractions, violations, or criminal convictions that occur under any of the remaining cannabis statutes. The department of criminal justice services shall publish reports on its findings annually and shall make the reports available to the public.

(iii) Reasonable costs incurred by agencies of the state, including the state university of New York to research and evaluate the implementation and effect of the cannabis law. No more than four percent of these monies may be used for expenses related to administrative costs of conducting such research, and to, if appropriate, make recommendations to the legislature and governor regarding possible amendments to the cannabis law. The recipients of these funds shall publish reports on their findings at a minimum of every two years and shall make the reports available to the public. The research funded pursuant to this subdivision shall include but not necessarily be limited to:

(A) the impact on public health, including health costs associated with cannabis use, as well as whether cannabis use is associated with an increase or decrease in use of alcohol or other drugs;

(B) the impact of treatment for cannabis use disorder and the effectiveness of different treatment programs;

(C) public safety issues related to cannabis use, including, but not limited to studying the effectiveness of the packaging and labeling requirements and advertising and marketing restrictions contained in the act at preventing underage access to and use of cannabis and cannabis products, and studying the health-related effects among users of varying potency levels of cannabis and cannabis products;

(D) cannabis use rates, maladaptive use rates for adults and youth, and diagnosis rates of cannabis-related substance use disorders;

(E) cannabis market prices, illicit market prices, tax structures and rates, including an evaluation of how to best tax cannabis based on potency, and the structure and function of licensed cannabis businesses;

(F) whether additional protections are needed to prevent unlawful monopolies or anti-competitive behavior from occurring in the cannabis industry and, if so, recommendations as to the most effective measures for preventing such behavior;

(G) the economic impacts in the private and public sectors, including but not necessarily limited to, job creation, workplace safety, revenues, taxes generated for state and local budgets, and criminal justice impacts, including, but not necessarily limited to, impacts on law enforcement and public resources, short and long term consequences of involvement in the criminal justice system, and state and local government agency administrative costs and revenue;

(H) the extent to which the regulatory agencies tasked with implementing and enforcing the marihuana regulation and taxation act have been able to implement the provisions of such act, consistent with its intent and purposes, and whether different agencies might be able to do so more effectively; and

(I) any environmental impacts and hazards related to cannabis production.

(f) Reasonable costs incurred by the state police and the department of motor vehicles to implement the provisions of section sixty of the marihuana regulation and taxation act, to expand and enhance the drug recognition expert training program and technologies utilized in the process of maintaining road safety.

(g) Reasonable costs, subject to available appropriations, incurred by the office of cannabis management, the cannabis advisory board, or the urban development corporation to administer grants for qualified community-based nonprofit organizations and approved local government entities for the purpose of reinvesting in communities disproportionately affected by past federal and state drug policies, in accordance with the allowable uses of moneys deposited in the New York state community grants reinvestment fund established by section ninety-nine-kk of this article.

(h) Reasonable costs, subject to available appropriations, incurred by the division of criminal justice services and the office of court administration to implement the expungement provisions of sections seventeen and twenty-four of the marihuana regulation and taxation act, as added by a chapter of the laws of two thousand twenty-one which added this section.

4. After the dispersal of moneys pursuant to subdivision three of this section, the remaining moneys in the fund deposited during the prior fiscal year shall be disbursed into the state lottery fund and two additional sub-funds created within the cannabis revenue fund known as the drug treatment and public education fund and the community grants reinvestment fund, as follows:

(a) forty percent shall be deposited in the state lottery fund for additional lottery grants to eligible school districts pursuant to subparagraph four of paragraph b of subdivision four of section ninety-two-c of this article, and shall be used to increase the total amount of funding available for general support for public schools; provided that notwithstanding any inconsistent provision of law, the amounts appropriated for such additional lottery grants shall be excluded from the calculation of: (i) the allowable growth amount computed pursuant to paragraph dd of subdivision one of section thirty-six hundred two of the education law; (ii) the preliminary growth amount computed pursuant to paragraph ff of subdivision one of section thirty-six hundred two of the education law; and (iii) the allocable growth amount computed pursuant to paragraph gg of subdivision one of section thirty-six hundred two of the education law;

(b) twenty percent shall be deposited in the drug treatment and public education fund established by section ninety-nine-jj of this article; and

(c) forty percent shall be deposited in the community grants reinvestment fund established by section ninety-nine-kk of this article.

State Finance Law § 99-jj. New York state drug treatment and public education fund.

1. There is hereby established in the joint custody of the state comptroller and the commissioner of taxation and finance a special fund to be known as the "New York state drug treatment public education fund".

2. Such fund shall consist of revenues received pursuant to the provisions of section ninety-nine-ii of this article and all other moneys credited or transferred thereto from any other fund or source pursuant to law. Nothing contained in this section shall prevent the state from receiving grants, gifts or bequests for the purposes of the fund as defined in this section and depositing them into the fund according to law.

3. The moneys in such fund shall be expended to the commissioner of the office of addiction services and supports and disbursed, in consultation with the commissioner of the department of health, the office of mental health, the office of cannabis management and the commissioner of education for the following purposes:

(a) Reasonable costs incurred, subject to available appropriations, by the office of addiction services and supports, to administer funds in accordance with the allowable uses in paragraphs (b), (c), (d) and (e) of this subdivision.

(b) To develop and implement a youth-focused public health education and prevention campaign, including school-based prevention, early intervention, and health care services and programs to reduce the risk of cannabis and other substance use by school-aged children;

(c) To develop and implement a statewide public health campaign focused on the health effects of cannabis and legal use, including an ongoing education and prevention campaign that educates the general public, including parents, consumers and retailers, on the legal use of cannabis, the importance of preventing youth access, the importance of safe storage and preventing secondhand cannabis smoke exposure, information for pregnant or breastfeeding women, and the overconsumption of edible cannabis products;

(d) To provide substance use disorder treatment programs for youth and adults, with an emphasis on programs that are culturally and gender competent, trauma-informed, evidence-based and provide a continuum of care that includes screening and assessment (substance use disorder as well as mental health), early intervention, active treatment, family involvement, case management, overdose prevention, prevention of communicable diseases related to substance use, relapse management for substance use and other co-occurring behavioral health disorders, vocational services, literacy services, parenting classes, family therapy and counseling services, medication-assisted treatments, psychiatric medication and psychotherapy; and

(e) To evaluate the programs being funded to determine their effectiveness.

4. On or before the first day of February each year, the commissioner of the office of addiction services and supports shall provide a written report to the temporary president of the senate, speaker of the assembly, chair of the senate finance committee, chair of the assembly ways and means committee, chair of the senate committee on alcoholism and drug abuse, chair of the assembly alcoholism and drug abuse committee, the state comptroller and the public. Such report shall detail how the moneys of the fund were utilized during the preceding calendar year, and shall include:

(a) the amount of money dispersed from the fund and the award process used for such disbursements;

(b) recipients of awards from the fund;

(c) the amount awarded to each recipient of an award from the fund;

(d) the purposes for which such awards were granted; and

(e) a summary financial plan for such monies which shall include estimates of all receipts and all disbursements for the current and succeeding fiscal years, along with the actual results from the prior fiscal year.

5. Moneys shall be payable from the fund on the audit and warrant of the comptroller on vouchers approved and certified by the commissioner of addiction services and supports.

State Finance Law § 99-kk. New York state community grants reinvestment fund.

1. There is hereby established in the joint custody of the state comptroller and the commissioner of taxation and finance a special fund to be known as the "New York state community grants reinvestment fund".

2. Such fund shall consist of all revenues received pursuant to the provisions of section ninety-nine-ii of this article and all other moneys credited or transferred thereto from any other fund or source pursuant to law. Nothing contained in this section shall prevent the state from receiving grants, gifts or bequests for the purposes of the fund as defined in this section and depositing them into the fund according to law.

3. The fund shall be governed and administered by the state cannabis advisory board as set out under article two of the cannabis law.

4. The moneys in such fund shall be awarded by the state cannabis advisory board and administered and disbursed by the office of cannabis management and/or the urban development corporation to provide grants for qualified community-based nonprofit organizations and approved local government entities for the purpose of reinvesting in communities disproportionately affected by past federal and state drug policies. Such grants shall be used, including

but not limited to, to support job placement, job skills services, adult education, mental health treatment, substance use disorder treatment, housing, financial literacy, community banking, nutrition services, services to address adverse childhood experiences, afterschool and child care services, system navigation services, legal services to address barriers to reentry, including, but not limited to, providing representation and related assistance with expungement, vacatur, substitution and resentencing of marihuana-related convictions, and linkages to medical care, women's health services and other community-based supportive services. The grants from this program may also be used to further support the social and economic equity program created by article four of the cannabis law and as established by the cannabis control board.

5. On or before the first day of February each year, the office of cannabis management shall provide a written report to the temporary president of the senate, speaker of the assembly, chair of the senate finance committee, chair of the assembly ways and means committee, chair of the senate committee on children and families, chair of the assembly children and families committee, chair of the senate committee on labor, chair of the assembly labor committee, chair of the senate committee on health, chair of the assembly health committee, chair of the senate committee on education, chair of the assembly education committee, the state comptroller and the public. Such report shall detail how the monies of the fund were utilized during the preceding calendar year, and shall include:

(a) the amount of money available and dispersed from the fund and the award process used for such disbursements;

(b) recipients of awards from the fund;

(c) the amount awarded to each recipient of an award from the fund;

(d) the purposes for which such awards were granted; and

(e) a summary financial plan for such monies which shall include estimates of all receipts and all disbursements for the current and succeeding fiscal years, along with the actual results from the prior fiscal year.

6. Moneys shall be payable from the fund on the audit and warrant of the comptroller on vouchers approved and certified by the office of cannabis management.

XII. Tax Law

ARTICLE 20-B. EXCISE TAX ON MEDICAL CANNABIS

Tax Law § 490. Excise tax on medical cannabis.

* NB Repealed July 5, 2028

1. (a) For purposes of this article, the terms "medical cannabis," "registered organization," "certified patient," and "designated caregiver" shall have the same definitions as in section three of the cannabis law.

(b) As used in this section, where not otherwise specifically defined and unless a different meaning is clearly required "gross receipt" means the amount received in or by reason of any sale, conditional or otherwise, of medical cannabis or in or by reason of the furnishing of medical cannabis from the sale of medical cannabis provided by a registered organization to a certified patient or designated caregiver. Gross receipt is expressed in money, whether paid in cash, credit or property of any kind or nature, and shall be determined without any deduction therefrom on account of the cost of the service sold or the cost of materials, labor or services used or other costs, interest or discount paid, or any other expenses whatsoever. "Amount received" for the purpose of the definition of gross receipt, as the term gross receipt is used throughout this article, means the amount charged for the provision of medical cannabis.

2. There is hereby imposed an excise tax on the gross receipts from the sale of medical cannabis by a registered organization to a certified patient or designated caregiver, to be paid by the registered organization, at the rate of seven percent. The tax imposed by this article shall be charged against and be paid by the registered organization and shall not be added as a separate charge or line item on any sales slip, invoice, receipt or other statement or memorandum of the price given to the retail customer.

3. The commissioner may make, adopt and amend rules, regulations, procedures and forms necessary for the proper administration of this article.

4. Every registered organization that makes sales of medical cannabis subject to the tax imposed by this article shall, on or before the twentieth date of each month, file with the commissioner a return on forms to be prescribed by the commissioner, showing its receipts from the retail sale of medical cannabis during the preceding calendar month and the amount of tax due thereon. Such returns shall contain such further information as the commissioner may require. Every registered organization required to file a return under this section shall, at the time of filing such return, pay to the commissioner the total amount of tax due on its retail sales of medical cannabis for the period covered by such return. If a return is not filed when due, the tax shall be due on the day on which the return is required to be filed.

5. Whenever the commissioner shall determine that any moneys received under the provisions of this article were paid in error, he may cause the same to be refunded, with interest, in accordance with such rules and regulations as he may prescribe, except that no interest shall be allowed or paid if the amount thereof would be less than one dollar. Such interest shall be at the overpayment rate set by the commissioner pursuant to subdivision twenty-sixth of section one hundred seventy-one of this chapter, or if no rate is set, at the rate of six percent per annum, from the date when the tax, penalty or interest to be refunded was paid to a date preceding the date of the refund check by not more than thirty days. Provided, however, that for the purposes of this subdivision, any tax paid before the last day prescribed for its payment shall be deemed to have been paid on such last day. Such moneys received under the provisions of this article which the commissioner shall determine were paid in error, may be refunded out of funds in the custody of the comptroller to the credit of such taxes provided an application therefor is filed with the commissioner within two years from the time the erroneous payment was made.

6. The provisions of article twenty-seven of this chapter shall apply to the tax imposed by this article in the same manner and with the same force and effect as if the language of such article had been incorporated in full into this section and had expressly referred to the tax imposed by this article, except to the extent that any provision of such article is either inconsistent with a provision of this article or is not relevant to this article.

7. All taxes, interest and penalties collected or received by the commissioner under this article shall be deposited and disposed of pursuant to the provisions of section one hundred seventy-one-a of this chapter, provided that an amount equal to one hundred percent collected under this article less any amount determined by the commissioner to be reserved by the comptroller for refunds or reimbursements shall be paid by the comptroller to the credit of the medical cannabis trust fund established by section eighty-nine-h of the state finance law.

8. A registered organization that dispenses medical cannabis shall provide to the department information on where the medical cannabis was dispensed and where the medical cannabis was manufactured. A registered organization that obtains cannabis from another registered organization shall obtain from such registered organization information on where the medical cannabis was manufactured.

Tax Law § 491. Returns to be secret.

* NB Repealed July 5, 2028

1. Except in accordance with proper judicial order or as in this section or otherwise provided by law, it shall be unlawful for the commissioner, any officer or employee of the department, or any officer or person who, pursuant to this section, is permitted to inspect any return or report or to whom a copy, an abstract or a portion of any return or report is furnished, or to whom any information contained in any return or report is furnished, or any person engaged

or retained by such department on an independent contract basis or any person who in any manner may acquire knowledge of the contents of a return or report filed pursuant to this article to divulge or make known in any manner the contents or any other information relating to the business of a distributor, owner or other person contained in any return or report required under this article. The officers charged with the custody of such returns or reports shall not be required to produce any of them or evidence of anything contained in them in any action or proceeding in any court, except on behalf of the state, office of cannabis management, or the commissioner in an action or proceeding under the provisions of this chapter or on behalf of the state or the commissioner in any other action or proceeding involving the collection of a tax due under this chapter to which the state or the commissioner is a party or a claimant or on behalf of any party to any action or proceeding under the provisions of this article, when the returns or the reports or the facts shown thereby are directly involved in such action or proceeding, or in an action or proceeding relating to the regulation or taxation of medical cannabis on behalf of officers to whom information shall have been supplied as provided in subdivision two of this section, in any of which events the court may require the production of, and may admit in evidence so much of said returns or reports or of the facts shown thereby as are pertinent to the action or proceeding and no more. Nothing herein shall be construed to prohibit the commissioner, in his or her discretion, from allowing the inspection or delivery of a certified copy of any return or report filed under this article or of any information contained in any such return or report by or to a duly authorized officer or employee of the office of cannabis management; or by or to the attorney general or other legal representatives of the state when an action shall have been recommended or commenced pursuant to this chapter in which such returns or reports or the facts shown thereby are directly involved; or the inspection of the returns or reports required under this article by the comptroller or duly designated officer or employee of the state department of audit and control, for purposes of the audit of a refund of any tax paid by a registered organization or other person under this article; nor to prohibit the delivery to a registered organization, or a duly authorized representative of such registered organization, a certified copy of any return or report filed by such registered organization pursuant to this article, nor to prohibit the publication of statistics so classified as to prevent the identification of particular returns or reports and the items thereof. This section shall also not be construed to prohibit the disclosure, for tax administration purposes, to the division of the budget and the office of the state comptroller, of information aggregated from the returns filed by all the registered organizations making sales of, or manufacturing, medical cannabis in a specified county, whether the number of such registered organizations is one or more. Provided further that, notwithstanding the provisions of this subdivision, the commissioner may, in his or her discretion, permit the proper officer of any county entitled to receive an allocation, following appropriation by the legislature, pursuant to this article and section eighty-nine-h of the state finance law, or the authorized representative of such officer, to inspect any return filed under this article, or may furnish to such officer or the officer's authorized representative an abstract of any such return or supply such officer or such representative with information concerning an item contained in any such return, or disclosed by any investigation of tax liability under this article.

2. The commissioner, in his or her discretion and pursuant to such rules and regulations as he or she may adopt, may permit the appropriate officers of any other state which regulates or taxes medical cannabis, or the duly authorized representatives of such officers, to inspect returns or reports made pursuant to this article, or may furnish to such other officers, or duly authorized representatives, a copy of any such return or report or an abstract of the information therein contained, or any portion thereof, or may supply any such officers or such representatives with information relating to the business of a registered organization making returns or reports hereunder. The commissioner may refuse to supply information pursuant to this subdivision to the officers of any other state if the statutes of the state represented by such officers, do not grant substantially similar privileges to the commissioner, but such refusal shall not be mandatory. Information shall not be supplied to the appropriate officers of any other state which regulates or taxes medical cannabis, or the duly authorized representatives of any of such officers, unless such officer or other representatives shall agree not to divulge or make known in any manner the information so supplied, but such officers may transmit such information to their employees or legal representatives when necessary, who in turn shall be subject to the same restrictions as those hereby imposed upon such officer or other representatives.

3. (a) Any officer or employee of the state who willfully violates the provisions of subdivision one or two of this section shall be dismissed from office and be incapable of holding any public office in this state for a period of five years thereafter.

(b) Cross-reference: For criminal penalties, see article thirty-seven of this chapter.

ARTICLE 20-C. TAX ON ADULT-USE CANNABIS PRODUCTS

Tax Law § 492. Definitions.

For purposes of this article, the following definitions shall apply:

(a) "Adult-use cannabis product" or "adult-use cannabis" has the same meaning as the term is defined in section three of the cannabis law. For purposes of this article, under no circumstances shall adult-use cannabis product include medical cannabis or cannabinoid hemp product as defined in section three of the cannabis law.

(b) "Cannabis" means all parts of the a plant of the genus cannabis, whether growing or not; the seeds thereof; the resin extracted from any part of the plant; and every compound, manufacture, salt, derivative, mixture, or preparation of the plant, its seeds or resin. For purposes of this article, cannabis does not include medical cannabis or cannabinoid hemp product as defined in section three of the cannabis law.

(c) "Cannabis edible product" means a product, containing either cannabis or concentrated cannabis and other ingredients, intended for use or consumption through ingestion, including sublingual or oral absorption.

(d) "Cannabis flower" means the flower of a plant of the genus cannabis that has been harvested, dried and cured but has not undergone any processing whereby the plant material is transformed into a concentrate, including, but not limited to, concentrated cannabis, or into an edible or topical product containing cannabis or concentrated cannabis and other ingredients. Cannabis flower excludes leaves and stem.

(e) "Concentrated cannabis" has the same meaning as the term is defined in section three of the cannabis law.

(f) "Distributor" has the same meaning as the term is defined in section three of the cannabis law.

(g) "Illicit cannabis" means and includes cannabis flower, concentrated cannabis, cannabis edible product and cannabis plant on which any tax required to have been paid under this chapter has not been paid. Illicit cannabis shall not include any cannabis lawfully possessed in accordance with the cannabis law or penal law.

(h) "Cannabis plant" means cannabis that has not been harvested, or undergone processing, drying or curing.

(i) "Person" means every individual, partnership, limited liability company, society, association, joint stock company, corporation, estate, receiver, trustee, assignee, referee, and any other person acting in a fiduciary or representative capacity, whether appointed by a court or otherwise, and any combination of the foregoing.

(j) "Sale" means any transfer of title, possession or both, exchange or barter, rental, lease or license to use or consume, conditional, or otherwise, in any manner or by any means whatsoever for a consideration or any agreement therefor.

(k) "Total THC" has the same meaning as the term defined in section three of the cannabis law.

Tax Law § 493. Imposition of tax.

(a) There is hereby imposed a tax on adult-use cannabis products sold by a distributor to a person who sells adult-use cannabis products at retail at the following rates:

(1) cannabis flower at the rate of five-tenths of one cent per milligram of the amount of total THC, as reflected on the product label;

(2) concentrated cannabis at the rate of eight-tenths of one cent per milligram of the amount of total THC, as reflected on the product label; and

(3) cannabis edible product at the rate of three cents per milligram of the amount of total THC, as reflected on the product label. This tax shall accrue at the time of such sale or transfer. Where a person who distributes adult-use cannabis is licensed under the cannabis law as a microbusiness or registered organization, such person shall be liable for the tax, and such tax shall accrue at the time of the retail sale.

(b) In addition to any other tax imposed by this chapter or other law, there is hereby imposed a tax of nine percent of the amount charged for the sale or transfer of adult-use cannabis products to a retail customer by a person who sells adult-use cannabis products at retail. This tax is imposed on the person who sells adult-use cannabis at retail and shall accrue at the time of such sale or transfer.

(c) In addition to the taxes imposed by subdivisions (a) and (b) of this section, there is hereby imposed a tax on the sale or transfer of adult-use cannabis products to a retail customer by a person who sells adult-use cannabis products at retail at the rate of four percent of the amount charged by such person for such adult-use cannabis product, which tax shall accrue at the time of such sale or transfer. The tax imposed by this subdivision is imposed on a person who sells adult-use cannabis products at retail, and shall be paid to the commissioner in trust for and on account of a city having a population of a million or more, and counties (other than counties wholly within such a city), towns, villages, and cities with a population of less than a million in which a retail dispensary is located.

(d) The taxes imposed by this section shall not apply to sales of adult-use cannabis to a person holding a cannabis research license under section thirty-nine of the cannabis law.

Tax Law § 494. Registration and renewal.

(a) (i) Every distributor on whom tax is imposed under this article and every person who sells adult-use cannabis products at retail must file with the commissioner a properly completed application for a certificate of registration before engaging in business. An application for a certificate of registration must be submitted electronically, on a form prescribed by the commissioner, and must be accompanied by a non-refundable application fee of six hundred dollars. A certificate of registration shall not be assignable or transferable and shall be destroyed immediately upon such person ceasing to do business as specified in such certificate, or in the event that such business never commenced.

(ii) Provided, however, that the commissioner shall refund or credit an application fee paid with respect to the registration of an adult-use cannabis business in this state if, prior to the beginning of the period with respect to which such registration relates, the certificate of registration described in subparagraph (i) of this paragraph is returned to the department or, if such certificate has been destroyed, the operator of such business satisfactorily accounts to the commissioner for the missing certificate, but such business may not sell adult-use cannabis products in this state during such period, unless it is re-registered. Such refund or credit shall be deemed a refund of tax paid in error, provided, however, no interest shall be allowed or paid on any such refund.

(b) (1) The commissioner shall refuse to issue a certificate of registration to any applicant and shall revoke the certificate of registration of any such person who does not possess a valid license from the office of cannabis management. The commissioner may refuse to issue a certificate of registration to any applicant where such applicant:

(i) has a past-due liability as that term is defined in section one hundred seventy-one-v of this chapter;

(ii) has had a certificate of registration under this article, a license from the office of cannabis management, or any license or registration provided for in this chapter revoked or suspended where such revocation or suspension was in effect on the date the application was filed or ended within one year from the date on which such application was filed;

(iii) has been convicted of a crime provided for in this chapter within one year from the date on which such application was filed or the certificate was issued, as applicable;

(iv) willfully fails to file a report or return required by this article;

(v) willfully files, causes to be filed, gives or causes to be given a report, return, certificate or affidavit required by this article which is false; or

(vi) willfully fails to collect or truthfully account for or pay over any tax imposed by this article.

(2) In addition to the grounds for revocation in paragraph (1) of this subdivision, where a person who holds a certificate of registration is determined to have possessed or sold illicit cannabis: (1) such registration may be revoked for a period of up to one year for the first such possession or sale; (2) for a second such possession or sale within a period of five years by such person, the registration of such person may be revoked for a period of up to three years; (3) for a third such possession or sale within a period of up to five years by such person, the registration of such person may be revoked for a period of five years. A certificate of registration may be revoked pursuant to this paragraph immediately upon such person's receipt of written notice of revocation from the commissioner.

(c) A certificate of registration shall be valid for the period specified thereon, unless earlier suspended or revoked. Upon the expiration of the term stated on a certificate of registration, such certificate shall be null and void.

(d) Every holder of a certificate of registration must notify the commissioner of changes to any of the information stated on the certificate, or of changes to any information contained in the application for the certificate of registration. Such notification must be made on or before the last day of the month in which a change occurs and must be made electronically on a form prescribed by the commissioner.

(e) Every holder of a certificate of registration under this article shall be required to reapply prior to such certificate's expiration, during a reapplication period established by the commissioner. Such reapplication period shall not occur more frequently than every two years. Such reapplication shall be subject to the same requirements and conditions as an initial application, including grounds for refusal and the payment of the application fee.

(f) Any person who is required to obtain a certificate of registration under subdivision (a) of this section who possesses adult-use cannabis products without such certificate shall be subject to a penalty of five hundred dollars for each month or part thereof during which adult-use cannabis products are possessed without such certificate, not to exceed ten thousand dollars in the aggregate.

Tax Law § 495. Returns and payment of tax.

(a) Every person on whom tax is imposed under this article shall, on or before the twentieth day of the month following each quarterly period ending on the last day of February, May, August, and November, respectively, file electronically with the commissioner a return on forms to be prescribed by the commissioner, showing the total amount of tax due in such quarterly period, and including such other information as the commissioner may require.

(b) Every person required to file a return under this section shall, at the time of filing such return, pay electronically to the commissioner the total amount of tax due for the period covered by such return. If a return is not filed when due, the tax shall be due on the day on which the return is required to be filed.

Tax Law § 496. Records to be kept; penalties.

(a) Records to be kept. Every distributor on whom tax is imposed under this article and every person who sells adult-use cannabis products at retail shall maintain complete and accurate records in such form as the commissioner may require including, but not limited to, such items as the total THC content of the adult-use cannabis products sold to or produced by such person; complete records of every retail sale of adult-use cannabis, and any other record or information required by the commissioner. Such records must be preserved for a period of three years after the filing of the return to which such records relate and must be provided to the commissioner upon request.

(b) Penalties. In addition to any other penalty provided in this article or otherwise imposed by law, every distributor on whom tax is imposed under this article and every person who sells adult-use cannabis products at retail who fails to maintain or make available to the commissioner the records required by this section is subject to a penalty not to exceed five hundred dollars for each month or part thereof for which the failure occurs. This penalty may not be imposed more than once for failures for the same monthly period or part thereof. If the commissioner determines that a failure to maintain or make available records in any month was entirely due to reasonable cause and not to willful neglect, the commissioner must remit the penalty for that month.

Tax Law § 496-a. Returns to be secret.

(a) Except in accordance with proper judicial order or as in this section or otherwise provided by law, it shall be unlawful for the commissioner, any officer or employee of the department, or any officer or person who, pursuant to this section, is permitted to inspect any return or report or to whom a copy, an abstract or a portion of any return or report is furnished, or to whom any information contained in any return or report is furnished, or any person who in any manner may acquire knowledge of the contents of a return or report filed pursuant to this article to divulge or make known in any manner the content or any other information contained in any return or report required under this article. The officers charged with the custody of such returns or reports shall not be required to produce any of them or evidence of anything contained in them in any action or preceding in any court, except on behalf of the state, the office of cannabis management, or the commissioner in an action or proceeding involving the collection of tax due under this chapter to which the state or the commissioner is a party or a claimant or on behalf of any party to any action or proceeding under the provisions of this article, when the returns or the reports or the facts shown thereby are directly involved in such action or proceeding, or in an action or proceeding related to the regulation or taxation of adult-use cannabis products on behalf of officers to whom information shall have been supplied as provided in this section, in any of which events the court may require the production of, and may admit in evidence so much of said returns or reports or of the facts shown thereby as are pertinent to the action or proceeding and no more. Nothing herein shall be construed to prohibit the commissioner, in his or her discretion, from allowing the inspection or delivery of a certified copy of any return or report filed under this article or of any information contained in any such return or report by or to a duly authorized officer or employee of the office of cannabis management; or by or to the attorney general or other legal representatives of the state when an action shall have been recommended or commenced pursuant to this chapter in which such returns or reports or the facts shown thereby are directly involved; or the inspection of the returns or reports required under this article by the comptroller or duly designated officer or employee of the state department of audit and control, for purposes of the audit of a refund of any tax paid by any person under this article; nor to prohibit the delivery to such person or a duly authorized representative of such person, a certified copy of any return or report filed by such person pursuant to this article, nor to prohibit the publication of statistics so classified as to prevent the identification of particular returns or reports and the items thereof. This section shall also not be construed to prohibit the disclosure, for tax administration purposes, to the division of the budget and the office of the state comptroller, of information aggregated from the returns filed by all persons subject to the taxes imposed by the article, whether the number of such persons is one or more. Provided further that, notwithstanding the provisions of this subdivision, the commissioner may, in his or her discretion, permit the proper officer of any county entitled to receive any distribution of the monies received on account of the tax imposed by subdivision (c) of section four hundred ninety-three of this article, or the authorized representative of such officer, to inspect any return filed under this article, or may furnish to such officer or the officer's authorized representative an abstract of any such return or supply such officer or representative with information concerning an item contained in any such return, or disclosed by any investigation of tax liability under this article.

(b) The commissioner, in his or her discretion, may permit the appropriate officers of any other state that regulates or taxes cannabis or the duly authorized representatives of any such officers, to inspect returns or reports made pursuant to this article, or may furnish to such other officers, or their duly authorized representatives, a copy of any such return or report or an abstract of the information therein contained, or any portion thereof, or may supply any such officers or such representatives with information relating to the business of a person making returns or reports hereunder solely for purposes of tax administration. The commissioner may refuse to supply information pursuant to this subdivision to the officers of any other state if the statutes of the state represented by such officers do not grant substantially similar privileges to the commissioner, but such refusal shall not be mandatory. Information shall not be supplied to the officers of any state that regulates or taxes cannabis, or their duly authorized representatives of any such officers, unless such officer or other representatives shall agree not to divulge or make known in any manner the information so supplied, but such officers may transmit such information to their employees or legal representatives when necessary, who in turn shall be subject to the same restrictions as those hereby imposed upon such officer or other representatives.

(c)(1) Any officer or employee of the state who willfully violates the provisions of subdivision (a) or (b) of this section shall be dismissed from office and be incapable of holding any public office in this state for a period of five years thereafter.

(2) For criminal penalties, see article thirty-seven of this chapter.

Tax Law § 496-b. Administrative provisions.

(a) The provisions of article twenty-seven of this chapter shall apply to the taxes imposed by section four hundred ninety-three of this article in the same manner and with the same force and effect as if the language of such article had been incorporated in full into this section and had expressly referred to the tax imposed by this article, except to the extent that any provision of such article is either inconsistent with a provision of this article or is not relevant to this article.

(b)(1) All taxes, interest, and penalties collected or received by the commissioner under this article shall be deposited and disposed of pursuant to the provisions of section one hundred seventy-one-a of this chapter, provided that an amount equal to one hundred percent collected under this article less any amount determined by the commissioner to be reserved by the comptroller for refunds or reimbursements shall be paid by the comptroller to the credit of the cannabis revenue fund established by section ninety-nine-ii of the state finance law. Of the total revenue collected or received under this article, the comptroller shall retain such amount as the commissioner may determine to be necessary for refunds. The commissioner is authorized and directed to deduct from the registration fees under subdivision (a) of section four hundred ninety-four of this article, before deposit into the cannabis revenue fund designated by the comptroller, a reasonable amount necessary to effectuate refunds of appropriations of the department to reimburse the department for the costs incurred to administer, collect, and distribute the taxes imposed by this article.

(2) All taxes, interest, and penalties collected or received by the commissioner under subdivision (c) of section four hundred ninety-three of this article shall be deposited and disposed of pursuant to the provisions of section one hundred seventy-one-a of this chapter, provided that an amount equal to one hundred percent collected under such subdivision (c), less any amount determined by the commissioner to be reserved by the comptroller for refunds or reimbursements, shall be paid to the comptroller and the commissioner shall certify to the comptroller the amount of tax, penalties, and interest attributable to retail sales within a city with a population of a million or more and counties (other than a county wholly within such city). Such amount will be distributed by the comptroller to such city and such counties. Such counties shall be entitled to retain twenty-five percent of the monies so distributed. Such counties shall distribute the remaining seventy-five percent of such monies to the towns, villages, and cities within such county in which a retail dispensary is located in proportion to the sales of adult-use cannabis products by the retail dispensaries in such towns, villages and cities as reported by a seed-to-sale system, provided, however, where a retail dispensary is located in a village within a town that both permit cannabis retail sales, then the county shall distribute the monies attributable to such retail dispensary to such town and village in such proportion as may be agreed upon by the elective governing body of such town and of such village or, in the absence of such an agreement, shall evenly divide such monies between such town and village. Such counties shall distribute the monies received for each quarter ending on the last day of February, May, August or November to such towns, villages and

cities no later than the thirtieth day after receipt of such monies from the comptroller.

Tax Law § 496-c. Illicit cannabis penalty.

(a) In addition to any other civil or criminal penalties that may apply, any person knowingly in possession of or knowingly having control over illicit cannabis, as defined in section four hundred ninety-two of this article, after notice and an opportunity for a hearing, shall be liable for a civil penalty of not less than two hundred dollars per ounce of illicit cannabis flower, five dollars per milligram of the total weight of any illicit cannabis edible product, fifty dollars per gram of the total weight of any product containing illicit cannabis concentrate, and five hundred dollars per illicit cannabis plant, but not to exceed four hundred dollars per ounce of illicit cannabis flower, ten dollars per milligram of the total weight of any illicit cannabis edible product, one hundred dollars per gram of the total weight of any product containing illicit cannabis concentrate, and one thousand dollars per illicit cannabis plant for a first violation, and for a second and subsequent violation within three years following a prior violation shall be liable for a civil penalty of not less than four hundred dollars per ounce of illicit cannabis flower, ten dollars per milligram of the total weight of any illicit cannabis edible product, one hundred dollars per gram of the total weight of any product containing illicit cannabis concentrate, and one thousand dollars per illicit cannabis plant, but not to exceed five hundred dollars per ounce of illicit cannabis flower, twenty dollars per milligram of the total weight of any illicit cannabis edible product, two hundred dollars per gram of the total weight of any product containing illicit cannabis concentrate, and two thousand dollars per illicit cannabis plant.

(b) No enforcement action taken under this section shall be construed to limit any other criminal or civil liability of anyone in possession of illicit cannabis.

(c) The penalty imposed by this section shall not apply to persons lawfully in possession of less than two ounces of adult-use cannabis or ten grams of concentrated cannabis in accordance with the cannabis law or penal law.

XIII. Vehicle and Traffic Law

Vehicle and Traffic Law § 1227. Consumption or possession of alcoholic beverages in certain motor vehicles.

1. The drinking of alcoholic beverages or consumption of cannabis, or the possession of an open container containing an alcoholic beverage, in a motor vehicle located upon the public highways or right-of-way public highway is prohibited. Any operator or passenger violating this section shall be guilty of a traffic infraction.

The provisions of this section shall not be deemed to prohibit the drinking of alcoholic beverages, the consumption of cannabis by means other than burning, or the possession of an open container containing an alcoholic beverage by passengers in passenger vehicles operated pursuant to a certificate or permit issued by the department of transportation or the United States department of transportation. Furthermore, the provisions of this section shall not be deemed to prohibit the possession of wine which is: (a) resealed in accordance with the provisions of subdivision four of section eighty-one of the alcoholic beverage control law; and (b) is transported in the vehicle's trunk or is transported behind the last upright seat or in an area not normally occupied by the driver or passenger in a motor vehicle that is not equipped with a trunk.

2. For the purposes of this section, a passenger vehicle shall mean a vehicle designed to carry ten or more passengers and used to carry passengers for profit or hire.

Part 2: Regulations

Title 1. Department of Agriculture and Markets

Chapter III. Plant Industry

SUBCHAPTER F. INDUSTRIAL HEMP

Part 159. Industrial Hemp Agricultural Pilot Programs

1 CRR-NY § 159.1. Definitions.

For the purpose of this Part, the following terms shall have the following meanings:

(a) Authorization holder means an institution of higher education that has been granted authority by the commissioner to acquire and possess industrial hemp to study its growth and cultivation.

(b) Commissioner means the Commissioner of Agriculture and Markets of the State of New York.

(c) Department means the Department of Agriculture and Markets of the State of New York.

(d) Dispose, and any variant thereof, means to render unusable for any purpose.

(e) Industrial hemp means the same as that term is defined in Agriculture and Markets Law section 505(1).

(f) Institution of higher education means the same as that term is defined in Agriculture and Markets Law section 505(2).

(g) Person means an individual, partnership, corporation, limited liability company, association, or any business entity by whatever name designated and whether or not incorporated, unless the context clearly indicates otherwise.

(h) Registered premises means any facility, location, or property owned, leased, or licensed, which is under the control of the authorization holder and certified by the commissioner as a site where industrial hemp may be grown or cultivated, harvested, stored, studied, or disposed of.

(i) Secured facility means a building or structure where access is restricted only to authorized persons.

(j) State means the State of New York.

1 CRR-NY § 159.2. Authorization to grow and cultivate industrial hemp.

(a) Industrial hemp and industrial hemp seeds may not be possessed, grown, cultivated, sold, distributed, transported, or processed unless an application therefor has been submitted to and authority has been granted by the commissioner.

(b) Only an institution of higher education may submit an application to the commissioner for authorization to grow, cultivate, possess, sell, distribute, transport, or process industrial hemp.

(c) Industrial hemp may only be grown, cultivated, or processed upon registered premises.

(d) An application to grow, cultivate, possess, sell, distribute, transport, or process industrial hemp ("application") shall be made upon a form prescribed by the commissioner and shall include an application fee of $500. Each application and renewal application shall provide the information deemed necessary by the commissioner for the administration of this Part, including but not limited to:

(1) a description of each premises where industrial hemp will be grown or cultivated, harvested, stored, studied, processed or disposed of, by physical address and by GPS co-ordinates;

(2) a diagram for each premises where industrial hemp is cultivated, possessed, sold to, distributed to, or transported from, that visually depicts the buildings, structures and improvements on the premises and identifies their use, and that sets forth the relevant activities conducted at the premises; and

(3) a detailed summary of the issues and matters that the applicant intends to study in conjunction with growing, cultivating, or processing industrial hemp which may include:

(i) the soils, growing conditions, and harvest methods suitable for the growth or cultivation of various types of industrial hemp in the State;

(ii) the cultivars suitable for the growth or cultivation of various types of industrial hemp, including the cost of each cultivar; the yield of industrial hemp attributable to each such cultivar; and the inputs required to assure that each such cultivar, when planted, results in a satisfactory yield of industrial hemp;

(iii) the markets that the applicant has identified, in consultation with appropriate commercial interests, that exist or that could feasibly be developed for various types of industrial hemp, including but not limited to markets for apparel, energy, food, paper, and tools;

(iv) the means and methods that could feasibly be used to process, market, advertise, expose, or publicize products that contain, in whole or in predominate part, industrial hemp, to facilitate the wholesale and/or retail sale thereof;

(4) a transportation plan, if industrial hemp will be moved from one location on the registered premises to another, from one registered premises to another registered premises, or from a registered premises to an unregistered premises, that sets forth information relevant to the security requirements set forth in section 159.6 of this Part;

(5) a security plan that sets forth the measures that the applicant intends to take to ensure that the security requirements set forth in section 159.6 of this Part are complied with.

(e) Applications shall be evaluated in the order in which they are received. In the event that two or more applications are received at the same time, the department will determine the order of receipt at random.

(f) The commissioner may decline to grant authority to grow, cultivate, process, sell, distribute, transport, and possess industrial hemp, and may revoke or decline to renew an authorization to grow, cultivate, possess, sell, distribute, transport, and process industrial hemp ("an authorization"), if he or she finds, after investigation and opportunity to be heard, that:

(1) the application does not set forth the information required pursuant to subdivision (d) of this section and fails to set forth such information within 20 days after the applicant has received notice that the required information was not set forth on the application; or

(2) ten authorizations to grow and cultivate industrial hemp have been issued and are in effect; or

(3) the applicant or authorization holder is not capable for whatever reason of complying, or has failed to comply, with the provisions of this Part or with State or Federal law relating to the possession, sale, cultivation, distribution, transportation and processing of industrial hemp; or

(4) the department determines, in its sole discretion, that it is or will be impracticable to regulate the

applicant's or authorization holder's adherence to the requirements set forth in this Part; or

(5) the authorization holder has not complied with the requirements set forth in section 159.3(e) of this Part.

(g) An authorization shall be for a period of three years from the date application therefor was approved by the commissioner. Notwithstanding the preceding, the commissioner may grant or renew an authorization for a period of more than three years if he or she determines that the issues and matters that the applicant or authorization holder intends to study or is studying cannot be adequately and fully studied within three years from the date that authorization is granted or renewed. An application for renewal shall be submitted to the commissioner no later than 30 days prior to the date that the authorization expires and shall include an application fee of $500.

(h) The commissioner may grant or renew an authorization with conditions, including but not limited to one or more of the following:

(1) industrial hemp is grown and cultivated on a limited number of acres;

(2) industrial hemp is grown and cultivated in a limited volume; or

(3) industrial hemp is not sold or distributed to a person(s) unwilling or unable to properly carry out the business of growing, cultivating, possessing, selling, distributing, transporting, or processing industrial hemp.

(i) An authorization holder may surrender its authorization at any time; however, the requirements set forth in section 159.6 of this Part shall remain applicable and binding upon such authorization holder until its authorization period would otherwise have expired.

1 CRR-NY § 159.3. Requirements.

(a) Studies and reports.

(1) An authorization holder shall, no later than three months after the date that his or her application was approved by the commissioner, furnish to the commissioner a report that provides, in detail:

(i) its findings and conclusions regarding the issues and matters set forth in its application; and

(ii) the name and address of each person who, as of the date of submission of such report, will receive industrial hemp or to whom industrial hemp will be sold or distributed to.

(2) An authorization holder shall every three months after furnishing a report of the type referred to in paragraph (1) of this subdivision, furnish a report that supplements, in detail, the information, findings and conclusions set forth in earlier report(s).

(3) An authorization holder may study issues and matters different from those set forth in its application, with the prior written approval of the commissioner, and all reports required pursuant to this section, furnished after the date of the commissioner's approval, shall set forth findings and conclusions regarding such different issues and matters.

(b) Except as provided in section 159.6(a) of this Part and in this subdivision, industrial hemp may be grown, cultivated or harvested only on the registered premises. Industrial hemp that has been harvested shall be stored in a secured facility except when it is being transported within the registered premises, to a laboratory for testing, or to another registered premises or facility approved by the commissioner.

(c) Industrial hemp may be transported only in an enclosed, locked compartment of a truck or van where it cannot be seen from the outside of the vehicle, the contents of the vehicle are not disclosed, and the operator of the vehicle has been approved by the authorization holder to transport industrial hemp, as indicated in the record required to be maintained pursuant to section 159.4(a)(1) of this Part.

(d) Testing and disposition.

(1) An authorization holder shall prepare, maintain, and make available to the commissioner, upon request, a record that sets forth an accurate inventory of industrial hemp plants and seeds and shall reasonably ensure that no plant is possessed or grown or cultivated that would not meet the definition of industrial hemp because it contains a concentration of more than 0.3 percent of delta-9 tetrahydrocannabinol, on a dry basis.

(2) An authorization holder shall ensure that a representative sample of plants grown or cultivated from each variety of seed used for the purpose of growing or cultivating industrial hemp is analyzed at a laboratory approved by the commissioner, to determine the concentration of delta-9 tetrahydrocannabinol therein. The authorization holder shall furnish a report that sets forth the results of analysis(es) to the commissioner promptly after such analysis(es) is made, in a form approved by the commissioner.

(3) An authorization holder shall dispose of all plants determined, after laboratory analysis, to have a concentration of more than 0.3 percent of delta-9 tetrahydrocannabinol on a dry basis, and shall prepare and maintain on the registered premises for a period of two years, a record that sets forth the information required in section 159.4(a)(4)(iii) of this Part. The authorization holder shall make available to the department such records upon request, in a form and at a location satisfactory to the commissioner.

(4) An authorization holder shall prepare a record that sets forth the name and address of each person who will receive industrial hemp or to whom industrial hemp has been sold or distributed and the volume of industrial hemp sold or distributed on each occasion when industrial hemp was sold or distributed.

(e) An authorization holder shall, no later than 15 days after having been granted authorization, notify, in writing, the applicable unit or units of law enforcement, including the unit or units of law enforcement in the political subdivision in which the registered premises is located, that it has received such authorization and shall provide such unit or units of law enforcement a copy of the security plan referred to in section 159.2(d)(5) of this Part. The authorization holder shall, no later than 15 days after having notified such unit or units of law enforcement, provide the department with a copy of such notification. An authorization holder shall adequately monitor registered premises under its control and shall notify the appropriate unit or units of law enforcement and the department regarding facts and circumstances that indicate that industrial hemp has been or may be held or possessed in violation of the provisions of this Part.

(f)

(1) Notwithstanding any provision of this Part to the contrary, an authorization holder may enter into a contract with a person for that person to be involved in growing or cultivating, harvesting, storing, studying, transporting, processing and/or disposing of industrial hemp, if:

(i) the contract has, prior to execution, been approved by the commissioner; and

(ii) the contract requires such subcontractor to comply with all relevant provisions of this Part.

(2) The commissioner may decline to renew or may revoke an authorization to grow and cultivate industrial hemp if he or she finds, after investigation, that such subcontractor has failed to comply with all relevant provisions of this Part.

(g) An authorization holder may sell and distribute industrial hemp to a person if:

(1) such sale or distribution is made pursuant to a contract that has, prior to execution, been approved by the commissioner; and

(2) such contract requires the person to whom such industrial hemp has been sold or distributed to maintain a record that sets forth the volume of industrial hemp received, the use to which such industrial hemp was put and the volume of industrial hemp allocated to each use, and the volume of industrial hemp disposed of.

1 CRR-NY § 159.4. Recordkeeping.

(a) An authorization holder shall create, maintain, and make available accurate records, in a form and at a location satisfactory to the commissioner, that set forth the following information:

  (1) a description of the registered premises at which industrial hemp is grown or cultivated that is in substantially the same form as the description required to be provided pursuant to section 159.2(d)(1) of this Part;

  (2) the name of the cultivar(s) grown and the volume of each cultivar purchased, acquired and/or used, for the appropriate growing season; and

  (3) the volume of industrial hemp grown or cultivated, for the appropriate growing season; and

      (i) the volume of industrial hemp harvested; and

      (ii) the volume of industrial hemp studied and the name and address of each person who or that has conducted or been involved in such study; and

      (iii) the volume of industrial hemp disposed of, the date and location of each disposal, and the method of each disposal;

  (4) the name of each person to whom industrial hemp is sold and/or distributed to, the date of each such sale or distribution, and the volume of industrial hemp sold or distributed, on each occasion when industrial hemp was sold or distributed.

(b) The records and materials referred to in subdivision (a) of this section and section 159.3(d)(4) of this Part shall be maintained on the registered premises, and the records and materials referred to in section 159.3(g)(2) of this Part shall be maintained on the premises of the person to whom industrial hemp has been sold or distributed, and all such records shall be made available to the commissioner for two years from the date they were made or prepared.

(c) Each record, material, and plan required to be prepared pursuant to this Part shall be revised, as frequently as necessary, so as to be accurate.

1 CRR-NY § 159.5. Inspections.

(a) The authorization holder shall inspect the registered premises as often as necessary to ensure compliance with the requirements set forth in this Part.

(b) The registered premises of an authorization holder are subject to inspection by the commissioner and by his or her authorized agents, employees, or officers, pursuant to Agriculture and Markets Law section 20, as often and to the extent necessary to ensure compliance with the provisions of this Part and State and Federal law relating to the possession, sale, or cultivation of industrial hemp. The commissioner may authorize agents, employees, or officers of the New York State Department of Health and/or local law enforcement to accompany him or her during an inspection of the registered premises of an authorization holder.

1 CRR-NY § 159.6. Security measures.

(a) An authorization holder shall take all actions necessary to ensure that industrial hemp is not acquired, possessed, grown or cultivated, harvested, stored, transported, sold, processed, distributed or disposed of except under conditions that ensure that it will not be used in violation of State or Federal law.

(b) The authorization holder shall take measures, satisfactory to the commissioner, to ensure compliance with the requirements set forth in subdivision (a) of this section, including but not limited to:

(1) restricting access to areas of the registered premises where industrial hemp is grown or cultivated; and

(2) posting signs, each of which set forth, in readily observable block letters, the words "NO TRESPASSING. FACILITY CONTAINS INDUSTRIAL HEMP. UNAUTHORIZED POSSESSION OF INDUSTRIAL HEMP IS SUBJECT TO PROSECUTION PURSUANT TO ARTICLE 220 OF THE PENAL LAW". A sufficient number of signs shall be posted so that a sign and the information required to be set forth on a sign can be read, from a distance of not less than 100 feet, from any location around the perimeter of the registered premises where industrial hemp is grown or cultivated, or held; and

(3) providing for equipment and/or other fixtures such as fences that are reasonably designed to prevent unauthorized persons from entering the registered premises and/or having their presence therein undetected.

(c) Nothing in this section is intended to apply to any finished or marketable product which contains industrial hemp but from which the hemp may not practically be extricated in the form of industrial hemp.

Title 9. Executive Department

SUBTITLE B. DIVISION OF ALCOHOLIC BEVERAGE CONTROL

Chapter II. Rules of the Office of Cannabis Management

PART 114. CANNABINOID HEMP.

9 CCR-NY § 114.1. Definitions.

For purposes of this Part, the following terms shall have the following meanings:

(a) Broad spectrum means hemp extract or cannabinoid hemp product containing multiple cannabinoids, but where Δ9-Tetrahydrocannabinol (THC) has been removed to non-detectable levels using a fit-for-purpose method, with a limit of quantification of less than 0.01% THC.

(b) Cannabidiol or CBD means the naturally occurring hemp-derived phytocannabinoid cannabidiol, but does not include synthetic cannabidiol.

(c) Cannabinoids means any hemp-derived phytocannabinoid, including but not limited to, Tetrahydrocannabinol (THC), tetrahydrocannabinolic acid (THCA), cannabidiol (CBD), cannabidiolic acid (CBDA), cannabinol (CBN), cannabigerol (CBG), cannabichromene (CBC), cannabicyclol (CBL), cannabivarin (CBV), tetrahydrocannabivarin (THCV), cannabidivarin (CBDV), cannabichromevarin (CBCV), cannabigerovarin (CBGV), cannabigerol monomethyl ether (CBGM), cannabielsoin (CBE), cannabicitran (CBT). Cannabinoids do not include synthetic cannabinoids, as that term is defined in subdivision (g) of section 3306 of the Public Health Law and section 9-1.1 of Title 10 of the Official Compilation of Codes, Rules and Regulations of the State of New York.

(d) Cannabinoid hemp product means hemp or any product manufactured or derived from hemp, including hemp derived terpenes, in its final form, used for human consumption. Cannabinoid hemp product shall not include cosmetics.

(e) Cannabinoid hemp retailer means a person licensed by the office to sell cannabinoid hemp products, including via the internet, to consumers in New York State.

(f) Cannabinoid hemp farm processor means a cannabinoid hemp processor that is licensed to cultivate hemp by the New York State Department of Agriculture & Markets and is permitted to manufacture cannabinoid hemp flower products. A cannabinoid hemp farm processor shall not:

   (1) produce more than 1,000 pounds of dried hemp annually;

   (2) purchase or sell hemp or hemp extract other than those produced from hemp grown on his or her own farm; or

   (3) perform extraction as defined in subdivision (l) of this Section.

(g) Cannabinoid hemp processor means a person licensed by the office to extract hemp extract and/or manufacture cannabinoid hemp products in New York State, whether in intermediate or final form, to be used for human consumption.

(h) Certificate of analysis means a certified report from an independent third-party laboratory meeting all of the requirements of section 114.10 of this Part, describing its analytical testing and results.

(i) Corrective action plan means a plan submitted by a licensee and approved by the office under this Part for the licensee to correct a violation or non-compliance with this Part.

(j) Cosmetic means a cosmetic meeting the requirements of section 321 of Title 21 of the United States Code and recognized as such by the office.

(k) Craft means a cannabinoid hemp product manufactured from hemp grown by a licensed hemp grower who grows less than 1,000 pounds of dried hemp annually and the hemp is hand trimmed, hang dried and if a cannabinoid hemp flower product hand packaged

(l) Distillate means hemp extract where a segment of one or more cannabinoids from an initial extraction are selectively concentrated through heating and cooling, with all impurities removed.

(m) Distribute means to offer or sell cannabinoid hemp products to a cannabinoid hemp retailer, for retail sale to consumers within New York state.

(n) Extract or Extraction means the process of concentrating or isolating one or more cannabinoids from hemp or cannabinoid hemp.

(o) Flower product means any form of cannabinoid hemp product consisting of the flower, buds, leaves, or stems of the hemp plant, including trimmings thereof, intended for retail sale to consumers with minimal processing. Provided, however that flower product shall not include:

   (1) any food, food ingredient, food additive, or items that are generally recognized as safe, pursuant to state or federal law; or

   (2) any other product, including microgreens, sprouts or certain hemp leaf products, as determined by the office.

(p) Full spectrum means hemp extract or cannabinoid hemp product containing multiple hemp-derived cannabinoids, terpenes, and other naturally occurring compounds, processed without intentional complete removal of any compound and without the addition of isolated cannabinoids, with a final Δ9-Tetrahydrocannabinol concentration of not greater than 0.3%.

(q) Hemp means the plant Cannabis sativa L. and any part of such plant, including the seeds thereof and all derivatives, extracts, cannabinoids, isomers, acids, salts, and salts of isomers, whether growing or not, with a Δ9-Tetrahydrocannabinol concentration of not more than 0.3% on a dry weight basis.

(r) Hemp extract means all derivatives, extracts, cannabinoids, isomers, acids, salts of isomers derived from hemp and used for human consumption, with a Δ9-Tetrahydrocannabinol concentration of not more than an amount determined by the office pursuant to this Part. Hemp extract shall not include:

> (1) any food, food ingredient or food additive that is generally recognized as safe pursuant to federal law; or

> (2) any extract derived from hemp that is not used for human consumption.

(s) Isolate means hemp extract or cannabinoid hemp product comprised of 95 percent or more of a single cannabinoid compound.

(t) Lot or batch means any cannabinoid hemp product produced during a period of time under similar conditions and identified by a specific code that allows traceability.

(u) Manufacture means to prepare, treat, modify, compound, process, package or otherwise manipulate hemp or hemp extract into a cannabinoid hemp product. Manufacturing shall not include:

> (1) growing, cultivating, cloning, harvesting, drying, curing, grinding or trimming when authorized pursuant to Article 29-A of the Agriculture and Markets Law; or

> (2) extraction as defined in subdivision (l) of this Section.

(v) New York Hemp Product means a cannabinoid hemp product that is derived from hemp exclusively grown, extracted and manufactured in New York, in compliance with section 114.13 of this Part.

(w) Person means an individual, partnership, corporation, limited liability company, association, or any business entity or institution of higher education, by whatever name designated and whether or not incorporated.

(x) Serious adverse event means a medical occurrence associated with the use of a cannabinoid hemp product in a human that results in one or more of the following outcomes: death, a life-threatening event, inpatient hospitalization or prolongation of existing hospitalization, a persistent or significant incapacity or substantial disruption of the ability to conduct normal life functions, or a congenital anomaly/birth defect.

(y) Total Δ9-Tetrahydrocannabinol concentration means [Δ9-Tetrahydrocannabinol] + (0.877 x [tetrahydrocannabinolic acid]).

(z) Used for human consumption means intended by the manufacturer or distributor to be:

> (1) used for human consumption for its cannabinoid content; or

> (2) used in, on or by the human body for its cannabinoid content.

9 CCR-NY § 114.2. Application for Cannabinoid Hemp Processor License.

(a) No person or entity shall extract hemp extract or manufacture cannabinoid hemp product, or hold itself out as a cannabinoid hemp processor, unless it is in compliance with Article 5 of the Cannabis Law and this Part and is licensed by the office as a cannabinoid hemp processor.

(b) An application for licensure shall be submitted to the office on a form prescribed by the office which shall include the following:

(1) the name, address, telephone number and email address of the applicant;

(2) identification of all real property, buildings and facilities that will be used in the extracting of hemp extract or manufacturing of cannabinoid hemp;

(3) the days and hours of operation;

(4) the Federal employer identification number of the applicant;

(5) for applicants extracting hemp extract, identification of all extraction methods that will be used to carry out the extracting;

(6) proof of New York State Workers' Compensation and Disability Insurance coverage, or a Certificate of Attestation of Exemption from coverage;

(7) a summary and description of the applicant's:

> (i) source(s) of hemp and hemp extract to be used by the licensee; and

> (ii) cannabinoid hemp products to be manufactured;

(8) a statement that the applicant's standard operating procedures will incorporate any language or requirements provided by the office and adequately address quality assurance, security, and a plan to ensure all hemp and hemp extract obtained by the applicant meets the requirements of this Part.

(9) evidence that Good Manufacturing Practices (GMP) will be used in the extraction of hemp extract and manufacturing of cannabinoid hemp products. Such evidence shall include one of the following:

> (i) proof of a qualified third-party GMP audit of the applicant's extraction and manufacturing processes; or

> (ii) a detailed plan for obtaining a qualified third-party GMP audit within six months of approval of the application and before beginning operations as a cannabinoid hemp processor in New York State;

(10) a copy and description of any other license(s) issued by state or federal authorities related to the operations of the licensee or the facility where licensed activity will occur;

(11) a description of any other businesses or business activities conducted on the premises to be licensed;

(12) copies of the organizational documents of the applicant;

(13) a statement attesting that the applicant and those in control of the entity, meaning a person that has the ability to direct the activity of the applicant or licensee, including principals, officers or others with such control, are of good moral character;

(14) a statement attesting that the applicant will comply with all applicable state and local laws and regulations relating to the activities in which it intends to engage under the license;

(15) a statement attesting that the applicant has the experience and competency to undertake the activities for which licensure is sought; and

(16) any other information as may be required by the office.

(c) The information required by subparagraph (b)(9) of this Section shall not be required for cannabinoid hemp farm processor applicants.

(d) Applications under this section shall be accompanied by a non-refundable application fee of $1,000 for extraction and manufacturing, $500 for manufacturing only and $100 for cannabinoid hemp farm processors.

(e) Applicants shall verify the truth and accuracy of the information contained in the application. The office, in its discretion, may reject or deny an application if it determines that information contained therein is false, inaccurate or omits a material fact.

9 CCR-NY § 114.3. Application for Cannabinoid Hemp Retail License.

(a) No person shall offer or sell cannabinoid hemp products to consumers in New York State, or hold itself out as a cannabinoid hemp retailer, unless it is in compliance with Article 5 of the Cannabis Law and this Part and is licensed by the office as a cannabinoid hemp retailer.

(b) An application for licensure shall be submitted to the office on a form prescribed by the office, which shall include the following:

(1) the name, address, telephone number and email address of the applicant;

(2) the physical address of any real property where the applicant intends to operate, the days and

hours of operation of such retail facility, and for any online retailer, the internet address of the applicant;

(3) the name, and license number to the extent practicable, of the manufacturer, packer, distributor, or cannabinoid hemp processor, and state or country where the manufacturer, packer, or distributor is located, for all cannabinoid hemp products the applicant intends to offer for sale;

(4) a summary and description of the types and forms of cannabinoid hemp products the applicant intends to offer for sale;

(5) a statement attesting that the applicant will not sell inhalable cannabinoid hemp products or flower products to consumers under 21 years of age;

(6) a statement attesting that the applicant and those in control of the entity, meaning a person or persons that have the ability to direct the activity of the applicant or licensee, including principals, officers or others with such control, are of good moral character;

(7) a statement attesting that the applicant will comply with all applicable state and local laws and regulations relating to the activities in which it intends to engage under the license;

(8) a statement attesting that the applicant will not distribute or sell any cannabinoid hemp product in the form of an injectable, inhaler, or flower product clearly labeled or advertised for the purpose of smoking or in the form of a cigarette, cigar or pre-roll or otherwise packaged or combined with other items designed to facilitate smoking such as rolling papers or pipes, or any other disallowed form as determined by the office;

(9) proof of a certificate of authority from the New York State Department of Taxation and Finance, as applicable; and

(10) any other information as may be required by the office.

(c) All applications under this section shall be accompanied by a refundable license fee of $300 for each retail facility to be licensed by the office.

(d) Applicants shall attest to the truth and accuracy of the information contained in the application. The office, in its discretion, may reject or deny an application if it determines that information contained therein is false, inaccurate or omits a material fact.

9 CCR-NY § 114.4. License Issuance and Denial.

(a) An application for licensure under this Part shall only be approved by the office if:

(1) a complete application has been submitted to the office, along with all necessary fees;

(2) the application demonstrates, to the satisfaction of the office, that the applicant will operate in accordance with Article 5 of the Cannabis Law and this Part;

(3) the applicant is ready, willing and able to properly carry on the activities set forth in the application; and

(4) the applicant is of good moral character.

(b) In determining whether to deny a license application, including an application for renewal, the office may consider the following factors with respect to the applicant, its owner(s) and any affiliated person, including parties with a controlling interest:

(1) false representation or omission of a material fact in filing the license application;

(2) failure to supply further information necessary to process the license application, within thirty days of the office's written request, without satisfactory explanation;

(3) conviction of any crime or sustained charges of administrative violations of state or federal laws, rules or regulations, related to the operation of a site growing, extracting, manufacturing or selling cannabis, hemp or cannabinoid hemp, in accordance with Article 23-A of the Correction Law. Convictions qualifying for expungement pursuant to section 160.50 of the Criminal Procedure Law shall not be considered for purposes of this subdivision;

(4) a pattern of deficiencies, including but not limited to:

(i) refusal or inability to produce records or reports as requested by the office;

(ii) failure to correct deficiencies in accordance with an approved corrective action plan;

(iii) deviation from regulations or standard operating procedures so as to jeopardize the quality of hemp extract or cannabinoid hemp products; and

(iv) refusal to provide office employees with access to the premises;

(5) knowledge of sale of cannabinoid hemp products not meeting the requirements of this Part; and

(6) general failure to comply with the requirements of this Part.

(c) Denial of a license shall preclude the applicant from being licensed as a cannabinoid hemp processor or cannabinoid hemp retailer, either directly or indirectly through any other person.

(d) No license application shall be considered for any applicant who is substantially the same as an applicant who has been denied a license within six months of a determination by the office denying such application. In the event an applicant receives two successive license denials, no license application shall be considered for that applicant within two years of the last determination by the office denying a previous application.

(e) The office will prioritize applications from applicants who previously held a valid research partnership agreement with the New York State Department of Agriculture and Markets pursuant to Article 29-A of the New York State Agriculture and Markets Law. All other applications will be reviewed in the order they are received by the office.

(f) For applicants seeking licensure as a cannabinoid hemp processor, the office may provisionally approve the application. Before a cannabinoid hemp processor license is issued, and the applicant can begin extracting or manufacturing, the provisionally approved applicant must first satisfy the following requirements:

(1) if for Extracting and Manufacturing or Manufacturing Only:

    (i) a copy of a certificate of occupancy, or its equivalent, demonstrating compliance with all local building codes; and

    (ii) a copy of the approved applicant's qualified third-party GMP certification.

(2) payment of licensure fee as follows:

    (i) Cannabinoid Hemp Processor – Extraction and Manufacturing: $3,500;

    (ii) Cannabinoid Hemp Processor – Manufacturing Only: $1,000; or

    (iii) Cannabinoid Hemp Farm Processor: $300.

(3) proof of sufficient product liability insurance for all manufactured cannabinoid hemp products; and

(4) evidence, to the office's satisfaction, that the applicant will be able to comply with this Part, which may include an onsite inspection.

(g) If a provisionally approved applicant fails to satisfy the requirements in subdivision (f) of this section within six months, the provisional approval will be revoked and the application denied; provided the applicant may request additional time and shall have the opportunity to demonstrate to the office a reasonable documented effort to complete the requirements of subdivision (f) of this section.

(h) Cannabinoid hemp processor licenses shall be valid for two years from the date of issuance of the license.

(i) A cannabinoid hemp processor seeking to terminate its license shall submit a withdrawal notice to the office at least 30 days prior to termination, along with a plan for shutting down operations at the licensed facility. Any licensing fees paid or invoiced prior to notice of withdrawal are not eligible for refund.

(j) Cannabinoid hemp retailer licenses shall be valid for one year from the date of issuance of the license.

(k) Cannabinoid hemp retailer applicants who submitted a completed application to the Department of Health on or before June 1, 2021 may sell cannabinoid hemp products at retail to consumers before having their license approved or denied by the office, provided that the cannabinoid hemp retail applicant adheres to all requirements of this Part.

9 CCR-NY § 114.5. License Renewal.

(a) An application to renew any license issued under this Part shall be filed with the office not more than 90 days nor less than 30 days prior to the expiration thereof. If a renewal application is not filed at least 30 days prior to the expiration thereof, the office may determine that the license shall expire and become void on such expiration date.

(b) Renewal applications shall be accompanied by a non-refundable application fee and a refundable license fee, as follows:

    (1) Cannabinoid Hemp Processor – Extraction and Manufacturing: $1,000 application fee, $3,500 license fee;

    (2) Cannabinoid Hemp Processor – Manufacturing Only: $500 application fee, $1,000 license fee; or

    (3) Cannabinoid Hemp Farm Processor: $100 application fee, $300 license fee;

    (4) Cannabinoid Hemp Retailer: $300 license fee per retail location.

    (5) the license fee shall be returned if the licensee's renewal application is not granted.

(c) The application for renewal shall be submitted to the office, in a manner prescribed by the office, and include such information as the office may require.

(d) The office shall determine whether to renew an applicant's license based on the relevant factors in section 114.4 of this Part.

9 CCR-NY § 114.6. Transferability, License Amendment and Change in Ownership or Control.

(a) Licenses issued under this Part shall be effective only for the licensee and shall specify the following information:

(1) name of the licensee;

(2) address of the real property, or if applicable the online retailer website, where the licensed activities may take place;

(3) date of issuance;

(4) date of expiration;

(5) license number; and

(6) list of activities the licensee is permitted to perform under the license.

(b) Licenses shall not be transferable or assignable without prior written approval of the office including, without limitation, to another licensee. A change in majority ownership or controlling interest in the license or person holding the license, shall constitute a transfer of the license.

(c) To obtain approval from the office for the transfer of a license, a transferee must submit an application to the office, in a manner prescribed by the office, demonstrating an ability to operate the license in compliance with this Part, along with an application fee pursuant to section 114.2 or 114.3, as applicable.

(d) The office may deny an application for transfer of a license if the application fails to demonstrate that the transferee will comply with all of the requirements of this Part, or if the licensee has a record of poor performance, meaning two or more violations pursuant to section 114.17 of this Part, within the past two-years.

(e) A licensee may amend a license to add or delete permitted activities or change the location of a licensed facility by submitting a written request to the office along with an application fee pursuant to section 114.2 or 114.3, as applicable.

(f) A request to add permitted activities shall be reviewed by the office in accordance with section 114.4 of this Part.

9 CCR-NY § 114.7. Requirements for Cannabinoid Hemp Processors.

(a) All cannabinoid hemp processors shall:

(1) extract hemp extract and/or manufacture cannabinoid hemp products to GMP standards and if applicable for the type of processor license, maintain a qualified third-party certification, to the satisfaction of the office, for the applicable GMP standard(s) for the duration of the license;

(2) maintain standard operating procedures and quality control standards to ensure consistency of hemp extract and/or cannabinoid hemp products, including but not limited to product purity, strength and composition;

(3) maintain sufficient records to demonstrate that any hemp or hemp extract used by the licensee was

grown, derived, extracted and transported in accordance with applicable laws and licensing requirements of the jurisdiction(s) from which such hemp or hemp extract was sourced. Such records shall include any pesticides used in the growing of such hemp, date(s) each shipment was received, adequate chain of custody to demonstrate from whom the licensee purchased such hemp or hemp extract, and certificates of analysis. For hemp received from an out-of-state grower, processors shall also maintain records of the out-of-state grower registration or license number in the respective jurisdiction;

(4) keep all designated extracting and manufacturing areas safe and sanitary, including but not limited to ensuring that such areas are adequately lit, cleaned, smoke-free, and no food is consumed in such areas;

(5) provide all employees performing extraction or manufacturing with adequate training and proper safety equipment;

(6) manufacture cannabinoid hemp products in accordance with section 114.8 of this Part;

(7) test a statistically significant number of cannabinoid hemp products per lot or batch at a thirdparty testing laboratory meeting all the requirements in section 114.10 of this Part, and maintain a certificate of analysis for all samples tested;

(8) maintain sufficient records pertaining to the calibration and inspection of instruments used in extraction and manufacturing of cannabinoid hemp products;

(9) report, in a frequency and manner prescribed by the office, the total production and sales of the licensee during such reporting period;

(10) ensure the security of the licensed premises to prevent unauthorized individuals from entering the facility and to prevent hemp extract and/or cannabinoid hemp products from being diverted from the facility;

(11) not use synthetic cannabinoids, or Δ8-tetrahydrocannabinol or Δ10-tetrahydrocannabinol created through isomerization, in the extraction or manufacturing of any cannabinoid hemp products;

(12) assign a lot or batch number to each lot of hemp extract or cannabinoid hemp product, extracted or manufactured by a licensee; and

(13) maintain any and all records required by this Part for at least three years and immediately produce such records upon request of the office.

(b) Possession and the intermediate sale of hemp extract by and between licensed cannabinoid hemp processors, is permitted, provided when such extract leaves the licensed premises it is accompanied by a certificate of analysis certifying that the extract is less than five (5) percent THC and a copy of the cannabinoid hemp processor's license, and further provided such hemp extract is only transported intra-state.

(c) Licensees shall monitor complaints from cannabinoid hemp retailers and consumers and have a mechanism in place to notify the licensee's supply chain to recall products when directed by the office or as deemed appropriate by the licensee. Licensees shall notify the office within 24 hours of learning of a serious adverse event.

(d) Licensees shall ensure the proper disposal, beyond reclamation, of any hemp extract or byproduct from the extraction and manufacture process with a total Δ9-Tetrahydrocannabinol concentration greater than three-tenths of a percent (0.3%) and which will not be used or subject to further processing. Such disposal shall render the hemp extract or by-product unusable for any intoxicating purpose. Licensees shall maintain records to document and track any Δ9-Tetrahydrocannabinol extracted from hemp or found within hemp extract throughout the extraction and manufacturing process, including records pertaining to the amount used in cannabinoid hemp products and the disposal of all hemp extract, Δ9-Tetrahydrocannabinol or by-product;

(1) licensees shall dispose of any cannabinoid hemp product that is outdated, damaged, deteriorated, contaminated or otherwise deemed not appropriate for sale; and

(2) licensees shall dispose of liquid, chemical and hazardous waste in accordance with applicable federal, state and local laws and regulations.

(e) The office may conduct random sampling and testing of hemp, hemp extract, cannabinoid hemp products, or any solvents, chemicals, or materials used by the licensee, unannounced, at any time during normal business hours of the licensee.

(f) If a cannabinoid hemp processor is authorized to perform extraction, the processor shall:

(1) only extract using methods approved by the office, on the licensed premises, and using employees and equipment sufficient to ensure safe extraction; and

(2) use only those solvents that are approved by the office. Solvent-based extraction must be completed in a commercial, professional grade, closed-loop system capable of recovering the solvent used for extraction.

9 CCR-NY § 114.8. Cannabinoid Hemp Product Requirements.

(a) All cannabinoid hemp products distributed or offered for retail sale in New York State shall:

(1) be manufactured in accordance with Parts 101, 111 or 117 of Title 21 of the Code of Federal Regulations, as appropriate for the type of product being manufactured and as otherwise determined appropriate by the office in guidance or future regulation.

(2) contain no more than three-tenths of a percent (0.3%) total Δ9-Tetrahydrocannabinol concentration. The office may through future regulation impose a total THC cap for the purpose

of protecting public health, which shall include detectable levels of total Δ9- Tetrahydrocannabinol, Δ8-Tetrahydrocannabinol and Δ10-Tetrahydrocannabinol in milligrams per serving and milligrams per package for cannabinoid hemp products based on the product form, volume, number of servings, and ratio of CBD to THC;

(3) not contain liquor, wine, beer, cider or meet the definition of an alcoholic beverage as defined in section 3 of the Alcohol Beverage Control Law;

(4) not contain tobacco or nicotine in the product;

(5) not be in the form of an injectable, inhaler, product including cigarette, cigar or pre-roll, or any other disallowed form as determined by the office;

(6) accurately reflect testing results and not contain less than 80 percent or more than 120 percent of the concentration of total cannabinoid content as listed on the product label;

(7) comply with packaging and labeling standards in section 114.9 of this Part;

(8) be prepackaged and not added to food or any other consumable products at the point of sale;

(9) comply with product testing standards in section 114.10 of this Part; and

(10) not contain synthetic cannabinoids, or cannabinoids created through isomerization, including Δ8-tetrahydrocannabinol and Δ10-tetrahydrocannabinol.

(b) If the cannabinoid hemp product is a food or beverage manufactured under Part 117 of Title 21 Code of Federal Regulations, it shall not contain more than 25 milligrams of total cannabinoids per individually packaged product. If the cannabinoid hemp product is a supplement manufactured under Part 111 of Title 21 Code of Federal Regulations, it shall not contain more than 3,000 milligram of total cannabinoids per product, with no more than 100 milligrams per individual serving.

(c) If the cannabinoid hemp product contains multiple servings which are not individually wrapped, premeasured, separated or delineated, it shall include a measuring device such as a measuring cap, cup or dropper with the product packaging. Hash marks on the package shall not qualify as a measuring device. This provision shall not apply to flower products.

(d) All inhalable cannabinoid hemp products shall meet the following additional requirements:

(1) be a closed system with a pre-filled disposable cartridge that attaches to a rechargeable battery, or a single-use product that cannot be recharged;

(2) electronic vaporization devices shall have internal or external temperature controls to prevent combustion and have a heating element made of inert material such as glass, ceramic or stainless steel and not plastic or rubber;

(3) except for hemp-derived terpenes, excipients and ingredients must be pharmaceutical grade unless otherwise approved by the office, and shall not include:

(i) synthetic terpenes;

(ii) polyethylene glycol (PEG);

(iii) vitamin E acetate;

(iv) medium chain triglycerides (MCT oil);

(v) medicinal compounds;

(vi) illegal or controlled substances;

(vii) artificial food coloring;

(viii) benzoic acid;

(ix) diketones; and

(x) any other compound or ingredient as determined by the office in regulation;

(4) not contain any flavors or flavoring agents, except for hemp-derived terpenes; and

(5) include an office approved symbol, as set out in future regulation, in a manner that is clear and conspicuous.

9 CCR-NY § 114.9. Packaging and Labeling of Cannabinoid Hemp Products.

(a) All cannabinoid hemp products distributed or offered for retail sale in New York State shall include the following information on the product label or packaging:

(1) if the cannabinoid hemp product is consumed through ingestion, comply with the requirements in Title 21 Code of Federal Regulations Part 101 and include a nutritional or supplement fact panel that is based on the number of servings within the container;

(2) a list of all ingredients in descending order of predominance by weight in the product;

(3) the number of servings per outer package or container, including the milligrams per serving of:

(i) CBD;

(ii) "Total THC" or "THC" which for the purposes of product labeling may be rounded and shall include detectable levels of total Δ9-Tetrahydrocannabinol, Δ8-Tetrahydrocannabinol and Δ10-Tetrahydrocannabinol; and

(iii) any other marketed cannabinoid;

(4) an expiration or best by date if applicable;

(5) a lot or batch number;

(6) the name of the cannabinoid hemp processor or out of state manufacturer, packer or distributor;

(7) a scannable bar code or QR code linked to a downloadable certificate of analysis, or linked to a website where the certificate of analysis can be downloaded;

(8) the state(s) or if outside of the United States of America, country of origin from which hemp used in the product was sourced;

(9) a means for reporting serious adverse events or side effects; and

(10) any other marking, statement or symbol as required by the office in regulation.

(b) No cannabinoid hemp product packaging shall imitate a candy label or use cartoons or other images popularly used to advertise to children or otherwise be marketed to anyone under 18 years of age, or for inhalable cannabinoid hemp products and flower product, to anyone under 21 years of age.

(c) All cannabinoid hemp products shall be packaged in tamper-evident packaging that minimizes oxygen and light exposure to prevent degradation of the product and cannabinoids.

(d) All cannabinoid hemp products shall be accompanied by recommended serving and clear usage instructions.

(e) All cannabinoid hemp products claiming to be craft "isolate," "full spectrum," "broad spectrum," or "distillate" shall comply with the applicable definition contained in this Part.

(f) All cannabinoid hemp products offered for retail sale shall include the following warnings on the product label or packaging, in a manner that is clear and conspicuous:

(1) keep out of the reach of children;

(2) that the product is derived from hemp and may contain THC which could result in a failed drug test. Provided however, this warning may be omitted for cannabinoid hemp products that are: topically applied; made exclusively using an "isolate;" or made from "broad spectrum" hemp extract;

(3) that the product has not been evaluated by the Food and Drug Administration for safety or efficacy;

(4) those who are pregnant or nursing should consult their healthcare provider before use; and

(5) if the product is an inhalable cannabinoid hemp product, a warning stating that smoking or vaporizing is hazardous to your health.

(g) No information required to be listed on cannabinoid hemp product labeling or packaging in accordance with this section shall be smaller than 4.5-point font.

9 CCR-NY § 114.10. Laboratory Testing Requirements for Cannabinoid Hemp.

(a) For purposes of this Section, the following terms shall have the following meanings:

(1) "Accreditation body" means an impartial non-profit organization that operates in conformance with the International Organization for Standardization (ISO) / International Electrotechnical Commission (IEC) standard 17011 and is a signatory to the International Laboratory Accreditation Cooperation (ILAC) Mutual Recognition Arrangement (MRA) for Testing.

(2) "Scope of accreditation" means a document issued by an accreditation body that attests to the laboratory's competence to carry out specific testing and analysis.

(3) "Testing laboratory" means an independent, third-party laboratory, contracted by a cannabinoid hemp processor to test cannabinoid hemp products.

(b) To be recognized as a testing laboratory for purposes of testing cannabinoid hemp products as required by this Part, a laboratory must either be approved to test medical marijuana pursuant to Section 55-2.15 of Title 10 of the Official Compilation of Codes, Rules and Regulations of the State of New York, Article 6 of the Cannabis Law, or meet all of the following minimum requirements:

(1) maintain ISO/IEC 17025 accreditation for the premises and for the testing of one or more of the following:

(i) Cannabinoids;

(ii) Heavy metals;

(iii) Microbial impurities;

(iv) Mycotoxins;

(v) Residual pesticides;

(vi) Residual solvents and processing chemicals; or

(vii) If tested, terpenoids.

(2) maintain a valid scope of accreditation, issued by an accreditation body, that attests to the laboratory's competence to perform testing of one or more analytes listed in subdivision (b)(1) of this section.

(3) maintain method validation reports for all testing performed; and

(4) maintain standard operating procedures for the sampling of cannabinoid hemp products.

(c) Cannabinoid hemp processors shall retain, and make available to the office upon request, all records associated with their testing laboratory's ISO/IEC 17025 accreditation, scope of accreditation, method validation reports and standard operating procedures for the sampling of cannabinoid hemp products, as required by this section.

(d) Cannabinoid hemp products shall be considered adulterated and shall not be sold within New York State, if contaminants are detected at levels greater than provided for by the office in this Part or issued in further guidance.

(e) The office shall have the ability to impose additional testing requirements including but not limited to, testing for additional analytes, setting stricter contaminant limits and mandating the use of specific sampling methodologies per lot or batch manufactured.

(f) Pesticide Limits. The following list of contaminants does not constitute authorization to use or apply any of the following during hemp cultivation or processing. If a pesticide is identified that is not listed here, the method limit of quantitation should be considered the maximum residue level for the unlisted pesticide:

1. Abamectin, 300 parts per billion.

2. Acephate, 3,000 parts per billion.

3. Acequinocyl, 2,000 parts per billion.

4. Acetamiprid, 3,000 parts per billion.

5. Aldicarb, 100 parts per billion.

6. Azoxystrobin, 3,000 parts per billion.

7. Bifenazate, 3,000 parts per billion.

8. Bifenthrin, 500 parts per billion.

9. Boscalid, 3,000 parts per billion.

10. Captan, 3,000 parts per billion.

11. Carbaryl, 500 parts per billion.

12. Carbofuran, 100 parts per billion.

13. Chlorantraniliprole, 3,000 parts per billion.

14. Chlordane, 100 parts per billion.

15. Chlorfenapyr, 100 parts per billion.

16. Chlormequat chloride, 3,000 parts per billion

17. Chlorpyrifos, 100 parts per billion.

18. Clofentezine, 500 parts per billion.

19. Coumaphos, 100 parts per billion.

20. Cyfluthrin, 1,000 parts per billion.

21. Cypermethrin, 1,000 parts per billion.

22. Daminozide, 100 parts per billion.

23. DDVP (Dichlorvos), 100 parts per billion.

24. Diazinon, 200 parts per billion.

25. Dimethoate, 100 parts per billion.

26. Dimethomorph, 3,000 parts per billion.

27. Ethoprop(hos), 100 parts per billion.

28. Etofenprox, 100 parts per billion.

29. Etoxazole, 1,500 parts per billion.

30. Fenhexamid, 3,000 parts per billion.

31. Fenoxycarb, 100 parts per billion.

32. Fenpyroximate, 2,000 parts per billion.

33. Fipronil, 100 parts per billion.

34. Flonicamid, 2,000 parts per billion.

35. Fludioxonil, 3,000 parts per billion.

36. Hexythiazox, 2,000 parts per billion.

37. Imazalil, 100 parts per billion.

38. Imidacloprid, 3,000 parts per billion.

39. Kresoxim-methyl, 1,000 parts per billion.

40. Malathion, 2,000 parts per billion.

41. Metalaxyl, 3,000 parts per billion.

42. Methiocarb, 100 parts per billion.

43. Methomyl, 100 parts per billion.

44. Methyl parathion, 100 parts per billion.

45. Mevinphos, 100 parts per billion.

46. Myclobutanil, 3,000 parts per billion.

47. Naled, 500 parts per billion.

48. Oxamyl, 500 parts per billion.

49. Paclobutrazol, 100 parts per billion.

50. Pentachloronitrobenzene, 200 parts per billion.

51. Permethrin, 1,000 parts per billion.

52. Phosmet, 200 parts per billion.

53. Piperonyl butoxide, 3,000 parts per billion.

54. Prallethrin, 400 parts per billion.

55. Propiconazole, 1,000 parts per billion.

56. Propoxur, 100 parts per billion.

57. Pyrethrins, 1,000 parts per billion.

58. Pyridaben, 3,000 parts per billion.

59. Spinetoram, 3,000 parts per billion.

60. Spinosad A & D, 3,000 parts per billion.

61. Spiromesifen, 3,000 parts per billion.

62. Spirotetramat, 3,000 parts per billion.

63. Spiroxamine, 100 parts per billion.

64. Tebuconazole, 1,000 parts per billion.

65. Thiacloprid, 100 parts per billion.

66. Thiamethoxam, 1,000 parts per billion.

67. Trifloxystrobin, 3,000 parts per billion.

(g) Residual Solvent Limits.

1. 1,2-Dichloroethane, 5 parts per million

2. 1,1-Dichloroethene, 8 parts per million

3. Acetone, 5,000 parts per million

4. Acetonitrile, 410 parts per million

5. Benzene, 2 parts per million

6. Butane, 2,000 parts per million

7. Chloroform, 60 parts per million

8. Ethanol, 5,000 parts per million

9. Ethyl Acetate, 5,000 parts per million

10. Ethyl Ether, 5,000 parts per million

11. Ethylene Oxide, 5 parts per million

12. Heptane, 5,000 parts per million

13. Hexane, 290 parts per million

14. Isopropyl Alcohol, 5,000 parts per million

15. Methanol, 3,000 parts per million

16. Methylene Chloride, 600 parts per million

17. Pentane, 5,000 parts per million

18. Propane, 5,000 parts per million

19. Toluene, 890 parts per million

20. Trichloroethylene (1,1,2-Trichloroethene), 80 parts per million

21. Xylenes, Total (ortho-, meta-, para-), 2170 parts per million

(h) Metals Limits.

1. Cadmium, 0.5 micrograms/gram for cannabinoid hemp products intended for ingestion. 0.2 micrograms/gram for cannabinoid hemp products intended for inhalation.

2. Lead, 1.0 micrograms/gram for cannabinoid hemp products intended for ingestion. 0.5 micrograms/gram for cannabinoid hemp products intended for inhalation.

3. Arsenic, 1.5 micrograms/gram for cannabinoid hemp products intended for ingestion. 0.2 micrograms/gram for cannabinoid hemp products intended for inhalation.

4. Mercury, 1.5 micrograms/gram for cannabinoid hemp products intended for ingestion. 0.1 micrograms/gram for cannabinoid hemp products intended for inhalation.

(i) Biological Limits.

    1. Shiga toxin-producing Escherichia coli (STEC E. coli) and other pathogenic E. coli, none detected in 1 gram.

    2. Salmonella, none detected in 1 gram.

    3. Total plate count for aerobic bacteria, <104 CFUs/gram.

    4. Total yeast and mold, <103 CFUs/gram.

(j) Mycotoxin Limits.

    1. Total Aflatoxin (B1, B2, G1, G2), 20 parts per billion.

    2. Ochratoxin A, 20 parts per billion.

(k) Cannabinoid Limits. The total Δ9-Tetrahydrocannabinol concentration for cannabinoid hemp products shall not exceed three-tenths of a percent (0.3%). If a cannabinoid hemp product fails, the processor may elect to re-formulate the failing batch to reduce the total Δ9- Tetrahydrocannabinol of the batch to not more than three-tenths of a percent (0.3%) total Δ9- Tetrahydrocannabinol. If the re-formulated batch still exceeds the three-tenths of a percent (0.3%) total Δ9-Tetrahydrocannabinol the processor shall destroy the batch in compliance with subdivision (d) of section 114.7 of this Part.

(l) If a cannabinoid hemp product is found to contain levels of any pathogen, toxicant, residual solvent, metal, or pesticide not enumerated in this section or by New York State law, then the product shall not be sold in New York State.

9 CCR-NY § 114.11. Requirements for Cannabinoid Hemp Retailers.

(a) Cannabinoid hemp retailers shall only sell cannabinoid hemp products manufactured, packaged, labeled and tested in accordance with this Part.

(b) Cannabinoid hemp retailers shall not offer or sell any cannabinoid hemp product clearly labeled or advertised for the purpose of smoking, or in the form of a cigarette, cigar, or pre-roll, or packaged or combined with other items designed to facilitate smoking such as rolling papers or pipes. Retailers shall have sufficient safeguards in place to verify that an individual presenting or submitting proof of age for an inhalable cannabinoid hemp product or flower product matches the identification and is 21 years of age or older.

(c) Cannabinoid hemp retailers shall post, visible to consumers, any and all signs or posted placards required by the office, including posting of the cannabinoid hemp retail license issued by the office, in a conspicuous location on the premises of each retail location.

(d) Cannabinoid hemp products shall be displayed in a manner that distinguishes them from noncannabinoid hemp products, to aide consumers in locating cannabinoid hemp products and avoid accidental purchase or consumption.

(e) Cannabinoid hemp retailers shall maintain sufficient records of where cannabinoid hemp products were purchased from for the license period, including the name of the cannabinoid hemp processor if applicable, and the wholesaler or permitted distributor if applicable.

(f) The office may inspect any retail location offering cannabinoid hemp products. This inspection may include taking samples of cannabinoid hemp products to ensure compliance with all the requirements of this Part.

9 CCR-NY § 114.12. Advertising Requirements.

(a) An advertisement for a cannabinoid hemp product, cannabinoid hemp processor or cannabinoid hemp retailer shall not:

(i) make any false or misleading claims or statements;

(ii) contain claims that cannabinoid hemp or a cannabinoid hemp product can, or is intended to, diagnose, cure, mitigate, treat, or prevent disease;

(iii) lead a reasonable person to believe that a cannabinoid hemp product is adult-use cannabis, marihuana, medical cannabis, or medical marihuana, or that a licensee is authorized to sell or dispense adult-use cannabis, marihuana, medical cannabis, or medical marihuana, as those terms are defined in Section 3 of the Cannabis Law and Article 33 of the Public Health Law;

(iv) have the purpose or effect of targeting or appealing to anyone under 21 years of age for inhalable cannabinoid hemp products or flower product. The use of images of children or minors consuming the product and the use of words, a design or brand that resembles a product that is commonly associated with children or minors or marketed to children or minors, is prohibited.

9 CCR-NY § 114.13. New York Hemp Product.

(a) A New York Hemp Product is a cannabinoid hemp product exclusively grown in New York State and processed in New York State by processors that are licensed under this Part and that demonstrate compliance with all requirements enumerated by the office;

(b) The office may establish standards and requirements above and beyond those established in this Part and use such standards and requirements to certify products as New York Hemp Product.

(c) The office may revoke a cannabinoid hemp product's status as certified New York Hemp Product, without a hearing, if it has reason to believe that such product no longer meets one or more of the standards or requirements established by the office.

(d) No cannabinoid hemp product sold in New York state may use the term "New York Hemp Product" or hold itself out as being New York Hemp Product, or approved or certified by the office in any way, unless such product has been certified by the office pursuant to this section, in which case the cannabinoid hemp processor and cannabinoid hemp retailer may portray such product(s) as being certified New York Hemp Product. A violation of this subdivision constitutes grounds for suspension or revocation of a license.

9 CCR-NY § 114.14. General Prohibitions.

(a) No licensee shall engage in any activity relating to the processing, packaging, labeling manufacturing, extracting, distributing, selling or laboratory testing of cannabinoid hemp extract or cannabinoid hemp that does not comply with the requirements of Article 5 of the Cannabis Law and this Part.

(b) No person shall extract hemp extract or manufacture cannabinoid hemp products in New York State unless licensed to engage in such activity by the office or otherwise authorized by the United States food and drug administration.

(c) Hemp extract shall be manufactured into cannabinoid hemp product before being offered for retail sale and shall not be distributed or sold directly to consumers within the state.

(d) No cannabinoid hemp product shall be distributed or offered for retail sale in New York State unless:

(1) it complies with the processing, packaging, labeling and testing requirements pursuant to sections 114.8, 114.9 and 114.10 of this Part; and

(2) is sold by a cannabinoid hemp retailer licensed under this Part;

(e) No person shall transport hemp extract within the state, unless:

(1) it is in a fully enclosed vehicle or container; and

(2) accompanied by a manifest or proof of ownership, documenting the name, physical address, lot or batch number, certificate of analysis and license number of the originating licensed cultivator or processor, and the name and physical address of the recipient of the delivery when transporting between non-adjoining facilities. When hemp extract is being transported to a laboratory for testing, a certificate of analysis is not required to accompany the shipment.

(f) Hemp extract shall not be shipped or transported into New York State unless:

(1) it is in a fully enclosed vehicle or container;

(2) accompanied by proof of origin with a hemp cultivation or processor license number, or equivalent, from the jurisdiction of origin; and

(3) accompanied by a certificate of analysis showing that the hemp extract has a total Δ9-Tetrahydrocannabinol of no more than three tenths of a percent (0.3%).

(g) No person shall distribute cannabinoid hemp products manufactured out of state, to a cannabinoid hemp retailer within New York State, unless permitted pursuant to section 114.18 of this Part.

9 CCR-NY § 114.15. Cannabinoid Hemp Processor Prohibitions.

(a) No cannabinoid hemp processor may transfer a license issued under this Part without prior written approval of the office.

(b) No cannabinoid hemp processor shall manufacture a cannabinoid hemp product that is a potentially hazardous food, as defined by Section 14-1.31 of Title 10 of the Official Compilation of Codes, Rules and Regulations of the State of New York.

(c) No cannabinoid hemp processor may conduct final product testing for the licensee's own products to meet the testing requirements of Section 114.10 of this Part. Nothing in this Part prohibits a cannabinoid hemp processor from performing internal testing for research and product development or for quality assurance prior to final product testing by a third-party laboratory.

(d) No cannabinoid hemp processor may sell cannabinoid hemp products to consumers for final retail sale without first obtaining a cannabinoid hemp retail license.

(e) No cannabinoid hemp processor shall sell hemp extract to anyone in New York State, unless such person is licensed as a cannabinoid hemp processor under this Part, registered as a registered organization under Section 3365 of the Public Health Law or Article 3 of the Cannabis Law.

9 CCR-NY § 114.16. Cannabinoid Hemp Retailer Prohibitions.

(a) No cannabinoid hemp retailer shall offer or sell cannabinoid hemp products in the form of an inhalable cannabinoid hemp product or flower product to anyone under 21 years of age.

(b) No cannabinoid hemp retailer shall sell a cannabinoid hemp product that is a potentiallyhazardous food, as defined by Section 14-1.31 of Title 10 of the Official Compilation of Codes, Rules and Regulations of the State of New York.

(c) Cannabinoid hemp retailers shall only offer and sell cannabinoid hemp products that meet all of the standards and requirements of Sections 114.8, 114.9 and 114.10 of this Part.

(d) Cannabinoid hemp retailers shall not offer or sell any cannabinoid hemp product to be added to food or other consumable products at the point of sale.

9 CCR-NY § 114.17. Penalties.

(a) Licensees under this Part shall comply with all applicable laws, rules and regulations as it relates to such licensure.

(b) Failure to comply with a requirement of Article 5 of the Cannabis Law or this Part may be punishable by a civil penalty, as follows:

> (i) a fine of up to $1,000 for a first violation;

> (ii) a fine up to $5,000 for a second violation within three-years; or

> (iii) a fine up to $10,000 for a third violation and each subsequent violation thereafter, within a three-year period.

(c) Where a licensee willfully violates, refuses or neglects to comply with one or more sections of this Part, the office may limit, suspend, revoke or annul a license after providing notice and an opportunity for a hearing to the licensee. However, a license may be temporarily limited, suspended, revoked or annulled without a hearing for a period not to exceed 30-days, upon notice to the licensee, following a finding by the office that the public health, safety or welfare is in imminent danger.

(d) A licensee who negligently violates this Part three times in a five-year period shall be ineligible to process or sell cannabinoid hemp for a period of five years beginning on the date of the third violation. The office, for good cause shown, may choose to impose a lesser penalty.

9 CCR-NY § 114.18. Cannabinoid Hemp Permits.

(a) The office may issue cannabinoid permits expressly authorizing a permittee to conduct one or more of the following activities:

> (1) distribute cannabinoid hemp products manufactured out of state, to cannabinoid hemp retailers within New York State;

> (2) deliver cannabinoid hemp products from a cannabinoid hemp retailer to consumers;

> (3) sell at retail cannabinoid hemp products for a limited duration;

> (4) continue operations for persons holding a valid CBD processor research partnership agreement with the New York State Department of Agriculture and Markets pursuant to Article 29-A of the New York State Agriculture and Markets Law;

> (5) any other activity as determined by the Cannabis Control Board.

(b) Applicants for a cannabinoid hemp permit must apply on a form prescribed by the office and submit a $100 application fee and permit fee as may be set by the office.

(c) Permits issued pursuant to this section shall be valid for one year from the date of issuance, unless the office prescribes a shorter time period for expiration.

9 CCR-NY § 114.19. Severability.

The provisions of this Part are severable. If any provision of this Part is found to be invalid, or if any application of this Part to any person or circumstance is found to be invalid, the invalidity shall not affect any other provisions or applications which can be given effect without the invalid provision or application.

9 CCR-NY § 114.20. Incorporation by Reference.

The provisions of the Code of Federal Regulations which have been incorporated by reference in this Subpart have been filed in the Office of the Secretary of State of the State of New York, the publication so filed being the booklet entitled: Code of Federal Regulations, Title 21, Parts 101, 111, and 117, revised as of April 1, 2012, June 25, 2007, and January 1, 2019 respectively, published by the Office of the Federal Register, National Archives and Records Administration. The regulations incorporated by reference may be examined at the Records Access Office, New York State Office of Cannabis Management, Harriman State Office Building Campus, Albany, New York, 12207 or can be directly obtained from the Superintendent of Documents, US Government Printing Office, Washington, D.C. 20402.

9 CCR-NY § 114.21. Effective date.

(a) The provisions of this Part are effective upon publication in the State Register; provided, however, that sections 114.9 and 114.10 shall not become effective until April 25, 2021.

(b) Notwithstanding subdivision (a) of this section, a licensed cannabinoid hemp retailer may continue to possess, transport, and sell cannabinoid hemp products in the retailer's inventory before the effective date of this Part, unless the cannabinoid hemp product:

> (1) is unsafe for consumption based on the presence or quantity of heavy metals, pesticides, harmful microorganisms, or residual solvents;

> (2) has a Δ-9 tetrahydrocannabinol concentration of more than 0.3 percent;

> (3) is a flower product clearly labeled or advertised for the purpose of smoking or in the form of a cigarette, cigar or pre-roll or otherwise packaged or combined with other items designed to facilitate smoking such as rolling papers or pipes; or

> (4) contains or was manufactured with Δ8-tetrahydrocannabinol or Δ10-tetrahydrocannabinol created through isomerization.

PART 115. PERSONAL HOME CULTIVATION OF MEDICAL CANNABIS.

9 CCR-NY § 115.1. Definitions.

(a) For purposes of this section, the following definitions shall apply:

> (1) "Cultivation" means growing, cloning, harvesting, drying, curing, grading, and trimming of the cannabis plant.

> (2) "Designated caregiver" means an individual designated by the certified patient. A designated caregiver is twenty-one years of age or older for purposes of this Part.

(3) "Immature cannabis plant" means a non-flowering female cannabis plant or a cannabis plant which does not have buds that may be observed by visual examination.

(4) "Mature cannabis plant" means a female plant that has flowered and that has buds that may be observed by visual examination.

(5) "Office" means the New York State office of cannabis management.

(6) "On the grounds" means the external areas of the private residence where the individual resides and has legal rights to use such external areas for their own purposes, including but not limited to, a backyard or any land adjacent to the private residence.

(7) "Personal Home cultivation" means growing, cloning, harvesting, drying, curing, grading, and trimming of cannabis plants for medical use that is subject to Cannabis Law Article 3 and Penal Law Article 222.

(8) "Private residence" means any building or part of a building, or structure designed and occupied for residential purposes, including but not limited to a private home; townhouse; condominium; co-op; apartment; or mobile home. For purposes of this Part, a hospital, hotel, motel, resort, or other similar public accommodation, shall not be considered a private residence, except as may be expressly allowed by the Board.

(9) "Process" or "Processing" means extracting, preparing, treating, modifying, compounding, manufacturing or otherwise manipulating cannabis for use to concentrate or extract its cannabinoids. For purposes of this section, processing does not include growing, cultivation, cloning, harvesting, drying, curing, grinding, or trimming.

9 CCR-NY § 115.2. Personal Home Cultivation of Medical Cannabis.

(a) Certified patients twenty-one years of age or older may cultivate cannabis for personal use pursuant to Section 115.2 of this Part.

(b) Designated caregivers twenty-one years of age or older, caring for a certified patient either younger than twenty-one years of age or whose physical or cognitive impairments prevent them from cultivating cannabis, may cultivate cannabis for use by such patient, provided that no patient may have more than one designated caregiver grow on their behalf.

(c) The personal home cultivation of medical cannabis may only occur in, or on the grounds of, a person's private residence.

(d) No certified patient shall plant, cultivate, harvest, dry, process or possess more than three mature cannabis plants and three immature cannabis plants at any one time.

(e) No more than six mature and six immature cannabis plants may be cultivated, harvested, dried, or possessed within any private residence, or on the grounds of any private residence at any one time.

(f) No certified patient or designated caregiver shall sell or barter any cannabis seeds, immature cannabis plants, mature cannabis plants, or cannabis, produced by a plant cultivated pursuant to this Part, to any other person. This subdivision does not prohibit the transfer, without compensation, to a certified patient or a designated caregiver twenty-one years of age or older, up to three ounces of cannabis and up to twenty-four grams of concentrated cannabis.

(g) A certified patient or designated caregiver may lawfully possess up to five pounds of personal home cultivated cannabis in their private residence or on the grounds of such person's private residence per section five of penal law section 222.15.

(h) Except as otherwise approved by the Office, no certified patient or designated caregiver shall process cannabis at home by means of any liquid or gas, other than alcohol, that has a flashpoint below 100 degrees Fahrenheit.

(i) Immature cannabis plants and mature cannabis plants must be stored in a secure location within a private residence or on the grounds of such certified patient or designated caregiver's private residence; and reasonable measures must be taken to ensure that such plants, and any cannabis cultivated from such plants, is not readily accessible to anyone under the age of 21. Such reasonable measures may include but are not limited to:

> (1) conducting cannabis cultivation in an enclosed area, which may not be plainly visible from public view, including from the street of the private residence or on the grounds of the certified patient or designated caregiver's private residence; and

> (2) locking and storing cannabis in a manner that prevents theft, loss, or access, which may include, but are not limited to locks, gates, doors, fences, and other barriers by an unauthorized person, including a person under the age of 21.

(j) Certified patients utilizing a designated caregiver shall identify a single site for cultivation of their medical cannabis.

(k) Designated caregivers growing on behalf of a certified patient may grow up to three mature cannabis plants and three immature cannabis plants for one certified patient. A designated caregiver that is also a certified patient shall not grow more than three mature cannabis plants and three immature cannabis plants for their own use, nor any one of their individual certified patient's use. Provided however, if a designated caregiver grows for two or more certified patients, which may or may not include themselves, they shall not grow more than six mature cannabis plants and six immature cannabis plants on their own private residence at any one time. A designated caregiver may grow on behalf of, but no more than, four certified patients at a time, which shall not include themselves if they are a certified patient.

(l) In addition to the requirements in Section 115.2 of the Part, designated caregivers shall:

> (1) keep any cannabis being cultivated for the designated caregiver's certified patient separate from any other cannabis being cultivated, and in a manner that can readily determine to whom such cannabis plants belong;

> (2) only receive reimbursement for the actual costs of goods, materials, or utilities for which they have incurred expenses directly related to the cultivation of cannabis for the certified patient, and not receive reimbursement or compensation for their time, knowledge, or expertise;

> (3) not sell any cannabis produced by any immature cannabis plant or mature cannabis plant which is or was cultivated for a certified patient, even if the certified patient no longer needs or wants such cannabis; and

> (4) only cultivate cannabis at, or on the grounds of, the designated caregiver's private residence or the certified patient's private residence.

(m) No landlord may refuse to lease, or otherwise penalize a certified patient or designated caregiver solely for engaging in medical cannabis activity as authorized by this Part and in accordance with Cannabis Law, except:

> (1) if failing to do so would cause the landlord to lose a monetary or licensing related benefit under federal law or regulations; or

> (2) if a property has in place a smoke free policy, it is not required to permit the smoking of cannabis products on its premises, provided no restriction may be construed to limit the certified medical use of cannabis.

(n) Section 115.2(k) of this Part does not exempt an individual from being liable for any property damage as outlined in their lease agreement.

9 CCR-NY § 115.3. Sale of Medical Cannabis for Home

Cultivation.

(a) No person or entity shall sell medical cannabis plants or seeds for home cultivation unless it has complied with the Cannabis Law, this Part, any other applicable federal and state rules, regulations and laws as amended for medical cannabis, and is a registered organization registered in accordance with Article 3 of the Cannabis Law or a licensee authorized by the Office of Cannabis Management. Applicable federal law or rules and regulation shall not be construed as to include any such federal law, rules or regulation that is contrary to, or otherwise conflicts with this Part or the Cannabis Law.

(b) Prior to selling medical cannabis for home cultivation, registered organizations or licensees shall update standard operating procedures to include activities related to home cultivation and furnish the standard operating procedures to the Office upon request.

(c) Packaging and Labeling requirements. Notwithstanding any other law or regulation, each cannabis plant or package of seeds for sale shall be labeled with an unobstructed and conspicuous label prior to being transported to the dispensing facility or delivered to the patient as follows:

  (1) Labeling shall include the following information:

      (i) strain name in bold type;

      (ii) product type (eg cannabis seeds, cannabis plant);

      (iii) potential potency, as confirmed by testing of the parent cannabis plant (THC:CBD levels);

      (iv) date of harvest;

      (v) unique identification number (UID);

      (vi) any pesticides used in the cultivation;

      (vii) name of the entity, licensed or registered with the Office, that cultivated the cannabis;

      (viii) name of the entity, licensed or registered with the Office, that sold the cannabis, if different from cultivator;

      (ix) for seeds, a seed count and net weight must be included on the packaging label in US customary units and metric;

      (x) a warning to "keep out of reach of children"; and

      (xi) any other information as determined by the Office.

  (2) The label shall be printed on or affixed to any package or container that is used to display the cannabis seed or cannabis plant for retail sale.

  (3) Packaging shall be in a manner that is not attractive to minors and that preserves the integrity of the cannabis. Seed packaging shall not be plastic.

  (4) Packaging and labeling shall not contain any untruthful or misleading statements including, but not limited to, health or benefit claims.

(d) Transport. Notwithstanding any other law or regulation, a registered organization or licensee shall transport medical cannabis for home cultivation in a manner determined by the Office and shall ensure that the following are provided to the dispensing facility, patient, or designated caregiver receiving the transport or delivery:

  (1) written instructions for basic care and environmental considerations for the plants (light, water, temperature controls) and the method for destruction if necessary, such as if the plants develop disease, or die;

and

(2) disclosure of any pesticide used in cultivation and a document signed by a duly authorized representative from the registered organization or licensee attesting that only pesticides that are registered by the New York State Department of Environmental Conservation or that specifically meet the United States Environmental Protection Agency registration exemption criteria for Minimum Risk Pesticides, and only in accordance with section 325.2(b) of title 6 of the NYCRR have been used;

(e) Storage at the dispensing facilities. Notwithstanding any other law or regulation, all medical cannabis seeds and immature plants shall be:

(1) stored in a secure area or location within the dispensing facility accessible to the minimum number of employees essential for efficient operation, to prevent diversion, theft or loss; and

(2) stored in such a manner as to protect against physical, chemical and microbial contamination and deterioration. However, a registered organization or licensees shall not apply any pesticides to live plants at the dispensing facility;

(f) Sales of medical cannabis for home cultivation. Registered organizations or licensees shall:

(1) only conduct sales of medical cannabis for home cultivation at their dispensaries or via delivery service to certified patients twenty-one years of age or older or their designated caregivers who are registered with the Office;

(2) sell seeds and immature plants only in quantities determined by the Office in guidance.

(3) provide certified patients or their designated caregivers with a safety insert at the time of sale consistent with guidance issued by the office. The safety insert shall include:

(i) the medical cannabis strain and potential potency;

(ii) information about contraindications;

(iii) warning of adverse effects and/or any potential dangers stemming from the use of medical cannabis;

(iv) instructions for reporting adverse events;

(v) a warning about driving and operation of mechanical equipment while under the influence of medical cannabis;

(vi) information on tolerance, dependence and withdrawal, and substance abuse, how to recognize what may be problematic usage of medical cannabis and how to obtain appropriate services or treatment;

(vii) language stating medical cannabis seeds and plants must be kept secure and out of reach of children;

(viii) language stating that the certified patient, or designated caregiver, may not distribute medical cannabis to anyone else;

(ix) language stating that unwanted, excess, or contaminated medical cannabis must be disposed of in a manner that makes it nonrecoverable beyond reclamation, except for stalks, stems, fan leaves, root balls, and soil media;

(x) language stating that medical cannabis for home cultivation is not required to be, and has not been, safety compliance tested; and

(xi) any other information as determined by the Office.

(g) Reporting and recordkeeping. Notwithstanding any other law or regulation, registered organizations or licensees shall perform seed to sale tracking of medical cannabis for home cultivation and submit seed to sale data from the registered organization's or licensee's system of record to the Office in a format as determined by the Office.

(h) Returns, complaints and adverse events.

   (1) Medical cannabis seeds or plants returned to the dispensing facility shall be securely stored separate from working inventory while awaiting disposal and disposed of as determined by the Office.

   (2) Registered organizations or licensees shall notify the Office within 24 hours of the following;

      (i) any adverse events that the registered organization or licensee is made aware of;

      (ii) any incident involving theft, loss or possible diversion of medical cannabis;

      (iii) any suspected or known security breach or other facility event that may compromise public health or safety, or which requires response by public safety personnel or law enforcement;

      (iv) any vehicle accidents or incidents occurring during transport of medical cannabis.

   (3) Within ten days of the occurrence of one of the events in paragraph (2) of this subdivision, the registered organization or licensee shall submit a complete written incident report to the Office detailing the circumstances of the event, any corrective actions taken, and where applicable, confirmation that appropriate law enforcement authorities were notified.

   (4) Quarantine any lot of medical cannabis returned or as directed by the Office, and not transport, distribute, dispense or destroy such lot unless prior approval is obtained from the Office.

   (5) Submit medical cannabis, samples and manufacturing materials to the Office upon request.

PART 116. CONDITIONAL ADULT-USE RETAIL DISPENSARY

9 CCR-NY § 116.1. Definitions.

For the purposes of this Part, the following terms shall have the following meanings:

(a) Act means the Marihuana Regulation and Taxation Act, Chapter 92 of the Laws of 2021.

(b) Aggregate ownership interest means the total ownership interest held by:

   (i) a legal entity and any legal entity in its multilevel ownership structure; or

   (ii) an individual and the spouse, domestic partner, civil union partner, child, sibling, or parent of such individual.

(c) Applicant means a person applying for a license under this Part.

(d) Board means the New York State Cannabis Control Board established pursuant to the Act.

(e) Bona fide labor organization means a local labor union:

   (1) that represents employees in this state with regard to wages, hours and working conditions;

   (2) in which officers have been elected by secret ballot or otherwise in a manner consistent with federal law; and

(3) that is free of domination or interference by any employer and has received no improper assistance or support from any employer.

(f) Conditional period means four years from the date the license is granted.

(g) Control means the power to order or direct the management, managers, or policies of a person.

(h) Eligible applicant means an applicant that satisfies all the required elements in section 116.4 of this Part.

(i) Financial institution means any bank, mutual savings bank, consumer loan company, credit union, savings and loan association, trust company, or other lending institution under the jurisdiction of the Department of Financial Services.

(j) Financial interest means any actual or future right to ownership, investment or compensation arrangement with another person, either directly or indirectly, through business, investment, spouse, parent or child. Person with a financial interest does not include a passive investor.

(k) Financier means any person, other than financial institution or government or governmental subdivision or agency, that provides capital as a gift, provides a grant, or lends capital pursuant to a secured or unsecured financing agreement. A financier may not receive an ownership interest, control of the business, a share of revenue, gross profits or net profits, a profit sharing interest, or a percentage of the profits in exchange for a gift, grant or loan, unless the financier receives prior approval from the Office.

(l) First renewal date means two years from the date the license is granted.

(m) Fund means a social and economic equity fund in which the state, any state agency, public authority, public benefit corporation, or division thereof has invested and is formed for the limited purpose of funding costs, which include, but are not limited to construction, renovations and equipment purchasing associated with establishing or developing adult-use cannabis operators.

(n) Justice involved means a person that satisfies the required elements in section 116.4(a)(2)(i) of this Part.

(o) License means a license issued pursuant to this Part and is conditioned on all requirements and prohibitions being met.

(p) Licensee means a person who has been granted a license to engage in the retail sale of cannabis products under this Part.

(q) Marihuana-related offense means a marihuana or cannabis offense defined under article two hundred twenty-one of the penal law prior to its repeal, any offense under article two hundred twenty or section 240.36 of the penal law prior to the effective date of article two hundred twenty-one of the penal law, where the controlled substance involved was marihuana, any offense that is eligible to be sealed or expunged pursuant to Chapter 131 of the Laws of 2019 or the Act or any offense identified by the Office to be a marihuana-related offense.

(r) Passive investor means a person that has an aggregate ownership interest of no more than five percent of the outstanding shares of an applicant or licensee whose shares are publicly traded, and such person does not have control over the applicant or licensee.

(s) Person means an individual, institution, corporation, government or governmental subdivision or agency, business trust, estate, trust, partnership or association, or any other legal entity.

(t) Primary residence means a dwelling where a person usually stays or stays more often than other locations with an intention to remain. The Office shall be authorized to select one or more, without limitation, of the following to verify an individual's primary residence:

(1) state or federal tax filing or return with proof of filing, including e-filing acknowledgements;

(2) a signed lease agreement, a property deed, a mortgage payment, or property tax statement that includes the

individual's name;

    (3) a letter addressed to the applicant from:

        (i) the public housing authority in New York State or New York City;

        (ii) a homeless shelter indicating the applicant currently resides at the homeless shelter;

        (iii) a nonprofit organization or religious institution that provides services to homeless individuals, indicating the applicant's lack of permanent housing;

        (iv) a domestic violence residential care program or organization that serves domestic violence survivors; or

        (v) a charitable organization registered with the New York State Attorney General that provided services to the applicant and for which eligibility was established prior to the nineteenth of April, two-thousand twenty-one, attesting to residence.

    (4) a voter registration card;

    (5) jury summons, court order, or other document from a court within New York State;

    (6) a government issued identification;

    (7) a paycheck stub;

    (8) a utility bill;

    (9) a health institution or insurance company statement, bill, or record;

    (10) a bank or credit card statement;

    (11) a document addressed to the applicant by a local government in New York State; or

    (12) any other proof of residency as determined by the Office.

(u) Qualifying business means a business as defined in section 116.4(a)(2)(iii) of this Part.

(v) Regional geographic zones means the zones established by the Office which represent the geographic area where conditional adult-use retail dispensaries will be located.

(w) True party of interest

    (1) includes, but is not limited to the following:

        (i) applicant or licensee's sole proprietor, partner (whether limited or general), member, manager, president, vice president, secretary, treasurer, officer, board member, trustee, director, or a person with equivalent title to each of the foregoing;

        (ii) stockholder of applicant or licensee, other than a passive investor;

        (iii) each person that makes up the ownership structure of each level of ownership for an applicant or licensee that has a multilevel ownership structure;

        (iv) person with a right to receive some or all of the revenue, gross profit, or net profit from the licensed business during any full or partial calendar or fiscal year;

        (v) person with a financial interest in the applicant or licensee;

        (vi) person that has authority to or exercises control over the applicant or licensee;

(vii) person that has membership rights in the applicant or licensee in accordance with the provisions of any articles of incorporation, bylaws, limited liability corporation agreements, partnership agreements, or operating agreement;

(viii) person that assumes responsibility for the debts of the applicant or licensee; or

(ix) spouse of any individual in sections 116.1(w)(1)(i) through 116.1(w)(1) (iii) of this part.

(2) does not include a person that, without limitation:

(i) receives payment for rent on a fixed basis under a lease or rental agreement relating to applicant or licensee. Notwithstanding, if there is a common ownership interest between applicant or licensee, and the entity that owns the real property, the Office may investigate all funds associated with the landlord to determine if the landlord is a financier. The Office may also investigate a landlord in situations where a rental payment has been waived or deferred;

(ii) receives a bonus or commission from the applicant or licensee based on the individual's sales, so long as the commission does not exceed ten percent of the sales of the applicant or licensee in any given bonus or commission period, unless otherwise determined by the Office. Commission-based compensation agreements must be in writing;

(iii) contracts with the applicant or licensee to receive a commission for the sale of the business or real property;

(iv) consults receiving a flat or hourly rate of compensation from the applicant or licensee under a contractual agreement;

(v) has an option to purchase the applicant or licensee, in the event the applicant or licensee is not an individual, or conditional adult-use retail dispensary, so long as no money has been paid under an option contract or agreement for such purchase or sale;

(vi) has a contract or agreement for services with an applicant or licensee, such as a branding or staffing company, as long as the applicant or licensee retains the right to and controls the business;

(vii) is a financial institution; or

(viii) is a passive investor.

9 CCR-NY § 116. 2. Application for Conditional Adult-Use Retail Dispensary License.

(a) Information Required to be Disclosed on Application. The application for a conditional adult-use retail dispensary license shall include the following:

(1) the legal name of the applicant;

(2) the name under which the conditional adult-use retail dispensary will operate or make sales if different than the legal name of the applicant, including, but not limited to, the assumed name, where applicable;

(3) the name, address, federal employment identification number, and date of birth, where applicable, of the applicant and each true party of interest of applicant;

(4) a copy of a valid photo identification containing the individual's date of birth issued by a local, state, or federal government for the applicant and each true party of interest of applicant, each of which shall be at least 21 years of age;

(5) a personal history disclosure for applicant and each true party of interest of applicant;

(6) submission of fingerprints for applicant and each true party of interest set forth in sections 116.1(w)(i) - (iii), on a form and in such manner as specified by the Office for purpose of obtaining a criminal history report from division of criminal justice services;

(7) the ownership structure of the applicant;

(8) the percentage of ownership interest held by each true party of interest in the applicant, and a description of any other interest held in the applicant;

(9) a list of all parent companies, subsidiaries, affiliates, predecessors, and successors of the applicant, including, but not limited to, all individuals of each entity at each level of ownership for the applicant that has a multilevel ownership structure;

(10) the name of every financial institution at which the applicant and each true party of interest of applicant that has or has had a personal and business account that is or was used to financially support the business in the past 3 years;

(11) a current organizational chart of the applicant that includes position descriptions and the names and resumes of persons holding each position identified on the organizational chart, to the extent those positions have been filled; to the extent not revealed by the resume, include additional information with each resume setting out the employee's particular skills, education, experience or significant accomplishments that are relevant to owning or operating a conditional adult-use retail dispensary. The organization chart should identify all officers with the authority to control and all business entities that through direct or indirect means, will manage, own or control the interests and assets of the license holder. If the business entities have boards, include all board members on this chart. If the business entity has a parent company, include the name of each parent company's principal officer(s) and the percentage ownership interest;

(12) organizational documents such as the certificates of incorporation, certificates of limited partnerships, articles of organizations, charter, by-laws, partnership agreement, agreements between any two or more persons of the applicant that relate in any manner to the assets, property or profit of the applicant, or any other comparable documents that set forth the legal structure of the applicant or relate to the organization, management or control of the applicant;

(13) if an applicant is not an individual, a description, beginning with the formation of the applicant, of any and all ownership changes between the formation of the applicant and the date the application is submitted, including, but not limited to, events such as asset sales and purchases, stock sales and purchases, mergers, business combinations, or consolidations involving the applicant, including all former names of the applicant;

(14) a copy of all compensation agreements between or among applicant and each true party of interest, or group of true parties of interest, whether direct or indirect, and to the extent such agreement is oral, a written description of the terms of such agreement with true parties of interest of the applicant;

(15) any proposed or executed contract, term sheet, agreement, or side letter between the applicant, true parties of interest of the applicant, or financier, and another party that relates to the ownership and control structure, assets, liabilities, real or intellectual property, revenue, funding or capitalization, royalties, or profit, or future profit, of the applicant or proposed licensee or comparable documents;

(16) the nature, type, terms, covenants and priorities of all outstanding bonds, loans, mortgages, trust deeds, pledges, lines of credit, notes, debentures or other forms of indebtedness issued or executed, or to be issued or executed, in connection with opening or operating the proposed conditional adult-use retail dispensary;

(17) audited financial statements of the applicant for the fiscal year ending one year prior to the date the application is submitted, which shall include, but is not limited to, an income statement, balance sheet, statement of retained earnings or owners' equity, statement of cash flows, and all notes to these statements

and related financial schedules, prepared in accordance with generally accepted accounting principles, along with the accompanying independent auditor's report. If the applicant was formed within the year preceding the application for license, provide certified financial statements for the period of time the applicant has been in existence and any pro forma financials used for business planning purposes;

(18) all sources of funding used to acquire, start, or develop the business for which the license is sought, and documentation concerning the source of the funds and copies of closing documents in connection with such acquisition or development;

(19) details of any state or federal, administrative or judicial proceeding in which the applicant or any of the true parties of interest of applicant:

(i) pled guilty, pled no contest, conditionally or otherwise, or were, convicted, fined, or the equivalent, or had a registration or license cancelled, suspended or revoked; or

(ii) managed or served on the board of a business or nonprofit organization that pled guilty or was convicted, fined, or had a registration or license cancelled, suspended or revoked.

(20) information relating to a business continuity plan;

(21) a certificate of status or good standing from the governing state agency of the state of formation, certificate of assumed name, a certificate of authority to do business in New York from the New York Department of State if the applicant is a foreign business, where applicable;

(22) if applicant or any true parties of interest of applicant are currently or have previously been licensed or authorized in another state or jurisdiction to cultivate, process, manufacture, distribute or sell cannabis products in any form, the following:

(i) a copy of each license or authorizing document verifying licensure in that state or jurisdiction;

(ii) a statement granting permission to contact the regulatory agency that granted the license to confirm the information contained in the application is true and accurate; and

(iii) if the license, authorization, or application was ever cancelled, denied, suspended, revoked or otherwise sanctioned, a copy of documentation so indicating, or a statement that the applicant or true party of interest of applicant was so licensed and was never sanctioned;

(23) any management agreement, contract, arrangement, or other type of formal understanding between a contractor and an applicant where the contractor will or does provide administrative, operational, financial, advisory, and/or management services to an applicant in exchange for remuneration and a list of all the parties that are contained in those agreements;

(24) a list of each vendor with which the applicant has entered into a contract, term sheet, agreement, or side letter;

(25) whether the applicant or any true party of interest of applicant:

(i) has ever filed a voluntary petition or had an involuntary petition filed against it for relief under the United States Bankruptcy Code;

(ii) is out of compliance with general obligations law section 3-503(2);

(iii) has been disciplined or sanctioned by a state or federal agency; or

(iv) has had any state or federal tax liens against any of their property;

(26) a list of each financier of applicant, and copy of all financier agreements, if any;

(27) a copy of each agreement between applicant and any person with a financial interest in the applicant;

(28) a list of any charitable contributions by the applicant in the last five years;

(29) a list of stocks, mutual funds or bonds held by the applicant;

(30) documentation acceptable to the Office that the applicant will be able to obtain insurance sufficient to indemnify and hold harmless the state and its officers and employees;

(31) information regarding any relationship, agreement, or arrangement that may exist between (i) the applicant or true parties of interest and (ii) any official or any other individuals with control over the approval of an application or license, including, but not limited to, employees of the Office and members of the Board;

(32) information evidencing compliance with the provisions set forth in section 116.4(a)(1) of this Part as required by the Office;

(33) information evidencing applicant's eligibility as set forth in sections 116.4(a)(2) or 116.4(a)(3) of this Part as required by the Office;

(34) designation of each portion of the application that applicant considers to be exempt from disclosure under the New York State Freedom of Information Law; and

(35) any additional information requested by the Office.

(b) General.

(1) Notification of the availability of applications, instructions for completion and submission of applications, and application forms will be posted on the Office's website at www.cannabis.ny.gov.

(2) The license application shall be submitted via forms provided by the Office. The forms will include instructions for their completion and submission. The application will reflect the information required of applicants by the Cannabis Law and this Part and will include requests for information in support of the application needed by the Office to ensure that the application submitted is complete. If all material, documentation, and information required by the application form is not submitted, the applicant shall receive a deficiency notice from the Office. The applicant shall then have 30 calendar days from the date the deficiency notice is sent to resubmit the application in its entirety. Applications that are still incomplete after this opportunity to cure will not be considered. Upon receipt of an application deemed to be complete, the Office will engage in no further communication with the applicant until after the selection process is completed.

(3) Only applications completed in accordance with this Part as determined by the Office and submitted in a timely manner shall be considered.

(4) Prior to the issuance of a license, an applicant may apply to amend its previously submitted true parties of interest; provided, however, that such amendment shall not violate the requirements as set forth in this Part. Failure to apply to amend may be deemed an inconsistent material statement in the application as to its true parties of interest and such failure may constitute grounds for denial of the application by the Board.

(5) There shall be a non-refundable application and license fee of $2,000 for applications submitted for a license under this Part.

(c) Continuing Duty to Disclose and Approval.

(1) The applicant shall have a continuing duty to disclose material changes in the information provided to the Office required in this Part.

(2) If an applicant is issued a license, this duty of ongoing disclosure shall continue throughout the licensed period and the following shall require prior written approval of the Office, including any changes thereto:

(i) ownership and control;

(ii) any financier arrangements;

(iii) any true party of interest;

(iv) location;

(v) management service agreements;

(vi) intellectual property agreements;

(vii) guaranty agreement; and

(viii) any other activity or agreement as determined by the Office.

9 CCR-NY § 116.3. Attestations.

(a) The applicant shall sign the proof of attestation, attesting that the applicant:

(1) has submitted an application that is complete and accurate;

(2) submits to jurisdiction of the courts of New York State and the application of all state laws, local laws and regulations of New York State, including, but not limited to, relating to the conditional adult-use retail dispensary;

(3) shall not sell any cannabis product to anyone under 21 years of age;

(4) shall not sell any cannabis product in any disallowed form, as determined by the Office;

(5) shall not give away any cannabis product as set forth in the Act;

(6) shall only acquire cannabis products from entities authorized to distribute cannabis products in New York State;

(7) shall ensure that the eligible applicant, upon being granted a license, shall maintain the minimum ownership and control requirements set forth in section 116.4 of this Part, and that noncompliance shall be deemed a surrender of license as determined by the Office;

(8) shall ensure that its true parties of interest are of good moral character;

(9) shall exercise reasonable care to confirm its information and the ability of each person to meet the requirements as set forth in this Part;

(10) shall provide the Office a complete disclosure that includes all true parties of interest and that each individual who is a true party of interest is at least 21 years of age;

(11) shall not attempt to conceal or disguise ownership or other control over its operations in its submissions;

(12) shall register with the New York State Department of Taxation and Finance for a certificate of adult-use cannabis registration and, if applicable, a certificate of authority should the applicant be granted a license;

(13) shall indemnify and hold harmless the State of New York for any and all civil or criminal penalties resulting from receiving a conditional adult-use retail dispensary license;

(14) has entered into a labor peace agreement with a bona fide labor organization and understands that the maintenance of such a labor peace agreement shall be an ongoing material condition of the license;

(15) shall comply with applicable state and local laws, regulations, and guidance; and

(16) shall submit any other information as required by the Office.

9 CCR-NY § 116.4. License Eligibility and Evaluation.

(a) Eligibility. The following minimum requirements must be met to become an eligible applicant for this license:

(1) an applicant must demonstrate:

(i) a significant presence in New York State, either individually or by having a principal corporate location in the state;

(ii) it is incorporated or otherwise organized under the laws of New York State; or

(iii) a majority of the ownership of the applicant are residents of New York State by being physically present in the state no less than 180 calendar days during the current year or 540 calendar days over the course of three years;

(2) if the applicant is an individual, or an entity with one or more individuals, at least one individual must:

(i) be justice involved, which means an individual that:

(a) was convicted of a marihuana-related offense in New York State prior to the thirty-first of March two thousand twenty-one;

(b) had a parent, legal guardian, child, spouse, or dependent who was convicted of a marihuana-related offense in New York State prior to the thirty-first of March two thousand twenty-one; or

(c) was a dependent of an individual who was convicted of a marihuana-related offense in New York State prior to the thirty-first of March two thousand twenty-one; and

(ii) provide evidence of the primary residence of the justice involved individual at the time of such individual's arrest or conviction; and

(iii) hold or have held, for a minimum of two years, at least ten percent ownership interest in, and control of, a qualifying business, which means a business that had net profit for at least two of the years the business was in operation; or

(3) if the applicant is a nonprofit organization, or wholly owned and controlled by one, the nonprofit organization must:

(i) be recognized as an entity pursuant to section 501(c)(3) of the Internal Revenue Code;

(ii) intentionally serve justice involved individuals and communities with historically high rates of arrest, conviction, incarceration or other indicators of law enforcement activity for marihuana-related offenses;

(iii) operate and manage a social enterprise that had at least two years of positive net assets or profit as evidenced in the organization's tax returns;

(iv) have a history of creating vocational opportunity for justice involved individuals;

(v) have justice involved individual(s) on its board or as officers; and

(vi) have at least five full time employees.

(b) Applicant Ownership and Control Minimums.

(1) At least 51% or more of the applicant shall be owned, in the aggregate, by:

(i) at least one individual that satisfies the requirements for an eligible applicant set forth in sections 116.4(a)(1) and 116.4(a)(2) or entity that satisfies the requirements for an eligible applicant set forth in sections 116.4(a)(1) and 116.4(a)(3) of this Part; and

(ii) any other additional individuals, if any, who are justice involved; and

(2) At least one individual that satisfies the requirements for an eligible applicant set forth in sections 116.4(a)(1) and 116.4(a)(2) or entity that satisfies the requirements for an eligible applicant set forth in sections 116.4(a)(1) and 116.4(a)(3) of this Part shall own at least 30% of the applicant and such individual or entity shall have sole control of the applicant or licensee.

(c) Evaluation. An eligible applicant shall be evaluated based on any of the following criteria which shall be weighted as determined by the Office:

(1) if the applicant is an individual, or an entity with one or more individuals, whether the justice involved individual was themselves convicted of a marihuana-related offense as set forth in section 116.4(a)(2)(i)(a) of this Part;

(2) the justice involved individual's primary residence at the time of such individual's arrest or conviction:

(i) relative to areas with historically high rates of arrest, conviction, or incarceration for marihuana-related offenses;

(ii) relative to areas with historically low median income; or

(iii) was provided by a public housing authority in New York State or New York City; and

(3) the qualifying business based on:

(i) the number of employees employed by the business;

(ii) the number of years the business has been in operation;

(iii) the profitability of the business;

(iv) type of business and whether the business was a retail business, or sold products or services directly to the end-consumer;

(v) whether the business had a physical location; or

(vi) whether the business received or resolved any violations, fines or fees assessed against the business by state or federal regulatory authorities; and

(4) any other factors as determined by the Office.

(d) The office may create regional geographic zones for the scoring of applicants. Applicants may be asked to rank a number of preferences of regional geographic zones to be considered for a license. For regional geographical zones where there are more applicants than available licenses, the Office may select from eligible applicants who indicated first preference for the given region based on weighted scoring of the evaluation criteria set out above. In the event there is a tie between two or more candidates or there are more applicants than available licenses after the evaluation criteria has been applied, the Office is authorized to use a random selection process to identify the final applicants to recommend to the Board for licensure.

9 CCR-NY § 116.5. Denials.

(a) Notwithstanding an applicant satisfying the requirements set forth in this Part, the application shall be denied where an applicant or eligible applicant, or any true party of interest of the applicant:

(1) has submitted an application that contains inconsistent information;

(2) failed to submit the materials required by this Part within the specified time allotted;

(3) failed to submit fingerprints for purposes of providing a criminal history report required pursuant to section 138 of the Cannabis Law;

(4) is a person forbidden to traffic cannabis as set forth in section 137 of the Cannabis Law;

(5) has demonstrated prior business practices and financial arrangements that may not comply with state and local laws incidental to the cannabis industry;

(6) has had a license associated with cannabis cancelled, revoked or suspended in any other state or jurisdiction;

(7) creates or enhances the dangers of unlawful practices, methods and activities in the cannabis industry, including, but limited to, product inversion or diversion;

(8) is delinquent in filing any required tax returns or paying any amount owed to any local, state or federal government;

(9) causes a violation of Sections 72 or 85 of the Cannabis Law; or

(10) is not a person of good moral character.

9 CCR-NY § 116.6. Application for Renewal or Transition.

(a) Renewal:

(1) Applicant shall comply with all applicable state and local laws, regulations, and guidance relating to the licensed activities for renewal of its license.

(2) Prior to the expiration of the first renewal date, licensee shall submit an application to renew the license as prescribed by the Office and include such information and fees, if any, as the Office may require.

(3) Upon request for renewal, the Office shall consider the licensee's history of compliance with the requirements of this part and applicable state and local laws, regulations, and guidance.

(4) The Board may deny a renewal after consideration of the licensee's history of compliance.

(b) Transition:

(1) After the conditional period, to continue to conduct the activities licensed under this Part, a licensee may apply to transition to an adult-use retail dispensary license issued by the Board.

(2) One hundred twenty calendar days prior to the expiration of the conditional period, licensee shall notify the Office of its intent to continue the activities licensed under this Part beyond the expiration of the conditional period.

(3) The Office shall consider the licensee's history of compliance with applicable state and local laws, regulations, and guidance, including, but not limited to, whether the applicant has served the community in which it is located, to determine whether the licensee may transition to an adult-use retail dispensary license approved by the Board upon the expiration of the conditional period.

(4) The review shall conclude prior to the expiration of the conditional period, unless otherwise extended by the Office.

(5) The Board may deny a transition after consideration of the licensee's history of compliance.

9 CCR-NY § 116.7. Requirements and Prohibitions for Conditional Adult-Use Retail Dispensary License.

(a) A conditional adult-use retail dispensary license shall have the same authorizations and conditions as an adult-use retail dispensary as defined by the Cannabis Law and regulations promulgated by the Board;

(b) Should an applicant be awarded a conditional adult-use retail dispensary license, provisions, including, but not limited to, the attestation in the application, become a mandatory condition of the license; and

(c) The following conditions shall also apply to the license:

(1) each licensee and true party of interest shall be at least 21 years of age;

(2) at least 51% or more of the licensee shall be owned, in the aggregate, by:

(i) at least one individual that satisfies the requirements for an eligible applicant set forth in sections 116.4(a)(1) and 116.4(a)(2), or entity that satisfies the requirements for an eligible applicant set forth in sections 116.4(a)(1) and 116.4(a)(3) of this Part; and

(i) any other additional individuals, if any, who are justice involved; and

(3) at least one individual that satisfies the requirements for an eligible applicant set forth in sections 116.4(a)(1) and 116.4(a)(2) or entity that satisfies the requirements for an eligible applicant set forth in sections 116.4(a)(1) and 116.4(a)(3) of this Part shall own at least 30% of the licensee and such individual or entity shall have sole control of the licensee;

(4) the percentage of ownership in the licensee of the individual or entity set forth in sections 116.4(a)(2) and 116.4(a)(3) of this Part shall be proportionate to their interest in the capital, assets, and profits and losses of the licensee;

(5) during the conditional period, the licensee shall maintain the minimum ownership and control requirements in the licensee as set forth in sections 116.7(c)(2), 116.7(c)(3) and 116.7(c)(4) of this Part;

(6) the licensee shall enter into and comply with all terms and conditions of any agreement with any fund, as defined by this Part, that has been approved by the Board and made available by the office, including, but not limited to, accepting a dispensary location identified by the fund or office, any loan agreement with such fund, any lease or sublease agreement with the State of New York or its agents, or any other such agreements into which the licensee enters;

(7) the licensee shall have entered into a labor peace agreement with a bona fide labor organization and each party to the agreement has signed such agreement prior to the license being granted;

(8) the licensee shall commence operations no later than 12 months from the date the license is granted, or as otherwise determined by the Office;

(9) the applicant is prohibited from leasing, assigning, or subcontracting, in whole or in part, the leased premises associated with the fund, as defined by this Part;

(10) A licensee or any true party of interest of the licensee shall not have a direct or indirect financial or controlling interest in more than three conditional adult-use retail dispensary licenses issued under this Part

until the expiration of the conditional period;

(11) A licensee or any true party of interest of the licensee shall not hold an adult-use cultivation, conditional adult-use cultivator, processor, microbusiness, cooperative or distributor license pursuant to article four of the Cannabis Law or be registered as a registered organization pursuant to article three of the Cannabis Law, except for such organizations licensed pursuant to sections 68-a and 68-b of this article;

(12) A licensee or any true party of interest of the licensee shall not be interested, directly or indirectly, in any cultivator, processor, distributor, or microbusiness operator licensed pursuant to this article by stock ownership, interlocking directors, mortgage, or lien on any personal or real property or by any other means. Any lien, mortgage or other interest or estate, however, now held by such licensee or true party of interest on or in the personal or real property of such manufacturer or distributor, which mortgage, lien, interest or estate was acquired on or before December thirty-first, two thousand nineteen, shall not be included within the provisions of this section; provided, however, the burden of establishing the time of the accrual of the interest comprehended by this section shall be upon the person who claims to be entitled to the protection and exemption afforded hereby;

(13) the licensee shall comply with any other requirements as may be promulgated by the Office; and

(14) after the conditional period, to continue to conduct the activities licensed under this Part, a licensee must apply to transition to an adult-use retail dispensary license approved by the Board.

9 CCR-NY § 116.8. Suspension, Revocation, and Surrender.

(a) The Board shall deliver a written notice to the licensee for failure to comply with this Part, applicable state and local laws, regulations, or guidance relating to conditional adult-use retail dispensary and adult-use retail dispensary, including those promulgated after applicant submits its application for a license. If no effort has been made to cure, the license shall be deemed surrendered 30 calendar days from the date of the written notice. Written notice shall be sent to the licensee's last known address on file with the Office.

(b) In the event that licensee elects to cease operation of all licensed activities or to surrender its license within the conditional period, the following shall apply:

(1) licensee shall notify the Office in writing at least 30 calendar days prior to the date licensee anticipates ceasing operations;

(2) the written notice shall include a proposed plan for closure. The plan shall be subject to Office approval and may include a recommendation of any individual or entity that would qualify under this Part; and

(3) upon surrender of the license or cessation of operation, licensee shall vacate the leased premises associated with the fund, as defined by this Part, within 30 calendar days of surrender or cessation.

(c) If a licensee fails to comply with standards and special conditions of the license, the Office may assess a penalty in addition to the surrender of the license pursuant to this Part.

9 CCR-NY § 116.9. Severability.

The provisions of this Part are severable. If any provision of this Part is found to be invalid, or if any application of this Part to any person or circumstance is found to be invalid, the invalidity shall not affect any other provisions or applications which can be given effect without the invalid provision or application.

PART 128. ADULT-USE PACKAGING AND LABELING (PROPOSED

9 CCR-NY § 128.1. Definitions.

For purposes of Part 128 and Part 129 of this Title, the following terms shall have the following meanings:

(a) Advertising means disseminating communications in any manner or by any means, for the purpose of causing, directly or indirectly, the purchase or use of a cannabis product brand or cannabis product, including but not limited to websites, social media, brochures, prints ads, TV, radio, streaming, out of home, and digital advertisements.

(b) Attractive to individuals under twenty-one means labeling, packaging, advertising and marketing that is pleasing or appealing to persons under the age of twenty-one by using or including, among other things:

(1) Cartoons;

(2) Bubble-type or other cartoon-like font;

(3) Bright colors that are "neon" in appearance;

(4) Similarities to products or words that refer to products that are commonly associated with or marketed in a manner so as to be attractive to individuals under twenty-one, including but not limited to, any imitation of food, candy, soda, drinks, cookies, or cereal, in labeling, packaging, advertising, or marketing;

(5) Terms "candy" or "candies" or variants in spelling such as "kandy" or "kandeez";

(6) Symbols, images, characters, public figures, phrases, toys, or games that are commonly used to market products to individuals under the age of twenty-one; or

(7) Images of individuals who could reasonably appear to be under the age of twenty-one.

(c) Board means Cannabis Control Board.

(d) Brand or Branding means the name, entity name, or doing business as name, registered trademark, logo, symbol, motto, selling message, recognizable pattern of colors, or any other identifiable marker that identifies one adult-use cannabis licensee or adult-use cannabis licensee's cannabis products as distinct from those cannabis products of other adult-use cannabis licensees and is used in, among other things, any packaging, labeling, advertising or marketing.

(e) Certificate of analysis means a certified report from a cannabis laboratory as set forth in Part 130 of this Title.

(f) Child-Resistant means special packaging for ultimate sale to a consumer that is:

(1) designed or constructed to be significantly difficult for children under five years of age to open and not difficult for adults to use properly as defined by 16 CFR §1700.15 for Poison Prevention Packaging Standards and 16 CFR §1700.20 for Testing Procedure for Special Packaging, as amended from time to time, and

(2) follows the packaging standards set forth in 16 CFR §1700.15 and the testing procedure set forth in 16 CFR §1700.20.

(g) Date of expiration means the date prior to which an unopened cannabis product meets applicable standards of identity, potency, and quality at the time of use, as determined by appropriate stability testing, subject to any storage conditions stated on the labeling.

(h) Exit package means a receptacle into which cannabis products within a retail package are placed at the retail point of sale. The exit package is optional.

(i) Health claim means any claim made on the retail package or marketing layer or in the marketing or advertising of a cannabis product, that expressly or by implication, including, but not limited to, by "third party" references, written statements (e.g., a brand name including a term such as "heart"), symbols (e.g., a heart symbol), or branding, characterizes the relationship of any cannabis product to a disease or health-related condition or symptom. Implied health claims include those statements, symbols, branding, or other forms of communication that suggest, within the context in which they are presented, that a relationship exists between the presence or level of a substance in the cannabis product to a disease or health-related condition or symptom.

(j) Licensee means an individual or an entity who has been granted a license for any activity under Article 4 of the Cannabis Law.

(k) Lot unique identifier or lot number or bar code means any distinctive combination of letters, numbers, or symbols, from which the complete history of manufacturing, testing, holding, distribution or recall of a lot of a cannabis product can be determined.

(l) Marketing means the activity or process for creating, communicating, delivering, and exchanging cannabis products.

(m) Marketing layer means packaging in addition to the retail packaging that is the outermost layer visible to the consumer at the point of sale. The Marketing Layer is optional, but if used it must be labeled according to the requirements in this Part.

(n) Non-consumer package means any container or wrapping used solely for the transport of cannabis or cannabis products in bulk and particularly a package intended solely for wholesale distribution as allowed in this Part.

(o) Office means the Office of Cannabis Management.

(p) Phytocannabinoids means any of the chemical compounds, excluding terpenes or any other compounds set forth by the Office, that are the active principles of cannabis sativa, including but not limited to tetrahydrocannabinol (THC) and cannabidiol (CBD), and does not include synthetic cannabinoids as that term is defined in subdivision (g) of schedule I of section thirty-three hundred six of the public health law.

(q) Post-consumer recycled material means new material produced using material resulting from the recovery, separation, collection and reprocessing of material that would otherwise be disposed of or processed as waste and that was originally sold for consumption. It does not include post-industrial material, or material generated by means of combustion, incineration, pyrolysis, gasification, solvolysis, chemical recycling and any high-heat or conversion process.

(r) Principal packaging display panel means the panel of the retail package or the marketing layer that the manufacturer or distributor intends to be displayed at retail.

(s) Resealable means a package that maintains its child-resistant effectiveness, as well as preserving the integrity of cannabis products for multiple servings.

(t) Retail package means a sealed, hard or soft-bodied, child-resistant receptacle in which cannabis product is for sale. Does not mean: (1) inner wrapping or lining; (2) an exit package; or (3) a non-consumer package used to transfer cannabis from one licensee to another.

(u) Reusable packaging is packaging made from durable material that is designed to be used repeatedly for a number of use cycles, is safe for washing and sanitizing, and is capable of being recycled at the end of use, with the exception of ceramic products.

(v) Use by date means the date prior to which an opened cannabis product meets applicable standards of identity, potency, and quality at the time of use, as determined by appropriate stability testing, subject to any storage conditions stated on the labeling.

(w) Tamper-evident means, with respect to a device or process, bearing a seal, a label or a marking that makes unauthorized access to or tampering with a package, product or container easily detectable.

(x) Total THC means the sum of the percentage by weight or volume measurement of tetrahydrocannabinolic acid multiplied by 0.877, plus, the percentage by weight or volume measurement of THC.

(y) Universal symbol means an image developed by the Office, and made available to licensees, that indicates that a retail package or product contains cannabis.

9 CCR-NY § 128.2. Cannabis Product Retail Packaging Minimum Standards.

(a) A retail package shall:

>   (1) be child-resistant;

>   (2) be tamper-evident;

>   (3) fully enclose the product, minimize oxygen exposure and prevent the contamination and/or degradation of the cannabis product; and

>   (4) not impart any toxic or deleterious substance onto the cannabis product.

(b) A licensee shall maintain a copy of the certificate showing that each retail package into which the licensee places cannabis or cannabis products is child-resistant and complies with the requirements of 16 CFR §1700.15 for Poison Prevention Packaging Standards and 16 CFR §1700.20 for Testing Procedure for Special Packaging, as amended from time to time.

(c) The exit package is optional and is not required to be labeled but may include the retail dispensary's name or logo, providing such that name or logo complies with the provision of section 128.6 of this Part.

9 CCR-NY § 128.3. Cannabis Product Retail Packaging Prohibitions.

(a) A retail package shall not:

>   (1) contain brand elements beyond one brand logo and the brand name (which has size restrictions but can be any font and color as set forth in this Part);

>   (2) contain any pictures, images, or graphics, other than what is required by the Office;

>   (3) contain any features that emit scent or sound;

>   (4) contain any features that change or alter a package's appearance through technology, other than for anti-counterfeiting purposes;

>   (5) be made attractive to individuals under twenty-one;

>   (6) be made of single-use plastic, unless containing a minimum 25% post-consumer recycled content; and

>   (7) violate any additional requirements as set out by the Office.

9 CCR-NY § 128.4. Retail Packaging Sustainability Program.

(a) A licensee shall submit an environmental sustainability program for cannabis product packaging as part of the application process, if applicable for the license type. Such programs may include but are not limited to reuse strategies collecting reusable cannabis packaging components to be sanitized and refilled or reused as cannabis packaging, or sustainable packaging strategies that use non-plastic, compostable or recyclable materials, or packaging materials exceeding 25% post-consumer recycled content. Within two years of issuance of the license, the licensee shall submit to the Board or Office a revised environmental sustainability product packaging plan.

(b) Retail packages can be reused after appropriate sanitation and based on visual inspection, if the retail package is in good working order and does not appear to pose a risk of unintended exposure or ingestion of cannabis products. The visual inspection must ensure such retail packages are not brittle or have chips, cracks, or other imperfections that could compromise the child-resistant properties of the retail package or otherwise pose a threat of harm to a consumer.

> (1) The retail packages shall be sanitized and disinfected either by a licensee or by a thirdparty to ensure that they do not contain any harmful residue or contaminants.

(c) Claims about recyclable or recycled content packaging shall comply with 16 CFR Part 260 regarding Guides for the Use of Environmental Marketing Claims.

(d) A licensee who packages products for retail sale shall annually report to the Office key metrics including but not limited to the total amount of packaging material, by weight, sold, offered for sale, or distributed into the state by the licensee in the prior calendar year; and the total costs of packaging material.

9 CCR-NY § 128.5. Cannabis Product Labeling Minimum Standards.

(a) Licensees authorized to package cannabis products for retail sale shall ensure that the principal packaging display panel shall have a white background with black text containing the following information:

> (1) milligrams per single serving of total THC (THC + THCA x 0.877), total CBD (CBD + CBDA x 0.877) content and any other marketed phytocannabinoids, or terpene profile;

> (2) milligrams per package of total THC (THC + THCA x 0.877);

> (3) the amount of total THC (THC + THCA x 0.877) and any other marketed phytocannabinoids as a percentage of volume, except if the cannabis product is in the form of an edible;

> (4) number of servings in total for the cannabis product except for cannabis flower and other forms of cannabis for vaporization;

> (5) weight of cannabis product; and

> (6) lot number.

(b) The retail package and any marketing layer shall contain the following information:

> (1) a list of all ingredients in descending order of predominance by weight in the cannabis product – both active and inactive. The ingredient list must include and separately list, in bold, any major allergens set forth in the Food Allergen Labeling and Consumer Protection Act of 2004, Title 21, as it relates to Food and Drugs, of the U.S. Code § 343, for misbranded food, as amended from time to time.

>> (i) Edible products and beverage products will include a nutritional label pursuant to Title 21, as it relates Food and Drugs, of the Codes of Federal Regulations §101.9(c) for nutrition labeling of food, as amended from time to time.

> (2) a list of any solvent used to produce the cannabis product, if applicable;

(3) the date of expiration of the unopened cannabis product;

(4) use by date;

(5) the proper storage conditions;

(6) name, address, license number, and contact information of the manufacturer or distributor;

(7) any one of the following three universal symbols on the upper left 25% of the marketing layer at a minimum size of 1.25 inch in height for the square symbol, 0.5 inch in width for the vertical symbol, and 0.5 inch in height for the horizontal symbol. The symbol must be made conspicuous by printing the symbol on, or outlining the symbol with, a contrasting color;

Image not shown. Refer to https://www.omarfigueroa.com/new-york-book/ or https://cannabis.ny.gov/system/files/documents/2022/06/part-128-and-129-plma-regs-final-draft-6-1-2022-v2.pdf

(8) total THC and CBD milligrams in bold on the principal packaging display panel or marketing layer;

(9) include clear usage instructions;

(10) a scannable bar code or QR code linked to a downloadable certificate of analysis, or linked to a website where the certificate of analysis can be downloaded; and

(11) any other information required by the Board.

(c) Required labeling text on the retail package or any marketing layer must be no smaller than 6-point font size. Labeling text on the retail package or any marketing layer must be clearly written or printed and in the English language. In addition to the required labeling in English, licensees may include an additional, accurate foreign language translation on the retail package that otherwise complies with this Part.

(d) The marketing layer is optional, but if used by a licensee in addition to the required packaging, it must be labeled according to the requirements in section 128.5 of this Part.

(e) The information required pursuant to section 128.5(a) of this Part must be unobstructed and conspicuous. A licensee may include the required information by printing the information directly onto the retail package or by affixing multiple labels with the information to the retail package, provided that none of the information is obstructed. For example, and not by means of limitation, the information may appear on labels that may be accordion, expandable, extendable, or layered to permit labeling of small retail packages.

(f) The retail packaging or marketing layer shall contain the following warnings:

(1) This product contains cannabis and THC;

(2) In all capital letters as indicated: "KEEP OUT OF REACH OF CHILDREN AND PETS. For use only by persons 21 years and older";

(3) Warning: Do not use if pregnant or nursing;

(4) National Poison Control Center 1-800-222-1222;

(5) For cannabis products intended to be smoked, inhaled, or vaporized: Warning: Smoking or vaping is hazardous to health;

(6) For cannabis products intended to be ingested orally: Warning: Effects of this product may be delayed by 4 or more hours;

(7) For all topical products: Warning: For topical use only. Do not eat or smoke; and

(8) Any other warning required by the Board.

(g) The warnings required pursuant to section 128.5(f) of this Part shall be displayed as follows:

(1) in the English language;

(2) in Times New Roman, Calibri, Arial, or Helvetica;

(3) in text no smaller than size 6 font;

(4) bolded;

(5) be legible, unobscured, and visible to the consumer; and

(6) in a bright yellow text box on the principal packaging display panel or marketing layer so as to stand out from other packaging and labeling. The use of a bright yellow color for the warning shall not render the retail package attractive to individuals under twenty-one as prohibited by section 128.3 of this Part. If the label or package are yellow in color, the text box shall be offset with a distinctive border so as to differentiate it from the surrounding label or package.

(h) In addition to the required warnings in section 128.5(f) of this Part, the retail packaging or marketing layer shall include any rotating health warnings as determined by the Office.

(i) Any research licensee conducting research approved by the Office involving human subjects shall comply with all packaging and labeling requirements, unless the licensee receives prior written approval for a waiver of specific packaging or labeling requirements in connection with any research approved by the Office. The waiver may extend to a licensee providing cannabis or cannabis products for an approved research study.

9 CCR-NY § 128.6. Cannabis Product Labeling Prohibitions.

(a) No retail package or marketing layer shall display any content or be labeled in any manner that:

(1) is made attractive to individuals under twenty-one as defined in 128.1(b) of this Part;

(2) includes any false or misleading statements including, but not limited to, any health claims;

(3) includes the term "organic";

(4) includes the term "craft" unless the processor meets the term as defined in Part 118 of this Chapter;

(5) causes a reasonable consumer confusion as to whether the cannabis product is trademarked, marked or labeled in a manner that violates any federal trademark law or regulation;

(6) contains any illustration or content that falsely portrays cannabis or cannabis products as being authorized under or part of Article 3 or Article 5 of the Cannabis Law;

(7) depicts cannabis, excluding the universal symbol as required by section 128.4 of this Part, cannabis products, or paraphernalia;

(8) promotes overconsumption;

(9) promotes price, price reductions, or any other discount or coupon;

(10) depicts a child or other person reasonably appearing to be under the age of twenty-one; and

(11) violates additional prohibitions as set out by the Office.

9 CCR-NY § 128.7. Retail Packaging and Labeling Violations and

Penalties.

(a) The Board may suspend, cancel, or revoke a license and impose any other penalties as authorized by Subchapter J of this Title and the Cannabis Law for the following violations:

>(1) failing to comply with this Part; and

>(2) transferring, selling, or offering to sell a cannabis product for retail sale to a consumer or to another licensee that is not packaged or labeled in accordance with this Part.

(b) If a licensee receives a cannabis product for retail sale that is not packaged or labeled in accordance with this Part, the licensee must immediately notify the Office and either:

>(1) return the cannabis product to the licensee who transferred the item or product to the licensee; or

>(2) in the event the cannabis product is packaged according to this Part but is not labeled according to Part 128, correct the labeling by adding only the information required to make the labeling compliant. If the noncompliance cannot be corrected by affixing a label with the required information, the cannabis product must be returned to the licensee who manufactured the cannabis product and transferred it to the licensee.

(c) If a licensee returns a cannabis product to the licensee who transferred the product, the licensee must document the return and the reason for the return in the inventory tracking system.

9 CCR-NY § 128.8. Referenced Material.

(a) Regulations included in Part 128 of this Title contain references to documents for information as to the standards to be met or guidelines and methodologies to be used in meeting the requirements of specific regulations. In addition, copies of referenced materials are available for public inspection and copying at the Albany office of the New York State Department of State.

Table 1

Regulation	Referenced Material	Availability
9 NYCRR Part/sec./etc.	CFR (Code of Federal Regulations) or other	
128.1(f)(1)	Title 16 §§ 1700.15 and 1700.20 (January 1, 2021)	*
128.2(b)	Title 16 §§ 1700.15 and 1700.20 (January 1, 2021)	*
128.4(c)	Title 16 CFR Part 260 (January 1, 2021	*

* Any printed editions of the Code of Federal Regulations (CFR) can be obtained by calling the Superintendent of Documents, U.S. Government Printing Office, at (202) 512-1800. Electronic copies of CFR sections may also be obtained at Government Printing Office (GPO) which contains the most recent revisions, can be searched directly at: https://www.ecfr.gov/

PART 129. ADULT-USE MARKETING AND ADVERTISING (PROPOSED REGULATIONS)

9 CCR-NY § 129.1. Definitions.

For purposes of this Part, the terms used herein shall have the meanings ascribed to them in section 128.1 of this Title.

9 CCR-NY § 129.2. Adult-Use Marketing and Advertising General Requirements.

(a) A licensee may use its brand on labeling, signage, and other material subject to Parts 128 and 129 of this Title.

(b) A licensee is permitted to develop advertising and marketing materials, provided the primary purpose of the advertising is to displace the illicit market and inform the consumer of the location of licensed retail dispensaries. A licensee may engage in reasonable advertising practices that are not otherwise prohibited in this Part, provided the marketing and advertising does not jeopardize public health or safety, promote youth use, or be attractive to individuals under twenty-one.

(c) Any marketing or advertisement of cannabis or cannabis products shall include the following statements, in a conspicuous manner on the face of the marketing material or advertisement or be read aloud clearly at the same volume and pace as the rest of the advertisement.: "For use only by adults 21 years of age and older. Keep out of reach of children and pets. In case of accidental ingestion or overconsumption, contact the National Poison Control Center hotline 1-800-222-1222 or call 9-1-1. Please consume responsibly."

(d) Any marketing or advertising of cannabis or cannabis products shall include one of the following warnings in a rotating manner as directed by the Office, in their entirety in a conspicuous manner on the face of the marketing material or advertisement:

(1) "Cannabis may cause impairment and may be habit forming.";

(2) "Cannabis can impair concentration, coordination and judgment. Do not operate a vehicle or machinery under the influence of cannabis.";

(3) "There may be health risks associated with consumption of this product.";

(4) "Cannabis is not recommended for use by persons who are pregnant or nursing." or

(5) Other warnings as determined by the Board.

(e) Warnings in print or digital advertisements pursuant to sections 129.2(c) and 129.2(d) of this Part shall be displayed as follows:

(1) in the English language;

(2) in Times New Roman, Calibri, Arial, or Helvetica;

(3) in text no smaller than size 6 font;

(4) bolded;

(5) be legible, unobscured, and visible to the consumer; and

(6) in a bright yellow text box so as to stand out from the surrounding advertisement. The use of a bright yellow color for the warning shall not render the advertisement attractive to individuals under twenty-one as prohibited by section 129.2 of this Part. If the surrounding advertisement is yellow in color, the text box shall be offset with a distinctive border so as to differentiate it from the surrounding advertisement.

(f) A licensee shall include the New York State HOPEline phone number, text number, and website or QR code on any advertising or marketing materials, by displaying the information on visual media or by reading the information in audio media.

(g) A licensee shall only advertise cannabis products, cannabis paraphernalia, or goods or services related to cannabis or cannabis products by means of television, radio, print, internet, mobile applications, social media, other electronic communication, or print publication if the licensee has reliable evidence that at least 90%, unless otherwise determined by the Office, of the audience for the advertisement is reasonably expected to be twenty-one years of age or older. The burden of proof of the audience composition lies with the licensee.

(h) A licensee shall maintain records and documentation to establish that its advertising and marketing meet the requirements of this Part.

(i) A licensee may sponsor a charitable, sports, or similar event provided however, a licensee shall not engage in advertising at, or in connection with, such an event unless the licensee has reliable evidence that at least 90%, unless otherwise determined by the Office, of the audience at the event and/or viewing advertising in connection with the event is reasonably expected to be twenty-one years of age or older. Advertising and marketing at eligible events must comply with this Part.

(j) A licensee shall limit the apparel displaying its brand and trademark used in connection with the sale of apparel displaying its brand to only adult sizes. Such apparel shall only be sold by the licensee within its licensed premises. The universal symbol as determined in Part 128.4(b)(8) of this Title cannot be used in branded apparel.

(k) A licensee shall accurately and legibly include its name and license number on all advertising and marketing for its products.

(l) A licensee who advertises via a website or digital application shall have a mechanism designed to keep those under the age of twenty-one from visiting the website or digital application.

(m) A licensee who has entered into an intellectual property licensing agreement, marketing or advertising agreement or any other agreement in which a licensee authorizes the use of its intellectual property, or allows a third party to market or advertise on its behalf, the licensee is responsible to ensure that such agreement, intellectual property use, marketing or advertising shall comply with Part 128 and Part 129 of this Title.

(n) Additional requirements as set out by the Office.

9 CCR-NY § 129.3. Adult-Use Marketing and Advertising Prohibitions.

(a) No marketing or advertising of cannabis products shall:

(1) depict cannabis not otherwise permitted by section 128.4 of this Title or paraphernalia;

(2) use or display images designed in any manner to be attractive to individuals under twenty-one;

(3) use audio that may be attractive to individuals under twenty-one, including but not limited to using children's voices or cartoon voices;

(4) be on or in the form of a billboard;

(5) use or display colloquial references to marijuana and cannabis or depictions or digital images or icons, whether animated or static, of cannabis, cannabis products, paraphernalia, or the imagery or action of smoking or vaping, including but not limited to "stoner", "chronic", "weed", "pot", or "sticky buds";

(6) be false or misleading, including making any health claims or a representation that use of cannabis has

curative or therapeutic effects;

(7) promote overconsumption or rapid consumption;

(8) promote product potency or THC concentration;

(9) promote price, price reductions, or any other discount, customer loyalty program, or coupon;

(10) falsely portray cannabis or cannabis products as being in compliance with Article 3 and Article 5 of the Cannabis Law;

(11) assert that cannabis or cannabis products are safe because they are regulated by the Board or Office;

(12) depict a child or other person under the age of twenty-one or reasonably appearing to be under the age of twenty-one. Talent portrayed in cannabis advertising should be a minimum of twenty-five years old, substantiated by proper identification;

(13) use the term "organic;"

(14) contain any obscene or indecent statement, design, or representation, picture, or illustration;

(15) be within or be readily observed within 500 feet of an elementary or secondary school grounds as defined in Education Law, recreation center or facility, childcare center, playground, public park, or library;

(16) disparage products of another cannabis business;

(17) encourage the transportation of cannabis across state lines or otherwise encourage illegal activity;

(18) be on or through handbills that are passed out in public areas including but not limited to parking lots and publicly owned property;

(19) a licensee's brand cannot include medical symbols that might reasonably lead a consumer to think the product is a medical product;

(20) sponsor an event using a licensee's brand, business, or trade name;

(21) utilize unsolicited pop-up or banner advertising on the internet other than on agerestricted websites for people twenty-one and over who consent to view cannabis-related material;

(22) produce any items for sale or promotional gifts, such as T-shirts or novelty items, bearing a symbol of or references to cannabis. This prohibition shall not pertain to cannabis paraphernalia sold to consumers;

(23) advertise through the marketing of free promotional items including, but not limited to, gifts, giveaways, discounts, points-based reward systems, customer loyalty programs, coupons, and "free" or "donated" cannabis products, except for the provision of branded exit packages by a licensee for the benefit of customers after a retail purchase is completed; or

(24) violate additional prohibitions determined by the Board or Office.

(b) A licensee shall not permit the use of their trademarks, brands, names, locations, or other distinguishing characteristics for third-party use on advertising in a manner that does not comply with this Part or any other statute, rule or regulation.

9 CCR-NY § 129.4. Outdoor Signage.

(a) Outdoor retail store signage for the purpose of alerting individuals to the location of an adult-use cannabis retail dispensary is permitted provided such signs:

(1) are limited to the following information:

    (i) business or trade name,

    (ii) business location, and

    (iii) the nature of the business;

(2) are affixed to a building or permanent structure;

(3) are both limited to sixteen hundred square inches;

(4) are not illuminated by neon lights;

(5) are not on vehicles;

(6) do not total more than two in number per licensee; and

(7) do not depict cannabis, cannabis products, or the imagery or action of smoking or vaping.

(b) Outdoor marketing or advertising is prohibited on signs and placards in arenas, stadiums, shopping malls, fairs that receive state allocations, and video game arcades, whether any of the foregoing are open air or enclosed, but does not include any such sign or placard located at an adult only facility or as further set out by the Office in guidance.

(c) Use of a commercial mascot is prohibited.

(d) A licensee shall remove the outdoor signage if the Office determines the outdoor signage violates the provisions of Cannabis Law and this Part or if the licensee fails to provide records to the Office upon request that establishes the outdoor signage meets the requirements of Cannabis Law and this Part.

(e) Outdoor retail store signage must comply with any additional requirements as set out by the Office.

9 CCR-NY § 129.5. Adult-Use Marketing and Advertising Violations and Penalties.

(a) A licensee shall immediately remove or discontinue advertising or marketing if the Board determines the advertising, marketing, or outdoor signage violates the provisions of Cannabis Law and this Part or if the licensee fails to provide records to the Office upon request that establishes the advertising and marketing meets the requirements of Cannabis Law and this Part.

(b) In the event a third-party has used a licensee's trademarks, brands, names, locations, or other distinguishing characteristics in an advertisement that does not comply with this Part or any other statute, rule or regulation, the licensee must immediately notify the Office, issue a ceaseand-desist notification to the third-party, and may pursue appropriate legal action.

(c) The Office may take any action against any licensee who fails to comply with this Part, including but not limited to recommendations to the Board for suspension, cancellation, or revocation of a license, imposition of any fees or fines, requiring a licensee to cease by a date determined by the Office the non-compliant marketing and advertising and requiring removal by a date determined by the Office of any marketing material or advertising still being published or displayed, and any other penalties set forth in Cannabis Law and Part 133 of this Title.

PART 130. CANNABIS LABORATORIES (EMERGENCY REGULATIONS)

9 CCR-NY § 130.1. Definitions.

For purposes of this Part, the following terms shall have the following meanings:

(a) Analyte means a contaminant, chemical and/or physical property, element, compound, organism, or group of any of the foregoing, the existence and amount of which a laboratory testing facility tests for or identifies in a sample.

(b) Analyte withdrawal means a cannabis laboratory's request to remove approval for an analyte or group of analytes, in total or in part.

(c) Approved method means an analytical method, including sample preparation, of proven reliability which has been approved or recognized by this Part, any New York State agency, or other regulatory program, for the specific purpose for which the method is to be used.

(d) Cannabis laboratory means a laboratory testing facility as defined in the Cannabis Law.

(e) Cannabis laboratory permit means a permit issued under this Part to a cannabis laboratory.

(f) Cannabis product batch means a uniquely defined quantity of medical cannabis or cannabis product; including pre-roll, that is uniform in processing, manufacture, and packaging within a concurrent time frame.

(g) Certificate of analysis means a certified report from a cannabis laboratory meeting the requirements of this Part.

(h) Data integrity training means training related to the following topics, among others: organizational mission and its relationship to the critical need for honesty and full disclosure in all sampling; transportation and analytical reporting; how and when to report data integrity issues; record keeping; and breaches of ethical behavior, including but not limited to, improper data manipulations, adjustments of instrument time-clocks, dry-labbing, and changes in: concentrations of standards, date and time of sampling, transport, and analysis.

(i) Gross Annual Receipts means:

(1) for an independent cannabis laboratory or cannabis laboratory operated within a facility which can segregate its laboratory income from total facility income, gross annual receipts means the total income of a cannabis laboratory from all sources for all laboratory tests performed pursuant to its permit under this Part, less any amounts paid to reference laboratories for such tests which are referred;

(2) for a cannabis laboratory operated by a facility which is reimbursed by third-party payors for laboratory services as part of an all-inclusive facility per diem rate and which cannot segregate laboratory income from total facility income, gross annual receipts means (x) the total annual cost of a cannabis laboratory multiplied by a fraction, the numerator of which is the gross revenue of the facility and the denominator of which is the gross cost of the operating facility, less (y) any amounts paid to reference laboratories for such tests which are referred; or

(3) for any other cannabis laboratory unable to segregate its annual income from tests performed pursuant to its permit under this Part, gross annual receipts means the amount a cannabis laboratory would have received had it billed the prevailing rate for such services. A cannabis laboratory must demonstrate to the Office its inability to segregate its annual income and obtain prior Office approval to use the approved method set forth in subdivision (c) of this section.

(j) Laboratory regulatory audit means an on-site or virtual assessment or audit conducted by the Office, or by a state regulatory program recognized by the Office pursuant to this Part.

(k) Lead technical director means a technical director or manager (1) that a cannabis laboratory designates to be directly responsible for overall administration of the technical and scientific operation of a cannabis laboratory, including the supervision of other technical directors or managers, and (2) whose name appears on the permit issued under this Part and on the application, proficiency tests and any laboratory regulatory audit materials submitted by a laboratory to the Office in connection with an application for a permit under this Part.

(l) Laboratory technician means a laboratory technician or analyst who is responsible for culturing, extracting or testing cannabis samples using analytical instrumentation including, but not limited to solid phase extraction, gas chromatography, liquid chromatography, inductively coupled plasma – mass spectrometry, and polymerase chain reaction.

(m) Permit year shall mean the approval year which is a period during which a cannabis laboratory is authorized to operate, commencing on April 1 and ending on March 31, unless otherwise renewed or extended as set forth in this Part.

(n) Phytocannabinoid refers to any of the chemical compounds, excluding terpenes or any other compounds set forth by the Office, that are the active principles of cannabis sativa, including but not limited to tetrahydrocannabinol (THC) and cannabidiol (CBD), and does not include synthetic cannabinoids as that term is defined in subdivision (g) of schedule I of section thirty-three hundred six of the public health law.

(o) Proficiency test (PT) means a test that requires a laboratory to produce analytical results within acceptable limits on an analyte or group of analytes of which the concentration and identity is unknown to the laboratory or its employees but known to a proficiency test provider.

(p) Proficiency Test Provider (PTP) means an entity with an ISO/IEC 17043 accreditation for cannabis testing and is independent of a laboratory for which it provides a proficiency test.

(q) Proficiency Test Provider Accreditor (PTPA) means an entity independent of the laboratory and proficiency test provider (PTP) that accredits the PTP to ISO/IEC 17043 accreditation.

(r) Proficiency test sample (PT sample) means a sample that a PTP provides to a laboratory to conduct a proficiency test.

(s) Quality assurance officer means a quality assurance director, quality assurance manager or any other individual who is responsible for an integrated system of activities involving quality control, quality assurance, and quality improvements to ensure that a service meets defined standards of quality with a stated level of confidence.

(t) Quality system means a structured laboratory management system that meets the standards for a quality system as determined by the Office.

(u) State reference laboratory means a cannabis laboratory with which the Office contracts, or a laboratory operated by the NYS Department of Health, that reviews or retests samples submitted by other cannabis laboratories.

(v) Technical director means an individual responsible for the technical and scientific operation of a cannabis laboratory, and who meets the minimum qualifications in this Part. If a cannabis laboratory employs more than one technical director, a cannabis laboratory shall designate one technical director as the lead technical director.

(w) True party of interest means a person that has direct or indirect interest in a cannabis laboratory or a cannabis laboratory sampling firm as set forth by the Office in applicable regulations under Title 9 or guidance.

9 CCR-NY § 130.2. Cannabis Laboratory Permit Application.

(a) No person shall be a cannabis laboratory authorized to test medical cannabis and adultuse cannabis and issue laboratory test reports required by the Cannabis Law unless they have been granted a cannabis laboratory permit. A laboratory certified by the New York State Department of Health to conduct medical cannabis testing shall be deemed a provisional permittee and must comply with this Part.

(b)(1) An application for a cannabis laboratory permit shall be submitted to the Office in a manner and format determined by the Board. The application shall be signed by technical directors of a cannabis laboratory, and the following individuals: (i) by the applicant (if an individual); (ii) by a managing member (if a limited liability company); (iii) by an officer (if a corporation), (iv) by all partners (if a partnership); or (v) by an officer, director or trustee if an institution, trust, estate, or any other legal entity.

(2) At the time of application for a cannabis laboratory permit, the Board may require information regarding a cannabis laboratory, including, but not limited to:

(i) proof of ISO/IEC 17025 accreditation;

(ii) ownership, true parties of interest, financiers, organization structure;

(iii) quality control systems;

(iv) proficiency testing program;

(v) the premises;

(vi) qualification of personnel;

(vii) training programs;

(viii) consumables including but not limited to reagents and standard reference materials;

(ix) laboratory equipment;

(x) method of reporting results; and

(xi) any other information as requested by the Office.

(3) An application for a cannabis laboratory permit under this Part shall be accompanied by a non-refundable application fee in the amount of $1,000.00. Prior to issuance or renewal of a permit, an application or renewal application fee of $1,000, and permit fee shall be paid, unless otherwise expressly authorized by the Board pursuant to this Part.

(4) For an analyte or group of analytes which the Office requires testing, an application for a cannabis laboratory permit shall specify an analyte or group of analytes that a cannabis laboratory is seeking approval for, the cannabis product or medical cannabis and any other intermediates or forms to be analyzed, and the approved methods to be employed for an analyte or group of analytes in cannabis product or medical cannabis, and any other intermediates or forms.

(c) Upon receipt of such application, the Office shall review a cannabis laboratory's performance on proficiency tests and proficiency test samples, quality system documentation, technical director credentials, performance in laboratory regulatory audit, if applicable, and any additional materials and/or information requested by the Office. The Office shall make a preliminary determination whether the applicant qualifies for a cannabis laboratory permit, the analyte or group of analytes for which the applicant has applied, and the application and permit fee to be paid. The Board will issue the final determination on whether or not to approve or deny a cannabis laboratory permit.

(d) For purposes of the application and permit process, testing facilities housed in separate buildings shall be considered separate cannabis laboratories and require separate cannabis laboratory permits, unless such facilities obtain a written waiver from the Office. The Office may provide a waiver if the Office determines that:

(1) effective supervision of the operation of all such facilities can be exercised by the same technical director;

(2) the facilities can share the same quality manual, standard operating procedures and record and reporting templates; however, the analytical, record keeping, and reporting results are not duplicative between the facilities; and

(3) the facilities are owned by the same legal entity or same individual.

(e) A cannabis laboratory applicant may withdraw an application at any time prior to the issuance or denial of a permit provided that:

(1) a notice to withdraw an application is submitted to the Office in writing, dated, and signed by the applicant.

(f) A cannabis laboratory applicant may reapply at any time following the withdrawal of an application and will be required to submit a new application and application fee prior to any deadline for such application.

9 CCR-NY § 130.3. Cannabis Laboratory Fees.

(a) Cannabis Laboratory Permit Fee. The fee for an annual permit under this Part shall be paid by an applicant. An applicant shall pay the appropriate cannabis laboratory permit fee based on its gross annual receipts determined by the Board.

(1) A cannabis laboratory which has no gross annual receipts because it did not operate in New York State the previous permit year shall pay a first-year permit fee of $1,000 regardless of the number of months remaining in the permit year. When applying for renewal of that permit, a cannabis laboratory shall report its gross receipts for the calendar months in which it operated, and these receipts shall be projected to a twelve (12)-month basis for the purpose of computing gross annual receipts.

(2) A cannabis laboratory that had gross annual receipts in the previous permit year, and applies for a permit after commencement of the permit year shall pay a fee computed as an annual fee but prorated for the months remaining in the permit year, or $1,000, whichever is greater.

(b) A cannabis laboratory that applies for additions to its current permit, adding an analyte or group of analytes for which approval is sought and any other changes, must pay an application change fee as determined by the Board.

(c) Any fee specified in this Part shall be paid to the New York State Office of Cannabis Management by the method approved by the Office at the time of submission of the application.

(d) Failure of a cannabis laboratory to pay the appropriate fee is grounds for denial, suspension, revocation pursuant to this Part.

9 CCR-NY § 130.4. Cannabis Laboratory Permit Renewal Application.

(a) A cannabis laboratory shall submit a renewal application with the Office in a manner and format determined by the Office.

(b) An application to renew a permit issued under this Part shall be filed with the Office not more than six (6) months nor less than four (4) months prior to the expiration thereof. If a renewal application is not filed within four (4) months prior to the expiration thereof, the Board may determine that the permit shall have expired and become void on such expiration date.

(c) An application shall be accompanied by an application fee, which shall be nonrefundable, and a permit fee as set forth in this Part. Only an application completed in accordance with this Part as determined by the Office and for which the application and permit fees have been submitted shall be considered if submitted in a timely manner. The permit fee shall be returned to the applicant if the applicant is not granted a renewal permit under this section.

(d) The Office shall consider applications for preliminary determination for renewal in accordance with the criteria set forth in this Part.

9 CCR-NY § 130.5. Cannabis Laboratory Permit Issuance.

(a) An applicant for a cannabis laboratory permit may be granted a provisional permit for a period not to exceed twelve (12) months, provided it has:

(1) obtained ISO/IEC 17025 accreditation, or accreditation that is based on ISO/IEC 17025 accreditation by any other laboratory accreditation authority approved by the Office;

(2) satisfied the technical direction staff requirements as set forth in Section 130.11 – 130.14 hereof;

(3) satisfied proficiency test requirements;

(4) satisfied all fee requirements; and

(5) satisfied any other requirements for approval pursuant to this Part other than completion of a laboratory regulatory audit.

(b) A cannabis laboratory with a provisional permit shall be granted final approval for an analyte or group of analytes for which it seeks approval provided:

(1) the results of a laboratory regulatory audit confirm compliance with the staffing, methodological and other requirements of this Part; and

(2) the cannabis laboratory demonstrates effective implementation of its quality system for (i) planning and assessing the work it performs, and (ii) conducting required quality assurance and quality control procedures to promote and maintain the accuracy and reliability of test results.

(c) A cannabis laboratory permit shall set forth the nature of the permit (provisional or final); an analyte or group of analytes that a cannabis laboratory is authorized to examine and identify; the approved testing methods; the name of the laboratory's technical director(s), including lead technical director if there is more than one; and the expiration date of the permit, which shall be March 31 of the permit year.

(d) A cannabis laboratory may make additions to its permit, adding an analyte or group of analytes for which approval is sought and will be required to submit an application and pay a fee for such addition.

(e) A cannabis laboratory permit and any appendices shall be posted conspicuously in a cannabis laboratory and on its website, and a copy shall, upon request, be provided by a cannabis laboratory to any person requesting the services of a cannabis laboratory.

(f) A cannabis laboratory permit shall be effective only for a cannabis laboratory to which it was issued.

(g) A cannabis laboratory permit is not transferable or assignable, including, without limitation, to another cannabis laboratory.

(h) A cannabis laboratory meets the requirements of a testing laboratory as set forth in section 114.10 of Title 9 of the Official Compilation of Codes, Rules and Regulations of the State of New York.

9 CCR-NY § 130.6. Cannabis Laboratory Permit Renewal Denial.

(a) A cannabis laboratory's application for a permit, or an application for a renewal of a permit, may be denied for the following reasons, among others:

(1) failure to submit a completed application;

(2) failure to pay an application fee;

(3) failure of laboratory staff to meet the personnel qualifications of education, training, and experience;

(4) failure to successfully analyze and report proficiency test results;

(5) failure to pass a required laboratory regulatory audit;

(6) failure to respond to a laboratory audit report with a corrective action report;

(7) failure to implement the corrective actions detailed in the corrective action report within the required timeframe;

(8) failure to implement a quality system;

(9) misrepresentation of any fact pertinent to receiving or maintaining a permit; and

(10) denial of entry during normal business hours for a laboratory regulatory audit.

(b) A denial of a cannabis laboratory's application for a permit, or an application for a renewal of a permit, including any notices and challenges thereto, if any, shall be pursuant to Subchapter J of Title 9.

9 CCR-NY § 130.7. General Cannabis Laboratory Requirements.

(a) A cannabis laboratory shall maintain ISO/IEC 17025 accreditation, or an accreditation that is based on ISO/IEC 17025 accreditation by any other laboratory accreditation authority approved by the Office.

(b) A cannabis laboratory shall participate in proficiency tests, if offered by an ISO/IEC 17043 approved proficiency test provider, at a frequency specified under this Part and have successfully passed two (2) out of the most recent three (3) proficiency tests as part of the permit requirements.

(c) A cannabis laboratory shall undergo a periodic laboratory regulatory audit by the Office as specified under this Part and provide any or all records associated with its ISO/IEC 17025 accreditation, or an accreditation that is based on ISO/IEC 17025 accreditation by any other laboratory accreditation authority approved by the Office.

(d) A cannabis laboratory shall employ qualified staff as set forth in this Part.

(e) A cannabis laboratory and its true parties of interest shall have no interest in a registered organization, adult-use cultivator, processor, distributor, retail dispensary, cooperative, microbusiness, delivery, nursery, on-site consumption, registered organization cultivator processor distributor retail dispensary, registered organization cultivator processor distributor, cannabinoid hemp processor, or any other license pursuant to the Cannabis Law.

(f) A cannabis laboratory shall have a continuing duty to disclose material changes in the information provided as required in this Part. Any changes to among other things, ownership, major instrumentation, technical direction, and location shall be subject to the requirements as set forth in Subchapter J of Title 9.

(g) A cannabis laboratory shall dedicate a percentage, as determined by the Board, of its testing capacity to licensees´ that are businesses with limited resources as determined by the Office, and to registered organizations for medical cannabis product testing pursuant to the requirements set forth in Subchapter B of this Title 9.

(h) A cannabis laboratory shall offer to businesses with limited resources as determined by the Office, terms and conditions for its services, including but not limited to pricing and priority of testing, that are at least as favorable as the terms and conditions granted by the cannabis laboratory to any other licensee or registered organization.

(i) A cannabis laboratory shall track and dispose of any quantity of cannabis product that is not consumed in samples used for testing. Disposal of cannabis shall mean that the cannabis has been rendered unrecoverable and beyond reclamation.

(j) Upon finding by the Board that the existing cannabis laboratory or cannabis sampling firm capacity is insufficient to meet the testing needs of the cannabis products manufactured, the Board may authorize the Office to take additional temporary emergency measures to reduce demand for laboratory testing services or increase laboratory testing supply to meet such needs.

(k) Notwithstanding provision (g) of this section, and to the extent practicable for efficient operations of the laboratory, all cannabis laboratories must test samples in the order they were received.

9 CCR-NY § 130.8. Required Cannabis Proficiency Testing.

(a) In connection with an application for a cannabis laboratory permit, a cannabis laboratory shall examine proficiency test samples supplied by a proficiency testing provider recognized by the Office, pursuant to this Part.

(b) Once a cannabis laboratory completes a proficiency test, a cannabis laboratory shall prepare a report for an analyte or group of analytes for which a cannabis laboratory is seeking approval and for which samples have been supplied.

(c) A cannabis laboratory shall submit the report directly to the proficiency testing provider.

(d) Upon the proficiency testing provider's review of a cannabis laboratory's report related to a proficiency test sample that a cannabis laboratory examined, a cannabis laboratory shall cause the proficiency test provider to provide the results of the proficiency test directly to the Office and in a manner and format determined by the Office.

(e) To obtain approval for a given analyte or group of analytes on its permit, a cannabis laboratory shall pass two (2) consecutive scheduled or unscheduled or supplemental proficiency tests. A cannabis laboratory may continue to attempt to obtain satisfactory performances beyond two (2) proficiency tests if the two (2) consecutive satisfactory performances are not obtained.

(f) To maintain approval for a given analyte or group of analytes on its permit, a cannabis laboratory shall attain satisfactory performance as determined by the Office, in at least two (2) of three (3) consecutive scheduled or unscheduled or supplemental proficiency test in which it has participated in an eighteen (18) month period.

(g) An unscheduled or supplemental proficiency test shall be at minimum seven (7) days from the close date of the prior scheduled or unscheduled proficiency test.

(h) At least one (1) of the two (2) of three (3) consecutive scheduled or unscheduled proficiency test in which a cannabis laboratory has participated in an eighteen (18) month period must be less than six (6) months old.

(i) A proficiency test that a cannabis laboratory completes must be administered by a proficiency test provider that:

(1) is accredited by a proficiency test provider accreditor to ISO/IEC 17043;

(2) offers scheduled tests on at least a semi-annually basis, and unscheduled tests on at least a monthly basis;

(3) agrees to supply the Office with proficiency test scores in a manner and format determined by the Office; and

(4) agrees to submit any other information and documentation requested to resolve any issues concerning compliance with this Part.

(j) The Office shall make available a list of proficiency test providers and the analytes to be proficiency tested on the Office's website.

9 CCR-NY § 130.9. Unsatisfactory Proficiency Test Performance.

(a) A cannabis laboratory's analyte or group of analytes approval status shall be deemed automatically unapproved for an analyte or group of analytes in the event:

(1) a cannabis laboratory fails two (2) out of three (3) most recent proficiency tests attempted for a particular analyte or group of analytes; or

(2) a cannabis laboratory fails to provide a corrective action report to the Office within thirty (30) calendar days of a request for a corrective action report from the Office.

(b) The Office shall change the approval status from unapproved to approved of a cannabis laboratory whose analyte or group of analytes is automatically unapproved, as specified above, when a cannabis laboratory re-establishes a history of two (2) successful proficiency test results out of the three (3) most recent attempts for an analyte or group of analytes tested.

9 CCR-NY § 130.10. Laboratory Regulatory Audit.

(a) A cannabis laboratory shall maintain an ISO/IEC 17025 accreditation, or accreditation that is based on ISO/IEC 17025 accreditation by any other laboratory accreditation authority approved by the Office.

(b) A cannabis laboratory shall have a laboratory regulatory audit every two (2) years during a cannabis laboratory's normal business hours.

(c) The factors to be considered during a laboratory regulatory audit shall include, but not be limited to, the competence and qualifications of staff as specified in this Part, adequacy of facilities and equipment, appropriateness of sampling protocols, use of approved methods, and a cannabis laboratory's quality system, including, but not limited to, quality assurance and quality control procedures, and record keeping and reporting practices.

(d) A cannabis laboratory shall demonstrate effective implementation of its quality system for planning and assessing work performed by a laboratory regulatory audit, and for conducting required quality assurance and quality control procedures to promote and maintain the accuracy and reliability of test results.

(e) A cannabis laboratory, following a laboratory regulatory audit, shall obtain an audit report which shall set forth any recommendations of the audit and any findings to be corrected.

(f) If findings are found during a laboratory regulatory audit, a cannabis laboratory may be granted a grace period not to exceed ninety (90) calendar days from the date of audit report to correct the findings, provided that, within thirty (30) calendar days of such audit report, a cannabis laboratory submits to the Office or another laboratory accreditation authority as approved by the Office performing the audit a written plan of correction to be implemented within ninety (90) calendar days from the date of audit report to correct the findings. If at the end of the grace period any of the findings remain uncorrected, the affected analyte or group of analytes pursuant to this Part will be unapproved.

(g) If the findings do not have an effect or do not have an immediate effect on either the accuracy or reliability of results, and if a cannabis laboratory demonstrates in writing that corrections of findings have been delayed for reasons beyond its control, the grace period granted pursuant to this subsection may be extended further for a period not to exceed ninety (90) calendar days. Such extension may not be extended further.

9 CCR-NY § 130.11. General Cannabis Personnel Qualifications.

(a) A cannabis laboratory shall:

(1) only employ persons who are eighteen (18) years of age or older;

(2) develop and implement an employee training program, which shall include but not be limited to, a training checklist, and an initial and continuing demonstration of capabilities, to ensure competency of a laboratory employee

for their assigned functions, which shall include, but not be limited to:

(i) health and safety training;

(ii) handling hazardous materials;

(iii) handling hazardous equipment; and

(iv) anything else as required by the Office.

(3) ensure and document that a laboratory employee meets the employee qualifications;

(4) ensure an employee completes data integrity training upon hire and annually thereafter, and evidence that such training was performed for an employee shall be documented and available upon request; and

(5) ensure an employee does not have a direct or indirect interest in a cannabis sampling firm, a registered organization or a cannabis permit, registration or license.

9 CCR-NY § 130.12. Cannabis Technical Director Qualifications.

(a) (1) A cannabis laboratory shall appoint one or more technical directors, who shall be fulltime members of the laboratory's staff, and who shall exercise actual supervision of laboratory operations, including the reporting of results from testing samples, during normal business hours. The designation of a lead technical director shall be documented; and

(2) a technical director shall have the requisite credentials and experience for an area of analysis, such as microbiology, analytical chemistry, organic chemistry, metals, inorganic chemistry, and physical analysis, and shall supervise only the areas of testing for which they meet the qualifications required by this section.

(b) A technical director's responsibilities shall include, but not be limited to, development and implementation of a quality system as defined in this Part, including: monitoring standards of performance in quality control and quality assurance; monitoring the validity of analyses performed and data generated to ensure reliable data; ensuring that sufficient numbers of qualified personnel are employed to supervise and perform the work of the laboratory; and providing educational direction to laboratory staff.

(c) A technical director may not serve as a technical director for more than one cannabis laboratory without written authorization from the Office. Circumstances to be considered in the Office's decision to grant such authorization may include, but not be limited to, the extent to which the operating hours of the laboratories to be directed overlap, adequacy of supervision in a cannabis laboratory, and availability of cannabis laboratory services in the area served.

(d) A technical director who is absent from a cannabis laboratory for a period of time exceeding fifteen (15) consecutive calendar days shall designate another full-time technical director, or where none is available, another staff member who meets the qualifications of this Part, to assume the responsibilities of technical director temporarily. Whenever the term of such temporary designation exceeds thirty-five (35) consecutive calendar days, the Office shall be notified in writing.

(e) A technical director of a cannabis laboratory engaged in organic chemical analysis shall be an individual with:

(1) an earned doctoral or master's degree in the chemical, environmental, physical or biological sciences, or engineering, with twenty-four (24) college semester credit hours in chemistry, or more, and one (1) or more years of experience in analysis of representative organic analytes for which the laboratory is permitted or seeking a permit; or

(2) a bachelor's degree in the chemical, environmental, physical or biological sciences, or engineering, with twenty-four (24) college semester credit hours, or more, in chemistry and two (2) or more years of experience in analysis of representative organic analytes for which the laboratory is permitted or seeking a permit.

(f) A technical director of a cannabis laboratory engaged in metals analysis shall be and individual with:

(1) an earned doctoral or master's degree in the chemical, environmental, physical or biological sciences, or engineering, with twenty-four (24) college semester credit hours, or more, in chemistry, and one (1) or more years of experience in analysis of representative metals analytes for which the laboratory is permitted or seeking a permit; or

(2) a bachelor's degree in the chemical, environmental, physical or biological sciences, or engineering, with twenty-four (24) college semester credit hours, or more, in chemistry and two (2) or more years of experience in analysis of representative metals analytes for which the laboratory is permitted or seeking a permit.

(g) A technical director of a cannabis laboratory engaged in inorganic chemistry analysis, other than metals analysis, and physical chemistry analysis, among other analysis, shall be a person with an associate's degree in the chemical, physical, biological or environmental sciences, or two (2) years of equivalent and successful college education, with sixteen (16) college semester credit hours, or more, in chemistry. In addition, such a person shall have two (2) or more years of experience performing such representative inorganic and physical chemistry analysis.

(h) A technical director of a cannabis laboratory engaged in microbiological and/or biological testing shall be an individual with:

(1) an earned doctoral degree or master's degree in the chemical, environmental, physical or biological sciences, or engineering, with sixteen (16) college semester credit hours, or more, in the biological sciences, including, for microbiological testing, at least once course having microbiology as a major component, and one (1) or more years of experience in analysis of representative microbiological analytes for which the laboratory is permitted or seeking a permit; or

(2) a bachelor's degree in the chemical, environmental, physical, or biological sciences, or engineering, with at least sixteen (16) college semester credit hours, or more, in the biological sciences, including, for microbiological testing, at least one course having microbiology as a major component, and two (2) or more years of experience in analysis of representative microbiological analytes for which the laboratory is permitted or seeking a permit.

(i) An individual who meets the experience requirements but not the educational and/or credential requirements of this Part, and is functioning in a technical director's capacity as subject to this section, including those individuals who are functioning in a technical director's capacity for those laboratories that were authorized to test medical cannabis products in New York State that existed prior to the effective date of these regulations, shall qualify as a technical director of that cannabis laboratory, or any other cannabis laboratory permitted by the Office and performing similar testing, provided such individual has been technical director in that cannabis laboratory for the previous twelve (12) consecutive months, or more, will oversee only those areas of testing for which they were a technical director for at the least previous twelve (12) consecutive months, and can demonstrate the ability to comply with the proficiency test and quality system requirements of this Part. An individual who is admitted as a technical director under these conditions, and leaves a cannabis laboratory, will be eligible for hire as a technical director for the same area of testing in another permitted cannabis laboratory.

9 CCR-NY § 130.13. Cannabis Quality Assurance Officer Qualifications.

(a) A cannabis laboratory shall appoint a quality assurance officer, who shall exercise oversight of a cannabis laboratory's quality system during normal business hours. The individual so appointed shall have documented training, and/or experience in quality assurance and quality control procedures; be knowledgeable in the required quality system; possess a general knowledge of analytical methods for which they perform data review; and have a bachelor's degree in the chemical, environmental, physical or biological sciences, or engineering, and two (2) or more years of experience in implementing a laboratory quality system.

(b) The quality assurance officer shall, at a minimum:

  (1) serve as the focal point for a cannabis laboratory's quality assurance and quality control, and be responsible for monitoring and/or review of quality control data;

  (2) evaluate data objectively and perform independent managerial reviews without outside influence;

  (3) arrange for or conduct annual internal audits of a cannabis laboratory's entire quality system and testing operation; and

  (4) notify cannabis laboratory management of any deficiencies in the quality system as part of an internal audit and monitor required corrective actions.

(c) The quality assurance officer shall have direct access to the highest level of management at which decisions are made on cannabis laboratory policy or resources, as well as to a technical director.

(d) The quality assurance officer shall fulfill their functions independently from cannabis laboratory operations for which they maintain quality assurance oversight.

(e) For cannabis laboratories with limited staffing, the quality assurance officer may also be a lead technical director or technical director; and an individual meeting the requirements of this section may not be the quality assurance officer of more than one cannabis laboratory without written authorization from the Office.

(f) An individual who meets the experience requirements but not the educational and/or credential requirements of this Part, and is functioning in a quality assurance officer's capacity as subject to this section, and is functioning in a quality assurance officer's capacity on the date a cannabis laboratory becomes subject to these regulations, shall qualify as quality assurance officer of that cannabis laboratory, or any other cannabis laboratory permitted by the Office and performing similar testing, provided such individual has been quality assurance officer in that cannabis laboratory for the previous twelve (12) consecutive months. An individual who is admitted as a quality assurance officer under these conditions, and leaves a cannabis laboratory, will be eligible for hire as a quality assurance officer in another permitted cannabis laboratory.

9 CCR-NY § 130.14. Cannabis Laboratory Technician Qualifications.

(a) A cannabis laboratory shall employ laboratory technicians. A laboratory technician shall have documented training or experience in laboratory procedures; possess a strong working knowledge of all methods for which they perform; and perform routine and non-routine sample preparations, tests, and analyses using the appropriate equipment, instrumentation, reagents, standards, and methods.

(b) A laboratory technician engaged in microbiology, analytical chemistry, organic chemistry, metals, inorganic chemistry, or physical chemistry testing shall have an associate's degree or two years of equivalent college or university studies in the chemical, environmental, physical or biological sciences, or engineering, and at least one (1) year of experience in testing of representative analyte or group of analytes for which the laboratory is permitted or seeking a permit

9 CCR-NY § 130.15. Approval of Laboratory-Developed Methods.

(a) A cannabis laboratory shall obtain approval from the Office prior to performing a laboratory-developed method, or other method not otherwise approved or given similar recognition as described in this Part. The Office may approve such a method, provided a cannabis laboratory submits data and other information as required supporting the technical merit of the method, and demonstrating that method's precision and accuracy are equivalent or superior to that of an approved method. Such data and information shall include, but not be limited to:

(1) a description of the method, including analyte or group of analytes, sample type, working range, reagents and their preparation, equipment specifications, analytical procedures, precision, accuracy, related calculations, intended purpose and pertinent literature citations;

(2) the anticipated date of method implementation;

(3) comparative data, if of the same technology, including: sample types, dates and times collected, and product or form, whether the sample was spiked, and, if so, the spiking procedure, and spiking samples at different concentrations; the approved method used; and analytical results for both the approved method and the method submitted for approval;

(4) data from two (2) or more proficiency tests;

(5) demonstration of capability data;

(6) limit of detection data, if applicable; and

(7) any other information pertinent to the Office's determination of the method's technical merit.

(b) Provided all other requirements of subdivision (a) above are met, the Office may approve a method for which reproducibility has not been demonstrated by inter-laboratory comparisons if a cannabis laboratory demonstrates that its performance of the method is technically acceptable for the intended sample types and analytical purpose. Such approval shall be limited to a cannabis laboratory which applied for such approval.

(c) In addition to the requirements of subdivisions (a) and (b) above, the Office may conduct a laboratory regulatory audit.

(d) The Office shall respond to a cannabis laboratory's request for method approval, notifying a cannabis laboratory of method approval, proposed denial of the request by the Office, or the need for further information.

(e) The Office may propose to deny a request for method approval if a method does not meet the established requirements. A cannabis laboratory shall be advised of a proposed denial and the reasons for the denial. A proposed denial shall become final thirty (30) calendar days from the date of notice of proposed denial, unless a cannabis laboratory submits, prior to the date that is thirty (30) calendar days after the date of such notice, a written request for reconsideration, including all documentation and rationale in support of such request. The Office shall consider a request for reconsideration and shall issue a final determination concerning the request for reconsideration.

(f) Notwithstanding the provisions of this Part, the Office may conduct an independent review of any approved method to substantiate or refute its technical merit. If the method's technical merit is found to be unacceptable, the Office shall notify a cannabis laboratory of its proposed determination that the method may not be performed under a New York State cannabis laboratory's permit, giving the reasons for such determination. Such proposed determination shall become final thirty (30) calendar days from the date of the notice of proposed determination, unless a cannabis laboratory offering such method submits, within thirty (30) calendar days of the date of the notice, a written request for reconsideration, including all documentation and rationale in support of such request. The Office shall consider a request for reconsideration and shall issue a final determination concerning the request for reconsideration.

(g) All information and data pertinent to method approval shall be documented and be made available for Office review at the time of a laboratory regulatory audit or upon request for a minimum of five (5) years after the date of the method's discontinuation.

9 CCR-NY § 130.16. Laboratory Sampling Firm Approval.

(a) No person may conduct sampling and transportation of cannabis product or medical cannabis and any other intermediates or forms for purposes of testing such cannabis product or medical cannabis by a cannabis laboratory unless they have been granted approval as a laboratory sampling firm; except where the registered organization or adult-use licensee, including conditional adult use cultivator and conditional adult use processor, is authorized to submit samples pursuant to Title 10 Part 1004, applicable regulations under Title 9, or the Cannabis Law.

(b) Prior to approval, a laboratory sampling firm shall submit a description of the sampling and transportation process describing how cannabis product or medical cannabis and any other intermediates or forms will be sampled and transported in the field or on premises, or a copy of the standard operating procedure addressing sampling and transportation.

(c) Approval of a laboratory sampling firm and its employees shall be conducted in a manner and format determined by the Office.

(d) Approval shall be effective for a period not to exceed two (2) years and shall expire on March 31.

(e) Approval of a laboratory sampling firm is not transferable or assignable, including, without limitation, to another laboratory sampling firm.

(f) A cannabis laboratory may receive conditional approval as a laboratory sampling firm with a written waiver from the Office. The Office may provide a waiver if the Office determines that a cannabis laboratory has met the conditions specified in sections 130.16 - 130.21 of this Part.

(g) A cannabis laboratory sampling firm and its true parties of interest shall have no interest in a registered organization, adult-use cultivator, processor, distributor, retail dispensary, cooperative, microbusiness, delivery, nursery, on-site consumption, registered organization cultivator processor distributor retail dispensary, registered organization cultivator processor distributor, cannabinoid hemp processor, or any other license pursuant to the Cannabis Law.

9 CCR-NY § 130.17. Laboratory Sampling Firm Fee.

(a) Laboratory Sampling Firm Application Fee and Approval Fee. A non-refundable application fee for a laboratory sampling firm is $500. The approval fee for the two (2) year approval period shall be $1000. The approval fee shall be returned to the applicant if the applicant is not granted approval under this Part.

(b) Any fee specified in this Part shall be paid to the New York State Office of Cannabis Management by the method approved by the Office at the time of submission of the application.

(c) Failure of a laboratory sampling firm to pay the appropriate fee is grounds for nonreapproval pursuant to this Part.

9 CCR-NY § 130.18. Laboratory Sampling Firm Reapproval.

(a) A laboratory sampling firm and its employees shall submit a reapproval application to the Office in a manner and format determined by the Office.

(b) An application to reapprove shall be filed with the Office not more than six (6) months nor less than four (4) months prior to the expiration thereof. If a reapproval application is not filed within four (4) months prior to the expiration thereof, the Office may determine that the firm's approval shall have expired and become void on such expiration date.

(c) An application shall be accompanied by a non-refundable application fee and approval fee as set forth in this Part. Only an application completed in accordance with this Part as determined by the Office and for which the application and approval license fees have been submitted shall be considered if submitted in a timely manner.

(d) The Office shall consider applications for reapproval in accordance with the criteria set forth in this Part.

(e) A denial of a cannabis laboratory sampling firm's application for a permit, or an application for a reapproval of a permit, including any notices and challenges thereto, if any, shall be pursuant to Subchapter J of Title 9.

9 CCR-NY § 130.19. Laboratory Sampling Firm Requirements.

(a) A laboratory sampling firm may only employ persons who are twenty-one (21) years of age or older.

(b) A laboratory sampling firm shall train all sampling and transportation employees on appropriate sampling and transportation procedures, and such training shall be documented.

(c) A laboratory sampling firm shall require all sampling and transportation employees to complete data integrity training upon hire and annually thereafter, and evidence that such training was performed for a sampling and transportation employee shall be documented and available upon request.

(d) An employee of a laboratory sampling firm shall carry a copy of the firm's approval and the copy shall, upon request, be provided to any person requesting the services of a laboratory sampling firm.

(e) A laboratory sampling firm shall conduct all sampling as set forth in this Part.

(f) A shipping manifest shall accompany every transport of cannabis product or medical cannabis and any other intermediates or forms from a registered organization, cultivator, processor, cooperative, microbusiness, or any other person licensed pursuant to the Cannabis Law or authorized to cultivate or process medical cannabis or adult-use cannabis pursuant to the Cannabis Law.

(g) While transporting cannabis product or medical cannabis and any other intermediates or forms, a laboratory sampling firm shall ensure the cannabis product or medical cannabis and any other intermediates or forms are not visible to and secure from the public:

> (1) The cannabis product or medical cannabis and any other intermediates or forms shall be locked in a fully enclosed box, container, or cage that is secured to the inside of the vehicle or trailer. No portion of the enclosed box, container, or cage shall be comprised of any part of the body of the vehicle or trailer. For the purposes of this section, the inside of the vehicle includes the trunk.

> (2) A vehicle and trailer transporting cannabis product or medical cannabis and any other intermediates or forms shall while left unattended be locked and secured.

> (3) A vehicle or trailer containing cannabis product or medical cannabis and any other intermediates or forms shall not be left unattended in a residential area or parked overnight in a residential area.

> (4) An employee of a laboratory sampling firm shall ensure that any vehicle or trailer used by the firm for transporting cannabis product or medical cannabis and any other intermediates or forms has a functioning alarm system.

> (5) An employee of a laboratory sampling firm shall ensure that packages or containers holding cannabis product or medical cannabis and any other intermediates or forms are neither tampered with, nor opened during transport.

> (6) An employee of a laboratory sampling firm, who is transporting cannabis product or medical cannabis and any other intermediates or forms shall only travel between the licensed premises and a cannabis laboratory, conducting testing.

> (7) An employee of a laboratory sampling firm shall not deviate from the travel requirements described in this section, except for necessary rest, fuel, or vehicle repair stops.

(8) An employee of a laboratory sampling firm may transport multiple cannabis product or medical cannabis and any other intermediates or forms obtained from multiple licensees at once.

(9) An employee of a laboratory sampling firm shall preserve the integrity of the cannabis product or medical cannabis and any other intermediates or forms during transport by maintaining environmental conditions that would not impact the cannabis product or medical cannabis, and any other intermediates or forms, including but not limited to, avoiding temperature and humidity extremes.

(10) Vehicles or trailers transporting cannabis product or medical cannabis and any other intermediates or forms are subject to inspection by the Office at any licensed premises or during transport at any time.

(11) No person under the age of twenty-one (21) years old shall be in a vehicle or trailer transporting cannabis product or medical cannabis and any other intermediates or forms.

(12) Only employees of a laboratory sampling firm shall be in any vehicle containing cannabis product or medical cannabis and any other intermediates or forms while being transported.

(h) Upon request, a laboratory sampling firm shall provide, at a minimum, the following transport vehicle information to the Office:

(1) A certificate of ownership or registration card issued by New York State Department of Motor Vehicles for a vehicle used to transport cannabis product or medical cannabis and any other intermediates or forms;

(2) The year, make, model, license plate number, and numerical Vehicle Identification Number (VIN) for a vehicle or trailer used to transport cannabis product or medical cannabis and any other intermediates or forms; and

(3) Proof of insurance for a vehicle used to transport cannabis product or medical cannabis and any other intermediates or forms.

(i) A laboratory sampling firm shall provide the Office with the information required by this section in writing for any new vehicle or trailer that will be used to transport cannabis product or medical cannabis and any other intermediates or forms prior to using the vehicle or trailer.

(j) A laboratory sampling firm's approval to conduct sampling and transportation shall be deemed retracted immediately upon a significant change in the sampling process or procedure, change in employees who perform sampling and transportation and change in vehicles used in transportation. However, provided a re-application has been made in writing to the Office within thirty (30) calendar days of the change, the Office may reinstate the firm's approval for a period not to exceed ninety (90) calendar days after any change in the sampling and transportation process or procedure.

9 CCR-NY § 130.20. Cannabis Sampling Technician Qualifications.

(a) A laboratory sampling firm shall employ sampling and transportation technicians. A sampling and transportation technician shall have documented training, and/or experience in sampling and transportation procedures; possess a strong working knowledge of all sampling and transportation methods for which they perform; and perform routine and non-routine sampling and transportation of cannabis product or medical cannabis and any other intermediates or forms using appropriate equipment, instrumentation, and methods.

(b) A technician of a laboratory sampling firm shall be an individual with, at minimum, a high school diploma or high school equivalency diploma.

(c) A technician of a laboratory sampling firm must be twenty-one (21) years of age.

9 CCR-NY § 130.21. Sampling of Cannabis Product and Medical Cannabis.

(a) A laboratory sampling firm shall obtain a representative sample of medical cannabis or adult-use cannabis as determined by the Office for testing by a cannabis laboratory.

(b) A laboratory sampling firm shall meet the standards for sampling cannabis product batch and harvest batch as approved by the Office.

(c) An employee of a registered organization, cultivator, processor, cooperative, microbusiness, or any other person licensed pursuant to the Cannabis Law or authorized to cultivate or process medical cannabis or adult-use cannabis pursuant to the Cannabis Law that has requested the sampling and testing of medical cannabis or adult-use cannabis shall be physically present to observe an employee of a laboratory sampling firm obtain the sample of cannabis product or medical cannabis and any other intermediates or forms for testing and shall ensure that the increments are taken from throughout the batch.

(d) The sampling shall be video-recorded with the batch number stated verbally or in writing on the video at the beginning of the video and a visible time and date indication on the video recording footage. The video recordings shall be maintained for at least ninety (90) calendar days by the licensee.

(e) After the sample has been selected by a laboratory sampling firm employee, both (1) the licensee requesting the sampling and testing, and (2) the laboratory sampling firm employee shall sign and date the chain of custody form as set forth in this Part, attesting to the sample selection having occurred according to the sampling process or procedure a laboratory sampling firm submitted to the Office pursuant to this Part and the requirements set forth in Subchapters B and E of Title 9.

(f) A registered organization, cultivator, processor, cooperative, microbusiness, or any other person licensed pursuant to the Cannabis Law or authorized to cultivate medical cannabis or adult-use cannabis pursuant to the Cannabis Law shall not assist a laboratory sampling firm employee nor touch the cannabis product or medical cannabis and any other intermediates or forms or the sampling equipment while a laboratory sampling employee is obtaining the sample.

9 CCR-NY § 130.22. Testing of Cannabis Product and Medical Cannabis.

(a) All testing of samples provided by a laboratory sampling firm to a cannabis laboratory shall be conducted by a cannabis laboratory employing methods approved by the Office and shall:

(1) be within the scope listed on the laboratory's current permit or on any appendices thereto; and

(2) require the prior completion of a demonstration of capability conducted at the same site where samples were prepared or analyzed using an approved method.

(b) Testing of the phytocannabinoid profile in cannabis product and or medical cannabis and any other intermediates or forms shall include, at a minimum, the analyte or groups of analytes specified under this Part.

(c) Testing for contaminants in cannabis product or medical cannabis, and any other intermediates or forms shall include, but not be limited to, microorganisms, foreign material, metals, moisture content and water activity, mycotoxins, pesticides, residual solvents, terpenoids, and any other analyte or group of analytes determined by the Office, consistent with the acceptable limits determined by the Office for each of the foregoing.

(d) The Office shall make available a list of required analytes, their acceptable limits and approved testing methods on the Office's website and in any other manner as determined by the Board.

9 CCR-NY § 130.23. Certificate of Analysis.

(a) Once a cannabis laboratory completes testing a sample, a cannabis laboratory shall prepare a certificate of analysis which shall include a summary of analytical results of the testing.

(b) A cannabis laboratory shall issue confidentially the certificate of analysis to a registered organization, cultivator, processor, cooperative, microbusiness, or any other person licensed pursuant to the Cannabis Law or authorized to cultivate medical cannabis or adult-use cannabis pursuant to the Cannabis Law on whose behalf a cannabis laboratory performed the testing.

(c) A certificate of analysis, that is issued by cannabis laboratory, shall be reported in a manner and format determined by the Office.

(d) A cannabis laboratory must report all results of tests that a cannabis laboratory performs directly to the Office in a manner and format determined by the Office. The results shall be reported to the Office within forty-eight (48) hours of release of the certificate of analysis to a registered organization, cultivator, processor, cooperative, microbusiness, or any other person licensed pursuant to the Cannabis Law or authorized to cultivate medical cannabis or adult-use cannabis pursuant to the Cannabis Law on whose behalf a cannabis laboratory performed the testing.

(e) A certificate of analysis shall include, but not be limited to, the following:

(1) a title;

(2) cannabis laboratory name, contact person, phone number, and address;

(3) office laboratory permit identifier;

(4) permit identifier issued by ISO/IEC 17025 accreditation, or accreditation that is based on ISO/IEC 17025 accreditation by any other laboratory accreditation authority approved by the Office;

(5) client name, contact person, phone number, and address;

(6) description or unique identification of sample(s) tested;

(7) methods used;

(8) analyte or group of analytes tested, analyte results and units of measurements;

(9) sample collection site, date and time;

(10) analysis date and time;

(11) any deviations from approved sampling, transportation and testing methods;

(12) reference to approved sampling and transportation operating procedures;

(13) name, signature and date of individual approving the release of the reported results;

(14) regulatory limits established by the Office;

(15) laboratory reporting limits;

(16) any non-approved methods or analyte or group of analytes reported;

(17) any methods used and analyte or group of analyte results reported by another OCM permitted cannabis laboratory;

(18) pagination of the report if greater than one (1) page in length; and

(19) any other information requested by the Office.

(f) An incomplete, verbal or informal certificate of analysis shall not be released by a cannabis laboratory without the written approval by the Office.

(g) Any amendments to a certificate of analysis after issuance shall be reported in a revised or amended certificate of analysis, and the amendments clearly noted and statement on the certificate to which report was superseded.

9 CCR-NY § 130.24. Cannabis Shipping Manifest.

(a) A laboratory sampling firm shall ensure and verify that the samples being taken into possession for transport at the originating licensed premises are as described and accurately reflected in the shipping manifest.

(b) A laboratory sampling firm is responsible for any discrepancies between the shipping manifest and the samples in its possession during transport, and may be subject to any enforcement or disciplinary action related to such discrepancy, including cancelation, suspension or revocation of its approval.

(c) A laboratory sampling firm shall not void or change a shipping manifest for samples after departing from the originating licensed premises with such samples.

9 CCR-NY § 130.25. Sample Chain of Custody.

(a) A cannabis laboratory shall develop and implement a chain of custody (COC) procedure to ensure accurate documentation is recorded for the sampling, transport, receipt, handling, storage, and destruction of samples.

(b) A COC procedure shall require the use of a COC form. A laboratory sampling firm employee shall use the COC to record, at a minimum, the following information for a sampled batch:

(1) permitted cannabis laboratory's name, permitted premises address, and permit number;

(2) date and time sampling started and ended;

(3) name of the licensee requesting the sampling, licensed premises address, and license number;

(4) batch number of the batch from which the representative sample was obtained and assigned unique sample identifier;

(5) sample type from cannabinoid hemp, cannabis product, or medical cannabis and any other intermediates or forms;

(6) total batch size, by weight, or unit count;

(7) total weight, or unit count of the representative sample;

(8) sampling and transportation conditions or problems encountered during the sampling and transportation process, if any;

(9) printed name and signature of the licensee requesting the sampling; and

(10) printed name and signature of the laboratory sampling firm employee and name of laboratory sampling firm.

(c) At each point a sample changes custody, is transported, or is destroyed, the date, time, and the names and signatures of persons involved in these activities shall be recorded on the COC form.

(d) Once the custody of the sample changes, the COC form for that change of custody may not be altered.

9 CCR-NY § 130.26. Record Retention.

(a) A cannabis laboratory shall retain the following records for no less than five (5) years and shall identify accurately and reliably:

    (1) the samples transported, collected, accepted, prepped, examined, and disposed of;

    (2) procedures used and personnel involved; and personnel training records;

    (3) document test conditions, observations, and results of analyses; and

    (4) all quality system related records including, but not limited to:

        (i) quality manual;

        (ii) standard operating procedures;

        (iii) internal audits;

        (iv) management reviews;

        (v) corrective action reports;

        (vi) analytical logbooks;

        (vii) equipment logs;

        (viii) consumable logs; and

        (ix) purchasing records.

(b) In the event a cannabis laboratory goes out of business or ownership is transferred to another permitted cannabis laboratory, a cannabis laboratory must have a plan or procedure in place to ensure all associated records are maintained for not fewer than five (5) years.

(c) A laboratory sampling firm shall maintain sampling and transportation records, including but not limited to, all employee training records, and standard operating procedures related to sampling and transport, for no less than five (5) years and shall identify accurately and reliably the samples collected and transported.

(d) In the event a laboratory sampling firm goes out of business or ownership is transferred to another approved laboratory sampling firm, a laboratory sampling firm must have a plan or procedure in place to ensure all associated records are maintained for not fewer than five (5) years.

9 CCR-NY § 130.27. Security, Safety and Storage of Cannabis.

(a) A facility operated by a cannabis laboratory shall have a security system to prevent and detect diversion, theft or loss of cannabinoid hemp, cannabis product, or medical cannabis and any other intermediates or forms, utilizing commercial grade equipment.

(b) A cannabis laboratory shall keep security equipment in full operating order and shall test such equipment no less than semi-annually. Records of security tests must be maintained for five (5) years and made available to the Office upon request.

(c) A cannabis laboratory must be securely locked and protected from unauthorized entry at all times.

(d) All cannabinoid hemp, cannabis product, or medical cannabis and any other intermediates or forms must be stored in a secure area or location within a cannabis laboratory that is accessible to a minimum number of employees essential for efficient operation, to prevent diversion, theft or loss.

(e) All cannabinoid hemp, cannabis product, or medical cannabis and any other intermediates or forms must be stored in such a manner as to protect against physical, chemical and microbial contamination and deterioration until extraction and analyses of the cannabinoid hemp, cannabis product, or medical cannabis and any other intermediates or forms begins.

(f) A cannabis laboratory shall ensure the safe and secure transport of cannabis product or medical cannabis and any other intermediates or forms as specified in this Part when subcontracting the analyses of any of the cannabis to another permitted cannabis laboratory.

9 CCR-NY § 130.28. State Reference Lab.

(a) If the Office suspects fraudulent, inaccurate or compromised testing of cannabinoid hemp, cannabis product, or medical cannabis, and any other intermediates or forms by a permitted cannabis laboratory, the Office may obtain the cannabinoid hemp, cannabis product, or medical cannabis, and any other intermediates or forms and request the state reference lab to perform testing on the cannabinoid hemp, cannabis product, or medical cannabis, and any other intermediates or forms in question.

(b) At the discretion of the Office, the Office may randomly pull samples of cannabinoid hemp, cannabis product, or medical cannabis, and any other intermediates or form directly from a registered organization, cultivator, processor, cooperative, microbusiness, or any other person licensed pursuant to the Cannabis Law or authorized to cultivate medical cannabis or adult-use cannabis pursuant to the Cannabis Law. The Office may pull such samples during hours of operation. The cannabinoid hemp, cannabis product, or medical cannabis, and any other intermediates or forms pulled will be tested by the state reference lab.

(c) The state reference lab may assist the Office in method development.

9 CCR-NY § 130.29. Summary Suspension, Suspension, Cancellation and Revocation.

(a) A cannabis laboratory's permit shall be deemed summarily suspended for the following reasons:

　　(1) failure to submit an application for a change in laboratory ownership, major instrumentation, technical direction, or location, and;

　　(2) failure to remit the annual permit fee.

(b) A cannabis laboratory's permit may be suspended in part or in full for the following reasons:

　　(1) a pattern of deficiencies on a laboratory regulatory audit or other demonstration that a cannabis laboratory lacks an effective quality system for planning and assessing work performed by the laboratory, and for conducting required quality assurance and quality control procedures to promote and maintain the accuracy and reliability of test results;

　　(2) except as provided in this Part, failure to undergo a laboratory regulatory audit or failure to demonstrate, during a laboratory regulatory audit so conducted: compliance with the staffing, methodological and other requirements of this Part; and effective implementation of a quality system for planning and assessing work performed by a cannabis laboratory and for conducting required quality assurance and quality control procedures to promote and maintain the accuracy and reliability of test results;

　　(3) failure of a cannabis laboratory technical director to meet the required qualifications of this Part;

(4) misrepresentation of any material fact pertinent to obtaining or retaining approval for any cannabis laboratory owned or directed by an owner or technical director listed on the application including, but not limited to, inclusion of false reports on or related to a laboratory analysis or submission of proficiency test results which were, in fact, generated by a laboratory other than the laboratory to which the samples were distributed;

(5) failure to remit the required application and permit fees;

(6) failure to respond to a laboratory regulatory audit report with a corrective action plan within the required thirty (30) calendar days after receipt of the audit report;

(7) failure to respond to a laboratory regulatory audit report with an acceptable corrective action plan within the specified timeframe; and

(8) failure to maintain ISO/IEC 17025 accreditation, or accreditation that is based on ISO/IEC 17025 accreditation by any other laboratory accreditation authority approved by the Office.

(c)(1) A cannabis laboratory's permit may be revoked in an affected analyte or group of analytes for reasons including:

(i) failure to respond to a laboratory regulatory audit report with an acceptable corrective action plan within the specified timeframe;

(ii) a pattern of deficiencies on a laboratory regulatory audit, or other demonstration that a cannabis laboratory lacks an effective quality system for planning and assessing work performed by the laboratory, and for conducting required quality assurance and quality control procedures to promote and maintain the accuracy and reliability of test results;

(iii) failure to implement the responsive actions detailed in the corrective action plan within the specified timeframe;

(iv) failure to correct the deficiencies meriting suspension within six (6) months of the effective date of the suspension; or

(v) for a cannabis laboratory suspended pursuant to this Section, unsatisfactory performance in the next proficiency test, resulting in three (3) consecutive failed proficiency tests.

(2) A cannabis laboratory whose permit is revoked pursuant to paragraph (1) above shall retain approval for an analyte or group of analytes for which it continues to meet Office requirements, and a cannabis laboratory may reapply for a permit once the deficiencies meriting revocation have been corrected.

(3) A cannabis laboratory's permit may be revoked, in total, for reasons including:

(i) failure to respond to a laboratory regulatory audit report which includes findings or deficiencies with a corrective action plan within the required thirty (30) calendar days after receipt of the audit report;

(ii) falsification of any report on or related to a laboratory test or analysis, including, but not limited to, submission of proficiency test results which were, in fact, generated by a laboratory other than the laboratory to which the samples were distributed;

(iii) misrepresentation of any material fact pertinent to obtaining or maintaining approval;

(iv) denial of laboratory entry to perform a laboratory regulatory audit during normal business hours;

(v) sustained charges of administrative violations of state or federal laws, rules and regulations related to the provision of cannabis laboratory services, or reimbursement for such services, against the owner or technical director, individually or jointly, or against any cannabis laboratory owned or directed by such individuals;

(vi) conviction of any crime, including, but not limited to, any offense related to furnishing of, or billing for, cannabis laboratory services, which is considered an offense involving theft or fraud;

(vii) failure to remit the annual approval fee, or, for partial fee payments, failure to remit such payments within the timeframes established by the Office;

(viii) aiding and/or abetting in the violation of any of the provisions of this Part; and/or

(ix) a finding by a municipality that a cannabis laboratory has violated a local ordinance related either to sampling, transportation and analysis of cannabis product or medical cannabis and any other intermediates or forms, or to reporting of results for analysis of such samples.

(4) If cannabis laboratory's permit has been revoked pursuant to paragraph (3) above and the Office finds that the violation was willful, or due to recklessness or gross negligence, no application shall be accepted, for a period of time to be determined by the Office from any person who was an owner or technical director of such cannabis laboratory on the date of notification of proposed revocation.

(d) A summary suspension, suspension, cancelation, or revocation of a cannabis laboratory permit, including any notices and challenges thereto, if any, shall be pursuant to Subchapter J of Title 9.

(e) In addition to summary suspension, suspension, cancelation, or revocation of a cannabis laboratory permit, a cannabis laboratory that fails to comply with this Part may be subject to any fines, fees or any other penalties pursuant to Cannabis Law.

(f) A person who does not hold a valid permit pursuant to this Part or who otherwise does not comply with this Part shall be subject to any fines, fees, or any other penalties pursuant to Cannabis Law.

Title 10. Department of Health

Chapter XIII. Medical Use of Marihuana

PART 1004. MEDICAL USE OF MARIHUANA

10 CRR-NY § 1004.1. Practitioner registration.

(a) No practitioner shall be authorized to issue a patient certification as set forth in section 1004.2 of this Part unless the practitioner:

(1) is qualified to treat patients with one or more of the serious conditions set forth in section 1004.2(a)(8) of this Part.

(2) is licensed, in good standing as a physician and practicing medicine, as defined in article 131 of the Education Law, in New York State, or is certified, in good standing as a nurse practitioner and practicing, as defined in article 139 of the Education Law, in New York State, or is licensed, in good standing as a physician assistant and practicing in New York State, as defined in article 131-B of the Education Law, under the supervision of a physician registered under this Part;

(3) has completed a two to four hour course approved by the commissioner as set forth in subdivision (b) of this section;

(4) has applied to the department for a registration or a renewal of registration to issue patient certifications in a manner and format determined by the commissioner; and

(5) has been granted such registration by the department.

(b) The commissioner shall approve at least one, if not more, courses for practitioners seeking to become registered, which shall be two to four hours in duration. The educational content of such course shall include: the pharmacology of marihuana; contraindications; side effects; adverse reactions; overdose prevention; drug interactions; dosing; routes of administration; risks and benefits; warnings and precautions; abuse and dependence; and such other components as determined by the commissioner.

10 CRR-NY § 1004.2. Practitioner issuance of certification.

(a) Requirements for patient certification.

A practitioner who is registered pursuant to section 1004.1 of this Part may issue a certification for the use of an approved medical marihuana product by a qualifying patient subject to completion of subdivision (e) of this section. Such certification shall contain:

(1) the practitioner's name, business address, telephone number and email address;

(2) the practitioner's license number as issued by the New York State Department of Education;

(3) the practitioner's drug enforcement administration registration number;

(4) a statement that the practitioner is licensed and in good standing in New York State and possesses an active registration with the drug enforcement administration;

(5) a statement that the practitioner is registered with the department to issue the certification;

(6) a statement that the practitioner is caring for the patient in relation to the patient's serious condition;

(7) the patient's name, date of birth, address, telephone number and email address if available;

(8) the patient's diagnosis, limited solely to the specific severe debilitating or life-threatening condition(s) listed below:

   (i) cancer;

   (ii) positive status for human immunodeficiency virus or acquired immune deficiency syndrome, provided that the practitioner has obtained from the patient consent for disclosure of this information that meets the requirements set forth in sections 2780 and 2782 of the Public Health Law;

   (iii) amyotrophic lateral sclerosis;

   (iv) Parkinson's disease;

   (v) multiple sclerosis;

   (vi) damage to the nervous tissue of the spinal cord with objective neurological indication of intractable spasticity;

   (vii) epilepsy;

   (viii) inflammatory bowel disease;

   (ix) neuropathies;

(x) Huntington's disease;

(xi) any severe debilitating pain that the practitioner determines degrades health and functional capability; where the patient has contraindications, has experienced intolerable side effects, or has experienced failure of one or more previously tried therapeutic options; and where there is documented medical evidence of such pain having lasted three months or more beyond onset, or the practitioner reasonably anticipates such pain to last three months or more beyond onset;

(xii) post-traumatic stress disorder;

(xiii) pain that degrades health and functional capability where the use of medical marihuana is an alternative to opioid use, provided that the precise underlying condition is expressly stated on the patient's certification; or

(xiv) substance use disorder; or

(xv) any other condition added by the commissioner;

(9) the condition or symptom that is clinically associated with, or is a complication of the severe debilitating or life-threatening condition listed in paragraph (8) of this subdivision. Clinically associated conditions, symptoms or complications, as defined in subdivision 7 of section 3360 of the Public Health Law are limited solely to:

(i) Cachexia or wasting syndrome;

(ii) severe or chronic pain resulting in substantial limitation of function;

(iii) severe nausea;

(iv) seizures;

(v) severe or persistent muscle spasms;

(vi) post-traumatic stress disorder;

(vii) opioid use disorder; or

(viii) such other conditions, symptoms or complications as added by the commissioner;

(10) a statement that by training or experience, the practitioner is qualified to treat the serious condition, which encompasses the severe debilitating or life-threatening condition listed pursuant to paragraph (8) of this subdivision and the clinically associated condition, symptom or complication listed pursuant to paragraph (9) of this subdivision;

(i) for purposes of this subdivision, a practitioner must hold a Federal Drug Addiction Treatment Act of 2000 (DATA 2000) waiver to be qualified to treat patients with substance use disorder or opioid use disorder;

(11) a statement that in the practitioner's professional opinion and review of past treatments, the patient is likely to receive therapeutic or palliative benefit from the primary or adjunctive treatment with medical marihuana for the serious condition;

(12) any recommendations or limitations the practitioner makes to the certified patient and/or the patient's designated caregiver concerning:

(i) the authorized brand, authorized form, administration method, dosage and any limitations in the use of the approved medical marihuana product; and

(ii) the total amount of usable approved medical marihuana product that may be dispensed to the patient, in measurable controlled doses, which shall not exceed a 30 day supply, if used as directed;

(13) a statement that the practitioner has explained the potential risks and benefits of the use of medical marihuana to the qualifying patient and has documented in the patient's medical record that such explanation has been provided to the patient;

(14) to the extent that a practitioner is seeking to authorize the use of an approved medical marihuana product by a patient who is under the age of 18 or a person who is otherwise incapable of consenting to medical treatment, the practitioner shall explain the potential risks and benefits of medical marihuana to the patient's parent or legal guardian, and if appropriate, to the minor patient. The practitioner shall document in the patient's medical record that such explanation has been provided as required herein; and

(15) a statement that the patient, or the patient's parent or legal guardian if applicable, has provided informed consent; and

(16) to the extent that a practitioner seeks to authorize the use of an approved medical marihuana product by a patient who temporarily resides in New York State for the purpose of receiving care and treatment from the practitioner, the practitioner shall so state on the patient's certification.

(b) Expiration of certification.

(1) The certification shall state the date upon which the certification shall expire, which shall be no longer than one year after the date it was issued, unless the patient is terminally ill.

(2) If the practitioner issues a certification to a patient who is terminally ill, the certification shall not expire until the patient's death or the practitioner revokes the certification.

(3) If the practitioner issues a certification to a patient who is not a resident of New York but is receiving care and treatment in this state, the certification shall be valid for a period of time which is no longer than the applicant is reasonably anticipated to be residing in New York State for the purposes of care and treatment, but in no event shall it be valid for more than one year after the date it was issued.

(c) Submission of certification to the department.

Practitioners shall utilize a form, which may be in an electronic format, developed by the department for the certification required in subdivision (a) of this section. The practitioner shall submit to the department, the information required by subdivision (a) of this section, in a manner determined by the department, including by electronic transmission through a secure website. In the instance that a practitioner submits this information to the department electronically, the practitioner shall retain, for a period of five years, a printed copy of the electronic certification that shall contain the information required in subdivision (a) of this section.

(d) Medical record retention.

The practitioner shall date and place his or her handwritten signature upon the printed certification, and provide the printed certification to the patient. The practitioner shall also maintain a copy of the signed certification in the patient's medical record.

(e) Consultation of prescription monitoring program registry.

Prior to issuing, modifying or renewing a certification, the practitioner shall consult the prescription monitoring program registry pursuant to section 3343-a of the Public Health Law for the purpose of reviewing a patient's controlled substance history. Practitioners may authorize a designee to consult the prescription monitoring program registry on their behalf, provided that such designation is in accordance with section 3343-a of the Public Health Law.

10 CRR-NY § 1004.3. Application for registration as a certified

patient.

(a) A person applying for issuance or renewal of a registration as a certified patient shall:

> (1) be a resident of New York State, or be receiving care and treatment in New York State; and

> (2) possess a certification issued by a registered practitioner.

(b) New York State residents.

An applicant shall demonstrate his or her New York State residency by submitting to the department a copy of information concerning his or her New York State driver's license or New York State identification card. If the applicant does not possess or cannot obtain a valid New York State driver's license or New York State identification card, the applicant shall submit a copy of one or more of the following forms of documentation to establish that he or she is a New York resident:

> (1) a copy of a government-issued identification card that contains the applicant's name and New York State address. If the applicant is under the age of 18, the parent or legal guardian applying on behalf of the applicant shall submit a copy of the parent or legal guardian's state or government issued identification and a copy of the applicant's birth certificate;

> (2) a copy of a utility bill or other document indicating an applicant's residency issued within the previous two months that contains the applicant's name and address;

> (3) a copy of a current lease or similar document indicating an applicant's residency within New York State; or

> (4) such other documentation as approved by the department containing sufficient information to show proof of residency in New York State.

(c) Non-New York State residents.

An applicant applying for registration who is not a resident of New York State but is receiving care and treatment in this state, may qualify for registration as a certified patient if the applicant otherwise meets the requirements of article 33 of the Public Health Law and this Part, and is temporarily residing in New York State for the purpose of receiving care and treatment from a practitioner registered with the department.

> (1) The applicant shall submit a copy of the following forms of documentation along with the application for registration:

>> (i) a copy of a State or government issued identification card that contains the applicant's name and permanent address. If the applicant is under the age of 18, the parent or legal guardian applying on behalf of the applicant shall submit a copy of the parent or legal guardian's state or government issued identification and a copy of the applicant's birth certificate;

>> (ii) proof of temporary residence in New York State, including, but not limited to a copy of a lease, utility bill, hospital bill, or such other documentation as approved by the department containing sufficient information to show proof of temporary residency in New York State. If the applicant is under the age of 18, the parent or legal guardian applying on behalf of the applicant shall submit a copy of such documentation to show sufficient proof of the applicant's temporary residency in New York State.

> (2) Nothing in this Part shall be construed to grant to the applicant authorization to transport approved medical marihuana products outside of New York State.

(d) Application for a registry identification card.

To obtain, amend or renew a registry identification card, a certified patient shall file a registry application with the department, on a form or in a manner determined by the department, which shall include:

(1) the documentation required in subdivisions (b) and (c) of this section, as applicable;

(2) the information required in section 3363 of the Public Health Law;

(3) for new applicants, if the applicant does not have a current valid New York State driver's license, New York State identification card, or government issued identification containing a photograph, the applicant shall provide a recent passport-style color photograph of the applicant's face, taken against a white background or backdrop. The photograph shall be a true likeness of the applicant's actual appearance on the date the photograph was taken and shall not be altered to change any aspect of the applicant's physical appearance. The photograph shall have been taken not more than 30 days prior to the date of the application. The photograph shall be submitted in a form and manner described by the department, including as a digital file (.jpeg) when appropriate, provided, however, the department may waive the requirements of this paragraph upon good cause shown. For amendments and renewal applications, the department may utilize a previously submitted photograph if the applicant attests it is a true likeness of the applicant on the date the amendment or renewal application is submitted;

(4) a nonrefundable application fee of $50; provided, however, that the department may waive or reduce the fee in cases of financial hardship as determined by the department; and

(5) acknowledgement that a false statement in the application is punishable under section 210.45 of the Penal Law;

(e) If the applicant for a registry identification card is under the age of 18 or a person who is otherwise incapable of consenting to medical treatment, the application shall be made by an appropriate person over 21 years of age. In preparing the application, the applicant may designate up to two proposed designated caregivers who shall be either: a parent or legal guardian of the certified patient; a person designated by a parent or legal guardian; or an appropriate person approved by the department upon a sufficient showing that no parent or legal guardian is appropriate or available.

(1) As a condition of registration of a certified patient who is a minor or is incapable of medical decision-making, the applicant shall consent, in a manner determined by the department, to the certified patient's use of an approved medical marihuana product, and shall acknowledge that the parent, legal guardian or other appropriate person, as applicable, will control the acquisition and possession of the medical marihuana and any device used for its administration.

(2) Once the certified patient who is a minor or is incapable of medical decision-making is registered, the proposed designated caregiver(s) may apply for and, if approved, receive a designated caregiver registration in accordance with the requirements of section 3363 of the Public Health Law and section 1004.4 of this Part.

(f) Prior to issuing or renewing a registry identification card, the department may verify the information submitted by the applicant. The applicant shall provide, at the department's request, such information and documentation, including any consents or authorizations to contact treating practitioners that may be necessary for the department to verify the information.

(g) The department shall approve, deny, or determine incomplete or inaccurate an application to issue or renew a registry identification card within 30 days of receipt of the application. If the application is approved within the 30 day period, the department shall issue a registry identification card as soon as is reasonably practicable.

(h) The department shall notify the applicant in writing, by email, by telephone, or in another manner as determined appropriate by the department, if an application is incomplete or factually inaccurate, and shall explain what documents or information is necessary for the department to consider the application complete and accurate.

(i) An applicant shall have 30 days from the date of a notification of an incomplete or factually inaccurate application to submit the materials required to complete, revise, or substantiate information in the application. If the applicant fails to submit the required materials within such 30 day time period, the application shall be denied by the department.

(j) Applicants whose applications are denied may submit a new application for an initial or renewal of a registry identification card, together with the applicable fee as set forth herein.

(k) A certified patient may designate up to two designated caregivers either on the application for issuance or renewal of a registry identification card or in another manner determined by the department. A designated caregiver may be either a natural person or a facility. For purposes of this section, a facility shall mean: a general hospital or residential health care facility operating pursuant to article 28 of the Public Health Law; an adult care facility operating pursuant to title 2 of article 7 of the Social Services Law; a community mental health residence established pursuant to section 41.44 of the Mental Hygiene Law; a hospital operating pursuant to section 7.17 of the Mental Hygiene Law; a mental hygiene facility operating pursuant to article 31 of the Mental Hygiene Law; an inpatient or residential treatment program certified pursuant to article 32 of the Mental Hygiene Law; a residential facility for the care and treatment of persons with developmental disabilities operating pursuant to article 16 of the Mental Hygiene Law; a residential treatment facility for children and youth operating pursuant to article 31 of the Mental Hygiene Law; or a private or public school. Further, within each of the facilities listed above, each division, department, component, floor or other unit of such facility shall be entitled to be considered to be a facility for purposes of this section. The application for issuance or renewal of a registry identification card shall include the following information:

(1) name of the proposed designated caregiver(s);

(2) address of the proposed designated caregiver(s);

(3) date of birth of the proposed designated caregiver(s), unless the proposed designated caregiver is not a natural person; and

(4) any other individual identifying information concerning the proposed designated caregiver(s) required by the department.

10 CRR-NY § 1004.4. Designated caregiver registration.

(a) A certified patient's designation of a designated caregiver shall not be valid unless and until the proposed designated caregiver successfully applies for and receives a designated caregiver registry identification card.

(b) A facility or natural person selected by a certified patient as a designated caregiver may apply to the department for a registry identification card or renewal of such card on a form or in a manner determined by the department. The proposed designated caregiver shall submit an application to the department which shall contain the following information and documentation:

(1) For a proposed designated caregiver that is a natural person, the individual shall submit:

(i) the applicant's full name, address, date of birth, telephone number, email address if available, and signature;

(ii) if the applicant has a registry identification card, the registry identification number;

(iii) a nonrefundable application fee of $50, provided, however that the department may waive or reduce the fee in cases of financial hardship as determined by the department;

(iv) a statement that the applicant is not the certified patient's practitioner;

(v) a statement that the applicant agrees to secure and ensure proper handling of all approved medical marihuana products;

(vi) acknowledgement that a false statement in the application is punishable under section 210.45 of the Penal Law;

(vii) proof that the applicant is a New York State resident, consisting of a copy of either:

(a) a New York State issued driver's license; or

(b) a New York State non-driver identification card;

(viii) if the documentation submitted by the applicant in accordance with subparagraph (vii) of this paragraph does not contain a photograph of the applicant or the photograph on the documentation is not a true likeness of the applicant, the applicant shall provide one recent passport-style color photograph of the applicant's face taken against a white background or backdrop. The photograph shall be a true likeness of the applicant's appearance on the date the photograph was taken and shall not be altered to change any aspect of the applicant's physical appearance. The photograph shall have been taken not more than 30 days prior to the date of the application. The photograph shall be submitted in a form and manner as directed by the department, including as a digital file (.jpeg);

(ix) identification of all certified patients for which the applicant serves, has served or has an application pending to serve as a designated caregiver and a statement that the applicant is not currently a designated caregiver for five current certified patients, and that he/she has not submitted an application which is pending and, if approved, would cause the applicant to be a designated caregiver for a total of five current certified patients.

(2) For a proposed designated caregiver that is an entire facility that is licensed or operated pursuant to an authority set forth in section 1004.3(k) of this Part, the designated caregiver shall submit:

(i) the facility's full name, address, operating certificate or license number where appropriate, email address, and printed name, title, and signature of an authorized facility representative;

(ii) if the facility has a registry identification card, the registry identification number;

(iii) a statement that the facility agrees to secure and ensure proper handling of all approved medical marihuana products; and

(iv) an acknowledgement that a false statement in the application is punishable under section 210.45 of the Penal Law;

(3) For a proposed designated caregiver that is a division, department, component, floor or other unit pursuant to section 1004.3(k) of this Part, the designated caregiver shall submit:

(i) the parent facility's full name, address, operating certificate or license number where appropriate, email address, and printed name, title and signature of an authorized representative of the parent facility and of an authorized representative of the division, department, component, floor or other unit;

(ii) if the parent facility, division, department, component, floor or other unit has a registry identification card, the registry identification number;

(iii) a statement that the parent facility, and the division, department, component, floor or other unit, agree to secure and ensure proper handling of all approved medical marihuana products; and

(iv) an acknowledgement that a false statement in the application is punishable under section 210.45 of the Penal Law.

(c) Prior to issuing or renewing a registry identification card, the department may verify the information submitted by the applicant. The applicant shall provide, at the department's request, such information and documentation, including any consents or authorizations that may be necessary for the department to verify the information.

(d) The department shall approve, deny or determine incomplete or inaccurate an initial or renewal application within 30 days of receipt of the application. If the application is approved within the 30 day period, the department shall issue a registry identification card as soon as is reasonably practicable.

(e) The department shall notify the applicant in writing, by email, by telephone, or in another manner as determined appropriate by the department if an application is incomplete or factually inaccurate, and shall explain what documents or information is necessary for the department to consider the application complete and accurate.

(f) An applicant shall have 30 days from the date of a notification of an incomplete or factually inaccurate application to submit the materials required to complete, revise or substantiate information in the application. If the applicant fails to submit the required materials within such 30 day time period, the application shall be denied by the department.

(g) Applicants whose applications are denied pursuant to subdivision (f) of this section may submit a new initial or renewal application for a registry identification card, together with the applicable fee as set forth herein.

(h) The department shall deny a registry identification card for an applicant who:

> (1) is already a designated caregiver for five currently certified patients or has an application pending that, if approved, would cause the proposed designated caregiver to be a designated caregiver for more than five currently certified patients; or

> (2) in accordance with subdivision (e) of this section, fails to provide complete or factually accurate information in support of his or her initial or renewal application.

10 CRR-NY § 1004.5. Application for initial registration as a registered organization.

(a) No person or entity shall produce, grow or sell medical marihuana or hold itself out as a New York State registered organization unless it has complied with article 33 of the Public Health Law and this Part and is registered by the department.

(b) In order to operate as a registered organization, an entity shall file an application on forms or in a manner prescribed by the commissioner. The application shall be signed by the chief executive officer duly authorized by the board of a corporate applicant, or a general partner or owner of a proprietary applicant. The application shall set forth or be accompanied by the following:

> (1) the name, address, phone and email address of the applicant;

> (2) identification of all real property, buildings and facilities that will be used in manufacturing, as defined in section 1004.11 of this Part, and dispensing of the medical marihuana products;

> (3) identification of all equipment that will be used to carry out the manufacturing, processing, transportation, distributing, sale and dispensing activities described in the application and operating plan;

> (4) an operating plan that includes a detailed description of the applicant's manufacturing processes, transporting, distributing, sale and dispensing policies or procedures. The operating plan shall also include:

>> (i) a detailed description of any devices used with approved medical marihuana products to be offered or sold by the registered organization;

>> (ii) policies and procedures related to security and control measures that will be in place to prevent diversion, abuse, and other illegal or unauthorized conduct relating to medical marihuana and are consistent with provisions set forth in this Part;

>> (iii) a standard operating procedure manual for all methods used from cultivation of the medical marihuana through packaging, sealing and labeling of each lot of medical marihuana product. The procedures shall include use of good agricultural practices (GAPs) and must conform to all applicable laws and rules of New York State. Standard operating procedures shall be able to be validated to

demonstrate that the applicant will be able to produce and dispense consistent and reproducible medical marihuana product such that, for each form of each brand produced, there is homogeneity, absence of contamination and reproducibility of the brand profile in each lot as defined in section 1004.11 of this Part;

(iv) quality assurance plans, including but not limited to plans to detect, identify and prevent dispensing errors;

(v) policies and procedures to document and investigate approved medical marihuana product returns, complaints and adverse events, and to provide for rapid voluntary or involuntary recalls of any lot of medical marihuana product. Such policies and procedures shall include a plan for any retesting of returned approved medical marihuana products, storage and disposal of marihuana and any manufactured medical marihuana products not passing requirements, and a requirement that adverse events and total recalls are reported to the department within 24 hours of their occurrence;

(vi) a quality assurance program to track contamination incidents and document the investigated source of such incidents, and the appropriate corrective action(s) taken.

(vii) detailed description of plans, procedures and systems adopted and maintained for tracking, recordkeeping, record retention and surveillance systems, relating to all medical marihuana at every stage including cultivating, possessing of marihuana, and manufacturing, delivery, transporting, distributing, sale and dispensing by the proposed registered organization.

(viii) proposed hours of operation for the manufacturing and dispensing facilities;

(5) copies of the organizational and operational documents of the applicant, including but not limited to, as applicable: the certificate of incorporation, bylaws, articles of organization, partnership agreement, operating agreement and other applicable documents and agreements, and all amendments thereto;

(6) the name, residence address and title of each of the board members, officers, managers, owners, partners, principal stakeholders, directors and any person or entity that is a member of the applicant. Each such person (if an individual, or lawful representative, if a legal entity) shall submit an affidavit with the application setting forth:

(i) any position of management or ownership during the preceding 10 years of a 10 percent or greater interest in any other business, located in or outside New York State, manufacturing or distributing drugs; and

(ii) whether such person or any such business has been convicted of a felony or had a registration or license suspended or revoked in any administrative or judicial proceeding. In addition, any managers who may come in contact with or handle medical marihuana, including medical marihuana products, shall be subject to a fingerprinting process as part of a criminal history background check in compliance with the procedures established by Division of Criminal Justice Services and submission of the applicable fee;

(7) documentation that the applicant has entered into a labor peace agreement, as required by subdivision 1 of section 3365 of the Public Health Law, with a bona-fide labor organization that is actively engaged in representing or attempting to represent the applicant's employees. The maintenance of such a labor peace agreement shall be an ongoing material condition of registration;

(8) a statement that the applicant is able to comply with all applicable State and local laws and regulations relating to the activities in which it intends to engage under the registration;

(9) copies of all applicable executed and proposed deeds, leases, and rental agreements or executed option contracts related to the organization's real property interests, that shows that the applicant possesses or has the right to use sufficient land, buildings, and other premises as specified in the application and equipment to properly carry on the activities for which registration is sought. In the alternative, the applicant shall post a

bond of not less than $2,000,000; provided, however, that if the applicant posts a bond in lieu of providing the documentation requested herein, the applicant's submission of the applicable executed deeds, leases and rental agreements shall be required prior to the issuance of a registration to the applicant, if selected; and, provided further that whenever any applicant proposes to lease premises for the activities described in its operating plan, the lease agreement shall clearly set forth as a purpose the manufacturing and/or dispensing of medical marihuana, as applicable, and include the following language:

"The landlord acknowledges that its rights of reentry into the premises set forth in this lease do not confer on it the authority to manufacture and/or dispense on the premises medical marihuana in accordance with article 33 of the Public Health Law and agrees to provide the New York State Department of Health, Mayor Erastus Corning 2nd Tower, The Governor Nelson A. Rockefeller Empire State Plaza, Albany, N.Y. 12237, with notification by certified mail of its intent to reenter the premises or to initiate dispossess proceedings or that the lease is due to expire, at least 30 days prior to the date on which the landlord intends to exercise a right of reentry or to initiate such proceedings or at least 60 days before expiration of the lease."

(10) a financial statement setting forth all elements and details of any business transactions connected with the application, including but not limited to all agreements and contracts for consultation and/or arranging for the assistance in preparing the application;

(11) architectural program and sketches of the applicant's proposed manufacturing and dispensing facility(ies) including the following:

(i) site plans;

(ii) schematic architectural and engineering design drawings and single line sketches in an appropriate scale showing the relationship of various buildings to each other, room configurations, major exit corridors, exit stair locations, and circulation along with existing buildings if additions or alterations are part of the project;

(iii) outline specifications for the type of construction proposed including a description of energy sources, type and location of engineering systems proposed for heating, cooling, ventilation and electrical distribution, water supply and sewage;

(iv) a security plan indicating how the applicant will comply with the requirements of article 33 of the Public Health Law, this Part and any other applicable law, rule, or regulation; and

(v) the registered organization shall submit detailed floor plans indicating the activities performed in each area and security plans (physical and cyber) consistent with the requirements of section 1004.13 of this Part;

(12) a construction timetable;

(13) a statement as to whether the applicant, any controlling person of the applicant, any manager, any sole proprietor applicant, any general partner of a partnership applicant, any officer and member of the board of directors of a corporate applicant, and corporate general partner had a prior discharge in bankruptcy or was found insolvent in any court action;

(14) if any controlling person of the applicant, any manager, any sole proprietor applicant, any general partner of a partnership applicant, any officer and member of the board of directors of a corporate applicant, or corporate general partner or a combination of such persons collectively, maintains a 10 percent interest or greater in any firm, association, foundation, trust, partnership, corporation, or other entity or if such entity maintains a 10 percent interest or greater in the applicant, and such entity will or may provide goods, leases, or services to the registered organization, the value of which is or would be $500 or more within any one year, the name and address of the entity shall be disclosed together with a description of the goods, leases or services and the probable or anticipated cost to the registered organization;

(15) if the applicant is a corporate subsidiary or affiliate of another corporation, disclosure of the parent or affiliate corporation including the name and address of the parent or affiliate, the primary activities of the parent or affiliate, the interest in the applicant held by the parent or affiliate and the extent to which the parent will be responsible for the financial and contractual obligations of the subsidiary;

(16) the most recent certified financial statement of the applicant, audited by an independent certified public accountant and prepared in accordance with generally accepted accounting principles (GAAP) applied on a consistent basis, including a balance sheet as of the end of the applicant's last fiscal year and income statements for the past two fiscal years, or such shorter period of time as the applicant has been in operation;

(17) if construction, lease, rental or purchase of the manufacturing or dispensing facility has not been completed, a statement indicating the anticipated source and application of the funds to be used in such purchase, lease, rental or construction;

(18) a staffing plan for staff involved in activities related to the cultivation of marihuana, the manufacturing and/or dispensing of approved medical marihuana products and/or staff with oversight responsibilities for such activities, which shall include:

> (i) a senior staff member with a minimum of one year experience in good agricultural practices (GAP);
>
> (ii) a quality assurance officer who shall exercise oversight of the organization's practices and procedures and who has documented training and experience in quality assurance and quality control procedures;
>
> (iii) a requirement that all staff be 21 years of age or older;
>
> (iv) a requirement that all staff involved in the manufacturing be trained in and conform to general sanitary practices; and
>
> (v) policies and procedures to ensure that the proposed registered organization shall not employ anyone who would come in contact with or handle medical marihuana who has been convicted of any felony of sale or possession of drugs, narcotics, or controlled substances in accordance with the requirements of section 3364 of the Public Health Law.

> (19) any other information as may be required by the commissioner.

(c) An application under this section may be amended while the matter is pending before the commissioner, if approved by the commissioner upon good cause shown.

(d) The applicant shall verify the truth and accuracy of the information contained in the application. The department, in its discretion, may reject an application if it determines that information contained therein is not true and accurate.

10 CRR-NY § 1004.6. Consideration of registered organization applications.

(a) Applicants for approval to operate as registered organizations shall submit an application to the department, containing the information required in section 1004.5 of this Part, in a manner and format determined by the department.

(1) Applications shall be accompanied by a non-refundable application fee in the amount of $10,000.

(2) The registration fee for the registration period shall be $200,000. Applicants shall submit the registration fee by certified check, or another method approved by the department, at the time of submission of the application. The registration fee shall be returned to the applicant if the applicant is not granted a registration under this Part.

(3) Only applications completed in accordance with this part as determined by the department and for which the application and registration fees have been submitted shall be considered if submitted in a timely manner. The department shall return the fee for $200,000 to all applicants who are not granted a registration.

(b) The department shall initially register up to five applicants as registered organizations. In deciding whether to grant an application, or amendment to a registration, the department shall consider whether:

(1) the applicant will be able to manufacture approved medical marihuana products, each with a consistent cannabinoid profile (the concentration of total tetrahydrocannabinol [THC] and total cannabidiol [CBD] will define the brand) and each able to pass the required quality control testing;

(2) the applicant will produce sufficient quantities of approved medical marihuana products as necessary to meet the needs of certified patients;

(3) the applicant will be able to maintain effective control against diversion of marihuana and medical marihuana products;

(4) the applicant will be able to comply with all applicable State and local laws and regulations;

(5) the applicant is ready, willing and able to properly carry on the activities set forth in this Part;

(6) the applicant possesses or has the right to use sufficient real property, buildings and equipment to properly carry on the activity described in its operating plan;

(7) it is in the public interest that such registration be granted;

(8) the number of registered organizations in an area will be adequate or excessive to reasonably serve the area, including whether there is sufficient geographic distribution across the State;

(9) the moral character and competence of board members, officers, managers, owners, partners, principal stakeholders, directors, and members of the applicant's organization;

(10) the applicant has entered into a labor peace agreement with a bona-fide labor organization, as defined in section 3360 of the Public Health Law, that is actively engaged in representing or attempting to represent the applicant's employees; and

(11) evaluation of the applicant's proposed operating plan and suitability of the proposed manufacturing and dispensing facilities, including but not limited to the suitability of the location and architectural and engineering design of the proposed facilities. Department approval of the applicant's operating plan and architectural and engineering design of the proposed facilities shall be required for issuance of a registration.

(c) The applicant shall allow reasonable access to the department and/or its authorized representatives for the purpose of conducting an on-site survey or inspection of the applicant's proposed manufacturing and/or dispensing facilities.

(d) If the commissioner is not satisfied that the applicant should be issued a registration, he or she shall notify the applicant in writing of those factors upon which further evidence is required. Within 30 days of the receipt of such notification, the applicant may submit additional material to the commissioner or demand a hearing, or both.

(e) Upon application to the department, a registered organization's registration may be amended to allow the registered organization to relocate within the State or to add or delete permitted registered organization activities or facilities. The department shall consider whether to grant or deny the application for amendment of the registration utilizing the criteria set forth in subdivision (b) of this section. The fee for such amendment shall be $250.

(f) Registrations issued shall be valid for two years from the date of issuance. To facilitate renewals of registrations, the commissioner may upon the initial application for a registration, issue some registrations which may remain valid for a period of time greater than two years, but not exceeding an additional 11 months. The registration fee will be prorated for the additional time exceeding two years.

10 CRR-NY § 1004.7. Applications for renewal of registration as registered organization.

(a) An application to renew any registration issued under this Part shall be filed with the department not more than six months nor less than four months prior to the expiration thereof. If a renewal application is not filed at least four months prior to the expiration thereof, the department may determine that the registration shall have expired and become void on such expiration date.

(b) Applications shall be accompanied by a non-refundable application fee in the amount of $10,000. Applications shall also be accompanied by a registration fee in the amount of $200,000 made by certified check. Only applications completed in accordance with this part as determined by the department and for which the application and registration fees have been submitted shall be considered if submitted in a timely manner. The registration fee shall be returned to the applicant if the applicant is not granted a renewal registration under this section.

(c) The application for renewal shall include such information prepared in the manner and detail as the commissioner may require, including but not limited to:

(1) any material change as determined by the department in the information, circumstances or factors listed in section 1004.5 of this Part;

(2) every known complaint, charge or investigation, pending or concluded during the period of the registration, by any governmental or administrative agency with respect to:

(i) each incident or alleged incidence involving the theft, loss, or possible diversion of medical marihuana manufactured, distributed, or dispensed by the registered organization; and

(ii) compliance by the applicant with local or State laws, or regulations of the department, including but not limited to, with respect to any substance listed in section 3306 of the Public Health Law;

(3) information concerning the applicant's ability to carry on the manufacturing and distributing activity for which it is registered, including but not limited to approved medical marihuana product shortages or wait lists occurring during the registration period; and

(4) a summary of quality assurance testing for all medical marihuana products produced in the prior year including but not limited to the percentage of lots of each brand and form passing all required testing, the percentage of lots failing contaminant testing, the percentage of lots failing brand requirements, all recalls of product lots and all adverse events reported.

(d) The department shall consider applications for renewal in accordance with the criteria set forth in section 3365 of the Public Health Law.

(e) If the department determines that the applicant's registration should not be renewed, the department shall serve upon the applicant or his or her attorney of record, in person or by registered or certified mail, an order directing the applicant to show cause why his or her application for renewal should not be denied. The order shall specify in detail the respects in which the applicant has not satisfied the department that the registration should be renewed.

(1) within 10 business days of receipt of such an order, the applicant may submit additional material to the department or demand a hearing, or both. If a hearing is demanded, the commissioner shall fix a date as soon as reasonably practicable.

(2) If the applicant fails to submit additional material to the department within 10 business days as requested, and the applicant does not demand a hearing within such time period, the application for renewal of

registration shall be denied.

10 CRR-NY § 1004.8. Registrations non-transferable.

(a) Registrations issued under this part shall be effective only for the registered organization and shall specify:

(1) the name and address of the registered organization;

(2) name of the contact person for the registered organization;

(3) the activities the registered organization is permitted to perform under the registration for each approved location; and

(4) the real property, buildings and facilities that may be used for the permitted activities of the registered organization.

(b) Registrations are not transferable or assignable, including, without limitation, to another registered organization.

10 CRR-NY § 1004.9. Failure to operate.

(a) A registration shall be surrendered to the department upon written notice and demand if the registered organization fails to begin operations, to the satisfaction of the department, of a manufacturing and/or dispensing facility within six months of the date of issuance of the registration.

(b) A registered organization who is required to surrender its registration in accordance with this section shall not be entitled to any refund of fees paid to the department.

10 CRR-NY § 1004.10. Registered organizations; general requirements.

(a) In addition to the requirements in Public Health Law and as otherwise set forth in this Part, a registered organization shall:

(1) make its books, records and manufacturing and dispensing facilities available to the department or its authorized representatives for monitoring, on-site inspection, and audit purposes, including but not limited to periodic inspections and/or evaluations of facilities, methods, procedures, materials, staff and equipment to assess compliance with requirements set forth in article 33 of the Public Health Law and this Part;

(i) any deficiencies documented in a statement of findings by the department shall require that the registered organization submit a written plan of correction in a format acceptable to the department within 15 calendar days of the issue date of the statement of findings. A plan of correction shall address all deficiencies or areas of noncompliance cited in the statement of findings and shall:

(a) contain an assessment and analysis of the events and/or circumstances that led to the noncompliance;

(b) contain a procedure addressing how the registered organization intends to correct each area of noncompliance;

(c) contain an explanation of how proposed corrective actions will be implemented and maintained to ensure noncompliance does not recur;

(d) contain the proposed date by which each area of noncompliance shall be corrected;

(e) address any inspection finding which the department determines jeopardizes the immediate health, safety, or well-being of certified patients, designated caregivers or the public. Such a finding shall be deemed a critical deficiency and shall require immediate corrective action to remove the immediate risk, followed by the submission of a corrective action plan within 24 hours of notification by the department of the critical deficiency. The department will acknowledge receipt within 24 hours and respond as soon as practicable to notify if the plan is accepted or needs modification. If the corrective action plan needs modification, the registered organization shall modify the plan until it is accepted by the department;

(ii) upon written approval of the department, the registered organization shall implement the plan of correction;

(2) only manufacture and dispense approved medical marihuana products in New York State in accordance with article 33 of the Public Health Law and this Part;

(3) only manufacture and dispense approved medical marihuana products in an indoor, enclosed, secure facility located in New York State which may include greenhouses;

(4) submit approved medical marihuana product samples and manufacturing materials to the department upon request, for but not limited to, quality assurance testing or investigation of an adverse event. A subset of each lot of medical marihuana product shall be retained by the registered organization to allow for testing in the future if requested by the department and shall be stored unopened as indicated on the label and in the original packaging. This subset of medical marihuana product must be readily identifiable as belonging to its specific lot. The quantity retained shall be a statistically representative number of samples to allow for complete testing of the product at least two times and shall be retained by the registered organization for at least 30 days following the date of expiration;

(5) implement policies and procedures to notify the department within 24 hours of the following:

(i) any adverse events;

(ii) any incident involving theft, loss or possible diversion of medical marihuana products;

(iii) any suspected or known security breach or other facility event that may compromise public health and/or safety, or which requires response by public safety personnel or law enforcement; and

(iv) any vehicle accidents or incidents occurring during transport of medical marihuana products;

(6) within 10 days of the occurrence of one of the above events, the registered organization shall submit a complete written incident report to the department detailing the circumstances of the event, any corrective actions taken, and where applicable, confirmation that appropriate law enforcement authorities were notified;

(7) quarantine any lot of medical marihuana product as directed by the department, and not transport, distribute or dispense such lot unless prior approval is obtained from the department;

(8) dispose of unusable medical marihuana products that have failed laboratory testing or any marihuana used in the manufacturing process pursuant to section 1004.24 of this Part;

(9) maintain records required by article 33 of the Public Health Law and this Part for a period of five years unless otherwise stated, and make such records available to the department upon request. Such records shall include:

(i) documentation, including lot numbers where applicable, of all materials used in the manufacturing of the approved medical marihuana product to allow tracking of the materials including but not limited to soil, soil amendment, nutrients, hydroponic materials, fertilizers, growth promoters, pesticides, fungicides, and herbicides;

(ii) cultivation, manufacturing, packaging and labeling production records; and

(iii) laboratory testing results;

(10) post the certificate of registration issued by the department in a conspicuous location on the premises of each manufacturing facility and dispensing facility.

(b) Registered organizations shall not:

(1) dispense approved medical marihuana products from the same location where the marihuana is grown or manufactured;

(2) grow marihuana or produce medical marihuana at any site other than a facility or site approved by the department and set forth in the registered organization's registration;

(3) distribute products or samples at no cost except as may be allowed by the commissioner;

(4) make substantial alterations to the structure or architectural design of a manufacturing or dispensing facility without prior written approval of the department;

(5) change the composition of the entity which is the registered organization, including but not limited to, a change in sole proprietor, partner, director, stockholder, member or membership interest of the registered organization without the prior written approval of the department;

(6) materially modify or revise its operating plan, including its policies and procedures related to cultivation, processing, manufacturing, distributing or dispensing policies or procedures, without prior written approval of the department;

(7) locate a dispensing facility on the same street or avenue and within 1,000 feet of a building occupied exclusively as a school, church, synagogue or other place of worship. The measurements in this paragraph of this subdivision are to be taken in straight lines from the center of the nearest entrance of the premises sought to be used as a dispensing facility to the center of the nearest entrance of such school, church, synagogue or other place of worship; or

(8) be managed by or employ anyone who has been convicted of any felony of sale or possession of drugs, narcotics, or controlled substances provided that this provision only applies to:

(i) managers or employees who come into contact with or handle medical marihuana; and

(ii) a conviction less than 10 years (not counting time spent in incarceration) prior to being employed, for which the person has not received a certificate of relief from disabilities or a certificate of good conduct under article 23 of the Correction Law.

(c) In the event that a registered organization elects to cease operation of all permitted activities and to surrender its registration, the following provisions shall apply:

(1) The registered organization shall notify the department in writing at least 120 days prior to the anticipated date of closure of the manufacturing and each dispensing facility.

(2) Such written notice shall include a proposed plan for closure. The plan shall be subject to department approval in accordance with department protocols, and shall include timetables and describe the procedures and actions the registered organization shall take to:

(i) notify affected certified patients and designated caregivers of the closure;

(ii) properly destroy, transfer or otherwise dispose of all the registered organization's supply of medical marihuana and medical marihuana products;

(iii) maintain and make available to the department all records required to be maintained under this part for a period of five years; and

(iv) maintain compliance with these regulations and any other conditions required by the commissioner until the approved closure date.

(3) A registered organization shall take no action to close a manufacturing and dispensing facility prior to department approval of the plan for closure.

(4) A registered organization's failure to notify the department of intent to cease any operations, failure to submit an approvable plan, and/or to execute the approved plan may result in the imposition of civil penalties, not to exceed $2,000, and shall be a basis for the department to revoke the registration of the registered organization under such terms as the department determines is appropriate based on public health and safety considerations. In addition, the department reserves the right to exercise any other remedies available to it.

(d) If a registered organization's application for renewal of registration is denied, the registered organization shall submit a proposed plan for closure in accordance with this section.

10 CRR-NY § 1004.11. Manufacturing requirements for approved medical marihuana products.

(a) Definitions.

Wherever used in this Part, the following terms shall have the following meanings:

(1) Approved medical marihuana product is the final manufactured product delivered to the patient that represents a specific brand with a defined cannabinoid content and active and inactive ingredients, prepared in a specific dosage and form, to be administered as recommended by the practitioner.

(2) Brand means a defined medical marihuana product that has a homogenous and uniform cannabinoid concentration (total THC and total CBD) and product quality, produced according to an approved and stable processing protocol and shall have the same inactive ingredients as that defined for that form of the brand.

(3) Form of medical marihuana shall be a type of a medical marihuana product approved by the commissioner and shall refer to the final preparation of an approved medical marihuana brand; for example, an extract in oil for sublingual administration, an extract for vaporization or an extract in a capsule for ingestion.

(4) Lot means a quantity of a medical marihuana extraction product that has a homogenous and uniform cannabinoid concentration and product quality, produced according to an approved and stable processing protocol specific to that brand and form of medical marihuana product, during the same cycle of manufacture.

(5) Lot unique identifier (lot number or bar code) means any distinctive combination of letters, numbers, or symbols, or any combination of them, from which the complete history of manufacturing, testing, holding, distribution or recall of a lot of medical marihuana product can be determined.

(6) Manufacturing shall include, but not be limited to cultivation, harvesting, extraction (or other processing), packaging and labeling.

(b) A registered organization shall use either carbon dioxide (CO_2, super-critical) or alcohol for cannabinoid extraction and shall only perform extraction of the leaves and flowers of female marihuana plants. A registered organization shall only use carbon dioxide that is of a supply equivalent to food or beverage grade of at least 99.5 percent purity; and alcohol used shall be of a grade that meets or exceeds specifications of official compendiums as defined in section 321 of title 21 of the United States Code (USC). 21 USC section 321 is available for copying and inspection at the Regulatory Affairs Unit, New York State Department of Health, Corning Tower, Empire State Plaza, Albany, NY 12237. A registered organization shall obtain prior written approval from the department if it seeks to use other extraction methods.

(c) A registered organization shall only produce such forms of medical marihuana as approved by the department according to the following requirements:

(1) Each registered organization may initially produce up to five brands of medical marihuana product with prior approval of the department. These brands may be produced in multiple forms as approved by the commissioner. Thereafter, additional brands may be approved by the department.

(2) Each medical marihuana product brand, in its final form, shall be defined as having a specific concentration of total Tetrahydrocannabinol (THC) and total Cannabidiol (CBD) and shall have a consistent cannabinoid profile. The concentration of the following cannabinoids, at a minimum, must be reported:

(i) Tetrahydrocannabinol (THC);

(ii) Tetrahydrocannabinol acid (THCA);

(iii) Tetrahydrocannabivarin (THCV);

(iv) Cannabidiol (CBD);

(v) Cannabinadiolic acid (CBDA);

(vi) Cannabidivarine (CBDV);

(vii) Cannabinol (CBN);

(viii) Cannabigerol (CBG);

(ix) Cannabichromene (CBC);

(x) any other cannabinoid component at > 0.2 percent, for which there is a certified standard available at a customary cost.

(3) The final medical marihuana product shall not contain less than 90 percent or more than 110 percent of the concentration of total THC or total CBD indicated on the label for this brand and shall have no more than 10mg total THC per dose. However:

(i) where the total THC concentration is less than 5 milligrams per dose, the concentration of total THC shall be within 0.5 milligrams per dose;

(ii) where the total CBD concentration is less than 5 milligrams per dose, the concentration of total CBD shall be within 0.5 milligrams per dose; and

(iii) the concentration of total THC and CBD in milligrams per single dose for each sample of a brand lot submitted for testing must be within 25 percent of the mean concentration of total THC and CBD in milligrams per single dose for that submitted lot with the exception that, for brands with a specified total THC and CBD concentration less than 2 milligrams per single dose, the concentration of each sample for that low concentration cannabinoid shall be within 0.5 milligrams per dose of the mean concentration.

(4) The registered organization shall offer and make available to patients at least one brand that has a low THC and a high CBD content (e.g., a 1:20 ratio of THC to CBD).

(5) The registered organization shall offer and make available at least one brand that has approximately equal amounts of THC and CBD.

(6) For each brand offered, the registered organization shall only utilize a distinct name which has been

approved by the department, consisting of only letters and/or numbers. The name shall not be coined or fanciful, and may not include any street, slang or other name. No reference shall be made to any specific medical condition.

(7) Each registered organization shall ensure the availability of at least a one year supply of any offered brand unless otherwise allowed by the department.

(d) The registered organization shall not add any additional active ingredients or materials to any approved medical marihuana product that alters the color, appearance, smell, taste, effect or weight of the product unless it has first obtained prior written approval of the department. Excipients must be pharmaceutical grade and approved by the department.

(e) A registered organization shall:

(1) use good agricultural practices (GAPs) and must conform to all applicable laws and rules of New York State;

(2) use water from a public water supply or present a plan, approved by the department, which demonstrates the ability to obtain sufficient quantities of water of equal or greater quality as that from a public water supply and to monitor the quality of such water on an ongoing basis;

(3) upon prior written notice to the department, only use pesticides that are registered by the New York State Department of Environmental Conservation or that specifically meet the United States Environmental Protection Agency registration exemption criteria for minimum risk pesticides, and only in accordance with section 325.2(b) of Title 6 NYCRR;

(4) process the leaves and flowers of the female plant only, in a safe and sanitary manner;

(5) perform visual inspection of the harvested plant material to ensure there is no mold, mildew, pests, rot or gray or black plant material;

(6) have a separate secure area for temporary storage of any medical marihuana or medical marihuana product that needs to be destroyed; and

(7) provide continual environmental monitoring for temperature, ventilation and humidity at all locations in the manufacturing facility where unprocessed leaf and flower material is stored, until further extraction or other processing is completed.

(f) Production of any approved medical marihuana product shall be in accordance with general sanitary conditions. Poisonous or toxic materials, including but not limited to insecticides, rodenticides, detergents, sanitizers, caustics, acids and related cleaning compounds must be stored in a separate area from the marihuana and medical marihuana products in prominently and distinctly labeled containers, except that nothing herein precludes the convenient availability of detergents or sanitizers to areas where equipment, containers and utensils are washed and sanitized.

(g) Approved medical marihuana products shall be limited to the forms of administration approved by the department, including but not limited to:

(1) metered liquid or oil preparations;

(2) solid and semisolid preparations (e.g. capsules, chewable and effervescent tablets, lozenges);

(3) metered ground plant preparations; and

(4) topical forms and transdermal patches;

(5) medical marihuana may not be incorporated into food products by the registered organization, unless approved by the commissioner;

(6) smoking is not an approved route of administration.

(h) The registered organization shall package the final form of the approved medical marihuana product at the manufacturing site. The original seal shall not be broken except for quality testing at an approved laboratory, for adverse event investigations, by the department, by the certified patient or designated caregiver, or by the registered organization for internal quality control testing or disposal.

(i) The registered organization shall package the approved medical marihuana product such that it is child-resistant, tamper-proof/tamper-evident, light-resistant, and in a resealable package that minimizes oxygen exposure.

(j) The registered organization shall identify each lot of approved medical marihuana product with a lot unique identifier.

(k) Each approved medical marihuana product shall be affixed with a product label. Medical marihuana product labels shall be approved by the department prior to use. Each product label shall be applied at the manufacturing facility, be easily readable, firmly affixed and include:

(1) the name, address and registration number of the registered organization;

(2) the medical marihuana product form and brand designation;

(3) the single dose THC and CBD content for the product set forth in milligrams (mg);

(4) the medical marihuana product lot unique identifier (lot number or bar code);

(5) the quantity included in the package;

(6) the date packaged;

(7) the date of expiration of the unopened product, based on stability studies in accordance with paragraph (m) (2) of this section, or a tentative expiration date approved by the department;

(8) the proper storage conditions;

(9) language stating:

(i) "Medical marihuana products must be kept in the original container in which they were dispensed and removed from the original container only when ready for use by the certified patient";

(ii) "Keep secured at all times";

(iii) "May not be resold or transferred to another person";

(iv) "This product might impair the ability to drive";

(v) "KEEP THIS PRODUCT AWAY FROM CHILDREN (unless medical marihuana product is being given to the child under a practitioner's care"); and

(vi) "This product is for medicinal use only. Women should not consume during pregnancy or while breastfeeding except on the advice of the certifying practitioner, and in the case of breastfeeding mothers, including the infant's pediatrician."

(l) For each lot of medical marihuana product produced, the registered organization shall submit a predetermined number of final medical marihuana products (e.g., sealed vials or capsules; with the number of samples submitted, based on statistical analysis, determined to be representative of the lot) to an independent laboratory/laboratories approved by the department. The laboratory verifying the cannabinoid content shall be approved for the analysis of medical marihuana product by the department in accordance with section 502 of the Public Health Law and Subpart 55-2 of this Title. Such laboratory, or approved laboratories cumulatively, shall certify the medical marihuana product lot as passing all contaminant testing and verify that the content is consistent with the brand prior to the medical marihuana product being released from the manufacturer to any dispensing facility.

(1) Any lot not meeting the minimum standards or specifications for safety shall be rejected and destroyed by the registered organization in accordance with section 1004.24 of this Part.

(2) Any lot not meeting the minimum standards or specifications for brand consistency shall be reported to the department and not dispensed by a registered organization without prior written approval from the department.

(3) The registered organization shall keep and maintain records documenting submission of medical marihuana products to approved laboratories as required herein, and the results of the laboratory testing. The registered organization shall provide the department with such records upon request.

(m) The registered organization shall demonstrate the stability of each approved medical marihuana product produced (each brand in each form) by testing both the unopened and opened product at an approved laboratory in accordance with section 1004.14(h) of this Title:

(1) the stability of opened products shall be validated under the conditions (light, temperature and humidity), specified for storage of the product and an expiration date for opened product shall be determined;

(2) the stability of unopened products (e.g., sealed packages or vials) shall be validated by ongoing stability testing and an expiration date for unopened products shall be determined;

(3) specifications regarding storage conditions must address storage at the manufacturing facility once the package is sealed, during transport, at the dispensing facility, in the patient's home and for samples retained for future testing.

(n) No synthetic marihuana additives nor any cannabinoid preparation not produced by a registered organization in an approved manufacturing facility shall be used in the production of any medical marihuana product; provided, however, that a registered organization may use hemp, or extracts derived from hemp, grown and processed under the authority of the New York State Department of Agriculture and Markets in the manufacturing of medical marihuana products.

(o) The registered organization's approved standard operating procedure for the aforementioned activities must be followed, unless otherwise approved by the department.

10 CRR-NY § 1004.12. Requirements for dispensing facilities.

(a) Medical marihuana products shall not be dispensed or handled unless an individual with an active New York State pharmacist license, as defined in article 137 of the Education Law, who has completed a four-hour course pursuant to section 1004.1 of this Part, is on the premises and supervising the activity within the facility.

(b) Dispensing facilities shall only sell approved medical marihuana products, related products necessary for the approved forms of administration of medical marihuana, and items that promote health and well-being subject to disapproval of the department and only in such a manner as does not increase risks of diversion, theft or loss of approved medical marihuana products or risk physical, chemical or microbial contamination or deterioration of approved medical marihuana products.

(c) No approved medical marihuana products shall be vaporized or consumed on the premises of a dispensing facility.

(d) Dispensing facilities shall not dispense approved medical marihuana products to anyone other than a certified patient or designated caregiver.

(e) When dispensing approved medical marihuana products, the dispensing facility shall:

(1) not dispense an amount greater than a 30 day supply to a certified patient, and not until the patient has exhausted all but a seven day supply provided pursuant to any previously dispensed medical marihuana

product by any registered organization;

(2) ensure that medical marihuana product packaging shall not be opened by dispensing facility staff;

(3) provide a patient specific log of medical marihuana products (brand, administration form, and dosage, and dates dispensed and any return of product) to the patient, the patient's designated caregiver, if applicable, or the patient's practitioner upon request;

(4) ensure the prescription monitoring program registry is consulted pursuant to 3343-a and section 3364 of the Public Health Law, prior to any sales transactions and dispensing of any approved medical marihuana products by the facility.

(f) The registered organization shall be responsible for maintaining the confidentiality of patients and the integrity of the security of the facility at all times. Access to medical marihuana storage areas and areas within the dispensing facility where security equipment and recordings are stored shall be restricted to:

(1) registered organization employees;

(2) employees of the department or its authorized representatives;

(3) emergency personnel responding to an emergency; and

(4) other persons authorized by a manager of the registered organization for the sole purpose of maintaining the operations of the facility.

(i) The dispensing facility shall maintain a visitor log of all persons, other than registered organization employees or emergency personnel responding to an emergency, that access these secured areas, which shall include the name of the visitor, date, time and purpose of the visit. The visitor log shall be available to the department at all times during operating hours and upon request.

(g) The dispensing facility shall affix to the approved medical marihuana product package a patient specific dispensing label approved by the department, that is easily readable, and firmly affixed and includes:

(1) the name and registry identification number of the certified patient and designated caregiver, if any;

(2) the certifying practitioner's name;

(3) the dispensing facility name, address and phone number;

(4) the dosing and administration instructions;

(5) the quantity and date dispensed;

(6) any recommendation or limitation by the practitioner as to the use of medical marihuana; and

(7) the expiration date of the product once opened pursuant to section 1004.11(m)(1) of this Part.

(h) The dispensing facility shall place the approved medical marihuana product in a plain outer package when dispensing to the patient or designated caregiver.

(i) The dispensing facility shall ensure that each patient receives approved medical marihuana product from no more than two distinct lots for any 30-day supply dispensed.

(j) The dispensing facility shall include with each product package dispensed to a patient, a department approved package safety insert. Information provided shall include but not be limited to:

(1) the medical marihuana product and brand;

(2) a list of any excipients used;

(3) a warning if there is any potential for allergens in the medical marihuana product;

(4) contraindications;

(5) more specific dosage directions and instructions for administration;

(6) warning of adverse effects and/or any potential dangers stemming from the use of medical marihuana;

(7) instructions for reporting adverse effects as may be determined by the department;

(8) a warning about driving, operation of mechanical equipment, child care or making important decisions while under the influence of medical marihuana;

(9) information on tolerance, dependence and withdrawal and substance abuse, how to recognize what may be problematic usage of medical marihuana and obtain appropriate services or treatment;

(10) advice on how to keep the medical marihuana product secure;

(11) language stating that the certified patient may not distribute any medical marihuana product to anyone else;

(12) language stating that unwanted, excess, or contaminated medical marihuana product must be disposed of according to section 1004.20 of this Part; and

(13) language stating that "this product has not been analyzed by the FDA. There is limited information on the side effects of using this product and there may be associated health risks."

(k) The dispensing facility shall store the medical marihuana product in a manner to ensure that there is no contamination or deterioration of the medical marihuana product or its packaging.

(l) If an approved medical marihuana product is returned to the dispensing facility, the dispensing facility shall:

(1) dispose of such product pursuant to section 1004.24 of this Part;

(2) provide the following information to the department:

(i) the name and registry identification number of the certified patient for whom the product was dispensed;

(ii) the date of the return;

(iii) the brand and form being returned;

(iv) the quantity and/or weight being returned;

(v) the reason for the return;

(vi) the name of the dispensing facility employee accepting the return; and

(vii) any other information required by the department;

(3) ensure the returned marihuana product is securely stored, separate from working inventory while awaiting disposal.

10 CRR-NY § 1004.13. Security requirements for manufacturing and dispensing facilities.

(a) All facilities operated by a registered organization, including any manufacturing facility and dispensing facility, shall have a security system to prevent and detect diversion, theft or loss of marihuana and/or medical marihuana products, utilizing commercial grade equipment, which shall, at a minimum, include:

(1) a perimeter alarm;

(2) motion detectors;

(3) video cameras in all areas that may contain marihuana and at all points of entry and exit, which shall be appropriate for the normal lighting conditions of the area under surveillance. The manufacturing facility or dispensing facility shall direct cameras at all approved safes, approved vaults, dispensing areas, marihuana sales areas and any other area where marihuana is being manufactured, stored, handled, dispensed, or disposed of. At entry and exit points, the manufacturing facility or dispensing facility shall angle cameras so as to allow for the capture of clear and certain identification of any person entering or exiting the facility;

(4) twenty-four hour recordings from all video cameras, which the manufacturing facility or dispensing facility shall make available for immediate viewing by the department or the department's authorized representative upon request and shall be retained for at least 90 days. The registered organization shall provide the department with an unaltered copy of such recording upon request. If a registered organization is aware of a pending criminal, civil or administrative investigation or legal proceeding for which a recording may contain relevant information, the registered organization shall retain an unaltered copy of the recording until the investigation or proceeding is closed or the entity conducting the investigation or proceeding notifies the registered organization that it is not necessary to retain the recording;

(5) a duress alarm, which for purposes of this section means a silent security alarm system signal generated by the entry of a designated code into an arming station in order to signal that the alarm user is being forced to turn off the system;

(6) a panic alarm, which for purposes of this section, means an audible security alarm system signal generated by the manual activation of a device intended to signal a life threatening or emergency situation requiring a law enforcement response;

(7) a holdup alarm, which for purposes of this section, means a silent alarm signal generated by the manual activation of a device intended to signal a robbery in progress;

(8) an automatic voice dialer or digital dialer, which for purposes of this section, means any electrical, electronic, mechanical, or other device capable of being programmed to send a prerecorded voice message, when activated, over a telephone line, radio or other communication system, to a law enforcement, public safety or emergency services agency requesting dispatch, or other department approved industry standard equivalent;

(9) a failure notification system that provides an audible, text or visual notification of any failure in the surveillance system. The failure notification system shall provide an alert to the manufacturing facility or dispensing facility within five minutes of the failure, either by telephone, email, or text message;

(10) the ability to immediately produce a clear color still photo that is a minimum of 9600 dpi from any camera image (live or recorded);

(11) a date and time stamp embedded on all recordings. The date and time shall be synchronized and set correctly and shall not significantly obscure the picture; and

(12) the ability to remain operational during a power outage.

(b) A registered organization shall ensure that any manufacturing facility and dispensing facility maintains all security system equipment and recordings in a secure location so as to prevent theft, loss, destruction or alterations.

(c) In addition to the requirements listed in subdivision (a) of this section, each manufacturing facility and dispensing facility shall have a back-up alarm system approved by the department that shall detect unauthorized entry during times when no employees are present at the facility and that shall be provided by a company supplying commercial grade equipment.

(d) A registered organization shall limit access to any surveillance areas solely to persons that are essential to surveillance operations, law enforcement agencies, security system service employees, the department or the department's authorized representative, and others when approved by the department. A registered organization shall make available to the department or the department's authorized representative, upon request, a current list of authorized employees and service employees who have access to any surveillance room. A manufacturing facility and dispensing facility shall keep all on-site surveillance rooms locked and shall not use such rooms for any other function.

(e) A registered organization shall keep illuminated the outside perimeter of any manufacturing facility and dispensing facility that is operated under the registered organization's license.

(f) All video recordings shall allow for the exporting of still images in an industry standard image format (including .jpeg, .bmp, and .gif). Exported video shall have the ability to be archived in a proprietary format that ensures authentication of the video and guarantees that no alteration of the recorded image has taken place. Exported video shall also have the ability to be saved in an industry standard file format that can be played on a standard computer operating system. A registered organization shall erase all recordings prior to disposal or sale of the facility.

(g) A registered organization shall keep all security equipment in full operating order and shall test such equipment no less than semi-annually at each manufacturing facility and dispensing facility that is operated under the registered organization's registration. Records of security tests must be maintained for five years and made available to the department upon request.

(h) The manufacturing facility of the registered organization must be securely locked and protected from unauthorized entry at all times.

(1) The registered organization shall be responsible for ensuring the integrity of the security of the manufacturing facility and the maintenance of sanitary operations when permitting access to the facility.

(2) The manufacturing facility shall maintain a visitor log of all persons other than registered organization employees or emergency personnel responding to an emergency that access any secured areas, which shall include the name of the visitor, date, time and purpose of the visit. The visitor log shall be available to the department at all times during operating hours and upon request.

(i) All marihuana must be stored in a secure area or location within the registered organization accessible to the minimum number of employees essential for efficient operation and in such a manner as approved by the department in advance, to prevent diversion, theft or loss.

(1) Registered organizations shall return marihuana to its secure location immediately after completion of manufacture, distribution, transfer or analysis.

(j) All medical marihuana must be stored in such a manner as to protect against physical, chemical and microbial contamination and deterioration of the product.

(k) All approved safes, vaults or any other approved equipment or areas used for the manufacturing or storage of marihuana and approved medical marihuana products must be securely locked or protected from entry, except for the actual time required to remove or replace marihuana or approved medical marihuana products.

(l) Keys shall not be left in the locks or stored or placed in a location accessible to individuals who are not authorized access to marihuana or manufactured medical marihuana products.

(m) Security measures, such as combination numbers, passwords or biometric security systems, shall not be accessible to individuals other than those specifically authorized to access marihuana or manufactured medical marihuana products.

(n) Prior to transporting any medical marihuana, a registered organization shall complete a shipping manifest using a form determined by the department.

> (1) A copy of the shipping manifest must be transmitted to the destination that will receive the products and to the department at least two business days prior to transport unless otherwise expressly approved by the department.

> (2) The registered organization shall maintain all shipping manifests and make them available to the department for inspection upon request, for a period of five years.

(o) Approved medical marihuana products must be transported in a locked storage compartment that is part of the vehicle transporting the marihuana and in a storage compartment that is not visible from outside the vehicle.

(p) An employee of a registered organization, when transporting approved medical marihuana products, shall travel directly to his or her destination(s) and shall not make any unnecessary stops in between.

(q) A registered organization shall ensure that all approved medical marihuana product delivery times are randomized.

(r) A registered organization shall staff all transport vehicles with a minimum of two employees. At least one transport team member shall remain with the vehicle at all times that the vehicle contains approved medical marihuana products.

(s) A transport team member shall have access to a secure form of communication with employees at the registered organization's manufacturing facility at all times that the vehicle contains approved medical marihuana products.

(t) A transport team member shall possess a copy of the shipping manifest at all times when transporting or delivering approved medical marihuana products and shall produce it to the commissioner, the commissioner's authorized representative or law enforcement official upon request.

10 CRR-NY § 1004.14. Laboratory testing requirements for medical marihuana.

(a) Medical marihuana products produced by a registered organization shall be examined in a laboratory located in New York State that is licensed by the department's Bureau of Narcotic Enforcement and approved for the analysis of medical marihuana by the department in accordance with article 5 of the Public Health Law and Subpart 55-2 of this Title.

(b) No board member, officer, manager, owner, partner, principal stakeholder or member of a registered organization, or such persons' immediate family member, shall have an interest or voting rights in the laboratory performing medical marihuana testing.

(c) For final product testing, the registered organization shall submit to the laboratory a statistically significant number of samples containing the final medical marihuana product equivalent to the sealed medical marihuana product dispensed to the patient (e.g., liquid extract in a sealed bottle or intact sealed bottle of capsules). Upon prior written approval of the department, a registered organization may submit to the laboratory the final medical marihuana product sample packaged in a quantity less than that which would be provided to the patient if the sample is prepared and packaged in the identical manner as the product provided to the patient.

(d) Testing of the final medical marihuana product is mandatory. However, at the option of the registered organization, testing may be performed on components used for the production of the final medical marihuana product including but not limited to water or growing materials. Testing may also be performed on the final marihuana extract e.g., for cannabinoid profile verification or contaminant testing.

(e) Sampling and testing of each lot of final medical marihuana product shall be conducted with a statistically significant number of samples and with acceptable methodologies, approved by the department, such that there is assurance that all lots of each medical marihuana product are adequately assessed for contaminants and the cannabinoid profile is consistent throughout.

(f) Testing of the cannabinoid profile shall include, at a minimum, those analytes specified in section 1004.11(c)(2) of this Part.

(g) Testing for contaminants in the final medical marihuana product shall include but shall not be limited to those analytes listed below. The department shall make available a list of required analytes and their acceptable limits as determined by the commissioner.

Analyte:E. coliPseudomonas (for products to be vaporized)Salmonella speciesEnterococcus speciesBile tolerant gram negative bacteria, specifically including Klebsiella speciesClostridium botulinumAspergillus speciesMucor speciesPenicillium speciesThermophilic Actinomycetes speciesAflatoxins B1, B2, G1, G2Ochratoxin AAntimonyArsenicCadmiumChromiumCopperLeadNickelZincMercuryAny pesticide used during production of the medical marihuana productAny growth regulator used during production of the medical marihuana productAny other analyte as required by the commissioner

(h) Laboratories performing final product testing pursuant to this section must report all results to the department, in a manner and timeframe prescribed by the department.

(i) Stability testing shall be performed on each brand and form of medical marihuana product as follows:

(1) For testing of open products, stability testing shall be performed for each extract lot, at time zero when opened and then, at a minimum, at 60 days from the date of first analysis. This shall establish use of the product lot within a specified time once opened.

(2) For testing of unopened products, until stability studies have been completed, a registered organization may assign a tentative expiration date based on available stability information. The registered organization must concurrently have stability studies conducted by an approved laboratory to determine the actual expiration date of an unopened product.

(3) For stability testing of both opened and unopened products, each brand shall retain a total THC and total CBD concentration in milligrams per single dose that is consistent with section 1004.11(c)(3) of this Part. If stability testing demonstrates that a product no longer retains a consistent concentration of THC and CBD pursuant to section 1004.11(a)(2) of this Part, the product shall be deemed no longer suitable for dispensing or consumption. The department may request further stability testing of a brand to demonstrate the ongoing stability of the product produced over time.

(4) The department may waive any of the requirements of this subdivision upon good cause shown.

(j) The laboratory shall track and use an approved method to dispose of any quantity of medical marihuana product that is not consumed in samples used for testing. Disposal of medical marihuana shall mean that the medical marihuana has been rendered unrecoverable and beyond reclamation.

(k) Any submitted medical marihuana products that are deemed unsuitable for testing shall be returned to the registered organization under chain of custody.

10 CRR-NY § 1004.15. Pricing.

(a) Definitions.

For purposes of this section, the following terms have the following meanings:

(1) Cost analysis shall mean the review and evaluation of the separate cost elements and profit of a proposed price and the application of judgment to determine how well the proposed costs represent what the price per unit for approved medical marihuana products should be, assuming reasonable economy and efficiency.

(2) Price shall mean the cost to manufacture, market and distribute approved medical marihuana products plus a reasonable profit.

(b) Department approval required.

A registered organization shall only charge a price for an approved medical marihuana product that has been approved by the department.

(c) Determination of price.

The department shall set the per unit price of each form of approved medical marihuana product sold by any registered organization, as follows:

(1) Registered organizations shall submit a proposed price per unit for each form of medical marihuana indicated in its registration. Registered organizations shall submit such information and documentation, in a manner and format determined by the department, sufficient for the department to perform a cost analysis of the proposed price. In particular, the registered organization shall, in a manner and format determined by the department, provide a detailed breakdown of, and submit information and documentation concerning, all costs it factored to arrive at its proposed price, including but not limited to its fixed and variable costs such as materials and services; direct labor; and indirect costs.

(2) The registered organization shall provide cost or pricing data that is accurate and reliable, and shall certify, at the time of submission of its price proposal, that to the best of its knowledge and belief, the cost or pricing data were accurate, complete, and current as of the date of submission.

(3) The department shall determine the reasonableness of the proposed costs. In making this determination, the department may consider whether the costs represent inefficient and uneconomical practices; are not costs appropriately attributable to the price; and/or are costs unsupported by sufficient documentation or information to justify their inclusion in the proposed price. If the registered organization has been granted a renewal of its registration, any relevant historical price, cost and/or sales data of the registered organization; and any other information the commissioner deems appropriate.

(4) The department may approve the proposed price, refuse approval of a proposed price, or modify or reduce the proposed price.

(d) Examination of records for determination of price.

The registered organization shall grant the department or the department's authorized representative the right to examine records that formed the basis for the proposed price, including the registered organization's books, records, documents and other types of factual information that will permit an adequate evaluation of the proposed price.

(e) Correction of insufficient price data.

If the registered organization or department determines that the cost or pricing data submitted is inaccurate, incomplete or noncurrent prior to the department's approval of the price, the registered organization shall submit new data to correct the deficiency, or consider the inaccuracy, incompleteness, or noncurrency of the data.

(f) Duration of price determination.

The department's approved price shall be in effect for the entire period of the registered organization's registration; provided, however, that at the conclusion of the first year of the registration period, or prior to that time based upon documented exceptional circumstances, the registered organization may request that the price be modified based upon a material change in the registered organization's costs. The registered organization shall fully support its request with sufficient information and documentation, in a manner and format determined by the department, to justify its request. If the department denies such request, the registered organization shall only charge prices previously approved by the department.

(g) Adjustments to determined price.

If the department has approved a price, the registered organization shall immediately notify the department of any cost or pricing data submitted that it determines was inaccurate, incomplete, or noncurrent as of the date of the department's approval of the price. If the registered organization provides such notice, or if the department independently learns of such inaccurate, incomplete or noncurrent data, the department may require the registered organization to provide new data to correct the deficiency, or consider the inaccuracy, incompleteness, or noncurrency of the data. The department may adjust the price per dose if the defective data significantly increased the price approved by the department.

(h) Audits.

The department may perform audits, which may include site visits. The registered organization shall provide reasonable access to the department of its facilities, books and records.

10 CRR-NY § 1004.16. Medical marihuana marketing and advertising by registered organizations.

(a) All physical structures owned, leased or otherwise utilized by a registered organization, including any dispensing facility, shall:

> (1) not advertise medical marihuana brand names or utilize graphics related to marihuana or paraphernalia on the exterior of the physical structures; and

> (2) not display medical marihuana products and paraphernalia so as to be clearly visible from the exterior of a physical structure.

(b) All restrictions listed in subdivision (a) of this section shall apply to any item located on any real property on which a registered organization's physical structures is located.

(c) All restrictions listed in subdivision (a) of this section shall apply to all vehicles owned, leased or utilized by a registered organization.

(d) All advertisements, regardless of form, for approved medical marihuana products that make a statement relating to effectiveness, side effects, consequences or contraindications shall present a true and accurate statement of such information.

(e) An advertisement does not satisfy the requirement that it presents a "true and accurate statement" of information relating to effectiveness, side effects, consequences, and contraindications if it fails to present a fair balance between information relating to effectiveness, side effects, consequences, and contraindications in that the information relating to effectiveness is presented in greater scope, depth, or detail than is the information relating to side effects, consequences and contraindications, taking into account all implementing factors such as typography, layout, contrast, headlines, paragraphing, white space, and any other techniques apt to achieve emphasis.

(f) An advertisement is false, lacking in fair balance, or otherwise misleading if it:

> (1) contains a representation or suggestion that one marihuana brand or form is better, more effective, useful in a broader range of conditions or patients or safer than other drugs or treatments including other marihuana brands or forms, unless such a claim has been demonstrated by substantial scientific or clinical experience;

> (2) contains favorable information or opinions about a marihuana product previously regarded as valid but

which have been rendered invalid by contrary and more credible recent information;

(3) uses a quote or paraphrase out of context or without citing conflicting information from the same source, to convey a false or misleading idea;

(4) uses a study on persons without a debilitating medical condition without disclosing that the subjects were not suffering from a debilitating medical condition;

(5) uses data favorable to a marihuana product derived from patients treated with a different product or dosages different from those recommended in New York State;

(6) contains favorable information or conclusions from a study that is inadequate in design, scope, or conduct to furnish significant support for such information or conclusions; or

(7) fails to provide adequate emphasis for the fact that two or more facing pages are part of the same advertisement when only one page contains information relating to side effects, consequences and contraindications.

(g) False or misleading information in any part of the advertisement shall not be corrected by the inclusion of a true statement in another distinct part of the advertisement.

(h) An advertisement for any approved medical marihuana product shall not contain:

(1) any statement that is false or misleading;

(2) any statement that falsely disparages a competitor's products;

(3) any statement, design, or representation, picture or illustration that is obscene or indecent;

(4) any statement, design, representation, picture or illustration that encourages or represents the use of marihuana for a condition other than a serious condition as defined in subdivision 7 of section 3360 of the Public Health Law;

(5) any statement, design, representation, picture or illustration that encourages or represents the recreational use of marihuana;

(6) any statement, design, representation, picture or illustration related to the safety or efficacy of marihuana, unless supported by substantial evidence or substantial clinical data;

(7) any statement, design, representation, picture or illustration portraying anyone under the age of 18, objects suggestive of the presence of anyone under the age of 18, or containing the use of a figure, symbol or language that is customarily associated with anyone under the age of 18;

(8) any offer of a prize, award or inducement to a certified patient, designated caregiver or practitioner related to the purchase of marihuana or a certification for the use of marihuana; or

(9) any statement that indicates or implies that the product or entity in the advertisement has been approved or endorsed by the commissioner, department, New York State or any person or entity associated with New York State provided that this shall not preclude a factual statement that an entity is a registered organization.

(i) Any advertisement for an approved medical marihuana product, which makes any claims or statements regarding efficacy, shall be submitted to the department at least 10 business days prior to the public dissemination of the advertisement.

(j) The submitter of the advertisement shall provide the following information to the department in addition to the advertisement itself:

(1) a cover letter that:

(i) provides the following subject line: Medical marihuana advertisement review package for a proposed advertisement;

(ii) provides a brief description of the format and expected distribution of the proposed advertisement; and

(iii) provides the submitter's name, title, address, telephone number, fax number, and email address;

(2) an annotated summary of the proposed advertisement showing every claim being made in the advertisement and which references support for each claim;

(3) verification that a person identified in an advertisement as an actual patient or health care practitioner is an actual patient or health care practitioner and not a model or actor;

(4) verification that a spokesperson who is represented as an actual patient is indeed an actual patient;

(5) verification that an official translation of a foreign language advertisement is accurate;

(6) annotated references to support disease or epidemiology information, cross-referenced to the advertisement summary; and

(7) a final copy of the advertisement, including a video where applicable, in a format acceptable to the department.

(k) Advertising packages that are missing any of the elements in subdivision (j) of this section, or that fail to follow the specific instructions for submissions, shall be considered incomplete. If the department receives an incomplete package, it shall so notify the submitter.

(l) No advertisement may be disseminated if the submitter of the advertisement has received information that has not been widely publicized in medical literature that the use of any approved medical marihuana product may cause fatalities or serious damage to a patient.

(m) A registered organization, its officers, managers and employees shall not cooperate, directly or indirectly, in any advertising if such advertising has the purpose or effect of steering or influencing patient or caregiver choice with regard to the selection of a practitioner. Nothing contained within this section prevents a registered organization from educating practitioners about approved medical marihuana products offered by the registered organization.

(n) The department may:

(1) require a specific disclosure be made in the advertisement in a clear and conspicuous manner if the department determines that the advertisement would be false or misleading without such a disclosure; or

(2) require that changes be made to the advertisement that are:

(i) necessary to protect the public health, safety and welfare; or

(ii) consistent with dispensing information for the product under review.

10 CRR-NY § 1004.17. Reporting dispensed medical marihuana products.

(a) A record of all approved medical marihuana products that have been dispensed shall be filed electronically with the department, utilizing a transmission format acceptable to the department, not later than 24 hours after the marihuana was dispensed to the certified patient or designated caregiver.

(b) The information filed with the department for each approved medical marihuana product dispensed shall include but not be limited to:

(1) a serial number that will be generated by the dispensing facility for each approved medical marihuana product dispensed to the certified patient or designated caregiver;

(2) an identification number which shall be populated by a number provided by the department, to identify the registered organization's dispensing facility;

(3) the patient name, date of birth and sex;

(4) the patient address, including street, city, state, zip code;

(5) the patient's registry identification card number;

(6) if applicable, designated caregiver's name and registry identification card number;

(7) the date the approved medical marihuana product was filled by the dispensing facility;

(8) the metric quantity for the approved medical marihuana product;

(9) the medical marihuana product drug code number, which shall be populated by a number provided by the department, to represent the approved medical marihuana brand that was dispensed to the certified patient or designated caregiver, as applicable;

(10) the number of days supply dispensed;

(11) the registered practitioner's Drug Enforcement Administration number;

(12) the date the written certification was issued by the registered practitioner; and

(13) the payment method.

(c) When applicable, a registered organization shall file a zero report with the department, in a format acceptable to the department. For the purposes of this section, a zero report shall mean a report that no approved medical marihuana product was dispensed by a registered organization during the relevant period of time. A zero report shall be submitted no later than 14 days following the most recent previously reported dispensing of an approved medical marihuana product or the submission of a prior zero report.

10 CRR-NY § 1004.18. Prohibition the use of approved medical marihuana products in certain places.

(a) Approved medical marihuana products shall not be vaporized in a public place. In no event shall approved medical marihuana products be consumed through vaporization in any location in which smoking is prohibited under section 1399 of the Public Health Law, including:

(1) places of employment;

(2) bars;

(3) food service establishments, except as provided in subdivision 6 of section 1399-q of the Public Health Law;

(4) enclosed indoor areas open to the public containing a swimming pool;

(5) public means of mass transportation, including subways, underground subway stations, and when occupied by passengers, buses, vans, taxicabs and limousines;

(6) ticketing, boarding and waiting areas in public transportation terminals;

(7) youth centers and facilities for detention as defined in sections 527-a and 503 of the Executive Law;

(8) any facility that provides child care services as defined in section 410-p of the Social Services Law, provided that such services provided in a private home are excluded from this subdivision when children enrolled in such day care are not present;

(9) child day care centers as defined in section 390 of the Social Services Law and child day care centers licensed by the City of New York;

(10) group homes for children as defined in section 371 of the Social Services Law;

(11) public institutions for children as defined in section 371 of the Social Services Law;

(12) residential treatment facilities for children and youth as defined in section 1.03 of the Mental Hygiene Law;

(13) all public and private colleges, universities and other educational and vocational institutions, including dormitories, residence halls, and other group residential facilities that are owned or operated by such colleges, universities and other educational and vocational institutions;

(14) general hospitals and residential health care facilities as defined in article 28 of the Public Health Law, and other health care facilities licensed by the State in which persons reside; provided, however, that the provisions of this subdivision shall not prohibit vaporization by patients in separate enclosed rooms of hospitals, residential health care facilities, and adult care facilities established or certified under title 2 of article 7 of the Social Services Law, community mental health residences established under section 41.44 of the Mental Hygiene Law, or facilities where day treatment programs are provided, which are designated as smoking rooms for patients of such facilities or programs;

(15) commercial establishments used for the purpose of carrying on or exercising any trade, profession, vocation or charitable activity;

(16) indoor arenas;

(17) zoos;

(18) bingo facilities.

(b) Vaporization of approved medical marihuana products shall not be permitted and no person shall vaporize an approved medical marihuana product within 100 feet of the entrances, exits or outdoor areas of any public or private elementary or secondary schools; however, that the provisions of this subdivision shall not apply to vaporization in a residence, or within real property boundary lines of such residential real property.

(c) Consumption of approved medical marihuana product shall not be permitted in any motor vehicle, either public or private, that is located upon public highways, private roads open to motor vehicle traffic, parking area of a shopping center or any parking lot, as defined in section 129 of the Vehicle and Traffic Law.

10 CRR-NY § 1004.19. Reporting requirements for registered practitioners, certified patients and designated caregivers.

(a) A practitioner shall report to the department, in a manner determined by the department, the death of a certified patient or change in status of a serious condition involving a certified patient for whom the practitioner has issued a certification if such change may affect the patient's continued eligibility for certification for use of approved medical marihuana product. A practitioner shall report such death or change of status not more than five business days after the practitioner becomes aware of such fact.

(b) If a practitioner re-issues a patient's certification to terminate the certification on an earlier date, then the registry identification card shall expire on such earlier date and shall be promptly returned to the department by the certified patient or designated caregiver.

(c) A practitioner shall report patient adverse events to the department, in a manner determined by the department, not more than five business days after the practitioner becomes aware of such adverse event, except that serious adverse events shall be reported not more than one business day after the practitioner becomes aware of such adverse event.

(d) A certified patient or designated caregiver, who has been issued a registry identification card, shall notify the department of any change in the information provided to the department not later than 10 business days after such change. A certified patient or designated caregiver shall report changes that include, but are not limited to, a change in the certified patient's name, address, contact information, medical status. A certified patient or designated caregiver shall report such changes on a form, and in a manner, determined by the department. Should a certified patient cease to have the serious condition noted on his or her certification, the certified patient or designated caregiver shall notify the department of such within 10 days and the certified patient's and designated caregiver's registry identification cards shall be considered void and shall be returned promptly to the department.

(e) If a certified patient's or designated caregiver's appearance has substantially changed such that the photograph submitted to the department does not accurately resemble such certified patient or designated caregiver, such person shall submit, in a timely manner, an updated photograph that meets the requirements set forth by the department.

(f) If a certified patient has a designated caregiver, that designated caregiver may notify the department of any changes on behalf of the certified patient using the same forms and process prescribed for certified patients.

(g) If a certified patient or designated caregiver notifies the department of any change that results in information on the registry identification card being inaccurate or the photograph needing to be replaced, the certified patient or designated caregiver shall obtain a replacement registry identification card. The department shall thereafter issue the certified patient or designated caregiver a new registry identification card. Upon receipt of a new registry identification card, the certified patient or designated caregiver shall destroy in a non-recoverable manner the registry identification card that was replaced.

(h) If a certified patient or designated caregiver becomes aware of the loss, theft or destruction of the registry identification card of such certified patient or designated caregiver, the certified patient or designated caregiver shall notify the department, on a form and in a manner prescribed by the department, not later than 10 days of becoming aware of the loss, theft or destruction. The department shall inactivate the initial registry identification card upon receiving such notice and issue a replacement registry identification card upon receiving the applicable fee provided the applicant continues to satisfy the requirements of section 3361 of the Public Health Law and section 1004.3 of this Part. Prior to issuance of the first replacement registry identification card, a certified patient or designated caregiver shall submit to the department a fee of $25, transmitted in a fashion as determined by the department. For each subsequent replacement registry identification card a certified patient or designated caregiver shall submit to the department a fee of $50, transmitted in a fashion as determined by the department.

(i) If a certified patient wishes to change or terminate his or her designated caregiver, the certified patient shall notify the department, in a manner determined by the department, and shall notify his or her designated caregiver as soon as practicable.

(1) The department shall issue a notification, in a format determined by the department, to the designated caregiver and the certified patient that the designated caregiver's registration card is invalid.

(2) In the event that the designated caregiver has no other active certified patients, the designated caregiver's registration card must be returned to the department within 10 business days.

(3) In the event that the certified patient has selected another designated caregiver, the proposed designated caregiver must register with the department as defined in section 1004.4 of this Part.

(j) If a designated caregiver wishes to terminate his or her relationship with a certified patient, the designated caregiver shall notify the department, in a manner determined by the department, and shall notify the certified patient, as soon as practicable.

(1) The department shall issue a notification, in a format determined by the department, to the certified patient and the designated caregiver that the designated caregiver has terminated his or her relationship with the certified patient.

(2) In the event that the designated caregiver has no other active certified patients, the designated caregiver's registration card must be returned to the department within 10 business days.

10 CRR-NY § 1004.20. Proper disposal of medical marihuana products by certified patients or designated caregivers.

(a) A certified patient or designated caregiver shall dispose of all approved medical marihuana product in the certified patient's or designated caregiver's possession no later than 10 calendar days after the expiration of the patient's certification, if such certification is not renewed, or sooner should the patient no longer wish to possess medical marihuana.

(b) A certified patient or designated caregiver shall complete disposal of approved medical marihuana products by one of the following methods:

(1) rendering the approved medical marihuana product non-recoverable beyond reclamation in accordance with the Department of Environmental Conservation's guidance; or

(2) returning the approved medical marihuana product to the dispensing facility from which it was purchased or any dispensing facility associated with the registered organization which manufactured the approved medical marihuana product, to the extent that the registered organization accepts product returns.

10 CRR-NY § 1004.21. General prohibitions.

(a) No person, except for a certified patient or designated caregiver, or an approved laboratorian shall open or break the seal placed on an approved medical marihuana product packaged by a registered organization and provided to the certified patient.

(b) No person associated with a registered organization shall enter into any agreement with a registered practitioner or health care facility concerning the provision of services or equipment that may adversely affect any person's freedom to choose the dispensing facility at which the certified patient or designated caregiver will purchase approved medical marihuana products.

(c) No approved medical marihuana product shall be sold, dispensed or distributed via a delivery service without prior written approval to the registered organization by the department, except that a designated caregiver may deliver the approved medical marihuana product to the designated caregiver's certified patient.

(d) No employee of a registered organization shall counsel a certified patient or designated caregiver on the use, administration of, and the risks associated with approved medical marihuana products, unless the employee is a physician, nurse practitioner, physician assistant or pharmacist with an active New York State license who has completed a four hour course pursuant to section 1004.1 of this Part, or the employee is under the direct supervision of, and in consultation with, such physician, nurse practitioner, physician assistant, or pharmacist on-site in the dispensing facility.

(e) No certified patient or designated caregiver shall be in possession of approved medical marihuana products without having in his or her possession his or her registry identification card. The certified patient or designated caregiver, upon request by the department or law enforcement, shall present such card to verify that the certified patient or designated caregiver is authorized to possess approved medical marihuana products.

10 CRR-NY § 1004.22. Practitioner prohibitions.

(a) A practitioner that is registered with the department shall not:

(1) directly or indirectly accept, solicit, or receive any item of value from a registered organization;

(2) offer a discount or any other item of value to a certified patient based on the patient's agreement or decision to use a particular practitioner, registered organization, brand or specific form of approved medical marihuana product produced by a registered organization;

(3) examine a qualifying patient for purposes of diagnosing a debilitating medical condition at any location owned or operated by a registered organization, or where medical marihuana products or related products necessary for the approved forms of administration of medical marihuana are acquired, distributed, dispensed, manufactured, sold, or produced; or

(4) directly or indirectly benefit from a patient obtaining a written certification. Such prohibition shall not prohibit a practitioner from charging an appropriate fee for the patient visit.

(b) A practitioner that issues written certifications, and such practitioner's co-worker, employee, spouse, parent, child, or sibling shall not have a direct or indirect financial interest in a registered organization or any other entity that may benefit from a certified patient's or designated caregiver's acquisition, purchase or use of approved medical marihuana products, including any formal or informal agreement whereby a registered organization provides compensation if the practitioner issues a written certification for a certified patient or steers a certified patient to a specific dispensing facility.

(c) A practitioner shall not issue a certification for himself/herself or for the practitioner's family members, employees or co-workers.

(d) A practitioner shall not receive or provide product samples containing marihuana.

(e) A practitioner shall not be a designated caregiver for any patients that he or she has certified under section 1004.2 of this Part. However, this shall not prohibit a facility, or a division, department, component, floor or other unit from being a designated caregiver pursuant to section 1004.4 of this Part.

10 CRR-NY § 1004.23. Designated caregiver prohibitions and protections.

(a) An individual shall not serve as a designated caregiver for more than five certified patients at any given time.

(b) A designated caregiver may only obtain payment from the certified patient to be used for the cost of the approved medical marihuana product purchased for the certified patient in the actual amount charged by the registered organization; provided, however, that a designated caregiver may charge the certified patient for reasonable costs incurred in the transportation, delivery, storage and administration of approved medical marihuana products.

(c) Designated caregivers, including employees of facilities registered as designated caregivers and acting within their scope of employment, shall not be subject to arrest, prosecution, or penalty in any manner, or denied any right or privilege, including but not limited to civil penalty or disciplinary action by a business or occupational or professional licensing board or bureau, solely for an action or conduct in accordance with this Part.

10 CRR-NY § 1004.24. Registered organizations; disposal of medical marihuana.

(a) The disposal of medical marihuana shall mean that the medical marihuana has been rendered unrecoverable and beyond reclamation.

(b) Registered organizations shall dispose of any medical marihuana that is outdated, damaged, deteriorated, contaminated or otherwise deemed not appropriate for manufacturing or dispensing, or any plant-based waste created as a by-product of the manufacturing processes. Registered organizations shall:

(1) obtain department approval of disposal methods; and

(2) dispose of liquid and chemical waste in accordance with applicable Federal, State and local laws and regulations.

(c) Registered organizations shall maintain records of disposal, which shall include:

(1) the type of plant material being disposed, if the material is a by-product of the manufacturing process;

(2) the brand and form of approved medical marihuana product being disposed, if a finished product;

(3) the weight of the disposed material, the number of plants, or in the case of a finished product, the quantity of the disposed product; and

(4) the signatures of at least two registered organization staff members who witnessed the disposal.

(d) All records of disposal shall be retained for at least five years and be made available for inspection by the department.

Part 3. New York State Bar Association Legal Ethics Opinions

New York State Bar Association Committee on Professional Ethics Opinion 1024

(9/29/14)

Topic: Counseling clients in illegal conduct; medical marijuana law.

Digest: In light of current federal enforcement policy, the New York Rules permit a lawyer to assist a client in conduct designed to comply with state medical marijuana law, notwithstanding that federal narcotics law prohibits the delivery, sale, possession and use of marijuana and makes no exception for medical marijuana.

Rules: 1.2(d), 1.2(f), 1.2 cmt 9, 1.16(c)(2), 6.1 cmt 1, 8.4(b).

FACTS

1. In July 2014, New York, following the lead of 22 other states, adopted the Compassionate Care Act ("CCA")[1], a law permitting the use of medical marijuana in tightly controlled circumstances. The CCA regulates the cultivation, distribution, prescription and use of marijuana for medical purposes. It permits specially approved organizations such as hospitals and community health centers to dispense medical marijuana to patients who have been certified by a health care provider and who have registered with the state Department of Health, and it further provides for the regulation and registration of organizations to manufacture and deliver marijuana for authorized medical uses.

2. At the same time, federal criminal law forbids the possession, distribution, sale or use of marijuana, and the federal law provides no exception for medical uses. The U.S. Department of Justice takes the position that the federal law is valid and enforceable even against individuals and entities engaged in the cultivation, transportation, delivery, prescription or use of medical marijuana in accordance with state regulatory law; however, the U.S. Department of Justice has adopted and published formal guidance restricting federal enforcement of the federal marijuana prohibition when individuals and entities act in accordance with state regulation of medical marijuana.

QUESTION

3. Under these unusual circumstances, do the New York Rules of Professional Conduct ("Rules") permit a lawyer to provide legal advice and assistance to doctors, patients, public officials, hospital administrators and others engaged in the cultivation, distribution, prescribing, dispensing, regulation, possession or use of marijuana for medical purposes to help them act in compliance with state regulation regarding medical marijuana and consistently with federal enforcement policy?

OPINION

4. Lawyers may advise clients about the lawfulness of their proposed conduct and assist them in complying with the law, but lawyers may not knowingly assist clients in illegal conduct. Rule 1.2(d) provides: "A lawyer shall not counsel a client to engage, or assist a client, in conduct that the lawyer knows is illegal or fraudulent, except that the lawyer may discuss the legal consequences of any proposed course of conduct with a client." Disciplinary Rule 7-102(A) (7), contained in the pre-2009 Code of Professional Responsibility, was to the same effect. As this Committee has

---

1 Laws of 2014, Chap. 90 (signed by the Governor and effective on July 5, 2014).

observed, if a client proposes to engage in conduct that is illegal, "then it would be unethical for an attorney to recommend the action or assist the client in carrying it out." N.Y. State 769 (2003); *accord* N.Y. State 666 (1994).

5. This ethical restriction reflects lawyers' fundamental role in the administration of justice, which is to promote compliance with the law by providing legal advice and assistance in structuring clients' conduct in accordance with the law. *See also* Rule 8.4(b) (forbidding "illegal conduct that adversely reflects on the lawyer's honesty, trustworthiness or fitness as a lawyer"). Ideally, lawyers will not only attempt to prevent clients from engaging in knowing illegalities but also discourage clients from conduct of doubtful legality:

> The most effective realization of the law's aims often takes place in the attorney's office,... where the lawyer's quiet counsel takes the place of public force. Contrary to popular belief, the compliance with the law thus brought about is not generally lip-serving and narrow, for by reminding him of its long-run costs the lawyer often deters his client from a course of conduct technically permissible under existing law, though inconsistent with its underlying spirit and purpose....

> The reasons that justify and even require partisan advocacy in the trial of a cause do not grant any license to the lawyer to participate as legal adviser in a line of conduct that is immoral, unfair, or of doubtful legality.

Am. Bar Ass'n & Ass'n of Am. Law Sch., Professional Responsibility Report of the Joint Conference, 44 A.B.A. J. 1159, 1161 (1958). The public importance of lawyers' role in promoting clients' legal compliance is reflected in the attorney-client privilege, which protects the confidentiality that is traditionally considered essential in order for lawyers to serve this role effectively. *See, e.g., Hunt v. Blackburn*, 128 U.S. 464, 470 (1888) (privilege "is founded upon the necessity, in the interest and administration of justice, of the aid of persons having knowledge of the law and skilled in its practice, which assistance can only be safely and readily availed of when free from the consequences or the apprehension of disclosure").

6. It is counter-intuitive to suppose that the lawyer's fundamental role might ever be served by assisting clients in violating a law that the lawyer knows to be valid and enforceable. But the question presented by the state's medical marijuana law is highly unusual if not unique: Although participating in the production, delivery or use of medical marijuana violates federal criminal law as written, the federal government has publicly announced that it is limiting its enforcement of this law, and has acted accordingly, insofar as individuals act consistently with state laws that legalize and extensively regulate medical marijuana. Both the state law and the publicly announced federal enforcement policy presuppose that individuals and entities will comply with new and intricate state regulatory law and, thus, presuppose that lawyers will provide legal advice and assistance to an array of public and private actors and institutions to promote their compliance with state law and current federal policy. Under these unusual circumstances, for the reasons discussed below, the Committee concludes that Rule 1.2(d) does not forbid lawyers from providing the necessary advice and assistance.

LEGAL BACKGROUND

7. Much has been written elsewhere about the interrelationship between federal criminal narcotics laws and recent state medical marijuana laws. For purposes of this opinion, only the following basic understanding is needed.

8. Under federal criminal law, marijuana is a Schedule I narcotic, whose manufacture, possession and distribution is prohibited, and for which there is no approved medical use. Further, individuals and entities are forbidden by federal law not only from violating these laws as principals, but also, under principles of accessorial liability, from intentionally aiding and abetting others in violating the narcotics law, counseling others to violate the narcotics law, or conspiring with others to violate the narcotics law.[2]

---

2 See, e.g., 18 U.S.C. §2(a)("Whoever commits an offense against the United States or aids, abets, counsels, commands, induces or procures its commission, is punishable as a principal."); 18 U.S.C. § 2(b)("Whoever willfully causes an act to be done which if directly performed by him or another would be an offense against the United States, is punishable as a principal."); 21 U.S.C. § 846 ("Any person who attempts or conspires to commit any offense defined in this subchapter shall be subject to the same penalties as those prescribed for the offense, the commission of which was the object of the attempt or conspiracy.").

9. For many years, states likewise criminalized the manufacture, possession and distribution of marijuana, allowing for concurrent federal and state enforcement of the criminal law. Most prosecutions of narcotics laws, especially with regard to marijuana, occurred at the state and local level. However, in recent years, more than 20 states have legalized marijuana for medicinal purposes to make it available by prescription. Colorado and Washington have gone farther, developing regulation permitting the sale and use of marijuana for recreational purposes.

10. The U.S. Department of Justice ("DOJ") takes the position that the manufacture, possession and distribution of marijuana remains a federal crime, and can be enforced by federal law enforcement officials, even when the conduct in question is undertaken in accordance with state medical marijuana laws. However, current federal policy restricts federal enforcement activity, including civil as well as criminal enforcement, concerning medical marijuana. The Deputy Attorney General's August 29, 2013 memorandum, titled "Guidance Regarding Marijuana Enforcement," acknowledges that "the federal government has traditionally relied on state and local law enforcement agencies to address marijuana activity through enforcement of their own narcotics laws," and the federal government has concentrated its effort in accordance with federal enforcement priorities, such as preventing the distribution of marijuana to minors, preventing revenue from marijuana sales from going to criminal enterprises, and preventing marijuana activity from being used as a cover for trafficking other drugs. The memorandum directs Department attorneys and federal law enforcement authorities to focus their enforcement resources and efforts on these priorities, which are less likely to be threatened "[i]n jurisdictions that have enacted laws legalizing marijuana in some form and that have also implemented strong and effective regulatory and enforcement systems to control the cultivation, distribution, sale, and possession of marijuana." Although the memorandum makes plain that it is not intended to create any enforceable substantive or procedural rights, the memorandum might fairly be read as an expression by the current Administration that it will not enforce the federal criminal law with regard to otherwise-lawful medical marijuana activities that are carried out in accordance with a robust state regulatory law and that do not implicate the identified federal enforcement priorities. Over the period of more than a year since the memorandum was published, federal law enforcement authorities have acted consistently with this understanding.

11. The CCA allows specified licensed New York physicians to prescribe, and patients to use, medical marijuana only in pill form or in a form that may be inhaled as a vapor, but not in a form that may be smoked. Medical marijuana may only be prescribed for identified, documented medical conditions categorized as "severe[ly] debilitating or life-threatening." The regulation of medical marijuana under the law will be overseen by the Health Department, which, among other things, will authorize and register a limited number of organizations ("Registered Organizations") to manufacture and dispense marijuana for medical use, will issue registration cards to patients or their caregivers certified to receive medical marijuana, and will set prices. The law restricts who may be hired by Registered Organizations, regulates their production and dispensation of medical marijuana, establishes a tax on their receipts, and criminalizes various abuses. *See generally* Francis J. Serbaroli, "A Primer on New York's Medical Marijuana Law," NYLJ, July 22, 2014, p. 3.

The potential role of lawyers in providing legal assistance regarding compliance with the medical marijuana law

12. Lawyers might provide a range of assistance to clients seeking to comply with the CCA and to act consistently with federal law enforcement policy. Among the potential clients are public officials and agencies including the Health Department that have responsibility for implementing the law, health care providers and other entities that may apply to be selected or eventually be selected as Registered Organizations authorized to manufacture and dispense medical marijuana, physicians seeking to prescribe medical marijuana, and patients with severely debilitating or life-threatening conditions seeking to obtain medical marijuana. Any or all of these potential clients may seek legal assistance not only so that they may be advised how to comply with the state law and avoid running afoul of federal enforcement policy but also for affirmative legal assistance. The Health Department may seek lawyers' help in establishing internal procedures to conduct the registrations and other activities contemplated by the law. Entities may seek assistance in applying to become Registered Organizations as well as in understanding and complying with employment, tax and other requirements of the law. Physicians may seek help in understanding the severe restrictions on the issuance of prescriptions for medical marijuana and in navigating the procedural requirements for effectively issuing such prescriptions.

13. Leaving aside the federal law, the above-described legal assistance would be entirely consistent with lawyers'

conventional role in helping clients comply with the law. Indeed, it seems fair to say that state law would not only permit but affirmatively expect lawyers to provide such assistance. In general, it is assumed that lawyers, by virtue of their expertise and ethical expectations, have a necessary role in ensuring the public's compliance with the law. "As our society becomes one in which rights and responsibilities are increasingly defined in legal terms, access to legal services has become of critical importance." Rule 6.1, Cmt. [1]. This is especially true with regard to complex, technical regulatory schemes such as the one established by the CCA, and where, as in the case of the CCA, noncompliance can result in criminal prosecution.

14. However, the federal law cannot easily be left aside. The question of whether lawyers may serve their traditional role is complicated by the federal law. Assuming, as we do for purposes of this opinion, that the federal marijuana prohibition remains valid and enforceable notwithstanding state medical marijuana law, then individuals and entities seeking to dispense, prescribe or use medical marijuana, or to assist others in doing so, pursuant to the CCA would potentially be violating federal narcotics law as principals or accessories; in that event, the legal assistance sought from lawyers might involve assistance in conduct that the lawyer knows to be illegal.

PRIOR ETHICS OPINIONS

15. Several other bar association ethics committees have confronted this problem but reached different conclusions under their counterparts to Rule 1.2(d). Most of these opinions pre-dated DOJ's August 2013 guidance, but took account of a 2009 DOJ memorandum suggesting that federal law enforcement would not be directed at patients and their caregivers who are in "clear and unambiguous compliance" with state medical marijuana laws.

16. In 2010, Maine's ethics committee took the view that although lawyers may assist clients in determining "the validity scope, meaning or application of the law," the rule "forbids attorneys from assisting a client in engaging in the medical marijuana business" because the rule "does not make a distinction between crimes which are enforced and those which are not. . . . [A]n attorney needs to . . . determine whether the particular legal service being requested rises to the level of assistance in violating federal law." Maine Op. 199 (July 7, 2010).

17. Connecticut's ethics committee similarly concluded that a lawyer may not assist a client insofar as its conduct, although authorized by the state's medical marijuana law, which created a broad licensing and registration structure to be implemented by the Department of Consumer Protection, violates federal law. Connecticut Op. 2013-02 (Jan. 16, 2013). The opinion noted that much of the legal assistance sought by clients seeking to comply with the law (e.g., patients, caregivers, physicians, pharmacists, distributers and growers), such as legal advice and assistance regarding the law's requirements and the rule-making and regulatory processes, would be consistent with lawyers' "traditional role as counselors" and "in the classic mode envisioned by professional standards." But some of that legal work might nevertheless constitute impermissible assistance in violating federal law.

18. More recently, in the context of Colorado's state law decriminalizing and regulating the sale of marijuana for recreational purposes, the state's ethics committee opined: "[U]nless and until there is a change in applicable federal law or in the Colorado Rules of Professional Conduct, a lawyer cannot advise a client regarding the full panoply of conduct permitted by the marijuana amendments to the Colorado Constitution and implementing statutes and regulations. To the extent that advice were to cross from advising or representing a client regarding the consequences of a client's past or contemplated conduct under federal and state law to counseling the client to engage, or assisting the client, in conduct the lawyer knows is criminal under federal law, the lawyer would violate Rule 1.2(d)." Colorado Op. 125 (Oct. 21, 2013). However, the committee recommended amending the state ethics rules to authorize lawyers to advise and assist clients regarding marijuana-related conduct, notwithstanding contrary federal law.[3]

---

3 Colorado added a new comments [14] to Rule 1.2 of the Colorado Rules of Professional Conduct, permitting a lawyer to counsel a client regarding the validity, scope and meaning of the Colorado marijuana law and to assist a client in conduct that the lawyer reasonably believes is permitted by that law, but the lawyer must also advise the client regarding related federal law and policy. Nevada adopted a new Comment [1] to Rule 1.2 that is substantively identical to Colorado Comment [14]. In Washington State, the King County Bar Association has urged the Washington Supreme Court to amend the Washington Rules of Professional Conduct to add a comment to Rule 8.4 and a new Rule 8.6, to make clear that conduct permitted by the state marijuana law does not reflect adversely on the lawyer's honesty, trustworthiness or fitness in other respects, and that a lawyer is not subject to discipline for counseling or assisting a client in conduct permitted by the state marijuana law, even though the conduct may

19. In 2011, Arizona's ethics committee reached a very different conclusion, however, based in significant part on the premise that "no court opinion has held that the state law is invalid or unenforceable on federal preemption grounds."

In these circumstances, we decline to interpret and apply ER 1.2(d) in a manner that would prevent a lawyer who concludes that the client's proposed conduct is in "clear and unambiguous compliance" with state law from assisting the client in connection with activities expressly authorized under state law, thereby depriving clients of the very legal advice and assistance that is needed to engage in the conduct that the state law expressly permits. The maintenance of an independent legal profession, and of its right to advocate for the interests of clients, is a bulwark of our system of government. History is replete with examples of lawyers who, through vigorous advocacy and at great personal and professional cost to themselves, obtained the vindication of constitutional or other rights long denied or withheld and which otherwise could not have been secured.

A state law now expressly permits certain conduct. Legal services are necessary or desirable to implement and bring to fruition that conduct expressly permitted under state law. In any potential conflict between state and federal authority, such as may be presented by the interplay between the Act and federal law, lawyers have a critical role to perform in the activities that will lead to the proper resolution of the controversy. Although the Act may be found to be preempted by federal law or otherwise invalid, as of this time there has been no such judicial determination.

Arizona Op. 11-01 (Feb. 2011). The opinion concluded:

• If a client or potential client requests an Arizona lawyer's assistance to undertake the specific actions that the Act expressly permits; and

• The lawyer advises the client with respect to the potential federal law implications and consequences thereof or, if the lawyer is not qualified to do so, advises the client to seek other legal counsel regarding those issues and limits the scope of his or her representation; and

• The client, having received full disclosure of the risks of proceeding under the state law, wishes to proceed with a course of action specifically authorized by the Act; then

• The lawyer ethically may perform such legal acts as are necessary or desirable to assist the client to engage in the conduct that is expressly permissible under the Act.

Id.

20. A recent opinion of the King County (Washington) Bar Association endorsed the Arizona committee's conclusion and much of its reasoning,[4] in the context of Washington's adoption of a state-regulated system for producing and selling marijuana for recreational purposes:

While the KCBA does not agree with all components of the Arizona opinion, its emphasis on the client's need for legal assistance to comply with state law accurately reflects the reality that Washington clients face in navigating the new Washington law. The initial proposed implementing regulations for I-502, for example, have added 49 new sections in the Washington Administrative Code encompassing 42 pages of text. These regulations are consistent with I-502's express goal of removing the marijuana economy from the province of criminal organizations and bringing it into a "tightly regulated, state-licensed system." In building this complex system, the voters of Washington could not have envisioned it working without attorneys. As the State Bar of Arizona recognized, disciplining attorneys for working within such a system would deprive the state's citizens of legal services 'necessary and desirable to implement and bring to fruition that conduct expressly permitted under state law.

---

violate federal law. Those proposals were still pending when we issued this opinion.
4 The King County opinion rejected the implication of the Arizona opinion that the propriety of the lawyer's assistance turned on the fact that the state medical marijuana law had not yet been invalidated or preempted.

KCBA Ethics Advisory Opinion on I-502 [Initiative 502 – marijuana legalization] & Rules of Professional Conduct (Oct. 2013). Following suit, the Washington State bar ethics committee recently proposed adding a Comment to the state's ethics code and issuing an advisory opinion authorizing lawyers to assist clients in complying with the state marijuana law at least until federal enforcement policy changes.

ANALYSIS

21. As Rule 1.2(d) makes clear, although a lawyer may not encourage a client to violate the law or assist a client in doing so, a lawyer may advise a client about the reach of the law. *See* N.Y. State 455 (1976) ("[W]here the lawyer does no more than advise his client concerning the legal character and consequences of the act, there can be no professional impropriety. That is his proper function and fully comports with the requirements of Canon 7.... But, where the lawyer becomes a motivating force by encouraging his client to commit illegal acts or undertakes to bring about a violation of law, he oversteps the bounds of propriety."). Thus, a lawyer may give advice about whether undertaking to manufacture, transport, sell, prescribe or use marijuana in accordance with the CCA's regulatory scheme would violate federal narcotics law. If the lawyer were to conclude competently and in good faith that the federal law was inapplicable or invalid, the lawyer could so advise the client and would not be subject to discipline even if the lawyer's advice later proved incorrect. *See, e.g.*, ABA Op. 85-352 (1985) ("[W]here a lawyer has a good faith belief ... that a particular transaction does not result in taxable income or that certain expenditures are properly deductible as expenses, the lawyer has no duty to require [disclosure] as a condition of his or her continued representation.... In the role of advisor, the lawyer should counsel the client as to whether the position is likely to be sustained by a court if challenged by the IRS, as well as of the potential penalty consequences to the client if the position is taken on the tax return without disclosure.").[5] As the Second Department recognized in dismissing a prosecution against a lawyer who allegedly gave erroneous advice about the lawfulness of the client's proposed conduct:

> We cannot conclude that an attorney who advises a client to take an action that he or she, in good faith, believes to be legal loses the protection of the First Amendment if his or her advice is later determined to be incorrect. Indeed, it would eviscerate the right to give and receive legal counsel with respect to potential criminal liability if an attorney could be charged with conspiracy and solicitation whenever a District Attorney disagreed with that advice. The potential impact of allowing an attorney to be prosecuted in circumstances such as those presented here is profoundly disturbing. A looming threat of criminal sanctions would deter attorneys from acquainting individuals with matters as vital as the breadth of their legal rights and the limits of those rights. Correspondingly, where counsel is restrained, so is the fundamental right of the citizenry, bound as it is by laws complex and unfamiliar, to receive the advice necessary for measured conduct.

Matter of Vinluan v Doyle, 60 AD3d 237, 243, 873 NYS2d 72 (2d Dep't 2009).

22. Further, Rule 1.2(d) forbids a lawyer from assisting a client in conduct only if the lawyer knows the conduct is illegal or fraudulent. If the lawyer believes that conduct is unlawful but there is some support for an argument that the conduct is legal, the lawyer may provide legal assistance under the Rules (but is not obligated to do so). *See* Rule 1.2(f) ("A lawyer may refuse to aid or participate in conduct that the lawyer believes to be unlawful, even though there is some support for an argument that the conduct is legal."); *see also* Rule 1.16(c)(2) ("a lawyer may withdraw from representing a client when ... the client persists in a course of action involving the lawyer's services that the lawyer reasonably believes is criminal or fraudulent").

23. The difficult question arises if the lawyer knows that the client's proposed conduct, although consistent with state law, would violate valid and enforceable federal law.[6] Ordinarily, in that event, while the lawyer could advise

---

5 Inasmuch as this Committee limits itself to interpreting the ethics rules, we take no view on whether a colorable argument can be made that the federal narcotics law is invalid or unenforceable in situations where individuals or entities transport, distribute, possess or use marijuana pursuant to state medical marijuana law. We note, however, that as a constitutional matter, duly enacted federal laws ordinarily preempt inconsistent state laws under the federal Supremacy Clause. We also note, in particular, that in Gonzales v. Raich, 545 U.S. 1 (2005), the Court rejected a claim that Congress exceeded its authority under the Commerce Clause insofar as the marijuana prohibition applied to personal use of marijuana for medical purposes.

6 Rule 1.2(d) allows lawyers to assist clients in good faith challenges to a law's validity, but that is not the situation posed here.

the client about the reach of the federal law and how to conform to the federal law, the lawyer could not properly encourage or assist the client in conduct that violates the federal law. That would ordinarily be true even if the federal law, although applicable to the client's proposed conduct, was not rigorously enforced and the lawyer anticipated that the law would not be enforced in the client's situation. *See* Charles W. Wolfram, Modern Legal Ethics 703 (1986) ("on the whole, lawyers serve the interests of society better if they urge upon clients the desirability of complying with all valid laws, no matter how widely violated by others they may be"); cf.Restatement (Third) of the Law Governing Lawyers § 94, Cmt. f (2000) ("A lawyer's advice to a client about the degree of risk that a law violation will be detected or prosecuted [is impermissible when] the lawyer thereby intended to counsel or assist the client's crime, fraud, or violation of a court order."). But the situation is different where the state executive branch determines to implement the state legislation by authorizing and regulating medical marijuana, consistent with current, published federal executive-branch enforcement policy, and the federal government does not take effective measures to prevent the implementation of the state law. In that event, the question under Rule 1.2(d) is whether a lawyer may assist in conduct under the state medical marijuana law that the lawyer knows would violate federal narcotics law that is on the books but deliberately unenforced as a matter of federal executive discretion.

24. This situation raises political and philosophical questions that this Committee cannot and need not resolve regarding how best to make and implement law in a federal system. Some may think it anomalous, where Congress has recognized no relevant exception to its narcotics prohibitions, for states to adopt medical marijuana laws that appear to contravene federal law and for the federal executive branch, through the exercise of prosecutorial discretion, effectively to carve out an exception for the implementation of these state laws. Others may think that DOJ's forbearance is consistent with its tradition, known to Congress, of exercising prosecutorial discretion to mitigate the criminal law's excesses, including where the criminal law reaches farther than its underlying purposes. We do not believe that by adopting Rule 1.2(d), our state judiciary meant to declare a position on this debate or meant to preclude lawyers from counseling or assisting conduct that is legal under state law. Rule 1.2(d) was based on an ABA model and there is no indication that anyone – not the ABA, not the state bar, and not the state court itself — specifically considered whether lawyers may serve in their traditional role in this sort of unusual legal situation. We assume for purposes of this Opinion that state courts will themselves serve in their traditional role: As issues of interpretation arise in litigation under the CCA, state courts will be available to issue interpretive rulings and take other judicial action that has the practical effect of assisting in the implementation of the CCA.[7] Serving this role will not undermine state judicial integrity. Similarly, we do not believe that it derogates from public respect for the law and lawyers, or otherwise undermines the objectives of the professional conduct rules, for lawyers as "officers of the court" to serve in their traditional role as well, if they so choose. Obviously, lawyers may decline to give legal assistance regarding the CCA.

25. We conclude that the New York Rules of Professional Conduct permit lawyers to give legal assistance regarding the CCA that goes beyond a mere discussion of the legality of the client's proposed conduct. In general, state professional conduct rules should be interpreted to promote state law, not to impede its effective implementation. As the Arizona and King County opinions recognized, a state medical-marijuana law establishing a complex regulatory scheme depends on lawyers for its success. Implicitly, the state law authorizes lawyers to provide traditional legal services to clients seeking to act in accordance with the state law. Further, and crucially, in this situation the federal enforcement policy also depends on the availability of lawyers to establish and promote compliance with the "strong and effective regulatory and enforcement systems" that are said to justify federal forbearance from enforcement of narcotics laws that are technically applicable. The contemplated legal work is not designed to escape law enforcement by avoiding detection. Cf. Rule 1.2 cmt. [9] ("There is a critical distinction between presenting an analysis of the legal aspects of questionable conduct and recommending the means by which a crime or fraud might be committed with impunity."); N.Y. State 529 (1981) ("[T]he Code distinguishes between giving legal advice and giving advice which would aid the client in escaping punishment for past crimes. EC 7-5 warns that 'a lawyer should never encourage or aid his client to commit criminal acts or counsel his client on how to violate the law and avoid punishment'"). Lawyers would assist clients who participate openly and subject to a state regulatory structure that the federal government allows to function as a matter of discretion. Nothing in the history

---

7 If the state courts were to nullify the CCA based on inconsistent federal narcotics law, the question addressed in this opinion would, of course, become moot.

and tradition of the profession, in court opinions, or elsewhere, suggests that Rule 1.2(d) was intended to prevent lawyers in a situation like this from providing assistance that is necessary to implement state law and to effectuate current federal policy.[8] If federal enforcement were to change materially, this Opinion might need to be reconsidered.

CONCLUSION

26. In light of current federal enforcement policy, the New York Rules of Professional Conduct permit a lawyer to assist a client in conduct designed to comply with state medical marijuana law, notwithstanding that federal narcotics law prohibits the delivery, sale, possession and use of marijuana and makes no exception for medical marijuana.

---

8 For essentially the same reason, we regard Rule 8.4(b) as inapplicable. Assuming that a lawyer's legal assistance in implementing the state medical-marijuana law technically violates the unenforced federal criminal law, we do not believe that the lawyer's assistance under the circumstances described here would amount to "illegal conduct that adversely reflects on the lawyer's honesty, trustworthiness or fitness as a lawyer."

New York State Bar Association Committee on Professional Ethics Legal Ethics Opinion 1177

(11/18/2019)

Topic: Counseling clients in illegal conduct; medical marijuana law.

Digest: The Committee reaffirms its conclusion in N.Y. State 1024 (2014) that a lawyer may ethically assist a client in conduct designed to comply with New York's medical marijuana law.

Rules: 1.2(d).

FACTS

1. In July 2014, New York, following the lead of 22 other states, adopted the Compassionate Care Act ("CCA"), a law permitting and regulating the cultivation, distribution, prescription, and use of marijuana for medical purposes. The CCA enables specially approved organizations such as hospitals and community health centers to dispense medical marijuana to patients who have been certified by a health care provider and who have registered with the state Department of Health, and provides further for the regulation and registration of organizations to manufacture and deliver marijuana for authorized medical uses.

2. Although federal criminal law forbids the possession, distribution, sale, or use of marijuana, the United States Department of Justice ("DOJ") does not enforce the law against individuals and entities engaged in the cultivation, transportation, delivery, prescription, or use of medical marijuana in accordance with state regulatory law. In 2013, the DOJ issued a memorandum (the "Cole Memo") restricting federal enforcement of the federal marijuana prohibition when individuals and entities act in accordance with state regulation of medical marijuana.

3. On September 29, 2014, this Committee issued Opinion 1024, which concluded that, "in light of current federal enforcement policy, the N.Y. Rules of Professional Conduct (the "Rules") permit a lawyer to assist a client in conduct designed to comply with state medical marijuana law, notwithstanding that federal narcotics law prohibits the delivery, sale, possession and use of marijuana and makes no exception for medical marijuana." Id. ¶ 26. Opinion 1024 said, too, that "[i]f federal enforcement were to change materially, this Opinion might need to be reconsidered." Id. ¶ 25.

4. In December 2014, as part of a spending measure subject to periodic review, Congress enacted the Rohrabacher-Farr amendment (now known as the Rohrabacher-Blumenauer amendment, hereafter the "Rohrabacher Amendment"), which prohibits the DOJ from using any of the funds appropriated by Congress to prevent states with medical marijuana laws "from implementing their own State laws that authorize, the use, distribution, possession, or cultivation of medical marijuana." https://www.congress.gov/amendment/113th-congress/house-amendment/748/text. The Rohrabacher Amendment was the basis of the decision in United States v. McIntosh, 833 F.3d 1163 (9th Cir 2016), which prohibited the Department of Justice from prosecuting defendants who complied with their respective states' medical marijuana laws. Since 2014, Congress has continuously renewed the Rohrabacher Amendment (by healthy bipartisan majorities) in subsequent spending measures. Although the Cole Memo was rescinded by former Attorney General Jeff Sessions on January 4, 2018, General Sessions' successor, William Barr, said during his confirmation hearing that he would not target state legal marijuana businesses, and would leave it to Congress to act.

QUESTION

5. Does the Committee adhere to its conclusion in Opinion 1024 that lawyers may assist clients in complying with New York's medical marijuana law?

OPINION

6. The Committee concludes that, notwithstanding the Attorney General's rescission of the Cole Memo, the guidance provided in Opinion 1024 remains sound because, in light of the Rohrabacher Amendment, federal law and enforcement practice continue to permit New York to implement its medical marijuana law.

7. After providing extensive factual and legal background, which we need not repeat here, Opinion 1024 focused on the application of Rule 1.2(d), which provides: "A lawyer shall not counsel a client to engage, or assist a client, in conduct that the lawyer knows is illegal or fraudulent, except that the lawyer may discuss the legal consequences of any proposed course of conduct with a client." We observed that, as a general matter, "although a lawyer may not encourage a client to violate the law or assist a client in doing so, a lawyer may advise a client about the reach of the law," and that therefore "a lawyer may give advice about whether undertaking to manufacture, transport, sell, prescribe or use marijuana in accordance with the CCA's regulatory scheme would violate federal narcotics law." N.Y. State 1024 ¶ 21. We observed also that "Rule 1.2(d) forbids a lawyer from assisting a client in conduct only if the lawyer knows the conduct is illegal or fraudulent. If the lawyer believes that conduct is unlawful but there is some support for an argument that the conduct is legal, the lawyer may provide legal assistance under the Rules (but is not obligated to do so)." Id. ¶ 22 (emphasis in original). We then turned to "[t]he difficult question [that] arises if the lawyer knows that the client's proposed conduct, although consistent with state law, would violate valid and enforceable federal law." Id. ¶ 23 (emphasis in original).

8. On that question, we said that "[o]rdinarily, . . . while the lawyer could advise the client about the reach of the federal law and how to conform to the federal law, the lawyer could not properly encourage or assist the client in conduct that violates the federal law. That would ordinarily be true even if the federal law, although applicable to the client's proposed conduct, was not rigorously enforced and the lawyer anticipated that the law would not be enforced in the client's situation." Id. We reasoned, however, that "the situation is different where the state executive branch determines to implement the state legislation by authorizing and regulating medical marijuana, consistent with current, published federal executive-branch enforcement policy, and the federal government does not take effective measures to prevent the implementation of the state law. In that event, the question under Rule 1.2(d) is whether a lawyer may assist in conduct under the state medical marijuana law that the lawyer knows would violate federal narcotics law that is on the books but deliberately unenforced as a matter of federal executive discretion." Id.

9. In concluding that lawyers may assist clients in complying with New York's medical marijuana laws, we explained in part (id. ¶ 24):

We do not believe that by adopting Rule 1.2(d), our state judiciary meant to declare a position on this debate or meant to preclude lawyers from counseling or assisting conduct that is legal under state law. Rule 1.2(d) was based on an ABA model and there is no indication that anyone – not the ABA, not the state bar, and not the state court itself – specifically considered whether lawyers may serve in their traditional role in this unusual legal situation. We assume for purposes of this Opinion that state courts will themselves serve in their traditional role: As issues of interpretation arise in litigation under the CCA, state courts will be available to issue interpretive rulings and take other judicial action that has the practical effect of assisting in the implementation of the CCA. Serving this role will not undermine state judicial integrity. Similarly, we do not believe that it derogates from public respect for the law and lawyers, or otherwise undermines the objectives of the professional conduct rules, for lawyers as "officers of the court" to serve in their traditional role as well, if they so choose. Obviously, lawyers may decline to give legal assistance regarding the CCA.

10. The DOJ's rescission of the Cole Memo does not meaningfully change federal law enforcement policy. If anything, the adoption, continued approval, and implementation of the Rohrabacher Amendment reinforces our earlier conclusion. Not only does the DOJ continue to permit states to implement their medical marijuana laws, but federal legislation now prohibits the DOJ from preventing states from doing so.

11. Accordingly, we reaffirm our earlier conclusion that the Rules permit lawyers to give legal assistance regarding the CCA that goes beyond a mere discussion of the legality of the client's proposed conduct. "Implicitly, the state law authorizes lawyers to provide traditional legal services to clients seeking to act in accordance with the state law. . . . Nothing in the history and tradition of the profession, in court opinions, or elsewhere, suggests that Rule 1.2(d) was intended to prevent lawyers in a situation like this from providing assistance that is necessary to implement state law and to effectuate current federal policy." Id. ¶ 25

CONCLUSION

12. In light of current federal policy, the Rules permit a lawyer to assist a client in conduct designed to comply with state medical marijuana law.

New York State Bar Association Committee on Professional Ethics Legal Ethics Opinion 1225

(07/08/2021)

Topic: Counseling clients engaged in recreational marijuana business; accepting partial ownership of recreational marijuana business in lieu of fee; personal use of recreational marijuana.

Digest: In light of current federal enforcement policy, the New York Rules of Professional Conduct permit a lawyer to assist a client in conduct designed to comply with New York's Recreational Marijuana Law and its implementing regulations, notwithstanding that federal narcotics law prohibits the activities authorized by that law. A lawyer may also use marijuana for recreational purposes and may, when the law becomes fully effective, cultivate an authorized amount of marijuana plants at home for personal use. Finally, subject to compliance with Rules 1.7 and 1.8(a), an attorney may accept an equity ownership interest in a cannabis business in exchange for legal services.

Rules: 1.1(a); 1.2(d); 1.3; 1.16(b)(2); 1.7; 1.8(a); 8.4(b); 8.4(h).

FACTS

1. New York legalized cannabis products for medical use in July 2014. On March 31, 2021, Governor Andrew M. Cuomo signed into law Chapter 92 of the Laws of 2021, entitled the "Marihuana Regulation and Taxation Act," creating a regulated recreational cannabis industry in New York (the "Recreational Marijuana Law"). Although marijuana possession and use were legalized for non-medical purposes effective immediately with the adoption of the Recreational Marijuana Law, the authorized commercial sale of cannabis products awaits various administrative rules and regulations and is not anticipated to begin before late 2022.

2. The regulatory framework established by the Recreational Marijuana Law bears many similarities to New York's regulation of alcohol by the New York State Liquor Authority under the Alcoholic Beverage Control Law. A Cannabis Control Board and the Office of Cannabis Management will control the issuance and revocation of licenses for retail dispensaries and on-site consumption establishments and will administer both the adult-use and medical-use programs, promulgating rules, issuing licenses, and investigating and enforcing violations. The cultivation, processing, distribution, and sale of cannabis products will be tightly controlled and, when the law becomes fully effective, individuals will be permitted to grow a limited number of plants in their homes for personal use.

3. Through local legislation that is subject to permissive referendum, the Recreational Marijuana Law gives cities, villages and towns the authority to "opt out" of allowing retail dispensaries and on-site consumption establishments to operate within their jurisdictions. These localities may also regulate the time, place and manner of the operation of these adult-use facilities, provided the Cannabis Control Board does not determine that such restrictions make such operations unreasonably impracticable. Cannabis businesses also remain subject to local zoning regulations.

QUESTIONS

4. The inquirer is an attorney who wants to provide legal services to a client engaged in the recreational cannabis business in New York. She poses three separate questions:

a. May an attorney ethically provide legal services to assist a client to comply with New York's Recreational Marijuana Law?

b. May an attorney ethically use marijuana recreationally and grow it at home for personal use?

c. May an attorney accept an equity interest in a client's cannabis business in exchange for providing legal services?

OPINION

Our Prior Opinions Regarding Rule 1.2(d) and New York's Medical Marijuana Law.

5. Rule 1.2(d) of the Rules of the New York Rules of Professional Conduct (the "Rules") provides:

> A lawyer shall not counsel a client to engage, or assist a client, in conduct that the lawyer knows is illegal or fraudulent, except that the lawyer may discuss the legal consequences of any proposed course of conduct with a client.

6. Notwithstanding Rule 1.2(d), following the enactment of New York's Compassionate Care Act (the "Medical Marijuana Law"), this committee held in N.Y. State 1024 (2014) that an attorney may ethically provide legal services and advice to doctors, patients, public officials, hospital administrators and others engaged in the cultivation, distribution, prescribing, dispensing, regulation, possession or use of marijuana for medical purposes to help them act in compliance with state regulation regarding medical marijuana, despite the federal narcotics laws that prohibit the possession, distribution, sale or use of marijuana and which provide no exception for medical uses.

7. We noted that the federal government had publicly announced that it was limiting its enforcement of federal narcotics laws and would not ordinarily prosecute individual actors and institutions who acted consistently with state laws that legalized and extensively regulated medical marijuana. Rather, the federal government said it would pursue enforcement only to further certain federal priorities, such as preventing the flow of revenue from marijuana sales to criminal enterprises and preventing marijuana activity from being used as a cover for trafficking other drugs. We reasoned that lawyers could provide a range of valuable assistance to clients seeking to comply with the Medical Marijuana Law consistent with this federal enforcement policy and, because a strong state regulatory system justified the federal policy of forbearance from the enforcement of federal narcotics laws, federal enforcement policy actually depended on the availability of lawyers to establish and promote compliance with a strong and effective state regulatory system.

8. Without minimizing the core tenet of Rule 1.2 (d) or a lawyer's fundamental duty not to counsel a client to violate the law or to assist a client in so doing, we concluded that "nothing in the history and tradition of the profession, in court opinions, or elsewhere" suggested that Rule 1.2(d) was intended in this "highly unusual if not unique" circumstance to "preclude lawyers from counseling or assisting conduct that is legal under state law" or to provide assistance "that is necessary to implement state law and to effectuate current federal policy" We identified that "highly unusual and unique circumstance" as "where the state executive branch determines to implement the state legislation by authorizing and regulating medical marijuana, consistent with current, published federal executive-branch enforcement policy, and the federal government does not take effective measures to prevent implementation of the law." (N.Y. State 1024 ¶¶ 6 & 23- 25; footnote omitted.)

9. We cautioned, however, that "If federal enforcement were to change materially, this Opinion might need to be reconsidered" (N.Y. State 1024 ¶ 25).

10. The federal enforcement policy we described in N.Y. State 1024 had been articulated in a Department of Justice memorandum issued August 29, 2013, known as the "Cole Memo" (named for then Deputy Attorney General James Cole, who was its author). On January 4, 2018, however, then Attorney General Jeff Sessions rescinded the Cole Memo. Accordingly, this committee, in N. Y. State 1177 (2019), reconsidered the conclusion we had reached in N.Y. State 1024.

11. N.Y. State 1177 adhered to the conclusion of N.Y. State 1024. We noted in Opinion 1177 that General Sessions'

successor, William Barr, had testified during his confirmation hearing that he would not target state legal marijuana businesses and would leave it to Congress to act. We further noted that during the interval between our release of N.Y. State 1024 in November 2014, and the rescission of the Cole Memo in January 2018, Congress had in fact acted. Specifically, in December 2014, Congress adopted legislation known as the "Rohrabacher-Blumenauer Amendment" that prohibited the Department of Justice from using any of the funds appropriated by Congress to prevent States from implementing their own State laws that authorized the use, distribution, possession or cultivation of medical marijuana. We reasoned that, in these circumstances, the rescission of the Cole Memo "does not meaningfully change federal law enforcement policy" (N.Y. State 1177 ¶ 9).

12. Accordingly, based on the state of federal law enforcement policy from 2014 through today, and subject to future changes in that policy, we decided in N.Y. State 1024 and affirmed in N.Y. State 1177 that a lawyer may assist a client in conduct designed to comply with the Medical Marijuana Law without violating Rule 1.2(d).

13. We now apply these same principles to answer the inquirer's three questions.

Assisting a Client to Comply with New York's Recreational Marijuana Law.

14. The inquirer's first question is whether an attorney may ethically provide legal services to assist a client to comply with New York's Recreational Marijuana Law. This question does not require us to analyze any change in federal enforcement policy since we issued N.Y. State 1177 (to our knowledge there have been no changes). Rather, the question is whether New York's broader legalization of cannabis for recreational use imports into the analysis any additional factors or competing considerations that would alter the conclusion reached by the committee in N.Y. State 1024 and 1177 regarding medical marijuana. For the reasons that follow, we believe it does not.

15. First, although the Rohrabacher-Blumenauer Amendment is specifically focused on marijuana for medical and not recreational purposes, over the course of three administrations -- Presidents Obama, Trump and Biden -- the Department of Justice has not, to our knowledge, taken any public position on federal enforcement that distinguishes between medical and recreational marijuana laws in the states. Indeed, unlike the Rohrabacher-Blumenauer Amendment, the Cole Memo (now rescinded) was not limited to medical marijuana. Inasmuch as 17 states, plus Washington, D.C., and Guam, have now legalized the recreational use of marijuana in some form, beginning with Colorado in 2012, it seems fair to say that for nearly a decade federal forbearance in the enforcement of federal narcotics laws has been equally applied to state laws legalizing recreational marijuana and to state laws legalizing medical marijuana.

16. Second, the comprehensive licensing and regulatory system that governs recreational use of marijuana in New York is clearly the type of robust and comprehensive state enforcement system that is squarely intended by federal enforcement policy to be an object of federal forbearance.

17. Third, the need for lawyer assistance to clients to assure compliance with state regulatory requirements in the medical marijuana industry, which justifies continued federal forbearance, applies with equal if not more force to recreational marijuana. For example, the licensing process under New York's Recreational Marijuana Law will function more expeditiously and with more consistency if lawyers can assist with preparing and submitting license applications and can counsel the regulators reviewing those applications. More generally, in a complex regulatory system where cultivation, distribution, possession, sale and use of a product are tightly regulated, legal advice and guidance has immense value. Without the aid of lawyers, the recreational marijuana regulatory system would, in our view, likely break down or grind to a halt. The participation of attorneys thus secures the benefits of the Recreational Marijuana Law for the public at large, as well promotes the interests of the private and public sector clients more directly involved in the law's implementation.

18. Fourth, as we observed in N.Y. State 1024, the tension created between federal and state narcotics laws remains a "highly unusual if not unique" situation that was never intended to fall within the blunt prohibition of Rule 1.2(d) against a lawyer counseling a client to engage in, or engaging in, conduct that the lawyer knows is illegal. The federal decision not to enforce narcotics laws against individuals and organizations engaged in conduct authorized by state law renders sui generis our determination of the issues presented by this inquiry, as well as in N.Y. State 1024 and N.Y. State 1177.

Ownership, Home Cultivation, and Personal Use by an Attorney.

19. The inquirer has been offered an equity stake in a client's cannabis business in exchange for legal services. She would also like to use cannabis products recreationally and grow lawful quantities of marijuana at home for personal use. She asks if this would be allowed under the Rules.

20. For many of the same reasons that lead us to conclude that an attorney may provide legal services to a cannabis business, we conclude that such ownership, home cultivation, and personal use, without more, would not violate Rule 1.2(d). We must, also, however, consider Rule 8.4(b) and (h), which provide:

> A lawyer or law firm shall not:
>
> (b) engage in illegal conduct that adversely reflects on the lawyer's honesty, trustworthiness or fitness as a lawyer;
>
> ***
>
> (h) engage in any other conduct that adversely reflects on the lawyer's fitness as a lawyer.

21. The first sentence of Comment [2] to Rule 8.4 provides:

> Many kinds of illegal conduct reflect adversely on fitness to practice law. Illegal conduct involving violence, dishonesty, fraud, breach of trust, or serious interference with the administration of justice is illustrative of conduct that reflects adversely on fitness to practice law.

22. Nothing the inquirer proposes to do involves acts of violence. Moreover, if the inquirer's ownership interest in a cannabis business, her home cultivation of marijuana plants, and her personal recreational use of marijuana comply with the Recreational Marijuana Law, they will fall within the scope of federal forbearance. For that reason, although those activities are technically illegal under federal law, they will not constitute illegal conduct that involves "dishonesty, fraud, breach of trust, or serious interference with the administration of justice." Accordingly, without more, such conduct would not adversely reflect on the inquirer's "honesty, trustworthiness or fitness as a lawyer" within the meaning of Rule 8.4(b).

23. The excessive use of marijuana, however, like excessive consumption of alcohol, may adversely impact a lawyer's ability to competently and diligently represent a client as required by Rules 1.1(a) and 1.3. It could also have more serious consequences and create a physical or mental condition that materially impairs a lawyer's ability to represent a client, requiring mandatory withdrawal from representation (see Rule 1.16(b)(2)). Nothing we say here connotes approval of such excessive use or establishes a protective shield for a lawyer who is facing disciplinary charges, malpractice claims, or other adverse consequences arising out of marijuana use.

24. The second sentence of Comment [2] to Rule 8.4 provides:

> A pattern of repeated offenses, even ones of minor significance when considered separately can indicate an indifference to legal obligation.

25. It is true that growing and harvesting marijuana, as well as repeatedly using marijuana, could be said to reflect a "pattern of repeated offenses" of the federal narcotics laws, but we reject the notion that it is a pattern that indicates an "indifference to legal obligation" where, again, the conduct falls squarely within the scope of federal forbearance and New York explicit authorization.

26. Federal forbearance policy is also relevant to Comment [4] to Rule 8.4, which provides in pertinent part:

> A lawyer may refuse to comply with an obligation imposed by law if such refusal is based upon a reasonable good-faith belief that no valid obligation exists because, for example, the law is unconstitutional, conflicts with other legal or professional obligations, or is otherwise invalid.

27. In our view, the scope of federal forbearance provides inquirer with a "reasonable goodfaith belief that no valid

obligation exists" to comply with federal narcotics laws that would otherwise prohibit her ownership of an interest in a cannabis business, her home cultivation of marijuana plants for personal use, and her recreational use of marijuana, where and when such activities are authorized by New York State law.

Additional Rules Relevant to Accepting an Equity Interest in Exchange for Legal Services.

28. Accepting an equity interest in the client's cannabis business as compensation for providing legal services also requires compliance with Rule 1.8(a) regarding a business transaction with a client. In N.Y. State 913, ¶¶ 6 & 10 (2012), we concluded "that Rule 1.8(a) applies to negotiation of a fee in which a lawyer is to receive an equity interest in a client or the client's company." Accordingly, "the terms of the transaction must be fair and reasonable to the client, fully disclosed and transmitted in writing in a manner that can be reasonably understood by the client, with the client being advised of the desirability of seeking independent legal advice and given a reasonable chance to do so, and the client signing a writing that describes the transaction and the lawyer's role in the deal, including whether the lawyer was acting for the client in the matter."

29. Further, the inquirer must consider whether acquiring or possessing an equity interest in the client's cannabis business will give rise to a conflict of interest under Rule 1.7(a)(2). A conflict will arise if there is a significant risk that the lawyer's advice or other legal assistance to the client will be adversely affected by the lawyer's financial self-interest. In that event, the lawyer may nevertheless proceed with the representation if (i) the lawyer reasonably believes she can provide competent and diligent representation despite the conflict and (ii) the lawyer obtains the client's informed consent, confirmed in writing. See Rule 1.7(b); N.Y. State 990 ¶ 26 (2013); N.Y. State 913 ¶¶ 13-14.

30. We caution that were the inquirer to engage in any cannabis related activity that constituted a serious violation of New York State law or of other federal laws, or in activity that would materially implicate federal enforcement priorities not subject to federal forbearance – for example, assisting in the transfer of sales revenues from recreational marijuana sales to criminal enterprises, or using a cannabis business as a cover for trafficking in other narcotics – her conduct would fall outside the safe harbor established by this opinion. In that case, her conduct would constitute violations of Rule 1.2(d) and Rules 8.4(b) and 8.4(h).

31. We further caution that law enforcement authorities may have views of their own on the reach of the criminal statutes they enforce, and whether the conduct we find here to be ethically permissible is within the prohibited scope of those statutes presents questions of law on which this committee does not opine. Our jurisdiction is limited to interpreting the Rules of Professional Conduct.

CONCLUSION

32. In light of current federal enforcement policy, the New York Rules of Professional Conduct permit a lawyer to assist a client in conduct designed to comply with New York's Recreational Marijuana Law and its implementing regulations, notwithstanding that federal narcotics law prohibits the activities authorized by that law. A lawyer may also use marijuana for recreational purposes and may, when the law becomes fully effective, cultivate an authorized amount of marijuana plants at home for personal use. Finally, subject to compliance with Rules 1.7 and 1.8(a), an attorney may accept an equity ownership interest in a cannabis business in exchange for legal services.

Part 4: Charts of License Types and Permits Under MRTA

Adult-Use Cannabis Licenses

License Type	Reference	Activities
Cultivator	CAN § 68 (Page 74)	planting, growing, cloning, harvesting, drying, curing, grading and trimming of cannabis
Registered Organization Adult-Use Cultivator Processor Distributor Retail Dispensary	CAN § 68-a (Page 75)	adult-use cultivator, adult-use processor, adult-use distributor and adult-use retail dispensary location of its adult-use dispensaries shall be limited to only three of the organization's medical dispensaries' premises and facilities may only distribute its own products shall maintain its medical cannabis license and continue offering medical cannabis
Registered Organization Cultivator, Processor and Distributor	CAN § 68-b (Page 75)	adult-use cultivator, processor, and distributor does not qualify for any other adult-use license may only authorize the distribution of the licensee's own products
Conditional Adult-Use Cultivator	CAN § 68-c (Page 75)	planting, growing, cloning, harvesting, drying, curing, grading and trimming of cannabis for a conditional period temporary authority to process and distribute cannabis products (cannabis flower) without adult-use processor or distributor license until June 1, 2023
Processor	CAN § 69 (Page 77)	blending, extracting, infusing, packaging, labeling, branding and otherwise making or preparing cannabis products
Conditional Adult-Use Processor	CAN 69-a (Page 78)	blending, extracting, infusing, packaging, labeling, branding and otherwise making or preparing cannabis products for a conditional period temporary authority to distribute cannabis products (cannabis flower) without adult-use distributor license until June 1, 2023
Cooperative	CAN § 70 (Page 80)	acquisition, possession, cultivation, processing, distribution and sale from the licensed premises of the adult-use cooperative by such licensee to duly licensed distributors, on-site consumption sites, registered organization and/or retail dispensaries; but not directly to cannabis consumers
Distributor	CAN § 71 (Page 81)	acquisition, possession, distribution and sale of cannabis from the licensed premises of a licensed adult-use cultivator, processor, adult-use cooperative, microbusiness, or registered organization to duly licensed retail dispensaries and on-site consumption sites
Retail Dispensary	CAN § 72 (Page 81)	acquisition, possession, sale and delivery of cannabis from the licensed premises of the retail dispensary by such licensee to cannabis consumers

License Type	Reference	Activities
Conditional Adult-Use Retail Dispensary	9 CRR §§ 116.1 to 116.9 (Page 239)	acquisition, possession, sale and delivery of cannabis from the licensed premises of the retail dispensary by such licensee to cannabis consumers for a conditional period
Microbusiness	CAN § 73 (Page 81)	limited cultivation, processing, distribution, delivery, and dispensing of their own adult-use cannabis and cannabis products
Delivery	CAN § 74 (Page 82)	delivery of cannabis and cannabis products by licensees independent of another adult-use cannabis license
Nursery	CAN § 75 (Page 82)	production, sale and distribution of clones, immature plants, seeds, and other agricultural products used specifically for the planting, propagation, and cultivation of cannabis by licensed adult-use cultivators, cooperatives, microbusinesses or registered organizations
On-site Consumption	CAN § 77 (Page 83)	licensed to sell adult-use cannabis for on-site consumption

Medical Cannabis Licenses

License Type	Reference	Activities
Designated Caregiver Facility	CAN § 33 (Page 60)	assists one or more certified patients with the acquisition, possession, delivery, transportation or administration of medical cannabis
Registered Organization	CAN § 34 (Page 60)	for-profit business entity or not-for-profit corporation organized for the purpose of acquiring, possessing, manufacturing, selling, delivering, transporting, distributing or dispensing cannabis for certified medical use
Cannabis Research License	CAN § 38 (Page 66)	produce, process, purchase and/or possess cannabis for the following limited research purposes: (a) to test chemical potency and composition levels; (b) to conduct clinical investigations of cannabis-derived drug products; (c) to conduct research on the efficacy and safety of administering cannabis as part of medical treatment; and (d) to conduct genomic or agricultural research.

Cannabinoid Hemp and Hemp Extract Licenses

License Type	Reference	Activities
Cannabinoid Hemp Processor	CAN § 92 (Page 96)	processing cannabinoid hemp or hemp extract used for human consumption
Cannabinoid Hemp Retailer	CAN § 93 (Page 96)	retailers selling cannabinoid hemp in final form to consumers within the state

Cannabis Laboratory Testing Permits

Permit Type	Reference	Activities
Independent Cannabis Testing Laboratory	CAN § 129 (Page 105)	test medical cannabis, adult-use cannabis and/or cannabinoid hemp or hemp extract

Special Use Permits

Permit Type	Reference	Activities
Industrial Cannabis Permit	CAN § 130 (Page 106)	purchase cannabis from one of the entities licensed by the board for use in the manufacture and sale of any of the following, when such cannabis is not otherwise suitable for consumption purposes, namely: (a) apparel, energy, paper, and tools; (b) scientific, chemical, mechanical and industrial products; or (c) any other industrial use as determined by the board in regulation
Trucking Permit	CAN § 130 (Page 106)	trucking or transportation of cannabis products, or medical cannabis by a person other than a registered organization or licensee
Warehouse Permit	CAN § 130 (Page 106)	storage of cannabis, cannabis products, or medical cannabis at a location not otherwise registered or licensed by the office
Packaging Permit	CAN § 130 (Page 106)	licensed cannabis distributor to sort, package, label and bundle cannabis products from one or more registered organizations or licensed processors, on the premises of the licensed cannabis distributor or at a warehouse for which a permit has been issued

Part 5: Office of Cannabis Management Guidance

Guidance for Adult-Use Conditional Cultivators

Originally Published: 3/14/2022

Updated: 8/16/2022

INTRODUCTION

Compliance with these guidance materials and any current and future state rules, regulations, guidance, and laws is required by licensees to remain eligible and in good standing with the Adult-Use Conditional Cultivator license program. Applicants who are not compliant with this guidance and any current and future state rules, regulations, guidance, or laws risk losing their conditional license and jeopardize their ability to secure a future Adult-Use Cultivator license. Templates for reporting requirements will be made available on the Office of Cannabis Management's (the "Office") website.

ADULT-USE CONDITIONAL CULTIVATOR KEY REPORTING DEADLINES TO THE OFFICE:

Within six months of licensure: Licensees are required to submit an Operating Plan for their business as outlined in this guidance document.

At the end of the first year of licensure: Licensees are responsible for submitting an Annual Cultivation Report to the Office indicating their compliance with the guidance outlined in this document. The Office will provide feedback to Licensees indicating any necessary changes to Adult-Use Conditional Cultivator grow operations and how to come into compliance with program standards.

Upon expiration of the Adult-Use Conditional Cultivator Program in two years: Licensees must submit updated records that will be used to evaluate whether the conditional licensee can transition to a full Adult-Use Cultivator license, pursuant to all applicable laws, regulations, and program guidance.

DEFINITIONS

1. Artificial Lighting. Horticultural Lighting Equipment (HLE) means any lighting equipment (e.g., fixtures, bulbs, ballasts, controls, etc.) that uses energy for the cultivation of plants, at any stage of growth.

2. Batch. A unit of adult-use cannabis produced during a period of time under similar conditions, identifiable by a unique code that allows traceability.

3. Corrective Action Plan. A plan submitted by a licensee and approved by the Office, for the licensee to correct a violation or non-compliance with this guidance or any rules, regulations, or laws.

4. Cultivation Cycle. Entirety of the cultivation period, including germination, seedling, cloning, vegetative and flowering stages of cannabis plant growth.

5. Energy Audit. An assessment of the licensee's cultivation operations that details energy consumption and identifies energy efficiency measures. EPA Energy Portfolio Manager is a resource that licensees can use to audit and track energy consumption.

6. Flowering Canopy. An area to be calculated in square feet and measured using clearly identifiable boundaries of all areas(s) that will contain flowering plants, including all of the space(s) within the boundaries. Canopy may be noncontiguous, but each unique area included in the total canopy calculations shall be separated by an identifiable boundary which includes, but is not limited to: interiorwalls, shelves, greenhouse walls, hoop house walls, garden benches, hedge rows, fencing, garden beds, or garden plots. An Adult-Use Conditional Cultivator licensee may cultivate up to 43,560 square feet (equal to 1 acre) of flowering canopy outdoors or 25,000 square feet of flowering canopy in a greenhouse. A cultivator may grow both outdoors and in a greenhouse, provided the flowering canopy in a greenhouse is equal to or less than 20,000 square feet and the total flowering canopy is equal to or less than 30,000 square feet. As part of the application process, Adult-Use Conditional Cultivators will have to submit to the Office a detailed site plan for each area where they plan to grow cannabis.

7. Greenhouse. A structure or thermally isolated enclosed area of a building that maintains a specialized sunlit environment used for and essential to the cultivation, protection, or maintenance of plants.

8. Independent Agricultural Safety Program. An organization promoting and advancing agricultural safety best practices through educational programs and training opportunities on topics including but not limited to agricultural worker health and hygiene, plant and soil management, pest management, land use, water management, waste management, and overall agricultural safety. An example of one such organization is the New York Center for Agriculture Medicine and Health (NYCAMH). The organization's website is https://www.nycamh.org/.

9. Integrated Pest Management (IPM) Principles. IPM principles (1) identify pests, their hosts, and beneficial organisms before acting; (2) establish monitoring guidelines for each pest species; (3) establish an action threshold for the pest; (4) evaluate and implement control tactics; and (5) monitor, evaluate, and document the results.

10. Lighting Energy Benchmarking Organization. A non-profit organization offering independent auditing, benchmarking, and advisory services related to improving energy efficiency, sustainability, and lighting quality for horticultural activities and the human experience in the built environment. An example of one such organization is the Design Light Consortium which can be used as a resource for licensees. The organization's website is https://www.designlights.org/.

11. Pests. Rodents, birds, insects, or other animals or organisms that present the threat of contamination to cannabis and cannabis products, especially drying, curing or in-process cannabis flower.

12. Photosynthetic Photon Efficacy (PPE). Photosynthetic photon flux divided by input electric power. In horticultural lighting, efficacy refers to micromoles of photon output per second, per watt of input power.

13. Plant Protection Products. Products applied during the cultivation of cannabis including insecticides, fungicides, herbicides, rodenticides, and plant growth regulators.

14. Processing. For the purposes of this guidance document "processing" includes the drying, trimming, curing, packaging and manufacture of cannabis flower products. Processing does not include extraction activities.

15. Production Cycle. The cultivation cycle and additional drying, curing, and on farm processing of cannabis.

16. Raw Product Samples. Samples of dried cannabis flower used for the purposes of analytical testing.

CONDITIONAL CULTIVATOR PROGRAM GUIDANCE

1. Recordkeeping and Data Collection Expectations and Requirements.

    a. Data Collection. Within six months of licensure, unless otherwise specified, Adult-Use Conditional Cultivator licensees must submit all elements of an Operating Plan to the Office consisting of the information in the Operating Plan section below. One year after issuance of the Adult-Use Conditional Cultivator license, the license holder is responsible for submitting to the Office an Annual Cultivation Report consisting of the information outlined below. Adult-Use Conditional Cultivator license holders are required to submit updated records to the Office upon request, and when the conditional license expires, to be eligible for a full Adult-Use Cultivator license. Compliance with practices outlined in this document will be used by the Cannabis Control Board (the "Board") to make licensing decisions.

b. Operating Plan. Cultivators must document, implement, and maintain to the satisfaction of the Office an Operating Plan that must include, at a minimum:

1. A site plan document indicating the activities performed in each area and detailing all physical boundaries, roads, and water crossings of the property, further outlined in Section 8 (Site Plan Modifications), **to be submitted to the Office within 30 days of licensure.**

2. A security and staff safety plan detailing risk mitigation and accident prevention plans resulting from a detailed risk assessment of all stages of cannabis production, **to be submitted to the Office within 30 days of licensure.**

3. A cultivation plan document that includes a detailed overview of all cultivation, processing, storage, and record keeping policies and procedures.

4. A soil preparation plan document that includes a plan or recipe for soil preparation and records of analysis or descriptions of soil quality and a plan to restrict the use of short lived or single use synthetic ground covers and/or mulches.

5. An environmental impact plan document that details the actions taken to maintain and improve ecosystem health and services with neutral or positive impact on biodiversity.

6. A pest management and control plan document based on Integrated Pest Management (IPM) principles that is adequate for the facility type and size and includes details on prevention, observation, and interventional steps and physical/mechanical/biological and chemical methods utilized that are consistent. The plan must demonstrate conformance with lists of authorized and prohibited products and materials as determined by the Office.

7. A cannabis sampling, analysis and testing plan document based on risks associated with materials or organisms normally present during the cultivation and production of cannabis.

8. A quality assurance plan document that establishes criteria to detect, identity, prevent, and track harvested cannabis contamination incidents.

9. A cannabis recall plan document that includes an annual mock recall test.

10. A sustainable water-use and conservation plan document that addresses water sources, quality, and use.

11. A sustainable energy use and conservation plan document that addresses the sourcing and use of energy and sets energy efficiency goals including timelines and benchmarks.

c. Annual Cultivation Report. Adult-Use Conditional Cultivators must maintain the following records in an Annual Cultivation Report for submission to the Office after one year of licensure and then upon license transition, as well as to be made available to the Office upon request:

1. An up-to-date site plan.

2. All physical inventory of cannabis, at any stage, and all associated labels, must be reflected accurately in an electronic inventory management system.

3. Traceability functionality must be capable of showing the complete production history of any cannabis in any stage, including cannabis that has been released for sale to allow for a total recall of all associated cannabis if necessary.

4. A detailed database for the tracking of all seeds, clones or other plant material used, which must include the source of the seeds, clones, or other plant material.

5. Detailed plant protection application records for any propagation treatments.

6. A detailed documentation of a soil, soil mixture or substrate material assessment including type, composition, and mineral content.

7. An agricultural input list that includes all agricultural inputs used or to be used. The list must include at a minimum: product name, active ingredient, purpose, application rate, timing within life cycle of plant and method, Material Safety Data Sheet, Certificate of Analysis, product labels, and history of application.

8. Water usage per cultivation cycle, as directed by the Office.

9. Record of a facility energy audit and Year 1 energy use report.

10. Records of scouting or monitoring for pests and diseases.

11. Records of submission of cannabis from each production cycle to a New York State cannabis testing laboratory approved by the Office for all required testing.

12. Lab results from a New York State cannabis testing laboratory approved by the Office for all required testing for cannabis from each production cycle.

13. Records of plant removal and destruction of all cannabis not meeting minimum quality, strain, and safety standards.

14. A list of all equipment used in the production of cannabis.

15. Equipment maintenance and upkeep records that include at a minimum: the type of maintenance performed, the name of the mechanic who performed the maintenance and the date the work was completed.

16. Records of all employees and independent contractors.

17. Staff health and safety procedures.

18. Signed consent forms from all employees and independent contractors involved in the cultivation, production, and distribution of adult-use cannabis that apply chemicals as part of their work activities.

19. Records of routine cleaning of all containers, tools, and equipment.

20. Records of routine cleaning and sanitizing of all sanitary facilities.

21. Records of routine cleaning and sanitizing of all areas of the facility where cannabis is produced, handled, or stored.

22. Pest management records that include: A map of all traps, types and coding/numbering system for the traps must be in place, records of routine trap maintenance, and record of any evidence of animal or insect presence including body parts, hair, or feces in cannabis handling areas.

23. Records of an annual mock recall.

24. Records of all complaints received which must include: a log of all complaints, defined timeline for response, persons responsible for complaint procedures and actions taken.

25. Production water analysis results.

26. Post-production water analysis results if there is any water runoff or discharge.

27. Waste disposal records including material resulting from the trimming process, as well as composting or other disposal or remediation methods, if applicable.

28. A visitor log of all persons other than employees, independent contractors involved in the cultivation, production, and distribution of adult-use cannabis, or emergency personnel responding to an emergency who access any production areas which includes at a minimum: the name of the individual, the company the individual works for, the reason for access, and the date and times the individual entered and exited the production area.

29. A signed copy of the labor peace agreement as required by the Cannabis Law and as detailed in Section 20 (Labor Peace Agreement), below.

d. Data and Record Submission. Record submission methods will be provided by the Office.

2. Inspections. The licensee shall make available to the Office data indicated under Section 1 (Recordkeeping and Data Collection Expectations and Requirements) of this document to ensure compliance with the program standards set forth by the Office. The Office maintains the rights to inspect licensees' facilities where cannabis operations are taking place. Inspections may be on-site or through remote technology. Inspections may be announced or unannounced. Applicants will be provided with an inspection evaluation report, including, if necessary, a Corrective Action Plan and related timeline to make any corrective actions.

3. Corrective Action Plan. Adult-Use Conditional Cultivator licensees issued a Corrective Action Plan must be held responsible for implementing the actions required by the Office in the time specified in the Corrective Action Plan or may risk losing their ability to maintain their license and further considerations for future licensing. The Office may conduct additional inspections to verify that actions required in a Corrective Action Plan have been implemented.

4. Data Collection and Submission. Adult-Use Conditional Cultivator licensees must be responsible for collecting and filing required data to the Office, including data related to the Operating Plan, Annual Cultivation Reports, Corrective Action Plans, and any other reports required for licensure and program compliance. The Office will provide more information about how licensees must submit data in the future.

5. Sampling and Testing. All raw cannabis product (flower) is subject to random sampling by the Office, or a party designated by the Office. The Office may provide updated sampling and testing guidance and regulations, including mandating requirements related to batch sizes, testing thresholds, and sampling procedures. The licensee is responsible for all related sampling and testing costs, as well as ensuring the following standards are met:

a. For each production cycle, cannabis must be tested by a New York State cannabis testing laboratory approved by the Office, for cannabinoid profile, pesticide residue, microbiological contaminants, mycotoxins, heavy metals, and any other required analytes as determined by the Office.

b. Cannabis must be stored in a clearly marked, separate, secure area while awaiting lab testing results.

c. Any cannabis not meeting the minimum standards for cannabis testing must be destroyed. Where there is no risk to humans and the environment, such cannabis may be remediated for other purposes or composted, with the permission of the Office.

d. Strain analysis must be performed on all cannabis produced in all production cycles.

e. Strain analysis must include, at a minimum, the levels of THC, THCA, CBD, CBDA, and CBN.

f. Strain analysis results must be linked by grower production coding system to individual strains.

g. All cannabis must meet established quality, strain, and safety standards prior to release for sale or consumption.

h. Any cannabis not meeting established quality, strain and safety standards must be rendered unrecoverable and beyond reclamation. On-site composting is a means of rendering any portion of the plant unrecoverable and beyond reclamation.

6. Prohibited Products and Materials. A public list of approved and prohibited products and materials for use in cannabis cultivation and growing activities will be provided by the Office and made available on the Office's website. The Office reserves the right to change or modify the products or materials considered approved or prohibited. Adult-Use Conditional Cultivator licensees may seek permission from the Office for the authorized use of a product or materials not contained in the list of approved Plant Protection Products and Materials.

> **a. Product Usage.** Application of agricultural inputs used by a license holder, such as plant protection products, fertilizers, and soil amendments, must be recorded. Licensees must develop and implement an input application recording system for each growing season. The input application recording system must include:
>
> > 1. Product name
> >
> > 2. Active ingredient
> >
> > 3. Purpose of use
> >
> > 4. Application rate
> >
> > 5. Timing within life cycle of plant and method
> >
> > 6. Material Safety Data Sheet, Certificate of Analysis, and/or product label information
> >
> > 7. History of application (if used in past production seasons)

7. Traceability. In time for the growing season, the licensee must have or develop an on-premises based identification and traceability system that allows the cannabis product to be traced back to the licensee and specific production site, to the block and bed level, and traced forward up the supply-chain to the next distribution point. The license holder must be able to link harvested cannabis product by batch number or harvest date to the production records. Such data must be made available to the Office upon request and in the Annual Cultivation Report.

8. Site Plan Modifications. The licensee is responsible for ensuring the Office has an accurate and up to date Site Plan. If any changes are made to the areas below, the licensee has an obligation to update the Office within 10 calendar days of any such change. Site Plans will also be required upon submission of the Operating Plan and Annual Cultivation Report. Instances of combined space usage must be disclosed in the licensees Site Plan with a plan to prevent cross-contamination related chemical use. Site Plans must include the following information:

> a. Flowering Canopy Area (Including aggregate square footage if the canopy areas are noncontiguous. All unique areas separated by identifiable boundaries must be clearly described and labeled in the premises diagram.)
>
> b. Area(s) Outside of the Canopy (Immature plants only) (if applicable)
>
> c. Pesticide and Agricultural Chemical Storage Area
>
> d. Drying Area
>
> e. Processing Area
>
> f. Harvest Storage Area
>
> g. Packaging Area (If applicable)
>
> h. Composting Area (If on-site)
>
> i. Secure Cannabis Waste Area (Not including composting areas)

j. Artificial Lighting used for Production of Cannabis (with wattage and Photosynthetic Photon Efficacy and placement)

k. Heating, HVAC (if relevant)

l. Sanitary Facilities

m. Parcel Boundaries

n. Perimeter Dimensions

o. Entrances to Both the Property and Premises

p. Exits to Both the Property and Premises

q. All Roads

r. All Water Crossings (includes seasonal streams)

s. Other Activities or Other Licensed Areas. **Conditional Cultivators must keep all areas used for adult-use cannabis operations, including any growing, harvesting, drying or storage areas separate and distinct from any area designated for hemp cultivation under the Department of Agriculture and Markets Hemp Licensing Program.**

9. Lighting. Applicants may use up to 20 artificial lights during the production of cannabis.

a. New Equipment. For new equipment, all fixtures must have a reported Photosynthetic Photon Efficacy of no less than 1.9 μmol/J. Equipment available on the Design Light Consortium list may also be used, as well as any other lighting equipment approved by the Office.

b. Existing Equipment. Existing horticultural lighting equipment can be used if already in place at the time of conditional licensure. Technical details (wattage input, Photosynthetic Photon Efficacy) related to existing equipment **must be submitted to the Office within 30 days of licensure.** For equipment that does not meet the minimum requirement of Photosynthetic Photon Efficacy 1.9μmol/J, a documented transition plan to more efficient lighting equipment must be in place by the conclusion of the first year in production under the conditional license. Applicants must have a plan to transition to a lower energy footprint system, as outlined in "part a" above (Photosynthetic Photon Efficacy of no less than 1.9 μmol/J), oriented toward a net zero emissions target after the conditional licensing period is over. The plan can include onsite renewable energy production, more efficient lighting equipment, carbon offsets as approved by the Office, and demonstrable carbon sequestration practices approved by the Office.

10. Sanitary Facilities. The license holder must ensure that all workers have access to hand washing and toilet facilities in all work areas; toilet units and hand washing units must be maintained in a clean and sanitary condition; and license holder must maintain records showing regular cleaning and sanitizing of all sanitary facilities. The license holder must require workers to wash and sanitize their hands before doing any work, after each visit to a toilet, after handling contaminated material, after smoking, eating, or drinking, and at any other time when their hands may have become contaminated, and there must be signage in restrooms to remind workers to wash/sanitize hands. Sanitary areas in this section must be marked in the licensees' Site Plan.

11. Facility and Equipment Cleaning and Maintenance. Licensees are responsible for the upkeep of their facilities and maintenance of all equipment used in the production of cannabis. In addition:

a. All containers, tools and equipment used in the production of cannabis must be well kept and maintained.

b. All containers, tools and equipment used in the production, packaging, labeling, and storing of cannabis must be designed, constructed, maintained, operated, and arranged as to protect against the physical, chemical, and microbial contamination and deterioration of the cannabis.

c. Containers used for the storage of cannabis must be food-grade or similar and must be clean, in good repair and suitable for the established use.

d. All areas of the facility where cannabis is handled must be well organized and routinely cleaned and sanitized.

e. All areas of the facility where cannabis is stored or handled must be maintained in a manner as to protect against the physical, chemical, and microbial contamination and deterioration of the cannabis.

f. All areas of the facility where cannabis is stored or handled must utilize continual environmental monitoring for temperature, ventilation, and humidity.

g. Areas and their intended purpose may be modified. All facility changes must be reported to the Office pursuant to Section 8 (Site Plan) of this guidance. Instances of a single space being used for multiple purposes must be disclosed in the licensees Site Plan and may be subject to approval from the Office.

12. Drying/Processing. The license holder must ensure that any drying or processing areas are clean, wellventilated, and free from condensation, sewage, dust, dirt, toxic chemicals or other contaminants. All buildings must provide adequate environmental controls to ensure product protection and be of adequate actual or proposed size to be able to properly dry the volume of cannabis produced. Photos or diagram of drying and processing area to be used for all product drying, processing and curing must be provided to the Office in the Site Plan, and notes on proposed staggered harvests and harvest window must be provided to the Office in the Annual Cultivation Report. Pursuant to the Cannabis Law an Adult-Use Conditional Cultivator is only permitted to process and distribute cannabis flower products without holding an AdultUse Processor or Distributor License, until June 1, 2023. The Office will be issuing additional guidance related to the processing and distribution of cannabis flower products for Adult-Use Conditional Cultivators. Conditional Cultivator's are not permitted to perform extraction activities without holding an Adult-Use Processor License.

13. Security. The license holder must install fencing, locked gates, secure doors, or other physical barriers sufficient to prevent unauthorized access to production and storage areas. Commercial-grade key or keypad equipped locks must be installed on all doors, fences, or other entries. Barrier design and installation should be context specific and account for risks posed by adjacent properties, persons, or activities.

a. All cannabis must be stored in a secure area or location within the production area accessible to the minimum number of staff necessary for efficient operation and in such a manner as to prevent diversion, theft, or loss.

b. Production areas must be securely locked and protected from unauthorized entry at all times.

c. The license holder must be responsible for ensuring the integrity of the security of the operational spaces and the maintenance of sanitary operations when permitting access.

14. Packaging. The license holder must comply with all relevant packing, labeling, marketing, and advertising standards as determined in the Cannabis Law and any future state laws, regulations, and guidance. Processing and packaging activities under the Adult-Use Conditional Cultivation license must take place at the licensed premise, or at the premise of another licensed adult-use cannabis processor.

15. Cannabis Waste Disposal. The license holder must dispose of any cannabis that is outdated, damaged, deteriorated, contaminated, or otherwise deemed not appropriate for further processing or manufacturing. The disposal of cannabis must mean that the cannabis has been rendered unrecoverable and beyond reclamation. For the purposes of this requirement, the stalks, stems, fan leaves, root balls, and soil media must be excluded from the requirement that they be rendered unrecognizable and beyond reclamation. On-site composting is a means of rendering any portion of the plant unrecoverable and beyond reclamation. No cannabis material must be intentionally diverted to a landfill. The disposal of any inputs including liquid or chemical waste must comply with applicable federal, state, and local laws and regulations. Regardless of the immediately preceding sentence, soaking cannabis in gasoline and then burning the cannabis is not an acceptable method of waste disposal.

a. Cannabis Waste Disposal Records. The Applicant must maintain records of disposal, which must include:

1. The type of plant material disposed;

2. The weight of the disposed material, the number of plants, or in the case of a finished product, the quantity of the disposed product, batch number; and

3. The signatures of at least two employees who witnessed the disposal.

16. Transportation. No license holder may transport cannabis outside of the licensed premises unless (1) it is in a fully enclosed vehicle or container; and (2) it is accompanied by a manifest or proof of ownership, documenting the name, physical address, certificate of analysis and license number of the license holder, and the name and physical address of the recipient of the delivery.

    a. Laboratory Transport. When cannabis is being transported to a laboratory for testing, a certificate of analysis is not required to accompany the shipment.

17. Plant Protection Products List. A list of Plant Protection Products approved by the Office for use on Cannabis will be available on the Office of Cannabis website.

18. Health and Safety Standards. Licensees will comply with all applicable federal, state, and local laws and regulations related to worker training, safety, health and pay including, but not limited to, the minimum wage, overtime, frequency of pay, posting requirements, pay equity, notice of pay rate, day of rest, meal periods, wage deductions, the employment of minors, paid sick leave, discrimination, and retaliation. Training materials should be available in the primary language of all employees or independent contractors involved in the cultivation, production, and distribution of adult-use cannabis.

    a. All employees or independent contractors involved in the production, cultivation and distribution of adult-use cannabis must receive safety and hygiene training, in line with standards of an independent agricultural safety programs.

    b. Safety data sheets for all chemicals must be on file and available to employees and independent contractors involved in the cultivation, production, and distribution of adult-use cannabis.

    c. Personal Protective Equipment must be assigned to employees and independent contractors involved in the cultivation, production, and distribution of adult-use cannabis as needed and must be in good working order.

    d. If respirators are required, staff must be trained in their proper use and respirators must be serviced and tagged to manufacturer's specifications.

    e. Information signs must provide clear instructions for material handling, equipment operation and general safety information for all operations.

    f. Warning signs must be posted in all areas of potential hazard.

    g. Employees and independent contractors involved in the cultivation, production, and distribution of adult-use cannabis must be trained to manage chemical and liquid spills.

    h. Emergency signage must be posted in all work areas.

    i. Someone onsite must be trained in First Aid and CPR.

    j. Well stocked first aid kits must be readily available in all operational areas.

20. Labor Peace Agreement. Within six months of licensure, the Applicant must enter into a labor peace agreement with a bona-fide labor organization, and a signed copy of the labor peace agreement must be provided to the Office. Maintenance of such labor peace agreement is an ongoing material condition of licensure. For purposes of this requirement, a "bona fide labor organization" is defined as a labor union:

a. That represents employees in this state with regard to wages, hours and working conditions;

b. In which officers have been elected by secret ballot or otherwise in a manner consistent with federal law, and;

c. That is free of domination or interference by any employer and has received no improper assistance or support from any employer.

21. Mentorship Program. As a condition of licensure, Adult-Use Conditional Cultivators must participate in a social and economic equity mentorship program, as determined by the Office. The Office will outline program standards and conditions. Cultivators may be asked to participate in a range of activities, including but not limited to pre-program surveys, mentorship activities, and related data reporting.

22. Transition to Adult-Use Cultivator License. License holders must be compliant with all sections above to be eligible for license transition under the Conditional Adult-Use Cannabis Cultivation law. The Office and Board will evaluate compliance with all relevant laws, regulations, and guidance, as well as information provided in the Annual Cultivation Reports. In determining allocations of larger flowering canopy in future licensing decisions, among the criteria the Board may consider is the extent that licensees demonstrate sustainable practices in the following areas:

a. Green-house Gas Emissions Reduction.

1. Low-carbon production goals, supported by an energy audit, including the use of energy efficient equipment.

b. Waste Reduction.

1. Removal, quarantine, and treatment of plants contaminated with pests and/or diseases.

2. Waste reduction through composting, recycling, and reusing cultivation materials

3. Water harvesting and reuse practices.

4. Energy reduction goals, supporting by an energy audit, including the use of energy efficient equipment.

5. Steps to further the promotion of biodiversity. Suggested methods include but are not limited to:

    a. Intercropping

    b. Cover cropping

    c. Crop rotation

    d. Planting, or promotion of native plants

    e. Providing habitat for native animals

    f. Planting or promotion of specific species that promote native pollinator activities

    g. Protecting native waterways through maintaining wild farm edges and removing invasive species.

c. Sourcing, Organic Principles and Waste.

1. On-farm compost and manure are the preferred method of soil fertility. Locally sourced, organic compost and manure are the next preferred method.

2. Cultivators are discouraged from utilizing substances, materials, or techniques that are incompatible with the general principles of organic production.

3. The Office will consider the life cycle (embodied energy) of packaging materials and whether packaging

is reusable, recyclable, or compostable. Plastic for packaging of consumer products is to be avoided, unless made with a minimum post-consumer content of 25%.

4. Locally sourced inputs are preferred

d. Water.

1. Implementation of efficient irrigation technology, equipment, and practices to reduce erosion, prevent runoff, and avoid polluting waterways.

2. Performance of regular documented maintenance on irrigation systems.

e. Additional Types of Consideration for Licensees in Transition Decision. Licensees may present to the Office sustainability practices and programs, such as:

1. Test soil at harvest for contaminants and residual nutrient buildup.

2. Provide a nesting or feeding habitat for bees and other wild pollinators through the season including at least 6% of all areas vested to pollinator beneficial planting.

3. Generate renewable power onsite.

4. Receive power from renewable energy sources such as solar panels, wind power, geothermal, or alternative energy co-op.

5. Buy carbon credits to offset their carbon footprint as may approved by the Cannabis Control Board, other State agencies, and consistent with environmental standards, such as the New York Climate Leadership and Community Protection Act.

Guidance for Adult-Use Conditional Processors

Updated: 9/23/2022

INTRODUCTION

Compliance with these terms and conditions and guidance and any future guidance, rules, regulations, terms and conditions, or laws is required of licensees to remain eligible and in good standing with the Adult-Use Conditional Processor license program. Applicants who are not compliant with these terms and conditions and guidance or any future guidance, rules, regulations, terms and conditions, or laws risk losing their conditional license and jeopardize their ability to secure a future Adult-Use Processor or other Adult-Use cannabis license. The Adult-Use Conditional Processor License is valid for up to two years from the date of issuance of the license. All Adult-Use Conditional Processor licenses become invalid after June 30, 2024.

ADULT-USE CONDITIONAL PROCESSOR KEY REPORTING DEADLINES:

Before beginning operations, all applicants must:

- Submit a complete Adult-Use Conditional Processor application with the required nonrefundable application and licensing fee and a signed copy of the terms and conditions page at the end of this guidance document.

- Schedule an inspection with the Office to inspect the licensed facility and verify compliance with Good Manufacturing Practices and this guidance.

- If the applicant or licensee is requesting to perform hydrocarbon extraction activities, including using volatile solvents such as propane and butane, the applicant must submit required materials and documentation on the application and provide a letter or equivalent document as determined by the Office from the jurisdiction's fire marshal, local building code authority, or its equivalent, stating that the facility is approved to conduct the proposed activities and that the processor has demonstrated compliance with all applicable fire codes and/or regulations.

Ongoing Reporting Responsibilities.

- Licensees must maintain a current list of processing activities and a list of any cannabis extracts or cannabis products to be produced at the facility. If a licensee is permitted to conduct extraction activities and requests to change such activities from what was provided on the application, the licensee must receive prior written approval from the Office. Notification of changes to extraction activities must be made no less than 30 days before commencement of planned activities.

- If the licensee is requesting to perform hydrocarbon extraction activities, including using volatile solvents such as propane and butane, the licensee must submit a letter or equivalent document as determined by the Office from the jurisdiction's fire marshal, local building code authority, or its equivalent, stating that the facility is approved to conduct the proposed activities and that the processor has demonstrated compliance with all applicable fire codes and/or regulations, upon any request to change the proposed extraction method.

- Licensees must benchmark annual energy and water usage in a manner consistent with EPA tracking and auditing formats. EPA Energy Portfolio Manager is a resource that licensees can use to audit and track energy consumption.

- Licensee who packages cannabis products for retail sale shall annually report through a method authorized by the Board, beginning one year after the date of licensure: the total amount of packaging material, by weight, sold, offered for sale, or distributed into the state by the licensee in the prior calendar year; the percentage of all packaging material sold, offered for sale, or distributed for sale in the state; and the total costs of packaging material.

Upon the expiration of the Adult-Use Conditional Processor Program:

- Licensees must submit, upon request, any records mandated herein, which will be used to evaluate whether the conditional licensee is eligible to transition to a full Adult-Use Processor license, pursuant to all applicable laws, regulations, and program guidance.

DEFINITIONS

1. Attractive to individuals under twenty-one means labeling, packaging, advertising and marketing that is pleasing or appealing to persons under the age of twenty-one by using or including, among other things: Cartoons; Bubble-type or other cartoon-like font; bright colors that are "neon" in appearance; similarities to products or words that refer to products that are commonly associated with or marketed in a manner so as to be attractive to individuals under twenty-one, including but not limited to, any imitation of food, candy, soda, drinks, cookies, or cereal, in labeling, packaging, advertising, or marketing; terms "candy" or "candies" or variants in spelling such as "kandy" or "kandeez"; symbols, images, characters, public figures, phrases, toys, or games that are commonly used to market products to individuals under the age of twenty-one; or images of individuals who could reasonably appear to be under the age of twenty-one.

2. Edible means food or beverage products that have been infused with cannabis extracts.

3. Extraction or Extracting means the process of concentrating or isolating one or more phytocannabinoids from cannabis.

4. Good Manufacturing Practices (GMP) means a quality control system for ensuring that products are consistently produced and controlled in accordance with current federal regulations 21 CFR Parts 111 or 117 established by the Food and Drug Administration (FDA).

5. Hazard Analysis Critical Control Point (HACCP) means a systematic approach that identifies, evaluates and controls hazards significant to product safety.

6. Inventory Tracking System means a system that is capable of tracking cannabis or cannabis product inventory. Licensees are required to maintain an inventory tracking system for all cannabis and cannabis products at their facility.

7. Lot unique identifier means any distinctive combination of letters, numbers, or symbols, or any combination of them, from which the complete history of production, manufacturing, testing, holding, distribution, or recall of a lot of adult-use cannabis product can be determined.

8. Phytocannabinoid means any of the chemical compounds, excluding terpenes or any other compounds that are the active principles of cannabis sativa, including but not limited to tetrahydrocannabinol (THC) and cannabidiol (CBD), and does not include synthetic cannabinoids as that term is defined in subdivision (g) of schedule I of section thirty-three hundred six of the public health law.

9. Pre-roll means cannabis that has been prepared in consumer-ready form for smoking.

10. Product Quality Plan means a product specific risk-based assessment of product safety hazards, and the preventive measures identified to prevent or mitigate each hazard.

11. Representative Sample means a sample of cannabis product of the same size and composition that is required for cannabis product testing by a cannabis laboratory that represents a unique lot of cannabis product processed. The representative sample(s) must be stored on-site at the licensee facilities and can be used as a replacement laboratory testing sample in the event the first sample is compromised, or the results of the analysis require that the lot be re-tested.

12. Sterile means free from bacteria or other living organisms, or totally clean.

13. Tincture means a liquid cannabis product usually made with alcohol or glycerin that is often dosed with a dropper. Tinctures can be flavored and are usually placed under the tongue, where they are absorbed quickly.

14. Topical means a type of cannabis product that is applied to the skin.

15. Total THC means the sum of the percentage by weight or volume measurement of tetrahydrocannabinolic acid multiplied by 0.877, plus, the percentage by weight or volume measurement of THC.

ADULT-USE CONDITIONAL PROCESSING GUIDANCE

1. Data Collection and Retention. Adult-Use Conditional Processor license holders are required to submit any records mandated herein to the Office upon request and in advance of transitioning to an Adult-Use Processor license. Compliance with practices outlined in this document will be considered in making licensing decisions.

2. General Record Keeping Requirements. A licensee must keep and maintain records required by this section for at least five years from the date of creation unless the Board requires the licensee to maintain records for a longer timeframe. Records must be legible and accurate and stored in a secured area protected from debris, moisture, contamination, hazardous waste, and theft. Intentionally misrepresenting or falsifying records may lead to penalties imposed by the Board, including but not limited to, suspension, cancellation or revocation of the Adult-Use Conditional Processor license, disqualification from future licensing opportunities, and fines. Licensees shall make its premises and all books, systems, and records readily retrievable and available upon request.

Records must account for all activities of the licensee, including but not limited to:

- architectural diagrams and floorplans of the licensed premises, including designation of functional areas and square footage available;

- for new construction and major renovation of a facility, certification by an NYS-licensed architect or engineer that the facility complies with the 2020 NYS Stretch Energy Code, or most recent version;

- annual benchmarking of energy and water usage, with the first report to be completed no later than one year after the date of licensure;

- a sustainable packaging plan as detailed in this guidance and annual reporting on the following, to begin one year after date of licensure: the total amount of packaging material, by weight, sold, offered for sale, or distributed into the state by the licensee in the prior calendar year; the percentage of all packaging material sold, offered for sale, or distributed for sale in the state through internet transactions; and the total costs of packaging materials;

- plans for the handling, storage, and disposal of waste, including plans for organic waste and for any hazardous waste;

- financial records in accordance with generally accepted accounting principles, including, but not limited to, ownership information of all individuals directly or indirectly involved with the license, capitalization tables, organizational charts, investment and financial agreements with any party, bank statements, sales invoices, receipts, and any other records maintained for tax purposes;

- personnel records, including each employee's full name, Social Security number or individual taxpayer identification number, date of employment, date of termination of employment (if applicable) background check and disciplinary actions (if applicable);

- training records including the content of the training provided and the names of employees trained;

- any contracts or agreements regarding the licensed cannabis activity including but not limited to real estate arrangements, financial loans, vendors or distributors;

- all records related to advertising and marketing required by the Board or Office;

- standard operating procedures, including a product quality plan;

- laboratory testing results for each lot or batch of cannabis or cannabis product produced;

- code of ethics;

- policies and procedures that notify persons with disabilities of their rights under applicable federal and state laws and regulations and includes provisions prohibiting discrimination and providing reasonable accommodations;

- policies and procedures demonstrating promotion of diversity in the workplace;

- all other documents prepared or executed by or for the licensee in connection with the license.

- any other records required by the Cannabis Law or as determined by the Board or Office.

The failure of the licensee to comply with the requirements set forth in this section may result in enforcement action, including but not limited to monetary fines and penalties, and license suspension or revocation.

3. Operating Plan. Processors must document, implement, and maintain an Operating Plan, which shall be made readily available to the Board or Office upon request, and that must include, at a minimum:

- A site plan indicating the activities performed in each area and detailing all physical boundaries, further outlined in Section 4.

- A security and employee training and safety plan that includes risk mitigation and accident prevention plans resulting from a risk assessment of all licensed activities.

- A product quality plan for each cannabis product produced by the licensee that addresses the risks and hazards associated with the premises and the processing process.

- A cannabis product sampling, analysis, and testing plan based on risks associated with materials or organisms normally present during the production of cannabis products and in accordance with any guidance or regulations issued.

- A quality assurance plan that establishes criteria to detect, identity, prevent and track cannabis contamination, mislabeling, and mispackaging incidents.

- A cannabis and cannabis product recall plan that includes an annual mock recall test.

- A sustainable energy-use and conservation plan that addresses the sourcing and use of energy and sets energy efficiency goals including energy tracking policies, timelines and benchmarks.

- A Sustainable Packaging Program as outlined in this guidance.

4. Site Plan. A licensee shall document, implement, and maintain a site plan, which must be submitted upon request to the Office consisting of the following information:

- architectural diagrams and floorplans of the licensed premises;

- activities performed in each area of the licensed premises including the identification of equipment used in the processing process;

- details of all parcel boundaries including but not limited to physical boundaries, roads, and water crossings of the property;

- sanitary facilities, as applicable;

- perimeter dimensions;

- entrances and exits to both the property and premises;

- a processor shall also include in its site plan the following additional information:

  - bulk packaging area;

  - composting area, if on-site;

  - cannabis waste area (not including composting areas); and

  - any other information as determined by the Office.

5. Environmental, Energy Efficiency, and Conservation. A licensee shall engage with energy efficiency programs as determined by the Board and must participate in an environmental sustainability program. The building envelope for all new construction or major renovation of licensed facilities shall meet minimum relevant requirements as set out in NYS Stretch Energy Code 2020 or most recent version or as determined by the Board.

6. Good Manufacturing Practices. All cannabis processing shall be in accordance with Good Manufacturing Practices (GMP) standards, pursuant to either Part 111 or Part 117 of Title 21 of the Code of Federal Regulations, as applicable for the type of product being manufactured or as otherwise determined by regulation and/or the Board. Licensees must demonstrate compliance with GMP by submitting in their application to the Office, proof of a qualified third-party GMP audit of the processor's extraction and/or manufacturing facility operations and any related certification or audit report. Licensees are required to maintain proof of a current GMP qualified third-party audit for the duration of the license and make evidence of such audit readily available to the Office upon request.

7. General Sanitary Practices. A processor must maintain all designated processing areas in accordance with general sanitary practices which are included in Good Manufacturing Practices as set forth in Part 111 or Part 117 of Title 21 of the Code of Federal Regulations. The licensee is responsible for the upkeep and maintenance of all facilities, containers, tools, contact surfaces, and equipment used in the processing, packaging, labeling, distribution, transportation, storage and sale of cannabis and cannabis products. All processors must:

- have floors, walls and ceilings constructed in such a manner that they may be adequately kept clean and in good repair;

- utilize containers, tools, contact surfaces, and equipment that are designed and of such material and workmanship as to be adequately cleanable and designed, maintained, operated and arranged as to protect against the physical, chemical, and microbial contamination and deterioration of the cannabis and cannabis products;

- use containers that are food-grade, or of a similar standard as approved by the Office, for the storage of cannabis and cannabis products. Containers shall be clean, in good repair and suitable for the established use;

- maintain all facilities, areas, containers, tools, contact surfaces, and equipment, in a clean and sanitary condition. Cleaning and sanitizing shall be as frequently as necessary to protect against contamination, using a sanitizing agent registered by the U.S. Environmental Protection Agency (EPA), in accordance with labeled instructions;

- maintain record of routine cleaning and sanitization of all facilities, containers, tools, contact surfaces and equipment and make records readily available to the Office upon request;

- provide adequate safety lighting in all processing, distribution, storage and sale areas, as well as areas where equipment, tools, containers, or contact surfaces are cleaned;

- provide sufficient space on the premises for placement of equipment and storage of materials as is necessary for the maintenance of sanitary operations;

- utilize appropriate environmental monitoring for temperature, ventilation, and humidity where cannabis or cannabis products are handled or stored so as to protect cannabis and cannabis products against their physical, chemical, and microbial contamination and deterioration;

- maintain records of pest management activities, including but not limited to the following information:

  a map of all traps, types, and coding/numbering system for the traps if applicable must be in place;

  a record of routine trap maintenance;

  a record of any evidence of animal or insect presence including body parts, hair, or feces in cannabis or cannabis product handling areas;

  properly remove and dispose of litter and waste so as to minimize the development of odor and minimize the potential for the waste attracting and harboring pests; and

  store poisonous or toxic materials, insecticides, rodenticides, detergents, sanitizers, caustics, acids and other related cleaning compounds in separate areas from cannabis or cannabis products, in prominently and distinctly labeling containers, except that nothing herein precludes the convenient availability of detergents or sanitizers in areas where equipment, containers, and utensils are washed and sanitized;

- protect cannabis and cannabis products from all sources of contamination or adulteration, by establishing precautions to protect against allergen cross contact and any other potential contamination, by microorganisms or foreign substances, of cannabis or cannabis products, noncannabis components, contact surfaces, and packaging materials that are used in processing, among others.

- Sanitary handling procedures. All licensees and their employees shall handle cannabis and cannabis products in a sanitary manner and comply with general sanitary requirements including but not limited to:

  maintaining adequate personal cleanliness;

  washing and sanitizing hands thoroughly in an adequate hand-washing area before starting work, after each visit to a restroom, after handling contaminated material, eating, or at any other time when hands may have become soiled or contaminated;

  licensees shall ensure that all workers have access to hand washing and toilet facilities on the licensed premises and shall maintain such facilities in clean and sanitary condition, maintaining records of regular cleaning and sanitizing of such facilities.

  - hand-washing facilities on the licensed premises shall be furnished with running water at a suitable temperature and shall be located in the licensed premises in any processing or production areas and where good sanitary practices require employees to wash and sanitize their hands.

  - effective hand-cleaning and sanitizing preparations and sanitary towel service or suitable drying devices shall be provided with the hand-washing facilities.

- signage shall be displayed in toilet facilities to remind workers to wash and sanitize hands. Sanitary areas in this section must be marked in the licensee's site plan.

- equipment, products and materials necessary for cleaning and maintaining the facility shall be stored in a space separate from the storage of any cannabis or cannabis products or any cash.

- plumbing shall be of adequate size and design, and adequately installed and maintained to carry sufficient quantities of water to required locations throughout the premises of the licensed entity. Plumbing shall properly convey sewage and liquid disposable waste from the premises of the licensed entity. There shall be no cross-connections between the potable and wastewater lines.

- hazardous waste handling, storage, and disposal must comply with New York State Department of Environmental Control standards.

8. Traceability. A conditional processor shall assign a lot unique identifier, and batch number where applicable, which allows for complete traceability of all cannabis and cannabis products processed during a specific period of time and under similar conditions. All cannabis products must be identified and categorized in a processor's inventory tracking system, which includes but is not limited to information detailing the milligrams of total THC in the cannabis product, to ensure compliance with Article 20-c of the Tax Law and any other information required by the Office. Licensees must report data from their inventory tracking system to the Office upon request and pursuant to regulation and further guidance when available.

9. Testing. Licensees must, prior to transferring cannabis product to a licensed distributor or if acting as a distributor, before selling cannabis product to a licensed retail dispensary, have a statistically significant sample of cannabis products from each lot produced, tested by a Board approved cannabis testing laboratory in accordance with other requirements as determined by the Board. Laboratory testing shall include but not be limited to, microorganisms, foreign material, metals, microbial impurities, moisture content and water activity, mycotoxins, pesticides, residual solvents, terpenoids, and any other analyte or group of analytes as determined by regulation. All cannabis product lots must pass required laboratory testing before being sold to a licensed distributor or if applicable, retail dispensary license. Licensees are required to retain a representative sample of each lot of final cannabis product tested to allow for testing in the future if required.

10. Requirements for Extraction. Only conditional processors approved to perform extraction activities can perform extraction activities under their Conditional Adult-Use Processor license. Unless otherwise approved in writing by the Board, a conditional processor authorized to perform extraction may only use the methods, equipment, solvents, gases, and mediums authorized under their existing hemp processing license when creating cannabis extracts and only in a manner exhibiting minimal potential for human health related toxicity. All extraction processes and activities must be conducted by employees adequately trained in the operation of the extraction equipment to be utilized, as well as in the emergency plan for incidents.

Licensees must be able to demonstrate control of all sources of ignition, and, if necessary, provide a spark- free environment where appropriate for the type of extraction method used. Licensees must ensure proper ventilation. Licensees must have ongoing equipment monitoring and maintain a record of regular maintenance of equipment based on equipment specifications and follow all applicable fire, safety and building codes, regulations, laws and guidance in the use and storage of solvents, including but not limited to, maximum quantities to be held onsite. Licensees must maintain evidence of the purity of any chemical solvents used, which must be at least 99% minimum purity, unless otherwise approved by the Board, and make any certificate of analysis or other documentation evidencing such purity readily available to the Office, upon request.

11. Acceptable Methods of Extraction. Unless a conditional processor obtains prior written approval from the Board, extraction shall only be conducted using the following methods:

- use of mechanical extraction methods, such as screens or presses, or heat, steam distillation, ice water and other methods without employing solvents or gases;

- use of a professional grade, closed-loop CO_2 gas extraction system that is of a supply equivalent to food or beverage grade of at least 99 percent purity;

- use of ethanol or alcohol-based extraction that must be of a grade that meets or exceeds specifications of official compendiums as defined in section 321 of Title 21 of the United States Code (USC);

- use of a volatile solvent or hydrocarbon extraction method, provided that the method:

  utilizes a commercial, professional grade closed-loop system designed to recover the solvent;

  or utilizes the following permissible volatile solvent-based or hydrocarbon extraction substances, which must be accompanied by a Certificate of Analysis that establishes that the substances have a minimum purity level of 99 percent.

- In addition, for all proposed hydrocarbon extraction, a processor shall submit to the Office, prior to receiving approval to commence extraction operations at a processing facility and on the application for licensure if applicable, documentation which demonstrates the following additional requirements for all designated extraction equipment, rooms, or other areas where volatile solvents used for extraction are handled or stored:

  A final certification letter from a licensed professional engineer or registered architect which certifies the completed installation of a professionally designed, commercially manufactured extraction system, that is compliant with all applicable state or local fire, safety or building codes;

  a letter or equivalent document as determined by the Office from the municipal jurisdiction's fire marshal, or their designee, stating that a final inspection of the facility has been conducted and that the processor has demonstrated compliance with all applicable fire codes and/or regulations; and

  a current certificate of occupancy, or equivalent document, from the local building official that all permits for extraction related rooms or areas have been closed as applicable.

12. Permitted Adult-Use Cannabis Product Types. A processor may produce the following types of cannabis products for retail sale:

- topicals;

- edibles (including single serving beverages, which may be sold in six packs);

- vaporization cartridges or single-use pens;

- concentrates;

- tinctures;

- capsules;

- tablets;

- cannabis flower products, including but not limited to whole flower, shake and pre-rolls; and

- any other product type or form with prior written approval of the Office. In determining whether or not to approve a new cannabis product type, the Office may request written submission by the processor of the proposal, including but not limited to the proposed manufacturing process, methods of administration and any other factors which assess risk to public health and safety.

13. Prohibitions and Prohibited Cannabis Product Types. A processor is prohibited from processing any cannabis products which:

- contain liquor, wine, beer, cider or meet the definition of an alcoholic beverage as defined in section 3 of the Alcohol Beverage Control Law;

- contain tobacco or nicotine in the product;

- exceed the maximum total THC per serving and per package limits set forth by the Board;

- are attractive to individuals under twenty-one or violate the Board's packaging, marketing, and advertising prohibitions or guidance;

- contain synthetic cannabinoids, as defined in schedule I of section thirty-three hundred six of the public health law;

- require manufacture under sterile conditions;

- are considered a potentially hazardous food as defined by Section 14-1.31 of Title 10 of the Official Compilation of Codes, Rules and Regulations of the State of New York;

- contain any non-phytocannabinoid ingredient that would increase potency, toxicity, or addictive potential, or that would create an unsafe combination with other psychoactive substances. This prohibition shall not apply to products containing naturally occurring caffeine, such as coffee, tea, or chocolate;

- are manufactured by application of phytocannabinoid concentrate or extract to commercially available candy or snack food items without further processing of the product. Commercially available candy or snack food items may be used as ingredients in a cannabis product, provided that they are used in a way that renders them unrecognizable as the commercially available items, and the label, including the ingredient list, does not note that the final cannabis product contains the commercially available item; and

- are in the form of an injectable, inhaler, suppository, transdermal formulations, or any other disallowed form, as determined by the Board, including a form allowed solely for medical cannabis use, unless otherwise authorized by the Board.

14. Requirements for Adult-Use Cannabis Products. All cannabis products intended for oral ingestion including but not limited to edibles, capsules and tablets shall not exceed more than 10 milligrams (mg) of total THC per serving and 100 mg of total THC per package, unless otherwise approved in writing by the Board. Any approved cannabis product exceeding the 10 mg total THC per serving or 100 mg total THC per package may be subject to additional safeguards and oversight required by the Board to protect public health and safety, including but not limited to, additional packaging, labeling or consumer education requirements. Topical cannabis products and tinctures are not permitted to contain more than 1,000 milligrams of total THC unless approved by the Board in writing.

- All cannabis products must:

  accurately reflect testing results and not contain less than 90 percent or more than 110 percent of the concentration of total THC, CBD, or any other phytocannabinoid and terpene content as listed on the product label. Any cannabis product not meeting this requirement must be relabeled with the accurate phytocannabinoid and terpene content;

  be prepackaged, tested and labeled;

  be shelf-stable, unless otherwise approved in regulation or by the Board, provided that nothing in this provision shall prohibit a processor from storing non-cannabis components or ingredients under refrigeration until use in product processing;

  cannabis products may contain only excipients or ingredients which are appropriate for the cannabis product type manufactured and are, at a minimum, food grade or considered generally recognized as safe; and be homogeneous, with phytocannabinoid content evenly distributed throughout the cannabis product. This requirement shall not apply to cannabis flower products.

For Vaporization Cartridges and Single-Use Pens:

- Cannabis vaporization devices shall be a closed system with a pre-filled single-use cartridge that attaches to a rechargeable battery, or a single-use product.

- Electronic vaporization devices shall have internal or external temperature controls to prevent combustion and have a heating element made of inert material such as glass, ceramic or stainless steel and not plastic or rubber.

- Except for cannabis or botanically derived terpenes, excipients and ingredients must be pharmaceutical grade and appropriate for the cannabis product, unless otherwise approved by the Board.

- Cannabis Vaporization Cartridges and Single-Use Pens shall not include:

  synthetic terpenes;

  polyethylene glycol (PEG);

  vitamin E acetate;

  medium chain triglycerides (MCT oil);

  medicinal compounds;

  illegal or controlled substances;

  artificial food coloring;

  benzoic acid;

  diketones; and

  any other compound or ingredient as determined by the Board.

- Cannabis products cannot exceed more than 10% total terpenes.

- Licensees must maintain records of all cannabis or botanically derived terpenes used in the cannabis product with full information on the source of botanically derived terpenes used, and provide this information upon request.

16. Packaging, Labeling, Marketing, and Advertising. Licensees must comply with all packaging, labeling, marketing, and advertising standards as set by the Board or in guidance from the Office.

17. Product Quality Plans and Batch Production Records. A processor shall implement and maintain a written product quality plan for each type of cannabis product processed at the licensed premises. Common plan types include a GMP Plan, Quality Assurance Plan, or Hazard Analysis and Critical Control Points (HACCP) Plan. The product quality plan shall address the risks and hazards associated with the premises and the manufacturing process that, if not properly mitigated, may cause the cannabis product to be adulterated or misbranded, or may cause the cannabis product to fail laboratory testing or quality assurance review. Each product quality plan must include a comprehensive assessment of the overall processing process, including all steps from component intake through transfer of product from the premises; evaluation of the potential risks associated with each processing step; and identification of preventive measures necessary to mitigate each potential risk identified, methods to evaluate the effectiveness of the preventive measure, and any action to take if a preventive measure was unsuccessful.

Such plan shall also include written protocols for each unique formulation of cannabis product manufactured, and for each batch size, to ensure uniformity in finished batches and across all batches produced. Such protocols shall include the following:

- the name and intended phytocannabinoid content of the cannabis product to be manufactured;

- a complete list of all ingredients to be used and the weight or measure of each ingredient, which may include the ability to adjust the weight or measure of phytocannabinoid-containing ingredients in order to account for the variability of phytocannabinoid content across different batches;

- the identity and weight or measure of each ingredient that will be declared on the ingredients list of the cannabis product, if different than above;

- the expected yield of the finished manufactured cannabis product, based upon the quantity of ingredients or packaging to be used in the absence of any loss or error in actual production, and the maximum and minimum percentages of expected yield beyond which a deviation investigation of a batch will be necessary;

- a description of packaging and a representative label, or a cross-reference to the physical location of the actual or representative label;

- the expected number of packages and labels to be used, if the cannabis product will leave the manufacturing premises in final form;

- written instructions for each point, step, or stage in the processing process; and

- written instructions for any action to mitigate risks identified in the product quality plan.

All licensees must have written procedures in place to track and ensure no cross-contamination between cannabinoid hemp and adult-use cannabis processing activities and products at the licensees processing facility. Processors must be able to always distinguish between cannabinoid hemp products and adultuse cannabis products. All record keeping and tracking activities as described in sections 2 and 8 must be applied to all cannabinoid hemp and adult-use cannabis processing. Upon inspection by the Office, licensees must be able to distinguish cannabinoid hemp extract and products from adult-use cannabis extract and products.

Licensees shall also maintain a written batch production record for every batch of a cannabis product manufactured, which shall include any batch specific remediation or relabeling. Records shall contain actual values and observations, as appropriate, during verification activities and be accurate and legible and be created concurrently with performance of the activity documented and include sufficient detail to provide a history of work performed, including the date each step was performed, and the signature or initials of the person performing the activity. The batch production record document shall also include, but not be limited to:

- lot number, or batch number as applicable, of the finished batch of cannabis product, and unique identification numbers or barcodes of all cannabis used in the batch as captured by the inventory tracking system of record;

- specific equipment and processing lines used in producing or remediating the batch;

- the identity and weight or measure of each component used;

- the actual yield and the percentage difference from expected yield at appropriate phases of manufacturing as identified in written protocols;

- the actual results obtained during any monitoring operation, if the product quality plan identifies any monitoring needed to ensure product safety at a specific manufacturing step;

- the date and time of when each step of the master manufacturing protocol was performed, and the initials of the person(s) performing each step;

- an actual or representative label or other identification of the label to be used for the cannabis product;

- the actual quantity of the packaging and labels used, and the difference from the expected number to be used, if the cannabis product will leave the manufacturing premises as a final cannabis product;

- documentation that quality control personnel reviewed the batch production record, including all required monitoring operations, test results for components, if applicable, and finished batches of cannabis product, and either approved and released, or rejected, the finished cannabis product, including any remediated, repackaged or relabeled cannabis product;

- documentation, at the time of performance, of any investigation identified in the product quality plan or written protocols, including investigations into deviations from the expected yield or package and label count.

Product quality plans and batch production records shall be readily available for employee reference and made readily available to the Board and Office upon request.

18. Inspections. The licensee shall make available to the Office data required by this guidance to ensure compliance with the program standards set forth by the Board. The Office maintains the rights to inspect licensees' facilities where cannabis operations are taking place. Inspections may be on-site or through remote technology. Inspections may be announced or unannounced. Applicants will be provided with an inspection evaluation report, including, if necessary, a statement of findings and related timeline to make any corrective actions and submit a corrective action plan to the Office for review and approval.

19. Corrective Action Plan. Any deficiencies identified by the inspection shall be documented in a statement of findings by the Office and require that the licensee submit a written plan of correction in a format acceptable to the Office within 15 calendar days of the issue date of the statement of findings. A plan of correction shall address all deficiencies or areas of noncompliance cited in the statement of findings and shall:

- contain an assessment and analysis of the events and/or circumstances that led to the noncompliance;

- contain a procedure addressing how the licensee intends to correct each area of noncompliance;

- contain an explanation of how proposed corrective actions will be implemented and maintained to ensure noncompliance does not recur;

- contain the proposed date by which each area of noncompliance shall be corrected;

- any other information as directed by the Office.

Any inspection finding which the Office determines jeopardizes the immediate health, safety, or wellbeing of the public shall be deemed a critical deficiency and shall require immediate corrective action to remove the immediate risk. The licensee shall submit a preliminary corrective action plan to the Office within 24 hours of notification by the Office of the critical deficiency.

The Office has the authority to determine whether a corrective action plan needs modification, and if the licensee must modify the plan accordingly. Upon written approval of the Office, the licensee shall implement the plan of correction. Failure by the licensee to comply with these requirements may result in suspension, revocation, and or a civil penalty pursuant to the Cannabis Law or any applicable rule or regulation.

20. Employee and Training Requirements. Licensees shall not employ anyone under the age of eighteen years. Licensees must use due diligence to ensure that all employees possess the necessary education and training for the duties they will be assigned.

Licensees shall be required to develop and maintain an employee training manual. The employee training manual must include, at a minimum, employee guidelines and safety procedures; security protocols; training on standard operating procedures for all staff involved in extracting, processing, and/or manufacturing cannabis or cannabis products, which includes, but is not limited to: training that is specific to the duties assigned, and the safe operation of the equipment, machinery, solvents, gases and systems to be utilized; and training on the hazards presented by use of chemicals and solvents, as described in the safety data sheet for each. An up to date, readily available, complete employee training manual shall be made readily available at each licensed location. Copies of this manual must be maintained and be made available to the Board or Office upon request.

Licensees shall train employees and contractors in accordance with an employee training manual, which shall be made available in a language of fluency or primary language of all employees or contractors involved in the production and distribution of adult-use cannabis. The act, omission, or failure of an agent, officer, representative, or other person acting for or employed by a licensee, within the scope of his or her employment or position, shall in every case be deemed the act, omission, or failure of the licensee. Signed and dated documentation demonstrating each employee's attestation of completion of the training shall be made readily available to the Office upon request.

Licensees must maintain safety data sheets onsite, readily available to employees, and to the Office upon request, including information regarding emergency operations, notification to emergency personnel and shutdown procedures and information on how to access current laws, rules and regulations, and any guidance or policy documents issued by the Board or Office.

21. Security. Licensees shall implement a security plan with sufficient security measures to deter diversion, theft or loss of cannabis and cannabis products or cash, prevent unauthorized entrance into areas containing cannabis or cannabis products, and to ensure the safety of the licensee's employees and the general public. In addition:

- Cannabis and cannabis products shall be stored in a secure, locked safe, vault or other approved equipment or location within the licensed premises accessible to the minimum number of employees essential for efficient operation, to prevent diversion, theft or loss, and in such a manner, as to protect against physical, chemical and microbial contamination and deterioration of the cannabis and cannabis products.

- All facilities operated by a licensee where cannabis or cannabis products are stored or handled shall have a security and surveillance system to prevent and detect diversion, theft or loss utilizing commercial grade equipment.

- The license holder must maintain full-time security camera coverage of all parts of the interior and exterior of the licensed premises. Such equipment may be motion-activated after hours of business operation. Such equipment must comply with any current or future standards as determined by the Board.

- Employees, visitors, and other persons at licensed premises, including persons engaged in the transportation of cannabis or cannabis products, must be able to provide identification to the Office, or other authorized enforcement official upon request.

- Licensees shall notify the Office in a manner prescribed by the Office, of any breach of security or other incident set forth in this subdivision immediately and, in no instance, more than 24 hours following discovery of the security breach or incident.

22. Quarantine, Remediation and Recalls. Licensees shall establish written policies and procedures to monitor and track all quality assurance concerns, and complaints from licensees and consumers, including, but not limited to, procedures for rapid notification to the licensees' supply and distribution chain to recall any lot of cannabis or cannabis product when directed by the Office, or as deemed necessary by the licensee. Such procedures must include notification to the Office with 24 hours of learning of a serious adverse event, quality assurance concern or initialing a recall.

Written procedures for recalling cannabis product, whether initiated by the licensee or mandated by the Office, shall include:

- identification of factors that necessitate recall and personnel responsible for implementing the recall procedures;

- notification protocols, including a mechanism to notify the Office within 24 hours of initiating a recall and to notify any licensee that supplied or received the recalled cannabis product;

- instructions to the general public and other licensees for the return or destruction of the recalled cannabis or cannabis products; and

- a requirement that all recalled products held by a licensee must be held in quarantine until the authorization of additional actions.

Licensees shall not sell or transfer cannabis or a cannabis product that has been placed on administrative hold by the Office, recalled, or ordered or otherwise required to be destroyed. Such cannabis or cannabis products shall be stored securely and separate and apart from other cannabis products while awaiting final disposition. All inventories, policies and procedures and other documents required by this section shall be maintained on the licensed premises and shall be made readily available to the Office upon request.

Licensees shall not sell or transfer cannabis product after the printed expiration date on the package.

23. Cannabis Waste Disposal. Licensees shall dispose of any cannabis or cannabis product that is outdated, damaged, deteriorated, contaminated, or otherwise deemed not appropriate for processing, distribution, or sale. This includes any plant-based cannabis waste created as a by-product of processing. All disposals must be conducted in compliance with all applicable state, and local laws, rules, regulations, and guidance. The disposal of cannabis shall mean that the cannabis has been rendered unrecoverable and beyond reclamation, by grinding and mixing the cannabis plant waste with other ground materials, so the resulting mixture is at least fifty percent non-cannabis waste by volume. The stalks, stems, fan leaves, root balls, and soil media of the cannabis plant shall not be required to be rendered unrecoverable beyond reclamation. Any other method used to render cannabis unrecoverable and beyond reclamation requires prior written approval of the Board.

Cannabis waste shall be maintained in a secured waste receptacle or secured area on the licensed premises until the time of disposal. All exterior cannabis waste receptacles located on the licensed premises shall be locked and secured to prevent unauthorized access. All cannabis waste and disposal shall be weighed, recorded and entered into the inventory tracking system prior to mixing and disposal. Cannabis waste may not be sold unless it is unrecoverable or beyond reclamation for use as a cannabis product.

Licensees shall maintain records of disposal for at least five years, and make available to the Board or Office for inspection, which shall include:

- the form (or type) of cannabis or cannabis product being disposed;

- the weight of the disposed cannabis material,

- the number of plants, or in the case of a cannabis product, the quantity of the cannabis product;

- the batch or lot number, as applicable, of the cannabis or cannabis product;

- the signatures of at least two of the licensee's employees who witnessed the disposal;

- the methods and destination/location of disposal, by waste type and weight, for each method of disposal; and

- any other information as determined by the Board.

For facilities generating more than a half ton of organic waste per week and within 25 miles of an organic recycling facility, the waste shall not be landfilled or combusted but must either be: 1) composted on-site or at an organic recycling facility; 2) used to produce energy through the process of anaerobic digestion; or 3) used as input by the licensee or a third party in the manufacture of other products, such as paper, packaging, or pet bedding.

24. Transportation. The transport of cannabis and cannabis products to an authorized licensee shall only be performed by a licensee or a licensee's authorized employee(s). Licensees shall ensure the safe and secure transport of any cannabis, or cannabis products, including the safety of those transporting cannabis. Cannabis and cannabis products shall be transported in a manner that will protect them against physical, chemical, and microbial contamination, and deterioration. All cannabis and cannabis products shall be transported in a secure manner in a fully enclosed vehicle, owned and operated by the licensee or hired and operated by the licensee from a trucking or transportation company. Cannabis and cannabis products being transported must be in a sealed package, which shall not be opened during transport.

Vehicles transporting cannabis or cannabis products shall be equipped pursuant to the Board's standards, including but not limited to:

- temperature controls designed, maintained, and equipped as necessary to prevent the cannabis and cannabis products from becoming unsafe during transportation;

- a secure lockbox or secure cargo area, which shall be used for the sanitary and secure transport of cannabis and cannabis products;

- an operational Global Positioning System (GPS) device, for identifying the geographic location of the vehicle, either permanently or temporarily affixed to the vehicle while the vehicle is in operation.

Vehicles shall bear no signs, markings, advertisements, or marketing that would either identify or indicate that the vehicle is used to transport cannabis or cannabis products. A licensee shall provide the Office, upon request, with information regarding any vehicles, including the vehicle's geographic location, make, model, color, vehicle identification number, license plate number, and vehicle registration. Transport of cannabis and cannabis products shall not be made through the use of an unmanned vehicle, such as a drone.

Any vehicle utilized for the purposes of transporting cannabis or cannabis products shall be considered an extension of the licensed premises and subject to inspection by the Office or authorized representative of the Office. Vehicles assigned for transportation may be stopped and inspected by the Office at any licensed location, or while on route during transportation.

25. Shipping manifests. Prior to transporting any cannabis or cannabis products, a licensee shall generate a shipping manifest to be submitted to the licensee, permittee or other authorized party that will receive the cannabis, or cannabis product. The shipping manifest shall contain, at a minimum, the following information:

- name, physical address, lot or batch number, and license or permit number of the originating licensee, permittee or other party authorized to receive cannabis or cannabis products;

- name, physical address, and license number, if applicable, of the receiving party;

- a certificate of analysis, except for those samples being transported to a permitted laboratory for

- testing by a permitted sampling firm;

- the unique identification numbers for all cannabis and cannabis products being transported;

- the cannabis or cannabis product name, item category and weight or count of cannabis or cannabis products;

- the estimated date and time of departure from the licensed premises;

- the estimated date and time of arrival at each licensed premises;

- the driver's license number of the employee transporting the cannabis or cannabis products;

- the make, model, and license plate number of the vehicle used for transport; and

- any other information as determined by the Office or Board.

The licensee receiving the delivery shall record acceptance or receipt of the delivery. The licensee shall record the receipt of delivery in the licensee's inventory tracking system.

Employees conducting the transport of cannabis or cannabis products shall possess a copy of the shipping manifest when transporting cannabis or cannabis products and shall produce it to the Office, the Office's authorized representative or law enforcement official upon request. A licensee shall not void, modify or change a shipping manifest or invoice after departing from the originating licensed premises. The licensee receiving and taking possession of cannabis or cannabis products shall ensure and verify that the cannabis or cannabis products being received and taken into possession for transport at the originating licensed premises are as described and accurately reflected in the shipping manifest. The licensee conducting the transport is responsible for any discrepancies between the shipping manifest and the cannabis and cannabis products in its possession during transport, and subject to any enforcement action related to such discrepancy. Shipping manifests and any invoices shall be made readily available to the Office, for inspection upon request, for a period of five years.

Employees of the licensee transporting cannabis and cannabis products shall:

- not make any unnecessary stops in between destinations;

- randomize transport times;

- have the ability to communicate with employees at the licensed entity at all times;

- only transport cannabis and cannabis products within the borders of New York State.

Where a transport is attempted and not completed and the cannabis or cannabis products remain in the possession of the employee conducting the transport, the employee shall return the cannabis or cannabis product to the licensed premises of the employee. The returned inventory may be restocked if the inventory is in a new, unopened condition and was handled in a manner that did not compromise the integrity of the cannabis or cannabis products. The cannabis or cannabis product inventory status must be updated in the licensee's inventory tracking system.

Only licensees, or employees thereof, may be in any vehicle as it is being used to transport cannabis or cannabis products.

26. Health and Safety Standards. Licensees shall comply with all applicable federal, state, and local laws and regulations related to worker training, safety, health, and pay. The licensee shall establish, maintain, and comply with a written alcohol-free, drug-free and smoke-free workplace policy.

Personal protective equipment must be assigned to employees involved in the processing of cannabis and cannabis products as needed and must be in good working order. If respirators are required, employees must be trained in their proper use and respirators must be serviced and tagged to manufacturer's specifications.

Licensees shall install informational signs that provide clear instructions for material handling, equipment operation, and general safety information for all operations. Licensee shall install warning signs in languages of fluency and the primary languages for the employees of the licensee in all areas of potential hazard.

Emergency signage must be posted in all work areas. At least one employee onsite must be trained in First Aid and CPR. Well stocked first aid kits must be readily available in all operational areas.

27. Labor Peace Agreement. Within six months of licensure, the applicant must enter into a labor peace agreement with a bona-fide labor organization, and a signed copy of the labor peace agreement must be provided to the Office. Maintenance of such labor peace agreement is an ongoing material condition of licensure. For purposes of this requirement, a "bona fide labor organization" is defined as a labor union:

- that represents employees in this state with regard to wages, hours and working conditions;

- in which officers have been elected by secret ballot or otherwise in a manner consistent with federal law; and

- that is free of domination or interference by any employer and has received no improper assistance or support from any employer.

28. Mentorship Program. As a condition of licensure, Adult-Use Conditional Processors must participate in a social and economic equity mentorship program, as determined by the Office.

29. Transition to Adult-Use Processor License. License holders must be compliant with all sections above to be eligible for license transition under the Conditional Adult-Use Processor law. The Board will evaluate compliance with all relevant laws, regulations, and guidance.

<u>Please Review and Sign on the Next Page and Upload the Signed Signature Page to Your Application on New York Business Express</u>

The terms and conditions and guidance of the adult-use conditional processor license are binding on an Applicant for an adult-use conditional processor license and a person, partnership, or entity that receives an adult-use conditional processor license (Applicant). In addition, all Applicants are bound by current and future state laws, rules, regulations, terms and conditions, and guidance, and an Applicant is subject to the same authorizations and restrictions applied to any adult-use processor pursuant to section sixtynine of the Cannabis Law.

By signing below, the Applicant understands and agrees to the following:

"I understand that the statements made in this application will be accepted for all purposes as the equivalent of an Affidavit and that any false statements, including omissions, made herein, in addition to being the possible basis for a revocation of any approval given as a result of this application, may be punishable as a misdemeanor under the provisions of Section 210.45 of the Penal Law of the State of New York."

Print: _____

Signed: _____

Date: _____

Packaging and Labeling Guidance for Adult-Use Licensees

Originally Published: 9/1/2022

Updated: 10/4/2022

INTRODUCTION

The Cannabis Control Board (the Board) has proposed packaging, labeling, marketing, and advertising (PLMA) regulations which are not yet effective. Once adopted and effective, the regulations will serve as the primary rules that all licensees must follow to remain compliant with the Cannabis Law. A copy of the final PLMA regulations will be available on the Office of Cannabis Management's website. In the interim, this guidance document provides the packaging and labeling framework that licensed Adult-Use Conditional Processors and Adult-Use Conditional Cultivators must use to guide the packaging and labeling of cannabis products before PLMA regulations are formally adopted.

Compliance with any current and future state rules, regulations and laws is required by all licensees to become eligible to transition to a non-conditional license and remain in good standing with the Office of Cannabis Management (the Office). This guidance document provides clarity on what the Office's expectations are in relation to those regulations and laws.

Adult-use cannabis licensees who are not in compliance risk their license being cancelled, suspended, or revoked or other enforcement actions as authorized by the Marihuana Regulations and Taxation Act (MRTA), Cannabis Law, and Title 9 of the New York, Codes, Rules and Regulations (9 NYCRR).

PLMA KEY REPORTING DEADLINES TO THE OFFICE:

Conditional Cultivators and Conditional Processors who package cannabis products for retail sale shall annually report:

- the total amount of packaging material, by weight, sold, offered for sale, or distributed into the state by the licensee in the prior calendar year;

- the percentage of all packaging material sold, offered for sale, or distributed for sale in the state;

- the total amount of packaging material, by the country of origin where the packaging was manufactured or sourced, sold, offered for sale, or distributed into the state;

- the total number of refillable containers reused for cannabis products sold, offered for sale, or distributed for sale in the state; and

- the total costs of packaging material.

This information shall be reported through a method authorized by the Board and shall begin one year after the date the license is issued. In anticipation of this reporting requirement, licensees should be tracking this information throughout the year.

DEFINITIONS

The Office will be using the following terms in describing requirements from Cannabis Law, and in this guidance document. The definitions below represent The Office's interpretation of these terms:

1. Attractive to individuals under twenty-one means labeling, packaging, advertising and marketing that is pleasing or appealing to persons under the age of twenty-one by using or including, among other things: Cartoons; bubble-type or other cartoon-like font; bright colors that are "neon" in appearance; similarities to products or words that refer to products that are commonly associated with or marketed in a manner so as to be attractive to individuals under twenty-one, including, but not limited to, any imitation of food, candy, soda, drinks, cookies, or cereal (with the exception of cultivar names) in labeling, packaging, advertising, or marketing; terms "candy" or "candies" or variants in spelling such as "kandy" or "kandeez" (with the exception of cultivar names); symbols, images, characters, public figures, phrases, toys, or games that are commonly used to market products to individuals under the age of twenty-one; or images of individuals who could reasonably appear to be under the age of twenty-one.

2. Board means the Cannabis Control Board of New York State as established by Article 2 of the Cannabis Law.

3. Brand or Branding means the name, entity name, or doing business as name, registered trademark, logo, symbol, motto, selling message, recognizable pattern of colors, or any other identifiable marker that identifies one adult-use cannabis licensee or adult-use cannabis licensee's cannabis products as distinct from those cannabis products of other adult-use cannabis licensees and is used in, among other things, any packaging, labeling, advertising or marketing.

4. Certificate of analysis means a certified report from a cannabis laboratory that meets the requirements of 9 NYCRR Part 130.

5. Child-resistant means special packaging for sale to a consumer that is:

> a. designed or constructed to be significantly difficult for children under five years of age to open and not difficult for adults to use properly as defined by 16 CFR §1700.15 for Poison Prevention Packaging Standards and 16 CFR §1700.20 for Testing Procedure for Special Packaging, as amended from time to time, and

> b. follows the packaging standards set forth 16 CFR §1700.15 and the testing procedure set forth in 16 CFR §1700.20.*

6. Date of expiration means the date prior to which an unopened cannabis product meets applicable standards of identity, potency, and quality at time of use, as determined by appropriate stability testing, subject to any storage conditions stated on the labeling.

7. Exit package means a receptacle into which cannabis products within a retail package are placed at the retail point of sale. The exit package is optional.

8. Health claim means any claim made on the retail package or marketing layer or in the marketing or advertising of a cannabis product, that expressly or by implication, including, but not limited to, by "third party" references, written statements (e.g., a brand name including a term such as "heart"), symbols (e.g., a heart symbol, plus '+' sign, caduceus, or other medical symbols indicating it is a health product), or branding, that characterizes the relationship of any cannabis product to a disease or health-related condition or symptom. Implied health claims include those statements, symbols, branding, advertisements, or other forms of communication that suggest, within the context in which they are presented, that a relationship exists between the presence or level of a substance in the cannabis product to a disease or health-related condition or symptom.

9. Licensee means an individual or an entity who has been granted a license for any activity under Article 4 of the Cannabis Law.

10. Lot unique identifier or lot number or bar code means any distinctive combination of letters, numbers, or symbols, from which the complete history of manufacturing, testing, holding, distribution or recall of a lot of a cannabis product can be determined.

11. Marketing layer means packaging in addition to the retail packaging that is the outermost layer visible to the consumer at the point of sale. The Marketing Layer is optional, but if used it must comply with all adult-use labeling requirements.

12. Non-consumer package means any container or wrapping used solely for the transport of cannabis or cannabis products in bulk between licensees and particularly, a package intended solely for wholesale distribution and not final retail sale.

13. Office means the Office of Cannabis Management.

14. Phytocannabinoids means any of the chemical compounds, excluding terpenes or any other compounds determined by the Office, that are the active principles of the cannabis sativa, including but not limited to tetrahydrocannabinol (THC) and cannabidiol (CBD), and does not include synthetic cannabinoids as that term is defined in subdivision (g) of schedule I of section thirty-three hundred six of the public health law.

15. Post-consumer recycled content means new material produced using material resulting from the recovery, separation, collection, and reprocessing of material that would otherwise be disposed of or processed as waste and that was originally sold for consumption. It does not include post-industrial content, or material generated by means of combustion, incineration, pyrolysis, gasification, solvolysis, chemical recycling and any high-heat or conversion process.

16. Principal packaging display panel means the panel of the retail package or the marketing layer that the processor intends to be displayed for a cannabis product at retail.

17. Resealable means a package that maintains its child-resistant effectiveness, as well as preserving the integrity of cannabis products for multiple servings.

18. Retail package means a sealed, hard or soft-bodied, child-resistant receptacle in which the cannabis product is offered for retail sale. Retail package does not mean: (1) inner wrapping or lining; (2) an exit package; or (3) a non-consumer package used to transfer cannabis from one licensee to another.

19. Reusable packaging is packaging made from durable material that is designed to be used repeatedly for a number of use cycles, is safe for washing and sanitizing, and is capable of being recycled at the end of use, with the exception of ceramic packaging.

20. Use by date means the date prior to which an opened cannabis product meets applicable standards of identity, potency, and quality at the time of use, as determined by appropriate stability testing, subject to any storage conditions stated on the labeling.

21. Tamper-evident means, with respect to a device or process, bearing a seal, a label or a marking that makes unauthorized access to or tampering with a package, product or container easily detectable.

22. Total THC means the sum of the percentage by weight or volume measurement of tetrahydrocannabinolic acid multiplied by 0.877, plus, the percentage by weight or volume measurement of THC.

23. Universal symbol means an image developed by the Office, and made available to licensees, that indicates that a retail package or the product contains cannabis.

ADULT-USE PACKAGING AND LABELING GUIDANCE

1. Required Documentation. Licensees are required to maintain a copy of the certificate showing that each retail package into which the licensee places cannabis or cannabis products is child-resistant and complies with the requirements of as defined by 16 CFR §1700.15 for Poison Prevention Packaging Standards Poison Prevention Packaging Standards and 16 CFR §1700.20 for Testing Procedure for Special Packaging, as amended from time to time*.

The Office may request a copy of this certificate at any time to ensure compliance with this provision.

2. Retail Package Minimum Standards. All retail packages must be child-resistant, tamper-evident, and fully enclose the product. The retail package must be sealed in a way that protects against light and other contaminations that may potentially damage the product during storage. The retail package must not pass on any toxic or harmful substance to the cannabis product. If the package contains multiple servings, the package must be resealable. A retail package is required. A marketing layer is optional.

3. Cannabis Product Packaging Prohibitions. Cannabis product packaging, which includes all packaging elements except non-consumer packaging, cannot contain:

- any components that may be attractive to individuals under twenty-one;

- any features that emit scent or make sound; or

- any features that change or alter a package's appearance through technology, other than for anticounterfeiting purposes, such as holographic features.

Cannabis product packaging **cannot** be attractive to individuals under twenty-one. As defined in the definitions section, packaging is attractive to individuals over twenty-one if it uses or includes:

- cartoons;

- bubble-type, or cartoon-like font, such as puffy, rounded block letters (see Appendix A);

- bright colors that are "neon" in appearance, including any color which, when listed in a form of hue, saturation, and lightness, has a saturation value greater than 60%. Examples of such colors are shown below in Figure 1;

**Image not shown. Refer to *https://www.omarfigueroa.com/new-york-book/* or *https://cannabis.ny.gov/system/files/documents/2022/10/packaging-and-labeling-guidance.pdf* **

- similarities to products or words that refer to products that are commonly associated with or marketed in a manner so as to be attractive to individuals under twenty-one, including, but not limited to, any imitation of food, candy, soda, drinks, cookies, or cereal (with the exception of cultivar names);

- terms "candy" or "candies" or variants in spelling such as "kandy" or "kandeez" (With the exception of cultivar names);

- symbols, images, characters, public figures, phrases, toys, or games that are commonly used to market products to individuals under the age of twenty-one; or

- images of individuals who could reasonably appear to be under the age of twenty-one.

Cannabis product packaging **cannot** be made of single-use plastic, unless containing a minimum 25% postconsumer recycled content. Licensees will have one year from January 1, 2023 to meet this requirement, unless otherwise authorized by the Board.

4. Cannabis Product Labeling Minimum Standards. There are minimum standards for cannabis product labeling. Appendix B shows an example of the retail package or marketing layer of a cannabis product intended to be ingested orally that is compliant with the Office's labeling standards.

4a. Principal Packaging Display Panel Minimum Standards. The principal packaging display panel is a panel of the retail packaging or marketing layer—if a marketing layer is used—which is intended to be displayed at retail.

The principal packaging display panel must be printed legibly and contain the:

- Milligrams per single serving of total THC,[9] total CBD,[10] and any other marketed phytocannabinoids,[11] (this information much be **bolded** on the principal packaging display panel);

- Terpene profile (*if the product's terpene content is marketed*)[11]

- Milligrams per package of total THC[9] and Total CBD[10] (this information must be **bolded** on the principal packaging display panel);

- Amount of total THC[9] and any other marketed phytocannabinoids as a percentage of volume (*except if the cannabis product is in the form of an edible*);

- Number of servings in total for the cannabis product and, if possible, the recommended size of the serving (*except for cannabis flower*);

- Weight of the cannabis product; and

This information must be unobstructed and conspicuous. Licensees may include this information by printing the information directly onto the retail package or by affixing one or more labels with the information to the retail package, provided that none of the information is obstructed. All required labelling text must be no smaller than 6-point font size. All required text must be clearly written or printed and in the English language. In addition to the required labeling in English, licensees can include accurate foreign language translation(s) of the required labels.

4b. Retail Package and Marketing Layer Minimum Standards. The retail package or, if a marketing layer is used, the marketing layer must contain a list of all ingredients in the cannabis product, other required information, and required warnings. Cannabis products are not required to contain a marketing layer in their packaging.

All required labelling text must be no smaller than 6-point font size. All required text must be clearly written or printed and in the English language. In addition to the required labeling in English, licensees can include accurate foreign language translation(s) of the required labels.

List of all ingredients in the cannabis product. This ingredients list must appear on the retail package or, if a marketing layer is used, the marketing layer. The list must include all active and inactive ingredients in descending order, by weight in the cannabis product. The ingredient list must include and separately list, in bold, any major allergens set forth in the Food Allergen Labeling and Consumer Protection Act of 2004, as it relates to Food and Drugs for misbranded food (21 U.S. Code § 343), as amended from time to time.

Edible products and beverage products must also include a nutritional label compliant with 21 CFR § 101.9(c), as it relates the labeling of food, as amended from time to time*.

Cannabis products marketed and sold as dietary supplements must also include a supplement fact panel compliant with federal codes for nutritional labels of dietary supplements (21 C.F.R. § 101.36) as it relates to the labeling of dietary supplements.

Other required information. In addition to a list of all ingredients, the retail package or, if a marketing layer is used, the marketing layer must contain:

- A list of any solvent used to produce the cannabis product, if applicable;

- The date of expiration of the unopened cannabis product;

- the use-by date;

- proper storage conditions;

---

9   Total THC is calculated as: total THC = THC + (THCA x 0.877)
10   Total CBD is calculated as: total CBD = CBD + (CBDA x 0.877); Total CBD is not required to be listed on products which contain <0.01mg CBD per package.
11   Marketed phytocannabinoids and marketed terpenes are any phytocannabinoids or terpenes that are mentioned on the cannabis product's packaging or labeling or otherwise associated with the cannabis product by the processor.

- Name, location (at a minimum, city and zip code), license number, and direct contact information[12] of the processor;[13]

- At least one of the three universal symbols (as shown in Figure 2 below). The symbol(s) must be at least 1.25 inches in height for the square symbol, 0.5 inch in width for the vertical symbol, and 0.5 inch in height for the horizontal symbol. Licensees cannot alter the colors of the symbol. The symbol must be made conspicuous by printing the symbol on—or outlining the symbol with—a color which contrasts with the symbol. Production-ready versions of the universal symbol in both CMYK and Pantone Matching System formats are available on the Office's website;

- Clear usage instructions;

- Lot unique identifier or lot number or bar code; and

- A scannable bar code or QR code linked to a downloadable certificate of analysis or linked to a website where the certificate of analysis can be downloaded.

Image not shown. Refer to *https://www.omarfigueroa.com/new-york-book/* or *https://cannabis.ny.gov/system/files/documents/2022/10/packaging-and-labeling-guidance.pdf*

Required Warnings. Either the retail packaging or, if a marketing layer is used, the marketing layer must contain the following warnings in **bold**:

- **"This product contains cannabis and THC."**

- **"KEEP OUT OF REACH OF CHILDREN AND PETS. For use only by persons 21 years and older"** (*NOTE: this warning must include the capital letters as indicated*)

- **"Warning: Do not use if pregnant or nursing"**

- **"National Poison Control Center 1-800-222-1222"**

- *For cannabis products intended to be smoked, inhaled, or vaporized*: **"Warning: Smoking or vaping is hazardous to health"**

- *For cannabis products intended to be ingested orally*: **"Warning: Effects of this product may be delayed by 4 or more hours"**

- *For all topical products*: **"Warning: For topical use only. Do not eat or smoke"**

These warnings must be printed in the English language in Times New Roman, Calibri, Arial, or Helvetica font as seen in **Appendix A**. Text must be no smaller than size 6 font, **bolded**, legible, unobscured, and visible to the customer. The word "Warning" does not need to preface each warning where indicated if it is clearly associated with the required warnings as a header.

Required Rotating Health Warnings. In addition to the required warnings described above, the retail packaging or marketing layer must include rotating health warnings as determined by the Office.

Rotating warnings must be printed in the English language in Times New Roman, Calibri, Arial, or Helvetica font. Text must be no smaller than size 6 font, bolded, legible, unobscured, and visible to the customer. Licensees may include this information by printing the information directly onto the retail package or by affixing one or more labels with the information to the retail package or marketing layer, provided that none of the information is obstructed.

The following warnings should be rotated:

---

12   A website alone will not suffice; licensees must include information that allows a consumer to directly contact them in the event of a contaminated product, such as a phone number or email address.

13   Adult-Use Conditional Cultivators (AUCC) have the ability to process and distribute cannabis flower products. For the purposes of this guidance document the term processor includes AUCC conducting this activity.

- "Cannabis can be addictive."

- "Cannabis can impair concentration and coordination. Do not operate a vehicle or machinery under the influence of cannabis."

- "There may be health risks associated with consumption of this product."

- *Other warnings as determined by the Office.*

Licensees shall label and package in a manner which ensures rotating warnings are randomly distributed and that each warning appears on an approximately equal number of labels within a given calendar year. Licensees may do this by printing an equal number of labels with each warning evenly across all product stock keeping units (SKUs) rather than within each SKU.

If additional warnings are added, the Office will provide advance notice to licensees in allowance for the time it will take to print new labels.

To permit labeling of small retail packages, certain required information may appear on labels that may be accordion, expandable, extendable, or layered, with the <u>exception</u> of:

- The principal packaging display panel minimum standards;

- At least one of the three universal symbols (**Figure 2**); and

- The following two warnings:

    "This product contains cannabis and THC."

    "KEEP OUT OF REACH OF CHILDREN AND PETS. For use only by persons 21 years and older"
    (NOTE: this warning must include the capital letters as indicated)

5. Labeling Prohibitions. A cannabis product package, including an exit package, shall **not** display any content or be labeled in anymanner that:

- Includes any false or misleading statements including, but not limited to, any health claims;

- Includes the term "organic", unless appropriately using the phrase "made with organic ingredients" as described below, since there is no organic standard yet established for cannabis recognized federally;

    <u>Please note:</u> This does not prohibit cannabis or cannabis products from being cultivated or processed using organic practices, being made using ingredients that are organic, otherwise being sustainably produced, or adding a statement to the label that the product is "made with organic ingredients".

    Licensees may use a "made with organic ingredients" statement if the product contains at least 70 percent certified organic ingredients (not including salt or water). These products may contain up to 30 percent of allowed non-organic ingredients (see 7 CFR § 205.600) Additionally, the label must identify the USDA-accredited certifying agent on the retail package or marketing layer.

- Includes the term "craft" unless the processor meets the term as defined by future regulation or guidance;

- Include the term "gluten-free" or imply the product is gluten-free, unless the product meets the term as defined in 21 CFR §101.91;

- Causes a reasonable consumer confusion as to whether the cannabis product is trademarked, marked or labeled in a manner that violates any federal trademark law or regulation;

- Contains any illustration or content that falsely portrays cannabis or cannabis products as being authorized under or of Article 3 (medical cannabis) or Article 5 (cannabinoid hemp) of the Cannabis Law;

- Depicts cannabis products or paraphernalia;

- Promotes overconsumption;

- Promotes price, price reductions, or any other discount or coupon;

  Please note: This does not prohibit a dispensary from lowering, or otherwise altering, the price of the cannabis product.

- Depicts a child or other person reasonably appearing to be under the age of twenty-six; or

- Violates additional prohibitions as set out by the Office.

A retail package or marketing layer shall not be made attractive to individuals under twenty-one. As defined above, labeling is attractive to individuals over twenty-one if it uses or includes:

- cartoons;

- bubble-type, or cartoon-like font, such as including puffy, rounded block letters (see **Appendix A**);

- bright colors that are "neon" in appearance, including any color which, when listed in a form of hue, saturation, and lightness, has a saturation value greater than 60%. Examples of such colors are shown below in **Figure 1**;

  Image not shown. Refer to *https://www.omarfigueroa.com/new-york-book/* or *https://cannabis.ny.gov/system/files/documents/2022/10/packaging-and-labeling-guidance.pdf*

- similarities to products or words that refer to products that are commonly associated with or marketed in a manner so as to be attractive to individuals under twenty-one, including, but not limited to, any imitation of food, candy, soda, drinks, cookies, or cereal (with the exception of cultivar names);

- terms "candy" or "candies" or variants in spelling such as "kandy" or "kandeez" (with the exception of cultivar names);

- symbols, images, characters, public figures, phrases, toys, or games that are commonly used to market products to individuals under the age of twenty-one; or

- images of individuals who could reasonably appear to be under the age of twenty-one.

6. Retail Packaging Sustainability Program. Conditional licenses are valid for up to two years, at which time, if a licensee is found to be in good standing with the Office, the licensee can apply for and receive a standard license. At that time, licensees will be required to submit to the Board or Office an environmental sustainability product packaging plan.

Such plans may include but are not limited to reuse strategies collecting reusable cannabis packaging components to be sanitized and refilled or reused as cannabis packaging, collection or redemption of batteries, cartridges, or vape pens, or sustainable packaging strategies that use non-plastic, compostable or recyclable materials, or packaging materials exceeding 25% post-consumer recycled content.

7. Reusable Packaging. Retail packages can be reused if appropriately sanitized and, based on visual inspection, if the retail package is in good working order and does not appear to pose a risk of unintended exposure or ingestion of cannabis products. The visual inspection must ensure such retail packages are not brittle and do not have chips, cracks, or other imperfections that could compromise the child-resistant properties of the retail package or otherwise pose a threat of harm to any individual.

Before being reused, retail packages must be sanitized and disinfected to ensure that they do not contain any harmful residue or contaminants. This sanitization and disinfection can be done by a licensee or by a third-party.

8. Recycled Content Packaging and Recyclable Packaging. Claims about recyclable or recycled content packaging must comply with 16 CFR §260 Guides for the Use of Environmental Marketing Claims*.

9. Correcting Noncompliant Packaging and Labeling. If a licensee receives a cannabis product that is not packaged or labeled in compliance with this guidance, and the licensee receives appropriate notification of verified noncompliance from the Office, a customer, or the licensee which processed or distributed the cannabis product, then that licensee must immediately notify the Office and the cannabis product must be returned to the licensee who transferred it to the licensee taking action. If a product is returned due to noncompliance, the licensee must document the return and the reason the product was noncompliant in the inventory tracking system.

If the noncompliance can be corrected by affixing a label with only the information required to make the labeling compliant, then the processor that packaged the product can affix such a label when it is returned to them.

10. Packaging and Labeling Violations. The Board may suspend, cancel, or revoke a license and impose any other penalties as authorized by Cannabis Law and current and future regulations, if the licensee:

- Fails to comply with packaging, labeling, marketing, and advertising requirements

- Transfers, sells, or offers to sell a cannabis product to another licensee that is not packaged or labeled in accordance with adult-use regulations or this guidance document.

* Any printed editions of the Code of Federal Regulations (CFR) can be obtained by calling the Superintendent of Documents, U.S. Government Printing Office, at (202) 512-1800. Electronic copies of CFR sections may also be obtained at Government Printing Office (GPO) which contains the most recent revisions, can be searched directly at: https://www.ecfr.gov/.

Appendix A (Fonts and Text Use) and Appendix B (Example of Compliant Labeling of an Edible Cannabis Product) are not included. Refer to https://www.omarfigueroa.com/new-york-book/ or https://cannabis.ny.gov/system/files/documents/2022/10/packaging-and-labeling-guidance.pdf

Adult-Use Conditional Cultivator (AUCC) and Adult-Use Conditional Processor (AUCP) <u>True Parties of Interest</u> Guidance & Frequently Asked Questions

Originally Published: 8/12/2022

Updated: 8/16/2022

The New York State Cannabis Law provides a statutory framework for individuals and entities with an interest in businesses licensed by the Office of Cannabis Management (Office). The Cannabis Law creates a two-tier market structure for the Adult-Use Cannabis Program, whereby individuals or entities having any direct or interest in a licensee authorized for the supply tier (cultivation, processing, distribution) are prohibited from holding any direct or interest in a licensee on the retail tier (dispensing, on-site consumption, delivery) of the market and vice versa. The Cannabis Law also includes prohibitions for individuals or entities with an interest in a registered organization or laboratory testing permit holder.

In contrast to the absolute prohibition on holding any direct or indirect interest vertically across the two tiers, the Cannabis Law allows for an individual or entity to have an interest in multiple licenses within the same tier, albeit with several significant restrictions designed to ensure increased competition and access to the industry.

The Office is issuing this guidance for conditional cultivator and processor licensees to provide additional information as they continue to grow their licensed businesses. Licensees are responsible for remaining compliant with this guidance and any future guidance, laws, and regulations governing conditional licenses. The Office reserves the right to review all agreements entered into by licensees.

DEFINITIONS

For the purpose of this FAQ, the following definitions shall apply:

Person means an individual, institution, corporation, government or governmental subdivision or agency, business trust, estate, trust, partnership, association, or any other legal entity.

Financial institution means any bank, mutual savings bank, consumer loan company, credit union, savings and loan association, trust company, or other lending institution under the jurisdiction of the Department of Financial Services.

Financier means any person, other than a financial institution or government or governmental subdivision or agency, that provides capital as a gift, provides a grant, or lends capital pursuant to a secured or unsecured financing agreement. A financier may not be a true party of interest in the licensee to which it is a financier.

TRUE PARTIES OF INTEREST (TPI)

1. What is a True Party of Interest (TPI)?

True Parties of Interest are those persons (whether individuals and entities) who have an interest in a cannabis license.

TPIs of Adult-Use Conditional Cultivators and Adult-Use Conditional Processors include persons who:

- are sole proprietors, partners, LLC members, LLC managers, shareholders of a licensed entity, or their spouses;

- exercise control over a licensee;

- hold an actual or future right to ownership or investment, or are the spouse of someone who holds such a right, including by stock, convertible bond, note, warrant, option, SAFE, or equity swap agreements over a licensee;

- serve in a leadership, senior, or control position, such as a manager, president, vice president, secretary, treasurer, officer, board member, trustee, director, or a person with an equivalent title or position in a licensee, or are the spouse of a person who holds one of these roles or titles;

- receive aggregate payments in a calendar year, as part of a flat fee consulting agreement or risk sharing agreement, that exceed the greater of:

    ten percent (10%) of gross revenue;

    fifty percent (50%) of net profit of a licensee; or

    $100,000;

- guarantee the debts of the licensee; or

- make up, or are the spouse of a person who makes up, the ownership structure of each level of ownership of a licensee that has a multilevel ownership structure.

Not all arrangements with a licensee make a person a TPI. Certain landlord relationships, realtors, consultants compensated with a flat fee, goods and services contractors, financial institutions, and financiers may not be TPIs in an applicant IF the arrangement does not cause the person to meet the TPI definition above.

Common consulting agreements or management service agreements include the provision of management, advisory, consultant, intellectual property, or other related services to assist in the growing, processing, distributing, or selling of cannabis or cannabis products under a licensee's authorization. For purposes of this FAQ, services agreements shall not include agreements procuring services exclusively for the following exempted services: accounting, recordkeeping, non-cannabis materials and goods from unlicensed persons, office supplies, leasing equipment, architect services, construction, heating, ventilating, air conditioning, refrigeration, plumbing, cleaning and janitorial, lighting, security, legal services, government relations (registered lobbyist), and license application preparation.

Applicants and licensees should be aware that any agreement that procures services beyond the scope of the exempted services listed above may be subject to TPI restrictions. In other words, any agreement combining elements of exempted and non-exempted services may be viewed by the Office as non-exempted in its entirety.

The Office reserves the right to review all agreements entered into by licensees.

2. Can a foreign national be a TPI in an adult-use license?

Yes, a foreign national can be a TPI. However, pursuant to Section 137 of the New York State Cannabis Law, the following must be US citizens or permanent residents:

- all members of a partnership; or

- if a corporation, each principal officer and more than one half of the directors.

3. Will the Office collect and review information about conditional licensees' TPI?

Yes. The Office plans on providing conditional licensees with a Personal Disclosure Questionnaire that will be required to be completed identifying all TPIs of the licensee at the time the conditional licensee applies to convert their conditional license to a full (non-conditional) cultivator or processor license.

The Office will only consider for a full license, applicants whose ownership structure does not violate any of the rules under the Cannabis Law, regulations, guidance, or FAQs, and that otherwise meets all regulatory requirements.

Conditional licensees are reminded that they risk losing their ability to continue their licensed activity upon the expiration of their conditional license period if their ownership structure is not fully compliant with all required ownership restrictions. Licensees are recommended to consult with their own legal counsel before entering into any agreements that may, for example, create TPI relationships, violate ownership rules, and result in denials of full licensure.

4. How will the Office calculate the percentage of shares that a TPI holds in a license?

The Office will consider a person's share in a license to be the greatest of that person's percentage share of:

- Current voting shares;

- Future voting shares;

- Current equity shares; or

- Future equity shares.

For the purposes of determining the total shares outstanding for future ownership, the Office will use a modified definition of fully diluted share count, calculating a TPI's future ownership interest based on the entity's fully diluted share count (inclusive of all restricted stock units, options, warrants, or any other units of ownership that can be converted into a share of voting stock or equity), LESS contingent or future shares owned by persons whose financial or controlling interest in an entity is active.

5. Can a licensee receive a gift, grant, or loan pursuant to a financing agreement from a financier or financial institution?

Yes. A licensee may borrow capital and enter into a financing agreement with a financier or financial institution. A financier or a financial institution may also give a gift, grant, or loan to **licensees across multiple tiers** (e.g. a cultivator and a retail dispensary). However, if the financier or financial institution giving such a gift, grant, or loan receives an ownership interest, control of the business, a share of revenue or net profits that exceeds the allowable thresholds (see question one) in exchange for the gift, grant, or loan, they become a TPI in the license and are subject to ownership prohibitions.

6. Can a management services provider to an AUCC or AUCP also provide services to a retailer, laboratory or registered organization?

No. Such a management services provider is prohibited from providing such services across the two tiers and cannot simultaneously service an AUCC or AUCP and an adult-use retail dispensary, delivery, on-site consumption, laboratory, or registered organization.

ADULT-USE CONDITIONAL CULTIVATOR

7. Can I be a TPI in multiple Adult-Use Conditional Cultivator (AUCC) licenses?

No, a person may not be a TPI in more than one AUCC license.

8. As a TPI in an AUCC, can I invest in other types of adult-use cannabis licenses?

It depends. Under no circumstances may a TPI in an AUCC have a direct or indirect interest in a license authorized to sell cannabis at retail (including retail dispensaries, delivery, and on-site consumption), a Registered Organization, or a cannabis laboratory or permittee. Such prohibited interests shall include lending, lease holding, or management services agreements. This means that a TPI in an AUCC may not, for example, be a landlord, lender, or consultant to a licensee authorized to sell cannabis at retail.

However, a TPI in an AUCC may invest in or have other arrangements with entities holding processor or distributor license and may enter into certain agreements with other cultivators.

No person may be a TPI in more than one cultivator license. Therefore, AUCC and their TPI should proceed with caution to ensure they are compliant with guidance, rules, and regulations when investing in other licenses and should maintain copies of all agreements for review by the Office.

For more information on Adult-Use Conditional Processors (AUCP) and their TPI, please see the section below.

9. Can an AUCC licensee gift, grant, or lend to another licensee pursuant to a financing agreement?

Any person giving a gift, grant, or loan to a licensee in which they are not a TPI is a financier.

Under no circumstances may an AUCC licensee, or a TPI in an AUCC, be a financier to a licensee authorized to sell cannabis at retail (including retail dispensaries, delivery, and on-site consumption), a Registered Organization, or a cannabis testing laboratory or permittee.

However, an AUCC licensee may be a financier for another cultivator, processor, or distributor licensee, as long as the AUCC does not become a TPI in the other licensee they are financing. The Office reserves the right to review all agreements entered into by the licensee for compliance with the Cannabis Law, rules, regulations, and guidance.

10. If I am an AUCC licensee, can I enter into a management service agreement or a goods and services agreement with another AUCC licensee?

An AUCC may enter into a management services agreement or goods and services agreement with another AUCC. However, a management services agreement must be based on a flat fee and may not result in a transfer of control from the licensee seeking the services. If the fee on a non-exempted services agreement exceeds, in a calendar year, the greater of: (1) $100,000, (2) 10% of the gross revenue of the licensed entity, or (3) 50% of net profit of the licensed entity, then the services provider becomes a TPI in the licensee.

No AUCC licensee, or its TPIs, can have a management services agreement with a licensee authorized to sell cannabis at retail (including retail dispensaries, delivery, and on-site consumption), a registered organization, or a cannabis laboratory or permittee.

11. Can an AUCC minimally process and distribute other peoples' cannabis products?

Yes, a conditional cultivator can minimally process and distribute other AUCCs cannabis products until June 1st, 2023. After that date, an AUCC is entitled to apply for and obtain an adult-use cannabis distributor license and will only be able to distribute its own products. However, any arrangement that would make a service provider a TPI in multiple AUCC licenses would not be allowed.

12. Can an AUCC rent space from another AUCC that also provides trimming and harvesting services? Can the AUCC pay for the space and services with a mix of cash and cannabis when harvested?

Yes, this agreement is allowed. A conditional cultivator licensee may rent space to another conditional cultivator licensee. In such a situation, the conditional cultivator landlord is permitted to include services in the terms of the agreement for a flat fee. As long as the conditional cultivator landlord is not taking on ownership or equity in the licensee, receiving a share of revenue or profit in excess of the thresholds described in question one, or controlling the tenant licensee, the conditional cultivator landlord is not a TPI in the conditional cultivator tenant. Payment to the landlord may be paid in cash or any legal alternative form of compensation, provided that such alternate forms of payment are valued at fair market value for the purposes of the transaction.

13. Can an AUCC have any interest in a Registered Organization?

No. Pursuant to the MRTA an AUCC or a TPI of an AUCC may not have any interest, direct or indirect, in a Registered Organization. In addition, an AUCC may not be a landlord or financier to, or enter into a management services agreement with, a Registered Organization.

Similarly, a Registered Organization may not be a landlord or financier to, nor may they enter into a management services agreement or similar agreement with, an AUCC.

Not all services agreements between AUCC and Registered Organizations are prohibited. For example, a Registered Organization holding a license pursuant to section 68-a or 68-b of the Cannabis Law may enter into a flat-fee for service agreement to process, manufacture and package cannabis for an AUCC.

ADULT-USE CONDITIONAL PROCESSOR

14. Can I be a TPI in multiple Adult-use Conditional Process (AUCP) licenses?

Yes, a person may be a TPI in more than one AUCP license.

15. As a TPI in an AUCP, can I invest in other types of adult-use cannabis licenses?

An investor in a licensee is a TPI in that licensee. A TPI in an AUCP license may also be a TPI in other entities holding cultivation, processing, or distribution license. However, TPIs should be aware of prohibitions on other licensees. For instance, the Cannabis Law allows a person to have a financial or controlling interest in only one cultivation license. If a person is an investor in an entity with a financial or controlling interest in, or that is holding both an AUCP and AUCC license, then they are a TPI in both license types and cannot be a TPI in another AUCC license.

Under no circumstances may a TPI in an AUCP have a direct or indirect interest in a license authorized to sell cannabis at retail (including retail dispensaries, delivery, and on-site consumption), a Registered Organization, or a cannabis laboratory permittee.

16. Can an AUCP licensee gift, grant, or lend to another licensee pursuant to a financing agreement?

Any person giving a gift, grant, or loan to a licensee in which they are not a TPI is a financier.

Under no circumstances may an AUCP licensee or its TPIs be a financier to a licensee authorized to sell cannabis at retail (including retail dispensaries, delivery, and on-site consumption), Registered Organization, or a cannabis laboratory or permittee.

However, an AUCP licensee may be a financier to a cultivator, processor, or distributor licensee, so long as the AUCP does not become a TPI in multiple cultivator licenses.

17. If I am an AUCP licensee or a TPI on an AUCP license, can I enter in a management services agreement or other similar agreement with another AUCP licensee?

Yes, an AUCP licensee or its TPI may enter into a management services agreement with other AUCP licensees.

However, an AUCP should be aware that while a person may be a TPI in multiple AUCPs, no person may be a TPI in multiple AUCC. As a result, an AUCP should be cautious in entering agreements with an entity holding both AUCC and AUCP licenses.

18. If I am an AUCP licensee or a TPI in an AUCP licensee, can I have a management service agreement or other similar agreement with an AUCC licensee?

An AUCP and its TPIs may enter into a management services agreement with an AUCC. However, any such agreement that qualifies the AUCP as a TPI in multiple AUCC licenses would not be permitted. An AUCP should refer to the TPI definition in question one for more information on the types of arrangements that would qualify them as a TPI in an AUCC.

19. If I am an AUCP licensee or a TPI in an AUCP licensee, can I have a risk sharing agreement with an AUCC licensee? Am I able to enter into risk sharing agreements with multiple AUCC licensees?

An AUCP licensee or its TPI may enter into a risk sharing agreement with an AUCC licensee.

While an AUCP and its TPI may enter into risk sharing agreements with multiple AUCCs, the conditions of such agreements may qualify that AUCP as a TPI in those licensees. As a person may only be a TPI in a single AUCC, an AUCP should be cautious when entering risk sharing agreements with multiple AUCC licensees.

An AUCP should refer to the TPI definition in question one for more information on the thresholds that would qualify them as a TPI in an AUCC.

20. If I am an AUCP licensee, can I distribute other peoples' cannabis products to adult-use retailers?

Yes, an AUCP may distribute other peoples' cannabis products until June 1st, 2023. After that date, an AUCP is entitled to apply for and obtain an adult-use cannabis distributor license and will only be able to distribute its own products.

21. AUCC A and AUCC B form a joint venture (with a 50/50 percentage split of ownership), and acquire an AUCP license together, forming AUCP C. AUCP C buys biomass from both AUCC A and AUCC B. As part of those purchasing agreements, AUCP C agrees to pay AUCC A and AUCC B a percentage of its revenue on those products. Is this arrangement allowed?

Assuming that there is no transfer of control, yes, this agreement is allowed. The ownership structure makes both AUCC TPI in the AUCP. Because the AUCCs are not sharing their revenue with the AUCP, the AUCP is not a TPI in either AUCC, and this arrangement would be allowed.

22. Using the same facts as above in question 20, if a fund purchases a stake in AUCC A, is the fund now a TPI in AUCP C?

Yes, the fund is a TPI in AUCP C.

AUCP C lists the Joint Venture between AUCC A and AUCC B as its 100% owner, which in turn lists AUCC A as its 50% owner. Therefore, OCM would go up the chain of ownership in AUCC A. Since the fund holds an interest in AUCC A, that fund's investors would be the natural persons that end the ownership chain. Such natural persons would be considered TPIs of AUCP C.

Question Not Answered Here?

If your question is not answered here, please contact the Office of Cannabis Management by e-mail at licensing@ocm.ny.gov.

Index

"board" refers to cannabis control board

A

B

C

D

E

F

G

H

I

M

motor vehicles

    medical marihuana use in (10 CRR-NY § 1004.18), 316

    operating while impaired (PEN § 222.05), 125

municipality involvement (CAN § 131; PEN § 222.15), 106, 126

municipality notifications (CAN § 76), 82

N

narcotics (EDN § 6815; PEN § 220.00), 116, 122

neglect (SOS § 488; SOS § 490), 185, 189

New York hemp product (PBH § 3398-p; 9 CRR-NY § 114.13), 182, 231

New York State Bar Association Committee on Professional Ethics Opinion 1024, 327

New York State Bar Association Committee on Professional Ethics Opinion 1177, 337

New York State Bar Association Committee on Professional Ethics Opinion 1225, 341

New York state cannabis revenue fund (CAN § 15; STF § 89-h; STF § 99-ii; TAX § 496-b), 53, 191, 192, 203

New York state community grants reinvestment fund (STF § 99-kk), 195

New York state drug treatment public education fund (STF § 99-jj), 194

nicotine, in cannabis products (CAN § 83), 87

not-for-profits

    grants for (STF § 99-kk), 195

    medical cannabis and (CAN § 34), 60

    registering for medical cannabis organization (CAN § 35), 63

    trafficking of cannabis and (CAN § 137), 110

nurseries

    definition of (CAN § 3), 41

    license (CAN § 75), 82

O

oaths, administering (CAN § 10; CAN § 17), 47, 54

office of addiction services (STF § 99-jj), 194

office of cannabis management. *See also* board, cannabis control

    advisory board and (CAN § 14), 52

    education campaigns and (CAN § 19), 55

    establishment of (CAN § 8), 46

    executive director of (CAN § 9), 47 (*See also* executive director, of office of cannabis management)

    functions, powers, and duties of (CAN § 11), 50

officials, elected, trafficking cannabis by (CAN § 137), 110

Olivieri, Antonio G., 173-175

on-site consumption

P

S

smoking and vaping near (PBH § 1399-o), 131

T

U

V

W

Y

www.ingramcontent.com/pod-product-compliance
Lightning Source LLC
Chambersburg PA
CBHW061758260326
41914CB00006B/1159